Labour and Sustainable Development

Labour, Education & Society

Edited by György Széll,
Heinz Sünker, Anne Inga Hilsen
and Francesco Garibaldo

Volume 26

PETER LANG
Frankfurt am Main · Berlin · Bern · Bruxelles · New York · Oxford · Wien

Francesco Garibaldo
Dinghong Yi
(eds.)

Labour and Sustainable Development

North-South Perspectives

PETER LANG
Internationaler Verlag der Wissenschaften

Bibliographic Information published by the Deutsche Nationalbibliothek
The Deutsche Nationalbibliothek lists this publication in the Deutsche Nationalbibliografie; detailed bibliographic data is available in the internet at http://dnb.d-nb.de.

Zugl.: Osnabrück, Univ., Diss., 2011

We gratefully acknowledge the support of:
Hans Böckler Stiftung and RLDWL Regional and Local Development of Work and Labour Global Network

Hans **Böckler**
Stiftung

D 700
ISSN 1861-647X
ISBN 978-3-631-61731-1

www.peterlang.de

Table of Contents

Introduction

This book is an outcome of the seventh Congress of the international network Regional and Local Development of Work & Labour/RLDWL,[1] which took place at Renmin University, Peking, P.R.C. from 10 to 13 June 2010. The book aims at a mixed audience of Western and Eastern readers, because it affords the topic of sustainability from the point of view of the main Asian countries, on the one side, and from European and some South American countries, on the other side. To the Westerners it offers the unique perspective of some insiders in the public life of China and India, academics and practitioners at the same time, on the topics of environmental and social sustainability of their societies. To the Easterners a thorough and a critical analysis of the European Union's social and environmental realities and policies, and some hints on the reality of South America. It gives the possibility of a global perspective to every reader.

The topics analysed in the book are related to the social and the natural environment's sustainability: innovation, research and education on the one side and the life of working people on the other side; it includes also the "invisible" people of the informal employment and the economic migrants, namely in Asia.

This book assumes a critical and realistic perspective on what is happening, avoiding hiding problems and difficulties, but communicating a positive message on the possibility to go further in achieving a better situation. In this perspective the analysis of the public policies is a key point; these policies, in the eastern as well as in the western countries show objective difficulties and social contradictions but also that a way forward is possible.

The initial chapter is fully devoted to analyse China from within, i.e. from the point of view of academic people, often involved in the practice of change, in their country; it represents a unique perspective on the Chinese situation on some relevant social and political questions. The following six chapters are on sustainable innovation, trade unions and sustainable innovation, migration, informal employment, social security and social sustainability, public employment, employee's participation, the role of education and research; for each article a broad list of references is available for students and researchers.

We would like to take the opportunity to thank all those who made the Congress possible and by it also this book.

Bologna & Peking, July 2011 — Francesco Garibaldo & Dinghong Yi

1 For more information please check our homepage: http://www.rldwl.uqam.ca/aboutus/manifestorldwl.html.

Chapter 1:
China from within

The Reform and Development of China's Trade Union System – Introspection of China's Current Unified Trade Union System

Liang Gaofeng
(College of Economic Law, Northwest University of Politics and Law)

Abstract

In a market economy, the nature of Chinesetrade unions that was once political groups in planned economy era has to be changed into private corporation organizations. Based on the analysis of the essential attribute that trade union organizations in a market economy should have, the paper puts forward that the key to the reform and improvement of Chinese trade union system lies in the return of essential attribute of the trade unions. In allusion to the practical development requirement of Chinese trade unions, the unified trade union system currently in effect should be reformed in order to meet the practical demand of workers in different levels, groups, or fields. The perfection of labor interest representation mechanism will allow the labor relations in domestic market economy to achieve dynamic balance and autonomy by effective group consultation, and will allow the government-trade union-enterprise tripartite coordination mechanism of domestic labor-capital relationship to achieve international integration with international market economy mechanism, resulting in the improvement of domestic harmonious labor relation system.

In August 2001, the Ministry of Labor and Social Security (MLSS), All China Federation of Trade Unions (ACFTU), and China Enterprise Confederation (CEC) established a national tripartite meeting system for coordination of labor relations. So far, China has established the communication channel and coordination mechanism for labor relations from nation to local governments. The mechanism provides an important approach to strengthen the communication and coordination, mutual understanding, and mutual support among government, capital, and labor. However, our current practice of running the tripartite mechanism has many problems. One of the important problems is the demand to enhance the representativeness of labor and capital in tripartite mechanism. (Wang, 2006).

Content

1. The historical origin and problems of currently domestic unified trade union system

1.1 Basic components of domestic unified trade union system

Unified trade union means that the form of trade union organization is unified. There is only one national legitimate trade union organization system, and there are no other trade unions except the only one that is accepted by law. Any unit or individual shall not establish, among the masses of workers, the same type of organizations as the trade unions that are independent of legitimate trade union system. The People's Republic of China Trade Union Law passed in 1950 defined the nature of trade union organization as: "mass organization organized by constitution and resolution that are passed by National Labor Congress and representative assemblies of specific industry trade union, which has independent and unified autonomous system, with ACFTU as its supreme leading organ"; In 1992, The People's Republic of China Trade Union Law regulated in Article 12 that the All-China Federation of Trade Unions shall operate uniformly at a national level, and in Article 13 that the establishment of a primary trade union, local all-level federation of trade unions or a national or local specific industry trade union must be reported to the trade union organization at the next highest level for approval. On October 27, 2001, amendment of Trade Union Law regulated in its Article 9 that trade union organizations at the various levels shall be established in accordance with the principle of democratic centralism, and trade union committees at the various levels shall be elected by their general assemblies or representative assemblies. No close relatives of the chief members of an enterprise may be candidates for members of the basic level trade union committee of the enterprise. Trade union committees at the various levels shall be responsible to and shall submit work reports to general assemblies or representative assemblies at their respective levels and shall be subject to their supervision. Trade union general assemblies and representative assemblies shall have the right to change or dismiss their elected representatives or committee members. Higher level trade union organizations shall provide leadership to lower level trade union organizations. Article 10 regulates that enterprises, public institutions, and government organs with more than 25 members shall establish primary trade union committee; those with less than 25 members shall independently establish primary trade union committee, and more than two units with less than 25 members shall jointly establish primary trade union committee, and one organizer shall be elected to organize activities for the members. Units with more female workers shall establish women trade union committee under the leadership of trade unions at their respective levels; those with less female workers shall set up female committee members in trade union committee. Towns or streets with many enterprise workers shall establish primary trade union associations. A locality at county level or above shall establish a local all-level federation of trade unions. Several enterprises operating in the same industry or in industries of a similar nature may establish a national or local specific industry trade union, depending on their requirements, and the All-China Federation of Trade Unions shall operate uniformly at a national level. Article 11 regulates that the establishment of a primary trade union, local all-level federation of trade unions or a national or local specific industry trade union must be reported to the trade union organization at the next highest level for approval. In sum, domestic primary trade union organizations shall be established at the approval of higher level trade unions, and the trade union organization system with strict hierarchies shall be established according to the number of members (in practice, the number is determined by the number of workers in enterprises or public institutions), and administrative levels. The establishment of trade unions or primary trade unions shall be approved by higher level trade unions. It can be perceived that China has a typical unified trade union organization system.

1.2 The historical origin of Chinese currently unified trade union system

There are two historical origins of Chinese unified trade union system currently in effect. (A).The first origin is the political environment in the early period after the foundation of People's Republic of China. In the early period after the foundation of People's Republic of China, facing the political instability, under the domestic and external threatens, the Chinese Communist Party had to unite the most reliable working class, through the national control, education, and advocacy, to prevent enemies to sow dissension among working class in against with the new socialist regime in China. Therefore, the unified trade union system became a good choice in order to protect the political stability. (B). The second origin is the economic environment in planned economy period. Chinese unified trade union system is determined by the political mechanism with the Chinese Communist Party as the only one ruling party, and is directly related to the characteristic that the social interest was integrated and the interest relation was adjusted by administrative means in planned economy. (Chang, 2007) In the planned economy period, means of production of enterprises were owned by the state and by the whole people, and the administrators, together with the producers directly possessed the means of production. The integration of interest between enterprises and workers, or between operators and workers determined that the trade union was the unified representative of labor interest. The planned distribution by state eliminated the differences in the distribution of profit in production; there was no mass division among workers, thus there was no diversified interest demand. Therefore, the unified trade union organization form met the social economy demand at that time.

1.3 Problems of currently Chinese trade union system

1.3.1 Failing to meet the diversified development in socialist market economy.

With the development of market economy,and the establishment and improvement of modern enterprise system, a new type of diversified labor relations is gradually formed on the basis of essential interest integration between enterprises and workers. The diversification of labor relations means that public-owned economy labor relation has lost the position of unifying the whole country.The labor relations formed in planned economy have been changed from administrative control to market regulation. In the market economy, it is impossible for the state to directly manage the labor relations. Labor relations will be directly handled by both bodies and be autonomously determined by market mechanism. The unified trade union system formed in planned economy based on the interest conformity of working class fails to adapt to the diversification of workers interest demand in market economy.

1.3.2 Failing to represent interest of workers in different labor relations

With the current economic globalization, many multinational companies have entered China. And at the same time, as the development and expansion of enterprise size and organization, labor relations at different levels have been formed in the same enterprise. A multinational company has more than several thousands or thousands of employees, but for the interior of the enterprise, the management level has senior executives in the board of directors, managers of high level, managers of middle level, and general managers. The workers can be further divided into technical workers, clerks, and general operating workers. In the new period of current market economy, some atypical employment relationships have emerged, such as labor dispatch, part-time employment, rural migrant workers in cities, employment for the duration fixed by completion of a certain amount of work, etc. In an enterprise, workers can be divided into those in different positions, different levels, and different groups, whose demand of interest differs. Therefore, it is doubtful whether the demand of interest of workers from different interest groups can be sufficiently realized by unified trade unions.

1.3.3 Failing to guarantee the independence of trade unions

Unified trade union system means mandatory enrollment in a sense. China's trade unions, representing the interest of all workers, count their members, and collect membership dues from employing units in accordance with the number of workers (the trade union law regulates that enterprises monthly allocate 2% of gross pay of all workers to trade unions as funds). Article 13 of the trade union law regulates that enterprises or public institutions with more than 200 workers can establish trade unions with full-time trade union chairman, whose full-time worker members determined through consultation between trade unions and enterprises or institutions. These regulations violate one nature of trade unions that trade unions are mass organizations formed by the working classes of their own free will and also violate the international standard that workers are not forced to join in the trade unions. Trade union leaders' dependence caused by the situation that the fund of trade unions is attached to enterprises directly leads to the passivity in rights protection. It is impossible to essentially judge the behavior of trade unions by whether members support the trade unions or not due to the unified trade union mechanism. Moreover, because it is the enterprises that pay the wages, enterprises will create obstacles for the trade unions by means of changing position, reducing wages, and delaying or scanting trade union fund, when it clashes with the enterprises' interest to protect the workers' interest. In reality, trade union leaders who dare to protect the workers' interest will meet the embarrassing situation that "I speak for the workers, but who will speak for me". The cost is unbearable personally when trade unions try to protect the workers' rights, and the fear of the unbearable personal cost determines that it is hard for workers to initiate rights protection. (Song, 2005)

1.3.4 Trade union enrollment standards are not clear

Article 3 of China's trade union law regulates the enrollment standards as: "All workers doing physical or mental work in enterprises, public institutions and government organs within Chinese territory who earn their living primarily from wages shall have the right to participate in and form trade union organizations pursuant to the law, regardless of their nationality, race, sex, occupation, religious beliefs or level of education.". In the law articles, the concept of workers has a broad definition. It is impossible to clarify the definition of workers in unified trade union mechanism; therefore, it is doubtful whether private entrepreneurs or high managers in foreign-funded enterprises can participate in the trade unions. (Huang, 2001) It is proposed that private economy has become an important component of China's socialist market economy; consequently, it is questionable that they still cannot join in the trade unions. It has been proposed that private entrepreneurs be permitted and encouraged to join in the trade unions, which is in favor of the improvement of the unity of labor relations, and strengthening the trade unions. However, this cognition is contrary to ILO conventions and China's law. The eighty-seventh convention, concerning solidarity and freedom, of ILO regulates that both workers and employers have the right to join in or set up trade unions or trade union organizations established by them, which requires no prior approval. In China's trade union organizations, administrators and workers of an enterprise or a public institution represent bodies of labor relation of different interest and different levels, therefore, when they exercise rights in the same trade union organizations, because of the different economic positions, the workers' rights are usually not sufficiently protected, and their interest demands are not smoothly expressed.

1.3.5 The rights of labor and capital to establish organizations are not equal

The law only requires that trade unions keep unified organization system, but the employer organizations are not restricted. China's present employer organizations, including national employer organizations, such as Association of Enterprises with Foreign Investment, Association of Private Businesses, China Entrepreneur Association etc., are established in accordance with the principle of diversification rather than unification. (Chang, 2007) This situation is not only inconsistent with the principles of labor legislation, but also violated the principle of general legislation. Under the circumstances that labors and capital have unequal right to establish organizations, the capital can have better communication to force the labors to accept unfavorable working conditions, such as fixed salary for the same professions, or unfavorable working environment, etc.

2. The nature of trade unions

Lenin had discussed the nature of trade unions, and traditionally we have been positioning trade unions in accordance with Leninist orientation. Lenin pointed out that trade unions are not nation organizations, and they are standing between the party and the country, if it can be put so, and it should be the gearing device linking the party and the mass. He said that the party led the country's entire political and economic work, and at the same time, the party must keep close contact with masses of the same class to realize the dictatorship of the proletariat by means of the gearing device, including Soviets, trade unions, and non-party workers and peasants representative assemblies, etc. The complex system formed by a number of gears is the structure of the basis of dictatorship of the proletariat. According to Lenin's theory, we can summarize the functions of trade unions as "two kinds of protection" (protecting the specific interests of workers and the interests of the state), and "three kinds of functions" (link, pillar, school), which is also named by us as "construction, participation, protection, and education". (Lenin, 1986) The positioning of the trade union adapted well to the political system in planned economy period. In planned economy, China's labor relation was essentially longitudinal administrative labor relation, in which workers, as the owner of production means, directly related to the government by means of enterprise administration, enterprises representing workers, county representing enterprises. Therefore, trade unions had not really entered into labor relations, nor become the representatives of workers in labor relations. Significance of trade unions showed in working as the party's mass work system, reflecting the working procedure, "from the mass, to the mass". (Chang, 2004) In the historical condition of that time, the political essence and political function of trade unions were stressed, which is compatible with the economic and political situation in planned economy period.

As the establishment of market economy system, the society has experienced an obvious differentiation of social structures and interest. It means that, in this kind of society, interest of different social groups differs, and even clashes; moreover, expression of different kinds of interest demands will become a regular social phenomenon. In the field of labor relations, the country and the enterprises have different function and interest orientation. A new kind of labor relation, that has clear subjects, equal positions (equity between capital property right and labor property right), fair competition, and diversified interest, has been formed based on the integration of fundamental interest of operators and workers. Construction of the interest expression mechanism for the workers, the disadvantaged groups in the new labor relations has been an important element to coordinate and standardize the labor relation in current market economy. In the market economy, capital and labor, or operators and workers, have been divided into different groups. The scarcity of capital in production means leads to the strong position of capital in labor relations. Facing the capital in the strong position, the workers receive help from the government that is also the government's responsibility on the workers, including formulating employment policy, and establishing social security system; the trade union organization becomes an important non-governmental organization in coordinating interest conflict between the capital and labor, safeguarding the workers' interest, and preventing enterprises' short-term actions. Admission of the legitimacy of trade unions spontaneously established by the masses, and granting the workers the right to establish trade unions and the right of collective bargaining have become an important guarantee to maintain and coordinate the labor relations.

Trade unions, as the product caused by the contradictory between capital and labor, are the mass organizations established for the survival and development of the workers. Beatrice. The Webbers regarded trade unions as organizations for the survival of workers, and for the maintenance and improvement of the workers' living and working conditions. The core function of trade unions can be defined as the anti-system to tackle with the obstacles deliberately put by employers when they are negotiating contracts with the workers. (Webber, 1959) Collective consultation and collective bargaining have become an effective mean to achieve this function. It can be perceived that the emergence of trade unions is based on the vulnerable position of the workers in labor relations. (Richard, 2004) Workers establish the trade unions to negotiate with the employers in maintaining their basic working conditions. It is the first purpose of trade unions to maintain the common economic and social benefit of the specific groups of workers. Establishing trade unions is one of the civil rights of association, which has essential difference with the political rights of association. From the perspective of the development history of trade unions, the core function of trade unions is to maintain the basic working conditions, to negotiate with the contrary party, the employers, to achieve the balance between capital property rights and labor property rights, and finally achieve the win-win situation. In a sense, the recognition of the workers' right to organize trade unions, namely, recognition of the subject status of the workers as the owner of the labor force is also the respect for the labor property right. Therefore, the trade unions have the following natures.

2.1 Trade unions are non-governmental organizations

The trade union law of the People's Republic of China regulates that trade unions are mass organizations of the working class that are established voluntarily. Workers voluntarily join in the trade unions and they are not profitable, no matter within the organizations or among the members. Meanwhile, trade unions are engaged in safeguarding the legitimate rights and interest of the workers, and their nature of public welfare is unquestionable.

In the tripartite coordination mechanism, government, as the representative of the country's interest, plays the role as the organizer, director, and coordinator in the tripartite coordination mechanism(Feng, 2003). Trade unions, as the representative of the interest of the workers (employees), express the workers' will. China's trade union law summarizes the functions of trade unions as participation, protection, construction, and education. In planned economy period, trade unions not only represent and maintain workers' interest, but also organize workers in production, which is determined by the consistency of interest between administrators and workers. However, in the market economy, trade unions seem to be a common interest representative of both administrators and workers, which change the tripartite coordination mechanism into bipartite supervision in market economy, and makes trade unions partly substitute some functions of government's administrative department of labor.

Meanwhile, China's trade union appears a serious tendency of administrative mode in terms of personnel, fund, formation, and running mode. Therefore, trade unions' representativeness of workers' interest is highly weakened, and has lost the workers' (employee) trust. (He & Luo, 2006) In the daily operations, trade unions are becoming a political organization, working in accordance with the orders from the top, which blocks the expression of the interest of the workers (workers).

2.2 The core function of trade unions is to express the interest of specific groups of workers.

Autonomy of capital and labor is the prevailing labor relation management mechanism in current market economy countries. The fundamental measure is to strengthen the workers' power by granting them right of organizing trade unions and collective bargaining, thus realizing the dynamic balance between capital and labor. The failure of effectively bringing the workers' collective bargaining right into effect is an important reason for the phenomenon in present China including the frequent mining accidents, failure to protect the rights of the rural migrant workers in cities, and the illegal working over time in enterprises, etc. In recent years, the country and the government have done a lot of work in punishing and supervising occupational safety and health, helping rural migrant workers in cities for wages, fighting against violations of labor standards, but achieved little success. The fundamental reason is that the adjustment over labor relations by external regulation mechanism, including law and government's supervision is very limited. When the enterprises violate the law or violate the workers' interest, the workers are not able to correct the behavior of the enterprises by means of effectively organizing trade unions and collective bargaining.

China's current interest expression system is not complete. Imbalance is the fundamental characteristic of the development of China's current interest expression organizations(Sun, 2006). The development of the interest expression organizations working for the disadvantaged groups lags behind, and by contrast the interest expression organizations working for the strong groups develop rapidly, showing that the disadvantaged groups have low degree of organization and weak autonomy.

In China's unified trade union system, employers and workers perform the expression of interest in the same trade union organization. Because of the different economic position and interest of all parties, the voice of the workers can be heard through trade unions, which is the key point that influences the healthy development of China's labor relations and social stability. In order to express their desires, workers are organizing organizations such as "Association of Employees", "Association of Fellows from the Same Hometown", etc.

As for the trade unions, in the same enterprise, the interest of workers who have different professions and the interest of managers who are engaged in different types of management differ.It should be noted that the social interest expression should have a diversified mechanism. The establishment and formation of diversified interest expression mechanism in the enterprise is of great importance.

2.3 Trade unions are private corporations

Trade unions are private corporations, the mass organizations that workers establish for their survival and development; they are essentially different from the political associations in the pursuit of political interest and the expression of political desire.

Trade unions are the product of social and economic contradictions, or to put it specifically, trade unions are the product of the contradictions of labor relations in the market economy. The purposes of trade unions are to maintain and improve the workers' working condition, to enhance the economic position of the workers in the enterprise, to supervise the legitimate operation of the employers inside of the enterprise, and to realize the democratically management and sustainable development of the enterprise. Trade unions, formed by the main body of specific mass of workers, in order to maintain their functions of protection and supervision, must possess the following conditions. a. Independence. It means that trade union must be independent of interference from a third party, including the government's administrative management of trade unions, and influence from the employers or the management layers. b. Purity. It means that the members, no matter materially or ideologically, must be independent of the employers or the association of employers. The task of the members or the representatives of trade unions must not be interfered by the employers or the association of employers. c. Workers team sense. It means that trade unions must work for the workers, as the representative of the interest of the workers (employees). Meanwhile, trade unions must be ready to put pressure on the contrary side so as to safeguard interest of the team or the members. d. Democracy. Workers should avoid be controlled by a minority of people. (Huang, 2003)

Trade unions' nature, private corporation, is manifested in the following two aspects. Firstly, workers voluntarily establish trade unions; they have the freedom to decide whether establish or do no establish the trade unions; workers have the freedom to join in or do not join in the trade unions; they are not influenced by any political forces. Secondly, the only purpose to establish trade unions is to study and protect the material or mental right and interest of their members (workers), no matter singly or collectively. Thirdly, except for the maintenance of workers' working condition and the protection of the workers' single or collective interest, including labor interest, social interest, and economic interest, trade unions' participation in any political or business activity is prohibited. For example, on April 10, 1998, the French Supreme Court judged the trade union called "Police National Front" as an illegal organization because its name was confused with the name of the party called "National Front". Trade union organizations' nature, private corporation, determines that they are essentially different from the political associations that aim to pursue political interest and the expression of political desires. (Wang & Li, 2001)

It should be noted that whether trade unions can play an important role in the market economy lies in achievement of the dynamic balance between capital and labor, regulation of the employers' legal operation, protection of workers' basic working conditions and survival guarantee, reduction of the government's positive supervision stress in the labor-capital relations, and in the framework of labor and capital autonomy, achieving the government-capital-labor tripartite coordination, and establishing harmonious labor relations. In China's unified legislative system, trade unions' coordination function is badly affected, resulting in the failure of expression of interest of a specific group of workers in the current trade union mechanism, consequently, some illegal organizations are emerging, such as "Association of Employees", "Association of Fellows from the Same Hometown", etc., and even mass disturbances break out. In order to achieve effective expression of the workers' interest and regulate workers' collective bargaining, the legality of the interest groups voluntarily established by workers only for social economic purpose should be recognized, which might be a useful approach to improve China's trade union system. The approach will achieve the diversification of the trade union organizations, giving workers of different groups or at different levels the opportunity to have their interest sufficiently be expressed.

3. The priority of the reform and improvement of trade union system is the return of its essential nature

In planned economy, China's labor relation was essentially longitudinal administrative labor relation, in which workers, as the owner of production means, directly related to the government by means of enterprise administration, county representing enterprises, enterprises representing workers. Therefore, trade unions had not really entered into labor relations, nor become the representatives of workers in labor relations. The significance of trade unions lies in that they are the link and bridge between the party and the mass, the basis and pillar of people's democratic dictatorship, and the big communist school to educate the masses of workers. (Chang, 2004) In the planned economy period, China's trade unions were mass organizations of the working class that were led by Communist Party of China and were established voluntarily by workers; they were important social political organizations working as the Party's mass working system. In the historical conditions at that time, the trade unions' political effect was more emphasized, which adapts to the political and economic system demand in the planned economy. China's unified trade union organization system fit the political and economic situation at that time, and played a positive social role in the planned economy.

However, with the establishment and improvement of modern enterprise system in the market economy, in line with the principle of "clearly established ownership, well defined power and responsibility, separation of enterprise from administration, and scientific management", the country and the enterprises have developed different functions and interest orientation; the labor and the capital have clear differentiation of the ownership of production means; the enterprises have become truly independent operating entities and economic organizations. A new kind of labor relation between enterprises and staff, or between operators and workers has been gradually formed. The new kind of labor relation has clear subjects, equal position, fair competition, and diversified interest. The situation in the planned economy that the demarcation line between subjects blurred, and interest relations confused has been thoroughly changed. The country, enterprises, and workers have become independent right subject and interest subject. The market mechanism will play a fundamental role in the allocation of labor resources, and the operation of labor relations will be adjusted by the market rather than be controlled by the county administration. On that occasion, the country cannot and will not need to directly intervene in labor relations. The right to directly handle the labor relations will, from the surface to the inside, be independently decided by both subjects of labor relations in accordance with the market rules. This independent decision right requires the relative balance between labor and capital, because the subordination nature of labor relations in reality strengthens the employers' dominance over the operation and development of labor relations. (Qiu, 2004) The relative balance between the power of labor and capital requires giving more support to the disadvantaged workers by granting them uniting right in order to enhance their position in labor relations and to strengthen their impact on the operation of labor relations. The workers' uniting right fundamentally appears to be the workers' right to establish trade unions. The nature of China's trade unions have to be changed from political organizations in planned economy to social economic organizations that are private corporations in the market economy.

Diversified interest demand is the essential manifestation and objective requirement of market economy. The main objective of the reform and improvement of current trade union system is to establish and improve the expression mechanism of interest for the disadvantaged groups. The reform and improvement of trade union system essentially requires the return of trade unions' essential nature. Some actions are important contents for establishing harmonious labor relations and harmonious society, including recognition of the legitimacy of the trade unions spontaneously established by workers, improvement of the purity of the trade union members, elimination of the employer trade union ("boss trade union'), improvement of the authenticity of the trade union representatives (to check whether the trade unions are true representatives of the specific worker groups' interest, and furthermore, to grant the trade unions the right of collective bargaining and consultation, to permit them to exercise the rights on behalf of the workers), recognition of the interest diversification of the worker groups, further recognition of the interest diversity of the different groups inside the enterprises and in social stratification, and improvement of the interest expression mechanism of the diversified trade unions. The author believes that as for an effective trade union organization form, the inevitable development goal of trade unions is the establishment of diversified trade unions. Indeed, in the market economy countries all around the world, all the trade union mechanisms are not diversified. However, influenced by the planned economy for a long time, China's trade union mechanism has a serious tendency of administrative mode. Factors, such as the administrative management and the forced enrollment, have severely damaged the trade unions' nature that trade unions are interest representatives of different interest worker groups. The saying that proper limits have to be exceeded in order to right a wrong, or else the wrong cannot be righted fits the current situation of the trade unions in China. An important approach of the reform of current trade union system is the implementation of diversified trade union mechanism, in which primary trade unions are established in the form of registration according to the need of the different interest groups of workers, for the purpose of fulfilling the interest expression of the workers from different levels, groups, and positions, finally resulting in that trade unions are true representatives of the workers' interest.

The core advantage of diversified trade union organization system lies in realizing the dynamic balance and autonomy of labor-capital relation, changing the government's positive position in labor-capital relation coordination, and preventing mass disturbance from happening. What the government should do is to follow the international trend of labor-capital relations autonomy, to grant workers true and complete right to organize trade unions, and to organize, lead, and coordinate the tripartite coordination mechanism. Our tasks include defining the member numbers of the trade union and the scope of the interest of the specific groups of workers that trade unions can represent, confirming and examining trade union's representativeness, examining the purity of the members of specific trade unions, eliminating employer trade unions and preventing a small amount of people from controlling or blocking the interest expression of workers group, setting up effective procedures for collective bargaining and tripartite coordination mechanism, regulating the operation of labor relations, realizing well-organized dynamic balance and autonomy of labor relations, and achieving harmonious and stable development of labor relations and social production economic relations.

References

Bao, L.C. Study on the Right Protection Function of Trade Unions in the Period of China's Economic Transformation [D]. Inner Mongolia: Inner Mongolia University.

Chang,K(2004). Study on Labor Rights-Legal Research on China's Current Labor Relations. China Labor and Social Security Publishing House.

Chang, K. (2007). Study on the Legislation and Implementation of China's Right of Unity [J].Modern Law Science, (1,121):48.

Douglas. L. Leslie. (1997). Translated by Zhang Qiang and Others, Labor Law Outline [M], Chinese Academy of Social Science, August, First Edition.

Feng,Y. J. (2003). Brief Introduction to the Study on Labor Rights.Social Science Front,1,172

He,Z.M.&Luo,P. (2006). Trade Unions' Protection of Labor Rights-Rights of the Disadvantaged and Non-government Organizations. Legal System and Society, 1

Huang,Y.G. . (2001). Organization and Function of Trade Unions in Private Enterprises[N]. Workers Daily, 2001-1-16.

Huang,Y.Q. (2003). New Study on Labor Law. China University of Political Science Press.

Qiu, X..P . (2004). Labor Relations.China Labor and Social Security Publishing House.

Hyman. R. (2004). Comparison of Trade Union Movement, Translated by Xu Jifeng and Wu Yuren, Taiwan Weber Publication International Ltd.

Sun,L.P(2006). Harmonious Society: Regulation of Interest Expression with System. Theory Reference,2.

Song,W.& Cheng, L.M. (2005). Legal System Arrangement for Trade Unions to Optimize Human Resource [J], Human Resource Development(1).

The Webbers. (1959). History of British Trade Union Movement, Commercial Press.

Wang,Y(2006). Status Quo, Problems, and Reform Ideas of China's Labor Relations Tripartite Coordination Mechanism.Review of Economic Research, Vol 44.

Wang,Z.R(2006). Problems in China's Current Interest Expression Mechanism. Theory Reference, 2.

Reconstitution of Chinese Labor Common Joint Action System Based on the Practice

Xu Ji-ping[1]
(School of Social Sciences, Shanghai University of Engineering Science, Shanghai 201620)

Zuo Ya-luo (Law School, Fudan University, Shanghai 200433)

Abstract

As China is still at the early stage of studying the common joint action system, little systematic probe and discussion has been given to the labor common joint action system. As a result, this has posed serious challenges to Chinese labor and judicial practice. It is quite necessary that starting from the actual practice of solving the group labor disputes and learning from the general principles in the common joint action system, China at present should reconsider and improve the arbitration and lawsuit proceedings of group labor dispute and thus reconstitute our labor common joint action system. In other words, the reconstitution will involve so many aspects as case jurisdiction, registration, trials, intercommunity principles of proposition and evidence, arbitration means and so on.

Content

1 Corresponding author. Tel.: +086-21-67791040, 138-17785550; fax: +086-21-67791040. E-mail address: rehcaetxu@yahoo.com.cn.

1. Introduction

Recently, the number of labor disputes has been soaring sharply, and therefore it becomes a hard nut demanding the quick crack of Chinese civil judicial department that how we can safely and efficiently solve the labor disputes. As a procedural regime that can save the judicial resources and improve the lawsuit efficiency, the common joint action system, widely accepted by many continental law countries, China included, has played a really positive role in solving civil disputes involving several parties. However, China currently is still at the preliminary level of studying common joint action system, the present theories can hardly be used to deal with the challenges posed in judicial practice, and the weakness is especially more obvious in solving the group labor disputes. This paper is a positive response to this situation from the writer in the hope that it can give some insight and make some contribution in certain respects.

2. Overview of Labor Common Joint Action System

2.1 Overview of Common Joint Action System

The common joint action system, also named as the unnecessary joint action system, means a certain litigant mode in which, there are two or more than two persons in one party or each side in the civil lawsuits, they have the same legal question and similar kind of lawsuits and therefore the two lawsuits being conducted separately can be carried through in the same lawsuit. [2]The diversity of one party and the unity of proceedings are the foundation of the joint action and the feature of the lawsuit as similar but not the same tells the difference between the common joint action system and the necessary joint action system[3]. It should be emphasized that the diversity of subject of litigation is the premise for the common joint action system. In the judicial practice, the central factors on which a judge decides to put certain separate lawsuits into one common joint action and hear it simultaneously are the relatedness of the cases, the possibility of hearing the cases together and the necessity of hearing them in the meantime. We believe that the combination of the three factors makes it possible that the related cases can break away from the former practice of hearing cases separately and follow

2 There is no convincible consensus on the definition of the common joint action system, and therefore the writer just presents the own idea, combining different thoughts from other fields.

3 The necessary joint action system means that the two persons or more in one party or each side identify the lawsuit as common and people's court should hear at the same time and give one verdict.

a new means of legal proceedings. In other words, the emergence of hearing the related case at the same time is not totally accidental but really on the inner bases, so this is a positive response from the legislative and judicial branches meeting the real needs of case hearing.

The common joint action system is basically characterized by the intercommunity of entities in the combined cases and the convenience of procedural handling. The intercommunity of entities is in the combined case the interconnection of the co-litigants' assertions and evidence to some extent and they not only influence other each and but also likely cite each other (although in the common joint action system, the intercommunity of entities is weaker compared with the necessary joint action system, but it is stronger than the real separate lawsuits). The convenience of procedural handling is an innovative procedure free from the traditional lawsuit mode rather than the simple duplication or overlapping of those single lawsuits. In comparison with the single lawsuit system, this procedure is more forthright and efficient.

Generally speaking, the common joint action system is presently applied to such fields as contract dispute (for example, property management) and tort dispute (for example, one certain deed leads to the damage to several people). As for the labor dispute, it is featured by the relative particularity[4] and the non-general application of the procedure, mainly to the occasional judicial practice, so there is almost no systematic theoretic statement or discussion[5]. In some way, this has turned out to be the basis for this paper.

2.2 Overview of the Labor Common Joint Action System

2.2.1 Definition and Features

This paper calls the common joint action system applied to the labor dispute the labor common joint action system and it is actually a special form of the common joint action system[6].There is need to state that owing to the particularity of the

4 Judging by the reality, with the practice of conducting the principle of the arbitration in advance in labor dispute cases, most group labor dispute lawsuit only linger at the stage of arbitration and not reach the judicial proceeding stage. Besides, in the legislative rules, on the one hand, China still has no Labor Procedure Law or Labor Common Joint Action Procedure Law; on the other hand, the seventh article in Chapter One in the newly-implemented Law on Labor Dispute Mediation and Arbitration merely mentions the arbitration and litigation systems of representatives.

5 By the time of presenting this paper, after typing the key words as labor joint action or the common litigation concerning labor on the CNKI, we can get no result.

6 In the labor common joint action system, the relatedness of cases is mainly reflected in the unity of labor contract as the basis to the labor relations and labor employment means. In general, the

system in solving Chinese labor disputes, the paper will widen the meaning of litigation in the labor common joint action system as two parts, including labor litigation in a narrow sense and labor arbitration.

On the whole, the labor common joint action system has the following features. First, the labor common joint action system is generally based on the reality of the employing companies, so the subjects of the lawsuits are unitary and the applied regulations are the labor laws and department rules, which determine that the type of the lawsuits needing resolving is intensive and it is beneficial for the arbitration department and people's court to sort out the type of lawsuits and handle them after concluding the experience. Second, different from other types of civil proceedings that stress the equal antagonism between plaintiffs and defendants, the labor arbitration or labor litigation quite emphasizes the protection of laborers' benefits in the legislative view, and therefore, in the labor common joint action system, the procedural design and entitative organization reflect the labor law's special protection for laborers[7]. Third, in the labor common joint action system, special attention will be given to the interconnection between labor arbitration and labor litigation, and the procedural arrangement will reflect that the people's court can review the arbitration process and results, and also can prevent the cases from the meaningless repetition in hearing to pave the way for the quick settlement of lawsuits. Fourth, in the process of applying the labor common joint action, considering the fact of one party including many laborers but with weaknesses in ability, the labor arbitration or labor litigation will pay special attention to the agreed assessment of all the evidence presented by laborers rather than simply conform with the old principle he who advocates should provide evidence. The evidence that can be favorable for the laborers, after the attestation process, should be applied to the whole laborers through some procedures. Besides, the hearing department will adopt the methods more reasonable and convenient than the methods of simple single litigation or combination of the same kind of lawsuits, ensuring the fast help to the laborers facing rights infringement and even threat.

---

employer will take the uniform model contract as the basis to change the labor relations of the company. Even in the real labor relations dispute, employer will take the uniform practice. The unity of these facts will objectively present the needs to give uniform legal and actual judgment to the related disputes, which serve as the basis for the relatedness of combining the joint action cases concerning labor. In addition, because of the unity of employers in the similar lawsuits, the combined hearing is faced with no obstacle to jurisdiction, and it is a feasible way of combining and hearing the similar cases. The necessity of combing cases is that whether the arbitrary department or labor department in people's court should solve labor disputes in the most forthright and efficient way to regain the harmony of enterprise labor relations and the whole society and make contribution to the sustainable development of the society and the country.

7 For instance, the procedural design in the labor common joint action system will better embody the procedural convenience so as to protect the delayed case from a second possible damage to laborers.

2.2.2 Main Types

In practice, there are majorly two types of the labor common joint action system; one is the lawsuit which several employees present on the same company for the salary, overtime pay or the due responsibility when the company refuses to sign the labor contract in accordance with the law or the company illegally terminates the labor relations. This kind of lawsuits occupies the main part of the group labor disputes. The lawsuits have the employing company as one party and the labor relations as lawsuits basis. Generally speaking, the same employing company takes the uniform standard contract to hire laborers, and even in the real situation of labor relations, the same employing company adopts the uniform system of labor employment, so this kind of the labor common joint action is put forward on the basis of the identical or similar facts. Although the lawsuits may be named differently, there is a good deal of similarity in the litigation opinions and evidence on the plaintiff's side, and therefore the intercommunity principle of evidence and assertion will be used in this kind. Because of the above reasons, the unity of lawsuit verdict can is very important. Different verdicts on the same kind of lawsuits will damage the judicial authority and cause bad influence to the social harmony, stability and sustainable development.

The other type is the lawsuit presented by the same employing company on several employees. In reality, this kind of lawsuits is often connected with the employees' behaviors such as the employees violate the confidentiality agreement or non-compete agreement, or the employees' malpractice lead to great damage to the company. This type is different from the first type. The co-plaintiffs in the first type will generally unite together to fight against the employing company and require to win the lawsuits, while the co-defendants in the second type will be likely to fight independently and shift the responsibility. Hence, the intercommunity principle of evidence and assertion should be used in certain scope so as to avoid the excessive negative effects.

3. The Current Operation State and Main Weakness of the Labor Common Joint Action System

3.1 Labor Arbitration or Litigation Not As the Priority to Solve Group Labor Disputes

At present, there are three ways to solve the group labor disputes in China. First is through the administrative coordination of labor supervision department, second is through the labor arbitration and litigation and third is through petition letters to the relative administrative departments asking the government for help. The labor supervision is one method of administration, by which laborers can inform the labor supervision department of the fact and ask them to intervene in the group labor disputes. As the intervention is quite arbitrary, the final result is usually the administrative penalty to the employment violation of the company, but the rights of employees is seldom fully relieved. Unless laborers harbor the idea of great losses to both parties, they will rarely choose this kind of help or will not take it as their priority. Of course, this method has its own relative advantage as the high efficiency, and employees can quickly get the result. Labor arbitration and litigation are the relief of quasi-judicial and judicial channels. Once laborers win the successful verdict or judge, relief will be fully given, but the relief calls for time and energy, especially in solving the group labor disputes, and therefore this method has not been the top choice to solve the disputes. The third method is the petition letters. There is no doubt that in the legal sense, labor disputes are not under the jurisdiction of administrative departments. It is interesting that most employing companies will choose to compromise after the administrative departments positively or negatively put pressure on the employing companies regardless of the aim. For this reason, most laborers will choose the petition letters or even make some trouble to solve the group labor disputes instead of the arbitration or litigation methods.

3.2 Main Weaknesses of Arbitration and Litigation Systems in Solving Chinese Group Labor Disputes

3.2.1 Jurisdiction

Nowadays, China adopts two stages to solve the labor disputes: labor arbitration and labor litigation. General lawsuits with little amount of money take such methods as arbitration award shall be final and binding, and few lawsuits will adopt the litigation proceedings with an aim to repeal the arbitration decisions owing to the flaws in the application or procedure of the law. But in a serious sense, the pure legal check is more a mechanism in judicial check and error correction than a procedure to solve disputes, so the paper will exclude it from discussion. The other is the labor dispute involving relatively large amount of money. After the decision of labor arbitration, the disputes can be put into civil proceedings. If one party is dissatisfied with the verdict of the court, they can continue the procedure of second instance.

The system designed to solve the labor disputes originally aims to help the labor arbitration department play a bigger role, leading them out of purely going through the procedure as a formality and turning them into an effective means to save the judicial resources. On the other hand, it helps the basic-level courts get away from the burdensome hearing of simple cases and concentrate on resolving big cases.

It has good intentions, but the problem is that legislators rely on the traditional thinking mode of single litigation while designing the system and they completely have no reasonable prospect of and response to the emergence and development of group labor disputes. For instance, when deciding whether to put the lawsuits into labor litigation after the arbitration, legislators merely consider the volume of subjects without thinking about the complexity of lawsuits. As there is almost no charge for labor arbitration or litigation in China, the charge fees entirely have nothing to do with the volume of cases and the amount has not been checked substantially at registration stage. In this way, while many laborers sue the employing company, they will raise the amount as large as possible in order to get one more chance of relief before the arbitration court gives the unfavorable verdict. In addition, the arbitration court usually takes the way of separate case registration. Even if too many persons get involved in the case and the amount exceeds the maximum of the law to apply for a single and final award, the case can not be put into the procedure of court hearing. The regulation actually is in contradiction with the hearing system of common civil litigation currently used in China. According to our code of civil law, the deciding factors of case hearing are the volume of cases, the influence and complexity of cases. The influence and complexity of group labor dispute cases can never be matched by the single labor dispute cases. There is no reason to put them into the procedure of a single and final award and they should be included into court hearing.

3.2.2 Registration Means

The registration here includes not only registration in court but also the registration in arbitration. As the difference between the two is not obvious, the paper will not make a clear distinction.

Because present registration of labor cases adopts the separate record registration and separate case number, the practice will never be changed even if several laborers come together to the arbitration court or court going through the process of putting the cases on record in hope that the arbitration court or court solves the concerned disputes altogether. This kind of registration means is really the infringement and even deprivation the right of choice enjoyed by the co-plaintiffs and co-parties in cases. Even though in many situations arbitrators or judges always hear the relevant cases at the same time, the temporary measure without the guarantee of the system will easily be handled with and accordingly the procedural protection of parties provided by law will not exist.

3.2.3 Hearing Ways

Both the Code of Civil Procedure Law or Law on Labor Dispute Mediation and Arbitration newly released and implemented do not mention too much about the hearing proceedings of labor common joint action and this has made it possible for the current chaotic prospect in labor judiciary.

From real experience of the writer, the arbitration court or the court just simply composes separate cases together as their way to solve the group labor disputes. For example, arbitrators or judges first ask the co-plaintiffs to read the pleadings respectively, and then check the basic facts one by one, and arbitrators or judges at most stress no repetition of the former content in the actual inquiry. The evidence presentation and evidence question are operated separately. Different parties don't cite the relevant evidence or assertion and the possibility that the universal evidence or assertion will influence the judges' free evaluation can't be ruled out. Finally, as for the affirmation of case facts, judges will try hard to maintain the unitary of fact evaluation in cases, but the contradiction in verdicts will occur sometimes.

The arbitrary hearing means of judges will ruin the official rules of procedure, damage the legal rights of co-litigants in reality, make the litigation proceedings more complex and non-transparent, weaken the credibility of hearing results and do harm to social harmony steadiness and sustainable development.

4. Reconstitution of Chinese Labor Common Joint Action System

In the light of current situation of Chinese arbitration and litigation systems in solving group labor disputes, we believe that it is necessary to reconsider the present labor common joint action system to ensure its sufficient scientific and reasonable spirits and at the same time, the group labor disputes can be solved more quickly and fairly under the new frame of the system. To be specific, the improvement should be reflected in the following parts.

4.1 Lawsuit Administration

The group labor disputes involve reversal litigants and the lawsuit is more complex than single labor disputes, and therefore all the disputes should be put into the examination of court. More specifically, after the arbitration department gives the verdict, all the litigants in the case should be allowed to present labor litigation and the volume of the single case should not be taken as the deciding factor to take a single and final award. There are three reasons for the practice. First, the litigants involved in the case are numerous with great social influence. If the labor litigation in the quasi-judicial procedure is adopted as the only way to give relief, it will be a little rash and be harmful to the final resolution of the case. After all, giving some more relief channels will open more opportunities for litigants to choose and actually provide the possibility of peacefully solving the case, and thus it will do good to resolve social contradiction. Second, the credibility of the court is superior to the labor arbitration department, so taking the disputes into the court examination will help establish a more objective image, give the parties another chance to check their own litigation and present the benefits of solving disputes in the mental state. Third, frankly speaking, our court is stronger in grasping the laws and regulations than the arbitration court and the court can quickly close the loopholes in the law through various methods to ensure the uniform application of the laws. Therefore, the guarding of the court is significant in improving the handling quality of the cases.

4.2 The Case Registration

The Code of Law on Labor Dispute Mediation and Arbitration has no rule about the combination of cases on labor arbitration at present, the case combination of labor arbitration is still not stipulated in law. This has posed a great challenge to the practice of arbitrating group labor disputes. We think in this situation where the clear law or regulation do not exist, the arbitration department should at least abide by the principle of convenience in case registration and give the relevant appealing documents to the party complaint about so that the overall assessment and reply about the case can be put forward. At the stage of labor litigation, the right of choice on whether to combine the cases or not should be given to the plaintiffs and the uniform registration should be permitted if plaintiffs apply for it or otherwise cases should be put on record separately.

4.3 The Intercommunity Rule of Evidence and Assertion

According to the general principles of the labor common joint action system, the proposal about the universality of cases should apply the intercommunity rule, meaning that giving the joint action is equal to presenting opinions on the same issue. We believe that we should stick to the intercommunity rule of evidence and assertion in the joint action concerning labor. For instance, in the case of pressing for the labor payment, it has been a common issue that the employing company doesn't legally give workers the payment and the assertion of the plaintiffs of the litigation should become the foundation of the court verdict whether they put forward it or not in fact. In other words, all the plaintiffs have the similarity on the assertion. Meanwhile, just as the writer has mentioned beforehand, in the labor common joint action system much evidence presented by the laborers actually can verify each other, but with the differences in the legal awareness and the ability in obtaining the evidence, some basic evidence can hardly be given by all the laborers. For all these situations, it is quite important to establish the intercommunity rule of evidence in this kind of cases. To be specific, the evidence that can reflect the universal fact[8] of the case should be cited by all the parties to help them accomplish the responsibility of producing evidence and the non-cited evidence should generally not be taken as the bases for verdict or judgment. Certainly, arbitrators and judges should clearly explain the rule in hearing cases so as to practically assist the concerned parties.

4.4 Hearing Procedure and Judging Modes

Commonly speaking, the labor arbitration or litigation includes such stages as the fact research, evidence providing and questioning, debating and closing statement. In the labor common joint action system, we believe whether arbitrators or judges should do investigation about the basic facts of the case. In the process, the common facts connecting the cases should be checked and the important individual facts[9] should be verified according to the case situations. With this method, the primary and the secondary can be distinguished and time can also be saved. At the stage of providing and questioning the evidence, the intercommunity rule of evidence should be made full use of in order to make the most of the evidence on hand and reproduce the facts in case objectively. The debate on the facts at the debating stage can be merged with the stage of providing and questioning evidence to save litigation time. If parties have controversy about the application of the law, it can be solved at the debating stage, and we believe we can take the mode of asking the representative of one party to make statements first and other parties to add, saving the unnecessary repetition. The closing statement can be undertaken in accordance with the single litigation. Besides, owing to the particularity of the group labor disputes, we think under the premise of the agreement

8 The facts used to prove the interconnection of cases.
9 The facts that reflect the individual situations of parties.

between co-litigants, the agreed combined judgment can be given, the handling results of the co-assertion can be written in the judgment and the individual problem can be responded. Thus it can save the trouble of service and help start the procedure execution as soon as possible when the employing company refuses to perform its duty and reverse the upside-down labor relations once again[10].

Acknowledgements

This paper is supported by the science & technology development fund item of Shanghai University of Engineering Science (Grant No. A-2500-10-01020).

References

Zhang W.S.(2009) .*On the Academic Analysis and Case Study of Foreign Group Action*. Beijing: Law Press, 2009.

10 Under the premise of the agreement of laborers, certain representatives can be appointed to sign in the verdict and the procedure execution can be started to avoid the unreasonable delay.

Professionalization of Employment: Perspectives on Improving the Quality of Employment

Ding Dajian
(School of Labor Relations and Human Resource, Renmin University of China)

Huang Xiaoyu
(China Institute for Employment Research, Researcher; School of Industrial and Labor Relations, Cornell University)

Abstract

This paper argues that the current labor market in China should not merely seek to expand its quantity of employment; instead it has reached a turning point where priority should be given to enhancing and improving the quality of employment. China's economic development is transforming from an outward extensive development model to an inward intensive one. Therefore, the employment development model in China must shift away from the previous one, which only focused on the number of employment, to the one which emphasizes on both quantity and quality of the employment. So, what is employment quality? Generally, a stable and safe job, a decent income, an adequate social security, as well as a harmonious labor relation constitute high employment qualities. This is the kind of employment laborers have expected. Such attractive conditions are for sure highly desired, and pursuing such high quality employments should be the common goal of the whole society.

Content

1. Introduction

A country focuses on different aspects of employment in different socio-economic development stages: sometimes it is more concerned with the quantity of employment and sometimes the quality, which reflects a pattern of employment development with respect to economic development. This paper starts with an analysis of the quantity and quality of China's employment, proceeds to explain the concept of professionalized employment, and then discusses how professionalized employment could contribute to better employment quality in China.

2. China's employment quantity – Has economic development driven employment growth?

For a long time, people in China have been mainly concerned with employment in quantitative terms such that the number of people employed and the unemployment rates are the highly sought-after statistics indicator. This is caused by China's long standing longstanding huge population and employment pressure as well as the economic reform and restructuring which intensify such pressure. The difficulties in employment have been demonstrated in great numbers, e.g. massive rural labor migration, laid-off workers in urban areas, and the increasing college graduate unemployment rate. Some scholars argue that China's labor supply is "massive" and "unlimited." Another widely accepted view is that since China started its economic reform, China's rapid economic growth has not brought about an increase in employment. Instead the economic development follows a pattern which is characterized by "jobless growth" or "low employment growth." The empirical evidence of such argument is that China's rapid GDP growth has been coupled with declining employment elasticity; therefore, "economic growth does not necessarily or automatically promote employment growth. In the 80s, China's economic growth rate was 9.3%, employment growth rate 3.0 %, employment elasticity 0.323%." (Hu, 2000)

During the 90s, the economic growth rate reached 10.4%, the employment growth rate was 1.1% and employment elasticity coefficient was 0.106, that is, each percentage point of economic growth could only drive 0.106 percent of employment growth. Compared to the number in the 80's, the labor-absorbing capacity dropped 2 / 3(Hu, 2000).Many foreign scholars also share this view on China's employment. For instance, the "2006 Asia-Pacific Human Development Report", issued by the United Nations Development Programme in June 2006, argues that behind East Asia's success story is the "jobless growth' challenges; young people and women are experiencing the 'no employment growth '. These judgments misled people to focus even more on the quantitative aspect of employment issues in China.

It should be noted that this view is theoretically incorrect: how can economic development be independent of the labor factor? The article "Does China have a jobless growth?" published by Wu Yaowu and Zhao Quan in 2006 analyzed the cause of this misconception comprehensively. It points out, "from the employment elasticity change in the secondary and tertiary industry, it is perceivable that 'jobless growth' in China since the economic reform has never occurred. Some scholars have neglected the job destruction caused by rapid industrialization and the transfer of labor departments and the adjustment of the labor market. Just from the poor 'total employment elasticity' phenomenon, they reached the 'jobless growth' conclusion." "China's economic growth has created a large number of non-agricultural employment opportunities, which not only absorbed surplus rural labor, but also the transferred labor from the primary industry to the secondary and tertiary industries, and gradually exhausted the 'reservoir' of surplus rural labor. The surplus labor force in urban areas – the informal sector, has also begun to decline." "The Chinese labor market has reached an equilibrium between demand and supply."

China's economic development absorbed a lot of labor; in terms of quantity it has greatly eased the employment pressure among the China's population. Some scholars conclude that for China's Employment: the "Lewis turning point has arrived" (Cai ,2006), i.e. our labor supply is no longer "unlimited". Another study on the rate of natural unemployment in China also shows that since 2000, "the structural unemployment and frictional unemployment have become the main parts of unemployment in China. The structural conflict is very prominent, and has become the biggest conflict in China's current unemployment problem." Zeng, 2006) i.e. the conflict in the total number of employment has been delegated to the second biggest conflict.

Although China's employment market suffered the impact of international financial crisis in 2008, under the influence of a strong economic stimulus by the government, economic recovery was fast. The Chinese economy maintained a relatively fast growth rate. As a result, the stagnant labor market from the fourth quarter of 2008 to the first quarter of 2009, saw "significant ease in employment pressure" (China's Employment Research Institute, 2010) during the first quarter of 2010. In some region, even a shortage of migration workers occurred. Excluding the short-term fluctuations in the employment market in China, in the broader view a gradual reduction in the supply of labor resources would accompany the economic growth, which will ease the longstanding employment pressure in China.

Should the term "the turning point" be employed to describe the current stage of economic development in China, perhaps the "turning point" could refer to a shift of focus from the quantitative aspect to the qualitative aspect of employment.

3. The current situation of China's employment quality

However, from the perspective of employment quality, the pressure faced by employment has not eased, but instead has exacerbated. We hear about frequent mining and industrial accidents, unpaid and below-minimum wages, the inadequacy and even the absence of welfare system, the growing non-regular employment which threatens to replace the regular ones, more and more dismissals of employees, and vice versa job-hopping by employees, unstable employment, the lack of standards and harmony in labor relations, the lack of responsibility and low efficiency at work, low quality of products and services, the lack of professional skills, professional ethics and the occurrences of professional corruption. Prevalence of these phenomena shows that the quality of employment in China is not optimistic.

In day-to-day conversation, high-quality employment usually refers to the "good job", meaning jobs that offer higher wages; better working condition, and which are respectable. However, this is only a partial understanding of the quality of employment. The definition of the quality of employment should include two main components: first, workers should be given their due by their employers and society, i.e. a stable job, decent income, safety, good benefits and working environment, comprehensive social security and harmonious labor relations, freedom of movement, of participation, of expression, equal employment opportunity (employment non-discrimination) and so on. This part is identical with the International Labour Organization (ILO)'s call for "decent work". Second, workers should contribute to their employers and society through work, namely: professional knowledge and skills, professional ethics and spirit, professional responsibility and job requirements, occupational standards and professional behavior, as well as the level of efficiency and the amount of output appropriate with their professional income.

The two parts in the definition of the quality of employment constitute employment inputs and outputs. Workers' due is what employers and society should pay; on the other hand, workers' contribution is what employers and society harvest. The so-called good quality of employment refers to the balance between high-quality employment input and output. It also represents the existence of a high-level harmony in labor relations.

At present, papers that evaluate and study the employment situation in China from the perspective of quality of employment are still rare. This paper is also lacking sufficient information and statistics to make an objective conclusion on the current quality of employment in China. Therefore, in this paper we discuss problems related to the two aspects of the quality of employment in China, through observation and by using general descriptive terms.

From the perspective of workers' due, that is, the basic content of "decent work" defined by the International Labour Organization (ILO), in recent years China has seen progress in the welfare system. In particular, the establishment of the rural welfare system and various insurance policies for migration workers, and the implementation of the Labor Contract Law and the Employment Promotion Law in 2008 improved of the quality of employment in China quite impressively. However, from the perspective of the requirement for "decent work", the quality of employment in China still has the following problems: low incomes, in particular for migration workers. Many employers use the minimum wage stipulated by the government as a reference, gives small or no increase of wage over long periods of time. Insurance plans are lacking, in particular for the vast migration workers; the bureaucracy in transferring insurance plans between different employments lead many migration workers to quit the insurance plans. Poor working conditions, compounded by the lack of safety measures, lead to frequent mining and industrial accidents. From 2000 to 2007, the million-ton level mines in China have an average death rate of 3.04, much higher than that of the United States (0.027) over the same period (Wei Gui-ling, 2009); employment is off standard, jobs become less secure, informal employment gradually replaces the formal ones, and even the college graduates are turning into migration workers.

Looking from the other perspective of quality of employment, i.e. workers' contribution, China's labor force has a low quality is an indisputable fact. The shortage of skills and professionals is a common phenomenon. Employees lack clear career orientations. The lack of professional spirit and ethics causes rampant corruption at workplace, and the lack of responsibility and efficiency leads to poor professional output.

Should the development of the Chinese economy be based on cheap labor only, that is, a large number of low-pay and hence low-quality employments, then China will never reach the XiaoKang (moderate prosperity) level, nor will there be any improvement on the quality of employment. From now on, improving employment should focus on improving the quality of employment. Government should bring society and media's attention to the quality of employment.

4. The only way to improve the quality of employment is professionalize employment

Improving the quality of employment is a broad topic. It includes observations and thinking that range macro to micro, from economic to social, legal, managerial, and ethical. It is hard to summarize all of them. However, a basic way of improving the quality of employment is to professionalize employment. We believe that the professionalization of employment is the necessary condition for improving the quality of employment.

What is professionalization?

Professions are the different categories of labor produced by the social division of labor.

The professionalization refers to the process of individualization of the characteristics of different professions, that is, the maturing of professions. The evaluation of professionalization usually has two aspects: 1. the amount of skills required by a profession, that is, skills that are based on the knowledge and experience acquired from training over a certain period of time. 2. The set of standards that a profession must follow. Specifically, the so-called "skills" include both vocational skills and managerial skills. Such skills could be derived from natural sciences, such as medicine, or they can also be derived from the humanities and social sciences, as long as these theories are widely accepted and applied, for example the law. The so-called "standards" include the professional conduct code, such as professional thinking, professional language, professional behavior etc., as well as professional conscience, such as professional ethics, professional attitude and so on. (Wilensky, 1964)

The professionalization of employment refers to the professionalization of the skills and the standards of professions, and applies to both the employees and the employers. Of employees it requires: knowledge and skills, work ethic and team spirit, professional responsibility, behavioral and operational standards, etc.; of employers it requires: the provision of professional reward, job security, vocational training, occupational benefits and social security, good working conditions, commensurate with their professions. Thus, the professionalization of employment is not just a requirement for workers and job-seekers, but also a requirement and constraint for employers. The professionalization of employment provides employers with professional and qualified workers, which in turn leads to high efficiency and output. For workers, it provides secure professional jobs and good professional welfare. Therefore, the professionalization of employment is a two-edged sword, simultaneously sharpening in the quality of employment from two aspects.

Among the many professions, certain professions are highly professionalized, such as lawyers, doctors, accountants, teachers, professional managers, etc. The degree of professionalization is low for some other professions, such as porters, cleaners, construction workers, baby-sitters, farmers, etc. Normally the latter type of work requires less knowledge and skills, the only requisite being physical strength. However, in a fully developed market economy, even these jobs that require relatively less skills will become professionalized. Speaking of the Filipino maids, everybody in world knows that they are very professional nannies; they are the model of professionalized nannies. There has been a well-known online article, "Disney turns cleaners to 'stars'". The article presents those professionalized cleaners in Disneyland who are dressed in beautiful attires and wheel shoes, who answer customers' questions with enthusiasm and always welcome customers with smiles. In the United States, Australia as well as many other developed countries, farmers are also a class of professionalized workers. They must take test to obtain professional certificates, which prove their professional knowledge and allow them to engage in their work.

The professionalization of employment can provide a clear career plan to workers. Workers entering the labor market could make human capital investment according to information provided by the society, such that they would be able to choose the profession which most reflects their own values, is compatible with their individuality, and allows them to realize their own potentials. "Professionalization has become a state of mind for the American society. Through professionalization, people can find their true selves, and their way of living, in harmony." (Li, 2006). It is clear that the professionalization of employment creates a win-win situation.

The professionalization of employment can also improve work efficiency, bring economic benefits, which have long been confirmed by a large number of studies on management, economics, and production practices. Just as Professor Zhang Weiying from Peking University put it, "professionalization is the core of enterprise development in China. "

5. Construction of China's professional employment system

A professionalized employment system is one that emphasizes the individuality of different professions and focuses on categorizing different professions. It can be described by the following diagram:

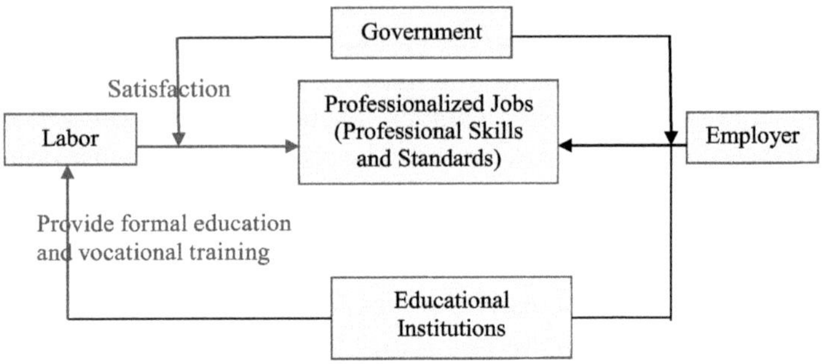

Figure 1: A professionalized employment system

Employment, in short terms, is the search and matching process between workers and employers. It is also the matching process between workers and professions. In a professional employment system, this matching process sets the professional skills and standards as the goal, and drives workers to undertake formal education and vocational training to meet these goals: skills and standards. Enterprises (employers) also recruit employees using skills and standards as their criteria. In this system, government plays the role of maintenance and reinforcing: maintaining the information on the skills and standards in professionalized professions, such that before workers and employees set to match themselves, workers could have a clear idea of the relation, characteristics, and requirement of different professions. This way, they can plan and foresee their career more clearly and easily, and know which professions are suitable for them. On the other hand, employers could also more easily know the kind of workers they need. Government's reinforcing role is manifested in creating laws and regulations related to employment, and ensuring that the employment system is functioning well. Educational and vocational institutions could provide education and training to workers, while promoting the further professionalization of employment by working with enterprise to innovate skills and standards. In this employment system, education, especially vocational education and training, plays a special role in promoting the professionalization of employment. Germany is a country with the one of the highest levels of professionalization; its vocational education system is precisely the main driving force behind the professionalization of employment.

At present, China's employment system is still far from being professional. China's employment system still focuses heavily on employee's identity (such as the household registration system), qualification (such as office position, title, education, etc.), and employer's reputation and industry.

Employee's identity: as a result of the household registration system, farmers who have entered the city and changed their occupations are forever entrenched in their household registration identity as farmers no matter whatever job they do. In many workplaces, the same department, and even the same role employs people of different household registration identities. They do the same job, but get different incomes, protected by different insurance plans, and enjoying different benefits.

Employee's qualification: regarding a job position, people are usually more attracted to its executive-level and professional title than its professional nature (nature of work). In general, within the same company or agency, a director could accept the role in the educational administration department, or the security department, or the capital construction department, as long as he or she can keep the director title.

Employer's reputation and industry: college graduates are most concerned with the company and the industry they go into, much more than they are concerned with the specific nature of the work.

Since the Chinese economy started its reform, the labor and human resource system in China has experienced the following reform: workers for the nation – employees for companies – people of society. Now it's time for us to turn into professionalized individuals. A domestic survey shows that 90% of the participating companies consider the biggest constraint on the development of the company to be the lack of high-quality professional staff. Therefore, improving the professionalization of employment in China is becoming a matter of urgency. However, building a system of professionalized employment is a long-term project that requires input and cooperation from government, society, enterprises and individuals. We have confidence that the professionalization of employment is an inevitable trend of social development. It will necessarily bring a win-win situation to everyone in society, and lay the cornerstone for a harmonious society.

6. Conclusion

This study allows one to conclude that the economic development doesn't follows the pattern which is characterized by "jobless growth" or "low employment growth" , an obvious conclusion if we take into account the job destruction caused by rapid industrialization and the transfer of labor departments and the adjustment of the labor market. Instead China's economic development absorbed a lot of labor; As a result, a shift of focus from the quantitative aspect to the qualitative aspect of employment arrived. However, the quality of employment in China is not optimistic. As we have analyzed, the only way to improve the quality of employment is professionalize employment.

References

Cai, F. (2005). Labor Shortage: Should we take precautions?. China Demographic Science.5, 11-16.

Chen, Y. & Li, S.L (2007). The German Labor Market "Professionalization" Trend and Impacts on Vocational Education. Vocational and Technical Education, 28, 85-87.

China's Employment Research Institute.(2010).China Quarterly Analysis Of The Employment Report.

Hu, A.G. (2000). China Must Implement The Development Strategy Of Giving Priority To Employment. Decision-Making Advice, 12, 5-6.

Li, X.G.(2006). Professionalism: Making the Lives Peaceful. People's Education, 22 , 5

Wei, G..(2009). Comparative Analysis and Warnings of Sino-U.S. Mine Disaster. Contemporary Economics, 1, 50-52

Wilensky, H. L. (1964).The Professionalization of Everyone?. The American Journal of Sociology, 70, 137-158.

Wu,Y. W & Zhao, Q. (2006).Does China Have "Zero Job Growth?" China Opening Heralde, 6, 57-62.

Zeng, X.Q&Yu, Y. (2006). Measurement of China's Natural Rate of Unemployment. Market-Oriented Measurement of Unemployment in China, Renmin University Press.

The effect of social capital and its localization on the nonfarm employment of rural labor: an empirical study in the western border areas of China[1]

Ying Chen[2], Xianming Yang and Yanping Zhou
(School of Development Studies, Yunnan University, China 650091)

Abstract

The social capital, as a non-market power, plays an important role for rural labors in making choices of employment in China western border areas, where employment information is incomplete. The study, using CGSS2006 survey data, discussed the effects of social capital and its structure on non-farm employment of rural labor force, and analyzed the trend of localization of social capital in the western border areas in China. It was found that social capital can facilitate rural labors to obtain nonfarm jobs; however, its role was constrained by the limited availability of social capital, unbalanced distribution of labor between farm and nonfarm production, and the localization of social capital.

Content

1. Introduction

At present, the main sources contributing rural labors' income growth are mainly nonfarm employment and increased production productivity in China, especially the former. Working in urban areas is the mainly source of farmers' nonfarm income. Since 1990s, tens of millions of rural labors have flowed rural areas to

1 The research was carried out with the financial support from the Social Science Fund of China Education Ministry (09XJC8400002)and the third phase of research grant of the "211" program of Yunnan University.

2 Corresponding author: Ying Chen, meagiezhucy@gmail.com

urban areas. According to the 1% sample of population survey in 2005, labor force mainly flowed from provinces in central and western China to coastal areas, especially Guangdong, Shanghai, Zhejiang and Beijing. As a result of labor mobility, the negative impacts of the outflow of human capital on the development of local economies are widely concerned. On one hand, the contribution of take-home income by farmer workers to the development of local economies in western china is limited because people's willingness to invest is low because of unfavorable investment climate (Du etc., 2010). On the other hand, in western border areas, apart from Guangxi that is the main province of labor outflow, other provinces including Yunnan, Inner Mongolia, and Gansu have a low mobility of labor outflows. In these areas, rural labor's income is mainly from agriculture. It is difficult to increase farmer's earnings by improving agriculture productivity in western border areas of china where rural labor quality and agriculture productivity are low. Thus, in the context of the limit external growth and poor internal pull, the employment of rural labors in western frontier is characterized by high proportion of local employment, low quality of labor force, high rate of returning migrant farmers, and weak willingness of working outside. Therefore, it is necessary to analyze the nonfarm employment choice of rural labor so as to solve the problem of low income circulation of rural labor force in western cross-border areas of China.

It is generally considered that individual and family characteristics are the chief factors affecting rural labors' employment choices. However, as is revealed in theory and reality, individual or family's social network contribute to employment by providing useful social resources to labor forces, and reducing cost in searching jobs. In the rural areas of China, the coverage of the family-centered social network is small, and the availability of employment information is limited. As a consequence, it is common for farmers to engage in agricultural production only in these areas. Therefore, social capital is usually confined in the local areas. What is the impact of social capital on individual or family's nonfarm employment decision in western border areas in China? Whether the feature of localization of social capital in the western border areas will restrict the decision of nonfarm employment?

2. The social capital and nonfarm employment decision: literature review

Once a rural labor decides to migrate for nonfarm employment, the dominant motive is the expected net earnings potentially from nonfarm job. In addition, labor force's individual characteristics and home characteristics such as family structure, age and gender, education are the important factors that affect non-farm employment decision of rural labor force (Zhao, 1999a,1999b).These results are base on the premise of complete information of occupation vacancy, so the scarce information in reality restricts the nonfarm employment decision. There are two channels to get the employment information for labor force usually, one is the public labor demand information issued in labor market, and the other is the private vacancy information passed among labor forces. The latter plays a significant role in the rural border areas in western China where absence of public employment information. The effective transfer of the personal information of vacancy among the different social groups helps to reduce the flow costs which caused by the insufficiency of public employment information.

Modern economics typically assumes that individual is not directly influenced by the action of others. Gary S. Becker (2000) thought that the social influences from others on behavior are common and even pervasive, which is called "social capital". Putnam et al. (1993) have defined social capital as the network, trust and norms which it can improve economic efficiency through coordinating behavior among different individuals. Zhang (2003) has proposed that the social network is one of the significant factors that promote nonfarm employment in rural areas. Getting the help from friends or family during the process of searching job will significantly increase the probability of nonfarm employment of rural labor force (Zhang, 2003). China's rural labor market has two important features (Zhang, 2003). First, there are very few public venues providing farmers with information about job and business opportunities. Second, there is a large surplus of rural workers in rural China and hence nonfarm employers are extremely selective. When work becomes scarce, social groups may provide jobs to their own members firstly (Banerjee, 1983). The rural people have more tightly networks of family members than urban people. The migrant workers who leave their hometowns become more depending on the social networks of kinship, especially native village social network (Li, 1996).

For less developed regions, especially for the rural labor force of western border areas in China, when they make their employment decision, tight relationship among family members which resulted from the diversity-orderly structure of Chinese rural society (Fei, 2007) has important influence. Once left hometown, the social capital which invested in original village relations will be lost, causing high depreciation rate of social capital. Therefore, on the one hand, social capital as an alternative channel of employment information will directly impact on the nonfarm employment decision of rural labor force through passing personal employment information, on the other hand, the diversity-orderly structure of rural society has formed the social network of extension of family-centered, in which the more tightly the relationship among local social networks is, the greater personal earning loss which caused by the depreciation of social capital while leave the hometown to nonfarm employment. So, staying in the hometown can reduce the risk and uncertainty of the nonfarm employment to other places, which means that the role of localization of social capital is obvious. As described by David (2008a), the localness of social capital may be a bottleneck impeding labor mobility and employment.

As the summary of literature mentioned above shows that the effects of social capital on rural labor force employment in China become more and more important. Family-level social capital of rural areas has significant influence on economic activities of individual family member. The characteristic that regarded family as decision-making unit in rural areas will bring differences between personal rural labor force and family nonfarm employment decisions. The first question will be answered in this paper is the effect of social capital and its contents on rural labor force employment decision at individual-level and family-level. And does the result is the same as the existing research? In addition, investing in local social network will reduce the risk and uncertainty of economic activity rural labor faced. The stability of the local social network will increase opportunity cost and reduce the possibility of rural labor force engaged in nonfarm employment. The second question will be answered in this paper is the extent of social capital localization and its effects in China western border areas.

3. Data and descriptive statistics

The study is based on data from the China Social Survey database (CGSS), which contains questionnaire-based survey data from a sample of 496 household from 49 villages in Yunnan, Guangxi, Gansu and Inner Mongolia. The data was collected by Chinese People's University in 2003, 2005 and 2006. In the study, the data of year 2006 was used to construct econometric model, while the data of Year 2005 was used as instrument variables to deal with the problem of endogenity.

It is necessary to make clear the quantitative methods of measuring social capital. Durkin (2000) reviewed the two proxy methods of measurement and discussed their deficiencies. One of the most commonly methods is that social capital is represented by the number of the memberships of the group or organization (Putnam, 1993, Glaeser et. al., 2002). The main disadvantage of this approach is that could not reflect the extent of the change of the group or organization. Another method is using the questionnaire survey to obtain the extent of trust. Despite of their disadvantages, both methods have been widely used. If one would like to identify how people get social resources through their social relations, it is important to find the dominant social networks. Durkin (2000) concluded that measures of trust and group memberships do not explain variation in accessing to social resources. But measures of the frequency of contact with family members and friends do explain variation in accessing to social resources. Thus, we can test whether measure of social capital can help explain rural labors' choice of nonfarm employment in China western border areas. The CGSS survey did not consider the two common used proxies of social capital, but discern the frequency of respondent's family interaction with different social relations, which is convenient to this study.

Based on questionnaire design and the objective of the study, we would not further explain the role of social trust and its structure in social capital. According to the CGSS questionnaire's contents, this paper uses the following proxy variables to measure social networks or social capital. First, we use family size and frequency of social interaction as proxies for social network. There is a questions in the questionnaire stating "how frequent does your family contact with the following personnel: … ". There are four options for each categorical personnel: never, seldom, sometimes and often. This proxy variable can identify the local social capital which is mainly formed by blood relationship and the professional social capital by organization relationship.

China's social network has the feature of "diversity-orderly structure", as Fei Xiaotong described. This paper tries to construct an overall social network evaluation indicator. According to KMO and Bartlett's test results, this paper use principal component method to construct the evaluating indicator of the stock of rural social network in western border areas by clustering respondent's family social interaction with these twelve personnel, to acquire the extent of interaction between family and social of interviewee family, treating family size and frequency of social interaction as interaction terms at the same time.

Furthermore, the "diversity-orderly structure" was embedded in the whole social structure and formed different levels of social capital. So, this paper classifies and groups together social capital in terms of frequency of social interaction, so as to reflect the influence of social capital's structure: (1) city residents, friends and relatives in city; (2) head of village and township head; (3) leadership and management of state-owned enterprises; (4) private business owners and managers as the peer group. Eight different types of social capital were identified, including SC1 the frequency of interaction with native village people, SC2 the frequency of interaction with the other local village people, SC3 the frequency of interaction with city residents, SC4 the frequency of interaction with village head, SC5 the frequency of interaction with the town and county magistrate, SC6 the frequency of interaction with professional personnel, SC7 the frequency of interaction with the leadership and management of state-owned or collective enterprises, and SC8 the frequency of interaction with owners and managers of private business. Therefore, selecting the proxy of two types of social capital respectively indicate the overall level of social network and the structure of social network.

Besides identifying the proxies of social capital, two kinds of control variables were also included. One is the individual and family characteristics of the rural labor force, including sex, age, education, per capita farmland area and the proportion of household nonfarm earnings etc. The other is the characteristics of villages in the sample areas, the majority of the rural labors are living in the mountainous or semi-mountainous areas, where the transmission of information is far lagged behind urban areas. Thus, the control variables include "are you living in mountainous area" and the distance from the village to the town.

Table 1 Descriptive statistics of factors affecting rural labor forces' employment decision

	Nonfarm employment		Farm production	
Observation of interviewee	149		347	
Observation of family	293		203	
Variables	Mean	S.e.	Mean	S.e.
Sctotal: The overall level of social capital	1.76	0.36	1.57	0.29
Sc1	0.95	0.14	0.98	0.10
Sc2	0.71	0.25	0.65	0.26
Sc3	0.50	0.27	0.36	0.24
Sc4	0.59	0.28	0.53	0.29
Sc5	0.29	0.23	0.21	0.21
Sc6	0.22	0.30	0.09	0.19
Sc7	0.16	0.30	0.05	0.14
Sc8 [t]	0.17	0.28	0.04	0.11
Household: whether the extended family	0.57	0.50	0.50	0.50

By comparing the data of social capital contents, it is obvious that the overall levels of social capital of those who engaged in nonfarm employment basically equal those who engaged in agricultural production. The social networks of those who engaged in agricultural production is chiefly with local people, while that of those who engaged in nonfarm production has more organization- and team-based social relationships. In general, social interactions are more frequent for family-centered network.

4. Model and Results

4.1 Model specification

This paper estimates rural labor force employment choice in Chinese border areas by referring to David (2008b) and Zhao (2003). We chiefly analysis the effect of the social capital on rural labor force's nonfarm employment choice in Chinese border areas and estimates the degree of the localization of social capital.

According to the CGSS, the employment status of individual or family is specified into two types, namely agricultural production and nonfarm employment. Accordingly, the model is specified as follows:

$$\Pr(employment = 1) = \Phi\,(\alpha + \beta_i sctotal + \beta_i X + \varepsilon) \qquad (1)$$

$$\Pr(employment = 1) = \Phi\,(\alpha + \beta_i sc_k + \beta_i X + \varepsilon) \quad k = 1 \ldots 8 \qquad (2)$$

Equation (1) and equation (2) are used to assess the effect of social capital and its structure on rural labors' nonfarm employment decisions, respectively. On the left side of equation (1) and (2), it is the probability of nonfarm employment of rural labors. For the independent variables, in equation (1) sctotal is used to measure the overall level of social capital; in equation (2) SCk is on behalf of eight different social capitals. X is the exogenous control variables, including individual characteristics, family characteristics and village type.

In addition, according to Quentin (2008), the more the labor's local social capital is, the more he/she loses as he/she leaves the area he/she was born or lived. In the short-run, social capital is predetermined to a large extent, but in the long run, it might be that individuals forecast future mobility episodes and so, endogenously determine their level of social capital. In this paper, the mobility variable take value 0 if the individual hasn't always lived in the same place and engaged in farming work without changing, and 1 in the opposite case. It means that the longer labors lived in the same place and engaged in farming work for rural labor force, the greater localness of social capital and the lower possibility of nonfarm employment. Therefore its specification is:

$$Social\ capital = \alpha + \beta_i liveplace + \beta_2 X + \varepsilon \qquad (3)$$

Where the Sc represents family social capital, liveplace represents the variable of whether individual has always lived in the same place and engaged in farming work. X represents other control variables including individual, family and village characteristics.

4.2 Empirical results

4.2.1 The effect of overall social capital on employment decision of rural labor force

To simplify the presentation, we only report the estimate results of social capital, family size and the interaction of social capital with family sizes from model (1). Judging by the value of LR and Pseudo-R2 reported in each table and those for the strict and non-strict model, the equation fits the data well. The estimates and test statistics for social capital are presented in table 2 and table 3, with the results of the restricted and non-strict model presented in the column.

The results show that the stock of social capital has a significant impact on nonfarm employment choice of rural labor force in Table2 (Model2b). Other things being equal, the probability of nonfarm employment choice at individual-level is 15.9% (not reported in Table 2). The result is similar to other research. Looking at the marginal effects of family size, one sees that given other things, the likelihood that the rural labor force in a large family participates in nonfarm employment is 37.7% higher than that for the rural labor in a core family. We next turn to the interaction of family size and we note that compared to that core family, the probability of rural labor force nonfarm employment for large family is significantly higher; the margin effect is 26.1%. In addition, the results of individual, family and village characteristics are similar to the other research.

Table 2 Probit model results on the effects of social capital on rural labors' nonfarm employment choice at individual-level

(Dependant variable: nonfarm employment = 1, farm production and other = 0)

Independent variables	Model 1		Model 2	
	Model 1a	Model 1b	Model 2a	Model 2b
Overall social capital	1.000***	0.550*	0.967***	0.509*
	(0.230)	(0.315)	(0.230)	(0.305)
Family size		-1.281*		-1.236*
		(0.759)		(0.728)

Family size & social capital		0.840*		0.836**
		(0.449)		(0.422)
Region dummy	No		Yes	
Observations	494	494	494	494
Log Lik	-234.6	-232.2	-233.4	-230.9
LR	90.97	84.26	141.3	146.4
Pseudo_R2	0.229	0.236	0.232	0.241

Note: (1) Robust standard errors in parentheses, *** p<0.01, ** p<0.05, * p<0.1; (2) As additional explicative variables, the above regressions include sex, years of education, age, marital status, house land, the distance from village to town, and village type.

There is an endogenous problem in the nonfarm employment decision regression, which is a result of mutual influence between social capital and nonfarm employment choice besides omitted variables. Introducing instrument variable to a two-stage regression is the common way to deal with endogenous problem. The instrument variables for social capital in the employment regression used in previous research include the past social capital value (Zhao, 2000), the average value of other family social trust except the respondent's family social trust value in the community (Gao, 2010), the current or past community social capital average level (Belot and Ermish, 2006; David et. al., 2008b). These four instrument variables are estimated respectively in this paper. But unfortunately, the estimate in this paper shows that they are weak instrument variable. It's necessary to find new way to treatment endogenous problem. Generally, the ways to solve this problem are to find new instrument variables or search the relations between variable on the base of theory.

We assessed the effect of social capital on family-level nonfarm employment choice and the effect of social network structure on individual-level and family-level nonfarm employment choice in this part. Further, the localization of social capital is to be discussed in the follows.

At present, we turn to examine the effect of social capital on family-level nonfarm employment. First, according to the CGSS survey, the social capital represents whole family social networks. Table2 estimate the effect of social capital on nonfarm employment choice at individual-level. In most cases, especially in China rural areas, the individual employment decision also depends on the other family members. And, it will be the important reason causing social capital endogenous problem. In Chinese western border areas, this feature will be prominent because it is impossible to separate rural production and consumption.

Will the effect of social capital on nonfarm employment be significantly positive while family joint labor supply decision is considered in the model? Table3 show that regional difference hasn't significant influence on the results between Model3 and Model4, but it improves the goodness of fit. Although the social capital impacts rural labor forces nonfarm employment at family-level significantly, these effects are not significant after introducing family size and it's interaction with social capital.

Table 3 Probit model results on the effects of social capital on rural labors' nonfarm employment choice at family-level

(Dependant variable: nonfarm employment = 1, farm production and other = 0)

Variables	Model 3		Model 4	
	Model 3a	Model 3b	Model 4a	Model 4b
Overall social capital	0.538***	0.395	0.613***	0.453
	(0.194)	(0.279)	(0.201)	(0.286)
Family size		0.181		0.131
		(0.646)		(0.653)
Family size & social capital		0.287		0.280
		(0.388)		(0.393)
Region dummy	No		Yes	
Observations	495	495	495	495
Log Lik	-304.2	-292.2	-299.1	-289.9
LR	47.71	73.05	60.12	79.81
Pseudo_R2	0.0920	0.128	0.107	0.135

Note: (1) Robust standard errors in parentheses, *** p<0.01, ** p<0.05, * p<0.1; (2) As additional explicative variables, the above regressions include sex ratio of family, average education years of family members, the mean age of family members, house land, the distance from village to town and other.

By comparing the results in Table3 and Table4, we find that the more social capital that family endowed, the greater social resources accessed to, the easier to access to nonfarm employment opportunity of rural labor force in the western areas. We also find that the collective labor supply of family decreases the effect of social capital on nonfarm employment of rural labor force. In a word, the accumulation of social capital will improve the opportunity of nonfarm employment in western China, when other conditions remain unchanged, while its effects will be not significant for the collective labor supply of family.

4.2.2 The effect of social capital contents on rural labors' nonfarm employment choice of force in western border areas of China

The social capital contents are not included in the above analysis. In general, the closer the interaction is with friends or organization, the more possibility of nonfarm employment for rural labor forces. If we want to know the influence of specific social network on the nonfarm employment choice at individual-level and family-level, then we would presumably want to show that the variables are related to most types of social interaction access to social resources.

The estimates in Table4 show that SC1, SC4, SC5, SC7 have negative impacts on the probability of nonfarm employment of rural labor force in western China; while SC2, SC3, Sc6, SC8 have positive impacts on the probability of nonfarm employment of rural labor force in western border areas of China.

From the estimates, we find that there are two kinds of social networks that have opposite impacts. One is composed of native village people—magistrate of village, town or county—managers of state owned enterprises; another is composed of other local village people—city residents—managers and owners of private enterprises. These two kind social networks are resulted from the diversity orderly characteristics of China, which is the relationship expanded from household to interact with other people. It is not only the way that individual and family contact with other people, but also the way that people is willing to provide resources to other with whom they have a relationship if they could reasonably expect that they will be compensated in the future (Fei, 2007). So, the relationship that can't compensate in the future will not provide enough employment information to access to job opportunity for rural labor force of western China. In addition, according to the discussion of Bian (2001), the effect of social network on occupation mobility does not weaken but strengthen in the transition economy of China. And especially the kinship relations have always kept its advantage.

The marginal effects in Table 4 show that the frequency of interaction with native village people decreases significantly one's probability of nonfarm employment by 58%, and the frequency of interaction with citizens such as relative or friends lived in city increase significantly one's probability of nonfarm employment by 37.7%; and the frequency of interaction with the manager or owner of private enterprises increases significant one's probability of nonfarm employment by 44.7%. In addition, the household characteristics is found to be statistically significant, one more laborer in the household increase one's probability of nonfarm employment of rural labor force of western China by 2.91%.

Table 4 Probit model results on the effects of social capital contents on rural labors' nonfarm employment choice at individual-level

(Dependant variable: nonfarm employment = 1, farm production and other = 0)

VARIABLES	Coefficient	S.e.	Marginal effects
Sc1	-1.797***	(0.651)	-0.580
Sc2	0.546	(0.343)	0.176
Sc3	1.168***	(0.375)	0.377
Sc4	-0.191	(0.329)	-0.0618
Sc5	-0.361	(0.470)	-0.117
Sc6	0.163	(0.273)	0.0526
Sc7	-0.0646	(0.510)	-0.0209
Sc8	1.386***	(0.499)	0.447
Family size	0.0901**	(0.0455)	0.0291
Region dummy	Yes		
Observations	424		
Log Lik	-189.8		
LR	102.8		
Pseudo_R2	0.285		

Note (1) Robust standard errors in parentheses, *** p<0.01, ** p<0.05, * p<0.1; (2) As additional explicative variables, the above regressions include sex, years of education, age, marital status, house land, the distance from village to town, and village type.

Similarly, we also estimate the effect of the variety of social capital on nonfarm employment choice. Table 5 shows that the effect of social network on nonfarm employment of rural labor forces at family-level is different with those at individual-level. Without controlling regional difference, the frequency of interaction with other local village people (Sc2) and managers or owners of private enterprises (Sc8) has significant positive impacts on nonfarm employment choice at family-level. From the marginal effects estimates, evaluated at the mean level, increasing the proportion of Sc2 and Sc8 by one increased the probability of nonfarm employment of rural labor force by 31.1% and 54.1%, respectively. It means that if those household devote more time to these two relationships, more information and higher possibility of nonfarm employment accessed without considering regional differences. But after controlling regional differences, there is only one variable that the frequency of interaction with magistrate of native village has significant impacts on nonfarm employment choice of rural labor force of western China, and increasing one percent point of the interaction frequency would decreases the possibility of nonfarm employment of rural labor force 22.9%. It means that the closer to interact with magistrate of native village, the more benefits of social and economic activity are obtained, the larger depreciate and risk of nonfarm employment decision, and the less possibility to choose nonfarm employment for the family's member. These two different results tell us that the region diversity make the effect of social capital ambiguous. In addition, the household characteristics is found to be statistically significant, one more laborer in the household increase one's probability of nonfarm employment of rural labor force of western China by 6.02%.

Table 5 Probit model results on the effects of social capital contents on rural labors' nonfarm employment choice at family-level

(Dependant variable: nonfarm employment = 1, farm production and other = 0)

Variables	Model 6a			Model 6b		
	Coefficient	S.e.	Marginal effects	Coefficient	S.e.	Marginal effects
Sc1	-0.473	(0.572)	-0.177	-0.686	(0.560)	-0.232
Sc2	0.638**	(0.311)	0.238	0.282	(0.295)	0.0954
Sc3	-0.115	(0.374)	-0.0429	-0.678*	(0.371)	-0.229
Sc4	-0.259	(0.322)	-0.0967	0.434	(0.285)	0.147
Sc5	0.168	(0.465)	0.0627	-0.232	(0.443)	-0.0786
Sc6	-0.150	(0.294)	-0.0560	-0.0769	(0.152)	-0.0260
Sc7	0.00743	(0.527)	0.00278	0.303	(0.508)	0.102
Sc8	1.441***	(0.541)	0.539	-0.615	(0.499)	-0.208
Family size	0.241***	(0.0570)	0.0900	0.178***	(0.0439)	0.0602
Region dummy	No			Yes		
Observations	425			425		
Log Lik	-219.8			-229.8		
LR	109.1			62.61		
Pseudo_R2	0.229			0.125		

Note: (1) Robust standard errors in parentheses, *** p<0.01, ** p<0.05, * p<0.1, (2) As additional explicative variables, the above regressions include sex ratio of family, average education years of family members, the mean age of family members, house land, the distance from village to town and other .

By comparing the results of Table 4 and Table 5, we find that: (1) the social network has significant different influence on the nonfarm employment for different labor supply agents; the close and stable kinship decreases the possibility of nonfarm employment significantly for the individual rural labor force, but the effect of social networks on nonfarm employment become unstable for the whole family; (2) due to opposite two power in the social networks, the effect of social network structure on nonfarm employment of rural labor force is uncertain.

4.2.3 The long-term accumulation of social capital in the western border areas of China

We will analyze the overall level of social capital and the long-term of its structure, and select equation (3) of the models to estimate, the results shown in table 6.

As illustrated in Table 6, the column of (1) indicates that the nonfarm employment of the rural labor mobility depreciate the social capital in the past, which means the social capital depreciate on the whole. The column of (2) ~ (9) indicates that the nonfarm employment of the rural labor mobility does not cause the depreciation of the social capital connected by relationships but the effect is not significant, and contributes to the depreciation of the social capital that family endowed such as the relations of friends and organization members; and also contributes to the depreciation of the social capital which interact with city residents, township head, professional personnel and managers of state-owned or collective enterprises. Generally speaking, the degree of the localization of social capital of family social capital is high in the western border rural areas, in other words, that the influence of the individual choice in local or foreign nonfarm employment on its social capital connected by relationships is small and not significant, while can weaken the effect of the social network of friendship or organization relationship. It means that the tendency of localization of social capital is increasing in terms of the social capital's accumulation in the western border areas of China in the long-term. It is the structure of the social network in transformation that makes the role of social capital has weaken possibility of nonfarm employment of labor force.

4.3 Summary

The main regression result indicates that the overall accumulation of social capital in the western border areas contributes to the nonfarm employment decision. However, the role of the structure of social capital is not obvious. The main performances are: (1) in the short term, the influence of the family-owned stock of social capital on the nonfarm employment of rural labor force is significant, while the influence on the nonfarm employment of family members is not significant. (2) In the short term, if the kinship in the structure of family-owned social network is closer and more stable will be going against the nonfarm employment of the rural labor force, otherwise will contribute to the nonfarm employment of the

Table 6 The OLS estimation results of social capital in western border areas in long-term

	(1)	(2)	(3)	(4)	(5)	(6)	(7)	(8)	(9)
Variables	Social capital	Sc1	Sc2	Sc3	Sc4	Sc5	Sc6	Sc7	Sc8
Not long lived in this village	-0.0907***	0.00678	0.0128	-0.0882***	-0.0351	-0.0602***	-0.108***	-0.0772**	-0.0344
	(0.0344)	(0.0154)	(0.0282)	(0.0275)	(0.0304)	(0.0228)	(0.0412)	(0.0302)	(0.0239)
Region dummy	Yes								
Observations	494	494	493	472	491	481	465	432	434
R-squared	0.150	0.064	0.066	0.182	0.076	0.151	0.137	0.102	0.120
F	9.032	2.410	3.379	9.327	3.674	10.05	6.281	4.158	4.064
R2	0.150	0.0642	0.0655	0.182	0.0761	0.151	0.137	0.102	0.120

Note: (1) Robust standard errors in parentheses, *** p<0.01, ** p<0.05, * p<0.1; (2) As additional explicative variables, the above regressions include sex ratio of family, average education years of family members, the mean age of family members, house land, the distance from village to town and other.

rural labor force. The role of the social network under the joint decision of the family becomes unstable due to the regional differences. (3) In the long term, the feature of localization of social network is distinctly in the western border areas of China. If the tendency of the localization of social capital decreases, the social networks should play an active promoting role to the nonfarm employment decision for rural labor force and their families.

5. Conclusions

Using data from the CGSS database, this paper assesses the factors affecting rural labors' decision on nonfarm employment in the western border areas. It is found that the social capital plays a positive role in affecting rural labors' decision on nonfarm employment in the border areas, where employment information is incomplete. After controlling the family size, the role of the social capital in the nonfarm employment decision of family members becomes insignificant due to the family joint labor supply decisions. Rather, the blood-based social network and the social network of friends and organizations interact with each other. The interaction will change the effect of social capital on rural labors' decision on nonfarm employment. The degree of the localization of social capital has negative impact on rural labors' decision on nonfarm employment in the western border areas. Therefore, with the influence of the localization of social capital and the diversity-orderly structure of rural society, the role of social capital in affecting rural labors' decision on nonfarm employment is not significant in the western border areas.

From the results, we got a deeper understanding of the role of social capital in affection rural labor's decision on nonfarm employment. First, in absence of effective public and private employment information, the role of social capital in overcoming the information asymmetry of employment in the western border rural areas is limited. Second, integrating the interaction of the personal labor supply decision and family joint labor supply decision, the available social resources that social network supplies to family members are limited in the western border rural areas. Third, the feature of the localization of social capital exists as a result of the diversity-orderly structure in the western border rural areas. As a consequence, the available information of employment and social resources are locally confined.

According to existing literatures, the expansion of social network can promote labor force to migrate. However, in rural China, based on the social trust, created through long-term interactions between people, reduces the uncertainty of living and working in the community faced by the labor forces, and increases the opportunity cost of labor mobility, and consequently impedes the outflow of labor (Gao, 2010). Nonfarm employment of rural labor has been proven to be an effective instrument for poverty alleviation. However, this paper deems that in the western border rural areas, if the limited family labor forces must be balanced between the agricultural production and nonfarm employment, the social network lacks of adequate and effective employment information, and the localness of social capital is the bottleneck of nonfarm employment, the attempt to change the exogenous factors such as the regulation of the urban labor market may only increase the share of inequality and informal economy, other than increase the nonfarm employment of rural labor force in these areas, which can effectively relieve the poverty in these areas. Therefore, it is concluded that improvement in agricultural productivity can increase the distribution efficiency of the rural labor force, strengthen the intermediary services of labor market in rural areas, overcome the information asymmetry, intensify the process of marketization, weaken the localization of social capital, and eventually prevent the nonfarm employment of rural labor from being trapped in a low level equilibrium under the in the context of urban-rural split in the western border rural areas.

References

Banerjee, B.(1983). The role of the informal sector in the migration process: A test of probabilistic migration models and labor market segmentation for India. Oxford Economic Papers, 35: 417-18.

Belot, M., &John, E.(2006). Friendship Ties and Geographical Mobility:Evidence from the BHPS, Dicussion paper No. 2209, http://www.iza.org/

Becker .G. S., & Murphy. (2000). Social Economics: Markets Behavior in a Social Environment, Cambridge, MA: The Belknap Press of Harvard University Press

Bian. Y.J. ,&Zhang. W.H.(2001). Economic Systems, Social Networks and Occupational Mobility, Social Sciences in China, 2,77-89

David .Q, & Janiak ,A. &Wasmer, E. (2008a) .Local Social Capital and Geographical Mobility: A Theory, Discussion Paper No.3668, http://www.iza.org/

David .Q, & Janiak ,A. &Wasmer, E. (2008b).Local Social Capital and Geographical Mobility: Some Empirical and a Conjecture on the Nature of European Unemployment, Discussio Paper No. 3669, http://www.iza.org/

Fei, X.T.(2007), Rural China, Jiangsu Literature Press, April 2007

Gao, H., &Lu,M. (2010). The Impact of Social Trust on Labor Migration-the Role of Rural Social Capital and Regional Differences, Chinese Rural Economy, 3,12-34

Glaeser, E. L., &David, L. and Bruce .S (2002).An Economic Approach to Social Capital, The Economic Journal, 112, 437-458.

John T. D., &Jr. ,(2000). Measure Social Capital and its Eocnomic Impact, Working Papers, No.0102, Harris School of Public Policy Studies, University of Chicago.

Knight, J., & Yueh ,L. (2002). The Role of Social Capital in the Labor Market in China, Oxford University, Department of Economics Discussion Paper.

Li, P.L, (1996), Social network and status of Migrant workers in China, Sociological Research, 4, 42-52

Lu M, &Zhang S.,(2008). The Effects of Labor Migration on Public Trust in Rural China, World Economic Papers, 4,77-87

Putnam, R.D., & Leonardi .R. & Nanetti..R.Y. (1993). Making Democracy Work. Civic Traditions in Modern Italy, Princeton University Press.

Wooldridge, J.M.,(2003). Introductory Econometrics, A Modern Approach, South-Western, Thomson Learning.

Zhang, S., &Lu, M., &Zhang Y. (2007)Does the Strength of Social Capital on Poverty Reduction Fall or Rise during Marketization?—Evidence from Rural China, China Economic Quarterly,Vol.6, No.2,539-560

Zhao.Y.H.(1999a). Leaving the Countryside: Rural-to-Urban Migration Decision in China.American Economic Review, 89(2), 281-286

Zhao.Y.Hi.(1999b). Labor Migration and Eaming Differenees: The Case of Rural China.Economic Development and Culture Change, 47(4), 767-782

Zhao.Y.H.(2003).The Role of Migrant Networks in Labor Migration: The Case of China, Contemporary Economic Policy, 21(4):500-511, 2003

Zhang,X.B., & Li.G. (2003). Does Guanxi Matter to Nonfarm Employment? Journal of Comparative Economics, 31(2): 315–331.

The Analysis of Channels and Possibility On Wage Data Collection in China

Weimin Zhang
(School of Economics, Central University of Finance and Economics)

Dinghong Yi
(School of Labor Relations and Human Resource, Renmin University of China)

Abstract

The paper investigated the channels and possibility on wage data collection in China. There are many channels to collect wage information in current China. According to the classification of agents to collect wage information, there are government, consulting firms, relevant websites, academia, trade associations, magazines and newspapers. The most important agents among them are government, consulting firms and relevant websites. The wage information can't satisfy the demand of China's social and economic developments as a whole. The paper also reviews the availability of China's wage information and their quality, and directs the ways of the future improvement of wage information collection in China.

With the gradual normalization of the labor market in China, the wage, as the signal of labor cost, is playing an increasingly important part in the operation of the entire market. The government needs the wage data to formulate macroeconomic policy, and then adjust the labor supply and demand, protect the disadvantaged minority. The firms need the wage data to frame their compensation strategies, and then meet the need of human resource competition. The academic community needs the wage data to study the labor market and the relevant institution. Individuals also need the wage data in the decision of human capital investment. On the other hand, although the wage data available in today's China can't fully meet the above requirements, the integrity and depth of the wage data has been constantly improving. Nowadays, the salary investigation has become a prospecting industry, attracting more and more agent joining in the survey activity. The purpose of this paper is to try to summarize the acquisition channel of Chinese wage data information, and give a brief analysis and evaluation on these data, in order to provide the basis work for academic research.

The agents of Chinese salary survey consist of the following categories: government, consulting firms, relevant websites, academia, trade associations, magazines and newspapers. More and more agents even cooperate to complete the salary survey at the present time. This paper is divided into four parts to introduce Chinese wage data information according to the agents. The first three parts focus on the government, consulting firms, and relevant websites; for they provide us the main resources of Chinese wage data, and each has unique characteristics. For other agents involved in fewer salary surveys, we discuss them in the fourth part.

Content

1. Analysis on Chinese Wage Data from Government Departments

There are three main wage data sources from Chinese government: firstly, statistics departments collect the payroll data from enterprises, public institutions & government administration through statistical reports every year, which is also the data published in statistical annual; secondly, the ministry of Human Resources and Social Security consigns its subordinate bodies to render enterprises wage data through SMIS software, which is published in The Guideline of Wage in Chinese Labor Markets; thirdly, other ministries of the government investigate the wage data from their subordinate units.

1.1 National Bureau of Statistics (NBS): Mainly Responsible for the Statistical Annual

The Wages and Social Security Office under the Department of Population & Employment Statistics in National Bureau of Statistics of China (NBS) is responsible for labor wage statistics. Provincial Bureaus of Statistics submit labor report to the State Statistical Bureau each year through the sophisticated form-reporting system. The uniform statistical report form, made by the NBS, is allotted and collected through email.

The coverage of form-reporting system is independent accounting units, including public institutions, government administration and enterprises, except private sector, township enterprises, and individual business. The samples of investigation are the units extracted from the economic census. Investigation method is overall statistic and multi-layer collecting. The problem in the implementation of this method is that there aren't scientific and accurate information channels for the investigation units on the entry and exit of coverage. Grass-roots units appear great arbitrariness in the completion of the collection and collation of data, and tend to be intervened by their administrative leaders. Moreover, the NBS can't monitor the investigation objects effectively, which may result in the omitted or false reporting from some grass-roots units.

The statistical indicator is the aggregate wages (payroll) of the investigation objects, without a breakdown of the various vocations, or a breakdown of the payroll. According to China Labor Statistical Yearbook, the aggregate wage means the total labor income paid by the unit in a certain period, such as time wages, piece-rate wages, bonuses, allowance, subsidies, overtime pays and wages for some special cases. The aggregate wage includes cash and commodity. The cash should remove labor protection fees and insurance costs (more than 14% excluding). The commodity should be converted to the form of money, in accordance with the purchase cost.

Grass-roots units tend to be intervened by their administrative leaders. And this may result in the omitted or false reporting. The NBS is not identifiable on data accuracy, and they only use common sense to delete some extreme abnormal samples. The NBS analyzes the datum, and then publishes Labor Statistical Yearbook, China Statistical Yearbook, statistical bulletins. These books are also available on the web site of the NBS.

At present, the NBS is promoting the use of "electronic account". This instrument can help enterprises get the integrate information on staff, and NBS acquires accurate wage information.

1.2 Ministry of Labor and Social Security (MLSS): Mainly Responsible for the Wage Guideline System

The Ministry of Labor and Social Security (MLSS) enacts the Notification on the Establishment of Labor Market Wage Guideline System in 1999, and investigates into the wage information for the wage guideline from then on. Sometimes the MLSS will do some internal investigations and make reports for certain special purposes. However, these data is generally not available for the public.

The MLSS Generally uses sampling survey methods to obtain wage datum. The datum is reported from the bodies in lower level to those in upper level. The coverage is all urban enterprises within administrative regions, including state-owned enterprises, collective-owned enterprises, enterprises from Hong Kong, Macao, foreign-invested enterprises and joint-venture enterprises, with under-scale (<100 persons) enterprises excluded. Then the above-scale enterprises are divided into large enterprises, medium-sized enterprises, and small business. The content of investigation is the annual wage income for workers of certain jobs during the whole last year, and the investigated jobs may have small changes every year. Wage income is collected in accordance with relevant state regulations calibers. In the aspect of sample-controlling, the response rate for sample is uncertain, since the MLSS has no power to force the selected enterprises to hand over tables on time.

Then the datum are aggregated and averaged by provinces, industry, firm size, the economic type, but the method of weighting is not used. Meanwhile, the wages of workers from the same occupation are listed in descending order. Then the MLSS can confirm the higher (simply average the top 5%), median (simply average the data in the middle of the list) and lower (simply average the 5% at the bottom of the list) levels of the regulated wage for particular occupations.

The MLSS makes public the regulated wages for all occupations through the published book named wage guideline in China. The data for various occupations may be different in detail. Some have the comprehensive price, some haven't; some have the information about the enterprise scale, some haven't. The subordinate units of MLSS in some provinces also announce provincial occupational wage guide.

1.3 Other Ministries

The Ministry of Personnel (MOP) also collects the institutional wages of the civil servants, but this data isn't available in the website of MOP, and the MOP just makes a presentation about the relevant policies and regulations on wages and welfare standards. And the State-owned Assets Supervision and Administration

Commission of the State Council (SASAC) also investigates the wages of the persons in charge in the state-owned enterprises. And the income of urban residents in the macroeconomic data from National Development and Reform Commission (SDPC) also contains the average wage datum. However, the wage datum from the above three ministries are confidential.

1.4 Evaluation on Government's Wage Datum

1.4.1 Advantages

The government formulates unified national statistical standards to standardize the conception of indicators, calculation methods, Categories, the survey forms, statistical coding and so on. And they have a large number of grass-roots survey teams, hence, they can provide datum from unparalleled extensive coverage. And they also have detailed information of workers' compensation, not only national, regional wage data, but also by industry, type of enterprises, occupations, etc. Sometimes the datum are categorized by industry and enterprise scale simultaneously.

1.4.2 Disadvantages

(A) Failing to satisfy survey coverage and the needs of economic development

Government wage statistics cover only employees in urban units, but employees in township enterprises, private enterprises and individual business are not included. With the development of township, private and individual economy, government statistics can't simultaneously reflect the situation of Chinese wages.

(B) Lack of scientific investigation methods: data accuracy can not be assured.

Generally, government departments collect statistics in the form of report form, relying on their administrative power. They can't monitor the process of investigation objects, the phenomenon of misstatement and omission occur from time to time.

(C) Statistical indicators too simple: definitions of wage in various departments are not unified.

Nowadays, the wage statistics usually contain the number of practitioners, annual aggregate wages, average wages and a few other indicators. When analyzing wage distribution relations, they can only compare the datum by industry or economic types. The wage guide of MLSS is refined to industry, but its survey coverage and posts are limited. Furthermore it hasn't refined wages or hourly wages statistics. Different departments have different definitions on wages.

(E) Awkward statistical reporting system with heavy workload.

Government statistics usually apply form-reporting system. The process includes the following steps: layout, collection, verification, and inputting to the summary report. Comparing with the international advanced statistical methods, the Chinese statisticians bear too much workload.

(F) Unscientific data processing and analysis methods.
Government statistics don't check the effectiveness of the samples before data analysis. When analyzing, they just aggregate or average the data rendered by the provinces, and have no scientific weighted system.

(G) The lack of data continuity makes it impossible to do the time-series analysis.
The statistical caliber of labor wage changed several times. And statistics stopped during the Great Culture Revolution. So now we can just get the datum since 1986. Moreover, The MLSS began the statistics of wage guideline after 1998, and there are not enough data accumulated.

(H) The lack of international comparability
Since statistical indicators, survey objects and job classification don't meet international standards, the datum is lack of international comparability.

2. Analysis of Wage Data from Consulting Firms

Wage information supplied by the consulting firms has played a large part in available wage information in the market. There are two types of such consulting companies: professional HR consulting company, such as Towers Perrin and Mercer HR consulting, and the consulting companies offering HR consultation and other business consultation, such as Deloitte Consulting. Chinese consulting companies have native advantages, which are easy for investigation in China, while foreign consulting companies have the leading analysis methods and comparable database.

2.1 Existing Wage Data

Let's start from the content of wage information. Judging from the wage reports released by the consulting firms, the wage information refers to aggregate compensation, that's to say, includes wage, welfare and so on, but there is no clearly distinction about the different compositions. However, some consulting firms concern about the employee's welfare changes, for example, Mercer released its annual employee welfare reports every year. Some firms would like to publish wage information for special groups. For example, Hewitt Associates focus on the high-level managers' wage, while Towers Perrin released global high-tech employees' wage report every year. The local companies also have unique advantages, e.g. CIIC management consulting company of China developed a special part for "the graduates" in its newly released wage investigation report, concerning the wage changes in graduates' first year and second year, and the talents' drain in the second year.

The forms for wage information can be divided into the following categories: wage databases (include the international and local wage database), annual wage reports, wage research reports, online wage appraisal systems, the pubic publications from the consulting companies (include the paper and electronic magazines), consulting activities and various wage forums hosted by consulting company.

A remarkable feature of the wage information from the consulting company is that it is easy to compare in the local or international dimension, because of formidable information collection network and definite position classification system. What's more, you can get additional information help the clients to make related decision. For example, the Hay Group wage database offers you macro-economic environmental information in your region or country, industry wage trend (seasonal data), wage practice, laws , regulations and policy about wage in you country, as well as the professional HR management advices according to the company's situation.

2.2 Data Sources

The consulting company has two sources to get wage information: by membership or non-membership. In practice, most of the consulting firms connect with the investigated enterprises by membership relation. That's to say, all the companies on their investigation list are their members. The enterprises have the responsibilities to render wage information by internet or questionnaire, and the investigation results are shared among these members for free or only charging little.

2.3 Survey Methodology

In order to get the comprehensive wage information, consulting companies apply varied methodology, such as paper questionnaire, internet, intranet or e-mail, face-to-face discussion or telephone survey. The most used instrument is internet and paper questionnaire.

Every consulting company also uses scientific and effective methodologies to maintain the competitive power. Hewitt Associates and many local companies bring in the Joint Investigation to wage survey. This method together with the employees' suggestion can avoid one-sidedness answers to the sensitive questions. The questionnaire requires the employee to select and express his opinion among kinds of wages instead of sensitive questions to enhance the validity and information scale.

2.4 Evaluation on consulting firm's Wage Data

2.4.1 Advantages

As a rapidly developing Asian country, China is playing a greater role in the world; there is an urgent demand for its wage information. Having introduced the existing wage information from the consulting firms, we can summarize their advantages over other agents:

(A) Powerful information collecting nets
The consulting company's information collecting nets have covered almost provinces in China, and now they are renewing unceasingly. Their wage information is usually more comprehensive than that in any other institutions or organizations. So there is richer wage information you can get in the local and international databases established on these nets.

(B) Consistent approaches
For the reason of data comparison, the consistent approaches are used in wage investigations around the world. When you get some wage data from some regions, you can use it to compare with other area if the position has no much difference.

(C) Analyzing and reporting system which has close ties with practices
The final intention of pay survey is not only to get the wage information, but to help make decisions for management. Now the information offered by the consulting company can supply some professional advices for enterprises with its analysis and report system.

2.4.2 Disadvantages

Strict and scientific methods are adopted in pay surveys launched by consulting companies, and the information from the surveys can meet the market demand to a certain extent. But there are also some shortcomings:

(A) Limited survey objects, and high cost
Consulting firms usually investigate the good-performance and large-scale enterprises. For example, Towers Perrin conducts a survey on high managers' pay in listed company in 2007, the objects are 290 biggest enterprises according to the market value, and the industries related contains transport, energy, mining and chemical, finance, information technology, consumer durables and real estate. The limited samples led to the limitations in wage data using. Moreover, as information processing technology doesn't mature enough, the majority of consulting firms have to use paper questionnaires, which are much more expensive than the internet survey. And these can increase the operation cost.

(B) Not refined job classification
Hay group, which has better job classification than others, just divides occupations into 13 categories. But there are much more complex categories in the occupation code. Refinement of the job classification is the key to improve the consistency and comparability of wage data.

(C) The lack of analyzing detailed pay classification
The definition of wage in consulting firms refers to the total compensation, including wages and benefits. But there is no analysis of detailed pay classification. We can't know about the information about statutory benefits, supplemental benefits, subsidies, allowances and basic wages.

3. Analysis of Wage Data from Website Surveys

Another collection channel for Chinese wage data is the website wage survey. These pay-survey websites can be divided into three categories: Firstly, various websites related with human resource management, such as www.chinahr.com, www.51job.com, www.sc.sh.cn, www.ChinaHRD.net, and so on. This kind of websites mainly supplies HR services, and wage survey is just used to provide information or other assistance for their main business (e.g., for increasing the visiting rate). Secondly, professional wage investigation websites. Pay survey is the only business of these websites. Xinchou114 (www.xinchou114.com) is the only website of this type in China now. Thirdly, professional investigation websites, such as 1diaocha (www.1diaocha.com). They investigate all kinds of hot topics which the enterprises or internet users are interested in, such as social news, social values and so on. So the pay survey is just one theme concerned.

3.1 Wage Data Available

Wage information available from website pay survey can be divided into the following categories in terms of form: firstly, wage report for sale. These wage data isn't publicly available, and can only be purchased from the website. Enterprises can also customize wage report according to their own needs. Secondly, wage report for free. For example, chinahr.com publishes annual "×× list of Chinese top ten high–paying occupations"; Zhaopin.com shows "2007 pay survey report for ×× industry". ChinaHRD.net published "2004 Chinese HR pay survey report" and so on. Thirdly, books and other publications, Such as the 2007 white paper on Chinese pay status.

Viewing from the contents, the current salary information available from the pay survey has the following types: Firstly, the regional wages data. For example, 2007 White Paper on China pay status announces the annual salary of 25-bit, 50-bit and 75-bit values in municipalities, provincial capitals, cities and other developed cities. Secondly, the industrial wages data. For example, xinchou114.com provides 10-bit, 25-bit, 50-bit, 75-bit and 90-bit wage data of real estate, manufacturing, leasing industry, IT, and financial sectors. Thirdly, jobs wage data, a significant portion of jobs data in the wage information for sale belongs to this type. For example, in the 51job's salary survey report, jobs pay data can be fractionized on industry, region, the nature of an enterprise, scale enterprises, and provides details of fixed pay, variable pay, subsidies, and other types of market conditions. This job wage data can provide a strong basis for enterprises compensation management.

From the view of scale and frequency, the survey samples in the network are increasing gradually, as technology of network wage survey matures, and popularity promotes. At the same time, investigation and release of wage information are more standardized in the website. For example, Chinahr.com launches a national pay survey every half year. Enterprises can sign up to participate and provide the salaries and fringe benefits paid to staffs in the past year. In the first half of 2007, the enterprise participants in the survey has increased to 11,700, covering different nature scale enterprises in 19 different industries throughout the country.

3.2 Data Sources

3.2.1 Personal data

Personal data forms in this way: firstly, participants submit their salary anonymously. The sponsors screen the samples according to their selection principle, and then they analyze the effective samples and submit the statistical results. A typical example of this type of survey is “2004 Accounting industry practitioners’ salary survey” initiated by esnai.com. ChinaHRD.net and other networks also hold such salary surveys.

Personal-data has lower costs, and can get large numbers of samples in a relatively short time. But there are also 3 shortcomings. Firstly, the samples representation is poor. The personal data source is unable to control the survey participants, which makes the survey results not be the true representation of the population. Secondly, the data has lower reliability. Because of the anonymity of the survey, it is not easy to give direct guidance to every participant, which may result in participants’ misunderstanding of the survey items as well as the maliciously cheating, and then makes data distortion. Although the survey sponsors try to find ways to solve this problem, such as putting all kinds of rules to exclude the unreasonable data, individuals can still fake deliberately. At the same time, personal data can easily overlook job- matching steps during the survey. It also affected the credibility seriously.

3.2.2 Enterprise data

Enterprise data forms in this way: the survey data is collected through voluntary enterprises involved in the wage investigation, whose human resource departments provide their current salary data directly. Enterprise data is the main source of network pay survey information in today’s China. For example, majority of the pay data, in Chinahr.com, zhaopin.com, xinchou114.com, comes from the enterprise side.

Compared with the personal data, enterprise data has the following advantages: Firstly, strong pertinence. Since these well-known survey websites usually have a rich source of customers, they can make these enterprises join in the survey heart-to-heart. Secondly, high reliability. HR manager take part in the survey and put in the wage data of their enterprise, and they usually has the best understanding of each employee’s compensation. Moreover, these enterprises involved in the data collection trust the survey agency and have the related legal protective means (such as confidentiality agreements), they are willing to fill in the actual and integrated salary information.

The disadvantages of enterprise data are as follows: Firstly, the high price of the report. Take the xinchou114.com for an example. Mmber enterprises must pay 4,000 Yuan to the survey agency to get the personalized wage report covering the whole city or broader area where the enterprise locates. Secondly, it will be hard for individuals to get his concerned pay data, since this information mainly services enterprises rather than individuals.

3.3 Survey Methodology

As a new channel for wage survey in recent years, network survey can save time and energy, be implemented more conveniently and updated more dynamically. At the same time, it also has some insurmountable shortcomings. On one hand, compared with other surveys, network investigations is more difficult to monitor, more likely to be faked (although authenticity of other surveys is also questioned). On the other hand, since network survey is difficult to control, the samples are difficult to overcome selection bias. Take the chinahr's pay survey from May 1, 2004 to January 18, 2005 as an example, despite the large number of samples collected (26,689), their distribution is not very uniform (mainly concentrated in a few metropolitans). The survey participants mainly distributed in Beijing (26%), other participants distributed more dispersedly, for whom the wage report may not be representative.

However, currently, every major site in China has unique survey and statistical technology to overcome the problems of cheat and selection bias.

(a) Job matching technology. As what is mentioned earlier, wage data without rigorous job matching is not valuable to market. Network pay survey will first make jobs sequence according to different industries characteristics. And then the website presents the jobs sequence together with the detailed standards for every job's duties (job description) to enterprises, to help them carry out their job matching. The enterprises involved in the investigation must first read the detailed job description seriously, and then examine their company's job responsibility. Ultimately they can match jobs in their company to the standard jobs sequence. Usually if 70% or more of the actual job duties are similar to the standards, we think they achieve a fine match. In a word, job matching can reduce the survey bias to some extent, but not completely eliminate the bias.

(b) Membership technology. The websites allow the individuals and enterprises investigated to be their members. Then the two sides form an interest community, thereby reducing the survey objects' false information motive. Because there are some contents in member's wage survey report about the comparison between self-information and statistical results, members normally do not spend time and effort to fill in false information to self-deception.

(c) Data filtering technologies. Before analyzing, all salary data submitted to the system have to go through a rigorous evaluation process: First, the system will examine the effectiveness and legitimacy of data, and illogical, inconsistent data will be excluded. Second, the system will check the reasonableness of the data according to the statistical result from the past survey, and those deviating from the experience will be removed. Thirdly, xinchou114.com has other channels and means to verify further the authenticity of data. Similarly, Chinahr.com also set

13 data screening rules to filter unreasonable data.

In addition, a variety of network system also has its unique investigative techniques to ensure the reliability of data. For example, xinchou114.com has an operative model of platform.

3.4 Evaluation on Website's Wage Data

Website pay survey has the merit of large samples just like the Government survey, at the same time its data is as professional and concrete as the consulting company. We believe that the networks wage survey will have greater development in the future, and make a greater contribution to Chinese wage data collection.

Of course, the survey data mainly aims to meet market demand, so the data usually aims at corporate employees in the mainstream labor market, and not directed against staffs at public institutions and state organizations, staff salaries. At the same time, for employees in non-mainstream labor market, because of their rare or seldom participation in the online survey, their wages data can be harder to be obtained through network investigation.

4. Analysis of Other Available Wage Data

Other pay survey agents include academia, trade associations, magazines and newspapers and so on. However, as having fewer resources, these agents' pay surveys are usually not continuing, cover smaller region, and have less datum. And they generally cooperate with government, consulting firms, and pay survey websites in data collection.

4.1 Pay Survey Held by Colleges

In the academic community, some colleges and universities, and scientific research units have special institutions devoted to employment, wages or income research, such as the Institute of Population and Labor Economics in Chinese Academy of Social Sciences (IPLE-CASS), Employment Institute in Renmin University of China, Income Distribution and Poverty Institute in Beijing Normal University and so on. Of course, the number of such institutions isn't very big.

What's more, due to being less likely to get wage data, the academia is lack of the motivation to survey. The wage data for academic research generally comes from second-hand information, especially from the government. Until now the independent pay surveys hold by the academia mainly include four income surveys since 1988 (the last one was conducted in August, 2007) hold by Income Distribution and Poverty Institute in Beijing Normal University. Wage data is also the main content in the Chinese labor market survey hold by IPLE-CASS in 2001.

At the same time, the wage data obtained by academic institute is generally used for their own research, and usually released in the form of academic reports and papers. For example, according to the wage data by IPLE-CASS, Meiyan Wang published Analysis of Employment and Wage Differences between Different Sexes in Chinese Urban Labor Market.

4.2 Pay Survey Held by Trade Associations

In order to know about the compensation situation in their own industry, some trade associations also launch pay survey sometimes. For example, in 2007, CFA (Chartered Financial Analyst) Institute launched pay survey for holders of the CFA certificate. Pay findings were released through the form of compensation report. This survey invited 1146 objects, and interviewed 123 persons, so the response rate was 11%.

4.3 Pay Survey Held by cooperative agents

As academia, trade associations, newspapers and magazines don't have many resources respectively, they tend to cooperate with other agents to carry out pay surveys.

For example, in 2007, Human Resource Service Center in Wujiang Economic Development Area, cooperating with Fudan Consulting Organization in Shanghai, initiated Wujiang Economic Development Area Enterprises Pay Survey in 2007, which contains 86 survey positions. And 80 enterprises, 85400 objects participated and submitted wage data. They completed 2007 Enterprises Pay Annual Report in Wujiang Economic Development Area.

Currently, xinchou114.com is initiating pay survey for various industries in Xinjiang, cooperating with Xinjiang consumption Morning News.

4.4 Evaluation on this agent's Wage Data

The wage survey channel plays a complementary role for the three channels mentioned above, aiming to meet the demand for special groups. From the overall perspective, these survey agents have limited resources respectively, and they can't manage large-scale and systematic wage surveys, which determines the wage data from academia, trade associations, magazines and newspapers will not be influential in the society. However, on the other hand, these survey agents usually controlled particular resources, and thus their wage data has the unique value.

5. Conclusion

In the 4 parts mentioned above, we introduced the formation process and status of Chinese wage data, and made an evaluation according to the different agents. After a broad understanding on Chinese wage data, now we gave an additional remark.

Firstly, the methods and results in different survey channels tend to be similar. Survey technologies used by different agents tend to be melted each other, and then maturing increasingly. Not only the investigation scale and methods, but also data structure is showing convergence. For example, consulting companies are having more customers and better survey methods, and thus the investigation scale is growing gradually to the level of Government and website. Government and consulting firms are using more electronic methods, or even directly apply the network survey methods. At the same time, government's electronic account can grasp the comprehensive information including basic salary, bonus, welfare, position, age, academic qualification and so on, which is gradually approaching the data depth in consulting firms and survey websites.

Secondly, current wage data in China can not meet the demand. The economic and social development calls for more sophisticated, professional wage survey. However, at present, this kind of data has small quantity and low quality. Again, Chinese current academic research on labor issues has shifted from general philosophy discussion to quantitative empirical analysis, so it urgently needs scientific, detailed and a large number of wage data. But the ideal wage data is not available now in China. Pay surveys that can meet the various demands are bound to develop very well in China.

Reference

Beijing labor and social security institute. The Regulated Wage of Beijing Labor Markets and the Firm's Labor Cost Condition: 2007.

Department of Population & Employment Statistics in National Bureau of Statistics of China.(2007). Labor Statistical Yearbook.

Pan, L.L.(2007).Problems and Advices of Current Employment Statistics. Zhejiang Statistics.April, 2007.

Mercer consulting (2007). "2007 worldwide pay survey".

Available: http://www.mercer.com/pressrelease/details.jhtml/dynamic/idContent/1242100

National Bureau of Statistics (2007). 2007 China Statistical Yearbook, Available: http://www.stats.gov.cn

Available: http://www.china.com.cn/zhuanti2005/txt/2006-03/17/content_6156348.htm.

Song, C. Q. Is the wage statistics exact in China? ", China Statistics, April, 2007.

Towers perrin.(2008).2008 global compensation planning report.Available:http://www.towersperrin.com

Towers perrin.(2007) Global high tech compensation planning report.

Available:http://www.towersperrin.com

Wang, M.Y. (2006) "Analysis of Employment and Wage Differences between Different Sexes in Chinese Urban Labor Market". China's Gender Equality and Women's Development Report 1995-2005.

Xinchou114.(2008). 2007 White Paper on China pay status. Available: www.xinchou114.com

Yue,X.Y.(2005). Problems of Current Employment Statistics in China. Economic Research Journal

1diaocha's web site: [www.1diaocha.com]

Haygroup consulting' web site: [http://www.haygroup.com/cn/]

Hewitt associates consulting' web site: [www.hewittassociates.com]

Labor statistics report-form institution of P.R.C., information from the web site[http://www.stats.gov.cn/was40/gjtjj_detail.jsp?searchword=%C0%CD%B6%AF%CD%B3%BC%C6%B1%A8%B1%ED&presearchw]

Ministry of Labor and Social Security' web site:[http://www.molss.gov.cn]

Statistics Law of PRC: [http://www.stats.gov.cn/tjfg/tjfl/t20030925_110606.htm]

Chapter 2:
Sustainable Innovation

Sustainable Development, Ecological Modernisation and Jobs: How quality of life is interlinked with nature conservation

Prof. Dr. Peter Hennicke, Dipl.-Vw. Tobias Schleicher
(Wuppertal Institute for Climate, Environment and Energy)

Abstract

This paper links the ecological, economic and social dimensions of sustainable development globally and for Germany referring to the **concept of decoupling** economic growth (quality of life) from the use of nature. The starting point is the severe crisis of the global financial and economic system as well as of the planet's ecosystems. To fight against a collapse of the international financial system with stimuli programs it has been argued that policies in favour of climate and resource protection have to be postponed. However, studies for Germany and the EU have shown that an opposite strategy might be valid: For Germany it has been demonstrated that win-win policies for economic recovery can be successfully combined with ecological modernisation, climate and resource protection.

There is some evidence that in general this **integrated strategy** can bring the world's economies closer to a sustainable development path by simultaneously approaching the ecological and economic challenges. Deciding for such a pathway implies changing gradually the traditional unsustainable investment, production and consumption patterns of the 20th century into consequent and comprehensive **investments in greener and cleaner technologies**. This structural change into more decentralized and renewable power systems is already happening in the energy sector of the EU. With supporting state frame conditions these policies can effectively create new business fields ("lead markets") and job opportunities and at the same time contribute to protect the planet's resources and climate.

However, a **technology and efficiency revolution** alone would not be enough. It is especially its combination with a fundamental socio-cultural change concerning consumption patterns as well as the perception of public and personal wealth that supports an **effective transformation** to a sustainable life-style. A broad scientific and political debate and concrete changes in the behaviour of consumers framed by appropriate policy guidelines and incentives are needed. Finally, this has to happen soon as some "planetary boundaries" (Rockström et al. 2009) are already exeeded whereas others (e.g. a challenging shortages of "critical metals") can be reached very soon.

Content

1. At the crossroads: What path do we choose?

After recovering from the world economic crisis of 2008/2009 the economic prospectives seem to brighten up though the risks of the financial sector have been widely postponed to the future and to the tax payers. At the same time the ecological crisis has been sharpened („Exceeding Planetary Boundaries“, Rockström 2009). Both developments fundamentally challenge equal living standards and the chances for future generations.

It might be useful as an introductory orientation to look into global alternative development paths up to the end of the 21st century. Is sustainable development still possible, what are the choices and how much time is available to change the unsustainable trends?

According to recently published global scenarios by the Tellus Institute (2010), it is possible for mankind to choose between bright or desastrous pathways for the next hundred years. The four scenarios presented range from an catastrophic and socially highly inequal scenario ("Fortress Scenario"), to conventional developments ("Policy Reform Scenario" and "Market Forces Scenario") up to an alternative scenario called "The Great Transition". Both conventional scenarios are based on an unchanged economic paradigm of "rising population, consumerism, universial convergence toward affluent life-styles and an incessant pressure for ever more energy and materials, land and food." While the "Market Forces Scenario" might lead to high social and environmental risks the "Policy Reform Scenario" might achieve a modest redirection of growth in a more sustainable way by politically coordinating an ambitous global action programme.

The most pessimistic scenario, the "Fortress World Scenario", paints the picure of steering into the risks of an historic descent of civilization. In contrast, the "Great Transition Scenario“ shows that humanity can build up a sustainable civilization by continously adapting to the basic environmental and social challenges of the 21st century. Basic features of this scenario are abondoning inequality and hunger, creating a dematerialized human life-style with a great reduction of resource and energy needs and emphazising sustainable development and individual fullfillment.

The common message of all scenarios, however, is that today's decision makers set the course on these pathways for the 21st century. That's why the metaphor of "historical crossroads" is used.

Based on comprehensive modeling[1] of various economic, ecological and social indicators figure 1 shows how "international equity" and the "number of people suffering from malnutrition" develops within the scenarios. It can only be reduced sufficiently in the scenario „Great Transition".

Figure 1: Four scenarios for international equity and the number of hungry people.

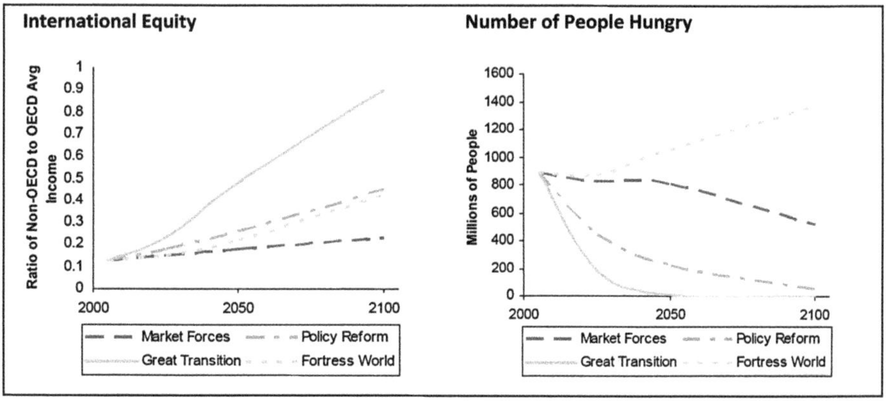

The „Policy Reform Scenario" models a 50 year delay reaching the latter not before 2100. The performance of this indicator in the „Market Forces Scenario" is very poor, the „Fortress World Scenario" even shows a dramatic increase in hunger.

Accordingly, figure 2 describes the expected development of total end-use energy demand and annual carbon dioxide emissions. In the "Great Transition Scenario" the global end-use energy peaks within the next two decades and then decreases continously. Emissions go down in both, the "Great Transition" and the "Policy Reform Scenario".

It is the intention of these scenario exercises to get a broad impression on how we could model feasible (not probable!) future developments and how to get a better orientation what the choises are or should be. The modelled developments show a strong interconnection of the environmental and the social challenges of

Figure 2: The Great Transition: Climate mitigation by an integrated strategy of

1 Concerning the definition and assumptions for all scenarios see Tellus (2010).

energy efficiency and renewables.

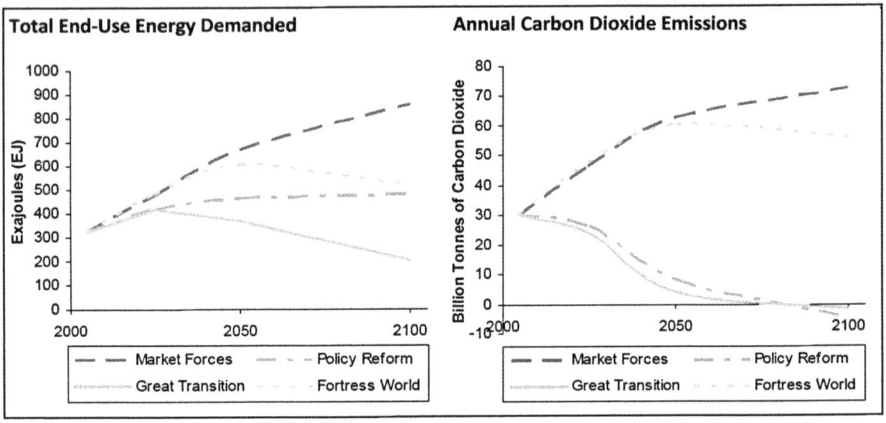

the 21st century. The sustainable pathway characterized by the "Great Transition Scenario" does not only refer to the resource and climate issue. Instead, the positive side effects of consequent resource and climate protection are the key for solving the social issues of the century as well. The other way round holds true as well: Without solving the social issues (e.g. equity; hunger alleviation) resource and climate protection will not be successful. It is a question of the political will what pathway will be chosen. The freedom and window of opportunity, however, to decide on these alternatives are not open indefinitely. Urgent strategic decisions have to be taken within the next two decades.

With this background the question has to be answered whether the unprecedented global programmes to fight the economic crisis have been used as a chance to steer the world economy in the direction of "The Great Transition".

2. Recovery Programmes and Green Modernisation

From the very beginning the economic crisis of 2008/09 changed the paradigm of deregulated markets and neoliberal policies to strong "emercency recovery programmes" in many countries. A considerable part of them, however, had the strucure of traditional, Keynesian type "deficit spendig" trying only to stimulate demand and consumption, without priorities for "green" investment. On the other hand it is nevertheless impressive how the concept of ecological modernisation has trickled down to established policies raising the "green"[2] share of recovery

2 There are questions and some critics about the concrete meaning of „green"; in our context it

programmes in some countries (e.g. S. Korea, China, US, EU). While traditional recovery programmes just stimulate the economies in the short term, investments in green technologies and energy and resource efficiency comes along with benefits not only for nature protection but also for the economy and the labor markets (see below).

Figure 3: Ratio of green stimulus of national recovery packages, absolute volumes in bn€ (Source: Schepelmann et al. 2009)

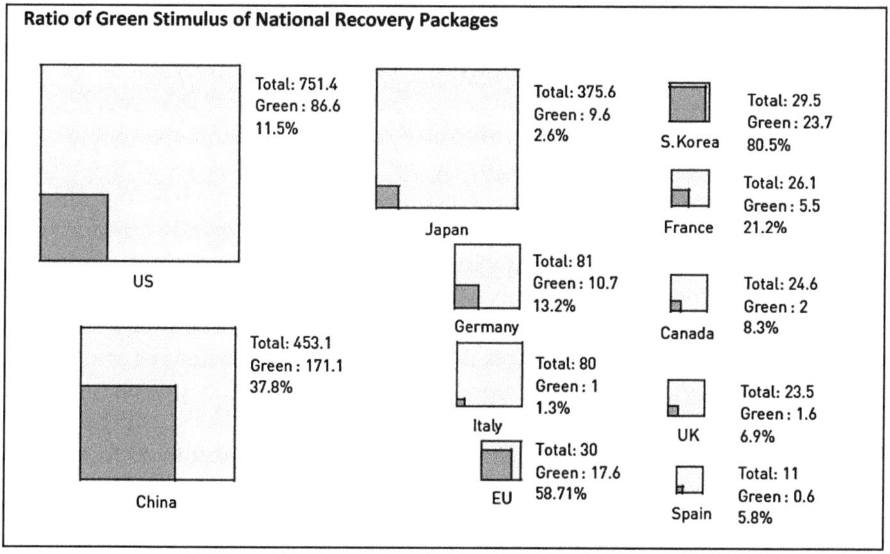

As figure 3 shows the shares of "green" stimuli of the overall national recovery packages were relatively poor compared to the potential benefits for the economies. Hence, many countries will be facing lost opportunities as they did not concentrate on long term investments in "green" technologies to foster the increase of energy and resource productivity, thus reducing import dependency and vulnerabilty by price fluctuations.

---

is the gradual departure from traditional Keynesian deficit spending which matters and which might be a turning point towards a new public „industrial ecological policy" (S. Gabriel, Former German Minister of Environment)

3. Decoupling: Part of the Solution

Increasing resource productivity by a factor of x is widely conceived as a necessary condition for worldwide sustainable development. In a certain respect this is a self-evident statement: As long as world population and world GDP are growing exponentially and the natural resources of the earth are finite it is common sense that only a massive increase of resource productivity and the decoupling of the quality of life (growth of GDP) from the use of nature can contribute to solve the apparent contradiction between man made growth and natural limits.

However, there are many different opinions concerning the precise understanding of „resources", the „scale of decoupling" (absolute or relative) and the ex post „statistical evidence" compared to ex ante „goals and policies" of decoupling.

For example: Even though an **absolute** decoupling and a tremendous increase of resource productivity might be the aim of national resource policies, counteracting social and economic reactions (direct/indirect rebound effects; growth, structural and quantity effects) can „eat up" even massive increases in specific or sectoral resource productivities. Therefore resource policies based on technology driven scenario analysis and respective policy mixes to overcome barriers and to disseminate advanced technologies should always be aware of these counterproductive side-effects. It is the triangle of **efficiency** („more with less"), **sufficiency** („less can be more") and **consistency** („better than more") on which policies and measures for decoupling should be based. At the end of the day, what counts from an ecological and ethical perspective is to **sustain ecosystem services for all countries and generations to come**[3]. This means on a worldwide scale that the necessary increase of well-being for a growing future world population (8-10 billions?) must not further increase unsustainable use of nature.

Concerning feasible worldwide decoupling scenarios two types of decoupling have to be distiguished. Firstly, **absolute** decoupling stands for reducing per capita resource consumption. This seems to be feasible in Industrialized Countries (ICs) only if the growth rate of resource productivity is higher than the increase of per capita affluence. In Developing Countries (DCs), however, only **relative** decoupling is possible which means a reduction of the growth rates of resource and energy consumption; e.g. most DCs and Countries in Transition the (Business as usual/BAU-) rate of electricity increase is high but can at least been halved in many cases by using more efficient electrical motors, pumps, pressurized air, air conditioning, appliances or lighting.

---

3 This simplified definition summarizes the often cited Brundtland definition of sustainable development; the strenght and impact of substitution between „nature" and „capital" (strong vs. weak concept of sustainability) can not be debated in this context.

Paul Ehrlich's formula I = P x A x T (I=Environmental Impact; P=Population; A=Affluence per capita; T= Technology) can be interpreted as follows: Taking resource use (R)4 as indicator for I, Y/P (per capita income) as indicator for "affluence" and T as indicator for resource intensity (reciprocal of resource productivity) then the relation R = P x Y/P x R/Y leads to a simple conclusion: With a positive growth rate of population (wP) and for per capita affluence (wA) the global environmental impact can only be constant if the resource intensity decreases by (wP)+ (wA).

Concerning the global environmental impact (I) diffentiated for industrialized and developing countries

- I_{IC} can be **absolutely** reduced in **industrialized countries** (IC; assuming constant population) if the growth rate of resource productivity is higher than the increase rate of per capita affluence
- I_{DC} can be **relatively** reduced in **developing countries** (DC; assuming growing population and high GDP-growth) if the growth rate of resource productivity is as high as possible to offset the necessary increase of per capita affluence.

Both parts of the world, ICs and DCs, have their respective duties for nature and resource protection according to their potentials and needs. This corresponds to the keyword "common, but differentiated responsibilities" from the climate debate. It also holds true for resource protection policies.

Figure 4: In an idealized development perspective ICs reduce their per capita resource and energy use more than it increases in DCs

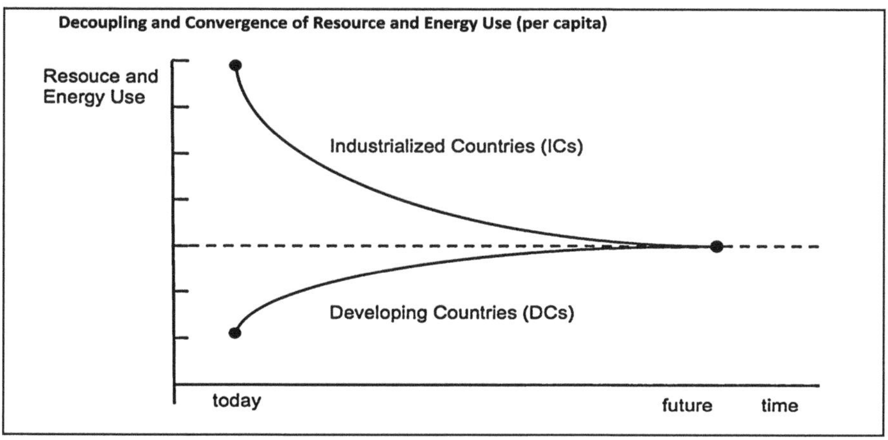

4 R may be measured by the TMR (total material requirement) as a common global indicator for the environmental impact of resource use.

The comprehensive concept of decoupling finally aims at convergence of resource and energy use to a sustainable level, whereas the convergence value should be compatible with the carrying capacity of the nature (e.g. bioshpere). Figure 5 visualizes the development paths of absolute and relative decoupling for the respective world regions. Eventually, the absolute reductions of resource use in the ICs and the relative reduction which is visualized by the flattening slope of the increase in DCs lead to convergence at a global sustainable per capita resource level (dotted line). It is obvious that the decrease of resource and energy use in ICs has to be faster than the increase in DCs. Hence, all countries face their feasible burden for climate and resource protection.

Summarizing, in reality green modernization can only be successful if investment and consumption patterns lead to absolute decoupling in ICs and relative decoupling in DCs.

The key word for relative decoupling in DCs is **"leap frogging"**. It implies that high efficient and clean technologies are implemented in DCs during their "take off" stage – instead of going through a "Kutznets Curve" development path: first beeing "clean and poor", than getting heavy polluted by increasing per capita income and later cleaning up when being rich. Fostering "leap frogging" and thus avoiding a resource and energy intensive development path by using cleaner technologies a priori has the potential to decrease the growth rates of energy and resource consumption.

For the Industrial Countries the feasibility of raising **energy efficiency** by a factor four (at least) has been demonstrated for many specific examples and with national and global scenarios (Weizsäcker/ Lovins / Lovins 1998 and Lovins/ Hennicke 1999; WBGU 2003 and Ecofys / DLR et al. 2007 and 2008). Especially the Swiss concept of a "2000 Watt per capita society" (see below; Jochem 2004) is interesting, because it includes a vision for the **combination of energy efficiency with material efficiency** as a goal.

Decoupling, leap frogging and socio-technical innovations is the basic rationale behind the concept of the "2000W per capita society" for OECD-countries. 2000W/cap (= 65 GJ/cap) corresponds to 1/3 of today's European per capita energy use. Enabling a GDP/cap growth of 2/3 up to 2050, the "2000W per Capita Society" implies a factor 4 to 5 increase of energy efficiency. Swiss research institutes have been working on this concept for many years demonstrating the technical feasibility of this challenging vision. As the world average energy consumption in the last two decades has been 70 GJ/cap one of the Swiss report's hypothesis is, that 65-70 GJ/cap could even be a future convergence value for a sustainable world energy system.

Thus, an ambitious increase in energy and material productivity, a complete change of the innovation systems, the exploitation of long re-investment cycles and the gradual structural change to more sustainable patterns of consumption and production are important preconditions for establishing a "2000 Watt per capita world society".

4. Germany: On the way to decouple GDP from resource use?

Up to now, the debate on resource efficieny is focussed on energy. Many detailed data bases and sophisticated scenarios are available, especially for Germany. Chapter 4.1. and 4.2. summarize some of the latest findings for the energy sector. Furthermore, in chapter 4.3. the key result of a scenario to foster the **combined increase of material and energy productivity** for Germany will be presented (Distelkamp / Meyer / Meyer 2010; see below).

4.1 A sustainable energy strategy for Germany

One detailed feasibility analysis of a sustainable energy system has been presented for Germany[5] in the so called "BMU Leitszenario" (see BMU 2008a) which serves as an orientation for energy, climate and resource policies advocated by the German Ministry of Environment. This scenario demonstrates that the phase out of nuclear power (up to 2023), the reduction of CO_2 by 80% (up to 2050), a moderate (green?) increase of GDP-growth (of 1,2% p.a.) and additional jobs are technically feasible and cost-effective for the society at the long run: the moderate additional societal costs for the energy system up to 2030 will be overcompensated by benefits until 2050. One crucial assumption is that (besides an ambitious increase of the share of renewables in all sectors) the energy productivity up to 2050 raises at least by a factor of four.

Figure 5 shows the "Lead Scenario" for Germany in which the primary energy productivity is increased by 3% per annum. Morevover, it demonstrates that in 2050 primary energy can be reduced by 40% (about 50% from renewable sources) compared with 2000. The scenario is strongly based on the **combination** of increased energy efficiency and a continous expansion of renewable energies in all sectors.

The combination of both is estimated to lead even in the short run to a reduction of primary energy consumption by 17% from the 2008 level in 2020. Accordingly, a 40% reduction of energy related CO_2 emissions by 2020 can be reached,

5 Sustainable world energy scenarios with comparable goals and results have been developed by Lovins / Hennicke 1999, WBGU 2003 and Ecofys / DLR et al. 2007 and 2008.

Figure 5: Absolute decoupling of GDP-growth and energy use in the German "Lead Scenario" 2008

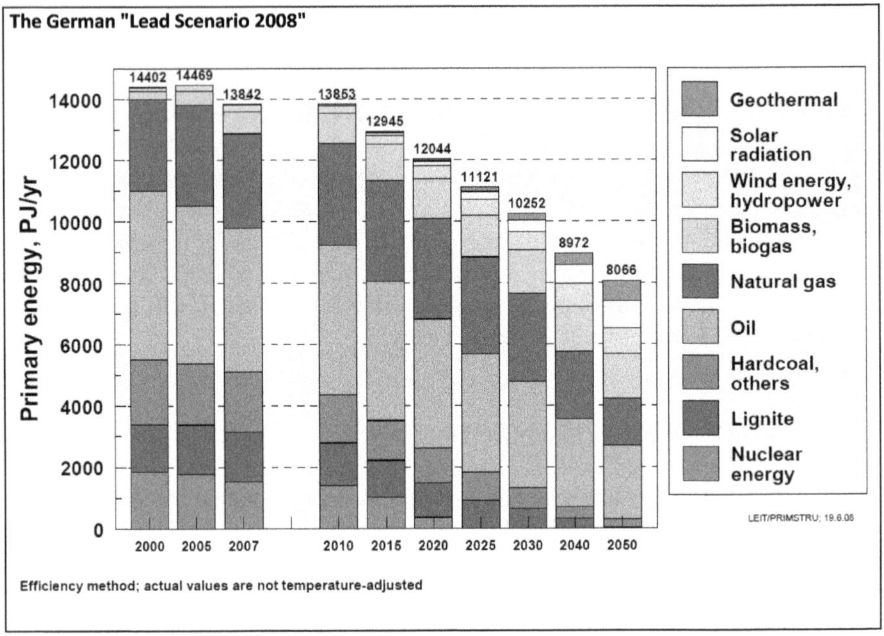

if (1) an additional significant increase in electricity efficiency is achieved and (2) the share of combined heat and power (CHP) production is raised to 25%.

Concerning the **transport sector** the "Lead Scenario" models a reduction of fuel consumption of the entire car fleet by 25% and of road freight by 20%. This leads to a reduction in overall consumption by 10% by 2020. In 2050 total energy demand in the transport sector drops to 73% of the 2005 level. In terms of fossil energy, then only 50% of the presently required quantity of fossil fuel is consumed.

Regarding the **electricity sector** the scenario at one hand demonstrates that "the future will be decentralized" (Siemens AG). On the other hand green centralized power (especially from offshore wind power) and green electricity imports cooperating with the northern part of Europe (Hydro Power from Norway) and North Africa (Concentrated Solar Power) is needed as well. About 15% of total electricity consumption will be imported in 2050.

It has been calculated that the **"break even point" for renewable electricity** in Germany will be about 15 years ahead. According to the "Lead Scenario" after 2025 average electricity prices from renewable sources will be more competitive than electricity from coal, gas or new nuclear (Source: German "Lead Scenario 2008")

It should be underlined that the implementation of this strategy in the long run depends on many uncertainties. But in the forseeable future (up to 2020) the goals of German energy policy are realistic. With the so called "Integrated Energy and Climate Program" (BMU/BMWi 2007; BMU 2008b) the German Government decided on two dozens policies and measures which up to 2020 aim to raise the share of renewables for electricity to 30%, for heat to 14%, the share of CHP for electricity to 25% and to save energy in all sectors; it is expected that with the help of the IECP and additional measures at least a 30% CO_2-reduction up to 2020 (and 40% reduction conditioned to ambitious goals of the EU27) can be reached.

The **Total Turnover** from renewable energy sources in Germany 2009 (investments and operation) adds up to 33.4 billion Euro (2009). The employment effect of the rapidly growing sector of renewable energy is shown by the following figure 6.

Figure 6: Jobs in the Renewable Energy Sector in Germany, Source: BMU 2010.

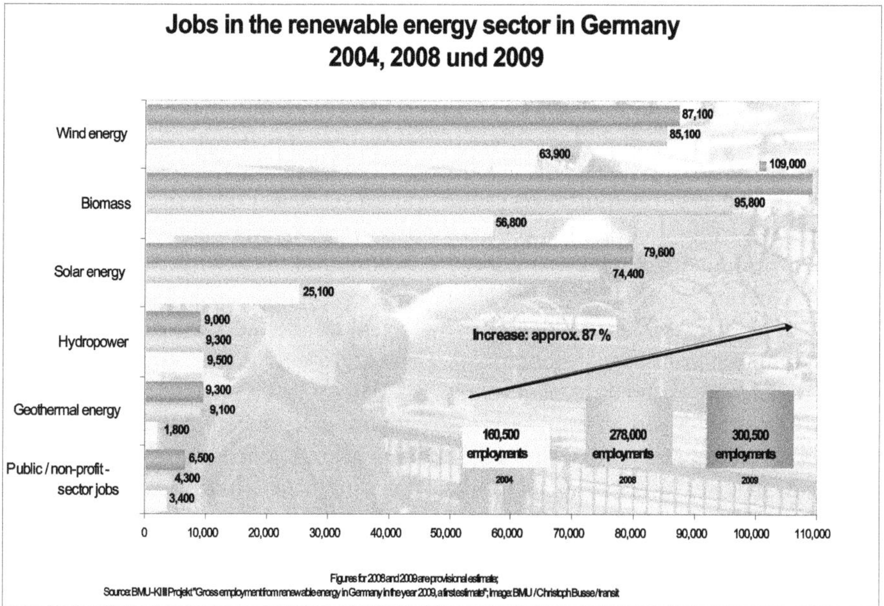

Looking only at the development of green electricity there is no doubt that Germany up to now is well under way. However, because of two main reasons this does not mean that the switch to a sustainable energy system has happened: Firstly, there are still heated debates about the role of nuclear and life time extension of existing nuclear power plans. Some people argue that sharing the extra profits between the public budget and the nuclear utilities (E.ON, RWE, EnBW, Vattenfall) could build a "bridge" to the solar age. Based on empirical evidence others are convinced that der opposite might be true: If the oligopolistic market power of the "Big Four" (current capacity share 80%) would be further strengthened by extraprofits, the entrance to the market and chances of decentralized green power would be weakened. Secondly, the implementation of energy efficiency strategies in all sectors (buildings, transportation, appliances) are lacking behind.

Therefore with existing policies the ambitious energy reduction goals and promising cost developments of the "Lead Scenario" will not be reached. This increases the risk, that avoidable incremental costs of fostering renewables without cost reduction by energy efficiency may prepare the ground for counterattacks against the transition to sustainable energy systems.

4.2 Lessons learned from restructuring the German energy sector

There are some key messages which can be derived from energy related scenario work and policies in Germany:

- **Sustainable energy systems presuppose advanced efficiency**
  From a technological and economic point of view, far-reaching efficiency improvements are possible. This has been proven by comprehensive analyses for the building and transportation sector and for electrical devices (e.g. appliances, motor drives, ventilation, pressurised air, lighting) and for integrated strategies to reduce material and energy consumption. Efficiency improvements for the period 2000 – 2050 of at least 2.6%/a for primary energy consumption (which almost doubles the long term historical trend) and 1.8%/a for electricity consumption has been demonstrated. **Thus an effective efficiency strategy is indispensable** if the reduction target for 2050 (80% CO_2-reduction compared to 2000) is achieved on time and in an economically acceptable way.
- **Decentralised electricity supply – cogeneration is one strategy pillar**
  One of the greatest challenges for the transition to sustainable energy systems is the tremendous structural change of electricity supply (decentralisation) and the interlinkages to reduced demand. This holds especially true during the first „decentralised stage" of a green power system and the conflicts with the existing highly concentrated supply. Compared with the reference case in which 65% of the additional capacity required by 2020, or some 45 GW, is produced by large (600 MW) condensing and a few CHP power plants, the structure of electricity supply on the way to green energy has to be changed in a systematic way: In a sustainable electricity sector up to 2020, roughly a quarter of the total electricity requirements (45 GW) can be (a) avoided by

improving end use efficiency and supplied (b) by distributed co-generation, (c) by renewable energy systems and (d) by large-scale condensing and CHP power plants.

- **Efficiency improvements can "buy down the costs" of renewable electricity supply**
  Speeding up improvements in efficiency for a certain amount of energy services is favourable from an economic point of view, since in many cases – calculated on a life cycle basis – saving energy is more cost-effective than producing additional energy. The „Lead Scenario" shows (compared to the reference case) rising macroeconomic energy costs up to 2030 and negative differential costs only after 2030 (at the earliest); in other words, after 2030 the total system costs for energy will be cheaper than an energy supply system that continues to be based on fossil energy sources. This has especially been shown for the electricity sector. The same holds true for the building sector, where active solar measures usually do not make sense until measures have been taken to improve the energy efficiency of buildings. **Thus, a strategy of increased energy efficiency has the macro-economic effect of compensating the additional costs for the forced market introduction of renewable energies.** For this reason, especially in the period 2000 – 2020, when the absolute additional differential costs of expanding renewables will be the greatest, highest priority should be given to a strategic initiative to raise energy efficiency e.g. by using Demand Side Management, Third Party Financing, Energy Saving Funds, Labelling and others (Hennicke, 2004).
- **A target and technology specific policy mix is needed to foster efficiency**
  The German Enquete-Commission on Sustainable Energy (EK 2002) recommended detailed strategies and instruments to implement a sustainable energy system (Hennicke 2004). The implementation process requires public support, incentive schemes, new organisations and guidelines especially for a *policy focussing on efficient energy use*. The "Integrated Energy and Climate Program" (BMU 2008b) has expanded this policy mix to 26 instruments.

Summarising the major findings of sustainability scenarios for Germany, one can conclude:

- A sustainable energy system is technically and economically feasible; many uncertainties exist, but a robust technological corridor (end use efficiency, CHP, renewables) should be used anyhow.
- There are moderate differential costs of a sustainable energy strategy compared to the business-as-usual case; positive employment effects and export advantages in growing world markets for renewables and efficiency equipment will be the benefits.

- A substantial increase in the conversion and utilisation efficiency of all energy sources is needed (e.g. factor of 3 to 4 up to 2050).
- Advanced efficiency improvements make it easier to finance and foster the market introduction of renewables.
- Within the next decades, a structural change of the power plant sector (e.g. decentralisation, diversification, participation) has to be managed.
- There is a need to speed up the market introduction of renewables: Timely integration into a supra-regional and trans-european system for importing electricity from renewable sources (e.g. solar thermal power plants in North Africa) is needed.
- It doesn't make sense to overspeed "hydrogen strategies from renewables" before 2030. There are cost effective alternatives which can pave the way to a "hydrogen economy" in the long run (2030 and beyond).
- A new policy mix of instruments is needed: Global, sector and technology specific instruments are necessary to overcome barriers and to combine the benefits of cost reduction from efficiency with cost degression effects of renewables (e.g. learning curves).

4.3 Integrating Material and Energy Efficiency Strategies

Up to now, policies and strategies to foster energy efficiency, renewable energies and climate mitigation are separated from activities to develop and disseminate material efficient production processes, products and services. Within enterprises an integrated accounting of energy and material flows is still an exemption. But from the **cost perspective** of enterprises as well as for the national economy there are close interlinkages if energy and material productivity is stepped up in an integrated way. In general, addressing resource productivity increase as a top priority seems to be a promising strategy for decoupling added value and economic growth from resource use and to create structural changes to new green patterns of growth.

To make it happen, this mainly technology and resource prices driven **eco-efficiency revolution** should be accompanied (see below) by a discourse and policies on more environmentally viable life-styles and on new patterns of sustainable consumption and production. In any case, the technological efficiency revolution only helps to gain time and must be supported by a structural change to new models of wealth.

The basic interlinkage between increasing resource efficiency and the labor market is implied by the fact that material and energy costs of firms are relatively high compared to other costs e.g. labor costs (see below; Hennicke / Kristof / Dorner 2009). A lower material and energy intensity, hence, lowers costs considerably and thus fosters productivity and competitiveness.

According to official statistics the average cost share of material throughput (about 45%) in the German processing industry is more than twice the labour cost share (See figure 7). Material costs include capital and labours costs of supplying raw materials within the production chain. Thus reducing the input of raw materials reduces simultaneously all cost items connected with the purchased raw material.

Figure 7: High shares of material (dark) costs compared to wages (bright) in relation to total costs in German Industry (Source: Hennicke / Kristof / Dorner 2009)

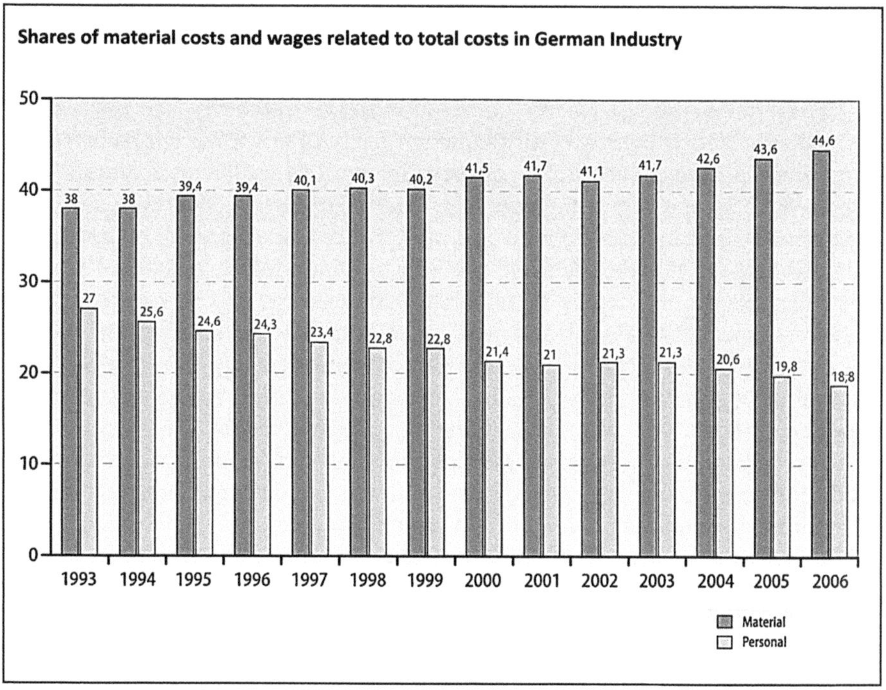

The energy cost share in processing industry in Germany thereby lies on average only at about 2 %. Thus, the cost factor „material“ is more important for the competitiveness of the economy and of enterprises than the labour and energy costs.[6] The same order of magnitude applies to other OECD-countries.

On the other hand raw material and energy prices (oil; gas) are mostly determined by the world market and thus will influence competitors all over the world in a more general and equalized way than domestic wages. Furthermore, concerning material and energy costs there are specific market failures and obstacles – also in the period of rapidly growing raw material and energy prices up to summer 2008 – why especially SMEs are reluctant to harvest even very cost-effective options for cost reduction. The lists of **obstacles** to realize cost effective **energy efficiency potentials** is long (e.g. deficits of awareness, information, market transparency and capital availability, missing life cycle-costs calculation, asymetric payback expectations, split incentives etc.) and will be certainly even longer and more complex when it comes to **material efficiency** (see Bleischwitz et al. 2008). Concerning materials the huge variety of raw materials, substances, composites etc. and of substitution or recycling options are the main reasons why without the help of a new policy mix (e.g. external experts, networking, information programs and incentives) high cost-effective potentials are not realized.

In this respect, it makes sense to ask how to jointly increase material and energy efficiency in practice by an integrated strategy and how to create positive incentives especially for small and medium enterprises. The management consultancy Arthur D. Little (AdL) assumes that companies can regularly reduce their material throughput costs by 20% by means of consulting by external experts. Experience shows that this annual reduction of costs can be achieved by non-recurrent expenditure that has an average payback of 12 months (AdL / ISI / WI 2006.) Reducing or using recycled material input avoids simultaneously energy input for transportation, processing and waste disposal.

The German Government decided in 2005 on a pilot phase for an “Impulseprogramme Material Efficiency” (see below) for testing instruments and for creating pilot projects and networks for SMEs and public enterprises.

---

6 To lower pressure on labour costs and to foster innovations are motives for the German Trade Unions (especially IG Metall) to engage in resource strategies on the enterprise level; see BMU / IGM / WI 2006.

Box 1: The Pilot Phase of the German "Impulse Programme Material Efficiency"

The Pilot Phase of the German "Impulse Programme Material Efficiency" (2005-2009)

- **Government target**: Raise resource and energy productivity by a factor of 2 (1990/1995-2020)
- **Overall economic goal**: Reduction of material and energy costs in the manufacturing industry and public sector
- Cost savings, new business fields, increased employment and competitiveness
- Minimization of resource use, residues, waste and emissions
- Pre feasibility study identified potentials, priority sectors for pilots (see: www.wupperinst.org)
- "German Material Efficiency Agency" (Deutsche Materialeffizienz Agentur/DEMEA) established;
- Financial support for **audits** (VerMat) and for establishing **networks** (NeMat) are offered for SMEs

The "German Material Efficiency Agency" (Deutsche Materialeffizienz Agentur/DEMEA) conducted and verified more than 400 audits on potential analyses. Among these an average annual cost saving potential of 200.000 Euro with short payback periodes (2 to 3 years) could be achieved. This corresponds on average to 2.4% of the total turnover and to an average saving per employee of 3.200 Euro per year (April 2010, demea 2010). Additionally the establishment of about 40 networks between SME for raising material efficiency were established. However, too many enterprises do not exploit these potentials for cost reduction.

In Northrhine Westfalia (NRW) the Efficiency Agency (EFA) was established in 2000 in Duisburg; since then the EFA supported more than 700 projects in NRW together with meanwhile 5 affiliates in other towns in NRW. A balance sheet of 140 realized projects summarizes that with an investment in resource efficiency technologies of 27.8 million € a cost reduction of 8.7 million € (average payback time of about 3 years) has been achieved.

Based on research and on these examples of good practice the German Ministry of Environment und the German Environment Agency decided to commit a 4 years research programme on material efficiency and resource conservation ("MaRess")[7]. Wuppertal Institute is coordinating this ambitious research pro-

7 See www.wupperinst.org

gramme in cooperation with a consortium of 30 partners from research institutes, universities and industry. The structure of the research project MaRess and its work packages (WP) is summarized in the following figure 8:

Figure 8: Structure of the project "MaRess".

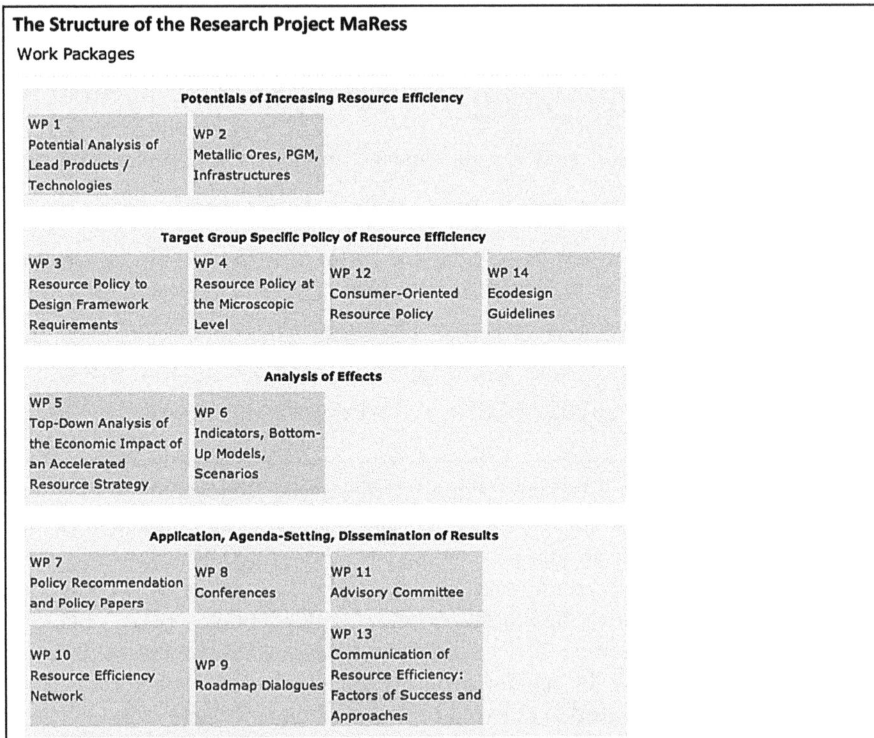

It is expected that a new policy mix for increasing resource productivity as key strategy of the new „Ecological Industrial Policy" will be the final outcome of MaRess.

Within the context of MaRess, Wuppertal Institute in 2008 suggested an „Innovation Programme Resource Efficiency" as a longterm part of a comprehensive German „Konjunkturprogramm" to mitigate the economic crisis[8]. The programme intended to foster ecological modernisation, create new business fields for GreenTech and (net) employment effects. It scales up existing experiences of the Demea and the Efa (see above) with financial support from the federal budget

8 See Hennicke / Kristof 2008.

for the SME-sector. It would be operated by a lean federal „Resource Agency“ together with a network of regional and local partners. The support for SMEs comprise a mixture out of impulse and indepth audits combinded with investment subsidies. The key rationale for this „Impulsprogramm“ is a **threefold integration:**

1. Integration of five key thematic strategies

- create sustainable markets, give innovations a direction
- establish strong institutions, build partnerships and networks to foster the diffusion of existing GreenTech
- develop sustainable products („craddle to craddle-approach“)
- use the market power of the state as a consumer
- create new thinking through training and education (e.g. „establish a Resource University“)

2. Integration of sectoral policies

At least the Ministry of Economics, the Ministry of Science and Education, the Ministry of Transport and Buildings and the Ministry of Environment should cooperate and harmonize overlapping and target oriented policies

3. The integration across technology and product development cycles

The program integrates target oriented R&D to raise material and energy efficiency with research, demonstration, pilots and market aggregation (fostering diffusion)

It has been estimated that (especially through this integrated approach) the programme would have a high self-financing effect for the federal budget and would contribute to defend and extend the world market position of German GreenTech industries. By the end of 2010 the MaRess consortium will publish the final reports. It will be available on the website (http://ressourcen.wupperinst.org) in January 2011.

One key result can be selected out of many detailed results of the MaRess project which is interesting from the perspective of decoupling and the macroeconomic benefits of integrated climate and resource protection strategies.

4.4. Economic benefits of integrated policies for climate and resource protection.

For a long time – especially among economists from the USA – concerning cost-benefit-analyses of climate change the perception dominated that ambitous climate protection would be more expensive and a strategy of „wait and see“ would be more advantageous comparatively (Nordhaus 2000; Hennicke 1998; Hennicke/Becker 1999). However, a rapidly growing number of national and international studies in the field of climate protection recently come to a consistent but opposite result: Reaching extensive Greenhouse Gas (GHG) reduction tragets and pushing structural change by ambitous climate protection is not only technically feasible but involves positive macroeconomic net effects also (UBA 2009, McKinsey 2009, WWF / Prognos / Öko-Institut / Ziesing 2009, ADAM 2009, RECIPE 2009).

Regarding the macroeconomic impact of integrated resource and climate policies first results from simulation calculations with the „Panta Rhei Model“ (Distelkamp / Meyer / Meyer 2010) show that already a limited implementation of resource policy instruments taken from the so-called „MaRess-Kit“ lead to the following effects for the target year 2030 – each compared to a reference path of an active climate protection that ensures reaching a 54% climate protection target in the year 2030:

- a considerable reduction of material consumption by about -20%,
- an increase of the Gross Domestic Product (GDP) by about +14%,
- an increase in employment by 1.9 % (considering demographic factors and a productivity-oriented trend in wages) and
- a reduction of the public deficit in 2030 by 30 bn €.

Following these results an integrated climate and resource policy would have a typical win-win-characteristic and a robust self-financing effect concerning the national budget.

Summarizing, the simulation calculation comes to the conclusion that „a consequent dematerialisation policy strenghtens Germany‘s international competitiveness ...“ (Distelkamp / Meyer / Meyer 2010). Thus, for the first time a complex model analysis demonstrated for a high-technology country that the „combination of an engaged climate protection policy with a policy aiming at increasing material efficiency can achieve an absolute decoupling from economic growth and resource consumption“.

This result is an exciting contribution for the recent debates on the limits of growth. On the one hand it has to be analysed in more detail whether the assumptions of the modelling approach could be translated into real models of change and into a societal transformation strategy. On the other hand the results are a challenge for a growing number of experts who believe that efficiency does not contribute to decoupling and even assume that further economic growth in IC is no more possible (see: new economics foundation 2010). At the heart of this discussion is the question whether and how far „GreenTech“ of „green“ growth can contribute to a more sustainable growth pattern.

5. “Green Tech”: Promising, but not sufficient!

Worldwide, green technology markets („GreenTech“) are developing very successfully (BMU 2009). A growing number of decision makers recognize this developments of „green lead markets“ as important levers for future green growth, for overcoming stagnation in other branches while facing the resource and climate crisis. The necessary new investment culture for green technologies has entered the literature by the keyword „Green New Deal“ (UNEP 2009, Schepelmann et al. 2009). Above all, the term refers to recovery programmes that concentrate on „green“ investments in products and services that simultaneously contribute to resource and climate protection.

Furthermore, it stands for a structural change in all fields of policy making for breaking up unsustainable structures and instead build up sustainable structures.

Estimates for the global market volume of the six GreenTech lead markets (energy efficiency, sustainable water management and mobility, environment-friendly power generation, material efficiency, waste management and recycling) total up to 1.4 trillion € for the year 2007 and 3.1 trillion € for the year 2020 (BMU 2009).

The share of turnover of the environmental technologies related to the total turnover of all economic sectors in Germany increases according to projections (BMU 2009) from 8% in the year 2007 (absolute numbers: about 150 billion €) to 14% in the year 2020 (absolute numbers: about 460 billion €) and by then exceeds the automobile industry (in 2020 about 390 billion €). For Germany alone, estimates by the German Federal Environenment Office for 2006 amount to 1.8 million employees in the environment sector. This means a share of 4.5 % of total employment; and this trend is rising rapidly .

What is the driving force behind these trends? The growing global scarcity of natural capital will trigger a historically unprecedented new quality and quantity of „clean“ innovations and **a new typ of a nature saving and (under specific conditions) labour augmenting technological progress**. This new direction of technical progress – raising resource and energy productivity – can be summarized under the popular slogan: “Make tons and kilowatthours redundant not people”.

If and to what extend social "win-win"-effects actually do result depends on a variety of determinants – not least on a forward-thinking climate and resource policy and on the design of a supporting framework and policy mix („carrots, sticks and tambourines").

The plausibility of win-win-effects of an integrated climate- and resource policy can be derived from the economic rationale of recent climate mitigation scenarios (see above) and the following list of driving forces. An integrated climate and resource policy

- induces and reinforces – in response to the secular scarcity of natural capital – a global innovation and investment push which is unique compared to other eras in history,
- guides capital – rather than into unproductive financial investments – into new, long-term and economically real investment dynamics which considerably increases the macroeconomic investment ratio and therefore triggers positive macroeconomic multiplier effects,
- promotes – by a targeted reduction of barriers – the dissemination of best available technologies (BAT) and simultaneously strengthens incentives for innovations concerning products (e.g. vehicles or consumer goods), production processes and infrastructures (e.g. buildings),
- thus increases resource costs savings and creates new business fields for producers with the effect of an increasing competitiveness, expanded or newly generated export markets and – under appropriate framework conditions – considerable positive employment trends,
- accelerates the subsitution of raw material imports (primarily energy, material) by efficiency and alternative technologies and therefore saves considerable import costs and contributes to the national value creation.

6. The importance of international cooperation: The case of „green buildings"

It remains an open question how the knowledge on the latest developments of GreenTech and integrated climate and resource protection policies can be transferred to the developing world. In the context of this paper a short view on the building sector will be chosen as an example. There is consensus between experts that green buildings have the greatest, but most neglected potential for costs and CO_2 reduction (IEA 2008). It has been calculated that almost 40% of the neccessary CO_2-reduction in 2050 could be realized by energy efficient buildings (see figure 9). On the other hand the building sector is highly complex and technology and know how transfer from ICs to the developing world on best available technologies (BAT) is still in its infancy, not to talk about the introduction of innovative financial mechanisms (e.g. CDM).

Figure 9: Energy Efficiency in Buidlings, Source: WBCSD (2009) / IEA (2008).

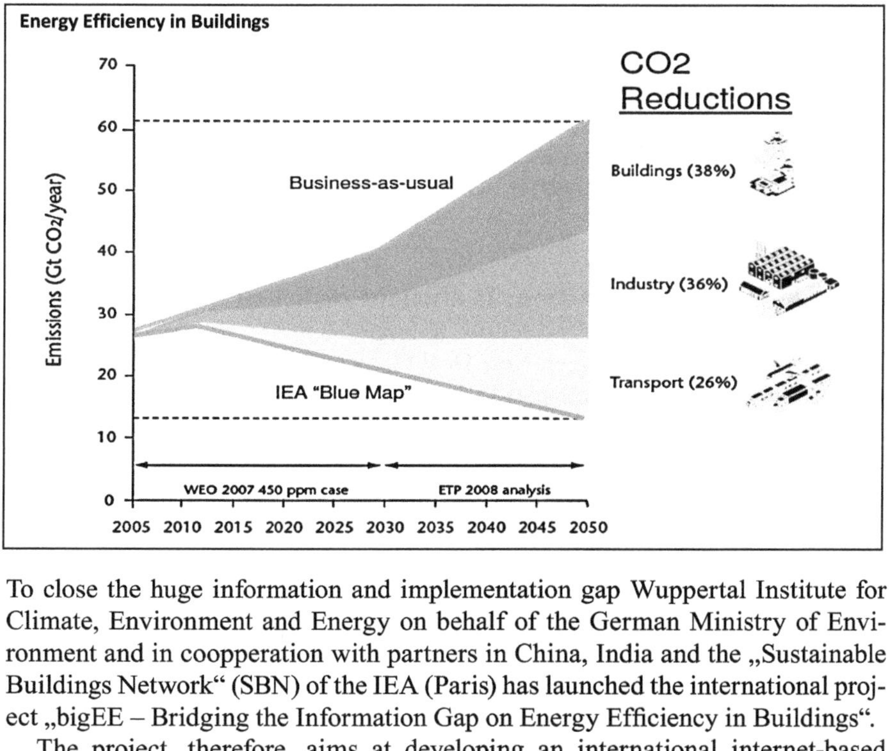

To close the huge information and implementation gap Wuppertal Institute for Climate, Environment and Energy on behalf of the German Ministry of Environment and in coopperation with partners in China, India and the „Sustainable Buildings Network" (SBN) of the IEA (Paris) has launched the international project „bigEE – Bridging the Information Gap on Energy Efficiency in Buildings".

The project, therefore, aims at developing an international internet-based knowledge platform for energy efficiency in buildings, building-related technologies and appliances. The platform will provide information on technical solutions, potentials, and cost-effectiveness of energy efficiency in buildings as well as information on policy instruments and good practices. All types of buildings (new/existing; commercial/residential) and four climate zones will be covered.

The pronounced goal and distinctive mark of bigEE is to address decision-makers, being private or public investors or policy makers in administrations and parliaments. The processing and presentation of information will be focused towards the background and practical needs of these target groups. Information will also be provided with a view to the specific conditions and needs of different countries. Therefore, bigEE is based on a network of institutions in partner countries, which will collect and actively disseminate information. (Wuppertal Institute 2010).

International cooperation and mutually social learning processes are the key to foster the global transfer of knowledge on (BAT) technologies, potentials, economics, policies and measures and good practice. This is also a precondition to bring the challenging concept of technological "leap frogging" down to implementation and action.

Furthermore, the lessons learned on **the integration of technological and social innovations** should be exchanged as well. At the end of the day, it is not technology which solves the problems but people who decide on sustainable production and consumption patterns. This brings us – last but not least – to the provoking question "Is efficient sufficient"?

7. An unconvenient question: Is efficient sufficient?

The main reason why a „Green New Deal" – focussing only on investment patterns towards „Green Technologies" – is not sufficient to protect the planet‘s ecosystems is that the underlying assumed efficiency drivers up to now do not effectively hold what they promise. While in many technology sectors (production processes, vehicles, buildings, household applicances) **specific energy efficiency increase** has made considerable progress, the sheer size of the applications overcompensated the relative efficiency gains realized during the last decade (ECEEE 2010). This holds true e.g. for buildings as the average size of living space in the developed countries increased considerably within the last decades (WBCSD 2009) and within this the respective heating, cooling and lighting energy. It also holds true for household applications like refrigerators or colour TVs and for car mobility (ECEEE 2010).

In the year 1955 a typical Volkswagen ("VW Käfer") with 30 HP[9] had an average fuel consumption of 7.5 litres per 100 kilometres while a modern "New Beetle" with 75 HP still needs 7.1 litres. In 1973 the german car fleet required 60 HP on average to enable car mobility. The corresponding value today is more than 100 HP. Colour TVs today – with a comparable diameter of its screens – are unequally energy saving related to earlier models, but the trend to very big flat screen TVs has overcompensated the energy efficiency gains (ECEEE 2010).

These developments have been summarized under the terms luxury, volume and rebound effects. Even if there are considerable relative improvements in energy efficiency the increasing size and absolute numbers of technological applica-

9 Horsepower (HP); 1 HP ≈ 735 Watt.

tions (e.g. cars, refrigerators, ICT-technologies etc) and of living space overcompensate the gains.

An appropriate policy measure confronting the described effects has entered the political debate in Europe by the keywords „Progressive Efficiency Standards“ (ECEEE 2010). Its fundamental difference to the conventional concept of *linear (relative)* efficiency standards with a certain value of energy consumption per unit of size is that such standards progressively demand a higher efficiency performance for increased application sizes. Hence, the "bigger" the application the higher the required efficiency indicator (instead of a linear growing indicator). If applications then (e.g. a colour TV) exceeded a specific limit of size the energy consumption would have to be within this absolute limit. It seems be useful to combine the introduction of progressive standards with a revenue neutral malus/bonus system.

For the EU and the member states it might also be necessary to focus **on absolute reduction targets of total energy consumption**. In its 20/20/20-decision the EU has decided on binding targets for renewables (20% of EU primary energy) and 20% CO_2-reduction up to 2020, but the 20% reduction of energy compared to baseline in 2020 is only an indicative goal. Additionally, it is important, to introduce incentive and awareness programmes to change life styles and consumer behaviour.

Based on existing technologies, products and services figure 10 demonstrates that an average European citizen today can decide to pratice a wasteful lifestyle emitting 14.5 tons of CO_2/a. If she or he switches to an efficient lifestyle the CO_2-emissions could be brought down to 5 tons/a even without any change in the structure of energy supply. However, looking into the underlying consumption patterns it is quite apparent, that e.g. air traffic, car transport, heating, food quality has to be adapted to a new life style. It remains to be seen whether and how these changes in consumer behaviour can be encouraged.

Nowadays, the discussion on this topic is getting more support in European countries. One reason for this possible behaviour shift is that the average citizen in Europe feels that – after a certain threshold of average per capita income – further increased income and general GDP growth does not really raise the citizen‘s life satisfaction („happiness“). Thus in many OECD countries (including Germany) the growth of GDP within the last three decades is correlated with a **stagnating indicator of life satisfation**. It has been argued that this striking development can be demonstrated for many countries in the world as well: After a certain threshold (about 9000 $ cap/a) there seems to be no more significant increase in life satisfation ("happiness") with growing income/cap (Jackson, 2009).

One underlying reason could be that for a typical citizen the statistical value of income/capita or GDP/capita (and GDP growth) is not an useful indicator of indi-

Figure 10: "European Lifestyle": The scope for different consumption patterns to reduce CO_2 in EU 25 (WI 2007).

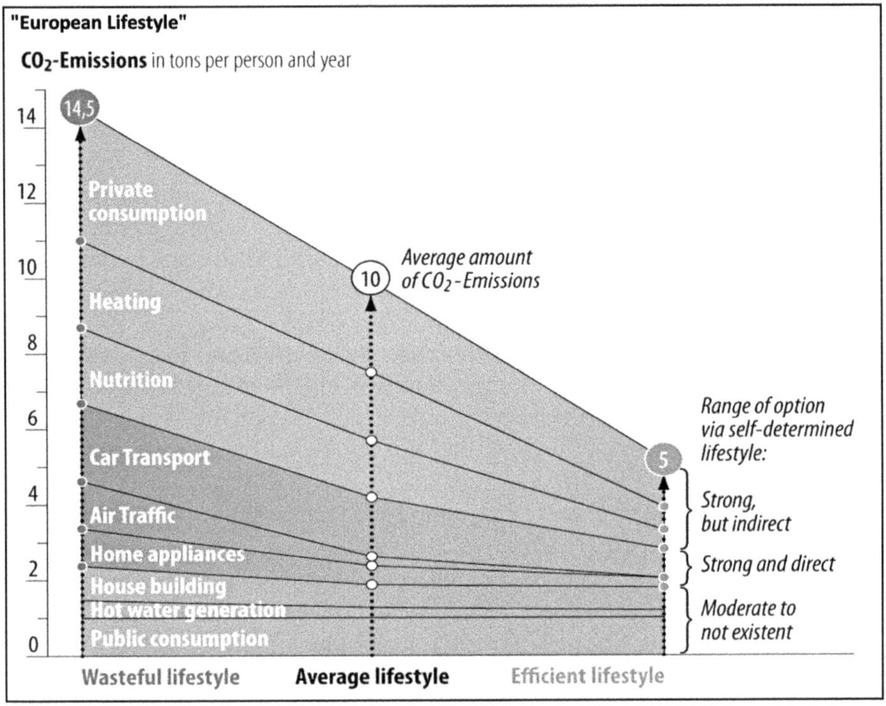

vidual welfare and quality of life. Many addional indicators have been developed to measure quality of life and new studies have been conducted (see Stiglitz / Sen / Fitoussi 2009) analysing the short comings of the GDP indicator.(Schepelmann, P. / Goossens Y. / Makipaa (2010)).

But up to now in official documents and in conventional policy thinking GDP growth is still the lead indicator of seemingly good economics and politics.

It is thus important to look deeper into the factors influencing people's personal feeling of happiness. Not going into the details of specific indicators, recent studies (Jackson, 2009) of factors influencing personal happiness give other features of living conditions a much higher priority than income or material consumption.

It might be argued that the debate on the limits of growth, sustainable patterns of consumption and life-styles is only important for the richer part of the world. This has been true for the past, but the general perception of the North („rich") and the South („poor") is changing and might be less valid in the years to come.

Figure 12: Factors influencing personal happiness, Source: Jackson (2009)

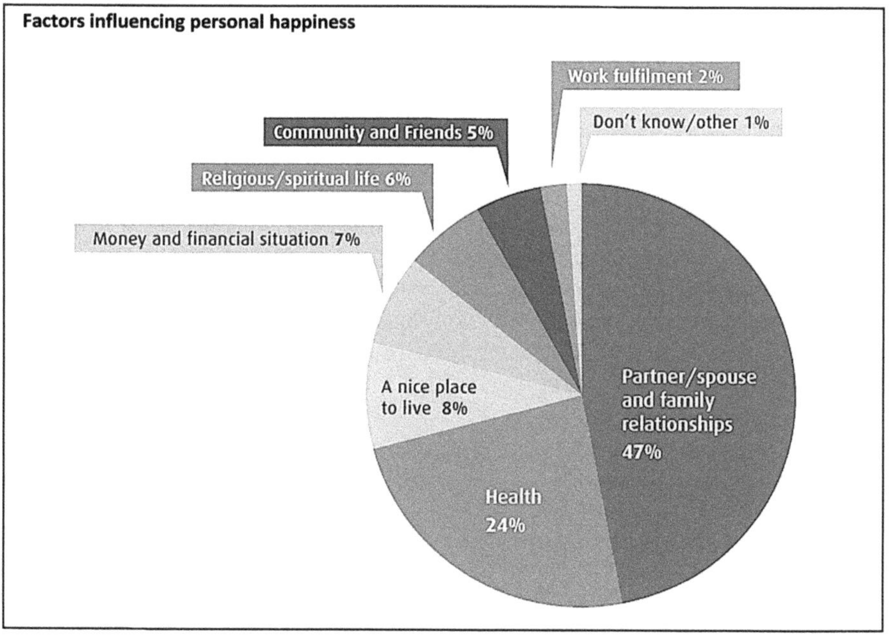

Growth, luxury and rebound effects[10], are not bound to national borders but they affect a growing share of the „new global consumer classes“ in a growing number of countries of the „South“ as well.

These effects especially gain a global momentum if the rapidly growing "new consumer classes" in Countries in Transition as well as in Developing Countries copy the materialistic and consumeristic model of life-style for which societies in industrializing countries serve as an example. Thus, the growth effects of unsustainable patters of consumption could be accelerated on a global scale. In 2002 the absolute numbers of the "new consumer classes" in China and in the USA had approximately the same size at around 240 million people. However, their share of the total population was only 19 % in China whereas 83% in the USA.[11] If the

10 These effects summarize all impacts reducing or even nullifying specific efficiency gains (e.g. household applications, information and communication technologies, vehicles, buildings) by more luxury, an absolute increase in quantity or resource intensive usages.
This also includes alternative usages of saved energy and material costs (e.g. more energy and/or resource intensive long-distance travels). For the definition of rebound effects from the perspective of the economic theory see Schettkat (2009).

11 Source: Bentley (2003) and Brot für die Welt, eed, BUND (eds.) (2008).

type and density of car mobility of the US would be transferred to China, the total oil production of the world/per day would be needed for China alone. What would happen if in the future 80% of the Chinese population would try to realize today's lifesytles and consumption behaviour of an average US (or European) citizen?

Apparently the globalisation of the western type of consumerism would „eat up“ all progress in resource efficiency. Therefore **an innovative and mutually interlinked type of "social leap frogging"** might be necessary. Again the North must take the lead to reduce its energy and material consumption per capita and to develop more sustainable consumption patterns and dematerialized models of wealth. But the „new consumer classes“ in the South must participate in this transformation. Therefore international cooperation not only on technology transfer is of utmost importance but know-how transfer on sustainable consumption patterns and new models of wealth as well. In this respect, the North might learn even more from the South.

Conclusions

It can be demonstrated by scenario analyses that (qualitative) economic growth can be decoupled from the use of natural resources by fostering energy and material productivity. However, this technically feasible **eco-efficiency revolution** must be accompanied by more environmentally viable lifestyles and new patterns of sustainable consumption and production. This challenging social transformation needs time – the scarcest factor of all. Thus in a global sense, gaining time may be the most important goal and "green and clean" technologies can contribute a lot to it.

References

ADAM (2009): ADAM 2-degree scenario for Europe – policies and impacts, Project No: 018476-GOCE, ADAM Adaptation and Mitigation Strategies: Supporting European Climate Policy Instrument: Integrated Project (IP), Global Change and Ecosystems, Deliverable D3 of work package M1 (code D-M1.3), http://adamproject.info/index.php/Download-document/473-D-M1.3.html (09/2009)

ADL / Wuppertal Institut / FhG-ISI (2005): ADL [Arthur D. Little GmbH], Wuppertal Institut, FhG-ISI [Fraunhofer Institut für System- und Innovationsforschung], Studie zur Konzeption eines Programms für die Steigerung der Materialeffizienz in Mittelständischen Unternehmen, Abschlussbericht: www.materialeffizienz.de/dateien/fachartikel/studie.pdf

Bentley, M. D. (2003): Sustainable Consumption : Ethics, National Indices and International Relations (Dissertaion), Paris

Bleischwitz et al. (2008): Ressourcenpolitik zur Gestaltung der Rahmenbedingungen. Wuppertal: Wuppertal Institut für Klima, Umwelt, Energie (MaRess Paper 3.1).

Bernard, S. / Asokan, S. / Warrell, H. / & Lemer / J. (2009): Which country has the greenest bail-out? Available online at: http://www.ft.com/cms/s/0/cc207678-0738-11de-9294-000077b07658.html?nclick_check=1.

BMU / BMWi (2007): Bericht zur Umsetzung der in der Kabinettsklausur am 23./24.08.2007 in Meseberg beschlossenen Eckpunkte für ein Integriertes Energie- und Klimaprogramm. http://www.bmu.de/klimaschutz/downloads/doc/40514.php

BMU (2008a): [Bundesministerium für Umwelt, Naturschutz und Reaktorsicherheit] (ed.): Lead Study 2008. Further development of the "Strategy to increase the use of renewable energies" within the context of the current climate protection goals of Germany and Europe. Berlin

BMU (2008b): Den Herausforderungen der Energie- und Klimapolitik erfolgreich begegnen. Hintergrundpapier zur Verabschiedung des zweiten Maßnahmenpaketes des integrierten Energie- und Klimaprogramms der Bundesregierung. http://www.bmu.bund.de/klimaschutz/nationale_klimapolitik/doc/41818.php

BMU (ed.) (2009): GreenTech made in Germany 2.0, Verlag Franz Vahlen München/Munich http://www.bmu.de/files/pdfs/allgemein/application/pdf/green tech 2009.pdf

BMU (2010): Gross employment from renewable energy in Germany in 2009 – a first estimate. Short- and long-term impacts of the expansion of renewable energy on the German labor market: third report on gross employment.
http://www.bmu.de/english/renewable_energy/documents/doc/45907.php

Brot für die Welt, eed, BUND (Hrsg.) (2008): Zukunftsfähiges Deutschland in einer globalisierten Welt. Eine Studie des Wuppertal Instituts für Klima, Umwelt, Energie. Frankfurt

Distelkamp, M. / Meyer, B. / Meyer, M. (2010): MaRess AP5-Kurzfassung: „Top-Down-Analyse der ökonomischen Vorteile einer forcierten Ressourceneffizienzstrategie"

ECEEE (2010): Is efficient sufficient? The case for shifting our emphasis in energy specifications to progressive efficiency and sufficiency, Prepared for the European Council for an Energy Efficient Economy (eceee) with funding from the European Climate Foundation and the U.S. Environmental Protection Agency's ENERGY STAR Program, Chris Calwell, 22 March 2010, http://www.eceee.org/sufficiency/eceee_Progressive_Efficiency.pdf

Ecofys / DLR et al. (2007): Ecofys; Deutsches Zentrum für Luft- und Raumfahrt et al. on behalf of Greenpeace International and European Renewable Energy Council (ed.): Energy (R)Evolution. A Sustainable World Energy Outlook. 2007 (available online at http://www.greenpeace.org/raw/content/international/press/reports/energyrevolutionreport.pdf).

IEA [International Energy Agency] (2007): World Energy Outlook 2008 OECD/IEA, Paris. http://www.iea.org/weo/2008.asp

Jackson, T. (2009): Prosperity without growth? The transition to a sustainable economy, Pu-blished by the Sustainable Development Commission, (05/2010), http://www.sd-commission.org.uk/file_download.php?target=/publications/downloads/prosperity_without_growth_report.pdf

Jochem, E.(ed.) (2004): Steps towards a Sustainable Development. A White Book for R & D of Energy-efficient Technologies. Zurich: Novatlantis. (available online at http://www.cepe.ethz.ch/publications/cepeBooks/WhiteBook_on_RD_energyefficient_technologies.pdf)

Lovins, A. B. / Hennicke, P. (1999): Voller Energie. Die globale Faktor-Vier-Strategie für Klimaschutz und Atomausstieg. Frankfurt/Main: Campus Verlag.

Hennicke, P. (1998): Climate Protection and the Economy, in: Toth, E. L. (Hrsg.): Cost-benefit Analyses of Climate Change, The broader Perspective, Berlin, 1998, pp. 67-86.

Hennicke, P./ Becker, R. (1999): Is Adaptation cheaper than Prevention?, The Applicability of cost-benefit Analysis to Global Warming, in: Hohmeyer, Olav (Hrsg.): Man-made Climate Change, Economic Aspects and Policy Options, Heidelberg, pp. 126-164.

Hennicke, P. (2004): Scenarios for a Robust Policy Mix, The Final Report of the German Study Commission on Sustainable Energy Supply, in: Energy Policy, Volume 32 (2004), No. 15, pp. 1673-1678.

Hennicke, P. / Kristof K. (2008): Impulsprogramm Ressourceneffizienz. Innovationen und wirtschaftlicher Entwicklung eine Richtung geben. Ein Vorschlag des Wuppertal Instituts. Wuppertal: Wuppertal Institut für Klima, Umwelt, Energie (MaRess Paper 7.2), 2008.

Hennicke, P. / Kristof, K. / Dorner, U. (2009): Ressourcensicherheit und Ressourceneffizienz – Wege aus der Rohstoffkrise; Policy Paper zu Arbeitspaket 7 des Projekts „Materialeffizienz und Ressourcenschonung“ (MaRess); RessourceneffizienzPaper 7.3, http://ressourcen.wupperinst.org

McKinsey Global Institut (2009): Advertising the next energy crisis: The demand challenge; MGI report, http://www.mckinsey.com/mgi/publications/next_energy_crisis (09/2009)

NEF [The new economic foundation] (2009): Growth isn't possible – Why we need a new economic direction, Website: www.neweconomics.org, ISBN

9781904882718, January 2010 http://www.neweconomics.org/sites/neweconomics.org/files/Growth_Isnt_Possible.pdf

Nordhaus, W. / Boyer, J. (2000): Warming the World: Economic Models of Global Warming; Cambridge MA: MIT Press

RECIPE (2009): Edenhofer, O. / Carraro, C. / Hourcade, J.-Ch. / Neuhoff, K. et al.: The economics of Decarbonization: Report on Energy and Climate Policy in Europe, http://www.pik-potsdam.de/members/edenh/publications-1/recipe_report.pdf

Rockström, J. et al. (2009): Planetary Boundaries: Exploring the Safe Operating Space for Humanity, published by the Resilience Alliance, Stockholm 2009; http://www.ecologyandsociety.org/vol14/iss2/art32/ES-2009-3180.pdf, Zusammenfassung: Nature 461, 472-475 (24 September 2009), doi:10.1038/461472a; Published online 23 September 2009

Schettkat, R. (2009): Analyzing rebound effects. – Wuppertal : Wuppertal Inst. für Klima, Umwelt, Energie, 2009 – (Wuppertal Papers ; 177). http://www.wupperinst.org/en/info/entwd/index.html?beitrag_id=1008&bid=43&searchart=publikationen_uebersicht

Schepelmann, P. / Stock, M. / Koska, T. / Schüle, R. / Reutter, O. (2009): A green new deal for Europe : towards green modernisation in the face of crisis ; a report by the Wuppertal Institute for Climate, Environment and Energy. http://www.greens-efa.org/cms/default/rubrik/16/16475.documents.htm

Schepelmann, P. / Goossens, Y. / Makipaa, A (ed.) (2010): Towards Sustainable Development. Alternatives to GDP for measuring progress. (Wuppertal Spezial 42). Wuppertal. http://www.wupperinst.org/publikationen/entnd/index.html?beitrag_id=1313

Stiglitz, J. / Sen, A. / Fitoussi J.-P. (2009): Report by the Commission on the Measurement of Economic Performance and Social Progress. www.stiglitz-sen-fitoussi.fr

Tellus Institute (2010): Rosen, R.A. / Electris C. / Raskin P. D. : Global Scenarios for the Century Ahead: Searching for Sustainability. Tellus Institute. Boston.

UNEP (2009): Barbier, E.D.: Rethinking the Economic Recovery: A Global Green New Deal. Report prepared for the Economics and Trade Branch, Division of Technology, Industry and Economics, United Nations Environment Programme

WBCSD [World Business Council for Sustainable Development] (2009): Energy Efficiency in Buildings – Transforming the Market. Geneva. http://www.wbcsd.org/Plugins/DocSearch/details.asp?DocTypeId=25&ObjectId=MzQyMDQ

WBGU (2003): German Advisory Council on Global Change (ed.): World in Transition. Towards Sustainable Energy Systems. Summary for Policy. Berlin.

Weizsäcker, E. U. / Lovins A. B. / Lovins L.H. (1998): Factor Four, Doubling Wealth – Halving Resource Use. The New Report to the Club of Rome. London: Earthscan

Wuppertal Institute (2010a): Project "bigEE – Bridging the Information Gap on Energy Efficiency in Buildings". http://www.wupperinst.org/en/projects/proj/index.html?projekt_id=310&bid=43&searchart=projekt_uebersicht

Wuppertal Institute (2010b): Project "Material Efficiency and Resource Conservation (MaRess)". http://ressourcen.wupperinst.org/en/home/index.html

WWF / Prognos / Öko-Institut / Ziesing (2009): [Prognos, Öko-Institut, Dr. Ziesing (2009)]: Modell Deutschland. Klimaschutz bis 2050: Vom Ziel her denken. Bericht für die WWF Umweltstiftung Deutschland. Basel/Berlin, 15.10.2009. http://www.oeko.de/oekodoc/948/2009-054-de.pdf

Transition to low-carbon economy and its impact on industrial jobs in Europe

Bela Galgoczi

Abstract

The aim of the paper is to take stock of the expected consequences of the transition to a low carbon economy on European employees and map the challenges trade unions are facing. For the framework for any restructuring scenario and its impacts, we need to take account of the climate policy targets and applied instruments and examine also where we currently are with the fulfilment of previously set policy targets.

We give a brief overview of European climate policy targets at the light of the EU 2020 Strategy and interpret the role the EU plays in global climate change mitigation policy.

The main focus of the paper will be the effect of the transition to low carbon economy on industrial jobs in Europe. Implementing climate targets will induce a restructuring process that will genuinely transform industrial jobs, in both quantitative and qualitative terms.

We take account of available literature and initiatives of the European Commission in mapping future employment impacts addressing also a number of open questions. Employment forecasts on particular industries will also be presented emphasizing however the uncertainty of such forecasts with main trends and challenges in focus.

Content

Policy background of mitigating climate change – promises

With the gradual easing of the dramatic and extraordinary pressures exerted by the 2008-2009 economic crisis long-term structural processes gain more and more attention to temporary crisis management measures. The next big restructuring wave will be the transition towards a low-carbon economy, also referred to as green transition or by certain authors as the third industrial revolution (Jänicke, M, Klaus, J, 2009).

The International Panel for Climate Change (IPCC, 2007) and the Stern Review (Stern, 2006) provide convincing evidence that the world is already experiencing global warming and that the human impact on climate greatly exceeds the impact from natural factors since the onset of the industrial era. As a result, deep and significant cuts in anthropogenic greenhouse gas (ghg) emissions are urgently needed if we are to avoid dramatic, irreversible and self-reinforcing changes in the world's climate.

In order to set an appropriate policy agenda an emission target should be agreed and then based on the current position the trajectory for reaching this target can be calculated. The G8 group of nations agreed in 2009 that the increase in global temperatures should be no more than 2°C above pre-industrial levels. To achieve that, according to the models on which the IPCC bases its calculations, global emissions will have to be cut to half their 1990 levels by 2050. For industrialised countries this would mean an 80% cut in their emissions by that date, a reduction to two tonnes of CO_2 equivalent per head per year. At present, emissions in America are around 24 tonnes per head; in Europe they are ten (Economist, 2009).

The European Union is committed to a 20% cut, rising to 30% if the rest of the world promises significant cuts. Japan's new government has promised a reduction of 25% on 1990, but has revealed little about how it might manage that. Australia's government struggled trying to get its legislation through parliament. Canada's emissions continue to grow.

The US would offer a 17% cut on 2005 emissions by 2020—the figure in the Waxman-Markey bill, which is around 4% below 1990 levels—well below the figure of 25-40% that is expected of developed countries.

According to the "road map" drawn up two years ago at the UNFCCC conference in Bali, developing countries are not required to come up with numerical targets for cuts, but they are required to propose "nationally appropriate mitigation and adaptation actions".

China has offered a 40-45% cut in the carbon intensity of its economy by 2020.

Getting to a globally applied and binding strategy for mitigating the effects of climate poses an unprecedented governance challenge. This is what we saw at the failure of the Copenhagen COP-15 Summit in December 2009.

Disappointing past performance

Past performance is not very convincing either. Regarding the performance of the EU, while the EU is still among the few regions that managed a greenhouse gas (ghg) emission reduction on the basis of 1990, it substantially lags behind the proportional fulfilment of the 2020 targets (Schepelmann, Ph. 2009). EU-15 ghg emissions were down by 5.3% in the period 1990-1999 and then by 1.4% between 2000-2007 as figure 1 shows. For the EU27 the reductions in the corresponding periods were 9.1% and 0.4% respectively. The single crisis year of 2008 contributed a larger decrease than the preceding eight years together, amounting to 1.8% in both the EU27 and the EU15.

If we add that the 9.1% reduction of ghg emissions by the EU-27 countries in the period 1990-1999 is mostly due to the collapse of the industry in CEE countries and in eastern Germany, it is a very disappointing result!

Figure 1 Reduction of greenhouse gas emissions in the EU15 and EU27, compared to 1990 levels (%)

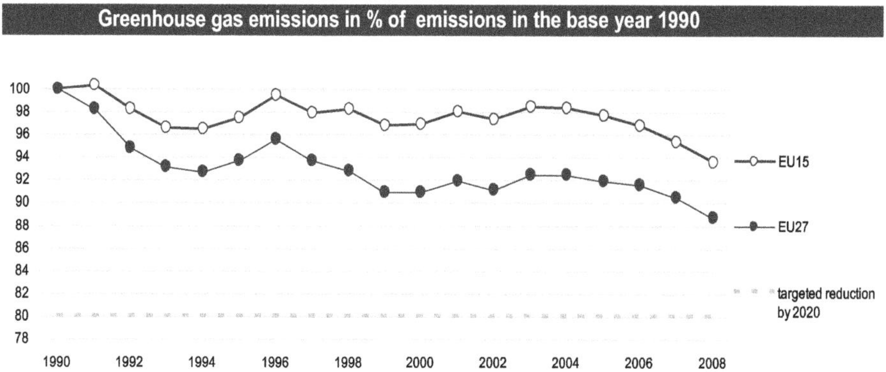

Source: EEA dataservice

The situation on global level is even more alarming. CO2 emissions by developed countries did not decrease in the period since 1990, while those of developing countries have substantially increased. The overall global balance is a 41% increase of emissions since 1990 (IGBP, 2008).

On the other hand, the necessary emissions reductions target would well be possible to meet on current technological basis. Economic history also delivers evidence that adjustments in economic performance of this magnitude had been taken place already.

Grossmann and Krueger (1995) adapted the Kuznets curve (originally interpreted in the context of equity) for environmental pollution during different stages of economic development by identifying phases, as 'clean and poor', 'rich and dirty' and 'rich and clean'. In regard to greenhouse gas emissions, this inverted U-shape curve development does not seem to apply. The most developed country, the US, is the greatest emitter of greenhouse gases. Economic history also shows that while labour productivity in developed economies grew to its 20 fold since 1850, resource efficiency only grew marginally. Compared to the tremendous increase of labour productivity during the industrial era, the current target of increasing resource efficiency by 20% does not sound extremely ambitious, or impossible to achieve.

The fundamental problem is that there are no inherent market economy incentives to raise resource efficiency. In order to correct this market failure, these incentives should come through regulatory intervention.

The ultimate policy challenge is to integrate the (full) costs of resource and energy use into the market prices through proper regulatory measures.

After the failure of the COP-15 Summit, the implementation and the applied policy tools are uncertain and the framework of the global climate policy regime after 2012 is unclear.

Still there is a wide consensus that measures against climate change are imperative and the basic framework of climate policy ambitions is given (80% decrease of greenhouse gas emissions by 2050).

The European policy framework

With all the uncertainties in implementation on global level, Europe must no doubt remain to be committed to its targets and apply the necessary policy measures to accomplish with its promised goals.

The EU 2020 Strategy with its triple priorities 'smart, sustainable and inclusive growth' has formulated its headline targets as 20% reduction of GhG emissions (possibly 30%), increasing the share of renewable energy to 20% of all energy generation and a 20% increase of energy efficiency, one of its 'flagship initiatives' being: 'resource efficient Europe`.

Implementation and economic instruments

Implementation is however the cornerstone of achieving climate policy targets. What we have now on European level, are mostly declarative objectives without a concrete roadmap and instruments of implementation. While economic actors are getting aware that the costs of using environmental resources will more and more appear in their operations, in lack of a concrete policy framework they are not able to plan the necessary adjustment.

The central issue is to have the 'carbon price' right. Economic policy instruments that determine the effective carbon price include 'cap and trade' policy (like emissions trading), a variety of carbon-related taxes and the direct involvement of the state through redistribution mechanisms (e.g. levies on carbon based energy generation and use, while subsidies for environmental innovation). None of these instruments alone would manage to transmit policy targets into business reality and none of them are without contradictions. What matters is an efficient policy mix of these instruments.

The European Emission Trading System clearly demonstrates the uncertainties and the distortions of the implemented policy instruments.

Generally speaking, the potential exposure level of industries or sectors to EU ETS can be assessed through three major factors: The CO2 intensity of production, the opportunity to abate carbon within the sector, and the ability to pass along carbon cost increases through to output prices. The economic impacts of the EU ETS scheme hinges to a certain extent on whether carbon costs are reflected in output prices, while the overall emission cap is of greatest importance in achieving lower emissions.

The Commission is currently finalising the design of the third trading phase of the ETS, which will begin in January 2013 and last until 2020. The Commission's stated objective is to increase the share of emission permits that are auctioned rather than allocated for free to installations covered by the ETS. A key concern will be the potentially negative impact of the next phase of the ETS on the competitiveness of affected businesses. Evidence from interviews with almost 800 managers in Europe shows that most industry sectors that will still be entitled to free emission permits would not face an increased risk of closure or relocation outside of the EU if they had to pay for permits (CEP, 2010). Another study on the potential effects of the EU ETS for industrial branches by the ZEW Institute concludes that some of the sectors analysed have the ability to pass through a portion of their carbon costs to the consumers. However, the results also indicate that the sectors cannot achieve a complete pass-through of their costs into output prices, with the exception of ceramic goods. Moreover, although generally accepted as an important indicator for competitiveness implications of EU ETS, the ability of sectors to pass-through costs also has its limits. Particularly, longer term impacts of sectors and firms attempting to passing through carbon costs, and the consequences for leakage remain uncertain (Oberndorfer, 2010).

The CEP paper argues that European governments improve the design of the ETS by limiting current exemptions and raise additional income of up to €7 billion annually. Rather than providing an unspecific subsidy for industry, this money could be earmarked to finance investments and R&D crucial for the transition to a low-carbon economy. It could equally be used to mitigate the possibly regressive effects of higher carbon prices on low-income groups.

There is thus substantial uncertainty about the third phase of EU ETS with a hardly calculable increase in EU ETS costs driven by an assumed increase in the price of allowances. Capital intensive industries need time to plan investments and to respond to policies where they can.

According to a study by the WWA consultancy group commissioned by the EIUG and the TUC, the forecast increase in the total energy bill, taking electricity, gas and emissions reductions schemes together is projected to be between 18% and 141%. These figures include the costs of EU ETS phase III and show an incredibly wide range (EIUG-TUC, 2010). Companies participating in this study reported increasing reluctance by their owners to commit to any investment given not only the scale of climate change costs, but the ongoing uncertainty surrounding the climate change regime and its impact on energy prices.

What is the target of climate policy?

It is a fundamental question of climate policy in what way it aims to achieve emission cuts; shrinking activities that are energy intensive or increasing the efficiency of energy intensive activities.

Government policies often do not target energy inefficiency explicitly so much as the amount of energy used. By doing this they do not recognise that many energy intensive products have a low life cycle carbon footprint, mainly due to their durability and recyclability. Energy intensive sectors, such as steel, chemicals and ceramics provide many of the materials and products that are essential for the transition to a low carbon economy (e.g. wind farms need steel, cement, carbon fibre and aluminium). These materials and industrial products may also help to reduce energy use by providing homes with energy efficient glass and insulation.

Energy intensity is not in itself bad for the environment, while energy inefficiency definitely is. Europe cannot produce low carbon energy or consume energy more efficiently without energy intensive products.

Consequently there is a great difference in adaptation strategies: do we want to downsize energy and resource intensive industrial activities (e.g. having financial services instead of manufacturing in the centre of economic activity), or increase the energy and resource efficiency of these activities while maintaining core industrial activities. These questions have remained open until now.

Employment effects

With all the uncertainties of policy tools and the implementation of climate change mitigation policies, it is important to examine the potential effects of these developments on industrial activity and employment in Europe both in quantitative and qualitative terms.

If we look at possible social consequences of a climate mitigation policy that is indeed being implemented and where the assigned economic instruments are actually applied (not the case up to now), we identify two major impacts. The one is the effect on employment, the other is the way a higher carbon price effects different income groups of society and has an influence on equity in society.

One thing is sure, with the implementation of climate targets industry and industrial jobs will be genuinely transformed, in both quantitative and qualitative terms:

There is a broad consensus in the literature that although climate policies would have no major aggregate impact on the number of jobs, a massive redistribution of jobs is to be expected:

- New jobs are being created,
- Existing jobs will be transformed (`greened' jobs in existing industries)
- Jobs will also disappear

With huge differences by region, branch and labour market segment!

There is also a clear consensus in the literature that jobs identified as 'green jobs' will be net beneficiaries of the process, although the contours of this category are not clearly defined (*often referred as jobs that contribute to preserving or restoring environmental quality; jobs that reduce energy, materials, and water consumption; jobs that contribute to de-carbonize the economy and minimize all forms of waste and pollution).* High energy intensity and carbon emission activities are on the other hand expected to suffer a decline and substantial losses of employment. This might effect regions, countries and industries unevenly and the resulting tensions need to be addressed.

In general, there is too much focus on the positive side of the green restructuring process on employment (`green jobs`) but less on employment risks and negative impacts at potentially shrinking activities. This is typically true for the Communication of the Commission, '7 measures for 2 million new EU jobs' (European Commission, 2009-1) that calculates the employment creation effect of the measures of the European Energy Efficiency Action Plan. The 'Employment in Europe 2009' report takes a more nuanced approach but puts the green job creation in the foreground (European Commission, 2009-2). A study by the UNEP and ILO (UNEP, 2009) takes into account the job creation potential of the green economy branch by branch. It takes an important distinction by saying that jobs which are 'green' in form of the end product are not always green in the procedure because of the environmental damage caused by inappropriate practices (e.g. in recycling industry). The report also addresses the issue of job quality in the context of green jobs.

A discussion paper by the King Baudouin Foundation goes further, as it addresses the implication of individual climate change mitigation measures on social justice and employment (Schiellerup et al, 2009).

Two examples where job creation effects are undoubtedly appear, but these cannot be seen as a long term and sustainable employment generation machine.

Retrofitting and insulation of buildings is indeed a great job creation instrument with tremendous potential for the construction industry that suffered particularly in the crisis. This very useful and important measure is of temporary effect on the mid-term, it can be seen as an extended element of green stimulus packages, but these are not jobs on the long-run horizon (when the overhaul of old building would be completed or the support for such activities runs out).

The other often raised argument is that the new green industry might become an export engine providing the rest of the world with some much needed green technology and equipment (the claim to become export leader in green technology appears mostly in Germany but also on European level). Developing green technology indeed has a great future job creation potential and exports might also play a key role. We should not forget however that exports on the global level (but also with the Eurozone) are a zero sum game, as we bitterly learned in the crisis.

All in all, the emphasis is mostly laid on the positive job creation effect of the climate policy measures. A more nuanced approach that addresses the complex effects of these policies with the full scale of expected quantitative and qualitative impacts on the labour market would actually not hinder but promote the transformation process.

Seeing the risks more clearly actors and policy maker would be more able to address these challenges by targeted policy measures.

Mapping branch level employment effects

When examining branch level employment effects of applied and planned climate policy measures the uncertainty is even greater than on higher level economic activities. We need to bear in mind however that most of the manufacturing emissions originate in primary production while most value added is concentrated in the downstream processing and application. According to a 2007 study of the UK based Carbon Trust estimates that the impact on carbon costs on these higher value added manufacturing activities would be small compared to differences in labour, energy and other input costs between EU and non-EU countries (Carbon Trust, 2007).

Significant impacts on international trade outside EU need to be only seriously examined for a highly concentrated number of industries eg. lime, cement, basic iron and steel.

A study commissioned by the ETUC and prepared by the Syndex consultancy agency (Syndex, 2009) took stock of potential employment effects for existing industries, emerging industries and of major infrastructure projects in the European context.

Energy generation plays a crucial role in climate policy and the renewable energy sector will be a future source of employment growth. Developing, installing, operating and maintaining renewable energy systems will create a vast amount of new jobs which at the same time are local in nature and not subject to relocation. According to the forecast of the study the sectors' 1.4 million jobs in Europe by 2005 would likely to increase by a further 760 thousand jobs until 2020. The Commission reckons with 2.3-2.8 million jobs in the renewable energy sector in Europe by 2020 (European Commission, 2009-2). The UNEP-ILO study on green jobs calculates with a potential of 20 million new jobs in the renewable energy sector worldwide by 2030 (UNEP, 2009).

The Syndex study warns however that the net job generation effect would be lower, as jobs in traditional forms of energy generation will be downscaled (e.g. by 80 thousand in coal mining and 20 thousand in related power plants)

There is a great employment creation potential in reducing emissions in the **housing and construction sector,** as the operation of buildings gives 40% of all energy use. Jobs are mostly to be created in the construction sector and the industries delivering the necessary technology overhaul. The Employment in Europe report of the Commission reckons that the directive on Energy Performance of Buildings will create between 280.000 and 450.000 new jobs in the mid-term. New jobs are linked to activities in retrofitting of buildings and energy management including related services (facility management, maintenance and control). Industries delivering domestic appliances, office equipment, air-condition, lighting and heating systems such as related ICT services will also benefit from the programme. It is estimated that each 1 million Euro invested into energy efficiency creates 12-16 new jobs. The part of stimulus packages spent for such projects have a high return not only in lowering emissions but also in creating jobs. The only question is for what period these public resources remain available.

The **information-communication technology (ICT)** sector will have a key role in improving energy efficiency with its potential of a 15% reduction in global

CO_2 emissions by 2020. De-materialisation of products and production processes is a key element in raising resource efficiency, where: software is replacing mechanical devices (embedded software), miniaturisation is driven by nanotechnology and fixed networks are changed for wireless networks. These processes will however also have employment consequences as ICT manufacturing is being replaced by ICT services, where software specialist replace hard-ware production workers.

Manufacturing industry as a whole is responsible for a third of global energy use and for 36% of global CO_2 emissions (International Energy Agency 2007).

Within manufacturing, **steel industry** gives 30% of industrial CO_2 emissions and employs 550 thousand employees in Europe after excess capacities have been eliminated through decades of restructuring. Steel industry is also a key innovator and supplier of several products of the green economy (wind mills), with lightweight steel solutions contributing to long lifetime buildings and better energy performance.

Over past 40 years CO_2 and energy consumption of the European steel industry decreased by 50% and 60% respectively. Almost all the steel of cars is being recycled and by 2015 95% of all car materials must be completely recycled.

The share of electrical mills that produce steel on basis of scrap has grown to 41%.

Even if steel industry belongs to the most energy intensive industrial activities, the lifecycle CO_2 footprint of its products had decreased dramatically and its energy efficiency has also improved. The contribution of the industry to further emission reduction is expected on basis of further energy efficiency improvements and not by further downsizing. The post 2012 EU ETS regime will be crucial for the steel industry in Europe. Under the current circumstances future employment effects on the industry are not foreseeable.

For other energy intensive sectors beside iron and steel, such as aluminium, cement and lime manufacture, pulp and paper making, basic inorganic chemicals, and nitrogen fertilisers an even greater uncertainty applies. Many of these industries are based in regions of relatively high unemployment and their continued operations are vital to the economies in which they are based.

Transportation is a particularly critical industry in both with view to its climatic effect and to its key role in the European economy. While efforts are being made to reduce the footprint of cars, public transport systems offer lower emissions and more green jobs.

Railways can generally be regarded as sources of green employment. In many countries, the trend over the last few decades has however been away from this mode of transport, and towards cars, trucks, and planes. Employment—both in the operation of railway lines and in the manufacture of locomotives and rolling stock—has fallen accordingly.

In the EU-25, a total of 8.2 million people were employed in all transport services combined in 2004. Railway transport accounted for just 11 percent, or 900,000 jobs. Rail employment has fallen in the last few decades and just the short period of time between 2000 and 2004, the number of jobs was cut by 14 percent. Road passenger and freight transport jobs, by contrast, number some 4.3 million, and air transport jobs number 400,000 (Syndex, 2009). According to the International Association of Public Transport (UITP), an estimated 900,000 people are employed in urban public transport in the 25 member states of the European Union.

The automobile industry and its supplying industries employ a total number of 12 million people in Europe by making it the backbone of the European manufacturing industry. 2,3 million employees are directly involved in the production of vehicles while the supplying industry has 10 million employees (ACEA, 2010). According to the already cited UNEP report only some 250,000 jobs are directly involved in the manufacturing of fuel-efficient, low-pollution and low-emissions cars and can be considered as green jobs within the European automobile industry (UNEP, 2009).

The automobile industry faces particularly high challenges in the next period in course of the transformation to a low carbon economy. The key process of the next decades will be the restructuring of the industry through environmental modernisation. Greening of the automotive industry by low-emission cars and its integration into an all-inclusive mobility system are the decisive elements of this strategy. top of the agenda. The aim is the innovation of products and services by deploying intelligent communications technologies, generating electric vehicles and exploring renewable energy sources (CLEPA, EUCAR, 2009).

There are two determining objectives for the automotive industry in regard to lower CO2 emissions: the reduction of emitted CO2 of cars and commercial vehicles in operation and the reduction of CO2 emissions in the production process of vehicles. CO2 emissions resulting from the production of passenger cars increased in sum between 2005 and 2007 at a rate of 1,4% due to the growing number of produced passenger cars. Efficiency rates that are measured by the amount of CO2 emitted per vehicle produced, fell by 5% to 0,83 tonnes CO2 in the same period (Syndex, 2009).

The greater challenge for the industry is however to meet the binding CO2 emission limits of passenger cars and light duty vehicles. The regulation of the European Parliament sets the binding limit of an average new car fleet CO^2 emission at 130g CO^2/km by 2012, with excess emissions premium fees imposed if the average CO2 emissions exceed its limit value in any year from 2012.

The long-term target of the Commission is 95g/km, specified for the year 2020.

It is worth mentioning that the binding regulation in 2009 came after 13 years of discussions on the reduction of CO2 emissions from passenger cars. In 1995, the European executive had indeed announced a 120g CO2/km target for 2005. In the meantime, the target had been postponed twice, once to 2010 and then to 2012. The automobile industry has failed to meet it voluntary targets resulting in the binding regulation.

Under these circumstances it is extremely difficult to give a forecast for the likely development of employment in the automobile industry in the next decade. The Syndex study calculated the employment effects of the conversion of car engines from conventional to electric engines. This calculation resulted in employment gains between 80,000 and 160,000 jobs until 2010 (Syndex, 2009). The conversion of conventional engines to hybrid engines was found as neutral for employment.

This calculation could not account for possible changes in the modes of transport, if the share of road and individual transport would lose on to rail and public transport.

The uncertainty of the expectable employment effects of the green transformation is not only true for the automobile industry but for the entire manufacturing industry, as well. Most available forecasts were based on at least a neutral overall employment effect, while putting the creation of new jobs in the green industries in the foreground.

Still, a recent Cedefop study reckons with a loss of nearly 2 million manufacturing jobs in Europe until 2020: '...although there might be expectations of an increasing share in manufacturing at national level, the total share of jobs in manufacturing and construction in EU-27 will decrease from 22.9 % in 2010 to 21.3 % in 2020..' (Cedefop, 2010).

Conclusions

We have shown the basic context of climate change mitigation policies with a focus on the European Union with the aim of mapping its potential employment effects for the European industry. There is a consensus in Europe that reversing climate change is the overall policy priority of the next decade and that the transformation towards a resource efficient and low-carbon economy will be the decisive trend of the future. Even if past performance in fulfilling previous targets is very disappointing, it can well be stated that the determination by European policy makers and economic actors to achieve a breakthrough in greenhouse gas emission cuts has undoubtedly become serious in the last years. The concrete economic tools and the economic fundaments of this process are however largely missing. Examples of the already existing economic instruments (like the EU ETS) clearly show this and lead to a situation where the effective carbon price in the future is still not calculable. On the one hand we have the ambitious targets and promises but it is still uncertain by what means and at what price these objectives could be achieved.

When addressing the issue of the employment impact of this transition process, the focus is generally put on the job creation effect in form of green jobs. It is not enough to talk about green jobs only, the challenges of the transformation of existing industrial jobs need to be addressed. If we have 10 million jobs in the automobile industry in Europe, out of which some 240 thousand can be classified as 'green jobs' for the moment, it absolutely crucial to discuss how the transformation of the rest of the jobs would proceed. Similarly, the future of the energy intensive industries in Europe should also be addressed.

It is clear that the transformation towards a low-carbon economy will encompass a full scale transformation of the whole economy with wide ranging employment impacts. Like it is the case with major restructuring processes, managing the transformation by appropriate policy instruments with the involvement of social partners will be a decisive factor in its final success. It is a crucial question how the costs of the transition will be distributed among the various actors and within the society.

This future restructuring process will be also unique in the sense that it is directly induced and shaped by explicit policy targets to mitigate climate change, implemented by means of a policy mix. This is genuinely different from restructuring processes that were driven by market forces (e.g. globalisation) and where the role of policymaking was more indirect in form of liberalisation and deregulation practices (without explicit policy targets). This is why 'anticipation' of change attached to this new restructuring wave can be more straightforward and explicit and responses to its challenges (above all related to employment) can even be planned and integrated into the policy framework right at the outset. Above all this would include the design of targeted labour market policies to ease necessary transitions and matching education and training measures. The most urgent step would be a proper assessment of the concrete and planned climate mitigation policy measures for employment.

It is also a vital question how to manage this process in a socially sustainable way, what role trade unions would have and what strategies they follow. One thing is clear however, a progress in emissions reduction that we saw in Central-Eastern Europe and the UK resulting from the collapse or downsizing of industrial activity is not the way to go for Europe.

References

ACEA, 2010: http://www.acea.be/index.php/news/news_detail/employment/

Carbon Trust, 2007: EU ETS Phase II allocation: implications and lessons, London, UK, www.carbontrust.co.uk/publications/pages/publicationdetail.aspx?id...

Cedefop, 2010: Skills supply and demand in Europe, Cedefop, http://www.cedefop.europa.eu/EN/Files/3052_en.pdf

CEP, 2010: Europe`s Emission Trading System: How European taxpayers are losing out to the industry lobby, Center for Economic Performance, 2010, London, UK

CLEPA, EUCAR, 2009: R&D Priorities for the Greening of Vehicles and Road Transport, Brussels, May 2009

Economist, 2009: A special report on climate change and the carbon economy, 3-rd December, 2009, London.

EEA dataservice: http://dataservice.eea.europa.eu/PivotApp/pivot.aspx?pivotid=475

EIUG-TUC, 2010: The Cumulative Impact of Climate Change Policies on UK Energy Intensive Industries – Are Policies Effectively Focussed? A summary report for the Energy Intensive Users Group and the Trades Union Congress Prepared by Waters Wye Associates, London. http://www.eiug.org.uk/publics/WWA%20Impact%20of%20Climate%20Change%20Policies%20EIUG%20TUC%202010723.pdf

European Commission, 2009-1: '7 measures for 2 million new EU jobs', Communication of the Commission, Brussels, 2009 http://www.euractiv.com/pdf/Draft_COM_IS_Oct2009-1%5B1%5D.pdf

European Commission, 2009-2: 'Employment in Europe 2009', European Commission Brussels, 2009, http://ec.europa.eu/social/main.jsp?catId=119&langId=en

European Parliament, 2009: Regulation (EC) No 443/2009 of the European Parliament and of the Council of 23 April 2009. http://eur-lex.europa.eu/LexUriServ/LexUriServ.do?uri=OJ:L:2009:140:0001:0015:EN:PDF

Grossman, G. and Krueger, A. 1995: Economic growth and the environment. *Quarterly Journal of Economics* 110, 353–77.

International Energy Agency, 2007: Tracking Industrial Energy Efficiency and CO2 Emissions.

IGBP, 2008: Global Carbon Project, http://www.igbp.net/page.php?pid=500

IPCC, 2007: Climate Change 2007: Synthesis Report http://www.ipcc.ch/publications_and_data/publications_ipcc_fourth_assessment_report_synthesis_report.htm

Jänicke, M, Klaus, J, 2009: A Third Industrial Revolution? Solutions to the crisis of resource-intensive growth, Berlin, 2009. http://www.polsoz.fu-berlin.de/polwiss/forschung/systeme/ffu/publikationen/2009/jaenicke_martin_jacob_klaus_2009/index.html

Oberndorfer, U. et al, 2010: Understanding the Competitiveness Implications of Future Phases of EU ETS on the Industrial Sectors, ZEW, Mannheim, 2010 ftp://ftp.zew.de/pub/zew-docs/dp/dp10044.pdf

Schepelmann, Ph, 2009: A green new deal for Europe, Wuppertal Institute for Climate, Environment and Energy. http://www.greens-efa.org/cms/default/dokbin/302/302250.pdf

Stern, N., 2006: Review on the Economics of Climate Change, report for the British government, London.

UNEP, 2009: Green Jobs: Towards decent work in a sustainable, low-carbon world, UNEP, ILO, Geneva, 2009 www.unep.org/labour_environment/features/greenjobs.asp

Syndex, 2009: Climate disturbances, the new industrial policies and ways out of the crisis, Brussels, 2009.

Regional Policy and Human Resource Development within the EU

Friedrich Fuerstenberg, Bonn University

Abstract

Harmonising regional disparities without giving up cultural identity is a fundamental prerequisite for peace and poses perhaps the greatest challenge of our time. Facing a wide diversity of both economic and social structures, the European Union meets the task of harmonising the development for future general improvement of living conditions. In spite of general progress in terms of GNP growth at national level, regional disparities show little convergence. Additionally, the integration of Eastern European states formerly marked by planned economies, poses enormous problems for HR development in the course of a transformation replacing authoritative regulations by market competition.

First, in view of the need for complex relationship between human capital and regional disparities, the need for multidimensional approaches is stressed. Then an outline of the administrative framework for regional and cohesion policy, promoted by the EU Commission, is given. The focus is upon the European Social Funds (ESF), its objectives, related strategies and implementations. The factors contributing to success or failure of projects related to HR development are then considered within a broader context of evaluation results, presented for the Italian mezzogiorno, the new Eastern German provinces and Eastern European transition economies. As an outlook, chances for a social dialogue to foster HR development, are discussed.

Content

Regional disparities and human capital

The social consequences of the evident economic disparities between regions, often resulting in subjective deprivations, are most obvious in labour market structures, especially wage differentials, differential employment rates and working conditions. On the other hand, there is wide agreement, that human resources, especially qualification by education and vocational training, are an important factor determining economic growth. A study by Rodriguez-Pose (2003), based upon regionalized microeconomic indicators extracted from the European Community Household Panel (ECHP) presents a descriptive analysis of this link by considering

- human capital and economic performance, taking the dimensions of educational stock as a measurement of the quantity, availability, and even quality of an areas human resources;
- the state of education referring to the current group of people taking part in some sort of education in the region;
- the matching of educational supply and the skills needed by regional economies;
- the relationship between migration and economic performance.

The relevant data are aggregated for four types of regions in terms of economic performance: winners, losers and regions catching-up or falling behind. The results are pointing towards a correlation between the endowment of human capital and regional economic performance. “This relationship tends to be clearer for winning and losing regions, than for those catching up and falling behind. Winning regions feature a better-educated stock of population, have a larger percentage of their population in full time education, and attract inward migration (although curiously not particularly job-related). Losing regions are characterised by a weaker stock of human capital, some evidence of mismatch between educational supply and labour demand, and lower than average inward migration. Catching up regions tend to attract workers from other areas, but still have a deficient stock of human capital and a relative shortage of people in full-time education. Finally, in the falling behind category, there are less signs of any link between their relative human capital endowment and economic performance. Not only do they have an average stock of education(..), but also manage to attract migrants across all categories and enjoy the highest level of job satisfaction” (p.18/19).

These conclusions certainly hint at a rather complex relationship between human capital and regional economic performance. A supply-side analysis needs to be augmented by demand-side investigations into the factors providing productive employment with competitive results. Regional policy by and within the EU, directed towards regional convergence and human resource development, therefore has a multidimensional structure.

The framework of regional policy in the EU

Article 130a (158 new version) of the Amsterdam Treaty states, that the "Community shall aim at reducing disparities between the levels of development of the various regions and the backwardness of the least favoured regions or islands, including rural areas". Accordingly, the purpose of EU Cohesion Policy is to provide EU Member States, and regions within Member States, with assistance to overcome structural deficiencies in order to reduce economic, social and territorial disparities and to enable them to strengthen their competitiveness and increase employment. For this purpose the EU Structural Funds have been established, consisting now of the European Regional Development Funds, the European Social Funds and the Cohesion Fund. A total of EUR 308.041 billion will be allocated to financing regional policy between 2007 and 2013. Three general objectives are set out for the next budgetary cycle:

1. The *Convergence Objective*, to support the economic convergence of poorer regions with a GDP per capita below 75% of the EU average. The fields of action will be physical and human capital, innovation, knowledge-based society, adaptability to change, the environment and administrative effectiveness.
2. The *Regional Competitiveness and Employment Objective*, to increase competitiveness, employment and attractiveness of regions other than those which are the most disadvantaged. This also refers to the development of inclusive labour markets.
3. The *Cooperation Objective*, to finance cross-border and trans-national cooperation projects.

According to Regulation (EC) No 1081/2006 of the European Parliament and of the Council of 5 July 2006 the *European Social Funds* (ESF) should strengthen economic and social cohesion by improving employment opportunities. Particular attention should be paid to the participation of target groups, the integration of migrants, including those seeking asylum, the identification of policy issues and their subsequent mainstreaming, innovation and experimentation techniques, methodologies for trans-national cooperation, outreach to groups marginalised in relation to the labour market, the impact of social issues on the internal market, and access to and management of projects taken on by non-governmental organisations.

The ESF should also act to tackle the relevant dimensions and consequences of demographic changes in the active population of the Community, in particular through lifelong vocational training. With a view to better anticipating and managing change and increasing economic growth, employment opportunities for both women and men, and quality and productivity at work under the

Regional competitiveness and employment and Convergence objectives, assistance from the ESF should focus, in particular, on improving the adaptability of workers and enterprises, enhancing human capital and access to employment and participation in the labour market, reinforcing the social inclusion of disadvantaged people, combating discrimination, encouraging economically inactive persons to enter the labour market and promoting partnerships for reform.

The *main regional foci of support* are the so-called Convergence regions – areas which have incomes per capita with less than 75% of the EU average. Regions qualifying for the status as convergence region status include nearly all the regions of the new member states, most of Southern Italy, East Germany, most of Greece and Portugal, and much of Spain and western and border regions of Great Britain.

Procedures for allocating funds are marked by five steps:

1. Considering the guidelines given by the Council of Ministers, the Commission attaches the means to different objectives; usually 77 % of available means are allocated to regional projects;
2. In conjunction with the Council of Ministers the Commission fixes benchmarks for each objective for the distribution among member states.
3. Member states submit regional development plans to the Commission for evaluation.
4. Following a process of negotiation and consultation the Commission presents a Joint Promotion Concept, fixing definitely the crucial points of transfer payments.
5. Finally, the financial framework is operationally related to concrete strategies.

Besides providing aid through the mentioned funds, investment in human capital is promoted through loans given by the European Investment Bank. In 2009 3.4 billion EUR were given by this institution as human capital loans, often with very long maturities, the main focus being the improvement of education infrastructure and healthcare.

It is quite obvious, that these funds and relevant transfer payments under a regional development label play a broader political role, e.g. in the context of side-payments between governments to reach agreements on other matters.

The allocation of means for inter-regional development needs to be justified in face of likewise *substantial intra-regional disparities* e.g. between urban and rural districts. The main argument is the promotion of economic and social cohesion, as has been stated in the European Commissions First Report on Economic and Social Cohesion: "Imbalances do not just imply a poorer quality of life for the most disadvantaged regions...but indicate an under-utilisation of human potential and a failure to take advantage of economic opportunities which would benefit the Union as a whole" (1996, 13).

The enlargement of the Union eastwards which came into effect 1st May 2004, and the affiliation of Romania and Bulgaria in 2007 have further increased economic and social disparities. The average income per capita for the acceding countries is around 50 % of the EU average at PPP terms. In order to handle regional subsidies within the given financial potential, the EU has introduced the rule that no country may receive means from EU Structural Funds above 4 % of its GDP. For the period 2007-2012 it is planned that the total budget for the Structural Funds will amount to 0.5 % of the EU GDP. For the period from 2007 to 2013 it is intended to spend 51,7% of available means within the previous EU-15 member states, 41,7% within the new EU-12.

Implementation problems

In order to make regional policy aiming at improving human resources effective, agreements for Joint Promotion Projects are crucial. Table 1 lists the links between targets, measures and groups concerned.

In view of the complexity and interdependence of intervening objectives and modes of action a multidimensional approach appears to be feasible. An example for such a Social Infrastructure Operational Programme related to Human Resource Development is given for Hungary in the Appendix. It is targeted to provide the infrastructure required for increasing employment and improving service quality, to develop the education infrastructure for the health care system, and to support labour market participation and social inclusion.

Table 1: Tailoring Programs to Objectives

Targets	Measures	Groups and areas
Moderate cyclical downturns	• Direct job creation (e.g., public works) • Wage subsidies • Training (subsidies or grants to workers or employers)	• Vulnerable groups (with least resiliency) • Hard-hit regions and industries • Employment services (counseling, job search assistance)

Reduce structural imbalances	• Employment services (e.g., information, Search • Mobility assistance • Training • Wage subsidies	• Proximate regions, industries, or occupations
Improve general labour market functioning	• Employment services • Training (e.g., apprenticeship, school to work transition	• All
Enhance skills and productivity	• Training and retraining (including in-service, apprenticeship)	• At risk or disadvantaged worker categories (especially for retraining)
Support disadvantaged or at risk workers	• Employment services (counseling, job search assistance) • Training (e.g., grants, subsidies) • Wage subsidies	• At-risk or disadvantaged worker categories

Source: Betcherman, Dar, Luinstra, and Ogawa (2000)

Human resource development as a component of regional policy within the EU needs to be considered within a broad frame of reference, taking into account basic factors of possible success or failure. In order to actually effect local decisions in accordance with regional policy objectives first the problem of dead-weight losses needs to be avoided: the use of transfer payments for investments, which would have taken place anyway. Thus the establishment of an organisational and institutional framework is necessary which guarantees proper allocation and use of available means. This also involves an adequate technical competence of local authorities. Likewise important is the neutralization of political networks of interest groups which might hamper the transparency of local decisions. A system of "countervailing power" as fundamental prerequisite for democratic decision-making may be lacking. While "the dominant factor in regional development is the quality of local institutions" (Hurst et al., 2000, p.28), negotiating power in order to overcome local lobbying is needed as well as the matching of self-interest with regional objectives. Therefore assessment by neutral outsiders may be required.

Evaluation of results

In order to better understand the factors contributing to success or failure of regional human resource development, three cases shall be considered in greater detail:

- the regional performance of the Italian mezzogiorno, contrasting the diverging development paths of Abruzzo and Sicily,
- the problem of Eastern Germanys convergence with special reference to labour market issues,
- and the evaluation of restructuring measures taken by Eastern European transformation countries to redress the massive misallocation of labour.

Case A: The development of the Italian mezzogiorno

Italian socio-economic structure is marked by a distinct North-South divide. According to Helg, Peri and Viesti (2000), in 1951 Abruzzos per capita income was 53 % of the Northern Italian one, while Sicilys was 56%. Both regions located in the Mezzogiorno had few natural resources, no large cities, and poor transportation infrastructure. One quarter of the population was illiterate. But over the following three decades, the performance of Sicily has steadily worsened, while Abruzzo has been the fastest growing Italian region. In 1994, while Abruzzo had grown to 76% of the average Northern Italian per capita income, Sicily had regressed to only 58 %. This diverging performance has been mainly based on putting a greater share of the population to work. Especially in competitive sectors, Sicily has not been able to generate sufficient employment, while Abruzzo could create more jobs in the industrial sector and in market services through generating steady productivity improvements. According to its geographical advantage, Abruzzo proved to be a suitable location for new plants, when in the 1970s labour disputes became widespread in the Northwest. For example, in Abruzzo clothing and furniture firms grew up mainly as subcontractors. They clustered in selected areas, especially along the coast and close to motorways. Gradually Abruzzo developed a dualistic industrial structure with large factories in mechanical engineering, transport equipment and telecommunication, together with small locally owned plants, often subcontractors of northern companies. Eventually industrial development became self-sustaining. New investment was attracted by the skills of the workforce and the availability of subcontractors. While Abruzzo has always been one of the Italian regions with the lowest crime rate, the role of organised crime in Sicily has remained important. The main factors explaining the divergences in regional development are summed up by Helg, Peri and Viesti as follows:

- In Abruzzo's success the development of a dynamic and competitive manufacturing industry played a major role.
- Compared to Sicily, a larger fraction of the Abruzzean work force became skilled and more resources were spent on research and development activities.
- Abruzzo benefited from a geographical advantage while there is little chance for Sicily to find adequate compensation.
- Sicily, being focused on high capital intensive industries, was not able to develop a diversified economic fabric. The industrial sector created less job openings than it destroyed. The public sector became an institution to absorb the otherwise unemployed.
- In Sicily, most public spending went to consumption and rent seeking activities and crime thrived.

This case shows clearly that an isolated human resource development program is likely to fail if it is not connected with a more complex socio-economic development granting fundamental productivity gains and competitive advantages. This will be even more obvious when discussing the Eastern German case.

Case B: The failure of Eastern Germanys fast convergence

The re-unification of Germany in 1990 started with a fundamental socio-economic reform within the new provinces, marked by immediate legal and institutional adaptation of Western German patterns, integration into world markets, rapid privatisation and price adjustment. As a consequence, a "high wage" strategy was adopted: While already by 1992 gross wages were comparable to those in the USA, productivity was at Mexican levels (Siebert, 1993).

Within the following years fiscal flows to Eastern Germany amounting to one-third of the former German Democratic Republics GDP and investment growth at a rate three times higher than in Western Germany provided equally new and modern capital equipment. This has contributed to quadrupling labour productivity in manufacturing between 1991 and 2002. Since then it is stagnating at 77% of the Western level. But this growth has been accompanied by massive labour-shedding. Labour costs in production stay at a level of 77 % of the Western German average (2007). Still there is no wage parity with Western Germany. The employment performance is poor with an unemployment rate of about 13,1% (2009) against 6,4 % in the West. Also the wage bargaining process still is deviating from the Western pattern due to "emergency provisions" (Oeffnungsklauseln), concession bargaining at firm level and fewer firms adhering to collective agreements. While around the turn of the century the overall picture presented growing concern about the continuity of Eastern German convergence (see Quehenberger,

2000, p.124ff.), ten years later the outlook appears to be less gloomy. The share of transfer-driven sectors like public and private services is shrinking, while the manufacturing sector is growing strongly. Nevertheless, structural convergence, also in terms of HR development, has to be conceived as a long-term process. The federal "solidarity pact" transfers expire in 2019.

Human resource development in Eastern Germany has to be seen against this background of a still heavily subsidized economy. An extensive Active Labour Market Program (ALMP) is being applied, mainly financed by the German government but also subsidised by the EU through its Social Funds. Its main components are:

- job procurement programs (ABM),
- measures for structural adjustment (SAM) aiming at re-employment through transitional labour markets, meaning new kinds of institutional arrangements for different employment statuses at the borderlines between gainful dependent labour and other productive activities,
- so-called incorporation and wage cost subsidies for regularly employed persons,
- further vocational training.

In 1999 2,66 bill. DM were spent for ABM and SAM, 2,09 bill. DM for incorporation and wage cost subsidies and 1,76 bill. DM for further vocational training, in total: 3,26 bill. EUR (Fitzenberger & Hugler, 2002, p.151). Recently these programs are focussing especially upon juvenile unemployed persons and incentives for job search, especially for the recipients of welfare payments and persons marked by long-duration unemployment. As far as concerns the efficiency of the programs in terms of employment promotion, evaluation results show considerable scepticism (Steiner & Hagen, 2002, p.192).

From a macroeconomic point of view, Calmfors (1994) differentiates between the following negative consequences:

- displacement effect (program participants occupy jobs otherwise held by non-participants),
- substitution effect (change in wage relations reduces demand for other types of non-participants),
- free rider effect (promotion of measures which would have been carried out anyway),
- taxation effect (financing ALMP also affects non-participants).

Case C: Active labour market policies in Eastern European transition economies

Similar observations (based upon the situation in 2001) have been made in evaluations of ALMP programs in Eastern European transition economies. Again we find a close link between the potential utilisation of human capital and an economic and institutional framework which promotes market-oriented investment.

In view of their formal affiliation to the EU, Eastern European economies face the challenge to create a dynamic labour market in order to redress still substantial misallocation and at the same time to grant basic worker protection against the risks of a market economy. Generally, real wages declined and wage inequality increased while at the same time a re-allocation of jobs between economic sectors as well a growth of the informal sector, due to increased self-employment (as an alternative to unemployment), took place. The reduction of employment was somewhat cushioned by social protection programs. But there are great regional differences. While in Estonia labour legislation imposes low termination costs for labour contracts with the result of higher labour flows and possibly higher job creation rates, in Poland and Slovenia labour market institutions are much more restrictive. Fixed-term contracts are limited in about one-third of collective agreements in Bulgaria, the Czech Republic, Hungary, and the Slovak Republic, and in almost half in Poland (Rashid & Rutkowski, 2001, pp.14-20).

In spite of trends towards a polarisation of earnings, the middle-paying jobs are still predominant. In Poland low- and high-paying jobs account for 19 % and 21% (Rashid & Rutkowski, p.10). Minimum wages (30-40% of average wage) exist in virtually all Eastern transition economies (Op.cit., p.21). In 2006 monthly minimum wages amounted to € 82 in Bulgaria, € 233 in Poland and € 512 in Slovenia (Eurostat). Labour market mobility is mainly concentrated within regions and sectors. International migration towards the West is still a major concern within the context of the EU extension, though a prognosis meets great methodological difficulties (Stepniak, 2001). Between 1989 and 2002 2,72 mill. Eastern European citizen came to Germany, and from this group 2,18 mill. persons left the country during the same period. This indicates, that due to immigration restrictions, migration from the East recently was a short term commuter phenomenon. For the coming 15 years estimates of net immigration from Eastern EU member countries to Germany range between 1,9 and 3,9 mill. persons (Dietz, 2004, pp. 43,47).

In European transition countries, education has become the key factor in explaining wage differentials and wage inequality. Like in Western Europe, the less educated are highly represented amongst the unemployed. Active Labour Market Programs (ALMPs) also are found in most transition countries. They comprise training, wage subsidies and public works programs in order to foster re-entry

Table 2: Evaluation Results of Active Labor Market Programs in OECD/Transi- tionCountries

Program	Appears to Help	Comments
1. Job-search assistance/ Employ.Services (19 evaluations)	Adult unemployed generally when economic conditions are improving; women may benefit more.	Relatively more cost-effective than other labor market interventions (e.g. training)-mainly due to the lower cost, youth do not benefit usually. Difficulty lies in deciding who needs help in order to minimize deadweight loss.
2. Training of long-term unemployed (28 evaluations)	Women and other disadvantaged groups.	No more effective than job-search assistance in increasing re-employment probabilities and post-intervention earnings and are 2-4 times more costly.
3. Retraining in the case of mass layoffs (12 evaluations)	Little positive impact – mainly when economy is doing better.	No more effective than job-search assistance and significantly more expensive. Rate of return on these programs usually negative.
4. Training for youth (7 evaluations)	No positive impact.	Employment/earnings prospects not improved as a result of going through the training. Taking costs into account – the real rate of return of these programs is negative.

5. Employment/ Wage subsidies (22 evaluations)	Long-term unemployed in providing an entry into the labor force.	High deadweight and substitution effects. Impact analysis shows treatment group does not do well as compared to control. Sometimes used by firms as permanent subsidy program.
6. Public Works Programs (17 evaluations)	Severely disadvantaged groups in provid ing temporary employment and a safety net.	Long-term employment prospects not helped: program participants are less likely to be employed in a normal job and earn less than do individuals in the control group. Not cost-effective if objective is to get people into gainful employment.
7. Micro-enterprise Development Programs (15 evaluations)	Relatively older groups, the more educated.	Very low take-up rate among unemployed. Significant failure rate of small business. High deadweight & displacement effects. High costs; cost-benefit analysis rarely conducted but sometime show costs to UI budget higher than for control group.

Source: Dar and Tzannatos (1998) "Active Labor Market Programs: A Review of Evidence from Evaluations." World Bank

into the labour market. However, they appear to reach their objectives only when the relevant economies are achieving economic growth and when they are targeted to particular groups. The latter holds especially true for job search programs. Public works programs do not provide greater employment or earning chances (Rashid & Rutkowski, 2002, p.26). In the long run, higher qualification and work competence by providing general skills and ability of analytical problem-solving will improve the human capital of a region better than the training in narrow vocational skills, as increased labour flexibility will be a main requirement for necessary structural adjustments. Main results of an evaluation of ALMPs by a World Bank research group are shown in table 2.

Conclusion: Chances for a social dialogue linked to regional human resource development

Improvements in regional policies aiming at human capital formation and utilisation are a fundamental prerequisite for a sustainable socio-cultural transformation in the 21st century. They are linked with the setting of objectives, the establishment of procedures, the mobilisation of actors and the evaluation of results.

The setting of objectives serving the formation of human capital requires several key data bases concerning the number and type of persons and groups concerned, the quality of measures taken into consideration, the duration of program participation and possible transition into employment. The actual definition of objectives certainly requires the monitoring of actual and prospective qualification needs (e.g. by Labour Market Surveys) as well as the matching of interests of participating parties and of course the matching of means and ends.

The establishment of procedures presupposes adequate administrative capacity and competent staffing. As procedures mainly are conceived as learning processes, proper motivation, communication and provisions for co-operative self-qualification must be incorporated. The choice of levels and sectors of action is very important.

The mobilisation of actors requires thorough situational knowledge and direct contact with participants concerned. Necessary incentives mostly will be the advantages of economic gains and the avoidance or reduction of risks, especially unemployment.

Finally, there must be a controlled feedback of program results by the way of independent evaluation in order to assess the impact of policy decisions and to enable their improvement.

First of all, however, the interdependence of political, economic and social factors determining human resource potentials requires a well functioning co-operative network of all parties concerned. Investment in human capital is strongly linked with macro-economic policy and labour market policies. An efficient co-ordination presupposes the matching of objectives bound to differing interests. Thus far, attempts of the EU Commission to introduce Social Dialogues have concentrated upon transforming a kind of tripartism of government, employers and unions at macro- and sector levels into "autonomous" joint problem-solving by trade unions and employers associations. The results have been not much impressive (Keller, 2003). Regional issues referring to human resource development are not mentioned in this context. Nevertheless the idea of establishing Social Dialogues at regional levels appears to be attractive in face of indispensable needs for co-ordinated if not concerted action in order to match differing interests in allocating available means.

Appendix: Social Infrastructure Operational Programme for Hungary

Source: European Commission, Regional Policy Inforegio (2007)

On 30 July 2007, the European Commission approved a Social Infrastructure Operational Programme for Hungary covering the period 2007-13. The Programme involves Community support for six regions of Hungary under the Convergence Objective, Transdanubia, Central Transdanubia, South Transdanubia, North Hungary, North Great Plain and South Great Plain regions. The total namely the Western budget of the Programme is approximately €2.3 billion and includes Community investment through the European Regional Development Fund (ERDF) of some €1.95 billion (approximately 7.7% of the total EU money invested in Hungary under the Cohesion Policy for 2007-13).

Human public services will benefit from support in an effort to provide the infrastructure required for increasing employment and improving service quality. The Programme also provides support for introducing structural reforms in the education, health, social and employment sectors, and contributes significantly to the revised Lisbon Strategy for growth and jobs.

The overall goal of the Programme is to increase labour market participation. To achieve this, two specific objectives have been established: (i) reducing territorial disparities in terms of infrastructure for human services, at the same time improving access to them; and (ii) improving the efficiency of human public services and ensuring that the reforms are fully introduced.

Priority 1: Development of the Education Infrastructure [approximately 27.8% of total funding]

This priority aims to improve the infrastructure for skill-based education and lifelong learning. The activities provide support for developing infrastructure related to formal and non-formal education, including ICT development in schools, development of higher education institutions, non-formal learning spaces and multi-functional community centres.

Priority 2: Development of Infrastructure for the Health Care System [approximately 50.1% of total funding]

The objective under this priority is to extend healthy lifetimes by establishing a more efficient, better quality and regionally more balanced health care network. The main activities include support for IT developments in the health sector and the development of regional out-patient care centres, in-patient care centres and infrastructure for specialised treatments.

Priority 3: Development of Infrastructure Supporting Labour Market Participation and Social Inclusion [approximately 18.5% of total funding]

This priority aims to improve access and quality in respect of services supporting labour market participation and social inclusion. Activities include the development of regional vocational training centres, an integrated employment and social service, institutions for social inclusion and elderly care.

Priority 4: Technical Assistance [approximately 3.6% of total funding]

Technical assistance will be provided for implementing the Programme. Financial support will also be available and will cover administration, monitoring and control.

References

Betcherman, G., Olivas, K., Dar, A. (2004): *Impacts of Active Labor Market Programs: New Evidence from Evaluations with Particular Attention to Developing and Transition Countries.* Wahington D.C.: World Bank Social Protection Unit. Human Development Network

Calmfors, L. (1994), *Active labour market policy and unemployment - a framework for the analysis of crucial design features.* OECD Economic Studies, 22, 7-47.

Commission of the European Communities (2009): *Report from the commission to the European Parliament and the council. Sixth progress report on economic and social cohesion.*

Commission of the European Communities (2010): *Regional Policy Info Hungary.*

Dar, A. & Tzannatos, Z. (1998), *Active Labor Market Programs: A Review of Evidence from Evaluations, Draft.* Washington D.C.: World Bank.

Dietz, B. (2004), Ost-West-Migration nach Deutschland im Kontext der EU-Erweiterung. *Aus Politik und Zeitgeschichte* B 5-6, 41-47.

Fitzenberger, B. & Hugler, R. (2002), Stand und Perspektiven der Evaluation der

Aktiven Arbeitsmarktpolitik in Deutschland. *Perspektiven der Wirtschaftspolitik* 3, 139-158.

Helg, R., Peri, G., Viesti, G. (2000), *Abruzzo & Sicily: Catching up and lagging behind. Papers 5(1).* Luxemburg: European Investment Bank, 61-89.

Hurst, Ch, Thisse, J.-F., Vanhoudt, P. (2000), *What diagnosis for Europe's ailing regions? Papers 5(1).* Luxemburg: European Investment Bank, 9-30.

Keller, B. (2003), Sektorale Sozialdialoge – vernachlässigte Bestandteile europäischer Arbeitsbeziehungen. *Industrielle Beziehungen* 10, 9-40.

Moucque, D. (2000), *A survey of socio-economic disparities between the regions of the EU. Papers 5(2).* Luxemburg: European Investment Bank, 13-24.

Quehenberger, M. (2000), *Ten years after: Eastern Germany's convergence at a halt? Papers 5(1).* Luxemburg: European Investment Bank, 117-136.

Rashid, M., Rutkowski, J. (2001), *Labor Markets in Transition Economies: Recent Developments and Future Challenges.* Social Protection Discussion Paper Series No.111. Washington D.C.: World Bank.

Rodriguez-Pose, A. (2003), *Human Capital and Regional Disparities in the EU.* Paper prepared for the Joint Conference of the European Commission and European Investment Bank on Human Capital, Employment, Productivity and Growth. Brussels: EU.

Steiner, V. & Hagen, T. (2002), Was kann die aktive Arbeitsmarktpolitik in Deutschland aus der Evaluationsforschung in anderen europäischen Ländern lernen? *Perspektiven der Wirtschaftspolitik 3*, 189-206.

Stepniak, A. (red.) (2001), *Die Freizügigkeit der Arbeitnehmer im Kontext von Polens Beitritt zur Europäischen Union.* Warschau: Regierungsbeauftragter für Verhandlungen über die Mitgliedschaft der Republik Polen in der Europäischen Union. Kanzlei des Vorsitzenden des Ministerrats.

Links:

www. Worldbank.org/sp. (Social Protection Discussion Papers).

www. Europa.eu.int/comm/eurostat (Statistics).

www. fuerstenberg-soziologie.de

Technology Innovation and Human Condition: Research and Development for Sustainable Economy in ECOWAS Region

Dr. Yunus Adeleke Dauda, Lagos State University, Lagos, Nigeria

Abstract

Sustainable economy is the one that satisfy the people without jeopardizing the prospect of the future generation. It relies on building environmentally sustainable economy. Gallopian and Raskin (2000) sees sustainable development as development "that seeks to meet the need and aspiration of present without compromising the ability to meet those of the future". Sustainable development policy process dated back to 1972 global conference on environment and development. The conference for the first time introduced sustainable development as a strategic concept. The conference recommendations led to establishment of many organizations to protect environment without undermining or reducing economic growth. Policies were made in advanced countries to protect the environment and lowered the consumption of non-renewable resources. Researches were directed to reduce oil consumption and alternatives and provide alternative to petroleum in commercial quantities.

Apart from its environmental hazards, it was also argued then that oil supply will only last for 36years if the present rate of consumption continues. The discovery of solar energy, wind energy and biofuels were the outcome of these researches. Two basic classes of solar power technology have earlier emerged; they are photorol-taic (PV) the technology that power spacecraft, watches and calculator where sunlight is turned directly to electricity and solar heating technology where heat from the sun generates energy. Researches in Europe and America starting from 1990 have led to the domestic and industrial uses of both and thousands of megawatts which are produced through wind and solar energy (Quinn, 2001).

Improved scientific and technological innovation that were the outcome of researches in most developed and some developing countries of the world have improved human condition. Douglas (1971) consider the benevolent aspect of science and technology to be the production of labor saving machines, promotion of wealth, improved method of production, provision of life saving miracle drugs, improved communication and greatly increased varieties of product and entertainment and others. Many scientists and researcher argued that technological revolution would lead to technological society where everyone would be wealthy and in which everyone will have unlimited pleasure to spend his wealth and where no one would die. But the uses of various methods and types of science and technology have no doubt improved human conditions in many aspects, but also led to the increased population and appropriation of earth natural resources that have changed the world ecosystem and endanger human condition.

Handim (1968) in his "tragedy of the common" thesis observed that the world population increase would lead to over exploitation and degradation of common resources that support human existence. These resources include water, trees, fisheries, public land use and air quality. Since then researchers have watched closely the trend in the depletion which support Handims thesis. They argued that 'the wise and unwise use of resources today directly affect the health and wellbeing of the present and next generations'. The developed countries are consider to be the greatest exploiter of world resources, but have also made efforts to use the same method she use to exploit the earth to control, ameliorate, and reduce its exploitation for sustainable development. The same science and technology that have been employed to exploit the earth resources is now being used to control and reduce its exploitation. Concrete efforts were made by them to ameliorate the effect of earth depletion in Europe, America and other emerging nations.

This paper examines the relationship between technology innovation, sustainable development, environment, resources depletion and human condition. The paper also seek to examine the processes and methods by which technologies are developed, used and managed to appropriate earth's natural resources for sustainable development and improvement of human condition in ECOWAS region.. The paper argued that despite the improvement in human condition through technology innovation most ECOWAS nation have not sufficiently benefited from technology innovation. ECOWAS nations have also witnessed problems of depletion of earth resources and ozone layer that were the result of the appropriation, use and misuse of technology and earth resources which now pose great danger to human condition, and sustainable development in the region.

Content

Environmental Threat and Human Condition

Unprecedented appropriation of the earth natural resources and emission of gases into the atmosphere and pollution of rivers and seas have caught the attention of environmentalist all over the world. The environment now faces the danger of destruction that was the outcome of its exploitation. The effect of these on atmosphere and the ocean have threatened the survival of human being, animals, fishes and all other living things in them. Glanz (2000) consider the atmosphere and the oceans as fluids that encircle the globe. In all days, years, centuries and from and up to millions of years, air and water circulate interactively irrespective of national boundaries and territorial claims.

Several types of human activity interacting with geographical process have disrupted the atmosphere and endanger human being and all others living things in the world. The atmosphere has been polluted by emission from automobile, air conditioner, home heating equipment, industrial process, war artilleries, bombing, electricity generation nuclear emission for peaceful purposes and others. In fact most of what we use to make the world easier and interesting to live and promote human condition endangers the atmosphere. Chlorofluorocarbons (CFC) are emitted into the atmosphere as a result of human activity which includes its use-in refrigerants, foam blowing agents and cleanser for electronic components.

Industrial economy is driven by fossil fuels which are carbon based like petroleum products, natural gas and coal. The environmental impact of extracting, refining, transporting and consuming petroleum product is obvious in developed countries and in oil producing countries. Oil pollution and spillage have damaging effect on land and ocean ecosystem. Gas flaring and pipeline leakages could result to air pollution and damaging of agricultural land, sea and river pollution and destruction of lives and properties. Human being now faced health and environment problem associated with the use of fuels in high tech industry and agricultural system.

Industrial processes have released pollutant that have interacted with atmosphere, which when washed by rainfall cause acid rain. The carbon dioxide also interacts with the sunlight or the heat radiated from the earth surface and cause global warming which is the cause of very high temperature in the world. Acid rain has caused health of forest to deteriorate in Europe, North America and Scandinavia. When air reached the atmosphere from a location in one country, it moves rapidly to another location within and outside the country. Tall smokes track used in industries send dispersed air farther from their source. This local air pollution could be turned into regional and global problems.

Environmentalists have attributed global warming to the change in the global climate, to industrial processes that produce large amount of carbon-dioxide (CO_2) which contribute to global warming or sculpture dioxide which contribute to atmospheric cooling or acid rain. Climate change has also change the location of extreme events such as droughts and floods. Emission of gasses especially CO_2 result from human activities such as the burning of fossil fuels tropical deforestation and food production processes. Scientists have argued that the emission of gases' into the atmosphere since 1700 have doubled and likely to double the pre-industrial level by 2050. The world oceans are also affected by pollutants from the earth and the atmosphere. Only small part of the ocean are under the control of different nation around them, more than 90% of the world oceans are not under any nation control or supervision. Human activities also polluted the ocean and current carry pollutant from the waters of one country into water of other, spread it to all parts of the world. Global fisheries, which provide people in all countries of the world with fish protein for domestic consumption, have been adversely affected.

Pollution and natural variability in physical environment have created conditions that have destroyed large number of fish species and greatly reduced their number and threaten the survival of the remaining ones. This has led to over exploitation of many species of fish all over the world. Co2 emission into the atmosphere increases its ability to trap and hold heat from radiant solar energy-which is regarded as the greenhouse effect. Research shows that global mean temperature has risen to about 1 degree centigrade in the last 100 years and reduces the ability of many plants and animals to migrate or adapt. (Krus et al 1992).

Global warming if it were to occur world could change rainfall and temperature pattern. Sea level rise will occur everywhere and low-lying coastal area all over the world will be endangered. Large percent of people lives around or at least about 100miles to the sea in developed and developing countries of the world are now threatened by ocean surge. Sea rise may also lead to the destruction of many islands all over the world. Some of them may even be submerged by modest increase of sea level. The disintegration of the West Atlantic ice sheet as a result of global warming would cause sea level to rise to an estimated eight meters if it broke away and fell into the southern ocean.

Many scientists now traced recent changes in spruce trees in many regions of the world to acid rain. Sulfur dioxide and nitrogen oxide are the two major pollutants. Sulfur dioxide raised to the skies from big industries, most especially electricity power plants, metal smelting industries and factory smokes track. The sulfur dioxide in the atmosphere mixes with moisture in the air and become a form of sulphuric acid, which falls back to the earth in acid rain. Motor vehicle exhaust and oil fired electric plants also send nitrogen oxide into air, and when it mixes with air moisture turn to nitric acid that fall to the earth as acid rain. Acid rain disrupts the life cycle of many living thins. Tree and lake dwelling animal suffer most from acid rain. Rivers and lake water becomes acidic and unsafe for human consumption.

Increasing human activities in the world have damaged the world ecosystem and endanger human and animal existence and condition. Vitousek et al (1986) observed that increased consumption of some species due to population increase and the cut of forest and cleaning of lands for crops have led to the depletion of species and lands. Brown (1986) catalogue lists and percentage of reptiles, amphibian birds, mammals and carnivores that are under extinction. He further assesses the world population and hectares of land that were cut in 1990. He projected to the year 2010 and found out that in spite of the destruction of hectares of forest and clearing of land for cultivation, the percentage of total and per-capital income change.

Many of Brown and World Watch Institute Report projection in table 1 have been witnessed and many of them are now happening. Every major indication shows a deterioration in natural systems; forests are shrinking, deserts are expanding, cropland are losing topsoil, stratospheric ozone layer continues to thin, greenhouse gases are accumulating, the number of plant and animal species is diminishing, air pollution has reached health threatening levels in hundred of cities and damage from acid rain can be seen from every countries traced to economy and ecology.

Table 1:Population Size and availability of renewable resources with projection for 2010

	1990 (in millions)	2010 in millions	Total change	Per capita change 10
Population	5290	1030	+33	-
Fish catch (tons)	85	102	+20	-12
Irrigated land (hectares)	237	277	+17	-12
Cropland (hectares)	1,444	1,516	+5	-21
Range and pasture (hectare)	3402	3540	+4	-22
Forests (hectares)	3413	3165	-7	-30

Source: State of the world 1994: World watch Institute Report

Technology Innovation and Sustainable Economy in ECOWAS Region

Economic Community of West African State (ECOWAS) consists of fifteen (15) independent West African Nations. ECOWAS was established in 1975 to promote socio-economic, political and educational development of these nations. As the organization develops these main goals and objectives were expanded and many areas of human endeavour were covered. Despite this sustainable economy and environmental technology were not given adequate consideration to promote human condition in the region. Technology innovation generally and research and development were mostly neglected as they are not part of major acts and agreements in the region. Most of the ECOWAS agreements were based on liberation of trade, immigration and emigration, free movement of persons and goods, monitoring co-operation, common convention and harmonization of economic and financial policies and others.

The ECOWAS region agreements and protocols also recognized the importance of the provision of infrastructural facilities such as transportation, communication, energy and others as vehicles for integration and improvement of people living condition. The major areas of technologies in which the ECOWAS integration focused are telecommunication, energy and transportation. Projects and programmes are directed to increase the telecommunication link and road traffic within ECOWAS. Modern and reliable energy, transportation and telecommunication services capable of offering a wide variety of services were embarked upon. Trans Sahara highways of 4,460km have been completed to ease transportation problems and promote trade and migration.

ECOWAS prepared master plan for the development of the energy potential of the region. The master plan covered hydroelectric dam sites, to be developed in the member states. Gas fueled thermal plants were constructed in Cote D'ivore and Ghana and that of Nigeria were rehabilitated to increase energy capacity in the region. But the enormous cost of 6.4billion dollar required for the project hindered the implementation of the thermal plants programme. Despite these, ECOWAS region has not been able to realize its potential in these areas.

At its twentieth session held in Abuja in July 1997 the organization adopted the political declaration and regional plan of action on drug control and the Inter-ministerial Drug Control Committees (IDCC). The committee meeting held in Banjul Gambia adopted the statutes of ECODRUG FUND to improve the production of drug in order to make it affordable to the people in the region. Protocol establishing, the West Africa Health Organisation (WAHO) was also adopted and Bobo Dioulasso (Burkina Faso) was selected as its headquarters. Regional strategy based on state intervention was implemented and private sector initiative was later introduced to improve science and agriculture.

Protocols were also adopted to improve industrialization through movement of trade and capital. Investors from all member nations were allowed to establish industries in any part of the region. This is to improve foreign direct investment (FDI). It is also to promote industrialization organized, provide quality goods and services, and to reduce unemployment and poverty in the region. The poverty level in most ECOWAS nation is very high. In most ECOWAS nations resources control and poverty have led to major crisis and war.

The domination of market economy has led to the problem of increasing gap between the income of the rich and the poor within the ECOWAS region. Multinational companies dominated the national economy of many ECOWAS nations. In the oil producing countries such as Nigeria, Cape Verde and Sao Tome environmental condition continue to worsen as a result of the oil exploitation leading to increased industrial activities and rising pollution. Rapid urbanization has led to the destruction of the ecosystem and threatened the environment. Deepening rural poverty accelerate soil degradation and deforestation. As population increases, freshwater become increasingly scarce and conflict over water emerge among countries that share rivers. Marine fisheries decline as a result of oil pollution and environmental problem along the coast depriving people of their primary source of protein.

Climate change causes hardship for subsistence farmers in ECOWAS region. Famine has become more frequent most especially in the Sahara desert belt the region and the response capacity of agricultural agencies and government could not cope with the magnitude of the problem created by famine. Mortality rate related to climate change increased as a result of poor health that are also environmental related. Unsanitary condition, excessive heat, flood, industrial pollution and others were responsible for unsafe and unhygienic conditions that are the causes of most of the diseases. Malaria parasite which is the greatest killers in the region could be traced to unhygienic conditions. Environmental degradation aids emergence of many new diseases, increases and lead to the resurgence of the old ones. Most countries in ECOWAS have not made concrete efforts to check the threat which these diseases posed to lives of the people. Resources depletion, environmental degradation and poverty become widespread and there were disconnections between production integration, industrialization, improved productivity, R&D and sustainable economy.

Shagbamah (2006) noted that unlike the ECOWAS, European Union (EU) has made consistent efforts at standardizing infrastructure and production integration to improve the regional economy for sustainable development. The EU has made conscious and collective efforts to standardize the development of roads, rail, air and water transportation, energy, water supply and communications for sustainable development and improved well being of the people. Development in these areas could be related and connected to production integration. Industries were rationalized and common sectoral policies that led to the establishment of many institutions, programmes and research development to promote industrialization and sustainable economy in European Union were established.

Individual nations in ECOWAS sub region have implemented some of the organisation of statues to promote infrastructure and industrial integration in the region but no concrete efforts have been made to integrate them. Dauda (2005) noted that lack of viable industry and infrastructural decay are the major causes of ECOWAS nation's underdevelopment and poverty. ECOWAS nation do not posses the political will to work towards socio-economic integration that could improve the living condition of their people. Unemployment, malnutrition, squalor, diseases, infant mortality and all other manifestation of subhuman existence has further marginalized many people in the ECOWAS regions. Member nations in the year 2001 jointly subscribe to the objective of reducing poverty by half by 2015, if such objective is to be met; there must be sustained annual per capita and GDP growth rates of 5.71% and 8.6% respectively the region (Dauda, 2005). But most ECOWAS are not working towards the achievement of these laudable objectives.

Energy crisis is one of the major problem facing industrialisation and economic development of most nations of the ECOWAS region, despite its energy production potential. Economic problems in Nigeria ECOWAS most populous nation form 1987 to date has been attributed to energy problem. ECOWAS region rank among the world lowest producer of energy. Incessant power failure and increasing cost of petroleum have led to increasing cost of production in most manufacturing industries which increases the price of the manufactured and make their goods less competitive in the national and international market. It has also led to the closure of many industries and further aggravates unemployment and poverty in the projects.

ECOWAS adopted master plan for the development of energy potential of the region in the 1980. The master plan covers the provision of hydro-electric site for ECOWAS nations to be developed Main in Ghana, Fomi in Guinea Saithno in Guinea Bissau, Bumbina in Sierra Leone, Martali in Mali, Garafuri in Guinea, and Adjarala in Togo. The development of these projects will increase the energy production in the sub region and promote industrialization and integration, but most of these projects were never undertaken.

Thermal construction of gas funded thermal plants in Cote d'Ivoire and Ghana and the rehabilitation of thermal plants and other were also proposed to increase energy capacity by 10,000 megawatts by 2015. The project is estimated to cost 6.4 billion U.S dollars. Electricity lines interconnecting ECOWAS nation to about 5,600Km was also part of the master plan. West African Gas pipeline project of 781km was also planned to provide supplement for hydroelectric energy. Benin, Ghana and Nigeria decided to construct a gas pipeline to utilize natural gas from Nigeria. Regional renewable energy programme was also planned. A regional programme for the utilization of renewable energy to provide energy needs of the people in the rural areas was also planned. This programme was to provide solar energy (photovoltaic) biomass, and energy conservation. The heads of state and government of ECOWAS nations accepted the principle of energy exchange programme. "Power Pool" directed to facilitate the exchange of electrical energy between countries with surplus supply and country in short supply was also planned.

Most of these laudable programmes were planned and many years after the planning, most of them were not executed or implemented. Poor financing of the project was attributed to lack of commitment by the individual nation. Lack of support from the developed countries of Europe and America were also considered to be the cause of non implementation of these laudable programmes.

Control of floating of weed plan which covered many rivers and lagoon in the coastline of ECOWAS state was put in place. The executive secretariat was directed by the heads of state to carryout the necessary fund mobilization for the programme. Support from ECOWAS country such as Benin, Ghana, Cote D'ivoire, Mali, Mauritania, Niger and Senegal have greatly reduced floating weed which threatened fisheries and environment in the coastal area. Member states have also promised to provide counterpart funding for regional meteorological programme. Synoptic observation system was prepared in collaboration with World Meteorological Organisation (WMO) and United Nations Development programme (UNDP). ECOWAS Heads of States and Government adopted a sub-regional action programme to combat desertification. Water resources management programme was also implemented as part of the integrated development plan for the region. But the failure of executing or completing most of these programmes and policies denied the ECOWAS nations of protecting her environment and promote the living conditions of her people.

The conflicts of social persistence of poverty, inequality and environmental depletion have consistently created socio-economic and political problems in ECOWAS region. These have undermined social cohesion, and put pressure and stress on security in ECOWAS region. Sociopolitical instability in many ECOWAS nations provide necessary condition for authoritarianism, the flaring of regional, ethnic and religious conflicts and suppression of democratic institutions. There was grown tension between the poor and rich as the poor in all nations of the region as the economy and democratic institution were manipulated to give power advantage to the business and political elites.

Research and Development in ECOWAS Region

Many ECOWAS nations established research and development (R & D) organization, in their countries in different areas of science and technology to promote innovation. Universities, colleges and schools also engage in research in different areas. The ECOWAS region proposed the harmonization of all courses taught at the universities and other higher and professional institutions to promote innovation. It was accepted that future plans and activities in R & D should be based on collaborative effort in order to guarantee more efficient allocation of resources. The region's R & D is to be based on area of priority to provide joint solution to problems, to avoid duplication of efforts and efficient use of resources. The ECOWAS decide to organize R & D based on that of the European Union that collaborate and engage in joint venture.

In most of the ECOWAS nations R & D organizations, universities and schools are not properly focused, funded and managed to promote and provide qualitative research in areas of science and technology. Most scientist and engineers are not innovative due to individual, organizational and national problems. Most organization and nations in the region could not provide enabling environment for effective and efficient creation of ideas and innovation across their organizations and nations.

Engineers and scientists are not properly motivated to be creative and innovative. They are not properly managed and were not provided with sufficient funds to make them effective. The chief executives and top manager often divert, misused, and misappropriate the R&D organization funds. They often turn research centres into army barrack where they give out order for the scientists and engineer to obey without questioning. (Dauda, 2009)They rely more on rigid rules and procedures rather than on flexibility and motivate their scientists and engineers. Under these conditions, there cannot be concrete technological innovation and breakthrough. In essence, ECOWAS regions basic research in science and technology are not developed to promote innovation for sustainable economy. Most universities, colleges, polytechnics and schools are not well equipped as to enable them to train their students to understand and use latest technology and be part of the global innovation process, which could only be made possible through education and development of trained people in science and technology (Utterback, 1979).

ECOWAS nations have also failed to tap and benefit from invention and innovation from other developed and developing countries of the world. Most of the ECOWAS nations have failed to initiate and improve upon existing technologies which many nations like the Japanese and other Asian nations such as Indonesia, Singapore, Malaysia and China are doing to develop their nations. Government policies and programmes that could improve venture capital formation and training and development of employee which could have significant effect on innovation were not undertaken by many industries in ECOWAS nations including the multi-national companies (MNC). Most MNC prefer to establish their R&D department or units in their countries of origin, and the processes of their researches were never transferred to their companies in the developing countries.

Research and development were not given adequate support by the ECOWAS. No major Heads of state resolution were provided to support R & D for sustainable economy despite the importance which world placed on it. Public utility and industry were mostly inefficient as a result of their failure to innovate. R&D neglect further lowered increased knowledge, proof of principle and commercial demonstration for improved technological innovation. These neglects have led to most of the ECOWAS nation's failure to check environmental threat and promote sustainable economy in ECOWAS nations. Laboratory and private investors were not supported by government to improve technology innovation.

Neglects of technology innovation through R&D have also denied them of the opportunities to determine the price and quality of their manufactured goods. Most of the consumer goods, machines and equipment are imported from the advanced countries of Europe and America. These importations have led to closure of many industries in ECOWAS sub region as they could not compete with good from advanced countries in term of their prices and quantities. Dauda (2009) argued that most developing nations are denied of determining the prices of their products, because of their inability to promote and manage technology innovation. They have to pay high prices for equipment and technologyt invented and manufactured in Europe, America, Russia and other developing nation such as China, Singapore, Taiwan and others. Many goods and services produced by their companies are much more expensive than those manufactured from the advanced countries.

Policy Options/Recommendations

In many advanced countries the use of process engineering whereby the use of energy and raw materials are minimized have lowered economic growth of many countries where these raw materials are produced. The uses of recycle and renewable materials, economical use of used material have reduced environmental problems. For example, technology innovation have also led to recovery possibilities of used air in oven to be re-used for the preheating of the combustion air and for the production for the heating energy for the operation rooms.

Brickwedde (1998) noted that continuous use of this method enable Germany to attain a 50% energy saving level. Process management in iron smiting industries and innovative energy saving devices have led to the production synthetic moulded parts and used papers for insulating materials have led to a considerable saving of energy.

Used materials such as papers and wastes were formerly burned which further increases environmental hazards. But the re-process and re-used of these material has led to reduction use of waste in Germany. Total amount of these materials industries have increased by 25% and increase the proportion of re-usable resources to 77%. Energy consumption has reduced by 36%, water input by 36% and consumption of raw materials 33%. 'Electronic nose' detector of harmful substance from up to one million of a gram per kilogram developed by Bruker Saxonia analytic GmbH is now being used to check environment hazards. But this is not the case in most developing countries. No frantic efforts have been made to promote the use of used materials and to save energy and raw materials in order to protect the environment.

While pollution and environmental degradation are kept low and controlled in the advanced countries multinational companies are operating in the developing countries in a way that endanger threatened the local people and their immediate environment. The Bhopal chemical leakage in India which killed more than 2000 people in 1981 is a clear example of the preference which multi-national companies placed on economic expediency or profit at the expense of people's lives and environment in the underdeveloped and developing countries of the world. The problem of oil pollution in Niger Delta of Nigeria could also be attributed to the appropriation of earth natural resources through the use of technology. Oil spillage and gas flaring have created so

In developed countries most technological innovation take place through industry based R & D, which its expenditure is related to its growth and profitability. Government policies have been used to stimulate innovation in three ways. The first approach is the encouragement of new firm by giving them various forms of assistance such as grant and tax relief to enable them to get enough fund to invest on improving the quality and quantity of their product or service through innovation.

The second approach is the support of the research and development for improved technology innovation to stimulate industrial innovation. There is need for government to assist or support industry in the production of quality goods and service that government purchase to enable government to produce quality service. Governments also provide the strongest patent protection to individual and industry and contribute or take part in activities that promote technological innovation.

The third approach is the provision of industrial standards that are related to produce and process of commerce to be set. In developing countries standard should not be set too early in the life cycle of a product so as not to limit innovation and should not be too late so as not to restrict the market and deny investors, some of the fruits of their investments support to be given to science by government. Science provides knowledge and understanding that will permit the improvement of the defense, health, industry, agriculture, and others.

Grants should be given to universities, polytechnics and colleges, secondary and primary school for the development in the major field of science. Laboratories should be established and their employees be supported through various grants to improve their know-how and to enable them move along or understand contemporary and latest scientific innovation. The scope of the scientific activity in a country may give an indication of its potential to contribute to its advancement. Government should also support industrial technology. The development of new technology comes largely through advances in understanding and expansion in development, manufacture and use of new products and processes. Basic technical area such as casting, welding machinery should be supported and grants and support to be provided to industry to enable them establish training outfit to attract the youth to these area.

Technology area such as pattern recognition, combustion, jet engines, integrated circuits, computer aided manufacturing, computer technology, aircraft, nuclear energy, space programmes and others to be supported by government to promote technology innovation in industry. Direct intervention in innovation should also be promoted by the government support product and process development should be provided to the industry, result of fully funded industrial research by the government should be made available to other small and medium sized firms. Special and guaranteed loans and subsidies should be given to industry to pursue research in the country area of needs or areas thought to be of importance to the national economy. Tax relief and grant in and should be provided. Industrial research associations, which aids the development and transfer of technology to firms in all the ECOWAS nations to be supported. The establishment of this association should be encouraged in all sectors such as pharmaceutical, rubber, mining petroleum, textile, and printing. Organization or institutes should be established to promote technology transfer from advanced countries through adaptation through dismantling of existing equipment and machineries in order to produce local Prototype or semblance.

Government should also provide assistance to reduce the market risk to the newly introduced commercial products that were the outcome of technology innovation or research. The market risk may be due to technical and uncertainties of the market. The government should help to arrange for industrial use of new product and guarantee a quantity of initial sales. There is need for government to determine the feasibility and range of possible cost of new process and reduce or restrict the importation and purchase of imported ones. Government should also help in reducing the adverse effect of technology innovation to industry. The introduction of new products and processes can displace existing products, techniques, labour, management forms and sometime whole industries. Major displacement of forms and their worker occur as a result of the spread and use of new products and processes. Adjustments may be difficult and traumatic. Govern may put in place to policies to ameliorate the problem such as protecting the workers, provide training and other incentives to management.

Sustainable development could also be achieved through the voluntary changing of the people's lifestyles to reduce the family size for population control. This will reduce the pressure and threat on the earth resources and people in ECOWAS region. Policy should be made to reduce waste and for the use of fuel efficiency automobiles and household appliances. Tax policies that could make industries to use environmentally friendly methods of production to be encouraged. Industries that engage in use and dumping of toxic materials and destructive activities to be sanctioned

Technological innovation changes value and alter the character of human relationship. It is the harbinger of progress and understanding. Significant economic development could only be achieved in any organization and nation through effective management and control of technological innovation. It is one of the major forces of change, economic growth and sustainability. Without technological innovation, it will be difficult for many developing nations to achieve sustainable economic development and improved and living condition of her people. But it has also influenced depletion and exhaustion of the earth resources, ozone depletion, tropical deforestation, global warming, proliferation of nuclear weapons, and others when it is not properly controlled and managed. Despite its advantages in prospecting and using of the earth natural resources it is equally necessary to check and control its uses without endangering the survival of mankind in the future.

While pollution and environmental degradation are kept low and controlled in the advanced countries, multinational and national companies are operating in ECOWAS in a way that have endangered and threatened the local people and their immediate environment. The oil spillages and gas leakages in the Niger Delta area of Nigeria and chemical leakages in industries in many ECOWAS nations have killed many people; destroy their soil, water, rivers and others. Many multi-national companies placed valued on profit and other on economic expediency, at the expense of people's lives and environment in the underdeveloped and developing countries of the world.

Governments in ECOWAS region have professed concern with environmental deterioration, but few have been willing to make basic changes needed to reverse it. Public understanding and consequences of the continuously rising global temperature is not yet sufficient to support effective policy in ECOWAS nations. It is imperative for all nations in the ECOWAS region to pursue technology innovation for economic growth without undermining the environmental and human condition now and in the future.

References

Ancker Johnson and Chang, D.B. (1974) Effect of International Technology Transfer on the U.S. Economy. Paper and Proceedings of a Colloquium July U.S Government Printing Office

Ancker-Johnson and Chang, D.B. (1970): Technological Factor in International Trade, Washington D.C. U.S. Government Printing Office.

Badawi, M.K. (1953) Why Manager Fail, Research Management Journal July-August pp. 28 – 35

Black, J. (2002) Oxford Dictionary of Economic, Oxford, Oxford University Press.

Brickwedde, F (1998) Environment and Work Innovative Environmental Technology as a Chance for Economy and Employment in Ways to Social Busch, K. et al (ed). Peace in Europe, Proceeding of International Congress in Osnabruck, Germany November 11 – 14 1998

Britannica internet guide – http://www.britanica.com

Burrows, B. et al (1991): A Handbook for Sustainable Future, Twickenham, U.K. Adamantie

Communication for Sustainable Future – grapher://csf.colorado.edu

Dauda, Y.A. (2009) Managing Technology Innovation: The Human Resource Management Perspective, Peter Lang Publisher, Frankfurt, Germany.

– (2009). Managing Technology Innovation: The Human Resource Management Perspective, Peter Lang, Frankfurt

– (2010): Between Economic Growth and Poverty: Assessment of Nigeria Urban Workers Wellbeing in AN Interdisciplinary Discuss on Human Condition, Ninalowo, M.A.B, et al (edited) Faculty of Social Sciences in Conjunction with Sociology Department, University of Lagos, Nigeria.

Dauda, Y.A (2001). Nigerian Telecommunications Industry and Challenge of Change Lagos, Nigerian This Day

– (2000) Investment in Technology Innovation and Improved Productivity of the Nigerian Telecommunication. A PhD Thesis submitted to the Faculty of Education University of Ibadan, Nigeria, Unpublished.

– (2005) Labour Relations in a Changing Global World: The ECOWAS Experience", Work Technology – Organisation – Society, Germany.

– (2005). Labour Relations in a Changing Globalised World, Work-Technology-Organisation-Society (30) Szell, G. (ed) Peter Lang, Frankfurt, Germany.

– (2006) Challenge of Global Capitalism to Industrial Relations in Nigeria: Investors, Union and Management Option Published in the Conference Proceedings of the 6th African Regional Congress of the International Industrial Relations Association (IIRA).

Dobbs, K. (1999). Knowing How to Keep Your Best and Brightest, Workface April pp. 75 – 90

Economic Community of West African States 2001 – 2008 Reports

Envirolink – http://www.envirolink.org

Flanders, A. (1965). Industrial Relations: What is Wrong with the System, London, Faber.

Fox, A. (1971). Sociology of Work in Industry, London, Collier Macmillan.

Friends of the Earth -http://www.foe.co.uk/index.htm/consumer/gec.index/html

Gallopian, G.C. et al (2010) Bending the Curve: Towards Global Sustainability: www.gsg.org

Gallopin, G.C. et al (1997) Branch Points: Global Scenarios and Human Choice, Stockholm, Sweden Stockholm Environment Institute.

Global climate change – http://www.puc.state.oh.us

Hardin, G. (1968). "The Tragedy of the Commons" Science, December (1) pp. 243 – 248

Hermon, L.R. (1956): Social and Technological Determinants of Creativity in Taylor (ed) University of Utah Research Conference on the Identification and Creative Talent 1955, Salt Lake University, Utah Press pp. 42-52.

Herera, A.D. et al (1976) Catastrophe or New Society? A Latin America World Model, Ottawa, Canada, International Development Research.

Hill, C.T. and Utterback, J.M. (1979). Technological Innovation for Dynamic Economy, New York Pergamon Policy Studies

International Monetary Fund (IMF), World Outlook, Global Economic Prospect and Policies Washington, DC.

Jenkins, T. (2000) Towards Broadbased Economy Published Online in Wiley Interscience (www.interscience.wiley.com)

Kast, F.E. and Rosenzweig J.E. (1979) Organisation and Management, A System and Contingency Approach New York McGraw Hill Book Inc.

Khalil, T (2000) Management of Technology: The Key to Competitive Wealth Creation, New York, McGraw Hill.

Lilly P. (1998) Social Representation of Environment in Italian Trade Unions in Ways to Social Peace in Europe, Busch, K ed. Proceedings of the International Congress in Osnabruck November 11 – 14.

Library of congress – http://nationalgeographic.com

Mathews, John A. (2008). Opinion is Growing Biofuels Crops is a Crime Against Humanity Published on line in Willey Interscience (www.intersceince.wiley.com)

Milbraith, L.W. (1989): Envisioning a Sustainable Society: Learning On Way Out, Albany, N.Y. Sunny Press.

Muller, M. (1998). Departure and Renewal – Perspective of a Policy of Sustainability in Ways to Social Peace in Europe, Busch, K. et al (ed) Proceeding of International Congress in Osnabruck, Germany November 11 – 14, 1998.

Norris, K. and Vaisey, J. (1973): The Economics of Research and Technology, London George Allen and Unwin

Ott, H.E (1998). "The Kyoto Protocol, Unfinished Business" Environment July/August

Quinn, R. (2001) Sunlight Brightens Our Future in Environment, in Environment 2000/2001 Allen, J.L (ed)

Rapacynski, W. (1992). Developing Technology with Human Face Research Technology Management May – June pp. 11-18

Rogers, D.M.A. (1996). The Challenge of the Fifth Generation Research and Development, Research Technology Management Journal July-August.

Sapp, M. (2008). California Carbon Crackdown, Published Online in Wiley Interscience (www.interscience.wiley.com)

School of Labour and Industrial Relations hot links – http://www./rl.msu.edu/hotlinks

Schwartz, M. and O' Connor, J. (1993) Exploring a Changing World, New Jersey, U.S.A Globe Company.

Shagbamah, E.I. (2006) Perspectives on the European Monetary Union: Lessons for the Economic community of West African States (ECOWAS). In cost and benefits of Economic Reforms: Selected Paper for the 2005 Annual Conference of the Nigerian Economic Society, pp. 705 – 745

Shrivastava, P. (1984). Technology Innovation in Developing Countries, Columbia Journal of World Business, Winter pp. 46-57

Takeda, Y. (1993) Managing Technology for the 21st Century in Research Technology Management Vol. 36 No. 6 November/December pp. 8-11.

Taylor, O.W (1958) Variables Related to Creativity and Productivity Among Men in Two Research Laboratories, University of Utah Creativity Research Report 1958.

The Hunger Project – http://www.thp.org

United Nations – http://www.unsystem.org

United Nations Environmental Programme – http://www.unep.ch

Utterback, J.M. (1979). The Dynamic of Product and Process Innovation in Technology Innovation for a Dynamic Economy Hill, C.T. and Utterback, J.M. (ed) New York, Perganon Press.

Chapter 3:
Trade Unions and Sustainable Innovation

Trade union implication in the sustainable development: global position and contingent situations[1]

Jocelyne Robert, HEC-Management School, University of Liege

Abstract

According to us, it matters to situate the sustainable development in relation to the social responsibility and to the question of the different actors. It is in this particular context that we will analyse the relationship between the trade unions and the sustainable development in Belgium. We will show the involvement of the trade unions in relation to the three areas which define the sustainable development: the environment protection, the work quality and its organization and the benefit notion. This implication depends on the relations between the actors: state, company, workers (notably the trade unions). The question of sustainable development is culturally rooted and is linked to a certain conception of the economy and of the social contract. Obstacles are liable to appear during the appropriation of the sustainable development by the trade unions. Management question is important and among others the one of corporate culture and the one of the negotiation. The trade union involvement depends on particular situations and specific contexts. We will therefore show that a systemic and contingent approach to the problem is required.

Content

1 All translations are by the author, if not indicated otherwise. Thanks to Zaineb Lazreq, assistant HEC-Management school at the University of Liege, for the translation of the French text into English.

Definition of sustainable development

The sustainable development as introduced by United Nations in 1987 is a model of development able to meet the actual needs without compromising the ability to address next generations requirements. Other definitions may appear, sometimes mentioning more specifically the environment, and sometimes highlighting the development of future generations. However, the concept of "sustainable development" is based on 3 main pillars: social development, economic development and the environmental aspects (Brégeon, 2004, p. 78).

According to Brégeon (2004, p.78), a project based on sustainable development must :

- Pursue social, economic and environmental objectives, in harmony and equilibrium;
- Respect democracy and good governance rules (precautionary, responsibility and equity principles, involvement in the decision making, and preventive integration…).
- Preserve the needs of future generations.

Sustainable development is based on the following principles (ibidem., p.83):

- Precautionary principle;
- Responsibility principle;
- Participation principle;
- Equity and solidarity principle;
- Preventive integration system;

Precautionary principle implies anticipating and finding solutions in a context of uncertainty. Responsibility principle involves taking into consideration the responsibility of all the actors involved in the process: citizens, companies, and governments. Participation principle emphasizes the participation of the various actors in the responsibility-making process. Information, transparency in the decision-making process, consultation and dialogue should be in the agenda. One of the main principles of sustainable development is equity, associated with solidarity between generations and people. Preventive integration implies anticipation, more by producing in a sustainable way, rather than taking corrective measures to reduce negative consequences of non-responsible activities.

Therefore, sustainable development is based on three major dimensions associated with three types of responsibility

- Economic efficiency to create profit/ value or value under certain conditions ;
- Sustainable environmental practices (Planet/ natural capital);
- Social equity (People/ human capital)

Three types of actors are highlighted: citizens and organizations; governments; companies.

Sustainable development and Business

If the concept of sustainable development seems more present and important in current researches, "this dimension has a relative importance, depending on its more or less strong integration in the management system. As far as, in the research field, the concept does not renew « the existing problems in management science ». "It allows the adoption of a new analysis' angle " (Krupicka & Dreveton,2005, p.1).

However, it seems that the implementation of sustainable development in companies « raises more problems than it solves ». There would be confusion between the sustainable development of society and the sustainable development of the business (ibidem, p.4)

After the Conference in Rio, the three axes mentioned above (social, environmental and economic aspects) are associated. Therefore, all the measures taken inside the company must include these three aspects. The pressures on companies are from three sources:

- Legal aspects and incentives (labels, charters, pollution quotas, etc.) ;
- Economic aspects: blurred organizations, the importance of the new information technologies, frequent contacts between the company and the social environment... constitute the context in which organizations evolve. These organizations communicate about their corporate social responsibility and « their economic, social and environmental performance » (Ibidem, p.5);
- Social commitment: citizen values, public opinion, but also investors and the company's social environment.

Inside the company, employees, trade unions and business groups influence the company policy and leads it « to take into account its social and environmental responsibility » (Ibidem, p.7).

It is interesting to notice that the motivations related to sustainable development practices may differ from one company to another, realities are different and should be set within the specific context of each company.

A.Krupicka, B. Dreveton (2005, p.8) suggest several reasons: « Legitimate companies with regard to investors and consumers; create a social climate; Positioning relative to competitors; Improve company's image; Perform internal processes: Customer loyalty; Comply with new regulation ».

However, beyond the adoption of charters, labels, social relations, it is useful to see how the issue of sustainable development is analyzed from the company's management perspective. It can be seen from the marketing, finance or human resources perspective. This will underline the question of change in the company, welfare and working conditions, employment, etc.

Sustainable development and trade unions

In Belgium, there is an agreement between trade unions highlighting the importance of environmental protection and the quality of work. The environmental aspect is unanimous. Some differences may arise between trade unions about the actions to be carried out (strikes, work stoppages) in order to ensure employment and the quality of work conditions. Some trade unions or political parties are waiting for a long-term commitment from multinational companies, others accept faster the reopening of the work sites focusing on short-term employment and postponing long term negotiations later.

The defense of maintaining the tool is part of the sustainable development approaches that allowing jobs development. Similarly, negotiations about CO2 quota ensure the quality of the environment.

Indeed, the objective is to "combine harmoniously »: economic growth, which aims to satisfy, particularly, the needs of poor people, human progress: social, educational, cultural, democratic, etc..,, protecting and safeguarding the environment " (Regards FGTB, 2002).

At the European level, the European Trade Union Confederation (ETUC, 2006) states: "The ETUC is determined to adopt a wider ranging approach on sustainable development. It sees the integration of economic, social and environmental objectives not as conflicting requirements but as complementary elements of a broadly defined improvement in job quality and development. The main trade union concern is to integrate social objectives into global strategies". At the national and international levels "workers and unions want to be fully recognised as major players in sustainable development strategies" (European Trade Union Confederation, 2006b).

The unions want to include actions related to sustainable development in collective agreements. The question social clauses is posited and linked to it, the question of interference in the management of companies located abroad (Béroud, 2003, p.25)

The trade union perspective

The trade union tradition is intrinsically linked to sustainable development, the answer to current needs and the preservation of future generations, to the extent that it seeks to protect employment security, welfare at work and production tool. Some positions will be evoked.

In Belgium, trade unions tend to resist to all precarious measures. However, the dilemma remains during the negotiations (such as the recovery of the high furnace) where sometimes the possibility of revival is related to a requirement for more flexibility at the employment level. Boosting the production tool gives more confidence for future employment. The question is then to make a concession and to ensure the improvement by renouncing to a certain quality of employment. The tool's revival is also always subject to negotiation with the government about CO2 quotas.

The objective is to ensure the « early retirement » when there is risk of unemployment and to be against measures that delay the retirement age, to maintain the quality's employment, to participate in important international meetings on environmental protection. The position of the two major Belgian trade unions is unanimous.

Trade unions defend the Tobin tax (taxation of speculative investments worldwide) as opposed to speculation. They wish to tax capital. Trade unions defend the solidarity and small incomes, wishing by this way, to increase the minimum wage.

The issue of sustainable development is thus asked, involving social, capital and environment.

Each of these measures could be discussed in terms of sustainable development. However, we can notice the unanimous position regarding the need of sharing wealth, the protection of the environment and the well being of individuals.

One of two major trade unions noticed:

> "In Belgium, we want to get involved in setting practice of an alliance for sustainable growth. For this, we challenge Belgian government (to establish a fund' solidarity and a better tax justice) ; regional governments (to develop innovation in industry and energy sectors) ;employers (at the inter-professional and sectorial levels and within companies) on their ability to develop innovative strategies that strengthen the economic structure, employment and reporting of how they spent the significant efforts that workers and government made for them (reductions of social contributions, taxes, ...) " (FGTB, 2009, p. 14).

It is both to answer to the international environmental agreements and CO2 quotas but also to respond to the objectives of growth and economic development set by Lisbon agreements. The trade unions wish a clarification of the relationship between these objectives and a « realignment and rebalancing of the social, economic and environmental dimensions ». The new EU Sustainable Development Strategy (ETUC, 2006b).

The statement of the international unions in Pittsburgh Summit (ITUC-CSI-IGB, TUAC, Global Unions, 2009) clearly highlights the importance of linking environmental protection and the preservation of decent social and economic conditions. This is to ensure a "fair transition".

"Just transition" requires governments to take steps to smooth the shift towards a more sustainable society by building the capacity of the "green economy" to sustain jobs and livelihoods for all. Just transition requires inter alia, major investments to develop long-term sustainable industrial policies, aimed at retaining and creating decent and "green"/sustainable jobs, "greening" all workplaces and developing and deploying technology; consulting with unions and employers; supporting training provision for workers; and the implementation of social protection and economic diversification policies. (ITUC-CSI-IGB,TUAC, Global Unions, 2009, p.11).

The recovery in the steel activity analyzed in terms of sustainable development

The question is then to consider the presence of these criteria in the business negotiations, based on specific situations.

The analyzed company was marked by the closure of one of its two high- furnaces. In 2007, many negotiations allowed the definition of new project plan for the high- furnace. For the trade unions, the main idea was to maintain the production tool and try to boost employment par restarting the steel activity. This was a sustainable development approach underlying the defense of the steel activity and the employment. The different stakeholders accepted to play their game. In 2008, long negotiations were necessary to find an agreement about who would pay the authorized pollution's quotas. At this level, a non-agreement could fail the project (Robert, 2009).

Unfortunately, the crisis prevented the reopening of the high- furnace and it freezes to operations for the both high-furnace. The current revival of the sector allows the possible reopening of one of the two high- furnaces. Lengthy negotiations have been taken in February 2010 to find an agreement between public authorities, company's representatives and trade unions. Public authorities have decided to extend to the company pollution quotas as long as the reopening of the two high furnaces, but this requires the company's commitment.

The analysis of the situation in the automotive sector (Perrat, 2009, p. 12) allows identifying different points of negotiation, also found in the case of steel sector:

- Contract of employment, flexibility, working conditions;
- Public intervention;
- Evolution of demand, strategic decisions;
- Technology investment;
- Social demands;
- Societal requirements in terms of sustainable development.

The importance of time and space in the trade union's approach of negotiations in the automotive sector is also crucial here. It concerns the development of a whole region, depending, however, of the world developments. The connection with time combines short-term to medium-term and long-term (ibidem):

- Contract of employment, flexibility, working conditions (very short term) ;
- Public intervention (short and medium term) ;
- Evolution of demand, strategic decisions (medium term)
- Technology investment (medium and long term) ;
- Social demands (medium and long term)
- Societal requirements in terms of sustainable development (medium and long term).

It is a system's approach involving social, economy and environment. The relationships between elements change the balance. The system is fragile and can be broken at any time. We have a feeling of progress, then status quo, and then a feeling of regress. It is urgency then nothing moves, waiting for decisions and urgency again.

One systemic approach

The sustainable development as a system

The three main pillars of sustainable development: economic, social and environmental, are combined in the definition of sustainable development. However, we notice that the environment seems to be argued as the main element. Nevertheless, the two other points are essential. The dangers associated to the environment request the survival of society and also our conception of the economic and social aspect.

"The environment" is rather the place of "perverse effects", "accidents" and other adverse and unanticipated events produced by the two other categories (social and economic aspect). These categories had been constructed with the objective to straight human activity in order to produce an environment of abundance. After the epic's development, mainly characterized by the growth of productive forces, human beings should enjoy an environment worthy of the Garden of Eden. However, it seems that some unforeseen and misunderstood problems arise (Flipo, 2004).

"The category "environment" is more all the "anomalous" phenomena than a clearly identified element. The environment is the place of failures growing for the two first categories " (ibidem).

The three elements are interrelated, and the environment finds its global meaning in reference to the economic and social aspects. Yet, the social aspect appears less often highlighted in the sustainable development approach, whereas it is better positioned in the "corporate social responsibility " approach. Belgian trade unions also emphasize the importance of considering the social aspect in the sustainable development approach. "There is no real sustainable development, if in the triptych: economy / environment / social, this latter one is sacrificed." (Regards FGTB, March 2007).

The company as a system

The company is based on the economic and social aspects and must increasingly take into account the environmental. The two major unions in Belgium: CSC (Confederation of Christian Trade Unions) and the FGTB (General Federation of Workers in Belgium) have created the Inter-union Network of Awareness for the Environment (RISE) which: « Has as primary objective to strengthen the position of workers and their representatives on environmental issues and encourage social dialogue in this area inside the businesses » (...). The workers, who are at the heart of production, are well located to influence a production respecting the environment, and acting everyday for its protection. (...) One of the main actions of RISE is the implementation and monitoring of pilot experiences inside the companies (Regards FGTB, September 1999).

The company's situation is like a system "that oscillates between opening and closing" (Desreumaux, 1998, p.24). Thus, over time, there is an alternation between order and disorder. This allows the survival of the organization. In order to survive, the company must "evolve according to events and changes occurring in its environment" while maintaining a certain order.

It seems that the negotiations related to the revival or not of the production tool, in a context of sustainable development, contributes to grant a certain unity on the organization operating in the way of order. These negotiations are long and difficult.

However, the position of the different stakeholders and the negotiation of the different points of view, suggests also that the organization would not be defined as a set of well-defined limits, but as a set of "contracts' nodes" between the contractor and all stakeholders involved in the process, without being more than this sum of contracts.

Difficulties of ownership for trade unions

According to Perrat (2009), in the automotive sector, trade unions are facing new questions, those about energy and technology constraints. Theses modifications bring institutional changes and also change in the hierarchy of relationships. Trade unions are facing internal changes, mainly related to middle management turnover.

Unions must master new issues and negotiate with new actors. Three elements are highlighted:

- The time mentioned above: short, medium and long term
- The space: international – national – regional – local professional organizations – businesses;
- Governance: institutional structures that coordinate the actors' actions; global, national, regional and by sector governance, or within the company (Perrat, 2009).

Unions must also negotiate with more partners: political authorities at various levels, civil society, and associations defending the environment. However, we notice that "Partnerships for sustainable development remain dominated by states and international organizations, and are predominantly led and populated by Northern actors. Participation of "major groups" is limited to stakeholders that have certain competitive advantages or useful resources, and traditional patterns of political exclusion of weaker groups tend to be reproduced at the transnational level of partnerships as well" (Biermann, Chan, Mert & Pattberg, 2007, p. 15).

New business models are established and new questions appear. The issue of long-term employment is debated during the negotiations: the objective is to promote flexibility in exchange for maintaining employment. Some sectors encourage the outsourcing associated with job creation and flexible work. The role of unions is sometimes challenged.

The studies conducted by industry, have shown: how a real policy of social responsibility may be unrealistic with regards to performance' constraints and short-term profit (Royle, 2005). This situation leads trade unions to adopt new strategies, to innovate (Turner, 2006).

As we have seen in Belgium, the two major unions join forces around the issue of environment. They participate with NGOs at international summits. They follow innovative projects. They want to be associated with sustainable development in the business.

Trade unions are not systematically involved in measures of "corporate social responsibility" or sustainable development. They are not always informed about procedures of certification. These do not necessarily depend on the HR department (Justice, 2002, p. 7). The actions of social responsibility and sustainable development could be the opportunity of the establishment of new union strategies. Finally, trade unions remain the « opposition unions » in Belgium. However, they are associated with different social and economic partners in order to find solutions to unemployment difficulties for example. Negotiation forums play a vital role in businesses.

The issue of sustainable development became a pressure tool for the maintenance and development of social dialogue.

Conclusion

Sustainable development focuses on meeting the current social, economic and environmental needs while insisting on the importance of respecting future generations. However, the environmental aspect seems to occupy a privileged position in the thinking related to sustainable development. This response must be ethical and democratic; it must follow different principles and involves citizens, associations, governments and businesses.

Nowadays, each company must take into account the external pressures (legal aspects, necessity of social responsibility, and value of citizenship) and internal pressures (stakeholders' considerations: unions, workers/ employees). Every enterprise faces a specific situation. The company is then required to implement changes and better consider the well being at work. Associated with social responsibility, certification's procedures introduce new procedures in the company.

At the Belgian and international level, trade unions support a sustainable development involving also the social perspective. Within the businesses, the unions want to be part of the thinking related to sustainable development. Their action is important in the negotiations upon the economic development and the maintaining of the employment's quality, as shown in keeping the steel business in Belgium. This last example illustrate that companies consider sustainable development, they experience similar situations and try to keep the balance between change and stability. They also attempt to reflect the views of different stakeholders – not always unanimous and they are more than ever internal and external « nodes of contracts ».

The involvement and the role of trade unions in sustainable development are not simple. The trade unions are experiencing a renewal of middle management. They must master the changes related to work organization and technology for example. They must also take on new responsibilities in international institutions; comprehend the rules of work in companies that became more and more international, work in the short, medium and long term and to be involved in the governance organizations. They have to develop new strategies of negotiation together with numerous players, over passing the conflicts, seeking for consensus, allying with different actors and new forms of solidarity. The Belgian experience of maintaining the steel business is a good example.

References

Béroud S. (2003). Clause sociale: limites et contradictions des réponses syndicales. In : *Mots. Les langages du politique* [online], 71 | 2003, retrieved from internet on may, the 05th, 2008. URL:http://mots.revues.org/index7743.html

Brégeon J. (2004). Développement durable versus responsabilité. In : J. Igalens (Eds), *Tous responsables*, Paris : Ed. d'Organsation.

Biermann F., Chan M.-S., MertA..,Pattberg P. (2007). Multi-stakeholder Partnerships for Sustainable Development: Does the Promise Hold? Paper presented at the 2007 Amsterdam Conference on the Human Dimensions of Global Environmental Change *Earth System Governance: Theories and Strategies for Sustainability*, VrijeUniversiteit Amsterdam, The Netherlands, 24-26 May.

CES. (2006). *Le CES acteur du développement durable*. Bruxelles. URL:http://www.etuc.org/a/500?var_recherche=developpement durable. Retrieved on April 12th, 2010.

European Trade-Union Confederation (ETUC) (2006a) : Actors for Sustainable Development.URL:http://www.etuc.org/a/140?var_recherche=SustainableDevelopment. Retrieved on April 12th, 2010.

Desreumaux, A. (1998). *Théorie des organisations*. Caen: Ed. Management Société (EMS)

European Trade-Union Confederation (ETUC). (2006b). *The new EU Sustainable DevelopmentStrategy*. June2006b. URL: http://www.etuc.org/a/2547?var_recherche=sustainabledevelopment. Retrieved on April 12th, 2010.

FGTB (2009). *La crise et les moyens de s'en sortir durablement*. Bruxelles. URL: http://www.abvv.be/code/fr/Documents/2009/c15_02e0100.htmRetrieved on April 12th, 2010.

Flipo, F. (2004). Les tensions constitutives du "développement durable ». In : *Développement durable et territoires* [En ligne], Points de vue, mis en ligne le 18 mars 2004, accessed from internet on November, 21th, 2009. URL:http://developpementdurable.revues.org/index1041.html.

ITUC-CSI-IGB, TUAC, Global Unions. (2009). *Déclaration syndicale internationale de Pittsburgh.* September, 24-25th, 2009. http://www.ituc-csi.org/920-Pittsburgh-mvst-be-a-jobs.html?lang=en. Retrieved on April 12th, 2010.

Justice, Dwight W. (2002). *Corporate Social Responsibility: Challenges and Opportunities for Trade Unionists.* Cornell University ILR School, This paper is posted at DigitalCommons@ILR.http://digitalcommons.ilr.cornell.edu/codes/9.

Krupicka, A. & Dreveton, B. (2005). Le développement durable : une problématique de gestion. *XIV° Conférence Internationale de Management Stratégique,* AIMS, Pays de la Loire, Angers. URL : http://www.strategie-aims.com/

Perrat, J. (2009). Crise conjoncturelle et structurelle de l'automobile et capacité syndicale d'anticipation. *Les 17èmes Rencontres Internationales Du GERPISA,* Paris, June, 18-20th, 2009. URL://www.gerpisa.univ-evry.fr. Retrieved on April 12th, 2010.

Pichon, A. (2008). Le Contrat à Durée Indéterminée dans la tourmente de la firme flexible. *Revue des Sciences de Gestion,* n°230 –spécial stratégie, pp 53-68.

Regards FGTB. (1999). *L'environnement, un défi syndical.* Bruxelles, september 1999. URL:http://www.fgtb-wallonne.be/TV/tv_199909.html. Retrieved on April 12th, 2010.

Regards FGTB (2002). *Le développement durable : un défi syndical.* Bruxelles, may 2002. URL:http://www.fgtb-wallonne.be/TV/tv_200205.html. Retrieved on April 12th, 2010.

Regards FGTB (2007). Freiburg : *Des syndicalistes à la rencontre du développement durable.* Bruxelles, march 2007. URL:http://www.fgtb-wallonne.be/TV/tv_200703.html. Retrieved on April 12th, 2010.

Robert, J. (2009). Negotiation and Transaction in the Context of Restructuring : Ethics, Trust and Social Responsibility. In: D. Harrisson, G. Szell & R. Bourque (Eds), *Social Innovation, the Social Economy and World Economic Development.* Frankfurt/M et al.: Peter Lang (vol. 17 in the Series Labour, Education, Society), pp.187-218.

Royle, T. (2005). Realism or idealism? Corporate social responsibility and the employee stakeholder in the global fast-food industry. *Business Ethics: A European Review,* vol. 14, pp. 42-55

Turner,L. (2006). Globalization and the Logic of Participation: Unions and the Politics of Coalition Building. *Journal of Industrial Relations.* Vol. 48, pp. 83-97.

Climate, labour market and industrial relations in the European Union – Responses to the climate challenge among trade unions and employers associations.

Carsten Strøby Jensen,
Department of Sociology, University of Copenhagen

Abstract

This article focuses on climate change and its impact on the work of labour market organizations especially in Europe (EU). It is based on the fact that we can observe a growing national and international political attention to climate issues and a desire by governments to reduce CO2 emissions in the face of global warming. Climate seems to be one of the major challenges for all societies in the 21st century. The question raised in the article is, 'What actions are trade unions and employers' associations taking in relation to the climate debate?' The hypothesis is that climate is now viewed by these actors as an issue that these social partners must deal with. Climate seems increasingly to be an area which is also taken up among the actors in IR systems. Hence, this article focuses on the way in which trade unions and employers' association relate to the climate issue as industrial relations actors.

Content

Introduction

A search of various business and employers' associations websites in Europe, shows that a large proportion now have climate high on their agendas.

For example, climate issues feature prominently on the website of the Confederation of British Industry, the British employers' organization (www.cbi.org.uk). The site provides references to additional information and publications about various aspects of the climate problem, such as how the UK can meet the internationally agreed CO2 targets or the question of how to ensure 'green growth' in Britain.

A similar priority on climate can be observed on the sites of other business- and employers associations in Europe. The climate issue is high on the agenda among those groups representing European business and employer interests.

Among the trade unions in Europe, the climate issue is also prominent on their websites. Here we can also observe references to issues such as the possibility of creating new green jobs. On the website of the English Trade Union, the TUC (www.tuc.org.uk), we can find references to projects for establishing 'green representatives' at workplace level. The intention is that the green representatives will help develop a more green and energy-conscious workplace culture, so that employees become involved in energy saving measures (www.greenworkplaces-southwest.org.uk). Similar initiatives can be observed on the websites of a number of trade unions in a wide range of other European countries.

This article focuses on climate change and its impact on the work of labour market organizations especially in Europe (EU). It is based on the fact that we can observe a growing national and international political attention to climate issues and a desire by governments to reduce CO2 emissions in the face of global warming. Climate seems to be one of the major challenges for all societies in the 21st century.

The question raised in the article is, 'What actions are trade unions and employers' associations taking in relation to the climate debate?' The hypothesis is that climate is now viewed by these actors as an issue that these social partners must deal with. Climate seems increasingly to be an area which is also taken up among the actors in IR systems. Hence, this article focuses on the way in which trade unions and employers' association relate to the climate issue as industrial relations actors.

Several types of data are used in the article. First, we use data from trade union and employers' association websites. The web texts are used to identify what kind of specific questions and concerns about climate are raised among the social partners.

Second, we use a number of observations (participant observation) made in connection with the UN Framework Convention on Climate Change Conference held in Copenhagen December 2009, which also included the Conference of the Parties or COP 15. While the Copenhagen COP 15 conference was dominated by government delegations and state leaders, business and trade unions interests were also represented. Under the auspices of the Danish main trade union LO, a number of trade unions held an independent conference on the climate issue related to COP 15. In this article, we discuss some of the observations from this conference.

Third, we also use publications and statements by various trade unions and employers' associations (or companies). The ETUC and Business Europe, for example, have formulated positions on the climate debate.

In the following section of the article, we introduce some of the key elements of international climate regulation, focusing especially on the EU. Climate issues are governed largely by international agreements. How and why, is discussed in this section. This is followed by a discussion of the specific aspects of the climate agenda which have engaged the trade unions and the employers' associations. In the final section of the article, we present some concluding remarks.

International climate regimes

The political institutional management of the climate issue is highly internationalized and supranational. We can identify what could be called a 'global climate change regime', with independent international and national actors, its own institutional structure (linked to the UN) and independent rules for decision-making (Thompson 2010).

The starting point for international cooperation on climate change is the United Nations Framework Convention on Climate Change (UNFCCC), adopted in 1992 in Rio de Janeiro. This convention includes targets for joint international initiatives aimed at reducing greenhouse gases in the atmosphere (Nedergaard 2009). Under the auspices of the UNFCCC, annual climate meetings were held, the Conference of the Parties (COP). The most recent of these meetings was COP 15, held in Copenhagen, which, after failing to agree on a binding treaty, ended with the 'Copenhagen Declaration'.

In 1997, the COP 3 meeting had reached agreement on the Kyoto Protocol. The Kyoto meetings formulated objectives for reducing CO2 emissions, and the Kyoto Protocol focused mainly on CO2 reduction among the industrialized countries. The Kyoto Protocol formally entered into force in 2005 in connection with Russia's ratification of the Protocol. It was only then that the terms of the Protocol achieved (at least 55 countries responsible for at least 55% of total global CO2 emission, should ratify) (Nedergaard 2009: 150, Howarth 2009).

In a European context, the political institutional handling of climate issues takes place predominantly in an EU context. In the climate area, the member states of the EU have delegated political competences to the EU level. On climate issues, the EU acts on behalf of the Member States in various international and national forums. The overall requirement to reduce greenhouse gas emissions in the EU is to international agreements (Kyoto) and is subsequently distributed among EU countries themselves.

Under the Kyoto agreement, the EU has committed itself to a total 8% cut in CO2 emissions over 1990 levels. The obligation to achieve this reduction is allocated to each Member State according to their level of economic development, energy efficiency, etc. Germany and Denmark must reduce their CO2 levels by 21% each, while Austria must reduce by 13%. Less developed EU countries such as Greece and Portugal have the opportunity to actually increase their CO2 emissions by 25% and 27%, respectively (Nedergaard 2009: 152-153).

The reduction in CO2 emissions can be achieved in various ways. Member states can either reduce their CO2 emissions directly or they can trade their CO2 quotas with other companies or countries (Howarth 2009).

EU has set some common goals in order to reduce the direct emission of CO2 coming from the member states. Hence, by 2020, 20% of the EU energy supply should come from renewable energy sources.

Trading of CO2 quotas in EU is regulated through an EU Directive (Emissions Trading System EU-ETS), which allows for the purchase of CO2 reductions from other countries. The intention of this directive is to ensure that investment in CO2 reduction is done in places where the potential reduction per Euro is greatest.

Generally, the climate policies of EU member states are well coordinated within the EU and connected to international climate agreements. The single member state has only limited ability to formulate its own climate policy.

If we examine what we have called the 'international climate regime', there are also other key climate players than nation states and the above- mentioned supranational organizations and institutions. Various NGOs also play a central role in the development of the international climate policy regime.

Among these NGOs, we can identify, firstly, environmental organizations that call for more action on climate policy and seek to mobilize political resources to promote their demands. Different types of national and international social movements also play a central role in relation to the climate policy agenda.

Second, there are business interest groups that argue that climate policy should be more restrained and take economic concerns into account.

Thirdly we can identify a knowledge-producing strata of scientists and experts who contribute to discourses about the need for climate regulation in light of increasing levels of CO2 emissions. In this context, the UN climate panel has played a crucial role as knowledge-producing body.

Overall, however, it is the nation states and the international organizations that are the most important actors in forming and maintaining the international climate regime. If the international climate regime is viewed from a realist international political theoretical perspective, it can be argued that it will be the most powerful states – or alliances of states – which will be the deciding actors in the climate regime. These states will set the framework for which climate targets to achieve and establish the rules and procedures for how to achieve them. The most important actors here seem to be EU (although not a state), the United States and China.

Industrial relations, labor market and climate

As suggested in the introduction to this article, trade unions and employers' associations have been increasingly preoccupied with climate issues. In this section, we discuss the key climate issues with which the industrial relations actors deal. Trade unions and employers' associations can be regarded as interest organizations representing employee and employer interests, both in relation to each other and to the surrounding communities (Hyman 2001, Ebbinghaus & Visser 2000).

IR systems are traditionally oriented towards managing relations between employees and employers. They operate within in national (and sometimes supranational) IR systems that manage different aspects of the employment relationship. IR regulation typically takes place through the conclusion of collective agreements between unions and employers, or through the use of different forms of government-driven regulation (often law-based) (Bamber et al. 2004).

Researchers in industrial relations are traditionally interested in analyzing the form of regulation or governance carried out in conjunction with the employment relation. However, the focus may also be on issues related to new technology, globalization and their impact on the employment relations.

This article examines the question of how climate problems and issues have affected and could further affect different IR systems and different IR actors. More specifically, we ask: 'How do IR actors seek to influence the climate debate and the various climate change initiatives coming from national and international authorities?'

The starting point for this analysis – beyond the introductory-mentioned observations about the climate policy agenda as indicated by their visibility on various websites – is that the climate challenge will come to affect the organization of production and labour in industrialized countries.

Companies are increasing expected to adapt their production and products to climate policy regulatory standards. Regulation of CO2 emissions seems to play an increasing role in the organization of work processes and in the way products are developed and produced.

The emergence of a climate challenge can be expected to affect the employee-management relations at enterprise level in a variety of areas. Some companies have sought to develop 'green' personnel policies, such that employees are encouraged to help reduce the company's CO2 emissions. Some employees have been subjected to increasing pressure on their skills and qualifications generated by the forecast of CO2 effects on the overall employment structure. Some types of jobs might disappear as society adapts to the climate challenge.

Both these examples show how the climate challenge could be an issue that IR actors must deal with, directly or indirectly. In the next section, we will focus on how trade unions and business associations have managed the climate challenge.

Labor markets in Europe could broadly expect to be affected by climate change in two ways. Firstly it is likely that over the long term, a number of industrial sectors would be directly affected by climate change. Several studies indicate that certain sectors and certain regions in Europe will be particularly hard hit by climate change. Agriculture, tourism, transport and water supply are some of the sectors that will be affected (Barker 2009, ETUC 2007). Similar predictions regarding specific regions in Europe – particularly in the Mediterranean region – indicate that they will be affected by changes in rainfall patterns, etc. Increased drought will alter the business environment and might lead to reduced employment opportunities. In contrast, other regions -- especially those in northern Europe -- might experience enhanced opportunities for production due to a warmer climate, e.g. in the agricultural sector (Barker 2009: 3).

Secondly climate change is expected to lead to different kinds of restructuring in certain sectors and within individual companies. In relation to the European situation, a report prepared for the EU Commission states:

> The changes needed to respond to climate change polices, to reduce CO2 emissions provide a clear example of a restructuring process. There are many opportunities – for example through the early adoption of innovative new technology – to place European companies ahead of global competitors that are slower to anticipate change. Conversely, a failure to anticipate by European firms may lead to hasty, reactive and forced later adjustment, which could damage companies and, leave their employees inadequately prepared, or trained, for alternative employment. Climate change will act as a key driver of evolution for the economic actors involved. … Companies will need to adapt their current products, processes and technology and to develop new innovative solutions, and workers will also need to acquire new skills. (GHK 2009: 2).

New sectors, such as those related to energy production, are likely to develop as a consequence of the increased focus on climate issues, while other sectors are likely to experience increased pressure to cut back or downsize.

In the following sections, focus will be on how trade unions and employers associations have reacted to the climate challenge.

Trade unions and climate

'Rather than being mere spectators, workers' representatives must become actively involved in the strategic guidelines defined and implemented to tackle emissions. A number of social dialogue and collective bargaining instruments and mechanisms should be introduced, and existing ones strengthened and updated ', (ETUC 2007: 180).

Safeguarding of employees' interests is carried out primarily done in relation to employers and to different political actors (the state) (Jensen 2006). In that context, trade unions play a special role. As actors in industrial relations systems, they often participate in collective negotiations (Müller-Jentch 2004). Trade unions have thus often close relationships (often in conflict with) businesses and their organizations. Key issues in the trade unions' agenda will often include topics such as how to create good jobs, how to increase wage levels, decrease working hours and other similar areas.

In the social science literature, it is argued that trade unions can be classified as belonging to what are called the 'first generation' of social movements in modern industrial society (Nash 2010). The trade unions captured the class-based interests of the employees in their relation to the employers. Today, the unions that were once social movements should be seen as part of an established system of relationships (e.g. the Industrial Relations context). This entails that trade unions tend to formulate their interests around the possibility for companies to create and ensure attractive jobs for the trade union members.

In the literature, however, it is also argued that since the 1960s, we can identify some new types of social movements, which see themselves as partly in opposition to the first generation of social movements represented by trade unions. Some of these new social movements have evolved around environmental issues and have tried to develop another kind of political agenda than that promoted by the trade unions. 'Post-material ideologies' have been one of the characteristics that have been attached to some of these 'second generation' social movements.

Observations, however, also stress that the 'old' trade unions and the 'new' social movements (e.g., environmental movements) represent different segments or classes in modern industrial (or post-industrial) society. Trade unions represent first and foremost the working class segments of society, while environmental movements primarily have middle class segments as their member base.

In the social science literature, some scholars have argued that significant differences could be identified in the interests and views expressed by the two types of social movements. The discussion of the relation between the 'old' social movements (e.g. trade unions) and the 'new' social movements (Melucci 1996) reflects the considerable tension between the views put forward by trade unions in light of their industrial relations position versus the views promoted by environmental organizations. This tension is particularly pertinent to views about how to handle the climate issue.

In the climate policy arena, trade unions find themselves in a field of tension between more traditional business interests (linked to cooperation and relations with business) and the desire of new social movements for significant (but often expensive and 'job lost costly') climate change initiatives.

In the following, we outline a number of empirical observations on the trade unions' involvement in various climate-related issues. In Table One, we present an overview of selected themes that trade unions are engaged in when they formulate climate policy oriented views. We also present an overview of the various 'arenas' (and actors) where trade unions deals with climate.

We distinguish between – on the one axis – different arenas of action starting with the 'local arena' (company level) proceeding up the 'global arena'. Further, we identify – on the other axis – the issues which trade unions have actively promoted in relation to the climate debate.

Table 1. Trade union activities related to climate issues

Issue / arena	Company level	Organizational Level (relation to employers' associations)	Regional/ local level	National level	International level (e.g. EU)	Global level (e.g. UN)
Green production/ Green jobs		E.g. joint statements or position papers. Influencing policy makers, etc.	Regional initiatives that can promote regional development of green jobs	Influencing national industrial policy	Statements or position papers about green jobs, e.g., influencing EU's industrial policy.	Statements or position papers about green jobs, etc.
Education/ training related to the possible restructuring of CO2-intensive sectors/jobs	Initiatives oriented toward increasing employee competencies and skills.	Agreements about general educational policy.	Regional initiatives that support regional restructuring.	Influencing national educational policy.		
Green representatives at workplace level	Green representatives at workplace level	Green representatives at workplace level				

Technological development	E.g., development of energy efficiency technology at company level	Joint support for general technology development		Positions about development of sustainable technology	Positions about development of sustainable technology	
Energy policy	Energy policy at company level	Recommendations about implementation of energy policies at company level		CO2 responsibility	CO2 responsibility	CO2 responsibility
CSR – Corporate Social Responsibility	CSR – Corporate Social Responsibility	Recommendations about implementation of climate policies in local CSR policies				
Social responsibility in relation to CO2 changes			Regional restructuring with social responsibility	Social and global responsibility toward the Third World.	Social and global responsibility toward the Third World.	Social and global responsibility toward the Third World.
CO2 – general policy development		Joint statements and views on CO2 policy		Influencing policy-making at national level	General views regarding EU climate policy	General views regarding UN climate policy development

Source: Web-pages from trade unions in Europe (observed in October and November 2009 – climate related issues was especially visible among trade unions in the following countries (English web-pages): Ireland, UK, France, Germany, Denmark, Sweden, Norway) , ITUC (2009), European Foundation for Improvement of Living Conditions (2009)

If we examine the themes discussed by the trade unions in more detail, they can be grouped into four major categories: (1) green businesses and green representatives at local level; (2) green jobs, green growth and green educational development; (3) sector and occupational restructuring; and (4) general energy and CO2 policy development.

Employer associations, business and climate

Business and employers' organizations appear to be a bit more active and visible in relation to climate policy issues than do trade unions, if we use climate visibility on web-pages as an indicator. There may be several explanations for this difference.

Firstly, business and employer associations are more directly affected by the various climate change initiatives. Climate regulatory initiatives often entail extra costs for companies (whether they think themselves as 'goods-producing' or 'employers'). Employees – and their interest organizations – are more indirectly affected by various climate-regulatory initiatives. Companies and organizations therefore have a more direct and immediate incentive to deal with climate policy initiatives.

Second, business and employers' association derive organizational benefits compared to the trade unions, insofar as they establish common views. Theories of collective action argue that business and employers' associations have more homogenous interests when compared to trade unions. The business community is defined largely in relation to economic parameters, by which common interests can be articulated. The literature describes a major heterogeneity of interests among the trade unions and the employees. This is a classic point in collective action theory (Offe & Wiesenthal 1980, Müller-Jench 2004).

In relation to climate policy issues, the main interests of business and employers' organizations are of two types: (1) the cost of climate regulatory measures for businesses should be as low as possible; and (2) the cost of climate-regulatory measures should not distort competition (between sectors, countries or regions).[1] The European business and employers' association, BusinessEurope, has argued for the need to establish a common global 'playing field' in relation to climate regulation in order to ensure fair competition under conditions of climate regulation. In a publication about climate issues, Business Europe writes:

> The more industrial production remains in Europe, the less greenhouse gases are likely to be emitted worldwide. In order for industry to be able to keep on investing within Europe, the cost of production must not rise disproportionately to the production cost of competitors outside Europe. Especially industry exposed to international competition need a global level playing field (Business Europe 2008: 7).

1 This view has to be modified specifically in relation to specific countries, sectors, etc. It is also possible that climate-regulating measures may be taken with the indirect aim of distorting competition and ensuring that specific sectors or nation-states obtain some comparative advantage compared to other sectors/countries. Business and employers' associations might therefore argue that certain types of climate regulatory measures should be implemented, the primary aim being that it meets their members' specific interests.

If we examine what types of initiatives have been taken by companies and employers' associations with regard to climate policy, the topics are very much similar to those identified in conjunction with the trade unions. We can observe statements about the need for 'green policies' at company level as part of CSR policy, meaning that employees should help develop the company so that CO2 emissions are reduced. And we can observe arguments about the need for developing green technologies, green production and green jobs (Business Europe 2008).

The European Foundation (2010) has in an analysis outlined a number of initiatives taken among various business and employers' organizations in the EU. Employers, like the trade unions, also seem to give attention to future opportunities to provide people with the right skill profile:

> In the UK, the employer organization, the Confederation of British Industry (CBI) highlights that skills are needed in areas such as science, technology, engineering and math, technical competencies and a range of new business skills. The CBI makes a range of recommendations on how to increase the number of workers with these skills: These include encouraging a greater focus on such skills in schools and proposing ways to encourage education providers to work with business to meet the demand for these types of skills (European Foundation 2010: 11-12).

Employers have also paid attention to the general conditions of the policy initiatives that have been put into place. Among the many business and employers' organizations, the argument was put forward that the market should be the most important regulatory factor in climate policy, rather than the market being subjected to direct policy decisions.

An important element of business and employers' handling of climate issues was that of developing local climate change initiatives. Companies brand themselves on climate topics by emphasizing their efforts in relation to climate. For example, a company such as Bayer AG has formulated its own climate policy. The aim is to contribute to the development of products that are climate friendly, and to undertake initiatives that will reduce its overall energy consumption (Bayer 2009). A company brochure describes 'the complex relationships that exist within our climate system, the impact on climate of human kind and the actions being taken to tackle climate change on a political level.' According to this brochure, 'Bayer's objective [is] to lead the way when it comes to climate protection.' Climate is largely a topic that also is subsumed within company policies.

The industrial relations actors and the climate regime actors

Let us focus on the types of climate political alliances that trade unions and employers associations could be involved.

It is possible to identify several climate policy actors who play an important role in the international climate regime. These actors are (1) state actors and supranational actors with state-like characteristics (EU, UN), (2) business and interest groups (including trade unions and employers' organizations), (3) environmental organizations (Thompson 2010).

The actors interact on many different levels, ranging from the local to the 'global' level and they use different types of representatives to articulate their interests (e.g., local unions, national unions, international unions, etc.).

We now present two cases which can illustrate how trade unions and business organizations interact with other actors in relation to the climate discussion. The cases show some of the differences in interests and positions among the industrial actors and other actors inside the 'climate regime', especially in relation to the environmental NGOs.

The first case is from Denmark and presents some of the conflicts between trade unions and the environmental movement in the issue of creating green jobs and green industries. The second case relates to France, and describes how trade unions have participated in a government-initiated project on climate and France.

The case reflects a broader conflict between environmental concerns (and alliances with social movements) and consideration for 'green jobs'. Denmark is a leading producer of wind turbines. The Danish company Vestas has been a leading player among wind turbine manufacturers, with a global market share of up to 35%. Increased attention to wind power generation has reduced Vestas global market position to about 15% in 2010. The emergence of a number of Chinese wind turbine manufacturers has increased the pressure on Vestas. However, Vestas has retained a significant production facility and research and development of wind turbines in Denmark. In addition, Siemens also has R&D activities in Denmark. In relation to – and linked to overall strategies to increase the amount of 'green jobs' in Denmark – the Danish government is seeking to construct a testing facility for wind turbines in the northern part of Denmark. The testing center is considered by the industry as a prerequisite for retaining wind turbine R&D departments in Denmark. However, the test center involves the construction of giant turbines, with a height of up to 250 meters, and this is expected to have significant environmental implications for the area in which they are sited. The professional organizations (and industries) are backing the construction of the testing center, while a number of environmental organizations have protested over the environmental consequences. The Danish Society for Nature Conservation (Dansk Naturfredningsforening), for example, has launched a petition and a number of demonstrations against the proposed location of the testing center (www.dn.dk). The conflicts between the trade unions, who are interested in 'green growth' and the environmental organizations – who prioritize environmental issues, are acutely visible in this case.

Some trade unions in Denmark have argued that the political commitment to 'green growth' should be increased, and that in certain contexts, green growth should have a higher priority than other environmental considerations. Moreover, this priority, they argue, should be implemented via the legislative and planning process. For example, the Danish Metalworkers' Union, Dansk Metal, in a leaflet on green growth, has highlighted the following:

> Although Denmark is the country in the world where there is proportionately the highest number of wind turbines, it is now difficult to obtain permission to set up new large turbine installations. However, there must be room not only for economic and knowledge-related space for energy venture in Denmark, there must also be physical space. Therefore, we propose the establishment of energy zones around the country. In the energy zones, we can create energy without unnecessary bureaucracy and with procedures for approval that are clear, simple and especially efficient. In energy zones, the construction of energy facilities should be given higher priority than other environmental concerns. This will make it easier to find investors and build testing and demonstration sites for renewable energy. Thus, we ensure a smooth transition as well as a market for new technologies '(Dansk Metal 2010: 8, my translation).

The above case illustrates some of the tensions between the social partners on the one side (trade unions and business companies) and environmental organizations on the other. The industrial relations actors argue that jobs and production should receive priority over specific environmental concerns. Denmark needs to develop competitive advantages on the 'green' production market. The environmental organizations – here represented by the Danish Society for Nature Conservation – argue that the consequences of building high turbines are too damaging to the local environment. This argument is put forward even though the testing center is expected to contribute – in the long run – to the reduction of CO2 emissions because it will help develop more effective wind turbines. The conflicts between the different types of actors and regimes are obvious.

The second case concerns the French Grenelle Environnement round table, a comprehensive energy and environmental policy national government initiative with the involvement of trade unions which took place in 2007.[2] Part of the GrenelleEnvironnement has been implemented in more concrete legislation in France during 2009 and 2010.

> Five parties were directly involved: NGOs, trade unions, employers, local authorities, and the national State. They where chosen for being actors in the civil society as well as for being closely related to environmental protection to different extents. It has been called the 'Dialogue of Five' (Vieira & Bétaille 2008: 202).

2 This Grenelle Environnement was presented at COP 15 in Copenhagen in connection with a conference arranged by several national and international trade unions.

The plans focuses on topics such as energy saving in houses and buildings, greener transportation, greener energy production with more focus on renewable energy and less on fossil fuels, agricultural-environment with less use of pesticides and respect for biodiversity (www.legrenelle-environnement.fr/ Grenelle-environnement). The process resulted in a large number of specific proposals, such as the establishment of a 'Transport Observatory', which could monitor and present ideas for energy efficient modes (The Grenelle Environnement 2007: 5).

Among the labour-related proposals are proposals to develop training programs to ensure skills that can facilitate the green economy. In one of the reports of the French round table, it is argued that

> The social partners have set up lifelong professional training tools: annual training plans, forward-looking employment management and skills management, validation of experience, sandwich training and the individual right to training, in particular. These tools should be mobilised to professional facilitate transitions linked to sustainable development (The Grenelle Enviroment 2007a: 9).

An overall evaluation of the process related to the Grenelle has been given by Vieira and Betaille, who conclude that

> The project had both positive and negative (critical) aspects. On the one hand, the *Grenelle* was a success in that it created an opportunity to exchange ideas about environmental problems faced by French society; the 'Dialogue of Five' has made possible for the first time the meeting of various key actors of the civil society; and new bi-lateral relations (e.g., NGOs and unions or NGOs and local governments) have been created and implemented. On the other hand, many criticisms must be expressed although the results cannot be evaluated as long as the implementation phase is not finished.' (Vieira & Bétaille 2008: 204).

Similarly, a press release formulated by the European Green Party in 2007 reveals some of the tensions present in the environmental policy development. The European Green Party, in connection with the French Grenelle Environnement, argued that although the initiatives taken by the French governments (and the parties involved) had some positive elements, that there were still considerable problems:

> The most serious difficulty posed by the forum's recommendations is related to the decision to keep nuclear power at the heart of France's energy policy. This is an irresponsible decision, as nuclear power is extremely dangerous and should not, under any circumstances, be seen as a viable way of combating climate change' (Press release by the European Green Party, 26 October 2007).

This second case can be seen as an example of how professional organizations seek to influence the general climate policy agenda through their participation in corporatively oriented national government initiatives.

What we have observed in these two cases is that there are numerous tensions between the industrial relations actors on the one side and the environmental organizations on the other. Trade unions, employers and business organizations have become more active in formulating policies and positions on climate issues. However, this has not meant that these actors have the same overall views about how to deal with the climate and emission problems as do environmental groups. Trade unions focus on how jobs can be preserved and developed in a world where climate has become a major issue. For their part, environmental organizations – not surprisingly – focus primarily on how to create a reduction in CO2 emissions.

Conclusions

In early 2010, the EU Commission launched its 2020 plan for the European Union. The plan sets out a number of key milestones in the economic development of Europe in the coming decade, among which are ensuring that climate concerns are taken into account In the words of the Commission:

> Europe must act: – Combating climate change: Achieving our climate goals means reducing emissions significantly more quickly in the next decade than in the last decade and exploiting fully the potential of new technologies such as carbon capture and sequestration possibilities. Improving resource efficiency would significantly help limit emissions, save money and boost economic growth. All sectors of the economy, not just emission-intensive, are concerned. We must also strengthen our economies' resilience to climate risks, and our capacity for disaster prevention and response (Commission of the European Union 2010: 13).

Climate issue is therefore expected to plan an even more central role in EU during the coming decade than has been the case so far.

As explained above, climate is also a major topic of discussion among the social partners in Europe. These discussions take place at both national and European levels. The main topics for debate and action – by both employers and unions – are economic restructuring, green growth, green business, green jobs and training and more general concerns in relation to different forms of energy- and C02 policy.

However, there is also – not surprisingly – a difference of interests between the industrial relations actors in relation to climate policy. There are differences between employers and employees, as well as among trade unions in different countries. European Foundation writes:

> While the green agenda is generally not a particularly contentious issue between the social partners, some differences in viewpoints have arisen between the trade unions and employers in a number of countries. For example, in Portugal, the employers are more sceptical of the green agenda, fearing that it will increase costs and therefore reduce competitiveness. Trade union concerns linked to the green agenda, on the other hand, are usually more related to employment levels and working conditions. Moreover, trade unions are often preoccupied with membership issues: on the one hand, trade unions in the UK see the emergence of new green

> industries as a recruitment opportunity; however, in other countries, trade unions fear the decline of more traditional industries with strong trade union membership and recognize that it may be harder to recruit members in new green industries' (European Foundation 2009: 11).

As we have seen, climate issues – despite differences in strategy – have rapidly become a field of concern for industrial relations actors. There is increasing pressure on the labor market parties ompelling them to formulate policies on various aspects of the climate debate. IR actors will be cnfronted with new expectations and demands both rom their members and their social environment.

References:

Bamber, G., Landsbury, R. & Wailes, N. (eds.) (2004): International and comparative employment relations – Globalisation and the developed market economies, (4th ed.). London, Sage.

Barker, T. (2009): Climate change and EU labour Markets. paper presented at Conference on 'Employment in Europe 2009', Bruxelles, Commission of the European Community.

Bayer AG (2009): The Bayer Climate Program. Leverkusen (www.bayer.com)

Business Europe (2008): Combating climate Change – Four Key Principles for a Successful International Agreement, Bruxelles, Business Europe.

Commission of the European Union (2010): Europe 2010 – A European Strategy for Smart, Sustainable and Inclusive Growth. Bruxelles, European Commission, www.ec.europa.eu/eu2020/

Dansk Metal (Danish Union of Metal Workers) (2010): Fra nulvækst til grøn vækst – Dansk Metals bud på grønne vækstinitiativer i Danmark. Copenhagen, Dansk Metal.

Det Økonomiske Råd (2010): Økonomi og Miljø – 2010. Copenhagen, Det Økonomiske Råd, (www.dors.dk).

Ebbinghaus, B. & Visser, J. (eds.) (2000): Trade Unions in Western Europe since 1945. Oxford, Macmillan Reference LTD.

ETUC (European Trade Union Confederation) (2007): Climate Change and Employment – Impact on Employment in the European Union-25 of Climate Change and CO2 Emission Reduction Measures by 2030. Bruxelles, ETUC.

European Foundation for the Improvement of Living and Working Conditions (2009): Greening the European economy: Responses and initiatives by Member States and social partners. Dublin, European Foundation for the Improvement of Living and Working Conditions.

European Green Party, press releases www.europeangreeens.org

GHK (2009): The Impact of Climate Change on European Employment and Skills in short to Medium-Term: A Review of the Literature – Final report vol 2. London, GHK (www.ghkint.com)
Howarth, D. (2009): Greening the Internal Market in a Difficult Economic Climate. Journal of Common Market Studies, 47, 133-150.
Hyman, R. (2001): Understanding European Trade Unionism – Between Market, Class and Society. London, Sage.
ITUC (International Trade Union Confederation) (2009): Trade unions and climate change – equity, justice & solidarity in the fight against climate change. Bruxelles, ITUC.
Jensen, C. Strøby (2006): Trade unionism: differences and similarities – a comparative view on Europe, USA and Asia. Journal of Industrial Relations, 48 (1): 59-81.
Jensen, C. Strøby (2009): Employer Associations in Europe: A comparative analysis of employer strategies in Denmark and UK. IIRA World Congress, Sydney, August, 2009.
Melucci, A. (1996): Challenging Codes: Collective Action in the Information Age. Cambridge, Cambridge University Press.
Müller-Jentsch, W. (2004): Theoretical Approaches to Industrial Relations'. In Kaufman, B.E. (2004): Theoretical Perspectives on Work and the Employment Relationship. Industrial Relations Research Association Series (pp. 1-40), Industrial Relations Research Association, University of Illinois.
Nash, K. (2010): Contemporary Political Sociology – Globalization. 2. edition, UK, John Wiley & Sons, Ltd.
Nedergaard, P. (2009): Nu taler politikerne også om vejret. In Marcussen, M. & Ronit, K. (eds.) (2009). pp. 144-170 in Globaliseringens Udfordringer – Politiske og administrative modeller under pres. Copenhagen, Hans Reitzels Forlag.
Offe, C. & Wiesenthal, H. (1980): Two logics of collective action: Theoretical notes on social class and organizations form. Political Power and Social Theory, 1, 67-115.
The Grenelle Environnement (2007a): Group 1- Combating climate change and controlling demand for Energy. (http://www.legrenelle-environnement.fr/grenelle-environnement/IMG/pdf/Groupe_1_Synthese_anglais.pdf.
The Grenelle Enviroment (2007b): Group 6:'Promoting ecological forms of development which are favourable to competitiveness and employment. (www.legrenelle-environnement.fr/grenelle-environnement/IMG/pdf/mini_ecol_group6_competitivite_emploi_gb.pdf)
Thompson, A. (2010): Rational design in motion: Uncertainty and flexibility in the global climate regime. European Journal of International relations, 16 (2): 269-296.

Vieira, R.S. & Bétaille, J. (2008): Grenelle de l'environnement: Is France making up for lost time?. In K. Bosselman, R. Engel, R, & P. Taylor, (2008). Governance for Sustainability – Issues, Challenges, Successes. IUCN Environment Law Center (pp. 201-208), Geneve.

An Emerging Social Innovation: Mutual aid Networks at Unionised Workplaces

Denis Harrisson and Maxime Bélanger
Crises-UQAM

Content

Introduction

The issue of mutual aid networks is part of an approach aimed at enhancing well-being and quality of working life by reviving links of solidarity among work colleagues. The development of this approach is closely associated with a deterioration of mental health at the workplace (Gabriel and Liimatainen 2000; Brun et al. 2003). Mutual aid networks created by local unions aim to help fix this hardship. The goals set for dealing with problems consist first of controlling, reducing or even eliminating the work factors that imperil mental health; next, of supporting employees through union involvement aimed at leading to a new type of relationship; and, finally, of defending their rights and facilitating their return to work under better conditions. It is a way of improving working conditions by introducing a type of relationship among the members that leads to rediscover the social dimension of human development, an answer to a need that becomes obvious in workplaces.

This article consists of showing how these networks play a part in union renewal. Mutual aid networks[1] are devised as a social innovation emerging from

1 In this article, unless indicated otherwise, "union mutual aid networks" are referred to simply as "mutual aid networks" to lighten the text. We are aware, however, that this use is more general and designates a mutual aid web that is much more complex than what we are dealing with here.

actions by employees associated with the trade-union and voluntary associations. Although networks are starting to develop a degree of self-reliance in terms of operations, outer connections are needed. We offer an understanding of how these networks are structured and inserted into unions' institutionalised activities. This involves analysing the process of their setting-up and the links that develop between agents as well as with principals and union representatives. The activities are set out based on the type of problem submitted to the network. The paper is divided into two parts. The first part presents what has emerged from rapid transformations in the labour world in terms of mental health, work organisation and the need for these problems to be handled through new union practices that complete the traditional course of actions. In the second part, we introduce the outcomes of our research by showing the structure-forming elements of mutual aid networks, in particular their internal organisation, their operations, the types of intervention and the conception of the role of mutual aid provider.

1. Research context and issues

Mental health problems currently represent one of the greatest causes of absence from work (Rhéaume et al. 2008; Rhéaume, Saint-Arnaud and Saint Jean 2003, Brun, Biron, Ivers and Martel, 2003; Vézina, 1996). The proportion of indemnified long-term absences due to mental health problems is thought to range between 30% and 50% in Canada (Filteau 2003). Three factors are identified in protecting the mental health of workers: recognition, autonomy in decision-making and social support at work. Recognition at work and autonomy in decision-making contribute to professional well-being and enable individuals to find sense in their work (Bourbonnais et al. 2000; Karasek and Theorell 1990). Social support contributes to enhancing human interrelationships, and it strengthens cooperation and serves to alleviate tensions found in the workplace. The absence of social support is associated with a contraction of social capital, i.e. the strength of the links that unite people in various arenas of social interaction, and with a lowering of trust between members of society in general (Putnam 2000). Corrosion of the social bonds contributes to the isolation of individuals, brought about by a form of conflict connected with individualisation (Hirigoyen 2007), loss of solidarity (Blais 2007) and greater social distance at work (Black 1993). Ambiguities at work flourish due to overwork, lack of recognition, distrust in relationships and minimal participation in decision-making.

With the abundance of problems associated with working life and personal life, a tightening of social links among peers is also part of the solution. This is why, in workplaces, mutual aid networks are called upon to act. Mutual aid is the basis of human solidarity and encourages values of sharing and assistance (Caillé 2000). Originally, these initiatives took shape around issues linked to alcoholism and drug addiction (Bacharah *et al.* 2001, Rhéaume *et al.* 2008). Given the scope of mental health phenomena experienced by workers, union members pointed out the relevance of expanding these networks' activities. Networks intervene among members suffering from the most serious social problems in current society: addiction problems (alcohol, drugs, gambling), long-term psycho-social problems (depression, schizophrenia, etc.), chronic physical illnesses, particular crises (death of a child, divorce, etc.), challenges to status (linked to sex, age, etc.) and, finally, situations in which individuals are affected by problems faced by family members or friends who are showing manic depressive traits, behavioural problems (Lavoie, 2001).

Mutual aid relies on community links that go beyond market or public accounts (expert-professional), with denial of an instrumental connection and of the utilitarian and rational paradigm (Romeder et al. 1989, Godbout 1994). Relationships between union members and representatives are generally organised along a service orientation and mutual aid links represents an alternative to the structuring of instrumentalised actions (Bacharach *et al.* 2001).

Mutual aid networks rely on the solidarity and cohesion of union's members, strengthening members' commitment at the local level. Ties of solidarity have long characterised unions. These links have gradually been eroded, however, by the logic of defending union members' socio-economic rights. Moreover, the state would be likely to entrust mutual aid responsibility and duties to voluntary organisations that operate at lower cost to society (Lévesque 2003). It is important to emphasise that the issue of mutual aid networks is "therapeutic" in itself, because it is conducted by volunteers who benefit just as greatly from the effects of what they give (Burnonville 1999).

In addition, the proposed approach breaks with the research that unions perform consisting of analysing the institutionalised practices of labour relations, and it also breaks with the emerging volunteer practices of social actors who, far from giving up in the face of an obstacle, succeed in changing their institutional environment, in creating new links and in gaining advantage from them (Harrisson et Klein 2007). The originality of our approach lies in dealing with the issue as a social innovation, a notion that enables the issue of social transformations to be dealt with through the analysis of new forms of conduct by social actors, who interact in highly institutionalised spaces. The preservation of the quality of working life and the protection of human integrity are parts of the sustainable development. Social innovation is a way of consolidating the social links between human beings and their environment by empowering their capacities.

1.1 Elements of theory

We conceive mutual aid networks in unions as being social innovations (Moulaert et al. 2005, Harrisson & Klein 2007), i.e. initiatives emerging from the interactions of local actors who form an alliance with actors from other areas of activity to resolve a problem. These networks rely on cooperation between a variety of actors when institutions cannot provide the resources for resolving the problem (Harrisson, Szell and Bourque 2009). To be effective, social innovations must arise from the base and be the object of a collective appropriation. Local solutions rub up against global elements of innovation and adjust themselves mutually based on context. In this perspective, innovation does not necessarily involve a radical development but rather a variety of new forms, values and standards that adjust themselves mutually (Campbell 2004). Actors exchange knowledge and ideas and become mobilised in legitimization activity. Contemporary mutual aid is a particular type of innovation. It responds to an ability to cooperate through exchanges and social ties that go beyond the quest for individual interest. Networks provide for relationships between peers who exchange knowledge, representations and emotions (Collins 2004). Human beings need attention from others and solidarity is an essential condition of social life (Blais 2007).

The case of union mutual aid networks involves analysing the emergence of networks as workers' self-organisation in creative tension with other parts of the union council (Croucher, Martens and Singe 2007). This is an addition to institutions, a dynamic social capital force that is mobilised by values of solidarity in a situation where representation about peculiar aspects (the employee's malaise) is not necessarily controlled by the union.

1.2 Methodology

Data were gathered by analysing documents on the mutual aid networks at the Confédération des syndicats nationaux (*Confederation of National Trade Unions*) (CSN) and through interviews with employees and CSN officials, with mutual aid providers and with resource persons forming the structure of the network.[2] We favoured qualitative research (semi-directive, individual or group interviews). A total of 24 persons were interviewed in a series of 17 individual interviews (six mutual aid providers, a president officer of the union executive, eight assisted persons and two mutual aid officers) and three group interviews involving six

2 Mutual aid networks have existed in the FTQ (Quebec Federation of Labour) since 1989, using the term "union counselors". Mutual aid networks in the CSN are more recent, dating back to the late 1990s.

mutual aid providers and a president of the union executive. The interviews with the mutual aid providers took place in six workplaces: two in the private sector and four in the public sector. The participants in the study were chosen for the diversity of the viewpoints that could be expressed. Their remarks were collected in semi-structured interviews based on questions devised especially for this project. Our basic corpus consists of about 20 hours of recorded interviews that were then transcribed and analysed by theme. A report was written and validated by the participants. A few corrections were made afterward. The following portions will set out the results that came from this study.

2. The structuring of the mutual aid network

At the network's beginning lies a recognition of the vacuum in the organisational structure for dealing with an upsurge in problems of mental health, tense relationships between people in the workplace or various forms of addiction. Organisations are poorly equipped, while the union is considered inadequate for handling these new elements of distress. Accordingly, the actors must innovate to deal with a growing problem, which also opens new perspectives for renewing union practices. An entirely new approach is created. As a mutual aid provider mentioned:

> "We have some major cases coming out, but in general it's much harder than before. Everything is harder than before [...], the shortage of employees in the organisation, [...] In terms of ambiance, we've always had people who were ill because of mental health problems. And that reaches 50%. So there are 50% off on disability insurance with problems related to mental health. It may be depression, or trouble adapting. There are a large number of people in depression. They were saying one in three. Among those who are off, half the cases are related to mental health."

Officials at the labour federation urge their members to identify risk factors in the organisation of work. The first factor is autonomy in decision-making, which consists of using an employee's knowledge and abilities as well as the decision-making power that provides meaning and leads to a sense of control. The second factor is social support in the form of interactions among the people who provide technical and emotional assistance.

In order to tackle these disorders, the network's cognitive aspects are based on Theorell and Karasek model (1991). The network is thus established from the start on validated knowledge that legitimises actions taken among union representatives and members. This is a robust source for structuring networks. These references to the scientific world, with the dual referral of knowledge dealing with connections between the work environment and mental health along with knowledge dealing with mutual aid networks, represent sources of legitimacy based on reason and scientific logic. They serve the logic of union action, which then creates its initiative on these knowledge-based arguments. This knowledge is taken up and interpreted so as to put it into action and connect it with experience.

Mutual aid exists in various forms, with most experiences never being reported because they occur informally. What is needed is to consolidate these informal networks and to structure them in a way that makes them sustainable. This is what CSN officials aim to do. They see mutual aid as a form of support based on voluntary commitment between different people. The network complements specialised professional assistance, but it is the union that will have to develop solidarity-based action. This action is then organised around mutual aid providers, who are volunteer unionised employees selected for their outstanding qualities. Their life experience at work and elsewhere is highly diversified. Some have experienced problems and overcome them, while others are involved in similar activities outside work in their communities. They all receive training to develop their relational abilities: knowing how to listen, being attentive to others, knowing institutional and community resources and being able to refer people to them. They share the mutual aid vision and are concerned with the quality of life in their workplace. Their actions play a role in deepening links of solidarity.

The network is created on a voluntary, selective and unconstrained basis among equals, with confidentiality guaranteed. It quickly stands out from other demands. From the start, this new arrangement is linked in a distinct and novel course of action within the union structure. A union representative explains clearly why this is the case:

> "...At the CSN, we have two fronts. The first one is the collective agreement, defending the economic interests of workers. The second front is the whole issue of the social and political order. At the union board, we work at mobilisation, and so we're not [involved] in collective agreements. When we're in contact with members, we see the social problems. This also began with drug addiction. Most of the mutual aid networks began with the issue of drug addiction. That's how it got started, and they were trying to scrape up a few pennies. But the CSN didn't want to put money into it because it already had its second front, which it handled politically. We knew United Ways [a charitable funding organisation] had [money] to redistribute to workers because they contributed heavily to the fund. This meant [amounts] were available. Mutual aid seems to come out of that.."

The mutual aid network also stands out from the union structure through the support it obtains from a charitable organisation such as United Ways. This non-profit organisation supports this project as regards mutual aid training and in covering the salaries of the two persons who handle the mutual aid file. The CSN endorses this project as a way of integrating it with the various levels of the union structure. Nevertheless, the CSN shows a willingness to develop and consolidate mutual aid networks through the hiring of an adviser of whose mandates is to promote and develop mutual aid everywhere.

Like any social innovation, the mutual aid network is not created entirely without previous links. While mutual aid is not new, it is taken up differently in a new context, and the receiving structures are solidly anchored in institutional terms, as a member of the union executive noted:

> "...because, as union officers, we are automatically approached to do counselling. [...] The advantage worth considering [in] the mutual aid network is that we are making a distinction there. It's really a matter of listening, mutual assistance, and that has nothing to do with the collective agreement. We're not talking about labour relations as such."

This innovation may help lead to a social transformation (at least in the labour relations area) if it is acknowledged as an element in a body of innovations that are structured coherently in terms of their effects in resolving problems, on governance, and on the rules and social norms that are created through interactions. This is why the making of the networks is considered so essential by the initiators who are well aware that its structuring is completely untested. Innovation is what is being disseminated, but above all everything is structured in a particular context rather than through systematically structured planning. Innovation is disseminated through the risky exercise of direct intervention among employees. Therefore, mutual aid networks are locally heterogeneous, with major differences appearing in their structures, in how they operate, and in the links uniting them with an employer or even the union. They are called by different names, and the practices of those involved are also different, as are the means of promotion and even the types of problems that mutual aid providers are able to consider. The reasons that lead activists to establish a mutual aid network also arise from concerns coming from the union executive committee as well as from members' personal experiences. This is what we will be examining in the next section.

2.1 Internal organisation of the mutual aid network

The mutual aid network setting-up follows observations of the extent of relational problems encountered in the workplace such as lack of cooperation among employees or between employees and management and also in indifference or a form of self-denial and neglect in facing the scope of the difficulties and their solutions. Some workplaces have undergone major structural modifications like change in management, reorganisation of work followed by a restructuring, job losses and new assignments, deterioration in the work climate causing stress, uncertainty, lack of recognition, or inadequate communication between various organisational levels. To this is added the social isolation felt by employees whose workplace is central to their lives, as mentioned by this employee:

"… I live alone. You get back home, and whom do you talk to about it? You can't talk to just anyone about it. And so you close in on yourself. You go back to work the next day, and it still hasn't been talked about."

The union executive committee becomes powerless in facing situations that may require concerted action with the employer, particularly in resolving problems associated with the organisation of work, the make-up of work teams, the workload, insecurity resulting from uncertainty and from reassignment of positions, and even disciplinary sanctions. The mutual aid network is one of the means of getting a handle on these problems and resolving them through the structuring of new means.

Unions are able to mobilise the experience of members. In each case, networks were initiated by employees who had gone through episodes of harassment or personal conflicts that affected their professional lives. The other enrolment measure consists of selecting persons who have union experience or who show considerable interest in the union movement and who share experience with natural forms of care. As mentioned by one of them:

"[…] People mention that I am very discreet and confidential. They trust me. When they know that they will be confiding things in me, they know it will not be repeated. It remains confidential. This is natural with me. I have always provided mutual aid. This is what it's called today, and I didn't know how else I could say it."

Networks are initiated by volunteer employees who seek support from their union. Other cases involve union representatives who take the initiative and develop the internal network among the members. Despite the expected benefits, the network does not spread as easily as it should. Some delays seem inevitable. Broadening the network is achieved following specific actions that encounter some obstacles. The first one involves the role of the employer, whose responsibility is significant. This role is variable, however. The employer is a vital go-between in the network and, although not involved in specific cases, remains an essential component for the network to be effective. This means the employer must admit the existence of this type of problem experienced by employees and recognise its contribution to resolving the problem together with the mutual aid networks. Not all employers are prepared to admit this. The reaction is uncertain: while some union representatives question their added value, others wonder if the network can continue without support from employers.

Then, the network is organised and structured around people who have an identity that can be modelled on union members' identities. In this regard, the network faces difficulties with the complexity of professional identities that become entwined with civic identities such as gender, ethno-cultural background, age, sexual orientation, etc. As noted by one person who was aided:

> "... In situations of stress or hardship, you're more likely to approach people who have affinities [a woman]. You'll feel you have greater affinity with her without even having seen her. You're more reassured, and this is more reassuring."

The network's strength depends on the confidence that develops among workers and the various persons who may be involved. Unions favour short networks even though they are aware that a network may remain unknown to most employees. The network relies on particular connections with people who are best known to their immediate colleagues in the same vocational group, with links of proximity developing. This is why groups, divisions, departments or work shifts without direct links to the network are more vulnerable, with workers tending not to meet someone unknown unless a strong reputation.

Some unions choose to elect network members in general meetings to regularise their status. This procedure is controversial, however. It does enable the mutual aid network to be recognised officially in the union structure and network members to become known in everyone's eyes as people to meet in case of need. As one mutual aid provider noted:

> "Not everyone has these qualities. Being a good business agent for a union does not mean you'll have these qualities. Thus, there is at least one person appointed by the executive who is able to convey expertise. [...] You really have to cut yourself off from your union functions to enter a completely different mode. It's a learning process, and there are frictions."

A mutual aid network is also structured horizontally through training, becoming a place for exchanges where mutual aid providers make use of the experiences of others, influencing each other in organising their own activities in their respective networks. Exchanges of experience are conducted in the form of descriptions, information exchanges and teamwork dealing with the various possible forms of mutual aid. This is an important area for structuring networks.

In short, the internal network is structured around five types of participants, with each having a defined role: the union, especially its executive committee members; the aid providers, who are trained volunteer members; the people who are assisted; work colleagues; and the employer. What sets the mutual aid network apart above all from the usual relationships between these actors are specific non-standard actions in the usual interventions between these actors, as we shall see in the following section, which also deals with roles performance.

2.2 The operation of a mutual aid network

A mutual aid network is structured on the basis of a certain number of criteria such as a set amount of leave, estimated at two hours per month. Some aid providers have been authorised by their employers to be away from their work area when requested by someone. In other cases, this presents a difficulty because they may hold a solo position and cannot easily get away without being replaced, meaning their action cannot be immediate. A third type of case involves freeing up time for aid providers to take part in a symposium, an information session or a conference without time being available to meet someone in distress. In this last instance, time is organised as if mutual aid were a usual union activity. Meetings take place during working hours without the employer being advised and in a very informal way, or else are held outside the workplace and outside normal hours. This makes it more complicated to organise the network and to recruit aid providers, as this union representative mentions:

> "The employer is [...] against this [the mutual aid network]. This cuts his wings, and union leave would be required to be able to assist them. Otherwise, you do this [outside] your work hours, or you do it clandestinely. This is another matter, and not everyone is prepared to do it during a time other than their work hours. At lunch hour, they don't want to. They don't want to be called at home. This becomes another problem."

Marginalisation or even exclusion of the mutual aid network is also exacerbated by the place that aid providers obtain with the employer and also with union representatives. Aid providers do not have specific facilities. Meetings must be held in union offices. The mutual aid network, while linked to the union executive, keeps a certain distance from the latter to preserve a relative independence and a level of autonomy in its operation. The union has the function of strenghtening the mutual aid network and promoting it, but in no case must it attempt to get involved in the internal organisation of meeting activities between an aid provider and a person in distress. This distance can be an issue, with some union representatives insisting on finding out what the network is doing and asking for the names of those who have been aided by their colleague.

The innovation here consists of transforming the usual roles and practices of union representatives who are inclined to know everything about fully controlled union activities. Some aid providers will nevertheless intervene with the employer to defend a person in difficulty and negotiate an arrangement that takes account of his or her particular situation. This practice is normally reserved exclusively for members of the union executive. However, they do it jointly with members of the union executive, and they acquire the necessary legitimacy, because the problem they face requires action on the fringes of the institutional framework of union intervention. It is difficult, however, for some of them to separate these two roles. As someone in charge of mutual aid emphasises:

> "Even with the training open, there are many [people] on grievance committees and the executive who come. But these are not necessarily the people who later serve as mutual aid providers. Sometimes, enforcing their collective agreement takes up too much [...] of their mind. It doesn't go together, and we need to try to separate them. I think it takes someone

> on the executive in charge of the mutual aid network who brings up this concern [...], which is open, and who supports the aid providers, and who raises the issue of quality working life from another angle. But there are difficult matches, between the grievance committee and the mutual aid network. It's hard to have an unbiased hearing in enforcing the agreement."

Interventions among members do not provide for comparisons with the work of a union delegate or employee representative. In this regard, it must be understood that the relationship between those who are aided and those who provide aid is created by "the lure of giving" and not by a utilitarian and economic conception of social exchanges dominated by the lure of profit. Mutual aid providers are captivated by the great ideal of intervention, as reported by one of them who earlier had suffered from problems of alcoholism and drug addiction:

> "It's like a way of thanking God for having helped me. I've been lucky, because I have good moral and a strong character. I didn't shot myself. I had the choice between that and going into therapy. [...] I didn't do it all alone. Someone somewhere is watching over me. It's my way of saying thank you. I had a way of getting out of it. If I'm able to help one of my workmates, to do the same, so much the better. I thank life for the gift it gave me."

Mutual aid providers are actors of a particular type, strongly marked by their own experiences, motivating their action which stands apart from regular union activities. Performing this role is thus solidly impregnated with non-institutionalised actions that lead to highly diversified practices of assistance.

2.3 Types of intervention

Practices may differ somewhat from one mutual aid network to another, with particular regard to decisions as to whether to intervene with colleagues in difficulty. Mutual aid providers will never act without those in difficulty having initially stated the need. They do not wish to rush things and make those in need more reticent to seek aid, whereas some others may attempt an approach even if a person has never asked for aid. In this regard, an aid provider emphasises:

> "It's a few years that I've been here. You get to know the people around you. When you see that there are sudden changes in attitude, that someone is becoming withdrawn[...]. As for us, we'll go and see them, we'll have a chat. I'll tell them straight off: I'm a little worried to see you letting go."

Two types of approach stand out in this taking of initiatives by mutual aid providers among their colleagues. The first approach is more aligned, whereas the second one is more indirect and clandestine. It casts light on the strength of the links between workers who turn out to be the key to the network's operation. The following example illustrates this clearly:

> "There are people who say to us: 'Martin seems to be down.' And then we say: "You work with him most often, go and find out what's going on. If there's something, talk about it with us.' We don't go out trying to take people by the hand. But we [want them] to act like proper people. You know him well. I don't know everyone here. We work well together in that way."

Mutual aid providers rely on relationships of proximity or even friendship among work colleagues, and they build the network on the strength of these relationships. Taking account of the links created by common identity and by the difficulty of revealing problems to people outside the circle of proximity, and relaying them to people identified as trustworthy, facilitates the work of aid providers, who can become involved once the link of confidence is established through a colleague's mediation. This collaboration leads to taking charge in a preventive way and not just to repair things. It leads workers to become more concerned with the well-being of others and to act more quickly with them. This action is also a factor in solidarity among work colleagues, helping to break down isolation, to create a space for bridging and to develop relational abilities concerning a request for assistance for their companions and workmates or for themselves. As a mutual aid provider remarked with great relevance:

> "This is helping your fellow workers at a difficult time in their lives, and this is also your whole entourage. In the end, I think this is an element that can strengthen solidarity and, I would say, even the cohesion of the group. Those who experience tough situations, those in a group who are vulnerable – you don't just let them fall down. In the same way, I think about when a company acts humanely toward someone in difficulty. People are grateful, and they say: I was in trouble, this could have crushed me, and I was helped. I also think, considering the purpose of a union, which is to help its members and improve their economic status – I think it falls directly within our mandate."

In this respect, one of the key effects of a mutual aid network involves raising workers' awareness with regard to relational difficulties or to the pain of living with others and with oneself. Of course this greater consciousness is stimulated by external factors such as the morals or culture of the moment but also by the daily work of aid providers in terms of awareness and day-to-day gestures. Mutual aid is applied in a spontaneous, natural and sustained manner, with the purpose being to succeed in creating an opening in case a colleague in difficulty wanted later to confide in a provider. Small day-to-day gestures in a friendly work climate can turn into preventive action in case this person experiences a problem one day and is thinking of calling upon an aid provider with whom he or she is in daily contact and finds agreeable. For example, an aid provider emphasises:

> « […] I like young people, and I talk to them. They're not accustomed to hearing a 45-year-old-woman tell them: 'You've been smoking some good stuff today.' I have fun. I make jokes, and they're open. […] I think this door is already open. I'm sure that, even with the joking, they know we're there. […] And let's hope this is a form of prevention."

This practice corresponds in any case to the goals of a mutual aid network, namely getting people to communicate and open up to someone else's point of view with the aim of solving the problem. The work of mutual aid providers also consists of doing research to document certain types of problems and to find professional referrals. Generally, three to four referrals are given for each worker requesting this.

2.4 Conception of the aid provider's daily role

Aid providers' practice consists of aid among equals conducted in a spontaneous, natural way and sustained through day-to-day interactions in their workplace. This form of social support enables individuals going through difficulties to feel accepted, understood, respected and listened to, and, above all, not to feel alone in facing their difficulties.

In this context, aid providers currently do little primary prevention in their workplace (requiring, for example, changes in work organisation or styles of management), in other words, improving working conditions or intervening in aspects that may engender or maintain personal problems or relational tensions. Accordingly, "a restitutive intervention, directly exclusively toward the person, will prove to be totally inadequate over the longer term. Helping individuals who are ill does not improve an organisation that bears the causes of certain problems" (Sylvestre and Rhéaume 1994, p. 387). Research work on mutual aid networks has shown that intervention by natural aid providers is still directed primarily toward individuals and reparation rather than toward the workplace based on a perspective of primary intervention. However, it is the union's role to intervene at this level, and this is really why mutual aid networks are associated with them. This is a long-term task relying on traditional union actions through representation with the employer. Still, the network acquires a legitimacy among employees.

The work of aid providers is also built through contacts with those who receive aid. In this regard, the people we met appreciate having received guidance at difficult times in their lives. Others were unhappy, having developed exaggerated expectations that went beyond what the network could provide. The cautious nature of interventions, along with anonymity and confidentiality, is among the network's most trustworthy elements. People who have not used it generally attribute this to weaknesses in these areas, or at least they have heard accounts that make them hesitate to use it.

The most consistent argument relies on the confidence that workers will show toward colleagues identified as aid providers. Indeed "natural aid providers" who have been able to gain the confidence of their peers by showing respect, listening to them, remaining discreet and responding to their needs gain the confidence of their peers. They break down the boundaries that crop up between them and the workers, whether it is a negative perception toward unions or barriers of identity. As explained by an employee who was aided:

> "I think the people who are here at present, they're close to us, they're well known and they've experienced things. When you approach them, there is already a sense of confidence because you've known them for years. You know how they act, and they're serious people. I think they have their place."

On another occasion, a person who was a victim of harassment went to see an aid provider, knowing that she had gone through a similar experience and that she might thus be of great assistance. As she emphasised:

> "I knew all the same that she had gone through things similar to me, and she was a good resource person for listening and giving advice and suggesting things to read. She had read quite a lot about harassment, and she had attended conferences. She had been very committed to this, and she talked to us about it. There were even special speakers who were invited here specially to talk about that. I had found this to be an excellent idea. To get people watching for what may look like psychological harassment in the workplace, you have to let people know about it."

When people are satisfied with the assistance offered by aid providers, word of mouth becomes a powerful means for persuading workers to use the mutual aid network that is accessible and close to them. People in distress admit that being heard by an aid provider is a great comfort. Being believed and supported by a competent person who can guide them brings a sense of peace. As noted by a victim of harassment:

> "[…] Just being believed and just saying: this is how it works, this is how it happens. It's also knowing that I'll be listened to. That takes 50,000 pounds off my shoulders. This is just what I was expecting. After this, I wanted to know if there was something to be done, because I didn't know."

By validating their perception of events, people in distress feel greater confidence. Turning to an aid provider who can recommend going to see a professional or a voluntary association can leave them with fewer prejudices and make them more open to the idea of using an outer resource.

Conclusion

Drawing up formal mutual aid network provides for the separation of mutual assistance (listening, support, referral) from traditional union activities (protection of workers' rights, enforcement of collective agreements, talks with employers).

With this aspect clarified, the workload of union representatives is lightened. It is a project under construction, which is being structured by concerted actions between local unions, community organisations and workplaces.

Achieving this seems all the more urgent, given an economic environment that favours phenomena such as mergers, restructurings, privatisation (in the public sector), mass lay-offs, outsourcing. These mutations in labour are reflected in management practices and work organisation (overwork, harassment, violence, organisational unfairness, social isolation, lack of autonomy, poorly defined roles), which often lead to deterioration in the work climate and aggravation of problems in work relationships. This misalignment is latent in a number of workplaces.

Actions in the form of mutual aid have an effect on social change and institutions. These are micro-changes that lead to a strengthening of internal identity forming the basis of relationships and leading toward social commitment. Several dimensions of innovation are fulfilled at the same time: a) there is a network formed with United Way, trade-unions, community groups; b) the mutual aid network is based on a novel form of governance within the union; it is autonomous and independent, open and transparent; c) aid providers acquire a distinctive identity based on experience and the maintenance of relationships of proximity; d) the mutual aid network has the effect of emphasising relational problems; it spreads in a state of tension with employers, who are invited to join the network; e) the mutual aid network is set through practices that are familiar to unions and are renewed by readapting values of solidarity.

This social innovation is not complete, however. It faces two types of difficulty that hold back its development and its broader dissemination. An initial difficulty is brought out by the problem of professional identity defined by trade, profession and seniority; then there are problems linked to civic identity: age, gender, family and personal situation, and sexual orientation. The effectiveness of mutual aid relies on the social support that the peer group provides. Workers bring several identities out in an exclusive way. The type of problems handled by the mutual aid group and the support provided by a relationship of confidence are based on proximity of identity. A second difficulty is added, namely building a mutual aid network that is closely associated with a union structure that differs totally in the way it operates. The network represents the strength of links formed by new sensibilities between colleagues. With the availability of aid providers being considerable even beyond workplace limits, this is a moral commitment that plays a role in union renewal toward members. Therefore, It is also a way of involving workers through sustainability of relationships by protecting and strengthening the social bonds.

Bibliography

Bacharach, Samuel B., Peter A. Bamberger et William J. Sonnenstuhl. (2001) *Mutual Aid and Union Renewal*, New York : IRL Press, 200 pages.

Brun, Jean-Pierre, Caroline Biron, Hans Ivers et Josée Martel. (2003) *Évaluation de la santé mentale : une analyse des pratiques de gestion des ressources humaines*, Montréal : IRRST, Coll. « Études et recherches » No. R-342, 88 pages.

Blais, Marie-Claude (2007) *La solidarité. Histoire d'une idée*, Paris, NRF, Éditions Gallimard.

Black, D. (1993) « Taking Sides » in Black, D. (ed) *The Social Structure of Right and Wrong*, SanDiego Academic Press.

Bourbonnais, Renée et al. (2000) Les impacts positifs et négatifs de la transformation du réseau de la santé sur la vie professionnelle la vie familiale et la santé des infirmières et des infirmiers de l'agglomération de Québec, ROPOST, Université Laval et Direction de la santé publique de Québec.

Burnonville, Francine(1999)« Des collectifs au travail, une pratique syndicale d'entraide», *Intervention*, no 109, avril, pp. 38-42.

Campbell, John (2004) *Institutional Change and Globalization*, Princeton University Press, Princeton and Oxford.

Caillé, Alain (2000) *Anthropologie du don. Le tiers paradigme,* Sociologie économique Desclée de Brouwer, Paris. 278 p.

Collins, Randall (2004) *Interaction Ritual Chains*, Princeton University Press, Princeton and Oxford.

Croucher, Richard, Helmut MARTENS et Ingo SINGE (2007) "A German Employee Network and Union Renewal : The Siemenskonflikt". *Relations industrielles*, vol. 62, no 1, pp. 143-169.

Confédération des syndicats nationaux (CSN) (2003) *Priorités 2002-2003, volet santé mentale au travail*, Plan de travail, Conseil fédéral, 11 et 12 juin 2003, 42 pages.

Filteau, Michel (2003) «Santé mentale au travail : la CSN passe à l'action», *Perspectives CSN*, septembre-octobre, 2003, 10-14.

Gabriel, Phyllis et Marjo-Riitta LIIMATAINEN (2000) « *Mental health in the workplace » Bureau international du travail*, Genève, octobre.

Godbout, Jacques (1994) « La sphère du don entre étrangers : le bénévolat et l'entraide », dans DUMONT, Fernand, LANGLOIS, Simon et Yves MARTIN, *Traité des problèmes sociaux,* Québec : Institut québécois de recherche sur la culture, pp. 981-994.

Harrisson, Denis et Juan-Luis KLEIN (2007) «Introduction : Placer la société au centre de l'analyse des innovations « dans Juan-Luis Klein et Denis Harrisson (sous la direction de), *L'innovation sociale : Émergence et effets sur la transformation des sociétés, Québec:* PUQ : p. 1-14.

Harrisson, Denis, Reynald BOURQUE & György SZÉLL (2009) "Social Innovation, Economic Development, Employment and Democracy" dans Harrisson, Denis, Gyoergy Szell et Reynald Bourque (Eds) "Social Innovation and Labour", Peter Lang: Bern, Berlin, Bruxelles, Frankfurt am Main, New-York, Oxford , Wien : 7–16.

Hirigoyen, Marie-France (2007) *Les nouvelles solitudes*, Paris, La découverte.

Karasek, Robert et Töres Theorell (1991) *Healthy Work, Stress, Productivity, and the Reconstructing of Working Life*, Basic books, NY.

Lévesque, Benoit (2003) « Fonctions de base et nouveau rôle des pouvoirs publics : vers un nouveau paradigme de l'État » *Annals of Public ad Cooperative Economics,* 74, 4 : 489-513.

Lavoie, Francine (2001) « Les groupes de soutien et les groupes d'entraide », dans F. DUFORT et J. GUAY (dir.), *Agir au c'ur des communautés. La psychologie communautaire et le changement social*, Québec : Les Presses de l'Université Laval, 410 p. Extrait : pp. 157-186.

Moulaert, Frank, F. Martinelli, E. Swyngedouw et S. Gonzalez (2005)« Toward Alternative Model(s) of Local Innovation », *Urban Studies, 42-11 : 1969-1990.*

Putnam, Robert D. (2000) *Bowling Alone: the collapse and revival of American community*, New York: Simon et Schuster, 541 p.

Rhéaume, Jacques, Louise Saint-Arnaud et Micheline Saint-Jean (2003). «De la désinsertion à la réinsertion professionnelle à la suite d'un arrêt de travail pour un problème de santé mentale», *Santé mentale au Québec*, vol. XXVIII, no 1, pp. 193-211.

Rhéaume, Jacques, Marie-France Maranda, Jean-Simon Deslauriers, Louise St-Arnaud et Louis Trudel (2008) « Action syndicale, démocratie et santé mentale au travail », *Nouvelles Pratiques Sociales,* 20 : 2 : 82-110.

Romeder, Jean-Marie et col. (1989) *Les groupes d'entraide et la santé, nouvelles solidarités.* Ottawa : Conseil canadien de développement social, 138 pages.

Sylvestre, Jean et Jacques Rhéaume (1994) « L'intervention en milieu de travail : des programmes d'aide aux réseaux d'entraide », dans P. Brisson (dir.), *L'usage des drogues et la toxicomanie*, Boucherville (Québec) : Gaëtan Morin, vol. 2, 549 p. Extrait : pp. 371-389.

Vézina, Michel (1996) « La santé mentale au travail : pour une compréhension de cet enjeu de santé publique », *Santé mentale au Québec*, vol. XXI, no 2, pp. 117-138.

Trade unions strategies, job precariousness and sustainable development: an analysis of the Portuguese case

Maria da Conceição Cerdeira
ISCSP/Technical University of Lisbon, SOCIUS and CAPP
João Dias
ISEG/Technical University of Lisbon and UECE

Abstract

The increasing tendency towards precariousness is a very important issue which, nowadays, challenges social cohesion and sustainable development in most developed societies. This tendency is inscribed in the de-territorialization of the economic processes, based on a liberalization logic and a new model of work organization which, in the name of competitiveness and international competition weakens job security and social rights.

In Portugal, job insecurity is a central issue that affects more than forty-five per cent of the active population. This figure includes only workers with fixed-term contracts, part-time employees, unemployed workers and self-employed with no employees. How are the Portuguese trade unions reacting to this heavy tendency in the Portuguese society? In order to protect from precariousness, is it enough to use the traditional strategy of political pressure? In particular, what type of relation do the Portuguese trade unions have with those workers most affected by precarious and flexible forms of work?

Content

1. Introduction: precariousness as an adverse factor for sustainable development

One of the basic assumptions of sustainable development is the capacity of societies to ensure decent standards of employment, for example, jobs with social rights, able to bring about cohesion, inclusion and social justice (ILO, 1999). However, the conviction held today maintains that changes taking place in advanced western countries over the last two decades are radically undermining the social and political balance established in the post-war period. Since the 1970s, countries have faced high levels of unemployment in conjunction with the steady erosion of the statutes of employees in terms of labour legislation and social rights. The surge in flexible, unstable and precarious employment practices currently represents a leading trend in labour markets. Flexibility, as an exacerbated division of social labour, resulting in what R. Castel terms "fragmentation of salaried conditions", hinders the founding of collective labour organisations, undermines the powers of trade unions and disorganises traditional labour relations institutionalised ever since World War Two (Castel, 1995, 2007; Traxler et al., 2001; Supiot, 2001; Hyman, 2001).

Some statistical data clearly point to the consequences of this social change. In the European Union, a quarter of the population lives below the poverty line, a level reduced only to 17% by social transfers. Poverty even impacts upon those in employment (8%), with particular incidence among those in non-standard jobs, including temporary work (13%) and part time working contracts (12%).

As shown below (table 1), within the European Union framework, Portugal is among those member states with the highest level of social inequality (placed 4th behind only Latvia, Rumania and Bulgaria), with high rates of both those living on the poverty line (3rd) and of working poor (4th).

These trends in western industrialised societies in general and Portuguese society in particular, running counter to the notions of social progress and democracy implicit to the development of the welfare state, are rooted in the economic transformations taking place globally and driven by the new production, information and communication technologies. De-territorialisation is a key facet to these economic processes based upon a logic of liberalisation and a new means of organising labour that, under the flag of competitiveness and international competition, undermines job security and working related social rights. The flexible company, perceived as the most appropriate model for the prevailing market instability and levels of competition, is hence that which combines, on a global geographic scale, differentiated employment strategies so as to obtain the maximum degree of flexibility, whether from the perspective of functionality, numbers employed, or costs.

However, comparative analysis show that, although it is true the processes leveraging flexibility, precariousness and deregulation are increasingly dependent on transnational or supranational levels, the dynamics of such phenomena display national and even sectoral based particularities. Therefore, given flexibility is a generalised phenomena, the social institutions and power relationships of trade union actors produce different practices and results in accordance with the prevailing national context. As Traxler et al. (2001) state, while pluralist systems quickly bow before the demands of neo-liberalism (market based governance, lack of salary policies, levels of negotiation centred on the company and the establishment) in accordance with a logic of exclusive negotiation, corporatist systems adopt features of lean corporatism (governance by networks, flexible wage policies, decentralised collective negotiation but without loss of central power over the field of activity), in conjunction with a logic of inclusive negotiation. Similarly, in contrast to those defending a convergence of labour relations, these authors highlight how the restraints of globalisation tend more to worsen than harmonise systems of labour relations (Traxler et al., 2001). As concluded over a decade ago by Locke, Kochan & Piore (1995) in their study of eleven OECD countries, while flexibility represents a general phenomenon, the characteristics of social institutions and actor strategies taking place within the respective national context lead to different results.

This article analyses the way in which Portuguese social actors, in particular trade unions, have been responding to market demands for employment flexibility. We specifically focus upon the perspectives of Portuguese trade unions on the flexibility of labour and employment practices as well as their support or opposition to strategies implemented for regulatory purposes. Closely bound up with this objective, our attention also extends to questioning the relationship between trade unions and workers with flexible contracts and in precarious positions of employment and questions whether or not these latter groups might provide the leverage to bring about the revitalisation of the trade union movement.

2. The notion of precariousness

One of the concepts deployed by sociology, in particular industrial sociology, to express the ongoing metamorphoses in labour and employment and the drop in levels of social protection and democracy in western countries is that of precariousness. The concept, along with others that are etymologically attached such as precarious and precarization is, however, fluid, complex, polysemic and has been subject to great debate among social analysts (Castel, 1995; Paugam, 2000; Cingolani, 2005; Le Lay, 2009; Appay, 2007).

Aballéa (2009) highlights the existence of at least three different but overlapping perspectives in sociological discussions of the term. The first, associated with the work undertaken as from the 1970s (Guilbert, Lowit & Creusen, 1970; Caire, 1973) and that we may identify with the idea of external numerical flexibility, referring to the statute of employment and new market regulations that expanded its scope over the course of time and weakened the working relationships built up by trade unions throughout the 20th century. This new regulation has emerged out of efforts by companies to rationalise their utilisation of human resources within an economic and political context unfavourable to workers. In sum, this approaches the fragmentation in employment conditions with the multiplication of "atypical" contracts in accordance with company needs: temporary workers, fixed term contracts, imposed part-time working contracts, false freelance working, etc.).

The second perspective introduces another concept: "labour precariousness". This derives from new patterns of organisation (networks of companies, subcontracting and outsourcing, etcetera) and/or new management methodologies (for example, project management) and downplays the quality of working conditions, the allocation of posts, hierarchical relationships, etcetera. Hence, there is no opportunity to build up a working collective able to inspire security. The very precariousness of employment means menial job content, poorly paid and badly recognised, thus tending to hinder investment in labour and personal fulfilment (Paugam, 2000). Within this scope, precariousness is also associated with a subjective component. In the majority of cases, the statute of precariousness combines working precariousness with economic and social vulnerability and, in the perspective of Gorz (1980), nurturing duality in society between, on the one hand, the traditional working class, designated the "privileged minority" and the "post-industrial neo-proletariat" on the other hand, without either status or class who take up precarious, auxiliary, temporary, part-time and similar positions.

Finally, the third perspective, which includes the works of Appay (1997) among others, moves on from the precariousness of employment and labour to the precariousness of wages. The characteristic features of this approach are the institutionalisation of instability, the return of individual responsibility for employability, the reduction of working contract social rights and individual risk management to the detriment of mutual solidarity. Precariousness is analysed "as a structural process transforming the structure of production and organisation of labour and as a process of recomposing systems of social rights affecting the protection of workers and their health and as a means of managing manual work" (Aballéa, 2009, p. 93).

In turn, Tuchszirer (2005) places emphasis on the importance of the national context when carrying out any comparative interpretation of precariousness related issues, or more precisely, employment flexibility between countries. In fact, the same numbers may indeed reflect very different realities of which part-time working in Sweden and Portugal would be one example. In Sweden, part-time working is generally an option taken by employees and falls within the scope of achieving a better balance between the individual's working and personal life. In Portugal, part-time working is imposed due to the lack of full-time employment opportunities. Correspondingly, while in the former, this employment regime bears no connotations of precariousness related issues while in the latter part-time working is bound up with low quality employment.

In this article, the concept of precariousness refers first and foremost to employment related problems (contractual relationships), given its association with low quality employment in the overwhelming majority of instances in Portugal. As we shall return to below, this precariousness concept has been prominent in social and political debate across Portuguese society.

3. Precariousness and employment flexibility: Portugal within the EU context

Within the EU context, Portugal displays above average economic and social weaknesses. After 2004, in the discourse of the first mandate of the Socialist government of José Sócrates, some concern was expressed about raising the lot of the poorest and resulting in a drop of two percentage points in the numbers of Portuguese citizens living in poverty. Nevertheless, despite efforts to strengthen social policies, and offset by the recession that the country is currently going through, the percentage of people living below the poverty line remains above the European average, a situation in common with other southern European states, specifically Spain, Italy and Greece.

Table 1: Inequality and poverty in the South of Europe and the EU (2008)

Indicators	Portugal	Spain	Greece	Italy	France	EU15	EU27
Inequality of income distribution (income quintile share ratio) (total)	6.1	5.4	5.9	5.1	4.2	4.9	4.8
At-risk-of poverty rate before social transfers (total)	25	24	23	23	23	25	25

At-risk-of poverty rate after social transfers (total)	18	20	20	19	13	16	17
In-work at risk of poverty rate (total)	12	11	7	9	7	8	8
In-work at risk of poverty rates permanent work contract	7	5	5	6	4	5	5
In-work at risk of poverty rates temporary work contract	11	14	16	16	12	13	13
In-work at risk of poverty rates working full-time	10	10	14	8	6	7	7
In-work at risk of poverty rates working part-time	27	15	26	13	11	11	12

Source: Eurostat

The table above shows how, similar to Italy and Spain, Portugal (12%) exceeds the European average (8%) of workers living below the poverty line. This situation impacts primarily on workers in non-standard jobs and particularly on part-time workers (27%). High levels of poverty are accompanied by high social inequality with Portugal returning the highest rate of the countries detailed in the table above (6.1% against 4.8% EU-27).

As regards developments in the labour market, the trend has been towards strong growth in non-standard employment. Between 1998 and 2009, permanent jobs rose by 4.6% while non-permanent jobs surged by 42.7%. The same period saw a 64.2% spike in fixed term contracts and a 5.7% rise in part-time employment to represent 11.6% in 2009. While this is not a particularly high level according to European Union averages, as aforementioned, in the Portuguese case, this is very much an imposition and not an option.

In the international context, recourse to fixed term contracts in Portugal is substantially higher than the EU-27 average. According to 2009 figures from Eurostat, fixed term contracts represent 22% of contractual employment in Portugal against an average EU-27 rate of 13.5%. Within the European framework, Portugal is 3rd highest behind Poland in first place (26.5%) and Spain (25.4%) in second. Spain and Portugal differ significantly as regards this flexibility indicator in relation to the other countries included in the table below.

Table 2: The labour market in southern European states and the EU (2009)

Indicators	Portugal	Italy	France	Spain	Greece	EU15	EU27
Total employment rate	66.3	57.5	64.2	59.8	61.2	65.0	64.6
Employees with a contract of limited duration (annual average)	22.0	12.5	13.5	25.4	12.1	14.1	13.5
Persons employed part-time	11.6	14.3	17.3	12.8	6.0	19.4	18.8
Unemployment rate	9.6	7.8	9.5	18.0	9.5	9.4	8.9
Total long-term un-employment rate	4.3	3.5	3.3	4.3	3.9	3.0	3.0

Source: Eurostat

Labour market flexibility in Portugal also contains other forms of employment including the rendering of services ("recibos verdes" (green receipts)) and self-employed freelance workers ("isolados") that together make up 18.4% of employees in 2006 and rising to 19% in 2009. It is currently estimated that over 30% of the active population experiences the effects of non-standard contracts in addition to an unemployment rate that stood at 10.6% in the first quarter of 2010.

Therefore, analysis of the labour market swiftly reveals a cleavage opening up over the course of two decades and separating "insiders" from "outsiders". The recession has only reinforced this cleavage as demonstrated by the rise in the average length of service among employees on permanent and open-ended contracts, up from 12 to 13 years between 2003 and 2009. This growth in length of service contrasts with the average duration of two years for term contracts and just over 4 years for those submitting "recibo verde" (Dornelas et al., 2010) requests for payment.

The "outsiders" also face wage inequality relating to "insiders" (which remain constant through to the middle of professional life (around 8% through to 40-45 years of age) and rising ever afterwards (to around 60% for those aged between 60 and 65)) and have lower support from the social security system (CMLB, 2007).

4. Trade unions campaigning against labour law reform and „flexibility at the margin"

Growth in "atypical" employment and the cleavage between "insiders" and "outsiders" has various explanations in the case of Portugal, three of them of particular relevance. The first relates to shortcomings in the private sector, mostly made up of small and medium sized companies lacking in capacity and managerial skills. These companies depend greatly on external numerical flexibility for their ability to survive in the marketplace. As the table below sets out, 97.8% of companies had less than 50 employees 2008, with a trend towards the atomisation both of the private sector as well as employment.

Table 3: The Portuguese business structure in 1998 and 2008

	1998		2008	
	Companies	Employees	Companies	Employees
1-4 persons	61.4	14.7	67.4	17.5
5-9 persons	20.9	14.4	17.6	14.7
10-49 persons	15.0	30.9	12.8	31.4
50-99 persons	1,6	11.7	1.3	11.2
100-499 persons	1.0	19.5	0.8	17.3
500 and more persons	0.1	8.8	0.1	7.9
Total	100	100	100	100

Source: Dornelas, 2010

The second derives from the difficulties experienced over the course of years in transposing the agreements reached in social concentration to the collective bargaining at the sectoral and enterprise level. Effectively, throughout its twenty-six years of existence, the CPCS-Conselho Permanente de Concertação Social (Permanent Council of Social Agreement) negotiated 21 agreements, of which only two have been bipartite agreements signed between trade union and business confederations, agreed in 2004 and 2005 for professional training and boosting collective contractual practices. However, the most representative trade union entity, the Confederação Geral de Trabalhadores Portugueses (CGTP – the General Confederation of Portuguese Workers), with a seat on this tripartite body did not sign up twelve of these tripartite agreements[1].

1 In addition to the CGTP, another confederation, the UGT (União Geral de Trabalhadores / General Workers Union) sits on the Conselho Permanente de Concertação Social. This confederation was the only trade union body that signed all agreements thus far negotiated.

This CGTP political choice and the ideological orientation within the framework of collective agreements leads onto the third explanation: the lack of consensus among social actors as to the way forward for the collective negotiation agenda. The divergence in opinions is partly due to the inflexible negotiating positions taken by trade unions making up this confederation, blocking recourse to collective contracts as a means of nurturing the internal adaptability of labour relations within companies.

Policies on the duration and organisation of the working schedule provide a key illustration of the point above. Given complaints from employer associations as to flexibility, adaptability and multi-tasking and trade union demands for a 40 hour working week, the 1990 social and economic agreement, which the CGTP did not sign up to, established that legislation would reduce working hours (as indeed happened) from 48 hours to 44 hours. The reduction from 44 to 40 hours was to come later, over a five year period, resulting from collective sectoral negotiations that would also stipulate the forms of working flexibility to be applied in each sector. Disagreement over adaptability resulted in one million workers still with working weeks in excess of 40 hours five years later[2]. The situation would only be resolved with a new tripartite agreement in 1996 with the short term social agreement that bound the government to legislating in favour of job flexibility and adaptability. This agreement encountered the opposition of the CGTP that staged a general strike against the principle of functional multi-tasking.

This difficulty of social actors to attain internal adaptability through collective negotiation "excused" employers over their frequent recourse to atypical forms of employment at levels far higher than the European average. In effect, legislative reform in Portugal followed a pattern similar to that which Regini (2000) characterised as "flexibility at the margins", in effect, a strategy designed to boost the flexibility of labour relations through facilitating recourse to atypical employment left exposed to the vicissitudes of the business cycle, while maintaining the protective terms and conditions for permanent employees (Dornelas, 2010).

In virtue of this strategy, within the international context, Portugal appears in an apparently paradoxical position: on the one hand, the country is considered by the OECD and other international institutions to have some of the most restrictive legislation in terms of compulsory redundancy (OECD, 1994, 1999, 2000, 2004, 2006)[3], on the other hand, some economic analysis relative to real salary elasticity reveals the Portuguese labour market to be among the least rigid in the

2 This happened primarily in labour intensive manual sectors, especially those with large percentages of females in the workforce with examples including the textile, clothing, footwear, electronics, restaurant and tourism sectors.

3 In 2003, the OECD placed Portuguese legislation at the top of the 28 countries analysed from the perspective of rigidity, a position the country shared with Turkey.

Eurozone (ECB, 2005; Centeno, 2005). In fact, Portugal records average rates of job creation and destruction similar to the United States, Canada and Sweden and higher than those of Finland, France, Germany and Italy even if below Denmark, New Zealand and the United Kingdom (CLBRL, 2007).

As Dornelas (2010) points out, Portugal has therefore created a triply penalising cycle: the formal rigidity of labour legislation contributed towards discouraging inward investment and "excused" recourse by employers to atypical levels of employment above European averages; the "flexibility at the margins" ensured workers in precarious position accumulate disadvantages in relation to those with permanent contracts; and the growth in unstable employment reaching very high levels according to European standards were leading to destabilisation of stable employment (Castel, 2007; Dornelas et al, 2010).

Against this backdrop, the Barroso Government tried to reform labour legislation for the third time[4] since the 1974 advent of democracy. This proved successful with the 2003 approval of the Código de Trabalho (Employment Code), which did have the merit of systematising the labour laws in effect. However, it did not attain one of its core objectives: a reduction in the level of the formal rigidity of Portuguese employment law (OECD, 2004). Furthermore, it fostered the aforementioned flexibility "at the margins" both through extending the period of fixed term contracts from 3 to 6 years and by the introduction of rules legally complicating the identification of contractual employment which combined with a strategy to drastically reduce the powers of trade unions, in particular, for collective negotiation. In the following year, the number of collectively negotiated conventions dropped significantly in conjunction with the number of employees covered by collective contracts (both dropped to less than half the figures recorded for previous years).

A new tripartite agreement was reached in 2008 (overall agreement on the regulation of employment, social protection and the labour market), which would result in the new 2009 Code, and reversed the logic underpinning the 2003 Code. Contrary to its predecessor, this rebalanced the powers of social actors and set restraints on external flexibility by three means: 1) a three-year cap on fixed term contracts, 2) penalties for non-permanent contracts in association with differential social security contributions, c) refining the assumption of the existence of juridical subordination and, hence, the contractual characterisation of employment contracts, sanctions on the undermining of employment contracts, that is, undue recourse to service rendered on a "recibo verde" basis, while also cutting deadlines and simplifying administrative procedures in cases of loss of job with-

4 The first attempt to enact change was during the government of Cavaco Silva in 1990 and the second in 1996, under the Socialist leadership of António Guterres, which included the tripartite commitment to proceed with analysis and systematise labour legislation.

out implying a loss of employee rights[5]. In addition, the legislative package established the foundations for improving negotiated internal adaptability, especially in terms of organising working schedules.

The introduction of opportunities for internal adaptation of working hours and the simplification of individual dismissal processes were among the arguments invoked by the CGTP for its refusal to sign up to the agreement and instead staged a series of protests against the new employment legislation. The short period of time since the 2009 Employment Code, in conjunction with the onset of recession, prevents any evaluation as to its impact across the main stated objectives: de-segmenting labour markets, fostering internal company flexibility and generating better social regulation of employee relations.

5. The decline of trade unions and the relationship between unions and precarious workers

Within the framework we have thus far analysed, characterised by ongoing developments in the labour market, and the notably defensive strategies deployed by the most representative trade unions for example, the tense relationships among actors over legislative reform meant the trade union movement could only have entered into decline. However, this is a trend that stretches right back to the first half of the 1980s, a period when the Portuguese level of union membership (59%) was among the highest of all OECD countries (Cerdeira, 1997). Recent surveys have put the rate of trade union membership at 18%, now amongst the lowest of European Union member states (Dornelas, 2007).

The precariousness of employment is an obstacle to union membership but the lack of trade union dynamism is a generalised phenomenon extending far beyond the young with workers experiencing simultaneously flexible and precarious working conditions. A recent study found that 63.2% of employees answering the questionnaire had never been trade union members and 14.2% had been but were no long members (Dornelas, 2009).

The trade union movement in Portugal is characterised by a dual cleavage: state institutions, public sector (or former-public) versus private sector, workers with a standard employment contract versus with atypical employment contracts. Trade union strongholds are above all among permanent civil service employees and the public and the former-public sectors. These are the sectors providing support and numbers to the movement, which, in turn, has been focused on category

5 Portugal dropped from first to seventh position in the OECD (2008), ranking of most rigid level of labour protection, above France and below Norway.

Table 4: Trade union membership according to contract type (%)

	Permanent full-time	Permanent part-time	Temporary work contract	Independent worker "recibos verdes"
Yes, I'm a union member	22.6	4.5	11.4	2.1
Not now, but yes in the past	14.2	4.5	11.4	8.5
Never a union member	63.2	90.9	77.2	89.4
Total	68.3	2.3	24.5	4.9

Source: Dornelas, 2009: 179

and corporative complaints of a fairly classical nature, without paying heed to the problems and challenges today facing companies and institutions not to mention the diversity of situations existing in the labour market.

The conflict over a more detailed system of teacher performance evaluation with implications for career progression, following over two years of fruitless negotiations between teacher trade unions and the Ministry of Education represents a relevant illustration of the narrow mindedness of the trade union outlook. In 2009, when the financial crisis, in conjunction with the already existing structural weaknesses, threw many thousands of workers out of their jobs and in a labour market in which over 30% of workers are affected by "atypical" forms of employment, it was the teaching sector conflict that attracted greatest trade union and political support.

Clearly, the theme of precariousness is not absent from trade union concerns and campaigns. In effect, denouncing precariousness and the consequent demand for due protection are relevant issues of any campaign, particularly when staged by the confederations. Following some autonomous protest movements against precariousness organised by youth groups, some trade unions have recently begun to make recourse to the new legal terms of the 2009 code and confront Government and the Labour Authority with illegal fixed term and/or "recibo verde" freelance working in some public institutions.

In addition to these specific situations, there is a relatively low level of importance attached to the particular situations of those facing precarious employment in the trade union campaigns and protests and particularly surprising given the extent of abuses across the restaurant, tourism and civil construction and public works sectors. Even in sectors and companies with high traditions of trade union representation (for example, telecommunications and banking), there has been relative trade union indifference to the introduction of precarious terms of employment. In general terms, working conditions in these sectors are above the national average, benefiting from their own healthcare system and complementary social protection, for example. In the case of the banking sector, the healthcare system is managed by the trade union themselves. However, contracted "call centre" workers are not directly employed by the banks and neither had access to social protection systems nor did they benefit from the terms and conditions of the collective contract in effect for the sector (Cerdeira 2005).

On the fringes of the traditional trade union movement, 2008 and 2009 saw the founding and developing of various organisations of young workers who, despite in their majority having university level education, are afflicted by precarious employment or belong to what is commonly referred to as the "€500 generation", a reference to their monthly salary payment. These organisations have taken up names that clearly identify the particular situation they are campaigning against, with the following some of the examples: FERVE (Fartos de Estes Recibos Verdes / Fed up with These Green Receipts), Precários Inflexíveis (Inflexible Precarious Workers), Intermitentes do Espectáculo (Performances Intermittent) and ABIC (Associação dos Bolseiros de Investigação Científica / Association of Scientific Research Grant holders).

These groups, with the exception of ABIC, are organised into the May Day movement and have demonstrated in the protest march held on May 1st as an independent block since 2007. More than staging demonstrations, these groups are network organised and live off the potential created by ICTs, especially the Internet. They use such means to denounce and appeal for "precarious workers" to put forward their experiences and question society in general and the institutional powers in particular as to the standards of living and working conditions that they have available to them. As one Precários Inflexíveis movement activist wrote: "My profession is journalism but I feel I better identify with the problems of others in precarious employment than with journalists with acquired rights. I would very much like to have the same priorities as those union members but, at this moment, my priority is knowing just how much I'll be getting paid".

6. Conclusions

The precariousness of employment in Portugal has advanced relentlessly and with it the rising economic and social fragility of the citizens affected. This development has understandably impacted negatively upon the trade union movement. Trade unions have already lost their place at the centre of a virtuous dynamic of employment statute stabilisation. The union strategy of denouncing and applying political pressure by the most representative sections of the union movement, within the tradition of campaigns undertaken during the corporative period, has in no way proven able to regain the resources and legitimacy as the collective representative of either contracted workers in general or those employed under precarious working conditions specifically. The trade union movement's option to turn away from the conditions now in effect for launching and closing companies, as well as its attachment to legislation dating to the early post-revolutionary period have indirectly contributed towards "excusing" the recourse by employers to atypical employment practices in the perspective of much of society.

To the aforementioned factors, there is the weak level of trade union representation in companies (26% according to Dornelas 2009), combined with an organisational and functional model that, based on companies and sectors, features a lack of adaptation to the rising mobility of precariously employed citizens. Furthermore, many trade unionists spurn any involvement in struggles on behalf of the precariously employed due to the stigma that precariousness represents to collective mentalities. Tending to be younger and with higher levels of schooling than permanent employees, the precariously employed are frequently perceived both by some activists and some with permanent contracts not as victims but as threats to their own job security.

However, trade union confederations have now undertaken strategies designed to reach out to precariously employed young workers and integrate some with trade union aspirations. In the case of the CGTP and within its traditional union culture of political mobilisation, this approximation has involved attempting to get such workers involved in the collective actions engaged in (strikes, demonstrations), as well as reporting incidences of false "recibo verde" working practices in the public and private sectors both to the media and the labour authorities.

The UGT, in turn, restructured its organisational and functional model to allow for the membership of "precarious" workers directly into the confederation and not in the sector or company trade union body as a means of overcoming sectoral borders and guarantee the continuity of trade union membership and protection, irrespective of the sector or company of employment.

To summarize, we conclude that the traditional strategies of trade unions are not fully aligned with the needs arising from certain changes, challenges and problems in the current labour market in Portugal. But it is also possible that these new problems may contribute to some revitalization of trade unions. Anyway, the solution to job precariousness and full alignment with sustainable development policies is particularly difficult in a situation of economic and financial crisis still persistent in Portugal and in several other countries.

References

Aballéa, F. (2009). La relation salariale éclatée, précarisation du travail e de l'emploi. In: B. Appay & S. Jefferys (Eds.), Restructurations, précarisation, valeurs (pp. 91-102). Toulouse: Octares Editions.

Appay, B. (2007). Précarisation sociale et restructurations productives. In: B. Appay & A. Thébaud-Mony, Précarisation sociale, travail et santé (pp. 509-553). Paris: Iresco.

Caire, G. (1973). Les nouveaux marchands d'hommes. Paris: Éditions Ouvrières.

Castel, R. (1995). Les métamorphoses de la question sociale. Une chronique du salariat. Paris: Fayard.

Castel, R. (2007). Au-delà du salariat ou en-deçà de l'emploi ? L'institutionnalisation du précariat?. In: S. Paugam (Ed), Repenser la solidarité : l'apport des sciences sociales (pp. 416-433). Paris, PUF.

Centeno, L. G. (Ed) (2005). Flexibilidade e Segurança no Mercado de Trabalho Português. Lisbon: DGEEP.

Cerdeira, M. C. (1997). A evolução da sindicalização portuguesa de 1974 a 1995. Lisbon: MTQE.

Cerdeira, M. C. (2005). Estratégias sindicais e precariedade do emprego. In: I. Kovács (Ed), Flexibilidade de emprego – riscos e oportunidades (pp. 91-125). Oeiras: Celta.

Cincolani, P. (2005). La précarité. Paris: PUF.

CLBRL (Comissão do Livro Branco das Relações Laborais) (2007). Livro Branco das Relações Laborais. Lisbon: MTSS.

Dornelas, A., Ministro, A., Lopes, F., Albuquerque, J., Paixão, M., & Santos, N. (2010), Emprego, contratação colectiva de trabalho e protecção da mobilidade profissional. Lisbon: MTSS.

Dornelas, A., Ministro, A., Lopes, F., Cerdeira, M., Galego, P., & Sousa, S. (2006). Livro Verde sobre as Relações Laborais. Lisbon: MTSS.

Dornelas, António (2009). Relações Laborais na Empresa. In: J. Freire (Ed), Trabalho e Relações Laborais (pp. 165-197). Lisbon: ICS.

ECB (2005). Real wages and local unemployment in euro area. WP nº 471.

Gorz, A. (1980). Adieux au prolétariat. Paris: Éditions Galilée.

Gorz, A. (1997). Misères du présent. Richesses du possible. Paris: Éditions Galiée.

Guilbert, M., Lowit, N., & Creusen, J. (1970). Le travail temporaire. Paris: Société des Amis du CES.

Hyman, R. (2001). The Europeanisation – or the Erosion – of Industrial Relations?. Industrial Relations Journal, 32, 280-294.

ILO (1999). Decent Work. Geneva: International Labour Office.

Le Lay, S. (2009) Contribution à une approche archéologique de la précarisation sociale. In: B. Appay & S. Jefferys (Eds), Restructurations, précarisation, valeurs (pp. 117-128). Toulouse: Octares Editions.

Locke, R., Kochan, T., & Piore, M. (Eds) (1995). Employment Relations in a Changing World Economy. Cambridge: MIT Press.

OECD (1994, 1999, 2004, 2006). Employment Outlook. Paris: OECD.

OECD (2008). Economic Surveys: Portugal. Paris: OECD.

Paugam, S. (2000). Le salarié de la précarité. Les nouvelles formes de l'intégration professionnelle. Paris: PUF.

Regini M. (2000), The dilemmas of labour market regulation. In: G. Esping-Andersen & M. Regini (Eds), Why Deregulate Labour Markets?. Oxford: Oxford University Press.

Supiot, A. (2001). Beyond Employment. Changes in Work and the Future of Labour Law in Europe. Oxford: Oxford University Press.

Traxler, F., Blaschke, S., & Kittel, B. (2001). National Labour Relations in Internationalized Markets. A Cross-national Analysis of Institutional Patterns, Change and Performance. Oxford: Oxford University Press.

Tuchszirer, C. (2005). Les différentes approches de la précarité de l'emploi en Europe, au Japon et aux Etats-Unis. Chronique internationale de l'IRES, 97, 23-32.

Chapter 4: Migration

From the Urban-Rural-Binary Labor Market to Urban-Internally-Binary Labor Market

Erduo Liu
(School of Labor Relations and Human Resource, Renmin University of China)

Abstract

The economy reform, started in 1979, has radically changed China's economy. It also changed China's labor market, making the frame of an urban-rural-binary labor market evolved into an urban-internally-binary labor market together with a rural labor market, which is deeply different from what it was before, though it still exists. The present frame of labor market of China defines to a great extent the present and future of China's economy, as well as China's employment policy. This thesis of mine will expound some questions concerned with the government's employment policy by analyzing some features of the national labor market via reviewing the evolution of this market.

Content

1. Centralized Economy and Binary Labor Market

The separate administering systems for the urban and rural areas began to take shape from in the late 1950s in the last century. In the early years of that period, peasants enjoyed the freedom and right of migration into cities and the government seldom intervened the process. During the period, the natural growing rate of city population was higher than that of the rural population, but the increase of city population during the period between 1950 and 1957 was not a natural result of population growing but was due to the population of migration from the rural area to the urban area, which was responsible for 60.8% increase in population in proportion to the total population increase. The trend satisfied a demand for labors for the large scale of city constructions and adapted to the economy. However, the uncontrolled influx to the cities from the rural gave rise to the tremendous burdens to the cities in terms of employment, housing, and food supply. It also had a negative effect to the agriculture. In direct to the situation, the government began to take control on the peasants' migration to cities. Actually, coming into the early 1950s, the government had began exert some constraints on that aspect. The state council promulgated even before 1953 Directions to the Blind Migration to Cities, and in 1957, the central committee of the Chinese Communist Party and the State Council promulgated Prohibit to the Rural Population Blind Exodus. Such measures were conducted as strictly prohibiting any rural enterprises from employing peasant-employees, setting up refuges to collect peasants staying in cities and send them back home. In 1958, the government promulgated Rules on Household Registration of the People's Republic of China by legislation. It is a turning point that in this law the nation definite divided the residents living either in the urban or in the rural areas into 2 categories: agricultural household and non-agricultural household and regulated it had to get approved by the concerned authorities in the city before an agricultural household holder could move into cities to live. This is an important event is history that a household registration system aiming to strict control a free-moving of residents in rural areas to cities was established formally. Later, in correspondent to the legislated household registration system, sub-systems for supplying materials needed to live in cities, employment, and welfare were established. Only a non-agricultural household status holder could be qualified enjoying the welfares regulated in these sub-systems. A barrier between the urban and rural thus came into being and so did a separated administration system for the urban and rural. Among the whole thing the most notable is that rural population could not move into urban areas freely.

What is in contrast to the situations of the rural was that, within an enterprise in the urban areas, the economy conducted an administrational philosophy that "each unit should be a society" in order to have a management and supervision to the enterprises, as well as to provide with various social and economic services to the urban citizens to facility their basic necessity. Under such a philosophy, each enterprise became a multi-functional synthetic entity. On the other hand, the economy also regulated the correspondent role, right, and status for each member in the enterprises for his/her behaviors, and the results are that each member had to be totally relied on the unit to survive in the society, for his/her personnel documentation were filed with the unit, he/she were accommodated according to its own principles by the unit in which he/she was employed. The unit or its up-level unit arranged even such affairs as his/her children's enrolling to kindergarten and school.

2. The Rural Labors Going Back into Urban Areas and the Urban-internally-binary Labor Market

The regime of the above urban-rural-separating management, based on the household registration system and the practice of "a unit, a society", has been changed with deepening of the economy reform of China. The changes were due to, on one hand, the government's loosening control the rural labors' migration to urban areas, and on the other hand, the agricultural economy reform started from in 1979, especially the adopted policy of making a contract of liabilities combining land cultivation and crops yields. The measures and the policy adopted raised the agricultural productivity and a lot of rural peasants became redundant labors as a result. At the same time, the economy reform conducted in cities and development of city economy had provided with a lot of employment opportunities to labor influx to urban area.

The migration of rural labors to urban areas was once described as "a flood of labors". Due to the restrictions of the household registration system, housing, and some other welfare conditions, only a very small part of the "flood", who possesses business ability or expertise and can generate a stable income and thus may be able to offer the accommodation, can stay in cities. Most of the them are belong to a type described as "a migratory bird", who, parallel those early peasant households in the history of Japan, go into cities when economy is booming engaging mainly in labor works or doing some business or involving in any professions that can bring them with income and retreat to their countryside homes when the economy is in a tough condition or when it is in a season to do farm works, such as collecting crops, inseminating, etc. They have become inalienable to the cities' prosperity and development, while at the same time the government does not take too much burden by taking up the responsibility for their social securities. This is the origin of the unique feature of the urban labor market – journeywork system.

This journeywork has something to do with the system of the state-owned enterprises, of which most are now under the contract of business operating liabilities. Under this contract, the salaries of the whole member, including the managers themselves, are combined with the growth of the unit's profit. This situation has left the interests of decision makers, staff and labors being agreed in most cases, though there may be conflicts sometimes when profit is distributed among the members themselves. It has made the maximization of the average income of members in a unit the only aim to pursue rather than stockholder's income growth in an enterprise under this situation, creating a barrier between labors' going in and out the enterprise and being the primer reason for the existence of journeywork and a binary labor management systems within an enterprise.

According to the concerned principles of labor economics, we assume, labors are homogenous, when enterprise behavior is maximization of its profit, labors will migrate from an enterprise with a lower rate of salary to that with a higher rate, the exodus of the labors will cause the marginal labor income of the enterprise with a lower rate of salary rising, thus raising its rate of salary to attract back labors, in contrast, the enterprise with a high rate of salary will decrease its marginal labor productivity because of the increase of labors, causing in the end the real rate of its salary decrease to reducing cost to increase profit, at this point, if labor mobility is free, the salary rate of labor markets will reach to a balanced point. But when enterprise behavior is maximization of average income of its members, enterprises with a low income will not allow labors in it to leave and those with high income not allow labors to join in if only the income has satisfied the aim set for the maximization, irrespective of whether there is a barrier or not the government has set for the labor mobility. Under the situation, a barrier between in and out comes into being, thus the differentia evidenced in the level of labors' salary income is sealed, the level of a labor's income is more determined by the performances of the enterprise he/she is working for than the level of his/her expertise or his/her efforts paid. But the performance to be achieved may be depended on whether the enterprise can dominate more assets actually belonged to the state, or may be its monopoly position in its industry, or the temporary shortage of its products on markets, so even if the government allows a free mobility of labors, the adjustment to the enterprise's labor input will not be by members formally employed but by the journeywork. This is because that according to the contract, formal members will share the bonus, while the journeywork will not, if only cost of employment to journeywork will not cause marginal income brought by journeywork less than salary paid to them, they can only bring income growth to average income of formal workers due to when calculate the average income, the net income created by the journeywork goes into the numerator, while the number of them will not go to the denominator. That is exact reason why a contracted state-owned enterprise comes to a situation when its formal workers are without much productivity and more than needed, it still employ a lot of journeyworks.

For most of these rural labors, the possibility getting an ideal job is much limited due to the existing discriminated treatment to the journeywork thus making them in a relatively unequal status compared with their local counterparts in terms of the household status, offspring enrollment to schools, housing, and social securities. In some of state-owned enterprises, there is even such phenomenon that formal workers stand by while journeyworks toil.

In addition to the practice of journeywork adopted within the state-owned enterprises, there are also among the rural labors some engaging in retail business in a small scale, doing labor works in construction industry or in service industry for city families. Just as rural labors working in state-owned enterprises, their incomes, obtained through their laboring, are extremely limited for subsistence. They constitute the other extreme in an urban-rural-binary labor market: i.e., one extreme is the labor market, constituted by labors from in urban enterprises or non-profit units, the market being called the first labor market, with stable jobs, good pay and working conditions, and opportunities of promotion, and the other extreme is being called the second labor market, constituted by the migrate rural labors, with less welfares, tough working conditions, and job mobility which means to the labors the breakdown of their career and they do not want. Instead of promoting opportunities, they often get arrogant management and supervisions in this second labor market. These labor markets together constituted, during the period from 1984 to 1992, based on the adoption of a system of urban-rural household separating registration, the urban-rural-binary labor market system, which persisted until later gradually evolved into urban-internally-binary labor market with a great number of laid-offs coming forth in state-owned enterprises.

3. The Laid-offs in State-owned Enterprises and Development of the Second Labor Market in Urban Areas

The above mentioned urban-rural-binary labor market became austere after 1992 due to more and more laid-offs come from state-owned enterprises. And in this year, the Chinese government formally sets its aim as a basic course to establish a socialism market economy system. For that, it began to experiment with establishing and promoting modern enterprise systems in the national-wide by founding some new type of enterprises. From then on, the problems hidden deeply in the bottom level of the workings of economy system became visible gradually. The state-owned enterprises, once as main conduits for absorbing newly added labors, now became large sources of delivering laid-offs and committed huge looses. Facing the pressures and competitions from the industrial structure transformation and market competitions and in order to adapt themselves to survive in the development of market economy, these traditional state-owned enterprises, long-term pursuing the maximization of average income of their members, had to establish modern enterprises system within their internal structure by conducting adjustments not having had in history. In this process, the hidden unemployment population that had been accumulated for many years appeared. From 1993, a large scale of laid-off workers started to be pushed society, causing the biggest laid-off-unemployment ever had in the history since the establishment of the People's Republic of China. According to the statistics from Ministry of Labors, the number of laid-offs in the urban areas nationwide reached 3 million in 1993, increased to 8.9 million in 1996, 11.51 million in 1997 and 12.1 million in 1999, the top level in the history, then decreased to 10.98 million in 2000. While same time, the unemployment population in the urban areas also increased gradually. According to the concerned statistics, the number of registered unemployment population in the urban areas was 3.639 million, the unemployment rate is 2.3%; 5 million in 1996 and 5.53 million in 1996 with an unemployment rate of 3%; 5.57 million in 1997, the unemployment rate being 3.1%; by the end of 2000, the figure reached to 5.95 million with a rate of 3.1%. Such a huge unemployment population was a tremendous impact to the urban labor market, which had already been in its tough time and caused the serious problem of social stability. Under the situation, the departments in charge of labor management in the various levels of governments, especially those in large and medium sized cities, thought even to prohibit the migration of rural labors to cities for the sake of solving rapidly the problem of laid-offs and people unemployed from the state-owned enterprises. On 17 November, 1994, the Ministry of Labor Affairs promulgated Temporal Provisions for the Management to the Rural Labors' Employment Crossing Provinces, in which there are a few restricting regulations to the employment of migrate people crossing provinces. In nature, these regulations are restrictions pointing to the employment of rural peasants going into cities. The Article 5 of the Provisions reads: an employing unit can employ rural labors only in case that the amount of labors of the local does not meet the local demand and at the same time in agreement with one of the following conditions: 1. Having been confirmed and approved by the local department charging of labors' employment affairs that the local area is primarily short of labors thus the unit needs to employ people across provinces; 2. The vocation, and the industry, to which it belongs, for both of which the employing unit needs to recruit labors, have been confirmed and approved by the local department charging of labors' employment affairs to be sound and have recruited a full quota of the local labors; 3. Does not belong to any one of the above 2 conditions, but the employing unit cannot recruit, any of, or to a full quota, the needed personnel, within the defined scope and period, or without any means to do so. It is not difficult to see, through this article, that the standpoint of various regulations is to restrict employing rural labors from other provinces and put as a priority the need for employing the local labors. For example, in May 1998 the government of Wuhan City decided to quit rural labors as a way of arranging laid-off workers. It regulated that 12 industries and 24 vocations were not opened to rural labors from other provinces. Those that had employed such personnel should quit them immediately. In 1999, the Beijing municipal government decided to tighten the approving procedure for employing personnel not from the local and reduced the amount of industries and vocations that were allowed to employ such people. The industries being influenced include: finance, insurance, post; the vocations being influenced include: management, salesman, businessman, staff, secretary, accountant, teller, cashier, shop clerk, driver, conductor, booker, checker, typist, steward, trainman, operator, telephonist, wireless operator, drawer, copyist, analyst, quality inspector, elevator operator, warehouse keeper, publisher, hotel service man and woman, office staff, etc. Such a detailed list, covering so wide range, is really to our surprise. In such an atmosphere, there was not much room left for a rural labor to have an idea for his/her choices to the professions. On the other hand, they were treated unequally with their urban counterparts in terms of salary, labor arbitration, as well as their lawful rights, which all had contributed to hurting their feelings and self-esteem. With those, and the nation's propelling to the process of market economy and reform of the household registration system, urban-rural-binary labor market, a product of era of centralized economy of China, has evolved into urban-internally-binary labor market. The status of urban laid-offs has got improved in this market compared with their rural counterparts. They can get some pay from the government as compensation and help from job-centers to find a new job. Still, the government, via the concerned financial institutions, can also provide them with some financial installment to help them carve out business. But we think that such goodness cannot last forever. With a unified management to the laid-offs and unemployment people and laws of market economy functioning, if they cannot find jobs in the first labor market, they have to enter into the second labor market. With a possibility that more and more laid-offs will go into the second labor market (for only a very small part of laid-offs can find jobs in the first labor market), the practice that "take jobs in elastic manner and irrespective of units" will become prevail, which will further increase labor supply to the second labor market, making the features of the urban-internally-binary labor market, having a root in the urban-rural household registration separating management system, become dim. The present condition of this labor market resembles that in the developing countries, which has caused attentions from the fields of economics and sociology and is becoming a new topic worthy of serious research.

4. The reform of Chinese Institutions and secondary labor market

After the year of 2005, with the mostly completion of the reform of state-owned enterprise, the laid-off workers from state-owned enterprises have been gradually absorbed by society. What influence the expansion of urban secondary labor market are three main factors: migrant workers, urban unemployed, as well as the possible laid-off workers for the reform of institutions. Migrant workers are still flowing into the city at 10 million per annum, and this process may continue for many years. The second factor which impacts the expansion of urban secondary labor market is the ongoing reform of institutions and the resulting diversion of labor issues. "Institutions" is a very Chinese characteristic concept, many experts and scholars attending international conferences often feel embarrassed for their translation. The institutions of China cover many areas such as science, education, culture, health, journalism, publishing, sports, environmental monitoring, urban construction and so on, in addition, there are subsidiary organs and legal services. Data shows that China currently has 1.3 million units of institution, the staff nearly 30 billion, and the proportion of their expenditure in the state financial expenditure is more than 30%. The organization and management of institutions have typical characteristics of government monopoly, and various utilities are generally the public sector, the assets belong to the country; the Government have right whether to set up, write off the institutions, and decide the quantity of staffs, the Government directly Organize and manage all kinds of activities of institutions; the funding for the activities are mostly from government grants or public funds. In China, the institutions are the extension or embodiment of central government or local government in the public service. Based on these institutional reasons, institutions had the same problem with the traditional state-owned enterprises, such as agency bloating, low efficiency and so on, making institutions difficult to adapt to the current needs of our market economy.

The reform of institutions will begin at the classification and function. Based on the principle of things which can be resolved by the market should submit to the market, the Government would strongly reduce the number of existing institutions and the number of employees to the appropriate level. Based on the function of the preserved institutions, we should re-design the institution's management model, clarify the range of self development and self pay of not full funding institutions, and change the employing concepts and personnel system, as well as properly divert surplus workers of institutions. As the reform of Chinese state-owned enterprise in 20th century 90's, we should revitalize the institutions by offering job-change, diversion and a variety of employment models, and, if possible, we should introduce more competition of market and privatization and some institutions will restructure as non state-owned "private non-enterprise units" or non-profit organizations engaged in non-profit social services. Only part of laid-off workers for the reform of institutions can have re-employment opportunities in the first labor market, while larger part of the laid-off workers will enter the secondary labor market looking for jobs. Thereby this situation strengthens the labor supply in Chinese urban secondary labor market.

5. The Expansion of Second Labor Market in Cities and Labor Market Policy

The formation of urban-internally-binary labor market is a new phenomenon in the development of China's labor market and this market will continually have an influence on the frame of China's labor market. With city labor market to develop towards becoming a perfect one, social installments in terms of, such as, housing, school enrolling, child care, etc. to become also commercialized, as well as welfare system to be accomplished going out from enterprise and institutions to become socialized, these privileges as affixed to the practice of household registration system have began falling into decay thus household registration system once as a means to restrict free mobile of the rural labors to cities will be defunct in the end. Another point which is worth noting is the process of the stratification of the urban labor market with economy reform deepening, causing more and more laid-offs from institutions joining in the second labor market. Those processes will propel the expansion of the second labor market. The phenomenon has caused our attention.

How to protect the right and interests of these labors who are at lower stratum in the labor market is a problem to be treated seriously when the urban-internally-binary labor market exits and the second labor market is under expansion. Most of these in the second labor market are rural labors, city laid-offs, and unemployments, who constitute "a weak group". Because in this market the labor supply is surplus, these people's relationships with employers may bear this influence that they may be in a less favorable condition. To protect these people's interests has become imminent which will involve further how to design patterns for the relationships between labor and employer in future. The government has noted this and premier Wen Jiabao in his Working Report of Government of this year raised the opinion to concern these weak-group people and support their employment.

When surveying to the expansion of urban-internally-binary labor market and the second labor market, not only should we pay attentions to making measures that protects the rights and interests of people of weak group, but also we should pay attention to labors' expertise structure witnessed in the second labor market and keep from duplicating a traditional labor market with lagged technical structure. According to the experiences of some countries in Africa and Asia, a professional structure with low level of technologies hinders the process of economy modernization, which, also a reason for the long-term existence of traditional industries.

Among other things, the expansion of the second labor market in cities also reminds us of the question of land tenure in the countryside. Some scholars argue that in order to let peasants input more on the farmland in a long term, we should promote tilling scale, even reform the current land tenure, until adopting privatization of land in the countryside. Set alone these a bit of ideological arguments, maybe, we think the system of contract of land-and-yield liabilities is of significance under the current situation in order to prevent the rural peasants from outflow to control the scale of the second labor market in urban areas. According to the experiences of the developing countries, a free mobile between the rural and urban will accelerate the process of citifying, however, it can also bring social problems such as too big unmanageable cities and paupers, which can never be ignored for the sake of social stable and economy development.

As such, while we are celebrating fast development of the economy and a free mobile of labors coming into being, we must keep a clear mind that the most challenge is coming from the gradual expansion in the second labor market in the urban areas. These will have an influence on our continued efforts to establish a rational and unified labor market irrespective of rural or urban areas. We must devote to establishing a system frame for the social stability, in which, the interests of labors, employer and employees, cooperation between workers and investors are wholly balanced. A right view about the current conditions of the second labor market in urban areas is no doubt a prerequisite for solving the problems involved in the process of urban second labor market expansion when we want to achieve that aim.

References

China Labor Market Information Networks and Supervision Center,(2002). Reports on the Re-employment of Laid-offs in China, 15.9.

Fan H.S, (2004). Thinkings about the reform of Chinese institutions, Chinese Economic Times, 12.4.

Liu E.D, (2002). Reform Our Household Registration System and Establish an Urban-rural Unified Labor Market. Labor Economy and Labor Relation (Publication Digest Center of the People's University of China), No.2;

National condition analysis and research group, (1998). China Academy of Sciences, Employment and Development, Liaoning People's Publish House, 12.

Wang L.M,(2010), Review of the Chinese institution's reform, Chinese executive management, 7.8.

Yang G,Z, & Liu E,D.(1990). Rational Labor Distribution and Mobile. Academic Field Publish House, 9.

Zhao L.K; &Yang T.R, (1988). The Reformation of the System of Labor Economy of China, Sichuang Science and Technology Publish House, 4.

Sustainable Development in Rural China. The Interrelation of Agriculture, Renewable Energy and Labour Migration

Sven Schaller
(University of Leipzig/Helmholtz Centre for Environmental Research, UFZ)

Abstract

The paper analyses the Chinese development scheme and the impact of renewable energy on rural employment and migration. It argues that, besides other measures, the supply of renewable energy could stimulate decentralised investment decisions, expanding national development to rural regions. By these means, rural employment opportunities may be created in industry as well as in a rural service sector. Labour migration to urban centres would decrease.

Content

Introduction

Although China ranks as biggest CO2-emittant in the World now, its CO2-emissions per capita (4.58 tonnes) are less than half of OECD average.[1] The poverty rate is eight percent and the average GDP per capita is 6,000 US-dollar. Economic and social welfare has remained very low, especially in rural regions. To achieve the United Nations Millennium Development Goals, China has to make further efforts for development. The question is if this development could be implemented in a sustainable manner.

Starting with the reforms in 1979, the Chinese development scheme has mainly focussed on urban industrialisation.[2] The special economic zones that served as a window to the global market, grew extremely fast. Rural regions scored some

1 See IEA (2009), p. 91.
2 See Murphy (2009); Bowlus/Sinclair (2003); Taylor/Rozelle (2003).

advances but showed only a very modest development. By these processes, the urban-rural income gap as well as the development gap widened more and more. The consequence was a huge stream of rural-urban migrants.

Throughout the 1990s and the beginning of the 21st century, the special economic zones that are mainly situated on the coast, got on with their unprecedented growth. This caused further inequalities. Although the rural-urban gap persisted, the coastal-inland disparity became now the largest component in the regional inequality decomposition.

The corresponding energy supply scheme was strongly related to that development line. Energy supply was to keep pace with the growing demand from industry. Another exigency was that it had to be cheap. Environmental aspects played a minor role. Coal is, therefore, still the single most important energy source in China. Its share of the total primary energy demand sums up to 62.8 percent in 2005. Oil counts up to 18.8 percent, water power to 2.0 percent, natural gas to 2.4 percent and nuclear energy to 0.8 percent.[3]

The Chinese government has realized the challenges that further economic development will entail. For the first time, energy security was established as official development goal in their XX. five-year plan (2001-2005).[4] The objective comprises the continuation of recent energy schemes, i.e. fossil fuels will continue to cover the main part of future energy needs. Nevertheless, the shift from fossil fuels to renewables seems to be a promising energy strategy for China, not only in remote areas[5] but also with regard to aspects of sustainability[6].

Although there is no systematic analysis of the correlation of access to renewable, decentralised energy and their impact on (rural) employment and labour migration, it will be argued in this paper that the installation of country-wide renewable and decentralised energy systems may have positive effects on employment, especially rural employment, and migration. The paper will provide some incentives for further empirical research on that topic. The underlying hypotheses, which are related to the structural change of energy supply, could be summarized as follows:

- Besides some important policy measures for rural development (e.g. rural financing, infrastructure, market access), renewable, decentralised energy supply is a prerequisite for investment decisions in rural regions.
- Sufficient access to energy in combination with adequate energy storage systems may thus permit permanent rural off-farm occupation and could be conducive to decrease rural migration to urban industrialised centres.

3 See IEA (2007), p. 262.
4 See Constantin (2005).
5 See Voravate/Barnes/Bogach, (2000).
6 See Scheer (2000).

The paper is structured as follows: Section 1 analyses the present development scheme focussing on urban industrialisation and its consequences, especially the rural-urban labour migration. Section 2 will give a brief overview over the energy system in China. Section 3 focuses on the interrelation of access to renewable energy, agriculture and rural employment. Section 4 summarizes the results.

1. The Chinese development scheme and labour migration

Since the launching of the Four Modernizations in 1978, that started the reform era, China has experienced an unprecedented economic growth.

In agriculture, the implementation of the household responsibility system enabled the farmers to retain surplus over their individual plots of land rather than working for the collective. Within only six years food production had increased dramatically. Recognizing that development, the Chinese government eliminated officially the people's communes that had been the hallmark of China's agricultural system for over twenty years. In some cases it established so called township and village enterprises (TVEs), i.e. industries owned by townships and villages. From the mid-1980s these TVEs showed a rapid growth. Ten years later, the TVEs for the first time produced more than the State owned enterprises (SOE). The new agro-industry-based rural development contributed to regional growth easing interregional disparities – at least in the early reform period.[7]

It is calculated that employment in the TVEs has expanded from 30 million in the early 1980s to about 130 million in the late 1990s. Additionally, over 40 million rural workers found a job in private business.[8] Other sources estimate that total off-farm labour increased from 80 million in 1988 to 154 million in 1995.[9]

Although very important in providing jobs for the rural labour force, the TVEs were confronted with some crucial limitations in transforming the rural regions from an agrarian society into a dynamic and industrialised community. These limitations consisted, above all, of their limited technological resources to become nationally and internationally competitive. These obstacles then led to a reduction in the TVEs' total employment from 135.1 million in 1996 to 127 million in 1999[10] with a further downward trend.

In view of these problems and a rural work force of approximately 350 million small farmers that still make up 43 percent of the total labour force, the new op-

7 See Kawakami (2004), p. 134.

8 See National Bureau of Statistics (2001): *China Statistical Abstract*, Beijing, p. 40, cited in Bowlus/Sicular (2003), p. 562.

9 See Rozelle et al. (1999), p. 368, p. 372.

10 See Yao (2002), p. 357.

portunities in rural off-farm employment were not sufficient to absorb the rural labour surplus. The problem of fighting back rural poverty and transforming rural society by the development of rural off-farm job opportunities has not been solved yet.

Despite these efforts for rural development, the Chinese economic development was pushed on mainly by urban industrialisation. This process became most illustrative when, starting in 1979, foreign capital inflows took a significant leading role for regional growth. These investments were initially limited to several small regions, the so-called special economic zones (SEZs). Most of them could be found along the coast, e. g., in the province of Guangdong (Shantou, Shenzhen and Zhuhai), in the province of Fujian (Xiamen), and on the island of Hainan. In 1984, the SEZ were extended to the 14 largest cities on the coast, including Dalian, Tianjin, Shanghai and Guangzhou. Encouraged by the success of the SEZs, the State opened the capital cities of inland provinces and autonomous regions for capital inflows from abroad in 1992. Additionally, the government established 15 free trade areas, 32 state-level economic and technological development zones and 53 specialized high-tech industrial development zones. All these zones focussed on urban growth and served as a window to the world. They played a dual role in an increasing foreign-oriented economy as they generated foreign exchanges for export products and facilitated the import of advanced technologies.

These enclaves enabled an accelerated inland economic growth through back-coupling and trickle-down effects. Some of the cities in SEZs experienced an average annual growth rate of 20 percent or more. The urbanization rate in China has increased from 17.4 percent to 41.8 percent between 1978 and 2005.

Private enterprises have played a crucial but not exclusive role in this process. From the start of the reform policy, enterprises were encouraged to produce for profit. Consequently, the role of the private sector increased. Nevertheless, the government maintained a decisive position in the urban economy and each significant economic sector is still supervised by State organisations or ministries.

Furthermore, China's economic growth does not come alone from private sector expansion in light industry for exports. The State, mainly through the 159 big State-owned enterprises (SOEs), had invested huge amounts in infrastructure and heavy industry in the meantime providing key inputs for development. Thus, the private sector's share of 70 percent of China's GDP in 2005 seems to overestimate its role in the country's economic development.

The concentration on rapid urban growth that accelerated with the establishment of the SEZ, was accompanied by various urban biased income transfer programs. For instance, urban price subsidies summed up in 1998 for 71.2 billion yuan, which was 7.6 percent of government's total budget.[11] Furthermore, subsi-

11 See Yang (2002), p. 332.

dies to the urban-based SOEs totalled 232.5 billion yuan for the years 1986-1990 and 206.1 billion yuan for 1991-1996, accounting for nearly 19 percent and respectively nine percent of state revenues in these two periods.[12]

As a consequence of the State's development strategy as well as its direct urban-specific fiscal transfers, rural income increases remained behind the urban gains. Rural-urban disparities widened and translated into an overall inequality. Especially during the 1990s, the progress of the reform became more and more uneven.

In the course of the reform process, the inequality got an additional dimension. In particular, only those regions where most TVEs and SEZ had established – mainly on the coast – showed rapid growth. The coastal-inland disparity increased dramatically due to these processes and became the largest component in the regional inequality decomposition.[13]

Rapid urban growth, underdeveloped agriculture and poverty evoked a rising rural-urban migration. It is estimated that since the 1980s over 80 million people have migrated from rural regions into the cities.[14] Newer statistics even report a total of 132 million rural-urban migrants.[15] Besides, China's urban population has more than doubled in 25 years, from 191 million in 1980 to 562 million in 2005.[16] By 2020, the urbanization rate could pass the 60 percent mark, an increase by 17.1 percent since 2005.[17]

When migrants leave for the cities to find a job, they are confronted with serious obstacles that prevent them from settling permanently in the urban centres.[18] These restrictions may be summarized as follows:

> "First, the urban segregated labor market sets barriers for migrant access to a variety of jobs and posts. Second, because of incomplete urban social service reform, outside workers are unable to obtain necessary housing, medical care, and children's education at reasonable prices. Third, migrants without local *hukou* are often dispelled by urban authority simply because they are outsiders and therefore may contribute to instability and crime."[19]

Consequently, without urban *hukou* registration, rural migrants are systematically denied access to better-remunerated and secure jobs or employment in State administration.[20] Only migrants who meet high skill requirements have the

12 See ibd.
13 See Kanbur/Zhang (1999), p. 694.
14 See Cai et al. (2002), p. 202.
15 See National Bureau of Statistics (2007): *Situation of Rural Migration in China in 2006*, Internal Research Report N° 18, Beijing, cited in: Démurger et al. (2009), p. 611.
16 See Yusuf/Nabeshima (2008), p. 8.
17 See Yusuf/Nabeshima (2008), p. 1.
18 See Zhang (2010), p. 51.
19 Cai et al. (2002), p. 202.
20 See Zhang (2010), p. 53. See Tuñón (2006), p. 11.

chance to get a "blue stamp" (comparable to the green card in the USA) and to get a permanent urban *hukou*.

Analysing migration, it was observed that migrants pass normally through various stages of labour mobility. In a first stage, they move out of agriculture to a local non-agricultural sector. A next step is the migration to more advanced rural areas and local small towns. Finally, they go to big industrialising cities.[21] These characteristics may explain why 68.4 percent of migration was intraprovincial and 80.4 percent intraregional (see Figure 1).

Figure 1: Intra- and interregional migration in China

Scope of migration cross regions in China (%), 1995

	Total	Rural to urban	Rural to rural
Intraprovincial	68.4	75.3	54.6
Intraregional	80.4	84.8	71.7
Of which			
Within east	93.1	95.1	87.2
Within central	67.7	72.7	58.6
Within west	72.4	75.6	69.0

Source: Cai et al. (2002), p. 202

Anyway, long-distance migration has risen sharply in the late 1990s.[22] For instance, the flow from the central regions to the eastern provinces has increased from 21.0 to 41.8 percent between 1990 and 2000. The province of Guangdong alone received 36.2 percent of total interprovincial migrants between 1995 and 2000.[23]

Despite of the still widespread migration into the cities, there are some rural villages where returning migrants settled down. After having worked for various years in urban centres, rural migrants return to their natal villages and contribute to the diversification of the rural economy by becoming self-employed or founding little enterprises. Estimations suggest that about a third of the rural migrants return to their native village.[24]

A study of two counties in south Jiangxi depicted the process of job creation by the returnees. It critically examines some structural problems that are related to this development. Many of the returning migrants stagnate with their entrepreneurships due to depressed market access, the lack of skilled labour force and the backwardness of their natal communities. This backwardness arises – not exclusively, but often – from the lack of energy.[25]

21 See Cai et al. (2002), p. 202.

22 See Rozelle et al. (1999), p. 375, p. 377.

23 See Fan, C. (2008), p. 73.

24 See Murphy (1999), p. 662.

25 See ibd., p. 667f.

Nevertheless, the development of the rural regions is essential to slow down the migration flows, bring to halt the unsustainable urban growth, to create job opportunities for the rural population, and to narrow the regional disparities. The importance of this policy gets empirical support from the finding that households from more industrialised villages produce fewer migrants.[26]

2. Energy

Until now, China's energy policy has been based on regional energy schemes . The lack of a unified national grid system did not pose any problems back in 1985 when China was still an energy exporter with a production of 855.5 million ton standard coal and a consumption of 766.8 million ton standard coal. It became problematic when the ratio changed during the following ten years. In 1995, a supply of 1290.3 million ton standard coal stands vis-à-vis a consumption of 1311.8 million ton standard coal. The gap has been widening since then, heightening the risk of localised shortages. When power demand increased by 15.3 percent in 2003, power supply could not keep pace with demand and China faced one of the most serious power shortages since its opening.[27] 21 out of 34 provinces (including the high-industrialised provinces of Beijing, Shanghai, Guangdong and Jiangsu) experienced wide-area outages[28] with far-reaching consequences.[29] Although some analysts warned that energy supply must grow faster if the country wants to sustain its rapid economic growth[30], energy supply in 2006 was 2210.6 million ton standard coal, but demand had grown to 2462.7 million ton standard coal.[31]

Despite the persistent gap between energy demand, especially that of the urban centres, and energy supply, the growth in electricity generation capacity is impressive. Electricity supply increased from 301 terawatt hours (TWh) in 1980 to 905 TWh in 1994[32] and to 3714 TWh in 2009.[33]

This growth in electricity supply was facilitated by huge investments in energy generation capacities. In the 1990s, for instance, the capacity of newly installed coal power plants alone was, on average, 11.5 GW per year. That is 6.4 percent of the total installed capacity of coal power plants in the country. By the 2000s,

26 See Taylor/Rozelle (2003), p. 86.
27 See Yang et al. (2007), p. 347.
28 See Cho (2004), p. 1.
29 See Cherni/Kentish (2007), p. 3617.
30 See Wu/Li (1995), p. 167.
31 See *China Statistical Yearbook 1996-2007*, Beijing, cited in: Ma et al. (2009), p. 42.
32 See Wu/Li (1995), p. 175.
33 See China Bureau of Statistics, online: http://www.stats.gov.cn/tjgb/ndtjgb/qgndtjgb/t20100225_402622945.htm (in Chinese), 22 March 2010.

new annual investments in coal powered plants reached 35.4 GW.[34] Since then, the trend has further accelerated. In 2008, China added in total over 90 GW of new capacity. That is the equivalent to the entire installed capacity of an industrialised country like Italy.[35] The total installed capacity for electricity generation accounted for 874 GW in 2009.

Analysing the energy mix, China's energy supply has been focussed on fossil fuels. The importance of coal is illustrated by its share of 76.7 percent of total primary energy production (TPES).[36]

Despite the widespread conception of the paramount significance of water power for China's energy supply, its share has remained relatively small. Nevertheless, it has grown rapidly during the last decade. Between 1993 and 1999, newly installed capacity of hydropower was, on average, 4.9 GW per year. In the 2000s, the newly installed capacity nearly doubled each year.[37] The supply of electricity by hydropower plants increased from 190.6 TWh in 1995 to 482.9 TWh in 2007.[38]

Renewable energy does not play a significant role in China's energy system.[39] For instance, the generation of non-hydro renewable energy worldwide showed an average increase by 52.4 percent in 2000-2005, but it grew by only 3.5 percent in China. It is estimated that China's potential of exploitable renewable energy sources amount to approximately 7.2 billion tonnes coal equivalent, while the current exploited renewable energy resource is only 0.1 billion tonnes coal equivalent.[40]

China's dependency on fossil fuels may cause serious ecological[41] and economic problems in the future. It is calculated, for instance, that China's fossil fuel reserves will only suffice for less than 50 years from now. Thus, coal reserves can be mined for another 48 years, while oil reserves will deplete in 12.1 years and natural gas in 41.8 years.[42]

The Chinese government seems to be aware of these problems. In 2006, it implemented a "Law on Renewable Energy"[43], accompanied by a number of ad-

34 See Ma et al. (2009), p. 11f.

35 See IEA (2009), p. 20.

36 See Ma et al. (2009), p. 22.

37 See ibd. (2009), p. 11f.

38 See ibd. (2009), p. 23.

39 See Shi (2009), p. 104.

40 Zhou, Fengqi (2006): *The Renewable Energy Development Strategy in China*, in: Strategy and Decision Making Research (in Chinese) 21, p. 287-294, cited in: Ma et al. (2009), p. 5.

41 See IEA (2009), p. 20. See Li/Oberheitmann (2009), p. 1421, p. 1416.

42 See State Council Information Office of the People Republic of China (SCIO) (2008): *China's energy conditions and policy white paper*, online: http://www.scio.gov.cn (in Chinese), cited in: Shi (2009), p. 95.

43 See Cherni/Kentish (2007), p. 3624ff., for a detailed analysis on the Renewable Energy Law.

ministrative decrees. In addition to these laws and rules, the government also took some economic incentive measures like tax concessions for the import of renewable energy equipment and a 50-percent reduction in the value-added tax for renewable energy production enterprises. Moreover, the government provides interest-discount loans for projects in rural areas, but mainly for large and medium-sized enterprises.[44] The success of the Renewable Energy Law and the other measures will depend heavily upon the degree of compliance with it.

Nevertheless, China is still limited in its capacity to cope with the gap between high-priced renewable energy and relatively cheaper fossil fuels. A fortiori, this is an important problem as renewable energy must enter the Chinese energy system through market mechanisms.[45] It is not clear, therefore, if renewable energy can replace fossil fuels, particularly in the short and medium term.

After the analysis of the framework of China's energy system, the structure of energy demand and the consequences of rapid urbanization will be set into the context of this paper. Available data show that China's industry demands the largest part of national primary energy. Although other sectors have expanded their share of TPES, industry accounted for 71.1 percent of TPES in 2006, followed by residents (10.3 percent), transportation (7.5 percent) and agriculture (3.4 percent).[46] As industry is concentrated in urban centres – especially on the coast – these figures indirectly illustrate once more that energy is unequally distributed across the country.

Although there are no detailed statistics for the regional level, demand by sector in the case of the main energy source (coal) suggests that the coastal provinces consume most of energy. In 1993, electricity generation by coal accounted for 403 million tonnes out of a total of 1135 million tonnes of coal, followed by industrial boilers with 330 million tonnes. Steel and coke production constituted for 167 million tonnes.[47] There is little reason to believe that these proportions have changed since then. As most of these industries are located in cities along the coast, the existing regional disparities in energy demand become obvious. In 2006, for instance, coal shipments (especially from the north to the south) accounted for 75 percent of total rail cargo with an average rail shipment of 760 kilometres. Major export provinces were Shangxi, Inner Mongolia, Henan and Shaanxi. On the other side, the provinces of Shandong, Hebei, Jiangsu and Zhejiang – all situated at the coast – imported most of the coal.[48]As a consequence of raw coal shipment, only a small amount of electricity is transmitted over long distances. On average,

44 See Shi (2009), p. 100f.
45 See ibd., p. 108.
46 See Chinese Energy Yearbook 2007, Beijing, cited in: Ma et al. (2009), p. 44.
47 See Wu/Li (1995), p. 171.
48 See Ma et al. (2009), p. 12 and p. 36.

more than 80 percent of electricity demand is met within provinces. Again, most electricity was imported by the industrialised coastal regions.[49]

The previous analysis suggests that the development of the energy system corresponds to the scheme of economic development. Both have a centralised focus. Huge power plants meet – with some problems – the rising demand of the industrialising cities. On the contrary, energy demand in rural regions has been of minor significance. The comparison between electricity consumption per capita in the cities (on average 370 kilowatt hours in 2006) and rural electricity consumption (190 kilowatt hours per capita) shows it quite clearly.[50]

Nevertheless, rural electrification, i.e. the provision of infrastructure for electricity supply, has advanced rapidly. In 1995, there were 16 counties, 828 townships and 29,783 villages, with an overall population of approximately 120 million people that had no access to electricity. By 2005, no county was without electricity and the number of people without access to electricity had reduced to 20 million.[51] Today, 98 percent of the Chinese population has access to electricity.[52]

Despite these impressive data, many problems for rural electrification are still unsolved. For instance, the presented figures include solar home systems (SHS) that provide current to the households. In most cases however, the SHS are too weak to serve for productive purposes. Moreover, electricity constitutes only a small part of total rural energy. Unprocessed biomass energy still accounts for 74 percent of total rural aggregate energy consumption.[53] The backwardness of the rural regions is even more illustrative in absolute terms. Utilization of rural biomass summed up to 280 million tonnes coal equivalent in 2006.[54] Total rural energy, i.e. the energy use of approximately 700 million people, accounted for only 378.4 million tonnes coal equivalent.

Nevertheless, biomass may play a crucial role for rural energy supply. Instead of the direct combustion of biomass, the construction of modern biogas plants should be advocated. Small hydropower stations will probably also gain importance for China's rural electricity supply. Even today, approximately one third of the counties and a quarter of the total population are dependent upon small-scale hydropower for rural electricity supply. The total installed capacity of small hydropower stations was 47 GW in 2006. The total generation of rural hydropower amounted for 148 TWh in 2006.

49 See ibd., p. 14.
50 See ibd., p. 27.
51 See Shi (2009), p. 102.
52 See ibd.
53 See Ma et al. (2009), p. 23.
54 See ibd.

In conclusion, it can be said that the energy pattern follow the scheme of economic development. The challenge will be to solve all the problems that emerge from that, i.e. unequal regional dispersion of growth and income, rural to urban and west-to-east migration, centralisation of energy demand in big cities, environmental distress, especially in the urban centres, and insufficient rural development.

3. Renewable energy, rural development and their impact on migration

Stable supply of enough energy for rural villages could stimulate decentralised investment decisions to expand national development increasingly to rural regions. Renewable, decentralised energy supply in combination with adequate energy storage systems would not only create new jobs in rural industries, e.g. in town and village enterprises (TVEs), but also permit permanent occupation. This seems to have a crucial impact on job and income securities for the rural labour force. For instance, the energy shortages that occurred regularly between 2003 and 2005 had had direct negative effects on production and industrial growth, as well as on agriculture and employment. Especially private enterprises had to stop their production. Consequently, many of them dismissed workers or offered them less payment.[55]

Therefore, access to electricity is regarded as a decisive prerequisite for rural industrialisation in China.[56] A study of Shiu and Lam (2004) shows that there is a causal connection between electricity consumption and the real GDP. These empirical findings for China's development during the period from 1971 to 2000 strongly support the standpoint of this paper that the provision of (renewable) energy to rural regions would foster economic growth through rural industrialisation and job creation. This finding becomes even more important in view of the fact that 70 to 80 percent of electricity demand is for industrial production.[57]

Furthermore, a rural service sector with communication services, retail shops, purchase or storage services may establish. Rural villages and small towns could run communal rural saving banks or health sanitation, extension and agro-technology services.

As a consequence of an accelerated rural growth, rural migration to urban industrialised centres as well as west-to-east migration would decrease. More off-

55 See Yang et al. (2007), p. 349.
56 See Lew (2000), p. 277f.
57 See Shiu/Lam (2004), p. 53.

farm job opportunities in local places, where the agriculturists have their *hukou*, are expected to detract incentives for long-distance and rural-urban migration. Rural labour force could find opportunities for income growth right on location or nearby.

Nevertheless, as mentioned earlier, rural energy supply alone is not sufficient to accelerate rural growth and to establish more off-farm job opportunities. Other policy measures must be taken. A serious problem that faces rural regions in China is the absence of credit markets. Even in better-off regions, banks have only gradually begun to extend credit to individuals. Earnings from migration or remittances, that reached nine percent of rural income in 2001[58], still constitute a crucial source for investment although it is used more for amelioration of housing than for self-employed businesses.[59] In the future, the Agricultural Bank of China and rural savings co-operatives[60] shall fill that gap.

This financial aspect could be accompanied by a State program to set up investment programmes for decentralised energy supply and storage capacities that serve for industrial purposes. If funding is secured, e.g. through rural saving banks, communal enterprises or rural energy cooperatives may establish themselves as integrated entities for local development. As they would be interested in environmental protection as well as in regional growth, investments in renewable energy capacities like wind power, small hydropower, biogas plants or even solar and solar thermal power plants are very likely to occur. Case studies in the South of Brazil illustrate the viability of such a development path.[61]

Other policy measures of the government should tend to increase the efficiency of farm supply and food markets. In this respect the consolidation of member-driven cooperatives may play a crucial role. Recent reforms are encouraging the growth of this type of farmer self-organisation, especially because there is a growing interest in market-driven business structures. It is estimated that 160 million households are currently members of the All-China Federation of Supply and Marketing Cooperatives.[62] Despite some problems in member operation or financial performance[63], the potential of cooperatives to foster rural development in China is enormous.

In the short run, this combined development scheme with rural financing, rural energy and rural market access as its core components would promise a growth of industries, services and employment opportunities. It is very likely that, as a

58 See Brauw/Rozelle (2008), p. 321.
59 See ibd., p. 322.
60 See Schaller (2009).
61 See Schaller (2008).
62 See Guo et al. (2008), p. 158-159.
63 See ibd., p. 169ff.

result of these measures, migration from rural areas (especially from the hinterland) would slow down because the rural population would eventually gain higher incomes locally. In the medium- and long-run, it promises more welfare for the State through the development of rural regions, less flexible costs in energy provision, higher energy security, more energy independence from abroad, higher revenues through more employment, less social conflict through harmonisation of urban and rural wages, and healthier environment.

Some pilot projects in China give empirical evidence of the general feasibility of such a way of development. A well-studied example is the rural development in the province of Yunnan that was for the most part enabled through the installation of biogas plants. Rural population in this region directly benefited with extra-incomes of 0.8 billion yuan per year.[64] A new programme based on combined renewable energy capacities is estimated to bring direct benefits of about 5 billion yuan to agriculturists.[65]As their incomes rise, it can be expected that a main cause for migration becomes obsolete. Nevertheless, the mentioned study does not analyse the impact of the access to renewable energy and regional growth on migration. As well as in other regions, a lot of field research has to be done.

Conclusion

The paper analysed the economic development in China since the opening in 1978, its relation to the energy system and migration. It argued that despite rapid progress in agriculture in the first years after implementing the reform, rural regions and rural development still limp behind the urban growth. The gap between rural and urban growth is even going to increase. The same applies to the incomes of the rural and urban labour force. Although the fast urban industrialisation has absorbed great quantities of former rural workers, there is still a huge potential of a rural proletariat that tries to enter the growing cities. Nevertheless, these migrants are faced with institutional constraints, especially the residence registration system (*hukou*) that complicates their search for well remunerated jobs in the cities. Since the establishment of the special economic zones (SEZs) that serve as a gateway between foreign high-tech-enterprises and the Chinese market, economic development has more and more concentrated in the coastal region. As a consequence, the coastal-inland disparities in economic terms became the largest component in the overall inequality. This unequal development constitutes a crucial pull-factor for migrants from the hinterland to the east.

64 See Li et al: (2005), p. 102.
65 See ibd., p. 107.

So far, the Chinese energy system has followed this path of economic development. Energy resources, especially coal, are shipped from the West and North to the coastal regions. As three-quarters of total energy supply are derived from the combustion of coal, the rapid urban industrialisation in the big cities of the east entails negative environmental aspects. On the other side, the historically unprecedented growth of energy capacities could not keep pace with the even more accelerated urban industrial growth and fast increasing energy demand. Hence energy shortages occurred periodically, especially between 2003 and 2005.

Rural regions, although showing a rapid increase in electrification, still lack access to sufficient energy for industrial purposes. The renewable, non-hydropower potential is huge, but underdeveloped. In view of the scarcity of their own fossil fuel reserves, China should shift to renewable energies and more decentralised energy systems.

The stable energy supply through decentralised, renewable energy capacities and storage systems would imply positive outcomes on rural development, especially to industrial growth, e.g. through the establishment of town and villages enterprises (TVEs). The emergence of a rural service sector could also be feasible. These new off-farm employment opportunities could slow down the stream of migration from the currently underdeveloped regions to the big cities and enable a sustainable rural development. However, energy supply is only one aspect in this context. The State should take further measures, such as improvement in infrastructure, education, market access, and a rural credit system, that are essential for a stable rural development process. The stable supply of enough energy to rural villages in combination with the other factors could stimulate decentralised investment decisions to expand national development increasingly to rural regions. Although the State should be the coordinator of such a development, it has not to fulfil all tasks by itself. It should rather encourage the foundation of member-driven rural cooperatives that would not limit their actions to agriculture but could also take a leading role in the development of rural renewable energy organisations. Instead of becoming "floating" people, local agriculturists might build up their own future.

References

Bramall, Chris (2007): *The Industrialization of Rural China*, Oxford.

Bowlus, Audra J.; Sicular, Terry (2003): *Moving Toward Markets? Labor Allocation in Rural China*, in: Journal of Development Economics 71, 2, (August), p. 561–583.

Cai, Fang; Wang, Dewen; Du, Yang (2002): *Regional Disparity and Economic Growth in China. The Impact of Labor Market Distortions.* in: *China Economic Review* 13, 2-3, pp. 197-212.

Cherni, Judith A.; Kentish, Joanna (2007): *Renewable Energy Policy and Electricity Market Reforms in China*, in: Energy Policy 35, 7, (July), p. 3616-3629.

Cho, Keii (2004): *Present Situation of Power Supply and Demand in China*, in: IEEJ Energy Journal, March, online: http://eneken.ieej.or.jp/data/en/data/pdf/243.pdf (22 March 2010).

De Brauw, Alan; Rozelle, Scott (2008): *Migration and Household Investment in Rural China*, in: China Economic Review 19, 2, (June), p. 320–335.

Démurger, Sylvie; Gurgand, Marc; Shi, Li; Ximing, Yue (2009): *Migrants as Second-class Workers in Urban China? A Decomposition Analysis*, in: Journal of Contemporary Economics 37, 4, (December), p. 610-637.

Du, Yang; Park, Albert; Wang, Sangui (2005): *Migration and Rural Poverty in China*, in: Journal of Comparative Economics 33, 4, (December), p. 688-709.

Fan, Cindy C. (2008): *Migration, Hukou, and the City*, in: Yusuf, Shahid; Saich, Tony (ed.) (2008): *China Urbanizes. Consequences, Strategies, and Policies*, World Bank, Washington, p. 65-90.

Guo, Xiangyu; Schmit, Todd M.; Henehan, Brian M. (2008): *Rural Supply and Marketing Cooperatives in China. Historical Development, Problems, and Reform*, in: Journal of Rural Cooperation 36, 2, p. 157-174.

Intergovernmental Panel on Climate Change (IPCC) (2007): *Climate Change 2007. The Physical Science Basis*, Contribution of Working Group I to the Fourth Assessment Report of the IPCC, Cambridge.

International Energy Agency (IEA) (2007): *World Energy Outlook 2007.China and India Insights*, Paris.

International Energy Agency (IEA) (2009): *CO2-emissions from fuel combustion*, Paris.

Kanbur, Ravi; Zhang, Xiaobo (1999): *Which Regional Inequality? The Evolution of Rural-Urban and Inland-Coastal Inequality in China from 1983 to 1995*, in: Journal of Contemporary Economics 27, 4, (December), p. 686-701.

Kawakami, Tetsu (2004): *Structural Changes in China's Economic Growth During the Reform Period*, in: Review of Urban and Regional Development Studies 16, 2, (July), p. 133-153.

Lew, Debra J. (2000): *Alternatives to Coal and Candle. Wind Power in China*, in: Energy Policy 28, 4 (April), S. 271-286.

Li, Yong; Oberheitmann, Andreas (2009): *Challenges of Rapid Economic Growth in China. Reconciling Sustainable Energy Use, Environmental Stewardship and Social Development*, in: Energy Policy 37, 4, (April), p. 1412-1422.

Li, Zhimin; Tang, Runsheng; Xia, Chaofeng; Luo, Huilong; Zhong, Hao (2005): *Toward Green Rural Energy in Yunnan*, China, in: Renewable Energy 30, 2, (February), p. 99-108.

Ma, Hengyun; Oxley, Leslie T.; Gibson, John K. (2009): *China's Energy Situation and its Implication in the New Millennium*, Motu Economic and Public Policy Research Trust, Wellington (online: http://motu-www.motu.org.nz/wpapers/09_04.pdf).

Murphy, Rachel (1999): *Return Migrant Entrepreneurs and Economic Diversification in two Counties in South Jiangxi, China*, in: Journal of International Development 11, 4, (June), p. 661-672.

Murphy, Rachel (Hg.) (2009): *Labour Migration and Social Development in Contemporary China*, London.

Park, Albert (2008): *Rural-Urban Inequality in China*, in: Yusuf, Shahid; Saich, Tony (ed.) (2008): *China Urbanizes. Consequences, Strategies, and Policies*, World Bank, Washington, p. 41-64.

Ravallion, Martin; Chen, Shaohua (2007): *China's (Uneven) Progress against Poverty*, in: Journal of Development Economics 82, 1, (January), p. 1-42.

Rozelle, Scott; Guo, Li; Shen, Minggao; Hughart, Amelia; Giles, John (1999): *Leaving China's Farms. Survey Results of New Paths and Remaining Hurdles to Rural Migration*, in: China Quarterly 158, (June), p. 367-393.

Schaller, Sven (2008): *Cooperativas y el sector de energía en Brasil. Posibilidades para un cambio hacia sistemas renovables y descentralizados*, in: Contexto & Educação 80, (Juli/Dezember), p. 93-125.

Schaller, Sven (2009): *The Development of Rural Regions in the Third World on the Basis of Decentralized, Renewable Energy*, in: Harrisson, Denis; Széll, György; Bourque, Reynald (Hg.): *Social Innovation, the Social Economy and World Economic Development. Democracy and Labour Rights in an Era of Globalization*, p. 105-119.

Scheer, Hermann (2000): *Solare Weltwirtschaft. Strategie für eine ökologische Moderne*, München.

Shi, Dan (2009): *Analysis of China's Renewable Energy Development under the Current Economic and Technical Circumstances*, in: China and Word Economy 17, 2, (March-April), p. 94-109.

Shi, Xiaoping; Heerink, Nico; Qu, Futian (2009): *The Role of Off-farm Employment in the Rural Energy Consumption Transition. A Village-level Analysis in Jiangxi Province*, China, in: China Economic Review 20, 2, (June), p. 350-359.

Shiu, Alice; Lam, Pun-Lee (2004): *Electricity Consumption and Economic Growth in China*, in: Energy Policy 32, 1 (January), S. 47-54.

Swee-Hock, Saw; Wong, John (Hg.) (2008): *Regional Economic Development in China*, Singapore.

Taylor, J. Edward; Rozelle, Scott (2003): *Migration and Incomes in Source Communities. A New Economics of Migration Perspective from China*, in: Economic Development and Cultural Change 52, 1, (October), p. 75-101.

Tuñón, Max (2006): *Internal Labour Migration in China. Features and Responses*, ILO Paper, April, Beijing, online: http://www.ilo.org/public/english/region/asro/beijing/download/training/lab_migra.pdf

Voravate, Tuntivate; Barnes, Douglas F.; Bogach, V. Susan (2000): *Assessing Markets for Renewable Energy in Rural Areas of Northwestern China*, World Bank, Washington.

Wang, Shaoquang; Hu, Angang (1999): *The Political Economy of Uneven Development. The Case of China*, Armonk.

Wu, Kang; Li, Binsheng (1995): *Energy Development in China. National Policies and Regional Strategies*, in: Energy Policy 23, 2, (February), p. 167-178.

Yang, Dennis Tao (2002): *What Has Caused Regional Inequality in China*, in: China Economic Review 13, 4, (December), p. 331-334.

Yang, Yanlin; Chen, Yin-e; Liu, Zhizhing (2007): *Energy Constraints and China's Economic Development*, in: Journal of Economic Policy Reform 10, 4, (December), p. 343-354.

Yao, Shujie (2002): *China's Rural Economy in the First Decade of the 21st Century. Problems and Growth Contraints*, in: China Economic Review 13, 4, (December), p. 354-360.

Yusuf, Shahid; Nabeshima, Kaoru (2008): *Optimizing Urban Development*, in: Yusuf, Shahid; Saich, Tony (ed.) (2008): *China Urbanizes. Consequences, Strategies, and Policies*, World Bank, Washington, p. 1-40.

Yusuf, Shahid; Saich, Tony (ed.) (2008): *China Urbanizes. Consequences, Strategies, and Policies*, World Bank, Washington.

Xiliang, Zhang; Rong, Chen; Jiankun, He (2005): *Renewable Energy Development and Utilisation in China. Opportunities and Challenges*, in: International Journal of Global Energy Issues 24, 3/4, p. 249-258.

Zhang, Huafeng (2010): *The* Hukou *System's Constraints on Migrant Worker's Job Mobility in Chinese Cities*, in: China Economic Review 21, 1, (March), p. 51-64.

Zhou, Zhongren; Wu, Wenliang; Chen, Qun; Chen, Shufeng (2008): *Study on Sustainable Development of Rural Household Energy in Northern China*, in: Renewable and Sustainable Energy Reviews 12, 8, (October), p. 2227-2239.

Labour Rights, Seasonal Migrant Women Workers in Sugar Industry and Sustainable Development in India

W.N. Salve
Associate Professor in Economics, Shri. Venkatesh College, Ichalkaranji 416115
Affiliated to Shivaji University, Kolhapur (Maharashtra), India

Abstract

On March 8, as we celebrate International women's day in each year. We have a chance to take stock of both the progress we have made and the challenges that remain and to think about the vital role that women must play in helping to solve the complex global challenges of the 21st century. According to Hillary Clinton, USA, (Sunday Times of India, March8, 2009), Today, more women are leading governments, business, and non-governmental organizations. But that good news has a flipside. Women still comprise the majority of the world's poor, unfed and unschooled. They are still subjected to rape as tactic of war and exploited by traffickers globally in a billion-dollar criminal business. Even in developed nations, the full economic power of women is far from being realized. Women in many countries continue to earn much less than men for doing the same jobs. Hillary Clinton pointed out that women offered a vivid portrait of the challenges women faced, employment discrimination, inadequate healthcare, domestic violence, antiquated laws that hindered women's progress.

Women constitute a significant part of the workforce in India. However, the work participation rate of women is still very low.In1993-94 the percentage of women in the workforce was 28.6 against 54.5 for males. The work participation rate of women is low as compared to U.S.A.42.7 percent and Italy 53.8 percent. (Joshi, 1999).Besides, more than 90 percent of the total workforce of the country is engaged in the unorganized sector (Salve.2002). Of the total employment of women, they comprise only 4 percent of the organized sector, and 96 percent women are employed in the so called unorganized or informal sector, which is unorganized, non-unionized, low waged and with unhealthy almost inhuman working conditions. Forty percent of these workers, who earn less than male workers in India. The size of the unorganized sector has been rapidly increasing with liberalization polices. (Haither, 1998).The government of India has been adopted the new economic policy since 1991 under LPG policy i.e. Liberalization, privatization globalization. After globalization, women are able to get more jobs but their jobs are more casual in nature. India is the first among countries to give women equal franchise and has a highly credible record with regard to the enactment of laws to protect and promote the interests of women, but women continue to be denied economic, social and legal rights and privileges. Though they are considered to be equal partners in progress, yet they remain subjected to depression, marginalization and exploitation (Singh Kulwant, 2005).

It is necessary to know the status of unorganized Indian working women in the labour market. What is the present position of seasonal migrant women workers in the sugar industry?

Objectives of the study:

The study is based on the following objectives:-

- To know policy of decent work adopted by ILO for workers in the world economy.
- To discuss about labour rights and standards of the workers.
- To study about sustainable development for the unorganized migrant labour in India.
- To know present position of the unorganized seasonal migrant women workers in the sugar industry of India.

- To examine working conditions of migrant women workers and the existing welfare facilities.
- To suggest measures in order to improve the working conditions of seasonal migrant Women workers.

In this paper, an attempt has been made to discuss about labour rights, Seasonal Migrant Women Workers in Sugar Industry and Sustainable Development in India. However, an attempt is made to examine the present position of the unorganized seasonal migrant women workers in the sugar factories of Maharashtra state. The study is based on both primary and secondary data. Personal data was collected through personal interviews at the time of survey. Secondary data was collected through the published sources like books, Journals and Reports of the governments and non government organizations.

Content

Sugar Industry in India

The sugar industry is claimed to be the second largest in the Indian economy ,being next only to the cotton textile industry .Besides the sugar industry is primarily ago- based because of its using sugarcane as the raw material . The annual production is in the range of 300 to 350 million tons of sugarcane, out of which ,about 30 percent is used for gur and chewing purpose and the balance for producing during of 2006-07 was a little over 28 million tons .Second only to Brazils production of about 33 million tons .There are 450 sugar mills in India ,out of which over 60 percent are either in the co- operative or government sector and the balance of about 40 percent in the private sector. Over 50 million farmers and dependents as also a large number of agriculture labourers are involved in sugar cultivatition, harvesting and ancillary activities (Joshi, 2008, Sanyal Bhagriya, 2008).

Sugar Industry is a seasonal character, seasonal factory is one which normally works for more than half the days of the year. (Government of India, 1931) the main feature of nearly all the seasonal factories is that the workers are still essentially agriculturists and the great majority live in their homes. The workers are generally quite unorganized and wages to be low. (Government of India, 1931) .There are more than 450 sugar mills in the country. In Maharashtra, there were171 sugar factories in the year 2007-08, out of which, 145 were cooperatives and 26 private sugar factories.

Sustainable Development

In the 21st century, human society faces the various problems. The new relationship is the best defined by "Sustainability" a question that has been emerged from analysis of the regional and global trends in population, development and the environment .Sustainability implies meeting current human needs while preserving the environment and natural resources needed by future generations. The world's human population has recorded 6 billion and by 2050 is expected to reach nearly nine billion. Hence reducing hunger and poverty will be the primary challenge. Table 1 is showing Global poverty trends. It indicates about share of people living on less than $ 1 a day from 1981 to 2001.Therefore.it is necessary to use science and sustainable technologies for ensuring food security for the future. (Vayalar Ravi, 2006).

Table 1: Global poverty trends in a Nutshell
Share of people living on less than $1 (PPPUS) a day (%)

Region	1981	1990	1996	2001
East Asia & Pacific	56.7	29.5	15.9	14.3
Europe & Central Asia	0.8	0.5	4.4	3.5
Latin America & Caribbean	10.1	11.6	9.4	9.9
Middle East	5.1	2.3	2.0	2.4
South Asia	51.5	41.3	36.7	31.9

Sub Saharan Africa		44.5	46.1	46.4
World	40.4	27.9	22.3	20.7

Sources: Human Development Report, 2005, Piya Mahtaney, Reflection on global trends and Sustainable Development Forum of free Enterprise, May, October, 2005, P.P.-12

Table 2: Human Distress in India (Figures in million) in 2001

Population	Total
Illiterate adult	291
Children out of primary schools	45
People denied access to primary health care	135
People without basic sanitation facilities	640
Number of people living in slums	512
Malnourished children under the age of five	62
Population below poverty line	325
Starving population	50
Pregnant women aged between 15 and 49 suffer from anemia (%)	88
Child labour	(Nearly one third of children under 16 forced into child labour)

Sources: University News 36, March30, 1998. University News, April13, 1998.
Outlook No.36, September 17, 2001.

Table 2 is showing human distress in India regarding illiterate adults ,children out of primary school ,people denied access to primary health care, people without safe drinking water ,people living in slums, population below poverty line ,starving population, malnourished children under the age of five, child labour etc.As far as literacy rate is concerned; literacy rate of these communities indicates that even planned intervention has not improved the educational level of the weaker sections.

According to Das and Satapathy (2007), the concept of dictionary meaning of sustainability is the amount or degree to which the earth's resources may be exploited without deleterious effects. Sustainable development requires that population resources and environment and development be fully recognized and brought into harmonious, dynamic balance. It is interesting to note that the millennium declaration 2000 by heads of states of 189 countries in the millennium Development goals stressed on eight dimensions. The goals are to be achieved by 2015 and give on education, environment, health care and sustainable development.

Decent Work of labour

The word decent means accepted moral standards, decent work; it shows an acceptable quality of work. let us say, workers are pleasant at work places and they are satisfied from any type of work due to decent conditions of life as well as decent working conditions of labour.It shows various types of freedoms and rights for men, women and children in order to maintain dignity of human life in the society, in other words, development of society, workers, as per labour standards.

According to Reddy,(2005), Decent work refers to work wider than job or employment including wage employment, self employment and home working and is based on the core enabling labour standards vie, freedom of association, collective bargaining, freedom from discrimination and child labour. Besides, Rodgers (2001) observes that the word decent too involves some notion of the normal standards of society, lack of decent work therefore has something common with concepts of deprivation or exclusion, but of which concerned with social and economic situations, which do not meet social standards. Decent work is a broad concept which is related to overall development of the society and workers. Rodgers (2001) says that decent work is a way of capturing interrelated social and economic goals of development. Development involves the removal of unfreedoms such as poverty, lack of access to public infrastructures or the denial of civil rights. Decent work brings together different types of freedoms. Such as labour rights, social security, employment opportunities etc. Therefore, there are four dimensions of decent work, (i) work and employment itself (ii) rights at work (iii) security (iv) representative at work dialogue. The goal of decent work is based on sound ethical principles of ILO.The main goal of decent work is to promote opportunities for women and men to obtain decent and productive work in conditions of freedom, equity, security, and human dignity.Mishra (2001) pointed out position of the population in the global economy, about three billion people today live on less than 2 dollars a day. It means that half of the global population is not even close to a decent standard of living. More than a billion people do not have enough to eat every day.

Unorganized Workers

The National Commission on enterprises in the unorganized sector(2004) has adopted a definition of the broader definition of the unorganized or informal workers .The unorganized workers consist of those working in the unorganized sector or households excluding regular worker with social security benefits ,and the workers in the formal sectors without any employment and social security provided by employers (IJHD ,January,2007, July ,2007.) The share of unorganized workers in the Indian economy that stands at around a whopping 92 percent of the total worker force .The most important characteristic of informal employment, as far as the workers are concerned, is the absence of any form of protection. An overwhelming majority of them have no facility for covering such as risks as ill-health, accidents, death and old age (IJHD, January, 2007). After independence, the government of India has been adopted various labour policies and enacted various labour laws, commissions since first five year plan. The first National Commission on labour was constituted on December 24; 1966.The Commission submitted its report in August 1969 after examining the relevant issues for labour in both organized and unorganized sectors. The Second National Commission on labour, 2002 submitted its report to the prime minister on June 29, 2002. The Commission stressed the need for an expanded social security network in the country to take care of workers interests. (Sury, 2004).

Seasonal migrant workers in India

Let us take the example of Seasonal Migrant workers in the Maharashtra state. During the year 2000-01, there were 7.6 lakh seasonal sugar cane cutters in the 132 sugar factories of Maharashtra state .Besides, 58 thousand bullock carts and 16 thousand truck and tractors were engaged through Mukadam / head of labourers team and contractors in the sugar factories of the Maharashtra state. However, sugar factories engage contract basis seasonal migrant workers, male and female workers, agricultural labourers, sugarcane cutters cane transports, bullock cart through Mukadam and contractors for crushing seasons. During the years 2008-09, there are about 12 lakh sugar cane cutters and cane transporters in the Maharashtra state .The average duration of the crushing season in the sugar factories is varied from 150 to 180 days in India.

Each sugar factory provides employment nearly about 5000 to 6000 harvesting labourers for the period of crushing season. However, indirect employment depends upon the size of sugar mill. Besides; agricultural labour is an essential requirement of the sugar factory. The male and female seasonal workers are mainly drawn from the villages within the district and from other districts of the state or other states for crushing season of the sugar mills. Agricultural labourers are recruited through contractors and mukadam.The contractor or mukadam occupies a key position in the organization of contract work in each sugar factory.

Mukadams are classified into two categories viz, those who hire labour teams together with bullock carts and other hand, those who hire labour teams as sugarcane koytas consisting of 15 to20 workers in each team of workers of the sugar factory. Besides, there are two types of contract basis work patterns in organization of the sugar factory. (i) Work on premises of the sugar factory (ii) work done outside the premises or in the area of operation of the sugar factory.

Sugar industry offers immense potentialities for developing by-products industries. Sugar is the main product, molasses is a by-product, and bagasse, filter mud and ash are waste products. It was found from the paper mills in sugar factories of Kolhapur district that women workers were mainly employed on contract basis work for collecting of rag, wastage paper and cleaning process, carrying bagasse bales in the premises of the sugar factories.

Generally, crushing season starts from October month and lasts up to the end of March month, sugarcane harvesting work is done by contract basis male and female agricultural labourers and harvesting work is performed according to a tight schedule of the sugar factory. However, it can be said that on an average the trucks and bulluckcarts make one or two trips a day from long distances. Sugarcane cutter and bullockcartman families harvest sugarcane and transport it to the site of the sugar factory; they stay in groups on the site of sugarcane farm. Every cart man is accompanied by nearly three to four family members who perform the role of cutters, loaders, cart drivers etc. (Rangaswamy, 1974, Jan, 1978). Generally, koyta includes a husband, and his wife and family, grownup children for harvesting and transporting of sugarcane. So far as women workers are concerned, women workers also perform the role of cane cutters, loaders, bullockcartdrivers etc,the campaign is programmed on the cutting and transporting of a fixed tonnage per day. It is based on the premises that one koyta can cut about one tone a day and that the maximum load of a bullock cart and a lorry is one and a ten tones respectively.

Labour Rights

Let us discuss aspect of labour rights, which is concerned with decent work. Social security is a fundamental right of workers. Which is guaranteed by law to all human beings, who live their own labour and who find themselves unable to work temporarily or permanently for their control .In terms of social security, the first beginnings were made at the time of French Revolution when a Declaration of the Rights of man was proclaimed. It served as a preamble to the French Constitution of 1793.Which stated; inter-alia public assistance is a sacred duty (Singh, 1997). According to Article 22 of the Universal Declaration of Human Rights, every member of society has a right to social security. The ILO declaration on fundamental principles and rights at work is a major step in this direction. Development must bring about an improvement in the living conditions of people. It should, therefore, ensure the provision of basic human needs at all. (Nayar, 2003).

The international covenant on economic social and cultural Rights of the United Nations is another international instrument bestowing workers with economic social and cultural rights. So that they enjoying these rights of self determination can freely pursue their economic, social and cultural development (Shyamsundhar, 2004). The Indian Constitution (GOI, 1991) provides for citizenship rights in part II. Citizenship rights are regarded as fundamental, because they are most essential for the attainment by the individual of his full intellectual moral and spiritual status. The guarantee of the minimum rights at the workplace will enable people to claim and realize a fair share of the wealth. The guarantee of these rights will ensure a process of translating economic growth into social equality. The development thus becomes synonymous with the agenda of integrated development. (Mishra, 2001).

According to the Directive Principles of State Policy of the Indian Constitution,(GOI 1991) The state is required to secure for the citizens ,both men and women to right to an adequate means of livelihood, 'equal pay for equal work for both men and women' protection against abuse and exploitation of worker's , economic necessity, protection of their health and strength, to secure for children opportunities and facilities to develop in a healthy manner and in conditions of freedom and dignity and protect children and a youth against exploitation and moral and material abandonment. The state is also required to secure equal justice and free legal aid, to make effective provisions for right to work, to education and to public assistance incases of undeserved want, to ensure just and human conditions of work and maternity relief, to secure work, a living wage and a decent standard of life to participation of workers in the management of industries.

However, citizenship rights are essential for the development of the citizens of the country. According to Thorat (2008),in complete citizenship or denial of civil rights (freedom of expression, rule of law, right to justice) political rights (right and means to participation in the exercise of political power),and socio-economic rights (right to property, employment, and education) are key dimensions of an impoverished life. Besides, Mishra (2001), states that we need to recognize that the right to move freely from one part of the territory of a country to another or one part of the globe to another is a basic right which should not be denied to workers.

The International Labour Organization (ILO) has played a significant role in promoting International Labour Standards. (ILS's).The ILO has formulated international labour standards at various conferences.

On International Women's Day, (IWD) India presents contrasting picture, while millions are shackled to a life of poverty and deprivation, others are going places where no woman has gone before. There are 61 women MP's (Member of Parliament) in the Loksabha or Parliament of India, out of a possible 543.Besides, out of 617 High Court Judges, in the country, only 45 are women, there is not a single woman judge in the Supreme Court. However, the present position of backward class' women's is worst in terms Judges and MP and other posts in India.55 of the 1000 girls born every year don't live beyond their first birthday and 77 per 1000 births don't live beyond the age of 5, this is the present position of women's in India.(The Times of India, March 8.2010).

We celebrate International Women's Day at the International level .The first National Women's Day (NWD) is observed across the united States on February, 1909.In 1913, International Women's Day (IWD) is moved to March 8 and this has remained the World's date with women ever since. More than one million women and men attend IWD Rallies campaigning for women's rights to work, vote, be trained, hold public office and be discriminated against no more.

So far as women's reservation Bill in India is concerned, it become clear the women's Reservation bill was brought to the Rajya Sabha on March 8, 2010, the 100th anniversary of international women's Day. Congress President Sonia Gandhi gave highest importance to the bill, which seeks to reserve 33% seats for women in the Loksabha and Sate Legislatures .For India, if the bill becomes law, it will set in turn one of the largest exercises in female empowerment any where in the world. However, it is necessary to observe the present position of backward classes' women's in India. But, how important is international women's day for the ordinary woman at work, at home, on city streets and in the villages. According to Insiya Amir, (The Times of India, March 8, 2010), There are still as many cases of rape as before. Domestic violence still goes largely unprotected. Women continue to be tortured, burned or murdered for dowry. Women can't reasonably expect to travel around most Indian cities alone late at night. It remains hard to find recommendation if you are a single woman, or worse, a single mother. The flipside is the need to dedicate one day to a basic truth, women are equal to men and should be treated accordingly. They need to know their rights and duties so that they can make the best choices. The Chief Minister of Uttar Pradesh state, Mayawati said that the Womens's reservation bill was against Dalit icon, Dr.B.R. Ambedkar's ideology of empowering women from all sections of society. " Dr.Babasaheb Ambedkar, the chief architect of the constitution of India, wanted empowerment of women from all sections of society, but the bill wouldn't benefit women from SC,ST,OBC, religious minorities and upper caste poor" said Mayawati, while addressing a meeting on Saturday, 27 March,2010.(The Times of India,March,30,2010).The party plans to hold the protests at the tehsil level and has asked its leaders to educate people about the "flaws" in the bill, which envisages 33% reservation for women in the legislature. Mayawati said the Bahujan Samaj Party (BSP) wasn't against the reservation, but wanted a sub-quota for the women from the weaker sections of the society. Mayawati said, Congress forced Dr. B.R. Ambedkar to sign the Poona pact under which Dalits had to give up the demand for separate electorate and agree to reservation of seats in the Legislative bodies. "The Hindu Code Bill drafted by Dr. Babasaheb Ambedkar as Union law Minister of India in the Prime Minister, Pundit Jawaharlal Nehru's Cabinet after Independence provided many rights to Hindu women, but he forced to resign following Stiff opposition by Congress leaders," she said.

Wage Rates

So far as wage rates of males and females are concerned, it was observed that women workers are paid lower wages than male workers in certain operations. Representatives of trade union of sugar factories reported that this difference on this count is mainly due to the difference in the capacity of the male and female workers to perform certain operations like bagasse bailing work in premises of the sugar factory. Therefore, it should be noted that the 'principle of equal pay for equal work' is not also strictly adhered to the fixation of wage rates for contract basis male and female seasonal migrant workers in the sugar factories as per the Equal Remuneration Act of 1926.The Act extends to whole of India and it is applicable to all establishments employing ten or more workers. The Act makes it obligatory on the part of the employers.

i) To pay equal remuneration to men and women for same work of similar nature and,
ii) To prevent discrimination against reduction in wages of any worker as a result of this legislation.

Salve (1990), pointed out that wage rates paid to contract basis male and female seasonal migrant workers in sugar factories found to be lower than wage rates paid to agricultural labourers in Maharashtra state and others states in India. (Joshi,1988).Vikhe Patil committee in Maharashtra State (Patil,1988) recommended insurance policy of Rs.3000/ for social security of farm workers, equal wages to male and female, work of eight hours with a break of an holidays with wages. The committee also recommended that the revision of wages should be done on the basis of dearness index. Such type of provisions of the minimum wages Act have not been still applied to contract basis seasonal migrant workers in the surveyed sugar factories of the Maharashtra .

Washing Facilities

The Factories Act of 1948, 1963, makes it obligatory on the employer to provide washing bathing facilities for workers. According to the contract labour Act of 1970,

i) In every establishment coming within the scope of the Act the contractors shall provide and maintain adequate and suitable facilities for washing for the use of contract labour employed their in.
ii) Separate and adequate screening facilities shall be provided for the male and female workers.

It was observed that washing and bathing facilities were totally absent for contract labour, where they did exist, other accessories for bathing were missing. Besides; it was found that more than 15 women workers were engaged in the premises of each sugar factory in the Kolhapur district of Maharashtra state for the contract basis work such as bagasse, bailing bagasse and carrying boiler ash etc.

Latrines and Urinals

So far as latrines and urinals are concerned, it was observed from surveyed sugar factories in Kolhapur district that latrines and urinals facilities were not existed for contract basis workers in the premises of the sugar factories. Besides, some sugar factories had made arrangements to erect temporary type of urinals with help of mats, which were not suited to provide them privacy, no water taps in or near the temporary urinals were found in the premises of the sugar factories. (Salve, 1990).

Crèches

As children are the future citizens of the nation. Child care in the crèche is not only benefits the working mothers but it is a definite benefit to the nation. (Moorthy, 1968, Sharma, 1981). As a result of the Factories Act of 1948, it becomes obligatory for all factories employing more than 50 women workers to maintain a crèche of a prescribed standard. According to Maharashtra contract labour Rules of 1971 (25) (vi) (a) In every establishment, where twenty or more women are ordinarily employed as contract labour, they shall be provided and maintained by the contractor a room or rooms for the use of children under the age of six years as may be required by the commissioner of labour and the standard of construction scale of accommodation and the facilities shall be such as may be specified by the commissioner of labour. Therefore, the provision of a crèche of prescribed standard is a statutory obligation in factories and other contract basis work employing 20 women. At the time of survey, it was found that (Salve,1990),none of the surveyed sugar factories had provided as such type of crèche facilities to cane harvesting women workers/working mothers in the sugar factories. It was observed that most of the children below the age of six years were found in sugar cane fields along with working women. Where binding sugarcane bundles were spread in cane field, children were trailing behind their working mothers. Infants were generally leftover a piece of cloth or sack under the shade of tree or a seasonal plant in sugarcane fields.Sometimes,they have to erect temporary crèches by binding three sticks/plant sticks together for the purpose of infants crèches in the sugarcane fields.

Medical Facilities

From women workers point of view, the major shortcoming detected in the existing medical facilities was the absence of qualified lady doctors in almost all surveyed sugar factories. Women workers who are, by and large, illiterate, feel shy of consulting male doctors especially in female diseses.Facilities for pre-natal and post-natal treatment were also inadequate and need to be improved.

Maternity Relief

In the case of illness arising out of pregnancy, delivery, miscarriage women workers, none of the surveyed sugar factories had provided medical facilities to women workers in pre natal and post natal stages. It was observed that pregnant women workers were found to be suffering from sickness like toxemia, nutritional anemia, trichomoniais etc. (Government of India 1958). It has been observed that factory owners and contractors allegedly exploit the women workers by paying them low wages. If a contractor thinks that a pregnant woman can not work to his satisfaction; she is retrenched without any retrenchment benefit. Sometimes, she is retrenched without even her full wages. (Manushi Journal, 1984).

Therefore, she works up to the day of delivery and goes back to work soon after; having no rest or care .This violation of the maternity Benefit Act goes unchallenged because there is no strong organization of contract basis male and female seasonal migrant workers in Maharashtra state.

Conclusion

After having known all the facts of contract basis male and female Seasonal migrant workers in the Surveyed Sugar Factories in India, it may be noted that these workers are unable to enjoy labour welfare facilities.

Even they do not get any of the minimum benefits according to laws viz.,The Factory Act,1948,.The Contract labour Act ,1970,Directive principles of state policy of the Indian Constitution, Human rights of UNO.It has been observed that the work of these seasonal migrant labourars may be agricultural, Industrial or some kinds of unskilled casual labour, they migrate from one Taluka to another taluka, or from one district to another district and even from one state to another for seasonal work in sugar factories in India. They migrate from drought prone areas through contractors and mukadam in the sugar factories for seasonal works. It was found that lower castes seasonal workers had almost migrated in large number in comparison with higher castes workers in surveyed sugar factories. Most of male and female workers belonged to scheduled castes and scheduled tribes, Craftsman, village artisans as well as socially economically lower caste group's workers. It should be noted here, that the propensity to migrate is more among scheduled castes and scheduled tribes workers due to the poverty and absence of productive assets in their native places. It has been observed that these migrant women workers are illiterate, ignorant and belong to schedule castes and scheduled tribe's community. They were not aware of their rights about labour welfare amenities available to them like education of workers children, medical, maternity benefits, provident funds, Employees state insurance scheme, crèche and others. How and when would be used these benefits to seasonal migrant unorganized women workers in the sugar factories of Maharashtra state as well as in other states in India.

It should be noted here that none of the sugar factories had provided labour welfare facilities to contract basis seasonal migrant male and female workers under social security scheme. These contract basis seasonal workers are migrated through contractors, who live under the deplorable conditions due to the illiteracy, ignorance and poverty and consequent to pitiable conditions. They do not know the constitutional provisions of the Indian constitution of India. The voice of the poor, are not heard or ignored, they are still in the shackles of poverty, illiteracy, bounded labour, ill health, blind beliefs, customs and manners .How to change this situation of working women today in the globalization era. Seasonal migration has not been beneficial to male and female workers, they have to face various problems such as inadequate earnings, health, education, the lack of bargaining power, absence of legal protection etc. It is necessary to implement various labour laws in order to improve the status of women workers in the labour market today. Unfair labour practices in the contract labour system should be abolished. Temporary or mobile crèches at the working places for the breast-fed babies and the infants of working mothers in cane harvesting, bailing bagasse and other works should be provided by each sugar factory. Women doctors should be employed for confinements in and child welfare work. The Minimum wages Act of 1948 should be extended to cover contract basis seasonal agricultural labourers, and contract labour in premises of the sugar factory in respect of hours of work, break the rest, leave and holidays, minimum wages, insurance policy, social security, equal wages for male and female for same work. Uniform standards, policies and procedures should be needed in all sugar factories to enable seasonal contract basis service to work as a well-knit and co-coordinated organization throughout the country.

Migrant women workers means, those workers, who migrate from one area to another area within the state or country in order to get seasonal or temporary or part time work in different sectors. Migrant workers, who are not organized under any trade unions and their labour standards, are not protected by the government as well as trade unions, these migrant workers are illiterate, ignorant, and belong to backward community .They do not get minimum wages stipulated under the Minimum wages Act. Today, the real issue is how to extend human rights to all segments of the labour market. There are many groups of workers in the unorganized sector or informal economy, like migrant workers in agriculture, building and road construction, brick kilns, sugar factories and others, for whom decent work is a very distant goal.

There are no strong trade unions of migrant workers in the unorganized sector. The bargaining power of these migrant workers is thus weaker than workers in the organized sector. After independence, India has been adopted various labour policies in order to improve working conditions of workers in the unorganized sector. There are also various labour laws for these workers. In fact, its implementation is mostly ineffective. Therefore, migrant workers and workers in the unorganized sector are struggling for their rights of workers and to implement the provisions of various labour laws as per International labour standards. Uniform labour standards in the context of unorganized sector workers, like migrant workers, should be implemented in rural and urban areas of India. It is necessary to protect migrant women workers and other workers in the unorganized sector by International labour standards as per principles of ILO.

References

Das and Satapathy (2007), "Education for sustainable development University News", No 49, December.

GOI, (1991), Our Rights and Duties two sides of the same Coin, Ministry of Information and Broadcasting, printing, Government of India, Calcutta.

Government of India (1931), Report of the Royal commission on Labour, .Govt. Press. Calcutta,

Government of India (1958), pure water for the villages, Govt .publications. New Delhi,

Government of Maharashtra, (1985) The Central Labour Regulation and Abolition Act, 1970, Rules, 1971, Govt.Central press. Bombay,

Government of Maharashtra, (1966) The Factories Act 1948 and the Maharashtra Factories Rules, 1963, Govt. Central Press. Bombay

Hillary Clinton (2009) invests in Women beat downturn, Sunday Times of India, March 8, 2009.

Haider Saraswati, (1998), All Women's Political party launched in UP, Economic and Political Weekly, No .8.

Insiya Amir,(2010),International Women's Day, The times of India ,March8,2010

Jan, Bremasn (1978), Seasonal migration and cooperative Capitalism, Economic and political weekly Vol.No. 31, 32, 33, August.

Joshi, A.V. (1988), Agricultural Wages in India, Economic and Political Weekly, Vol.No.26, June.

Joshi Sharad., (2008), Sugar Issues, Yojana, April.

Joshi Vasant (1999), Book Review, Human rights and working Women, Yojana, (Marathi).Vol.No.1.

Mishra Lakshmidhar (2001), Can Globalization and Labour Rights co-exist? The Indian Journal of Labour Economics , Vol.44 No.1 January -March.

Moorthy, M.V. (1968), Principles of labour Welfare, Gupta Brothers. Vishakapattam

Nayar Deepak (2003), Work, livelihoods and Rights, The Indian Journal of Labour Economics, Vol .46 No.1, January –March.

Patil, R.B. (1988), Minimum Wages for farm Workers in Maharashtra, Rural India, Vol.No.52. September.

Piya Mahtaney (2005): "Reflections on Global trends and Sustainable Development" Forum of Free Enterprise, May-October, Mumbai.

Rangaswamy Amrita, (1974), Maharashtra Contractors Opera, Economic and Political Weekly, February, 2.

Reddy Narasimha (2005), Challenges of Decent Work in the Globalizing Word, The Indian Journal of labour Economics, Vol.48 No.1, January –March.

Rodgers Gerry (2001), Decent work as a Development Objective, The Indian Journals of labour Economics, and Vol .44 No.1, January -March.
Salve, W.N. (1990), A Socio-economic Study of seasonal migrants in the Co-operative sugar factories with special reference to Kolhapur district, un published Ph.D. Thesis of Shivaji University, Kolhapur.
Salve,W.N.(2002),The Status and position of Indian working Women, S.Murthy, (ed. 2002),Women Work Participation and Empowerment, problems and prospects.RBSA ,publishers,Jaipur.
Sanyal N.B,Bhagria R.P,.Ray SC(2008), Indian Sugar Industry,Yojana,April.
Sharma, A.M., (1981), Aspects of labour Welfare and Social Security, Himalaya Publishing House limited, Bombay
Shyamsundhar K.R. (2004), The Issue of Right to Strike, Report on Four Consultations, The Indian Journals of labour Economics, New Delhi.
Singh kulwant, (2005) Globalization and employment status of women in India. V.subbulakshmi, (ed. 2005) Globalization Indian experience, ICFAI, University press, Hyderabad.
Singh Parduman (1997), Social Security Systems in Developing Countries, Friedrich Ebert Stiftung, New Delhi.
Sury, S.S. (2004), Indian economy in the 21st century, New Century Publications, New Delhi
Thorat Sukhadeo (2008), Labour Market Discrimination Concept ,forms and remedies in the Indian Situations, The Indian Journal of Labour Economics, Vol.51, No.1,January- March.
Vayalar Ravi, (2006). "Knowledge and Sustainable Development". University News, No.51, December.

Journals

Manushi No 23, 1984.
University News 36, March 30, 1998.
University News, April13, 1998.
Outlook No.36, September 17, 2001.
Indian Journals of Human Development, (Documentation on NCEOS, Report) volume 1 Number 1,January, 2007, Number 2, July, 2007
The Times of India, March 8, 2010
The Times of India,March30,2010

Chapter 5:
Informal Employment, Social Security and Social Sustainability

Voluntary Poverty and the Moral Economics of Development: The Gandhian Paradigm

Anup Dash , Utkal University, Bhubaneswar (Orissa), India

Abstract

The deepening civilizational crisis has already brought us to the point of structurally irreversible limits. As the great lessons from the 20th century teach us, it seems impossible that we can solve the problems of development, environment, human security and social peace through application of conventional wisdom by making simple "make shift" policy changes at the global level or merely changing the "forms" in the dominant paradigm. Therefore, as we enter into the 21st century, we ought to search for answers beyond the Capitalist-Socialist divide, or the State-Market dichotomy in a globalized world. Essentially, both are two different faces of the same paradigm of violence – based on violence of man by man and violence of nature by man. At the root of this paradigm is the acquisitive, self-seeking, utility-maximizing, atomistic, instrumentally rational, and anthropocentric *homo oeconomicus*. In our search for another world, we ought to look for radical alternatives to this very foundation of the present paradigm, and build up an agenda for a peaceful social transformation through a human revolution. Against this backdrop, this paper examines the Gandhian Paradigm of Non-Violent social transformation as an alternative to create a sustainable society, ensuring human wellbeing at the micro level and peace at the macro level, through a moral transformation of the anthropological monster, the *homo oeconomicus*.

Content

The Wall Street Model in Crisis

With the fall of the Berlin Wall in 1989 and the subsequent collapse of the Socialist empire, the long ideological battle between laissez faire and dirigisme was globally believed to be over. Market fundamentalists celebrated the "ultimate victory" of the Wall Street model of the economy. But, barely twenty years on, in 2008, had the Wall Street become bankrupt. The financial crisis, which led to the most severe global recession since the Great Depression, damaged the global economy, and brought it under terrible stress with "cracks in the system". The "Wall Street Model" failed yet once again. While the causes and the magnitude of the crisis, its consequences, and strategies for its prevention in future continue to be the center of intense public debate, and as governments try hard to recover from it, we now realize that some of the basic "truths" on which market fundamentalists base their arguments are too naïve and fatally flawed. The events leading to the global crisis do confirm that market can not be left to itself, and we need in-built devices within the system to ensure macroeconomic stability. The economy needs regulation, management, and intervention. The Keynesian view of the macro relationships between the market and the government broadly held sway in most western countries up until the 1980s when Milton Friedman questioned the efficiency and the ability of the (already failing) governments to deliver public goods, and championed the ideology of market fundamentalism. The recent global crisis has once again brought Keynes back to the center of public policy. We have turned back again to the "Big Government" – not only for a rapid economic recovery through "bail out" and stimulus packages, but also as the "Lender of Last Resort" for regaining public confidence in the economy.

Clearly, the crisis has shown the limits of the current regulatory and supervisory frameworks. The challenge is therefore to design new rules and institutions that reduce systemic risks. Corporate gurus emphasize the need for the introduction of more stringent regulations, stronger risk management, and better board oversight with a robust consolidated supervision framework as the bottom line for the global corporate governance. While there are serious efforts to re-engineer the economy by incorporating the above elements into the grand architecture of the speculative financial market – prone to naturally occurring ponzi processes – so as to contain the "greed" in the system that drove the run up to the Wall Street crisis, the present paper argues that the present model is itself flawed, based on distorted logic and we need to rethink the economic paradigm itself. As David Korten (2009) says, "[t]his crisis may be our best chance to build a New Economy" – a new economy "that puts money and business in the service of people and the planet", not the other way around.

The celebration of the present economic model and its mantra of "growth" mask the fact that a "phantom-wealth" economy is unsustainable. Illusory assets based on financial bubbles, abuse of the power of the banks to create money from nothing, corporate asset stripping, baseless credit ratings, manipulative accounting, and the predatory behaviour led to the financial breakdown (ibid.). The Current proposal which are advanced for dealing with the economic crisis fall far too short, leaving the deep conflict of values and interests at the core of the current system untouched. Therefore, in our search for answers to the present crisis, we need to deepen the debates, and question the very foundations of the present paradigm and the economic logic that drives it The answer to the problems created by the market is certainly not more market, nor can solutions to these problems be found within the market economy, we need to search for answers to these problems outside the market economy.

Wealth vs. Wellbeing: The "Easterlin Paradox"

No doubt, the new capitalist economy today has enormous capacity for wealth creation. The "New Economy" today produces enormous global prosperity. Globally, we produce more wealth, more food, and more consumer goods. Average disposable income has significantly increased in recent years. The World Bank's World Development Indicators recorded the world GDP In 1960 at US$1.35 trillion. By the year 2000, it rose to US$ 32 trillion; and within a span of eight years it had again nearly doubled crossing US$61 trillion in 2008, thanks to the "New Enlightenment" – market-led globalization as the road to prosperity. But, with all this "new wealth", we don't experience greater happiness. Happiness and Wellbeing research has proved economists wrong. The literature on the happiness and wellbeing research in the developed countries shows discrepancies between income measures and reported (subjective) measures of wellbeing (Graham, 2005). Layard (2005) concludes his study in his book on Happiness that over the last fifty years Western man has failed to find greater happiness despite remarkable growth in material prosperity. The single minded obsession to earn more has led to deterioration in things that are really more important for human happiness: stable families, job satisfaction and quality of working life, good relations with friends and neighbors, healthy communities – all of which are so obvious from the growing statistics on divorce, work-related stress, crime, and suicide. Veenhoven's longitudinal study on happiness over the world shows that the correlation between money and happiness is extremely weak. People, who get more money, experience an instant but very short-lived sense of happiness which vanishes quickly. He discovers a clear difference between the developed and developing countries – in the latter an increase in income leads to a greater and more lasting feeling of happiness than in the developed countries. This difference disappears when the per capita GDP exceeds a level between 20,000 and 25,000 dollars (2009). Earlier research in this area, pioneered by Richard Easterlin, confirms that the average happiness levels do not increase as countries grow wealthier or as people become richer – widely known as the "Easterlin Paradox".

The new (global) economy, highly efficient as it is in terms of wealth creation, produces ever growing global prosperity, but also creates a serious social divide. In 2005, the Forbes recorded the number of officially known billionaires in the world at 691, which increased to 793 in 2009; and within the next one year (2010) another 218 world celebrities joined the billionaires' club. But, alongside this growth in affluence (of the few), poverty and inequality are also growing alarmingly. Almost half of the population of the world (2.8 billion) is poor living with less than $2 a day, of whom1.2 billion live in conditions of extreme poverty and misery unable to earn even $1/day. They are mostly concentrated in Sub-Saharan Africa and South Asia, but poverty, unemployment, and social exclusion are also growing as problems in the developed North. We have today a world order structured around the Pareto Law. 20% of the world's population enjoys 80% of the world's wealth. One-fifth of the global population monopolizes four-fifth of its resources. We live in a "one-fifth society".

But, poverty is not just material or economic, we should emphasize its plurality and speak of poverties (Max-Neef, et.al.,1989: 21): poverty of subsistence (due to insufficient income, food, shelter etc.), poverty of protection (due to bad health, violence, arms race etc.) , poverty of affection (due to authoritarianism, oppression, exploitative relation with the natural environment etc.), poverty of understanding (due to lack of education), poverty of participation (due to marginalization and discrimination), poverty of identity (due to cultural hegemony, imposition of alien values, forced migration, political exile etc.). Again, these are not just different forms of poverty, they are much more than that – each of them generates their own pathologies and brings painful miseries. Obviously, as a result, human misery is on the rise everywhere, so much that many social scientists now use the "Human Misery Index" to evaluate the present growth-centric process of development. Deepening poverty, growing inequality, social exclusion, disintegration, unemployment, loss of livelihoods, hunger, and the resultant increase in crime, violence, terrorism etc. add new dimensions to the growing problem of human security. Human security has become a major issue all over the world, as the people across countries feel more and more vulnerable to the complex of interrelated threats associated with civil war, genocide, and displacement of the populations. But, the problem of insecurity is far greater than just war, genocide, crime, violence and terrorism, because threats of insecurities are strongly associated with poverty, lack of State capacity, and various forms of socio-economic and political inequality as well as disasters – both natural and man-made. As the Commission on Human Security, in their 2003 report, Human Security Now argue, the threat agenda should be broadened to include hunger, disease, natural disasters because these kill far more people than war, genocide, and terrorism combined. Thus, there is now a serious policy debate as achieving human security (understood both as "freedom from fear" and "freedom from want") poses growing challenges for State institutions.

Therefore the French President Nicholas Sarkozy, unsatisfied by the present GDP-centric system of measurement of economic performance and progress, set up a Commission in 2008 on the Measurement of Economic Performance and Social progress (CMEPSP, with Joseph Stiglitz as its President and Amartya Sen as the advisor) with the aim to identify the limits of GDP as an indicator of development and assess more relevant alternatives. As the Commission observe, with excessive focus on the GDP metrics, those "attempting to guide the economy and our societies are like pilots trying to steering a course without a reliable compass" (2008: 9). The unifying theme and a key message of this report is that "the time is ripe for our measurement system to shift emphasis from measuring economic production to measuring people's well-being. And measures of well-being should be put in the context of sustainability" (p.12, emphasis in original). Wellbeing, as the goal of economic activities, ought to be at the center of development. Wellbeing is multi-dimensional, and is deeply embedded not merely in the material-physical but also (and even more powerfully) in the emotional-psychic, social-relational and moral-spiritual levels of our existence. These different dimensions reinforce each other and need to be considered simultaneously with a composite index of objective as well as subjective wellbeing of the people. On a broader scale, the European Commission, realizing the inadequacies of the GDP-centric approach to meet the present challenges, recently organized a conference on "Beyond GDP" (together with the European Parliament, the Club of Rome, the WWF and the OECD) with a purpose to evolve improved indicators by incorporating environmental and social issues to reflect the new political and technical context, which may contribute to setting new strategic goals for the post-2010 Lisbon Strategy (Commission of the European Communities, 2009).

With the growth in the standard of living, social values are breaking down. Family as an institution is collapsing with serious consequences for the social and emotional wellbeing of the people. A growing number of children do not live with both parents, divorce rates are reaching alarming proportions, various forms of child abuse and torture, teen age pregnancy, problems of drug addiction and suicide, the rising levels of crime and violence are no longer isolated cases of "deviance" in our (otherwise normal) society; but are hard facts of a morally eroding and disintegrating society – which we feel in our very bones in everyday life. There is a growing deficit of trust in our social life, an erosion of values as well as an institutional decline. These are the "unintended social consequences" of an economy which is spreading its "wings" to go global without any moral "roots". Economic expansion equals to Social recession. Market is inversely related to morality. The more we live in the world of objects, the more we destroy the world of relationships, the less we belong to ourselves. This is the paradox, the zero-sum relationship between, what Erich Fromm (1976) described as "To Have" and "To Be". The homo oeconomicus is eating into the homo humanis, their relationship has been made zero-sum.

The immoral basis of "Eco-no-mics"

In the same way, the relationship between Economy and Ecology is also zero-sum. The greenhouse effect, the ozone layer, pollution, and depletion are the results of the paradigm which does not take into account the goods and services provided by the natural ecosystem. The overall success, if any, of this paradigm is, in fact, dependant on externalizing the costs of the environmental destruction they produce. The earth's economy as a whole is collapsing without fertile soil, fresh water, clean air, and an amenable climate, driving us towards an ecological bankruptcy and a resultant rise in human misery.

This has brought the question of sustainability to the center of debate as we move closer and faster to the natural "limits" of growth, both in environmental and social terms. In 1960, mankind's global footprint (a measure of the pressure human activity exerts on the resources of the earth) was only 40 per cent of the earth's capacity to renew itself. Today it has reached 140 per cent. Since the late 1970s humanity has been in ecological overshoot with the annual demand on resources exceeding what the earth can regenerate each year, and today we use the equivalent of 1.4 planets to provide the resources we consume and absorb the waste we produce. It now takes the earth one year and five months to regenerate what we use in a year, thanks to the "magic of growth" (Global Footprint Network, 2010). As the Indian management advisor Arun Maira says, "[w]e are no longer living off the earth's revenue account. We are eating into its capital" (2008:14). Overshoot is a serious threat to human wellbeing and the health of the planet, which has been underestimated by development planners under the monopoly of the neo-classical economics.

The recent global initiative, known as The Millennium Ecosystem Assessment, in its effort to document the contribution of ecosystems to human wellbeing, has calculated and put a price tag of US$ 33 trillion a year (nearly twice the value of the global GNP) on these fundamental ecosystem services, which are taken for granted because we get them free from nature. Thus for example, the cycling of essential nutrients like nitrogen and phosphorus in soil formation, which is never reflected in any nation's GNP, accounts for US$ 17 trillion of these US$33 trillion in annual ecosystem services. Similarly ecosystem services like pollination and carbon storage is assigned a monetary value of US$ 400 billion. These are only approximations, as acknowledged by the research team, but we think that it is better to give a rough estimate than to say these things are worth nothing. They do point to a very important aspect of our current process of development and its vulgar economism. Imagine that if we were to buy these services from nature, we would have to pay US$33 trillion a year to produce a global GNP of US$ 18 trillion!! (Costanza, et. al. 1997:259; quoted in World Resources Institute, 1998). This is the environmental cost of our development; add to it the social costs inherent in this process of environmental degradation. This is the "cost-benefit" analysis of our development. Would any economist advising policies and planning for development call it "efficient" and "rational"? And, with ecosystem degradation, these costs are sharply rising, because our development planning is rapidly eating into the stock of the natural capital. The earth's ecological infrastructure, the global commons, and the public goods – the very foundation of our life and wellbeing – do not enter into the current economic standards of calculation of profit and loss and thus seriously distorts our balance sheets of development. "More Growth", the economists and planners keep saying, is the answer to solve all our problems. The truth, however, is that growth is not the answer, but is itself the very cause of these problems.

The homo oeconomicus: an Anthropological Monster

The ideological roots of the centrality of money and monetary standards, the assumptions behind the logic of growth as well as the epistemological foundation of the Rational Choice theory, the ontological basis of the homo oeconomicus are all too naïve and misplaced. At the root of the present economic system is to be found the homo oeconomicus – the building block of the huge edifice of capitalism, its micro foundation. S/he is autonomous, instrumentally rational, psychologically self-sufficient, "under socialized" and motivated into action by the utilitarian principle of maximizing pleasure. Insofar as man is under constant fear of not getting enough of what he wants, or of losing what he already possesses, the meaning of homo oeconomicus reduces to an anxiety-ridden hunt for pleasure. Social order is the result of either a deliberate contract among these "free-standing" individuals or a natural result of 'the invisible hand". Emphasis on self-interest and maximization as prime movers of human action governed by the principle of competition strip the homo oeconomicus of any morality and substantive rationality. The homo oeconomicus is a "a kind of anthropological monster" (Bourdieu,1997:61), who has learnt that the way to prosperity is to impoverish the others, and who gets bigger and meaner, dominating more and more our cultural life.

A fundamental problem with the concept of homo oeconomicus is its underlying assumption of the linearity of human needs. Human needs are better understood through a systemic approach – the dynamics of which does not obey hierarchical linearity (Max-Neef, et.al. op. cit: 44). Unlike the linear approach, no need is per se more important than any other, nor is there a fixed order of preference in the actualization of human needs. Simultaneities, complementarities and trade offs are key features of the system's behaviour. When the possibilities of satisfying the subsistence needs are severely impaired, all other needs remain blocked, and a single drive prevails intensely. But this is also equally the case with other needs. For example, the total lack of affection, or the loss of identity, may lead people to the extremes of self-destruction.

Atomistic individuals, self-interests, competitive and calculative rationality, accumulation and expansion as goals, all add up to corrupt the substantive rationality of social institutions, erode the moral foundation of the society, fail as a means to provide for human needs, and create conditions of dangerous social irresponsibility. Many social critics advance the theory of performativity – to argue that economics as a discipline (through its conceptual tools) has shaped the world of (global) corporate capitalism the way it has emerged with its "unacceptable face". Thus, E.F.Schumacher, in his foreword to a book on the Gandhian idea of Trusteeship, very eloquently writes: " If you want a good society, you must appeal to the goodness that is in people, to provoke it, stimulate it, to take it for granted, and acclaim it . . . The more we assume that economics and politics are about nothing else than gain and power, the more this becomes true, and the better instincts of the people are being suppressed instead of encouraged"(quoted in Diwan and Lutz, eds. 1985:p.20). The worst excess of neo-classical economics is the loss of the "moral minimum" from our economic life. One of the corollaries of the marginal utility theory has been the shift in focus – economics changed from being a theory of the material world to becoming a theory of human nature, with scarcity no longer located in material life, but rather in our minds as a function of infinite human desires. The consumer choice ceased to be a moral category, it did not matter whether the good desired was good or bad, just that the consumer was willing to pay for it (Gagnier, 2000).

Um outro mundo é possível

Already the search for another world is on. With optimism and hope, the World social Forum proclaims: um outro mundo é possível. The failure of socialism has added a new seriousness in this search. But, socialism is essentially not an alternative to this hegemonic economic order, as it too is based on domination and control and is equally rooted in anthropocentrism. As Erich Fromm puts it, socialism promises the same material comfort for all what capitalism has brought only to a few. However, the search for another world, in effect, translates into a search for another economy. It is a search for another economy which could create a better society – an inclusive and morally integrated society, free from poverty and unemployment, expanding opportunity to meet social needs, and an economy that does not subjugate but emancipates the socially marginalized to be free from the structures of subordination, live a life with a sense of dignity and self confidence, and realize a "positive freedom". The crisis has brought us to the point of structurally irreversible limits and now appears to be impossible to solve through application of our conventional wisdom by making simple "make shift" policy changes or merely changing the "forms" in the dominant paradigm. In order to fight with the disease (and not merely with the symptoms), we ought to look for ways to design radical alternatives to the very core of this paradigm. There is thus a need to construct a coherent theoretical framework based on an alternative philosophical foundation to restructure the debates around the complex interrelationships between environment, development, poverty, sustainability, world peace, and social wellbeing. It is against this backdrop, the paper examines the Gandhian Paradigm of Non-Violence as an alternative to create a sustainable society with a firm basis for world peace.

Gandhian Paradigm of Non-Violence as an Alternative

Mohandas Karamchand Gandhi (1869 -1948), philosopher and a rare blend of a saint and a politician, developed an alternative philosophical foundation that challenged the science and craft of neoclassical economics built around the homo oeconomicus. At the theoretical level, there are fundamental epistemological and normative divides between Gandhian and the neoclassical economics, and in their ontological claims. Gandhi offers a theory of contrastive explanation of the "human agency", which rejects the ontological construct of the homo oeconomicus as an atomistic individual, "under-socialized" and exclusively self-regarding, autonomous, and instrumentally rational to maximize utility. Gandhi's theory of action and social order represents a "paradigm of reversals", which strikes the dominant neoclassical economic paradigm at its very ontological roots. The Gandhian paradigm seeks to bring about a societal self-reorganisation from within through a moral transformation of the homo oeconomicus. The Gandhian strategy for creating an alternative sustainable future is essentially based on the ethical transformation of the human agency awakened to a different law – the Law of Non-Violence – governing human life and structuring human relationships.

Gandhi had seen around him both capitalism and communism at work in different parts of the world; and both, according to Gandhi, were the obverse and reverse of the same coin – violence. Neither had been able to solve the problem of exploitation and domination. On the other hand, both the systems together have produced the present day world reality through a complex historical process based on highly managed and centralized violence. The institutional structure of contemporary societies plays a part both in stimulating and reproducing the ideology of violence notwithstanding the existing differences in their political arrangements.

As an alternative to this violence-ridden socio-cultural and ideological order, Gandhi developed a paradigm of non-violence. "What is happening today", Gandhi once wrote, "is the disregard of the law of non-violence and enthronement of violence as if it were an eternal law" (Harijon, 11.2.1939. p.8). Non-violence is the law of the human race and is infinitely greater than and superior to brute force (i.e., violence). The spirit lies dormant in the brute and he knows no law but that of physical might. The dignity of man requires obedience to a higher law – to the strength of the spirit, or soul. Non-violence is the force of the soul. All society is held together by non-violence, even as earth is held in her position by gravitation. Non-violence is the road to Truth. Without non-violence it is not possible to seek and find Truth. Truth and non-violence are inseparable. Non-violence is not a cover for cowardice, but it is the supreme virtue of the brave. The path of true non-violence requires much more courage than violence. Non-violence is an active force of the highest order. It does not work in the same way as violence As Gandhi says:

> *Violence, like water, when it has an outlet, rushes forward furiously with an overwhelming force. Non-violence cannot act madly. It is the essence of discipline. But, when it is set going, no amount of violence can crush it (Harijon. 21.3.1939, p.33).*

Non-violence, as Gandhi explains, is not a cursory reference at moments of unease, but it is a continuous process towards living and evolving. The non-violent approach demands that its adherents must possess positive values of courage, absence of ill-will against the adversary, self-control, and self-abnegation. Its aim is not to defeat and humiliate, but to guide the adversary out of his wrong choice of values. Non-violence is a social instrument in the struggle for freedom and justice. It is a way of thinking and living. The faith in non-violence therefore can only stem from feelings of solidarity of the whole mankind and universal brotherhood as well as a unity of existence with nature and the values of trans-generational, and trans-species democracy.

The Unity of Existence

Gandhi begins by transforming the homo oeconomicus and seeks to (re)construct the society based on Peace, Harmony, and Non-violence. In the Gandhian conception, the process of the politico-economic transformation of the society is inevitably linked to the individual (spiritual and moral) transformation. It is one of an integral transformation of man and society. The Gandhian man is an integral man and the Gandhian society is an integral society. The Gandhian paradigm is characterized by its "Unity of Existence" and this unity we find at several levels : unity of the individual and the social order, unity of the private and public life, unity of religion and politics, unity of man and nature, and above all, unity of theory and practice (praxis). It is this "Unity of Existence" which is fundamental to the understanding of Gandhian thought in all its dimensions. It is the dimension of individual spiritual transformation in which society becomes a necessary "field" to work out and develop the individual as well as the collectivity, spiritually. In the process, Gandhi resolves all the problems and issues those social scientists and democratic reformers are faced with: the question of private ownership, unemployment, technology, poverty, inequality, environment etc. These issues are automatically resolved in the Gandhian society where non-violence is a living force, a creed, the only law.

Paradigm of Ethical Holism and Gandhian Praxis

Gandhian philosophy assumes even a greater significance, providing an alternative model that offers answers to the contemporary crises especially when the global socio-economic order is showing signs of aging. His ideas cut across ideological boundaries. Like Liberals he prized freedom and self-direction. Like Radicals he condemned economic exploitation and all that creates hiatus between man and man. Ethics is an integral part of his philosophy as he considers reality not merely as a natural order but also a moral order, Unlike the Marxian thought (in which the economy was the foundation), the ethical-moral system in Gandhian thought constituted the foundation while the socio-political-economic system forms the super-structure governed by the base-structure of the ethical-moral system.

Gandhi combined theory and practice in a very creative way. A man committed to the unity of theory and practice (praxis), for him thought and action were two sides of the same coin. Gandhian thought is holistic in nature and its nucleus lies in the ethical conceptual trinity of Truth-God-Nonviolence. His own life-long struggle is best described by him as a story of his experiments with truth. Truth was not merely to be debated in abstract, but more concretely discovered in one's own life in everyday living. Thus, for Gandhi, Truth was to be lived – i.e., it was to be practiced in our everyday lives in body, mind, and soul. He formulated "Truth" and "Non-Violence" as absolute entities. A seeker of Truth, Gandhi has overcome the means-ends dichotomy by maintaining that ends (truth) and means (non-violence) are convertible terms. It is very important to emphasize here that, due to the holistic nature of Gandhian thought, decomposition and analysis of its separate aspects and elements would blur our understanding of the Gandhian system.

The Gandhian Man (Satyagrahi): Micro foundations of a Non-Violent Society

Man, according to Gandhi, is a homo duplex – a divided self. In the western philosophy we find similar conceptions of Man in the deontological philosophy. Kant, for example, distinguishes between "two men" found within each of us. One is instrumental, seeking efficient means, directly observable. The other is the seat of free-will and values, the world of "reason", which leads to recognition of moral imperatives. The first "man" acts out inclinations, the second, in pursuit of what is right. Gandhi calls the first as the "ego" (or the "small self"), and the second as the "Self" (the bigger self). Such a man is in perpetual conflict between different orders of desires, quite akin to Freud's distinction between id and super-ego which are in perpetual conflict between instinctual urges and socially introduced morality. Now, Gandhi claims that what distinguishes man from other animals is their ability to transcend their "lower order desires" and form "higher order desires", – a process which Gandhi calls as "Self realization". Such a man, motivated to actions by the "soul-force", constantly seeking to purify himself and to transcend the "lower order of desires" in the pursuit of the "higher" ones, is a seeker of the "Truth" – a Satyagrahi.

Thus the Gandhian Man is a moral-ethical being and a multidimensional personality pursuing his own Self-realization (homo humanis). And the "Self" that is being realized is distinct from the ego (or, the "small self"). The process of self-realization (which is central to Gandhian economics) is a process of the growth and expansion of the "Self" and correspondingly a shrinking of the "ego", a process through which ultimately the ego consciousness totally yields to Self, God, or Truth consciousness. The homo oeconomicus in conventional economics on the other hand suffers from a limited consciousness. He is only aware of his ego and is motivated to action by the utilitarian principles of pleasure. Governed by the principle of maximizing behaviour, any action, regardless of how altruistic it may seem, is ultimately determined by the maximization of use value, or utility (i.e., by self interest). In other words, morality only exists if it is in our rational self-interest to have it exist and the so-called altruism is nothing but the result of calculated maximization of some kind of a utility index. As has been mentioned above, insofar as man is under constant fear of not getting enough of what he wants, the meaning of the homo oeconomicus reduces to an anxiety-ridden hunt for pleasure. The conventional economics, thus, in emphasizing on self interest and maximization as the prime-movers of human action, strip the homo oeconomicus off the (Gandhian)"Self" and maintains that the only interest is ego-type self interest. Clearly then, from the Gandhian perspective, the homo oeconomicus is at a very low level of human development.- In his construction, Gandhi ennobles man by endowing him with a higher "Self' (synonymous with Truth, Perfection, and above all, God) and by makes him capable of its realization. Overcoming the conflict between ego-interested motivation (i.e., maximization) and Self- interested motivation (pursuit of higher order goals) takes the centre stage in the moral transformation of the homo oeconomicus.

The concept of rationality is to be found at the very core of the Gandhian economics. Rather than mere cognitive calculation of means, Gandhi broadens the concept to involve harmonious action of body, mind, and soul. The truly rational individual, in the Gandhian model, will be guided not by rational calculations but by his conscience which he equated with what he called the inner voice. Gandhi's conscience is rational to the extent that it is critical. In other words, even though an action is pursued regardless of its consequences to one's self, we do have to critically examine the consequences ex post and readjust our inner values, and our conscience in the process. As Gandhi said, this way even the mistakes committed while seeking the pure path take us a step forward in the quest. Thus personal growth consists essentially in response to conscience, in an ever-renewed choosing between love-based action leading to Truth and selfish undirected action based on fear and greed, leading to violence. Ahimsa (non-violence) is the very key to moral growth and self actualization. The Satyagrahi is driven by the internal self-direction "to be", rather than lured by the outer world "to have".

The etiological meaning of Satyagraha is "holding on to Truth", hence "Truth-Force". Gandhi also called it "love-force" or "soul-force". In contrast to the homo oeconomicus, who is guided by the "brute-force", the Satyagrahi (one who holds on to Truth) is guided by the "soul force" (the force of love and non-violence) and lives a very rigorous life by practicing the following vratas (meaning "vow" for the Hindus, non-negotiable principles of life, which for the Satyagrahi are the "sacred commandments") in his daily life. It is only through the practice of these principles in our everyday lives, can we transcend from our brute-force, be awakened to the soul-force, and experience the emancipatory process for Self-realisation.

Sacred Vratas	Secular Principles
Satya	Truth/Objectivity/Holism
Ahimsa	Non-Violence/ Reverence for Life and Nature
Brahmacharya	Self-control/Celibacy
Aswad	Control over Consumption
Abhaya	Freedom from fear/Citizen Activism
Kaayak Shram	Dignity of labour
Sarvadharma Sambhava	Religious harmony
Namrata	Non-Dominance/Curbing of ego-pride
Swadeshi	Self-reliance/ Non-exploitation
Aparigraha	Non-possession/Freedom from envy and covetousness
Astheya	Non-Stealing

(Source: Kishore Saint, 1993)
Manifesto of the Moral economics

With his Satyagrahi Gandhi erects a new normative economics which goes beyond the self interest-based economics, or "egonomics". With the rejection of the homo oeconomicus, Gandhi rejects the economics that is built around the abstract notion of atomistic "rational economic man" who ceaselessly calculates the pros and cons of actions to determine when his own advantage is maximised. The distinctive feature of Gandhian economics is that it is fundamentally a means to promote higher human (moral) capacities.

This perspective in economics does not advocate actions (and policies) that lead to material economic advancement at the cost of moral and spiritual impoverishment. Public good is not secured by maximization of private self-interests but by self-restraint or even self-sacrifice. In this context the Gandhian doctrine of non-possession (based on the principle: "Enjoy your wealth by renouncing it") derive meaning and significance. The utilitarian maxim – "the greatest good of the greatest number" – as enunciated by Jeremy Bentham in the nineteenth century, is replaced by Gandhi by his concept of Sarvodaya (a Sanskrit word meaning "uplift of all"). But the Gandhian concept of Sarvodaya means much more than the commonly held view of "the welfare of all" – it means the development of every person and the whole person. It comes close to what Ruskin tried to communicate through his Unto This Last, but goes beyond in scope by focusing on the need to give the rich an opportunity for (nonmaterial, moral and spiritual) upliftment too. Thus the Gandhian model is built around the principles to develop and encourage a higher overall quality of man.

Table I

(Voluntary) Poverty and self-sacrifice might purify and ennoble man	**High Quality of Man**		*Assumptions that growing affluence fosters higher*
Low Quality of Life Life	Inverse relationship between low quality of life and high quality of man	Direct positive relationship between quality of life and quality of man	**High Quality of**
	Direct relationship between low quality of life and low quality of man	Inverse relationship between high quality of life and low quality of man	
Corrupting impact of poverty	**Low Quality of Man**		*Possible orruptinginfluence of abundance*

The concept of "quality of life" in the Gandhian sense is quite different from the generally accepted view in conventional development economics. Unlike the conventional view, where the concept is used to refer to material and economic well-being of the individual, "quality of life" in the Gandhian sense essentially refers to the quality of the man, i.e. man's spiritual and moral wellbeing (and perfection). The Gandhian concept, as distinct from the standard view, could be best explained using Oleg Zinam's (1989) four-fold classification of the potential relationship between Quality of Life and Quality of Man as depicted in the table –I.

The generally accepted conventional view (in Development Economics) implicitly assumes a direct positive relationship between quality of life and quality of the person (here again the concept of the "quality of the man" is narrowly defined, devoid of such key elements as human dignity unlike the Gandhian concept of the total moral and spiritual well-being of the person. The emphasis is on the thesis that poverty corrupts and destroys human dignity. A higher material wellbeing (= quality of life) improves human dignity (= quality of the man) in a mutually self-reinforcing manner. On the basis of this assumption of a direct positive relationship between the "quality of life" and the "quality of man", conventional economics defines " Development" as a progress along the III à I axes, which is sought to be achieved through the "revolution of rising material expectations", The domain assumptions in the alternative Gandhian paradigm are based not on this direct positive relationship but on the inverse relationship between the quality of life and the quality of man. Growing affluence and improvement in conventionally accepted indices of quality of life (economic wellbeing and material progress) contributes to the decay in the moral values of a society. The ultimate purpose of improving quality of life is the moral perfection of the individual and "Self-realisation" through the gradual ascendance of the person toward an ideal state of homo humanis.

Development through Voluntary Poverty

Development, in the Gandhian paradigm is defined as progress along the II à IV axes. In living a life of "a semi-naked fakir" (as described by Winston Churchill), Gandhi himself demonstrated a concrete empirical evidence to this theoretical plausibility of an inverse relationship between the "quality of life" and the "quality of man" and sought to bring about a human revolution through transforming the homo oeconomicus into a moral-ethical man whom he calls the Satyagrahi – the follower of "Truth", governed by the innate dynamics of "Self-realisation" through observance in their daily lives of the eleven commandments (vratas) listed above. Gandhi personally practiced Satyagraha and lived a very austere life, and made it a principle for his Ashram as well – demonstrating that his ideas are not utopian.

There is a strong positive correlation between voluntary poverty and the development of the soul. Enforced poverty and compulsory reduction to a subhuman level of subsistence corrodes the soul and minds of men, but superabundance of wealth cramps the soul and vulgarizes our mind even more dangerously through a diminishing return of happiness. Men must be ensured a minimum standard of living, but must limit their wants through self-discipline. We must deliberately and voluntarily cultivate a Spartan life. Voluntary poverty is, for Gandhi, essential for one wishing to serve both the God and humanity. The adoption of voluntary simplicity and an austere life is necessary – as we find increasingly with the passage of time – not merely for individual good, but for corporate good also. It promotes real happiness, peace, and the capacity for service. Gandhi's own ambition was to identify himself with the poorest of the poor.

Voluntary poverty and a minimizing behaviour is the natural result of a life based on the values of a Satyagrahi (namely, self-control, control over consumption, curbing of ego-pride, non-exploitation, non-stealing, and non-possession). The Gandhian doctrine of voluntary poverty is both a challenge and a response to our "acquisitive society". It is a challenge because it proposes a radical transformation of society through the transformation of the individual. It is a response because it suggests a way to fill one of the most serious gaps in modern society, i.e. the moral gap. It is clear that the Gandhian doctrine of non-possession is offered as an indictment of one of the most powerful drives in the modern (capitalist) society: the drive for multiplication of wants, fuelled by an insatiable propensity for what Thorstein Veblen termed as "conspicuous consumption". To Gandhi, it was essentially a moral issue. He believed that possession of Goods, beyond the limits of need (as distinguished form want), is a form of theft and, therefore, immoral. A Satyagrahi has to pursue the principle of non-hoarding or non-possession. As total non-possession is unattainable (since our body is also a possession in the strict sense of the term), Gandhi suggests that in observing the vow of non-possession, the main thing to be borne in mind is not to store up anything which we do not require. The golden rule is "to refuse to have what millions cannot". One has to make a movement towards the ideal of non-possession through the process of gradual reduction of wants and minimization of consumption. In this regard, minimizing behaviour and a progressive simplification of one's life (as against the maximizing behaviour of the homo oeconomicus) emerges as one of the cardinal principles of the Gandhian model. The doctrine teaches that every one should limit his own possession to only what is needed by him and spend the rest for the welfare of others.

From the point of view of the homo humanis, non-possession, i.e., voluntary self-denial (voluntary reduction of wants and spending the rest towards altruistic goals) would purify and ennoble man, lead him to higher levels of moral perfection (i.e. a high quality of man). This promotes real happiness and contentment among individuals and ensures social peace. From the point of view of the society, non-possession is conceived as a desirable, non-violent method of reducing inequality of income distribution and maldistribution of wealth (through the Gandhian principle of "to each according to his need" on a voluntary basis). Gandhi would put utmost reliance on the individual's own moral awakening to bring about radical changes in the distribution of income and wealth in society.

Gandhi wants to bring the right to private property under the guidance of the soul force of men. This means that private wealth is only legitimate, subject to the condition that any excess wealth is used for the welfare of all. This is the essence of the idea of trusteeship. The spirit of voluntary poverty on the part of the rich is a means of realizing economic justice, and of removing the involuntary poverty that huge masses of people are suffering from. While Gandhi saw that structural changes were necessary if the welfare of all was to be attained, he saw two things even more clearly. First, that these changes have to be brought about voluntarily, and second, that if they are to be brought about voluntarily, the soul had to be reformed first. Each individual has to come to terms with his/her possessive instinct through self control. This is the essence of Gandhi's concept of Swaraj (self-rule) – the self has to gain control over itself. For Gandhi, no transformation of the society can be possible without the transformation of the individual.

Non-Violent Production

While voluntary poverty and reduction of wants lead to non-violent consumption, Gandhi also strongly argues for creating an economy based on non-violent production. Modern industrial societies have institutionalized exploitation, particularly in the process of the production of goods and services (exploitation of both man and nature). In view of the inequalities and the prevalence of alienation, the very concept of market may be exploitative. Exploitation is violence, for one cannot exploit without doing violence. Non-exploitation follows directly from the concept and principle of non-violence.

Contemporary social developments are increasingly dominated by a series of technological developments, or, the "high-tech" revolution, which has pervasive effects throughout our economic and socio-cultural life. Technology, although of course the creation of man, tends to develop by its own laws and principles, and these are very different from those of human nature. For instance, technology recognizes no self-limiting principles especially in terms of size, speed, or violence (i.e., it evolves towards ever-greater size, ever-higher speed, and ever-increased violence). As Schumacher makes it succinctly clear, the modern world, shaped by modern-technology, finds itself involved in three deep crises simultaneously: (i) human nature revolts against inhuman technological, organisational and political patterns, which it experiences as suffocating and debilitating: (ii) the living environment which supports human life aches and groans and gives signs of breakdown; and (iii) it is clear by now that the inroads being made into the world's non-renewable resources are such that serious bottlenecks and virtual exhaustion loom ahead in the quite foreseeable future (Schumacher, op.cit.:137). A way of life that bases itself on materialism, i.e., on permanent, limitless expansionism in a finite environment, cannot last long. Apart from the ecological doom, Gandhi also emphasized that modern technology cannot really help us to alleviate poverty, not to mention the problem of unemployment.

However, Gandhi was not against all machinery. His objection is directed to the "craze for machinery" and its indiscriminate multiplication. He, therefore, would impose limitations on it. Gandhi would welcome the machine that lightens the burden of millions of men living in cottages, but he set his face against all machinery which turns men into 'robots' and as a result, ousts human labour. The Gandhian paradigm is therefore based on a different kind of technology, a technology with a human face (it is a human centered approach to technology), which, instead of making human hands and brains redundant, helps them to become far more productive than they have ever been before.

As Gandhi said, the poor millions cannot be helped by mass production, but only by production by the masses. The system of mass production, based on sophisticated, highly capital-intensive, high energy-input dependent, and human labour-saving technology. presupposes that you are already rich for a great deal of capital investment needed to establish one single workplace. The system of production by the masses, on the other hand, mobilises the priceless resources which are possessed by all human beings. their clever brains and skilful hands, and supports them with first-class tools. The technology of mass production is inherently violent, ecologically damaging, self-defeating in terms of nonrenewable resources, and stultifying for the human person. The technology of production by the masses, making use of the best of modern knowledge and experience, is conducive to decentralization, compatible with the laws of ecology, gentle in its use of scarce resources. and designed to serve the human person instead of making him the servant of machines (Schumacher, ibid. : 143). As Gandhi observes:

> *Men go on 'saving labour' till thousands are without work and thrown on the open streets to die of starvation. I want to save time and labour, not for a fraction of mankind, but for all. I want the concentration of wealth, not in the hands of the few, but in the hands of all. Today, machinery merely helps a few to ride on the backs of millions. The impetus behind it all is not the philanthropy to save labour, but greed. It is against this constitution of things that I am fighting with all my might (Young India, dt.13.11.1924: 378).*

Gandhi rightly argues that the craze for mass-production through modern technology is responsible for the present world crises. Granting for the moment that machinery may supply all the needs of humanity, still it would concentrate production in particular areas, so that we have to go in a roundabout way to regulate distribution. Whereas, if there is production and distribution both in the respective areas where things are required, it is automatically regulated. Therefore, Gandhi envisages mass-production, but certainly not based on violent, dehumanizing technology. After all the message of the spinning-wheel is exactly that. It is mass production, but mass-production in people's own homes. If you multiply individual production to millions of times, would it not give you mass-production on a tremendous scale? Gandhi asks (Harijan, dt.2.11.1934:302). At the heart of this system of non-violent production by the masses, is a human-centered, non-exploitative technology. The Gandhian technological system (non-violent, non-exploitative, human centered), as we find, satisfies four basic conditions:

i. the operator must have control of the technology,
ii. the technology must not replace the worker,
iii. the technology must increase the productivity of the worker, and
iv. it mlust be productive of goods and services needed by the worker and useful for the society.

Village Republics, Swadeshi, and Trusteeship

In the context of the present mega trends and processes, forces and policies driving the process of globalization, it is very useful to look at the Gandhian model of village republics as self-reliant and self-governed units. Centralization, as a system, is inconsistent with the non-violent structure of society. According to Gandhi, centralization, the source of all social contradictions, has two major loci: (i) the sphere of production (market), and (ii) the sphere of power (state); which are correlated. Centralism in production leads to exploitation and centralism in power leads to oppression. The two centralisms reinforce each other. Therefore, the Gandhian paradigm, based on non-violence, is essentially decentralized in nature.

The primary behavioural-organisational unit in his model is the individual man and the household, and the primary structural-organisational unit is the village. For, as Gandhi says, society based on non-violence can only consist of groups settled in villages in which "voluntary cooperation is the condition of dignified and peaceful existence" (Harijan, dt.13.1.1940, pp.410-11). It is essentially a decentralised system, where the fundamental economic decisions are to be made at the micro- level -- i.e., the village communities. The Gram Panchayat (the village council) is the nucleus. The individual, village, and the community of villages do not suggest a hierarchical ordering in a vertical structure; rather they expand and evolve through horizontal cooperation in a federated structure. As Gandhi says:

> *In this structure, composed of innumerable villages, there will be ever-widening, never-ascending circles. Life will not be a pyramid with the apex sustained by the bottom. But it will be an oceanic circle whose center will be the individual, always ready to perish for the village, the latter ready to perish for the circle of villages, till at last the whole becomes one life composed of individuals, never aggressive in their arrogance, but ever humble, sharing the majesty of the oceanic circle of which they are integral units. Therefore, the outermost circumference will not yield power to crush the inner circle but will give strength to all within and will derive its own strength from it (Quoted in Prabhu, 1947 : pp.26-27).*

The village republics can only flourish as self-reliant and independent units if they are embedded on the spirit of Swadeshi, which in the Gandhian paradigm defines the relation of the individual to the society and the larger world in terms of socially responsible economic behaviour. As Gandhi says :

> *Swadeshi is that spirit in us which restricts us to the use and service of our immediate surroundings to the exclusion of the more remote . . . In that (the domain) of economics, I should use only things that are produced by my immediate neighbuors . . . Much of the deep poverty of the masses is due to the ruinous departure from Swadeshi in the economic and industrial life . . . I think of Swadeshi not as a boycott movement undertaken by way of revenge. I conceive it as a religious principle to be followed by all (Gandhi, 1958, vol 13 : 219-20)*

Economic activity is not to be carried out simply for maximizing one's own benefits, but to promote the social interests as a whole from the very bottom upwards. A people-centered, socially useful, locally oriented economy, in the Gandhian thinking, aims at, not enhancing private goods but, enhancing public goods. However, Gandhi also makes it clear that Swadeshi did not mean exclusiveness, isolation, and non-involvement with the rest of the world. On the contrary, he considered it to be the proper and firm starting point and the foundation of global cooperation. Local self-reliance stimulates regional self-reliance, which, in turn, fosters national self-reliance. Relationships of self-reliance have greater synergic and multiplying effects when they flow from the bottom upwards. Self-reliant processes originating from the micro spaces are less bureaucratic, more democratic, and more efficient in marrying personal growth with social development. He visualizes cooperation between the primary units leading up to an integrated national economy and the emergence of a global economy based on mutual cooperation on term of equality between nations. The global economy will be equitable and just only when it had its roots in communities where the human values that were to animate were nurtured. The basic mantra is : Think globally, Live locally.

Gandhi gives the concept of "Trusteeship" as a way to transform the present capitalist order of society into an egalitarian one. Gandhi's concept of "Trusteeship" is linked to his concept of 'non-possession' and is aimed at achieving the socialist ideal (economic equality and elimination of exploitation) through nonviolence. Through his concept of "Trusteeship" he resolves the capitalist-socialist controversy over the issue of ownership through a moral transformation of the homo oeconomicus. Gandhi's approach to trusteeship is all-comprehensive, based as it is, on his approach to life and society. It has been one of his major contributions to the ideology of the new (moral) economic order. It seeks to achieve the goal of abolition of private property without sacrificing the advantages of individual initiative. In the formulation of his concept of trusteeship, he was influenced by the Indian spiritual wisdom: Tena Tyaktena bhunjithah (enjoy your wealth by renouncing it); expanded it means: "Earn your crores by all means. But understand that your wealth is not yours; it belongs to the people. Take what you require for your legitimate needs. And use the remainder for society". The capitalist may possess millions, but he may not own any wealth. He may only hold it in trust. Thus, those who own the capital are asked to behave like trustees, holding their riches on behalf of the poor. A trustee has no heir but the public. A violent and bloody revolution is a certainty one day, unless there is a voluntary abdication of riches and the power that riches give and sharing them for the common good. To quote Gandhi:

> *Supposing I have come by a fair amount of wealth – either by way of legacy or by means of trade and industry – I must know that all that wealth does not belong to me; what belongs to me is the right to an honourable livelihood, no better than that enjoyed by millions of others. The rest of my wealth belongs to the community and must be used for the welfare of the community (Harijan, dt.3.6.1939 : 145).*

Private ownership is incompatible with non-violence and non-exploitation. Economic equality is the master key to non-violent independence. Working for it means abolishing the eternal conflict between capital and labour. Gandhi, with his emphasis on individual freedom and non-violence, enunciated his theory of "Trusteeship" at a time when the socialist theory was advanced in respect of the possessions held by the landlords, the ruling chiefs, and the rising industrial class. They would do away with these privileged classes. There are two ways of removing the disparities of inequality. One is by lopping off the tall poppies – liquidating of the owning class and redistribution of its assets; the other, through State action. Now, leveling down can achieve a dead uniformity, but it does not add to anybody's stature. This dead uniformity, thus achieved, can only be transitory. Inequalities are bound to crop up as often as they are removed owing to the natural differences in the talents and capacity of different individuals. The other way is through state ownership. Gandhi says, is better than private ownership. But that, too, is not acceptable on the ground of violence. The State represents violence in a concentrated and organised form. The individual has a soul, but the state is a soulless machine. It can never be weaned from violence – to which it owes its very existence. Hence Gandhi advocates "Trusteeship" as a third alternative to the issue of ownership.

> *By the non-violent method, we seek not to destroy the capitalist, we seek to destroy capitalism. We invite the capitalist to regard himself as a trustee for those on whom he depends for the making, the retention, and the increase of his capital. Nor need the worker wait for his conversion. If capital is power, so is work. Either power can be used destructively or creatively. Either is dependent on the other. Immediately the worker realises his strength, he is in a position to become a co-sharer with the capitalist instead of remaining his slave (Quoted in Prabhu and Rao, 1987 : 257-58).*

In this, Gandhi says, the capitalist has nothing really to lose and everything to gain. There is no other choice than between voluntary surrender on the part of the capitalist of the superfluities and consequent acquisition of the real happiness (and human development along the II-IV axes shown in the above figure) on the one hand, and on the other the impending chaos into which, if the capitalist does not wake up betimes, awakened but ignorant, famishing millions will plunge the country and which, not even the armed force, that a powerful government can bring into play, can avert (Young India, dt. 5.12.1929 : 396). Thus Gandhi says:

> *As for the present owners of wealth, they will have to make their choice between class war and voluntarily converting themselves into trustees of their wealth, they will be allowed to retain the stewardship of their possessions and to use their talent to increase the wealth, not for their own sakes, but for the sake of the nation and therefore, without exploitation. The state would regulate the rate of commission which they would get commensurate with the service rendered and its value to society. Their children would inherit the stewardship only if they proved their fitness for it (Harijan, dt.31.3.1946 : 63).*

Again, as Gandhi says :

> *My theory of 'trusteeship' is no make-shift, certainly no camouflage. I am confident that it will survive all other theories. It has the sanction of philosophy and religion behind it. That possessors of wealth have not acted up to the theory does not prove its falsity. It proves the weakness of the wealthy. No other theory is compatible with non-violence. In the non-violent method the wrong-doer compasses his own end, if he does not undo the wrong. For, either through non-violent non-cooperation he is made to see the error, or he finds himself completely isolated (Harijan, dt.16.2.1939 :376).*

What is significant in Gandhi's model is that it gives a chance to all possessors of property (prospective trustees) voluntarily to liquidate their rights of exclusive ownership and identify with the people. If they don't do so voluntarily, according to Gandhi's suggestions, there would have to be social sanctions like non-cooperation and Satyagraha to convert private ownership to Trusteeship. Conversion is Gandhi's weapon of choice, and conversion must precede legislation. Eventually, however thus, he also foresaw compulsion by legislative action. Gandhi preferred the ancient socialism of the Hindu ethics to the modern compulsory form of expropriation, as he believed it would keep the "geese" alive while taking the eggs.

The debate around economic democracy has always had a very emotional, political, and ideological character. This is especially so with regard to the issue of ownership. Since the early utopians, most social revolutionaries were concerned with questions of ownership. The central feature of the development of bourgeois society and capitalism is the private ownership of the means of production. Through the socialist revolution, abolition of private ownership (not only of the means of production) was realised. But with the collapse of the really existing socialist societies, there is again a return of work and production to capitalism and with it to private ownership, and that too, on a global scale, with the resultant problems assuming global magnitude, much beyond the capacity of the national state to solve. Against these developments the Gandhian concept of "Trusteeship" assumes a special significance as an alternative paradigm for the management of capital within a completely different value and power structure than those obtaining today.

Concluding Remarks

Gandhi sought to combine Lincoln's love of liberty with Marx's urge for equality without resorting to "the barrel of the gun". Western democracy is on its trial, if it has not already proved a failure, according to Gandhi. It has germs in it, certainly of the true copy. But it can only come when all violence is eschewed and malpractices disappear. Indeed, malpractice is a species of violence. The western paradigm is essentially one of violence and systemic exploitation, rooted in the very instinct of acquisition of the homo oeconomicus, and is thus logically oriented towards capitalist expansion, domination, and hegemony. This is true of both capitalism and socialism as both have developed from the same homo oeconomicus. Thus, if in capitalism capital exploits the labour, in socialism it is the other way round (i.e. the labour exploits the capital). The violent way of liquidating the rich will not necessarily mean the eradication of the instinct for possessiveness and acquisitiveness, and hence is not a real permanent, enduring solution to the problem. Both share the same anthropocentric view of nature, and thus do violence to the nature. In fact, our experiences from the cold war era, strongly suggest that, at the global level, both systems escalated violence and the threats of war to expand their power and control over the globe. Therefore, both are based on the same paradigm of violence. Merely changing forms does not eliminate the cause.

Gandhi's paradigm is sometimes treated as "utopian". But Gandhi would emphatically say, it is immaterial whether many live up to it or only one man lives up to it. The question is of conviction. If you accept the principle of ahimsa (non-violence), you have to strive to live up to it. There is nothing in this theory which can be said to be very difficult for practice. If people meditate over it constantly and try to act up to it, then life on earth would be governed far more by love than it is at present. If we strive for it, we shall be able to go further in realising state of peace on earth than by any other method. For, as Gandhi says, it is certain that if you use violence today, you shall doubtlessly be faced with greater violence tomorrow. With non-violence as the rule, life will no doubt be a series of compromises. But it is better than an endless series of blood-thirsty clashes.

The difference between what exists today and what is possible (economically, socially, politically, culturally, ecologically, and morally), the gap between the problem and the solution, has never been as great as it is today. We have come to a point where we need to take a 'U' turn. The hope and the answer lie in Gandhi. Take care of the tree and the woods will take care of itself. Take care of the man and the society will take care of itself, Gandhi believed. No system can be transformed unless its seed is transformed. Gandhi emphasized on the transformation of the homo oeconomicus – the seed of the present global system. Through that the goals that Gandhi set for a restructured society and an economy were the end of exploitation, economic equality, harmony with nature and a world order free from war and violence. Gandhi's value lies in pointing out the direction. His greatest achievements are still to come. Gandhi is the guide to the 21st Century.

The global society today suffers from serious crises, which emanate from four major problems: i. growing violence in our social, economic, political and religious lives within and between nations, ii. growing problems of poverty, exclusion, unemployment, and social disintegration, iii. Increasing degradation of the environment and the erosion of resources, and iv. growing degeneration and decay in standards of moral conduct. As Hay (2000) argues, following Gandhi's example, we can really create a sustainable and peaceful social order in the future only if we can fill the world with billions of morally reformed, self-disciplined, empathetic, loving and caring individuals – voluntarily minimizing their material needs in pursuit of a simpler living with higher thinking, living the life of a satyagrahi, restoring a unity of existence, in obedience to the law of non-violence, and continuously maturing on the path of "Self-realisation" – who alone can be the seeds of change to create another society based on the ethics of wellbeing. But, the critical question in the process of this peaceful social transformation is: How? Gandhi's answer is: "Be the change you want to see".

References

Bourdieu, Pierre, 1997. "Le champ economique", Actes de la recherché en sciences sociales, 119, pp.48-66.

Commission of the European Communities (2009), GDP and Beyond : Measuring Progress in a Changing World, Communication from the Commission to the Council and the European Parliament, COM(2009) 433, 20.8.2009, Brussels, www.beyond-gdp.eu

Dash, Anup (1994), "Economic Democracy : A Conceptual Analysis of The Gandhian Model", paper presented at the International Political Science Congress, Berlin, August.

Diwan, Romesh and Mark Lutz (eds) (1985), Essays in Gandhian economics, New Delhi, Gandhi Peace Foundation.
Fromm, Erich (1976), To Have or To Be?, New York, Harper and Row.
Gagnier, Reginia (2000), The Insatiability of Human Wants : Economics and Aesthetics in Market Society, Chicago, The University of Chicago Press.
Gandhi, M.K. (1958), The Collected Works of Mahatma Gandhi, Ministry of Information and Broadcasting, Government of India, Ahmedabad, Navjivan.
Global Footprint Network (2010), "World Footprint : Do we fit on the planet?", www.footprintnetwork.org
Graham, Carol (2005), "Globalization, Poverty, Inequality, and Insecurity", Research Paper No. 2005/33, Helsinki, UNU-WIDER.
Hay, Stephen (2000), "Gandhi : Guide to a Better Human Future", in Anthony J. Parel (ed.), Gandhi, Freedom, and Self-Rule, Boston, Lexington.
Korten, David (2009), "Why This Crisis May Be Our Best Chance to Build a New Economy", YES! Magazine, posted June 19, 2009. www.yesmagazine.org/issues/the-new-economy
Layard, Richard (2005), Happiness: Lessons from a New Science, London, Penguin.
Maira, Arun (2008), "Let's Revisit Capitalism", The Times of India. 16 April, p.14.
Max-Neef, Manfred, et.al. (1989), "Human Scale Development : An Option for the Future", Development Dialogue, I.
Prabhu, R.K. and U. R. Rao (eds.) (1987), The Mind of Mahatma Gandhi, Ahmedabad, Navajivan.
Report by the Commission on the Measurement of Economic Performance and Social Progress, (2008), www.stiglitz-sen-fitoussi.fr
Saint, Kishore (1993), "Hindu View of Ecology", Caritas India Bulletin, No.2.
Schumacher, E.F. (1973), Small is beautiful, London, Blond and Briggs.
Veenhoven, R (2009), World Database of Happiness, Erasmus University Rotterdam. Available at: http://worlddatabaseofhappiness.eur.nl
World Resources Institute (1998), "Valuing Eosystem Services", EarthTrends : The Environmental Information Portal, www.earthtrends.wri.org/text/economics-business
Zinam, Oleg (1989), "Quality of Life, Quality of the Individual, Technology and Economic Development", American Journal of Economics and Sociology, January.

A Minimum Wage For Malaysia: An Analysis Of The Arguments And Recent Policy

Marian Whitaker and Idaya Husna Mohd
Flinders Business School, Faculty of Social Sciences,

Abstract[1]

For more than a decade, the Malaysian Trade Union Congress (MTUC) has demanded the introduction of a minimum wage. This demand was recently presented again to the Malaysian government with a proposal for a minimum monthly wage of RM 900 (US$264) plus RM 300 (US$88) cost of living allowance. In considering this proposal, the government's response was to reject the idea of a national minimum wage covering all workers. Instead, through the National Wage Council, the government has decided upon sectoral minimum wages covering four groups of workers: Security guards, Clinic assistants, Hotel and Catering workers and General workers from small holdings. As at January 2010, the National Wage Council has agreed upon the amount of RM 575 per month (US$169) for Hotel and Catering workers. This paper analyses the arguments surrounding the introduction of a national minimum wage for Malaysia and recent policy developments from a variety of perspectives. It reports on recent data gathered through a series of interviews held with representatives of the National Wage Council for the hotel and tourism industry – a tripartite body comprising employers, trade unions and government officials. The paper concludes with a discussion about the implications of the proposal of a national minimum wage and the recent policy developments for sustainable employment in the Malaysian hotel sector.

This research is concerned with an analysis of the Human Resource Management and Industrial Relations implications associated with the proposal of a minimum wage in Malaysia. Specifically, the research will gather data from the hotel sector, a part of the leisure and tourism industry characterized by low wages. At present, Malaysia does not have a national minimum wage. A case for the introduction of this new wage policy has been proposed by the Malaysian Trade Union Congress (MTUC) and this proposal is being considered by the Malaysian Government. This potential change in wage policy in Malaysia provides an opportunity to research the human resource and industrial relations implications in the hotel sector. Data are gathered through a series of interviews held with representatives of the National Wage Council for the hotel and tourism industry – a tripartite body comprising employers, trade unions and government officials. Survey questionnaires are also distributed among 30 hotel employers in Kuala Lumpur to further explore the potential implications of a new minimum wage rate for the hotel sector. The nest stage of the research is to examine the attitude of the hotel employees towards minimum wages and their preparedness to engage with productivity enhancing changes.

Content

1 Thesis title: Minimum Wage And Employment: Perspective on the Implications for the Malaysian Hotel And Tourism Industry. Supervisors: Dr Marian Whitaker and Emeritus Prof. Keith Hancock of Flinders University, South Australia

Introduction

This paper explores and analyses the arguments surrounding the introduction of a national minimum wage for Malaysia and recent policy developments from a variety of perspectives. It reports on recent data gathered through a series of interviews held with the representatives of the National Wage Council for the hotel and tourism industry – a tripartite body comprising employers, trade unions and government officials. The paper concludes with a discussion about the implications of the proposal of a national minimum wage and the recent policy developments for sustainable employment in the Malaysian hotel sector.

1. Is Malaysia an unusual case?

Malaysia is certainly unusual in not having a national minimum wage policy (Malaysian Employment Act, 1955)[2]. The reasons for this are embedded in Malaysian industrial policy which, over several decades of national economic planning, has emphasised the pursuit of economic growth through attracting foreign direct investment in manufacturing, and the export of manufactured goods (Ninth Malaysia Plan). The success of this strategy has been dependent on maintaining a labour cost advantage (Ninth Malaysia Plan). It is also evident in the national economic planning documents that the dominant ideology tends towards neo-classical principles. That is, there is a preference to allow market forces to determine wages and conditions, and disapproval of government interventions except in so far as regulating to limit or eradicate factors that might damage competitiveness or discourage foreign investment e.g. the banning of trade unionism in the electronics sector. Neighbouring Singapore also has no national minimum wage policy. In Singapore, Wages are set through collective bargaining based on recommendations from the National Wage Council (NWC) *(World Bank, Data*

2 In fact, Malaysia had previously enacted minimum wages for four groups: cinema workers, Penang stevedores, shops assistants and hotel staff, but these minima were set at such an extraordinarily low level that they became ineffective.

and Statistics,2008). According to the Singapore Employment Act, the NWC recommendations are "gazetted", and they are used by negotiating parties during the setting of wages.[3]

Figure 1.0 GDP and the total number of local and foreign workers in each of the states in Malaysia

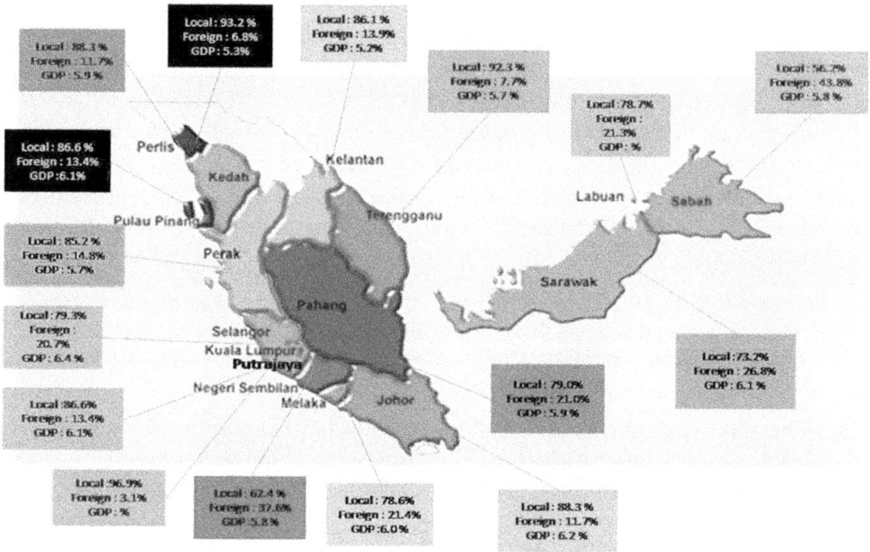

Source: Ninth Malaysia Plan (2009)

An unusual feature of Malaysia concerns its development status. The economic geography of the country shows marked divisions between the highly industrialised peninsula, especially Kuala Lumpur and Johor, and the under-developed regions of Sabah and Sarawak as shown is figure 1.0 above. It is difficult, therefore, to think of Malaysia as an underdeveloped, developing, or developed nation. It is simultaneously all three. Devising national policies that are appropriate for the needs of all Malaysians is a distinct challenge.

This paper analyses the arguments surrounding the introduction of a national minimum wage for Malaysia and recent policy developments from a variety of perspectives. It reports on recent data gathered through a series of interviews held with representatives of the National Wage Council for the hotel and catering sector – a tripartite body comprising employers, trade unions and government officials.

3 Based on the Employment Act, Article 49, retrieved from http://statutes.agc.gov.sg

2. Minimum Wages and Wage Councils in Malaysia

The minimum wage has always sparked debate amongst academicians, employers, & economists, policy makers and trade unionists (Neumark,Washer,2006). As explained by Neumark and Wascher (2008), the minimum wage has been a core element of public policy for more than a century. Originating in the 1890s in New Zealand and Australia, minimum wages spread to the United Kingdom in 1909 and to nearly one-third of U.S. states during the next two decades. In 1938, the U.S Congress passed a federal minimum wage law as a part of the Fair Labour Standards Act. Since then, minimum wages have been introduced in some form or another in numerous other industrialized countries, as well as in many developing countries. By the 1990s, minimum wages existed in well over one hundred countries and the International Labour Organization (ILO) has designated the minimum wage as an International Labour Standard (ILO 2006) which defines a minimum wage as :

> "The lowest level of remuneration permitted.... Which in each country has the force of law and which is enforceable under threat of penal or other appropriate sanctions. Minimum wage fixed by collective agreements made binding by public authorities are included in his definition"[4]

The minimum wage places a legal floor on the rate that employers must pay to workers. In other words, the minimum wage is the lowest standard rate to be paid to employees. Chandarot (2005) explains that there are numerous variations between countries, in terms of the minimum wage rate and the way in which it is determined, depending largely on nations' respective policy objectives, e.g. to reduce inequality; the eradication of poverty. Saget (2005) identifies four approaches to the setting of minimum wages: (i) a base rate for the whole country or per region, with the state as the key decision maker, (ii) multiple rates that vary by sector and / or occupation, with the state as the key decision maker, (iii) A base rate for the whole country or per region, determined by collective bargaining, and (iv) multiple rates that vary by sector and/or occupation, determined by collective bargaining.

Generally, in Malaysia, salaries and wages are set at the discretion of the employer. It is a matter to be agreed between employer and employee and also stated in a contract of employment as per the employment Act 1955. According to Malaysian Standard Industrial Ctassification (MSIC) 2000, in line with the International Classification Standards, wages, income and basic wages are defined as follows :

4 ILO: Minimum wages: Wage-fixing machinery, application and supervision, Report III (Part 4B) (General Survey), International Labour Conference, 79th Session, Geneva, 1992.

(i) Wages: Any cash payments made to the employees according to the works / jobs performed.
(ii) Income: The amount earned which includes basic salary, wages, overtime, incentives, and other additional benefits such as meals, uniforms and accommodations.
(iii) Basic Salary: The emoluments paid to the employees based on the work time unit performed not including the premium, allowances, and other additional benefits.

Malaysia does not have a national minimum wage provided for all workers. However, the Wage Council Act of 1947 provides the authority for specially constituted Wage Councils to set minimum wages for certain industries. These Councils play a role in recommending minimum wage rates to the Government for enacting a Wage Regulation Order.

Before 2009, Wage Councils existed covering the following groups: cinema workers (RM175) (USD$54), shop assistants (RM 250)(USD$78), hotel and catering industry workers[5] (RM185) (USD$57) and port of Penang stevedores (RM 120)(USD$37) (Aminuddin, 1991, p. 90). These are industries in which workers find it difficult to group themselves into unions and fight for their own rights. For sectors not covered by the minimum wage, collective bargaining between the employer and trade union can be used for setting a minimum rate, except where trade unionism is banned e.g. in the electronics sector.

Not only was the coverage of these councils very limited, but the minimum wages being set were infrequently upgraded. For instance, the catering and hotel wages council had last amended its regulations in 1982. The minimum wage set for the workers in this sector was RM 185 per month (for those over 18 years of age). It is stipulated in the Wage Council Act 1947, Act 195 (revised 1977), Section 13(2) and Section 13(6) that, failure to pay minimum wage rates as established by wages regulation orders may result in the employer being ordered to pay the difference between the amount the worker ought to have been paid and the amount actually paid. The employer is also liable to a fine not exceeding RM500 for each offence. In practice, the minimum standard wage as mentioned above fell into disuse as employers found it necessary to raise the rate of pay in order to attract and retain the workforce (Aminuddin, 2006).

The national minimum wage issue in Malaysia has stimulated debate between trade unionists, government ministers, employers, employees, academics and the

5 According to the Wages Regulation (Catering and Hotel) order, 1967, PU 288/67, Section 2, Hotel and catering workers are the workers within certain jurisdictions who are engaged in the business to supply meals, refreshments or alcohol to the public for consumption on the premises engaging in hotels, lodging houses, restaurants and premises used for the sale of alcohol.

people at large. The key questions are: should there be a national minimum wage or not? If so, at what rate should it be introduced?

3. The Proposal for a National Minimum Wage

In 2007, The MTUC (Malaysian Trade Union Congress) proposed a national minimum wage of RM 900 (US$264) plus a cost of living allowance of RM 300 (US$88) per month in its memorandum to Malaysia's former Prime Minister, Datuk Seri Abdullah Ahmad Badawi. Shown in Figure 1.1 below is the segregation of the RM 900 proposed based on the essential and basic needs of a single person.

Figure 1.1 MTUC's proposal of RM 900 based on the essential and basic needs of a single person

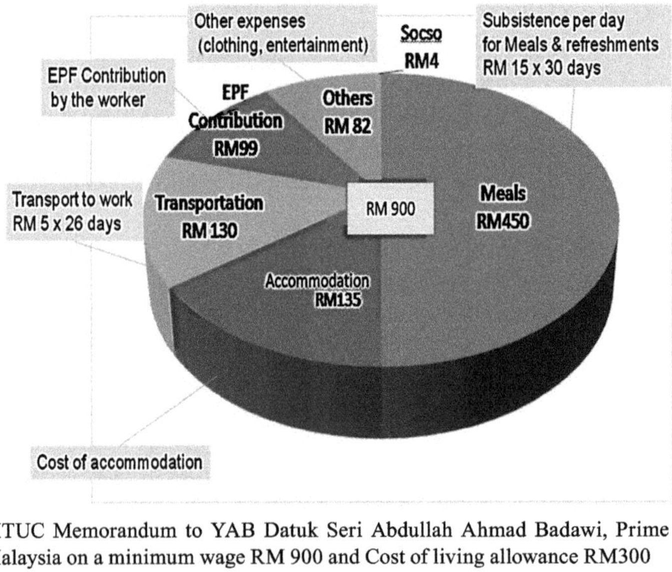

Source: MTUC Memorandum to YAB Datuk Seri Abdullah Ahmad Badawi, Prime Minister of Malaysia on a minimum wage RM 900 and Cost of living allowance RM300

In concluding the 2007 memorandum for a minimum wage, the MTUC expressed the hope that by setting and implementing a minimum wage of RM 900, the Government would be able to deal effectively with the following:

Industry's need for manpower
Reduced dependency on foreign labour
Eradication of poverty
Strengthening manufacturing and facilitating economic growth

See Mohd (2009) for an analysis of these claims from a trade union perspective.

In 2008, the government agreed to consider the MTUC's proposal through the Economic Planning Unit with the caveat that they had to act responsibly in managing the economy and would only implement what was good and feasible. However, prior to 2008, the government had generally been resistant to the idea of a national minimum wage. One of the reasons offered was that, the cost of living varies from state to state (between the Peninsular Malaysia and also Sabah and Sarawak) (Aminuddin, 2006). As mentioned earlier, Malaysia is rather unusual in its development status where it is highly industrialised in the peninsular especially in Kuala Lumpur and Johor while areas like the east coast and Sabah and Sarawak are considered to be underdeveloped regions. Setting a high wage would be too expensive for employers in small, less developed states. On the other hand, a low minimum wage would be meaningless to the states with higher costs of living. With regards to this statement, the MTUC has expressed its disagreement saying that the price of consumer goods remains the same all across Malaysia.

The Government generally believes that wage levels should be left for the market to determine, through negotiations and collective bargaining. However, it was clear that in certain sectors of the economy, workers needed greater protection from exploitation and that low wages were failing to attract good quality local staff, particularly graduates.

In considering the proposal for a national minimum wage, the Malaysian government in 2008 has established several commissions of inquiry and wage councils to review the minimum wage of security guards, clinic assistants, hotel and catering staff and general workers in small holdings. The wage councils were later expanded to include electronics and textile workers.

This paper concentrates on the analysis of the arguments for a national minimum wage in Malaysia and follow up on recent policy developments on the minimum wage issue in hotel and tourism industry in Malaysia. The analysis considers the arguments from the Malaysian Government, the Malaysian Trade Union Congress and the Malaysian Employers Federation.

4. Findings and Discussion

4.1 Should Malaysia Legislate a National Minimum Wage?

As mentioned above, the MTUC has been fighting for a National Minimum Wage for more than a decade. The idea of having a national minimum wage for Malaysia has sparked a heated debate among key players in industry, most notably:

(i)The Malaysian Employers Federations (MEF), and (ii)The Malaysian Trade Union Congress (MTUC)

The Malaysian Trade Union Congress (MTUC) is a federation of trade unions and registered under the Societies Act, 1955. It is the oldest National Centre representing the Malaysian workers. The Unions affiliated to MTUC represent all major industries and sectors (where Trade Unionism is permitted) with approximately 500,000 members[6].

The Malaysian Employers Federation (MEF) is the central organization of private sector employers in Malaysia recognised nationally, regionally and internationally. Established in 1959, MEF promotes and safeguards the rights and interest of employers.[7]

Foreign Direct Investment

In terms of foreign direct investment issues, MTUC feels that having a national minimum wage would attract more investors. However, MEF disagree with this idea. As an employer, MEF feels that to operate within a competitive scenario and to consider the cost of doing business is a vital factor in setting up a business. If the labour cost is higher than what is considered acceptable, employers might close business and move to other countries which the labour cost is lower. What is preferable is that, in terms of wage policy, the objectives should be to encourage the global investment in the Malaysian economy, help companies regain their cost competitiveness, and to preserve jobs for employees and minimise unemployment.

The government on the other hand are more concerned with employees' skills and productivity improvement.Despite impressive economic growth and rapid development since independence overall productivity and wages of Malaysian workers remains low. It has been agreed that the real reason is not because Malaysian workers are not productive. It is that employers were so successful in suppressing wages that there is no incentive to invest in research and development for productivity improvement (The Star, 25 April 2008). It is more profitable for employers to employ lowly paid workers (including foreign workers) than to invest in modern technology and machinery which will indirectly contribute to greater productivity.

Productivity Link Wage System

The introduction of a national minimum wage would represent an increase in employers' labour costs and a shift in the relative prices of capital and labour.

6 www.mtuc.org
7 www.mef.org.my

If labour is more expensive, capital becomes relatively less expensive and we can expect firms to seek opportunities to invest in labour saving capital. While this may produce an unemployment effect, it is also an important step towards modernisation. Other productivity improvements might also be achieved through greater efficiency, reduction of waste, and work intensification.

As mentioned by Goh (2009), labour productivity is relatively important in influencing wage increases in the labour market. The Malaysian government has recognized that wage levels must be increased in order to improve living standards and in terms of reducing poverty. Increasing wages without a concomitant increase in productivity would result in a build up of inflationary pressures and may weaken the country in terms of attracting foreign investment. There are studies concerning the link between productivity and wages, however, most of this research is based on the manufacturing sector rather than the service sector. In Malaysia itself, there is a lack of local studies on the relationship between productivity and real wages, except for Ho and Yap (2001). Ho and Yap (2001) found a positive relationship between productivity and wages for Malaysian manufacturing industry,

In terms of the service sector, the Malaysian government has come up with a scheme called Productivity Linked Wage System (PLWS). The PLWS is a strategic tool for enhancing business efficiency as it links the payment of wages to productivity. The PLWS aims to enhance competitiveness and promote employment stability in the private sector. The PLWS system aims to ensure that companies adopt a systematic approach to linking wages to productivity, to sustain labour cost competitiveness (National Human Resource Institute, Ministry of Human Resource, Malaysia, 2009).

According to the government, through the implementation of PLWS, employers will be able to develop performance measurements for improving productivity to ensure that productivity increases are the foundation for determining wage increase. The government has placed much emphasis on productivity improvement and this is a desired national goal. Their preferred approach has been to exhort employers to adopt the PLWS which establishes a closer link between wages and productivity so as to enhance competitiveness at firm level. It will also enable employers to develop a wider and systematic approach towards improving productivity and wages through the active involvement and co-operation of all employees.

In May 2009, as the Malaysian Employers' Federation (MEF) responded to the government and expressed their opposition towards having a national minimum wage, claiming that employers are 'allergic" to the minimum wage issue and strongly oppose to the MTUC's proposal. In fact, MEF thinks that the wages are to be tied with productivity as according to them, it is the most equitable and fair system being practised universally. MEF further comment that that in order to increase productivity, the workers had to be retrained and the companies had to acquire new machinery and equipment. Other than retraining, the qualifications of the employees also need to be certified in order to make it easier for the industry to emplace them in the correct salary scale.(The Star, May 2009) MEF on the other hand also finds that it would create a positive direction in wage negotiation when it is being linked to the productivity. MEF has always supported the productivity linked wages system which takes into account the performance of employees which contributes to the performance of the organization as a whole.

The PLWS is said to have a positive effect on employees in that they are encouraged to be more productive, and to perform better, knowing that they will be able to receive a fair share of the gains through their efforts. Basically, it is a win – win situation for both employers and employees as both works together to enhance performance of the firm.

However, although the government is promoting the PLWS among the private sector employers, this move seems to not be getting their attention. According to the results shown in the 2008 National Employment Report, of 337,473 private sector employers throughout Malaysia, only 71,547 (21.2%) practices the Productivity Linked Wage system (PLWS) (2008 National Employment Report, Ministry of Human Resource). It seems clear that it will take more than exhortation to stimulate productivity enhancing change in the Malaysian private sector.

In addition to the arguments about improving productivity, there is also the impact of an increase in wages on local purchasing power. This could be expected to stimulate spending and some savings, which, in classic Keynesian analysis, would generate demand, stimulating the demand for labour, and contribute to economic growth. Since the minimum wage would affect the purchasing power of lower paid workers we might expect that the increase in spending power would be confined to the local economy with limited leakage to imports and savings. At the household level, we might also expect that an increase in wages will enable more families to support children into further education.

Reduce Dependency On Foreign Labour

The government rejected the MTUC's proposal in 1997 giving the reason that the implementation of a minimum wage would have a negative impact on the nation's industrialization and the privatization policy that was being implemented during the administration of Tun Dr Mahathir Mohamad.

According to the MTUC, there is no reason for the government to delay further the passing of national minimum wage legislation to be applicable to all workers. By enforcing a decent minimum wage, government will be able to attract more

Malaysian workers and reduce dependency on foreign labour. However, the former Human resource Minister Datuk Seri Dr. Fong Chan Onn says that a RM 900 minimum wage would lead to an inflow of migrant workers from the neighbouring countries as Malaysian wages would rise well above the average pay in those places (Asia Times, 2007).

The former minister also expressed his concern that a national minimum wage would push up operating costs and drive foreign investors to Indochina, China and India. Although the government are concerned over the workers' wages, the government also must also ensure that Malaysia remains competitive in the global context.

According to the Ministry of Human Resources, the Malaysian economy registered near full employment with the unemployment rate at 3.5 percent in 2005 and even lower at 3.32 percent in 2007. Labour shortages especially of low skilled workers, resulted in the increase demand for foreign workers. Foreign workers with work permits increased to 1.7 million in 2005 with the manufacturing sector as the largest employer (Labour Situation in Malaysia : overview 2008/2009, Ministry of Human Resource,Malaysia).

The intake of foreign workers into Malaysia was legalized after 1992, although initially it was limited to the construction and plantation sectors. In 2000, however the intake was extended to include the manufacturing and services (including hotel and restaurant) sectors as well. In 2002, the intake was liberalized further, being extended to all economic sectors. The more liberal policy towards employment of foreign workers was attributed to the rapid economic growth enjoyed by the country, driven largely by rapid industrialization. An upward surge of foreign workers' employment in Malaysia has been recorded since the early 1990s which further accelerated during the 8th Malaysia plan period (2001-2005). In 2000 there were 807,096 foreign workers but by 2006, the foreign workers registered in employment were 1,869,209. In 2007, the number breached the 2 million mark for the first time (see figure 1.3). Thus, over the 2000-2005 periods, the proportion of foreign workers in Malaysia climbed from 8.5 percent in 2000 to 16.1 percent in 2005 and 17.2 percent in 2007.

Figure 1.3 Foreign Workers Employment in Malaysia as at 2007

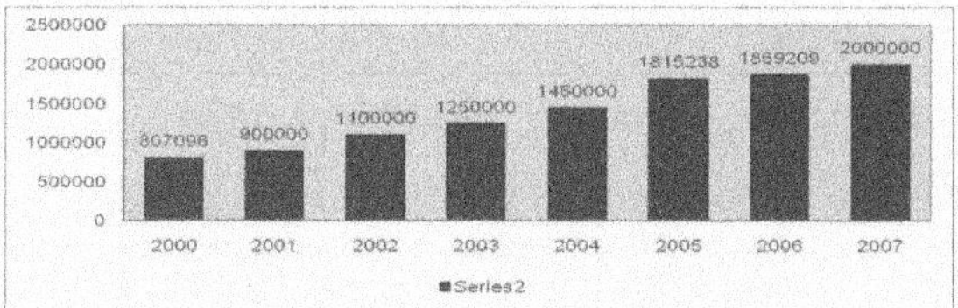

Source: Labour Department, Ministry of Human Resources, Malaysia

In terms of sectors, foreign workers are predominantly employed in the manufacturing sector followed by the plantation sector. These sectors, in 2007 accounted for 36 and 24.6 percent of foreign workers respectively. Foreign workers were also common as domestic helpers (15.7 percentage) and in the construction industry (14.2) percent (refer table 1.0). From 2006 to 2007, the total number of foreign workers in the Malaysian labour force increased by more than 151,000.

Table 1.0 Foreign workers Employment by Sector in Malaysia, 2006-2007

Sector	2006		2007	
	No.	%	No.	%
Manufacturing	545,412	34.58	726,561	35.95
Plantation	477,497	25.55	498,858	24.58
Construction	257,809	14.33	285,943	14.15
Services	166,829	8.93	192,200	8.51
Domestic Helpers	310,562	15.51	317,537	15.71
Total	**1,869,209**	**100**	**2,021,099**	**100**

Source: Labour Department, Ministry of Human Resources, Malaysia

In the 2008 National Employment Report, a survey conducted by the Ministry of Human Resources amongst a sample of 337,473 employers, the total number of foreign workers working in a specified sectors was as follows :

Table 1.1 Total amount and percentage of employees in Malaysia as at 2008

Area	LOCAL WORKERS		FOREIGN WORKERS		Grand Total	
	AMOUNT	%	AMOUNT	%	AMOUNT	%
Peninsular	2,492,008	84.3	***464,687***	15.7	2,956,695	100
Sabah	209,354	65.6	***109,776***	34.4	319,130	100
Sarawak	238,143	80.3	***58,472***	19.7	296,615	100
MALAYSIA	**2,939,505**	**82.3**	***632,935***	**17.7**	**3,572,440**	**100**

* the report is based on a survey conducted on 337,473 participating employers
Source: National Employment Report, 2008, Ministry of Human Resources, Malaysia

Table 1.2 Total amount and percentage of employees in Malaysia according to sector as at 2008

Sector	Local		Foreign Labour	
	Total	%	Total	%
Agricultural	231,225	7.9	185,231	29.3
Fisheries	6,521	0.2	3,105	0.5
Mining	16,438	0.2	1,582	0.2
Manufacturig	***777,278***	***26.4***	***284,780***	***45***
Electricity, Gas and water	37,074	1.3	2,738	0.4
Construction	127,552	4.3	31,984	5.1
Entrepreneurship, Retail trade	656,408	22.3	44,567	7
Hotel and Restaurant	144,364	4.9	27,855	4.4
Transportation	113,563	3.9	9,999	1.6
Finance	385,622	13.1	1,057	0.2
Real estate	223,132	7.6	16,408	2.6
Education	30,901	1.1	908	0.1
Health and social work	43,969	1.5	2,374	0.4
Community/social service	145,377	4.9	20,334	3.2
Others	81	0	13	0
Total	**2,939,505**	**100**	**632,935**	**100**

* the report is based on a survey conducted on 337,473 participating employers
Source: National Employment Report 2008, Ministry of Human Resource, Malaysia

MTUC in its proposal has stated that, with the implementation of the minimum wage policy, there should be reduced dependency on foreign labour. This argument is debatable although the growing number of foreign workers in Malaysia is indeed a growing concern and creates social pressures in the country. In economic terms, the introduction of minimum wages and applying it to foreign workers as well will more likely increase the supply of foreign workers rather than decrease it.

The MTUC arguments for reducing the dependency on foreign labour by the implementation of minimum wage is also debatable because the foreign labour in Malaysia does much of the dangerous, difficult and demanding (3Ds) work in sectors such as manufacturing, plantations and construction. From the MTUC's perspective, not only will the minimum wage reduce the dependency on foreign labour, but also legislating on health and safety policy will attract locals to fill in the gap. However, again, this depends on the local employees' willingness to do the 3Ds job as mentioned above. It could be argued that the dependencies on foreign labour will persist as long as there is demand for the kind of work that they perform. The Master Builders Association of Malaysia has expressed its concern over this matter. According to the president of the association, Ng Kee Leen, foreign workers would be needed in the construction industry until a time came when locals were able to replace them. 95% of the workers in the construction industry in the Klang Valley alone were foreign workers. During the industry's negative growth in 2006, it still employed about 300,000 foreign workers. Hence, Ng concludes that if we put a stop to foreign workers, then the industry will also stop unless the locals have an incentive to replace them.

It is the intention of the Ninth Malaysia Plan that, "the number of foreign workers will be reduced gradually to provide greater employment opportunities to local workers and to reduce administrative costs as well as the outflow of foreign exchange." However, there is no strategy on how the target can be achieved provided in the Ninth Malaysia plan. It does mention that "local labour, particularly graduates, will have to change their mindset so as not to be too choosy in selecting occupations." (Ninth Malaysia Plan). Employers will have to look and compare the cost of hiring local and foreign labour should the minimum wage being implemented. Hiring foreign labour would become more costly than local staff because of the transaction costs involved with work permits, visas, and other additional on-costs. This should switch demand in favour of local workers.

Eradication of poverty

According to the MTUC, the increased salary of the public sector workers has affected both public and private sector workers. The MTUC claims that the private sector workers especially the lower rankings are still living in poverty due to low wages. According to the MTUC's 2006 survey, the current lowest wages recorded in the private sector are those of Security guards with a monthly wage of RM 600 (Aud 210.33) , factory workers RM 300 (Aud 105) and plantation workers and cleaners RM 450 (Aud 157). Those workers tend to have a second job to support their daily lives, which causes problems not only for their respective families but also socially.

The monthly minimum wage rate of RM 600 was decided by MTUC in 1996 after taking into consideration current costs, and the rate was considered the most realistic in order to safeguard the private sector worker's living and welfare at that time. In 2008, the proposed rate of RM 600 was raised to RM 900 a month. This was considered reasonable to cater for a worker and family at the current cost of living. Furthermore, the rate proposed would allow higher contributions towards the monthly employees' provident fund and also the social security fund. The higher monthly contributions would make employees better prepared for retirement.

According to Saget (2002 p.67), as for governments, a major purpose of the minimum wage is to contribute to alleviating poverty. The minimum wage can act as a social safety net in countries where social security is as yet little developed. Saget (2002 p.67) further explains that:

Governments have also used the minimum wage to redistribute income in society, to promote productive employment and to enhance demand driven growth, this is because low-income families tend to consume more and save less, in proportion, than do higher-income families. In developing countries, the minimum wage is often at the core of social dialogue. Removing it may amount to seriously damaging the quality of social dialogue.

Saget (2002 p.67)

Furthermore, according to Saget (2008, p.68) quoting from the ILO's *Organization, bargaining and social dialogue in a globalizing world 2000* , in some countries where waged employment is developed, increasing the minimum wage may lower wage inequality and thus help to reduce income inequality. Most economists would agree that inequality affects the growth of the economy through a combination of inequality of access to credit markets, asset inequality and human capital inequality. In these countries, coordinated wage bargaining also acts as an important tool to achieve low inflation combined with low unemployment when the growth of the economy leads to pressure on wages to increase.

MTUC's main expressed concern is that, if the government keeps on refusing the proposal for a national minimum wage, it will contribute to serious social problems among the low income families.

Although MTUC argues that minimum wages would help in eradicating poverty, the official poverty rate in Malaysia is very low at 2.7%. However, it has been suggested that the poverty line in Malaysia has been drawn at an unreasonably low level (Musa, M.Bakri, 2007). However the poverty rate is relatively lower than in neighbouring countries e.g. Indonesia and Thailand.

Furthermore, it could be argued that the poverty level might be better attacked using different policies, e.g investment in education, support for single parents and orphans and special programs targeted on specific impoverished groups such as the bumiputera minorities in Sabah and Sarawak and also the *Orang Asli* (Malaysian indigenous people).

Impact on Small and Medium Enterprises (SMEs)

In reviewing the MTUC's proposal for a national minimum wage with the suitability of the current situation, MEF would prefer if the present Malaysian economic structure be looked at first. Businesses in Malaysia is made up of 99% of small and medium enterprises (SMEs) varieties ranging from a small food and beverage kiosk, provision shops, coffee shops, servicing shops (mechanics, laundry service and health care),petrol kiosk and medium enterprises.

According to MEF, the implementation of a national minimum wage would force many of the SMEs to close down their business. As these SMEs are the key players in boosting up the Malaysian economic development, their development and performance should be assisted and monitored rather than having their effort and survival dampened with the implication of a national minimum wage. Rainnie (1989) in Arrowsmith, Gilman, Edwards, Ram, (2003), explained that employment in small firms is likely to be harsh as a result of exposure to more competitive markets and dependence on large firms as customers which resembles the fragmented "price taking' model of firms in the tradition of neoclassical economics. As mention by Arrowsmith, Gilman, Edwards, Ram, (2003), small firms not only operate in a highly competitive market, but are also incapable of influencing their environment. Thus, wages in small firms are expected to be relatively low, and are more vulnerable to regulatory shocks. This is supported by Edwards and Gilman (1999) as orthodox economic theory predicts that any regulatory interference which raises the labour cost above market equilibrium will lead to unemployment.

Wage Determination

As mentioned above, the Government generally believes that wage levels should be as follows; (i) left for the market to determine, (ii) through negotiations and (iii) collective bargaining. However, it was clear that in certain sectors of the economy workers needed greater protection from exploitation and that low wages were failing to attract good quality local staff, particularly graduates.

At present, wages in Malaysia are determined by the market forces and where workers are unionised, the management negotiate with the unions in terms of wage settlement. Having to have these ways of determining wage, it makes it possible to have wage differences among different types of economic activities regardless of firm sizes, locations and the nature of business itself in which leads MEF as the representative of employers in Malaysia to strongly disagree on having a national minimum wage as the present wage determination system are said to be far more efficient.

In terms of having to have the market to determine the wage or it falls on the employers to set wage, as explained by Card and Krueger (1995) the assumption that employers can hire all the workers they want at the going wage rate is widely adopted in modern discussions of the labour market. This assumption is the key player of the standard labour market and gives proper reasoning that each worker is paid on his/her "marginal product". The generalization of the standard model gives rise to what is known as the monopsony model. Card and Krueger further explains that in a monopsony situation, firms usually operate with ongoing vacancies. Different firms might choose to pay different wage rates, depending on the sensitivity of the recruiting effort to the level of wages. While some firms would choose to offer a lower wage and to operate with higher vacancies and higher turnover, others would choose a higher wage and to operate within lower vacancies and lower turnover.

According to Card and Kruger (1995), monopsony carries an interesting aspect where it can reserve the predicted adverse employment effect of an increases minimum wage. In a monopsony situation, a slight increase in the minimum wage will lead employers to increase employment. This is because; a higher minimum wage enables formerly low wage firms to fill their vacancies more quickly.

Management-Employee Flexibilities

One of the arguments brought up by MEF against the national minimum wage proposal was that having a national minimum wage would only introduce inflexibilities into the system and interfere with management-workers relationships.[8] From the viewpoint of MEF, the present system of industrial relation in Malaysia allows parties to resolve issues themselves and also through conciliation services. Should it fail to reach resolution, the Industrial Court will hear the matter and will hand down an award that binds the parties and more importantly prohibits industrial action.

"Decent Wage" As A Tool

MEF discard the idea that a national minimum wage would promote a decent wage that will eliminate wage exploitation, reduce poverty and ensuring equal pay for equal work. MEF also believe that, all the objectives mentioned above could not only be met when the economy prospers instead, continuous economic development will help improve the welfare of wage earners because the increase prosperity will make possible increase in wages. Therefore, MEF believe that a minimum wage will not ensure the economic expansion needed which is contrary to MTUC's believes.

According to the ILO, a minimum wage is introduced to "secure workers a reasonable standard of life as this is understood in their time and country" (ILO 1992). This form of minimum wage is usually referred to as a "safety net". Another policy reason for setting a minimum wage can be to ensure that income and profit are fairly distributed to workers (Chandarot, 2006)

8 www.mohreng.blogspot.com

4.2 Fixing Minimum Wage Level

In terms of setting up a minimum wage for a country, using Saget's (2008) criteria, the rate proposed by MTUC would fall into the category of a 'maxi minimum wage' i.e. one that is 60% or more of the average wage for an economy[9].

Countries are classified as being in a situation of "mini minimum wage" if their ratio of minimum wage to GDP per capita is less than 0.30, and as being in a situation of "maxi minimum wage" if their ratio is above 0.60. These two figures are used as cut-off points, in an arbitrary way, based on the distribution of ratios of the minimum wage to GDP per capita (Saget, 2008).

When a country sets their minimum wage at a high price, too high in fact to be called a real minimum wage, then it is called a 'maxi minimum wage"(Saget,2008). It is considered high because the minimum wage legislation amounts up to average wage fixation. Usually, having poorly developed collective bargaining is the factor behind the "maxi minimum wages" occurrence. Thus, making the minimum wage consultations as the only forum where trade unions can make their demands known, with the danger that the resulting minimum wage is not a genuine threshold, but rather the actual wage earned by most formal workers (Saget, 2008).

Saget (2008, p.38) argued that some developing countries have gone from negotiating a minimum wage to negotiating a kind of average wage. A close examination of the legislation in some Asian countries indicates that in a number of cases the minimum wage is not really a minimum wage, but rather the effective wage paid to most unskilled or semi-skilled workers for example the Philippines, Indonesia and Thailand fall in this category.

Saget also suggested that there are some disadvantages of setting a national minimum wage at a relatively high level in developing countries: (i) it will result in displacement of workers from the formal to the informal sector where the increased supply of labour will cause wages to fall; (ii)it will discourage workers from joining trade unions and keep collective bargaining weak; (iii) the minimum wage will be unaffordable for some employers (especially small firms) who will demand exemptions thus weakening the coverage of the minimum wage; (iv) and there will be a high level of non-compliance requiring strong enforcement of the policy. It is further argued that the increase in wages, if not corrected by corresponding productivity increases, will result in inflation that impacts most on low income groups which is in line with the Government's concern over the inflation issues.

9 Based on a minimum wage of RM900 + 300/1731.66 (monthly GDP per capita as at first quarter est 2007) = 0.63

4.2.1 Coverage Of The Proposed Minimum Wage

The MTUCs claim is for a national minimum wage covering all workers (including foreign workers), in all industrial sectors, and all regions. The advantages of this blanket approach to minimum wage policy are that : (i) All employers will experience the same increase and there will be no opportunity for undercutting' (ii) Entitlements to the minimum wage are easily understood and well known making compliance more likely.

The disadvantages of comprehensive coverage are: (i) some employers, especially SMEs may find the increase unaffordable. (ii) regional disparities in purchasing power exist. (iii) the supply of foreign workers will increase.

For these reasons, some governments have chosen policy options that are less than comprehensive by targeting minimum wages at certain groups and industries, or excluding certain categories of employment. These include:

Excluding young workers and apprentices: thought to be most exposed to potential unemployment. Some governments have opted to set a lower minimum wage for young workers to make them more attractive to employers who may then be persuaded to offer training places;

Excluding foreign workers: this might be justified on the grounds that an increase in the minimum wage would attract more foreign workers willing to work for that minimum. This excess supply might have the impact of dragging wage levels down to the minimum such that the minimum wage begins to look like the maximum. However, the consequences of exclusion are likely to push up the demand for foreign labour by employers who seek to undercut competitors. Any exclusion of foreign workers under the minimum wage policy would need to be accompanied by some form of quota regulation e.g. stipulating that no more than 10% of an employer's workforce may be registered as foreign workers and stronger border controls. In practice, the exclusion of foreign workers is likely to have many unintended consequences.

Targeting particular occupations or industrial sectors: this has the attraction of attacking existing low paid occupations and industrial sectors that suffer from a shortage of local labour supply. It is this approach that has found favour with the Malaysian government with its recent introduction of minimum wages in four sectors. This will be discussed further later in the following section.

4.3 Recent Policy Developments

In 2008, the Malaysian Government announced that several commissions of inquiries and wage councils had been formed to look into minimum wages of security guards, clinic assistants, hotel and catering staff and general workers from small holdings. The wage councils were later established for workers from the electronics and textile sectors. This is prior to the MTUC's proposal for a national minimum wage and it will take roughly six month to one year for the wage council to do their research and come up with a specific rate (The Star, October 2008).

As mentioned above, the sectors taken into the consideration of the wage councils are security guards, clinic assistants, hotel and catering staff and general workers from small holdings and also the electronics and textile sectors. The sectors above especially security guards currently receive as low as RM 400 (USD$125) per month as their basic wage plus supplements made up of overtime and other benefits. The current pay for security guards is said to be inadequate for survival. They are being paid at low rate for a high-risk job. In a survey by the wage council for security guards, even food stall assistants and foreign security guards get paid more. One of the other reasons to introduce a decent minimum wage for security guards is to cope with the problem of outsourcing the licence to the outsider or foreign workers.

Clinic Assistants receive low levels of pay given the work burden they carry. According to the Wage Council's report on a minimum wage for clinic assistant, not only the starting salary, but also their rest days and annual holidays are inadequate. (Wage Council's report for a minimum wage for clinic assistant, Ministry of Human Resources, Malaysia, 2007)

There is a minimum wage set for the hotel and catering sector, however, it is fairly low and was set over 25 years ago at the rate of RM185 (USD$57). This amount is highly irrelevant for the current living condition. Although most hotel employers pay more than the minimum wage rate, the hotel and catering staff indeed needs a better wage so as for them to cater with their living. A new minimum wage rate will also boost up their morale to work and provide better services in the hotel and catering sector as the Tourism Industry is booming since a few years back. (Ninth Malaysia Plan)

The minimum salary for the textile and electronic sectors on the other hand, will be reviewed for it to be in tune with the current economic situation.

4.3.1 New Minimum Wage Rate for Hotel and Catering Sector

The recent policy development revolves around the minimum wage rate setting which covers the setting up of wage council for the hotel and catering staff. The wage council for the hotel and catering staff includes the representative of the following bodies : (i)Ministry of Human Resources, (ii)Malaysian Trade Union Congress, (iii)Association of Hotel Employers, (iv)Malaysian Association of Hotel Owners, (v) Malaysian Employers Federation, and the (vi)National Union of Hotel, Bar and Restaurant Workers.

In January 2010, the ministry announced that the rate for the new minimum wage for hotel and catering employee will be announced in March 2010. To date (June 2010), no announcement has been made just yet. However, the rate being discussed among the wage council members for the hotel and catering sector are RM575 (US$169).This section provides some interview results with the wage council committee members for the hotel and catering sector.

As the ministry has mentioned in January that this new rate will be announced in March, however, according to the National Union of Hotel, Bar and Restaurant Workers, the rate is yet to be finalised and the possibility of the government announcing the new rate in March was highly unlikely. The Union body agrees to the rate being discussed although they still think that further discussion is needed as there are many different categories of hotels ranging from 2 to 6 stars located in the various states in Malaysia. One standard rate might be to high or too low according to the categories.

In terms of the rate discussed, the MTUC still argue that the rate should be higher to provide the worker with the "safety net" and decent wages. MTUC are still pushing for a national minimum wage instead of a sectoral minimum wage. As mentioned earlier, MTUC disagree with the statement saying that cost of living in various states in Malaysia varies and believes that the consumer goods across the country are similar.

According to the Malaysian Association of Hotel Owners (MAHO), they agree to have a decent amount of wage to be paid to the hotel employees. They provide two reasons for this statement :(i) in the recognition of the increasing cost of living, (ii) to attract a better quality workforce. However, they would prefer that any increases in wages should be performance based rather than a standardised rate base. A small increase (standard wage) in wages either in the private or public sector, would lead to increase of price in consumer goods as well which would bring no meaning to the increase in wages. In order for the employees to survive, it does not only depend on the employers to provide appropriate and decent wage but the government should play an important role in monitoring the price of consumer goods.

Therefore, MAHO highly recommend the government to further look into this issue where it concerns the controlled price of good, so that people at large would not have to pay for the unnecessary cost. MAHO also strongly believe that employees should be rewarded for their performance and productivity not merely to cover the cost of living. Having to have a standardised increase in wages is not effective as it would draw the employee out of the commitment to their work. Especially in the hotel and tourism industry where most of the jobs in this industry are labour oriented such as the doorman, housekeeper, waiter and waitresses and others. These jobs are not low rated jobs but the hotels could not afford to pay high wages for these jobs. Instead, employees in this sector are compensated with service charges which provide them a better take home salary although their basic salary is low. Although the basic salaries of the employees are low, the hotels provide all the workers with the "payment in kind".[10] The hotels in Malaysia practices PLWS in their approach to wage determination. In the PLWS system, productivity is defined as the outcome and the achievement of performance achieved out of the work done. This system combines fixed and variable components illustrated in the following example of pay for a hotel receptionist:

Example calculation:

Hotel receptionist

Fixed components
Basic wage = RM 302 / month
Yearly wage increment = RM 34.00 / year (the increment is based on what is specified in the employment contract or the collective agreements)

Variable Components
Monthly service points
Points = 2.0 *
Monthly point value
= 2.0 x RM 100 **
=RM 200.00/month

* *a service point of this particular employee depends on the length of years of work, experience or the work performance and service points amount is obtained through the division of total payment of the accumulated service charge for a month duration with the total service points of all employees.*

** RM 9000/90 points = RM 100

Eg : accumulated service charge is RM 10,000 and 90% of it (RM 9,000) will be distributed to the eligible employees. If the accumulated service points for the eligible employees are 90 points, therefore the service points for the month is RM 100 (RM 9,000 / 90)

Overall total

= Basic wage + monthly service points

= RM 302 + RM 200

= RM 502[11]

---

10 Payment in kind includes the free meals, free transportations, free accommodations and other benefit that hotels provide their employee with.

11 This amount does not include other payment in kind such as Free meals, free transportation, and others

MAHO are also concerned about getting the locals to work in the hotel and catering industry, with attractive salary scale, it would attract the locals especially the graduates. From the interview data, MAHO agreed that they would support any proposal to remunerate the employees because it is important to attract good employees, good remuneration system would help in retaining employee and reduce the amount of turnover and good remunerations will help the employees to increase their productivity. However, there are two issues being brought forward in determining the new wage rate for the hotel and catering sector namely : (i) The service charge issue and (ii) Employee's saving issues.

The service charge issue

Among other issues that arise in determining the new minimum wage rate for the hotel and catering sector are the service charge issue. Both MAHO and AHE agree that the ministry should amend the definition of basic wages to a new proper definition that exclude the service charge. Currently, service charges are excluded from the basic wage definition but it is included alongside the basic wage in terms of calculation of take home pay. The wage system in the hotel industry in Malaysia comprises of the basic wage plus service points. Service points as defined by the Ministry of Human Resources are as follows:

Service points: Rewards points fixed by hotels / bars / restaurants as a method to allocate to the employees the accumulated amounts collected through the *service charge* imposed.

Service Charge: The total amount of service charge collected from the customers will be disbursed to the employees according to the point system used.

(Translated from *Sistem Upah yang Dikaitan dengan Produktiviti*, Industrial Relations Department, Ministry of Human Resources, 2008)

The service points however, vary according to hotels' standards and fluctuate monthly. Most hotel employees earn their highest service points during peak holiday seasons. Therefore, the government should consider the definition of wages along with the new minimum wage rate to be set.

Employee's saving Issues

MAHO and AHE also reject the saying that hotel employees in Malaysia are poorly paid and the employer's EPF[12] contribution based on the low basic wage are too low that it does not help in the future. Rejecting MTUC's earlier statement on low rates of minimum wage, according to MAHO and AHE, hotel em-

12 EPF (Employee's Provident Fund) are savings for the employees upon retirement. Employees contribute 11 percent of their monthly income to the EPF, and the employer will contribute another 12 percent or more. These contributions are made by employees for their retirement benefit.

ployees in Malaysia are not poorly paid as they received the service charge, "payment in kind" and other various benefits as explained in the previous section. However, they agreed that the EPF contributions are fairly low but the employees should be able and should be able to afford enough to save up their take home pay which includes the service point that would rise up to RM 2000 per month on peak season. Employees must also have their own awareness in terms of savings rather than depending on the EPF itself and consider all the benefits and payment in kind that they get. However, this issue will be further ventured in the future research.

5. Conclusion

The MTUC's case for a national minimum wage is compelling in some respects: (i) addressing the differential between public and private sector workers; (ii) Stimulating productivity enhancing activity in the private sector and facilitating economic growth. There are also strong arguments to be made that national minimum wages are consistent with the nation's objectives to become an advance industrial economy with decent living standards [13](Vision 2020).

In general, a minimum wage is consistent with the objective of Malaysia's Vision 2020 which aims mainly at improving the life of all Malaysians, protecting the dignity of the ethnic groups and safeguarding them from oppression by others (Chamhuri and Hassan, 1999).

Upon analysis, it is evident that the arguments about reduced dependency on foreign labour are misleading. If anything, a comprehensive national minimum wage will increase the supply of foreign labour. If the minimum wage applies to foreign labour, other policy including a higher level of border protection will be required. However, the MTUC has been successful in drawing attention to what they perceive to be a problem with the growing number of foreign workers in Malaysia. A stronger argument might be developed in support of raising standards of health and safety at work and other policies designed to eliminate 3D's jobs and create jobs that are more attractive to the locals.

The argument about the eradication of poverty is relatively weak. Malaysia shows limited poverty exists and where it does exist, other policies measure might be more successful. It remains to be seen at what level the government will set the new sectoral minimum wages.

13 Vision 2020, was first mentioned in 1991. It was introduced by our former Prime Minister, Mahathir Mohamed during the tabling of our Sixth Malaysian Plan. Vision 2020 aims at self-sufficient industrial developed nation, complete with an economy, in 2020 that will be eightfold stronger than the economy of the early 1990s.

The MTUC's demand for a national minimum wage may present difficulties in that it would be possible for employers to exploit the situation by raising working hours. Therefore, the minimum wage would need to be accompanied by formal limits on working time or specified as an hourly rate.

In our analysis, Malaysia is a special case. Within the region, it is unusual in being one of the few countries that does not have a minimum wage of some type. What is particularly unusual is its development status. Malaysia is simultaneously a highly developed, developing and underdeveloped nation. It is therefore extremely difficult for any government to devise policy that meets the needs of all Malaysians. In terms of the new minimum wage rate policy development, the differentials in cost of living between the regions are important. Any attempt to set a standard minimum wage across the nation or sectoral based would likely result in dislocation in local economies. An absolute bare minimum poverty line standard could be declared and a set of calculations based on purchasing power parity could be devised for each region. This is hazardous and would need very careful research and management.

There is probably never going to be a perfect time to introduce a major policy intervention such as national minimum wage. It would be understandable, if a government chose to delay policy in the light of recent turbulent economic conditions. However, the notion of decent living standards fits with the grand vision for Malaysia. In determining an appropriate time for the introduction of a national minimum wage, it may be helpful to generate a set of economic conditions e.g. desired levels of unemployment and inflation that, once satisfied and aligned, would give the green light for the introduction of new wage laws.

References

Aminuddin,M,2006 *"Malaysian Industrial relations and Employment Law"* Mc Graw Hill (Malaysia) Sdn. Bhd.

Aminuddin M, 1991 *"An A-Z of Malaysian Employment Law"* Mc Graw Hill (Malaysia) Sdn. Bhd.

Boal,W. and Ransom M, 1997, *"Monopsony in the Labour Market"* Journal of Economic Literature Vol. XXXV (March 1997), pp. 86-112

Arrowsmith,J, Mark,G.Edwards,P and Ram,M , 2003*"The Impact of the National Minimum Wage in Small Firms"* British Journal of Industrial Relations 41:3 September 2003 0007–1080 pp. 435–456

Arrowsmith,J, Mark,G.Edwards,P.Ram,M, 2002 *"Pay determination in small firms in the UK: the case of the response to the National Minimum Wage"*

British Journal of Industrial Relations 41:3 September 2003 0007–1080 pp. 435–456 Industrial Relations Journal 33:1 ISSN 0019-8692

Card, D. and A. B. Krueger 1995, "*Myth and Measurement: the New Economics of the Minimum Wage*" (Princeton, Princeton University Press).

Chandarot,K: Daney Liv, 2006 *"Comparative Study on Minimum Wage Provisions in Selected ASEAN and Asian Countries,"* Cambodia Institute of Development Study

Gunderson,M.2005 *"Miminum Wages In Canada: Theory, Evidence And Policy"* Federal Labour Standards Review Commission

ILO Minimum Wage Database: http://www.ilo.org/travaildatabase

ILO. 2000. *Organization, bargaining and social dialogue in a globalizing world.* Geneva.

ILO,2009. *Update on Minimum wage Developments*, BG.304/ESP/3, Geneva

ILO: Minimum wages: Wage-fixing machiinery, application and supervision, Report III (Part 4B) (General Survey), International Labour Conference, 79th Session, Geneva, 1992

Malaysian Employers Federation www.mef.org.my

Malaysian Trade Union Congress www.mtuc.org.my

Malaysia, 2008, *" National Employment Report 2008."* Ministry of Human Resources of Malaysia

Malaysia, 2008, *" Labour situation in Malaysia : overview 2008/09."* Ministry of Human Resources of Malaysia

Malaysia, 2008 "*Sistem Upah Yang Diakaitkan Dengan Productiviti*" Industrial relations Department, Mininstry of Human resources of Malaysia

Malaysia 2006 *"Ninth Malaysia Plan"* Economic Planning Unit, Prime Minister's Department.

Malaysia 2007 "*Wage council report on a minimum wage for clinic assistant*" Ministry of Human resources of Malaysia

Malaysian Employment Act 1955

Malaysian Wage Council Act 1947

Ministry of Human Resources of Malaysia (2001), *Guideline on Wage Reform System, 2001.* Retrieve from http://www.mohr.gov.my/mygoveg/makluman/bullel.htm

Mohd, 2009 "A critical Analysis of the case for a national Minimum wgae for Malaysia" PhD Conference in Economics and Business, University of Western Australia, Perth, Australia. www.business.uwa.edu.au/__.../Mohd_Husna_Perth_conference_UWA.pdf

Musa, M. Bakri (2007). "Towards A Competitive Malaysia." Petaling Jaya: Strategic Information and Research Development Centre. pp. 124. ISBN 978-983-3782-20-8

MTUC. 2007, Memorandum to YAB Datuk Seri Abdullah Ahmad Badawi, Prime Minister of Malaysia on a minimum wage RM 900 and Cost of living allowance RM300

Netto, A. (2002). "*Minimum Wage Row Splits Workers*". *Asia Times*. Retrieved November 18, 2005, from http://www.atimes.com/seasia/BE12Ae02. html

Neumark, David and William Wascher, 2008, "*Minimum Wages*" Cambridge, Mass.: MIT Press ISBN 9780262141024

Neumark, David and William Wascher, 2000, *"Minimum Wages and Employment: A Case Study of the Fast-Food Industry in New Jersey and Pennsylvania: Comment," American Economic Review* 90(5), 1362–1396.

Neumark, David and William Wascher, 2002 *"Do Minimum Wages Fight Poverty?" Economic Inquiry* 40(3) 315–333.

Ninth Malaysia Plan

Saget, C (2008)."*Fixing minimum wage levels in developing countries: Common failures and remedies*"*International Labour Review*, Vol. 147 (2008), No. 1

Saget, C. 2006. "*Wage fixing in the informal economy: Evidence from Brazil, India, Indonesia and South Africa*." Conditions of Work and Employment Series No. 16. Geneva, ILO.

Saget, C.2006 *"Fixing minimum wage levels in developing countries; common failures and remedies"* Jakarta, International Labour Organization,

Saget, C .2002. "*How to get the maximum out of the minimum wage*" Labour Education 2002/3, No. 128

Saget, C. 2001. *"Poverty reduction and decent work in developing countries: Do minimum wages help?"*, in *International Labour Review*, Vol. 140, No. 3, pp. 237–269.

Saget, C. (2001). *Is the Minimum Wage an Effective Tool to Promote Decent Work and Reduce Poverty? The Experience of Selected Developing Countries* (Employment Paper 2001/13).

Saget, Catherine. 2000. *"Can the level of employment be explained by GDP growth in transition countries? Theory versus the quality of data"*, in *Labour*, Vol. 14, No. 4 (Dec.), pp. 623–643.

Singapore Employment Act, http://statutes.agc.gov.sg

U.S. Embassy (2001). *Singapore's Wage System*. http://singapore.usembassy.gov/

World Bank, Data and Statistics, Country Groups: http://www.worldbank.org/data/countryclass/classgroups.htm#High_income

In-between: Illegality and Legitimacy of the Off-the-Books Self-employment of Urban Youth in Sofia

Tanya Chavdarova
Department of Sociology, St. Kl. Ohridski University of Sofia

Abstract

This article deals with the off-the-books self-employment – a wide-spread phenomenon in Bulgaria nowadays. It is defined as an engagement in the production and sale of goods and services which is unregistered by, or hidden from, the state for tax, social security and/or labour law purposes but which is legal in all other respects. This type of self-employment especially concerns the young people (aged 18-24) being the biggest group among the unemployed people in the country. The article's central thesis is that informal self-employment is more and more functioning as every other legal business which is to be explained primarily by the increasingly unquestioned legitimacy of the informal economy in Bulgaria. The article draws on results from a qualitative empirical research done in 2008. The dataset is composed by 24 semi-structured interviews with informally self-employed young workers in Sofia, the capital city of Bulgaria.

Democratic upheaval and transformation of the economic system in Central and Eastern Europe brought about a rapid growth of interest in self-employment. One of the major roles of self-employment is generating employment and thereby absorbing labour surpluses which result from economic restructuring. The boom of emerging small firms substantially contributed to the introduction and institutionalization of market mechanisms in the economy. Alongside with the transformation of socialist planned economy into market economy, the informal economy has been transformed, too. The informal self-employment in particular became a widespread phenomenon in post-socialist societies (see Earle and Sakova 1999; Hanley 2000; Saar and Unt 2008).

The informally self-employed are autonomous workers in a market economy who work for themselves, whose line of business is the production and sale of goods and services, who for tax, social security and/or labour law purposes are unregistered or hidden from the State, but whose activities are legal in all other respects. Their *means* are illegitimate, not the *ends* (goods and services) themselves. As such, informally self-employed workers are party to either corporate tax evasion and unemployment benefit frauds or labour legislation elusion, including insurance coverage or certain safety or other standards in the workplace. They could be either full- or part-time self-employed or officially registered unemployed who are actually self-employed whilst claiming benefits. Together with off-the-books wage-workers and informal employers, informally self-employed workers are main agents in the underground economy.[1] The line of work of these three categories is fully socially unprotected and not subject to social regulations.

Due to the illicit nature of informal self-employment, even an approximate estimation of its occurrence[2] and its study through quantitative sociological methods is extremely difficult, if not

1 Underground economy is an essential part of informal economy. The informal economy itself is not a homogeneous concept; in fact, there are many informal economies which could be distinguished according to the degree to which they are integral or an alternative to official institutions and to their legal vs. illegal status (Henry 1981: 6ff). In this understanding, the underground economy is illegal and alternative to the official economic institutions.

2 The estimations are done most often with various economic methods and concern the share of the informal economy as a whole in GDP (for a worldwide comparative analysis, see Schneider

impossible. That is why it has been very rarely sociologically studied (see Williams 2006) and in Bulgaria, in particular, it has never been a special subject of sociological research. This article seeks to address this lacuna by focusing on the interplay between the illicit nature of informal self-employment and its growing social legitimacy. The qualitative study that this article is based on concentrates on young, mostly highly educated, informally self-employed workers in Bulgaria's capital Sofia. It aims at revealing how their social legitimacy is becoming possible. The first part of the article discusses the basic hypotheses on the background of some European surveys related to the issues of undeclared work and social networks, its second part presents the specificities of the studied target group, and in the third part the main finding are analysed.

Content

1. The growing market anonymity of the informal self-employment

Economic life is substantially shaped by networks (Granovetter 1985, Smith-Doerr and Powell 2005). Field research on informal self-employment in particular (see e.g. Williams 2006) clearly shows that it is embedded in informal networks and closely bound to local communities; hence it is normally limited to local markets. Its illicit nature restrains the anonymous market action.

Generally, buyers and sellers in the informal economy are typically connected via bonds of interpersonal trust and also typically they are not legal entities. Evidence in support of these observations is provided by the data of the Special Eurobarometer on *Undeclared work in the European Union* (2007) describing the relationships between buyers and sellers of goods and services – products of undeclared work. They show that sales of products from undeclared work in the European Union occur, firstly, through *strong* ties (Granovetter 1973), which are the most important hotbed of undeclared work (40% of the exchange is via friends, relatives, neighbours, see table 1). Secondly, it occurs through *weak* ties with other private persons or households, working most probably on the off-the-book basis (28%) and, thirdly, through officially registered market players (19%).

2007). According to Schneider and Buehn's estimations, the Bulgarian informal economy forms average 35.4% of GDP in the 1999-2006 time spans. (Schneider and Buehn 2009: 24)

Table 1. Sellers of goods and services* – products of undeclared work

Sellers	EU (27)	BG
Friends, colleagues, relatives, neighbours	40	16
Other private persons or households	28	34
Firms or businesses	19	39
Others, refusal, DK (spontaneous)	13	11
Total:	100	100

* Base: Those who have acquired goods or services from undeclared activities, having in mind the most important good/service bought during the last 12 months.

Source: European Commission. 2007. Special Eurobarometer. Undeclared Work in the European Union: 14.

In the European comparative perspective, the Bulgarian situation is quite atypical. Almost 40% of Bulgarians who buy goods or services from undeclared activities buy them from firms and business, i.e. via registered economic agents[3]. This is the highest share all over the EU (Special Eurobarometer 2007: 14). These data indicate that underground economy in Bulgaria presupposes a much greater use of the anonymous market mechanisms than the EU average. This is evidence in favour of the idea that the official business is heavily afflicted by informal practices and that economic informality in Bulgaria could make use of the anonymous exchange in the same way as the official activities do.

The importance of the Bulgarian private persons and households (most probably informally self-employed) in selling products of undeclared work nears the one of the firms or businesses (34%), which implies a widespread practice of informal self-employment.

Informal networks with strong ties come last on this list, quite opposite to the EU situation in general. On the one hand, this finding additionally reinforce the research question about the ways in which market action and network action are combined in the case of informal self-employment. On the other hand, this is in contrast to some previous results of research done on Bulgarian social networks, which depicted them as dense and quite important for the economic life (see e.g. Chavdarova 1996; Benovska-Sabkova 2004, 2007; Petrova 2008).

It seems that social networks have been undergoing a process of general slackening in Bulgaria. Indirect evidence in this regard is provided by the European Social Survey conducted in 2007, part of which is devoted to studying of social networks and social trust. It shows that the density of social contacts in Bulgaria is below the European average for 23 European countries (mean of 4.75 vs. 5.01 on average, see table 2). Social gatherings with friend, relatives,

3 They are serial and continuous users of underground transactions in their formal business. Typically, they provide services, part of which are on off-the-book basis.

colleagues etc. which makes social networks run smoothly and leads to social capital accumulation seem to have become thinner at least for certain social groups[4] in Bulgaria.

It might be suggested that the process of slackening concerns in particular the economic significance of the strong social ties. The socialist "economy of shortage" (Kornai 1980) and the socialist "second" economy that both maintained social networks' high economic value went in the past and hence one of the important reasons to invest in social capital dropped out. In view of undeclared economic activities, however, social networks should be expected to play an invaluable role in keeping those activities hidden from authorities and in generating trust between suppliers and customers of the goods and services produced in the informal sector of economy.

The discussed data provide arguments for suggesting that two tendencies are in play in the contemporary Bulgarian socio-economic context. Firstly, economic informality has gained social legitimacy and could make use of the anonymous exchange in the same way as the official activities do.

Table 2. Meeting friends, relatives or work colleagues socially in comparison (2007)

Country	Mean	Std. Dev.	Country	Mean	Std. Dev.
Portugal	6,11	1,363	Slovakia	4,97	1,646
Norway	5,61	1,278	Ireland	4,86	1,573
Spain	5,51	1,444	Estonia	4,83	1,649
Netherlands	5,46	1,325	Bulgaria	4,75	1,774
Denmark	5,34	1,252	Germany	4,73	1,466
Switzerland	5,32	1,221	Slovenia	4,56	1,588
Sweden	5,30	1,324	Ukraine	4,52	1,678
Austria	5,25	1,446	Russian Federation	4,47	1,784
Belgium	5,20	1,450	Poland	4,28	1,692
France	5,16	1,402	Cyprus	4,23	1,739
Finland	5,11	1,380	Hungary	3,71	1,792
UK	5,10	1,551	Average EC (23)	5,01	1,595

Note: The question is: "How often do you meet socially with friends, relatives or work colleagues?" ("Meet socially" implies meet by choice rather than for reasons of either work or pure duty). The applied scale has seven answers form 1 – "never" to 7 -"every day")

Source: European Social Survey 2007. Round 3. http://www.europeansocialsurvey.org.

4 It should also be pointed out that the standard deviation for Bulgaria - 1.774 is the third highest one in the sample (after Hungary and Russia.), i.e. Bulgarian society is highly split on this issue. It is a question for further investigation to determine the most important factors and lines of this division.

Secondly, the importance of strong ties (family, friends, relatives, etc.) in economic life in Bulgaria is diminishing. Could these tendencies be relevant in the context of a concrete economic field such as off-the-books self-employment? The study of young informally self-employed workers tries to test the following hypotheses, formulated on the background of the assumed tendencies: (1) Though its illicit nature, off-the-books self-employment is socially legitimate and because of this it could freely make use of the anonymous market exchange; (2) The weak ties (acquaintances or "friends of friends") are more important than the strong ties (family, friends, relatives, etc.) for doing business informally.

The applied qualitative methods make the findings valid only for the studied group of respondents; consequently, the conclusions must be accepted as hypotheses requiring further verification.

2. The data

Twenty four in-depth interviews with informally self-employed persons – mostly *young, highly educated, single and living in Sofia* – were conducted from January to February 2008. Nineteen of the respondents live in Sofia, two of them in big cities and another three in a small town. Only three of them are more than 30 years old, while the rest is relatively equally divided into two groups – between 21-24 years (11 persons) and 25-29 years old (10 persons). Most of the interviewed are single (19 of them) and either students (11 altogether) or already have a higher education diploma (10 persons). Only three of them have completed secondary school. Not surprisingly, 15 of the self-employed workers practice activities that require high qualification, while another 5 are artisans.

What do they do? Graphic and web designers form the largest group (5). The group of the engineer- and computer scientists (5) consists of two hardware specialists and "computer doctors", two audio and video specialists, one dealing with computer programming; two women teach foreign languages, while the following activities are represented by one respondent: scientific worker/inventor, journalist, construction entrepreneur, internet (online) trader, jazz singer, tour operator, building facade renovator, fabrics trader, bag manufacturer, dressmaker, goldsmith and jeweller.

Informal self-employment is practiced either in addition to the official job (13 persons) or as a sole (9 persons) employment. In another two cases respondents have officially registered their firms but employ workers without labour contract.

Bearing in mind the young age of the respondents, it is noteworthy that about one third (7) of them have also had previous informal work experiences, in some cases three, even four informal jobs. Aside from this *continuous* informality, the research provides evidence of *double informality*: besides being informally self-employed, some of the respondents are simultaneously wage-workers employed with a fake labour contract, which most often states that they receive minimum wages, while actually receiving what are known as "envelope wages" on a cash-in-hand basis from their formal employer, as has been previously discovered in Romania (Neef 2002), Latvia (Sedlenieks 2003), Ukraine (Williams and Round 2008). This is done as a favour to the formal employer, who thus pays the lowest possible social security tax for his worker while the worker as well benefits since s/he does not pay the full amount of income tax.

3. The conflict between illegality and legitimacy of informal self-employment

The macro-picture of the flourishing informal economy in Bulgaria is corroborated by the study's results. What the interviewed persons see around them is widespread economic informality: (1) all of them have acquaintance(s) who work informally; (2) almost half of them (11 out of 24) state that at least one member of their families has worked or is now working informally; (3) most of them have business connections with other people engaged in informal activities or firms that do not require any receipts and invoices, thus practicing double-entry in their bookkeeping. They share the opinion that working informally in Bulgaria is quite a normal and socially unquestioned practice. As they often put it in the interviews, going informal is not a matter of discussion; it is just "a fact", "a datum" of the country's economic landscape.

> *No, I am doing nothing wrong; I have already told you that in my case [giving private foreign language lessons] even the law is on my side, so I have an easy conscience. ... I do think that [practicing non-registered activities] goes on all over the place and most of the people do not ponder at all on the question of whether it is right or not. It is already a datum. (17, female, 24 y.)*

In this perspective, it was not surprising to see that three of the respondents operate on the national market and even more –six of them– work internationally. Two points should be made in this regard: first, the new technologies, where the young generation has definite priority, allow working globally; second, the young autonomous workers in big cities do not solely rely on informal networks for their informal activities but can well make use of atomised market action.

The dissemination of economic informality seems to be related to the level of confidence in the reliable functioning of the State as a key economic player that sets the rules of the game. All respondents, without exception, express their negative attitudes towards the State institutions, which is the strongest indicator of the lack of *system trust* (Luhmann 1982). They all think that the State institutions do not work properly and blame them for: – bureaucracy often combined with corruption (6 respondents); – incompetence and low quality of public services (5); – lack of any concern for the micro- and small enterprises (3); – lack of any control (2)[5]. An indirect confirmation of the lack of efficient State control is the fact that only four respondents acknowledge that there is a *danger* – a *small* one mentioned by three of the interviewed and a *big* one, pointed up only by one person – to be caught by the State authorities. Most of them have no idea what kind of sanction is provided by the law in such cases. Three respondents think that the informal self-employment is fineable, and another one thinks there are no fines.

The combination between viewing economic informality as a widespread and normal phenomenon and the firm conviction in the State's inability to provide qualitative public services and to control the economic activities can explain the respondents' belief in social legitimacy of their informal self-employment. It clarifies why nearly all (20 out of 24) respondents express an unquestioned conviction that what they are doing is quite socially acceptable (although illicit). Two of the interviewed cannot even see what is wrong at all with his/her activity (see the cited excerpt).

The justification of informality is typically related to the perception that there is a reciprocal relation between the citizen and the state and if the state does not perform its obligation, the citizen should have no obligations either. Most often this concerns the opinion that the state is to be blamed for low incomes and poverty:

> *I do not think that the state institutions are functioning as they should, if everybody – well, at least these are my observations – everybody looks for any kind of additional, non-registered activity. It is more convenient, it is paid better. I... when I know what the teachers in my High School of Music are paid, I am getting sick... They (the state institutions) could not care less for such [people] like me... I do not think that I am engaged in something wrong, this [she sings in clubs] in not socially irresponsible, this employment is extremely helpful for my development. I know that people are delighted with me and they don't care how exactly I earn my money. How should you earn your own living in any sphere of art in Bulgaria, if you do not find such activities? (15, female, 21 y.)*
>
> *Yes, of course, it is connected [his decision to be informally self-employed with the state action]... since it just could not be that I, as an electronics engineer, receive such a low salary, while I need additional incomes, I must for all that get by. (3, male, 27 y.)*

With regard to the second cited respondent, it is indicative that the state has never been his employer. He had changed several jobs in the private sector. At the time

---

5 The study could not provide firm evidence about the extent to which these attitudes are grounded in respondents' personal negative experience with official authorities. They might well be subjective justification of a socially deviant behavior. Even so, of importance here is the fact that they indicate a total lack of system trust.

of the field work, he unofficially provided technical support to taxi radio stations. His official job as an engineer was again in the private sector where he got part of his salary "in an envelope", i.e. he worked with a fake labour contract. The fact that the respondent readily blames the state rather than his employer in this case, may indicate that he is satisfied with such a form of salary payment, as he also does not pay the full extent of income tax. This worker–employer "partnership" is a good manifestation of the deep estrangement from the state.

Health and pension insurance are important aspects of the reciprocal relations between state and citizen. They are viewed by the respondents as practically senseless for the time being since free health care is considered very low-quality and pensions in the distant future are expected to be so low that they could not secure a normal existence anyhow.

Concerning taxation, the shocking fact is that some of the respondents do not have any idea of the level of taxation [6], even when they foresee a registration of their business shortly:

> *I think, we are capable enough to make it and to pay taxes... but I am not so sure, since, if they are about 40% of our profit, as I have heard that some firms pay 40% taxes on their profit, I am not sure that we will not use those [accountancy] instruments [for avoiding taxation]... especially for this project [creation of a computer game] we have been working on for two years which is going to generate profit – I do know why, why must we give [anything] to the state, how did the state help us during the elaboration of... let's say, this project? (21, male, 25 y.)*

All four of the informally self-employed who still see their activity as *illicit and illegitimate* are older and have been operating on the market for more than three years. Two of them are among the three respondents who are over 30 years old, so age may play a role. Another important factor points to the respondents' perceptions about which of their business relations is most important. While those who see their activity as legitimate lay stress on the (typically informal) relation with customers as the most important one, those who regard themselves as illegitimate mostly mention the relation with other partner firms and persons. Apparently those who have been involved more intensively and for a longer time in the anonymous market transactions have developed a sense of irregularity that does not prevent them from insisting upon their economic interests:

> *Yes, I do something wrong, there is a law after all. And it says: you are doing business, you are getting money, and you must declare it. But at the moment that does not suit me. (19, male, 30 y.)*

The self-confessed illegitimacy is not accompanied by any effort to justify one's own behaviour. In one case only the process of legalizing the business serves as justification:

---

6 A flat rate of 10% corporate and individual taxes is in force in Bulgaria, the lowest in Europe in 2008 when the survey was conducted.

Sometimes [I think that I am incorrect being illegal] but we are on the point of legalizing our activity, which, I hope, will happen in the shortest time. (8, male, 24 y.)

Principally, one may obey a social order because one believes in its legitimacy or because one believes that others accept it as legitimate, or one could obey it by calculating the consequences of its imposition (Lewine 2005). None of these reasons to comply with the legal order seems to be present according to the study results. What reason then could there be to believe in the legality of rules set by a specific order that claims thereby to be legitimate? The core of Weberian understanding of the relation between legality and legitimacy is his concept of formal (rational) law (Weber 1956: 122-176). He argues that the legal order generates its own legitimacy by sticking to strict legality (which, in turn strengthens the belief in a given legal order) (ibid.). Weber seems to indicate that believing in legality is based on an instrumental rationality as the predominant social action orientation. Yet, the question remains about whether legitimacy by legality is actually a sound argument, or whether Weber implicitly relies on moral arguments to back his legitimacy concept (Lembcke 2007). In societies characterised by high mistrust in public institutions there is a conflict between legality and legitimacy (Giordano 2006: 210-211). In such societies the official economic order might be legal but not legitimate, whereas the socioeconomic practices, norms and conventions, even when they are (partly) illegal, gain legitimacy (ibid.: 211).

This conflict of legality and legitimacy in the case of Bulgaria and the unquestioned legitimacy of informal economic activities in the respondents' opinion could be viewed as a sign of economic informality's deep-seated permeation in the official market economy, which could be due to the enduring estrangement from the State. These processes on its part explain the compatibility between going informally and taking anonymous market action.

The research also provides some hints about the changes in the character and functioning of the young autonomous workers' social networks. The economic action of two-thirds of them is deeply embedded in informal social networks. *The respondents mentioned four types of informal networks*: friends (including colleagues who appeared in the interviews only in their quality of friends), acquaintances (friends of friends), family members, and neighbours[7]. They carry a very different weight and the kind and level of embeddedness differ depending on the stage of business development (see table 3). All four types of networks are active mostly as *customers'* networks. As the vast majority of self-employed workers are engaged in providing small-scale services, their contact with customers seems to be crucial to the success of the business venture. And indeed, the respondents'

7 Neighbours were mentioned only in two cases (a dressmaker and a dress-shop owner) as important customers.

focus during the interviews was chiefly on the relationship with the customer[8], which will be at the centre of further analysis.

Friends constitute the economically most significant network. They appear in all interviews without exception and are definitely the most important social capital for the young self-employed, even more important than the economic capital.[9] They are the first customers and "advertising agents", sometimes also the first partners in setting up the business. By spreading information about their friends' services they guarantee the transitive trust and thus further the venture's establishment. In the course of business development the role of friends diminishes while the role of the "friends of friends" gains importance. Most of the respondents stated that once the informal self-employment had been established, reputation comes into play. Almost all of the interviewed said that the most intensive way of expanding their customer network is the principle of "word of mouth" recommendation, which speaks about the effectiveness of the transitive trust.

Table 3. Networks vs market in finding and expanding the customers' circle

Business set up Finding customers through:		Established business Expanding the circle of customers through:	
Only friends and neighbours	8	Only friends and neighbours	4
+ Acquaintances (friends of friends)	5	+ Acquaintances (friends of friends)	10
++ Market (anonymous)	4	++ Market (anonymous)	5
Only market	4	Only market	2
Missing	3	Missing	3

Family members appear in whatever direct role only in about one-third (9) of the interviews. The family is typically a provider of financial help for setting up the business, in terms of quite small investments as already mentioned. In the initial phase the family also plays an important indirect role by leading the young generation into the informal economy; almost half of the interviewed persons "have already tasted" the environment of informality through their families since at least one family member is working or has worked informally. Family members rarely appear as either somebody who lends a hand with his/her labor or as providers of contacts with potential customers. In one case only the off-the-books

8 In five cases the focus was also on the relationship with their business partners or collaborators who are either wife/husband or friends, including colleagues.

9 The vast majority of the respondents (19 out of 24) have invested not more than 1500 Euro in their activity.

self-employment was developed as a family business (of two computer specialists – programmer and graphic designer both working on a computer game project).

While in the group of those for whom the informal self-employment is an additional job there is no or a quite limited involvement of family members in one's informal self-employment, more than half (5 persons) of the solely informally self-employed receive some kind of help from their families. The family participates most often by providing financial support (subsistence and/or investment) and rarely by securing customers/contacts and labor.

It is very indicative that no relatives of any kind were ever mentioned in the interviews. This finding prompts to the need of further detailed investigation of the, probably diminishing, role that the extended family plays in various aspects of economic life in Bulgaria.

The described tendencies in the functioning of such strong ties as the friends and the family members lead to a correction of the second hypothesis which implied a greater importance of the weak ties for the informal employment. Those tendencies indicate that the strong and the weak ties have different importance in the different stages of the informal business venture. While the strong ties are crucial for embarking on informal self-employment by securing customers and start up capital, in the consecutive phase of business establishment they are gradually replaced, in terms of significance, by the petty entrepreneurs' weak ties with various circles of acquaintances.

Along with the exchange within the informal networks of family, friends and "friends of friends", the anonymous market exchange is also important for informal self-employment. One-third of the respondents rely on a combination of informal networks and atomised market mechanisms for finding and expanding their customers' circle. Most often this is done through adds on the internet and newspapers and in some cases the adds are disseminated on the street. There are even some respondents that rely only on the market method to perform their activities, especially at the beginning. The two outlined groups of solely and additionally self-employed differ in relation to the scope of their atomized market action. It is noteworthy that those employed only informally do not solely make use of the market mechanisms and are much more dependent on the dense informal networks. This is due to the fact that they are younger, with limited work experience and still get financial help from the family.

In conclusion

Over the last twenty years, informal economy has become an inherent part of Bulgaria's socioeconomic landscape. Informal self-employment, in particular, is flourishing both as a main and as an additional employment. The entrepreneurial spirit of post-communist capitalism often finds its hotbed precisely in off-the-books self-employment. Many factors have contributed to the social situation by which it is experienced as a quite legitimate albeit illicit economic activity. Besides the fact that economic informality is widespread in society, a culture of its denunciation is missing. There is no fear that someone (client or neighbour, etc.) would report the informally self-employed workers to the authorities. This is why these activities are not perceived as risky ones. Risk in this form of employment is perceived to be a matter of bad luck or unlucky coincidence.

The relatively large involvement of pure market mechanisms in the informal exchange contrasts the *normative* expectation that, since informal self-employment is illicit, the fear of prohibition ought to prevent the economic action of becoming atomised. Because such fear, as already discussed, is not present, and because of the low level of confidence in the proper functioning of market regulations in Bulgaria, the informal and the officially registered entrepreneurs operate in similar market conditions. This is especially visible in the case of business contracts, whose enforcement is not perceived as guaranteed by the legal system. Registered and informally operating businesses are thus functioning in similar conditions; it does not matter whether or not their owners have signed written business contracts as they do not believe that the legislative power would defend them when needed. There is a conflict between illegality and social legitimacy of the informal employment. Being illicit, it is, however, perceived as socially acceptable and unquestioned which contributes to the "normalisation" of the informal economy. In these circumstances formal and informal self-employed workers are on an equal standing. The anonymous market action was thus able to gain an importance, although informal self-employment is still heavily embedded in social networks.

References

Benovska-Sabkova, M. (2004). "Social Networks, Coalitions and Clientelism at the Place of Work in the 1960-1989 Period in Sofia". In: Roth, K. (Hg) *Arbeit im Sozialismus – Arbeit im Postsozialismus*. Freiburger Sozialanthropologische Studien. Lit Verlag, Münster, pp. 109-128.

Benovska-Sabkova, M. (2007). "Friendship and Friendly Coalitions and Groups. Friendship as a Pattern of Social Relations". In: Roth, K. (Hg.) *Soziale Netzwerke und soziales Vertrauen in den Transformationsländern*. Ethnologische und soziologische Untersuchungen. Freiburger Sozialanthropologische Studien, Bd. 15. LIT, pp. 143-156.

Chavdarova, T. (1996). „Informelle Netzwerkhilfe und Strategien der wirtschaftlichen Aktivitäten in Bulgarien". In: W. Glatzer (Hg.) *Lebensverhältnisse in*

Osteuropa. Prekäre Entwicklungen und neue Konturen. Frankfurt: Campus Verlag, pp. 237-46.

Earle, J. S. and Z. Sakova. (1999). *Entrepreneurship from Scratch: Lessons on the Entry Decision into Self-Employment from Transition Economies*. IZA. Discussion Paper No. 79, Bonn, Germany: Institute for the Study of Labour.

Eurobarometer 62. (2004). *Obstestvenoto mnenie v Evropejskia Sujus. Nazionalen doklad Bulgaria. (Public Opinion in the EU. National Report Bulgaria.)* Autumn. http://ec.europa.eu/public_opinion/archives/eb/eb62/eb62_bg_nat.pdf

Eurobarometer 68. (2007). *Obstestvenoto mnenie v Evropejskia Sujus. Nazionalen doklad Bulgaria. (Public Opinion in the EU. National Report Bulgaria.)* Autumn. http:/ec.europa.eu/public_opinion/archives/eb/eb68/eb68_bg_nat.pdf.

Eurobarometer 68. (2007). Public Opinion in the European Union. December. http://ec.europa.eu/public_opinion/archives/eb/eb68/eb68_first_en.pdf

European Social Survey (2007). *Round 3*. http://www.europeansocialsurvey.org

Giordano, C. (2006). Vlast, Nedoverie I Nasledstvo. Skeptichna Antropologia (Power, Distrust and Legacy. Sceptical Anthropology). Sofia: Polis.

Granovetter, M. (1973). The Strength of Weak Ties. *American Journal of Sociology* 78(6): 1360-1380.

Granovetter, M. (1985). Economic Action and Social Structure: The Problem of Embeddedness. *American Journal of Sociology*, Vol. 91, 3, pp. 481–510.

Hanley, E. (2000). Self-employment in Post-Communist Eastern Europe: A Refuge from Poverty or Road to Riches? *Communist and Post-Communist Studies*, 33, 3: 379-402.

Henry, S. (1981). "Introduction." In: Henry, S. (Ed.). *Informal Institutions. Alternative Networks in the Corporative State*. New York: St. Martin‘s Press.

Kornai, J. (1980). *Economics of Shortage*. Amsterdam: North Holland.

Lembcke, O. W. (2007). *From Belief to Obedience: Max Weber on Legitimacy and Legality*. Paper presented at the annual meeting of the Law and Society Association, TBA, Berlin, Germany, 25 July.

Levine, B. B. (2005). "Legitimacy and the Process by Which It Is Pursued." In: Beckert, J. and M. Zafirovski (eds.) *Encyclopaedia of Economic Sociology*. London: Routledge.

Luhmann, N. (1982). *The Differentiation of Society*. New York: Columbia University Press.

Neef, R. (2002). Aspects of the Informal Economy in a Transforming Country: The Case of Romania. *International Journal of Urban and Regional Research* 26(2): 299–322.

Petrova, I. (2008). „Aufbau von sozialem Kapital im sozialistischen und postsozialistischen Betriebsumfeld." In: K. Roth (Hg.) *Sozialkapital – Vertrauen*

– *Rechtssicherheit. Postsozialistische Gesellschaften und die Europäische Union*. Berlin: LIT Verlag, pp. 125-139.

Saar, E. and M. Unt. (2008). Selective Mobility into Self-employment in Post-socialist Transition: Early Birds, Later Entrants, Quitters and Shuttles. *International Small Business Journal*, 26(3): 323 – 349.

Schneider, F. and A. Buehn. (2009). Shadow Economies and Corruption All Over the World: Revised Estimates for 120 Countries. *Economics. The Open-Access, Open-Assessment E-Journal*, Vol. 1, 2007. http://www.economics-ejournal.org/economics/journalarticles/2007-9

Sedlenieks, K. (2003). ''Cash in an Envelope: Corruption and Tax Avoidance as an Economic Strategy in Contemporary Riga.'' In: Arnstberg, K.-O. and T. Boren (eds.) *Everyday Economy in Russia, Poland and Latvia*. Stockholm: Almqvist & Wiksell, pp. 37–52.

Smith-Doerr, L. and W. W. Powell. (2005). "Networks and Economic Life." In: Smelser, N. J. and R. Swedberg (eds.). *Handbook of Economic Sociology*, Second Edition. Princeton, NJ: Russell Sage Foundation/Princeton University Press, pp. 379-402.

Special Eurobarometer. (2007). *Undeclared Work in the European Union*. European Commission. http://ec.europa.eu/public_opinion/archives/ebs/ebs_284_en.pdf.

Weber, M. (1956). *Wirtschaft und Gesellschaft*. Tübingen: J. C. B. Mohr und Siebeck Verlag.

Williams, C. and J. Round. (2008). A Critical Evaluation of Romantic Depictions of the Informal Economy. *Review of Social Economy*, 66(3): 297-323.

Williams, C. C. (2006). The Hidden Enterprise Culture: Entrepreneurship in the Underground Economy. Cheltenham: Edward Elgar.

Management and Strategies for Sustainable Development of the Labour Force in the Rubber Plantation Sector in India

Y.Annamma Varghese
Former Joint Director, Rubber Research Institute of India, Kottayam 686009, Kerala, India

Joseph P.Varghese
Former Professor of Botany, CMS College, Kerala, India

Abstract

The Government of India through constitution of the Rubber Board in 1947 (the Rubber Act 1947) provides institutional support for the rubber plantation industry. A range of welfare measures covering basic amenities at work place, paid holidays, annual leave, medical care, canteen, residential quarters, educational facility for children, etc. are obligatory under the rules.

The rubber act 1947 provides, amongst other functions, that it shall be the duty of the Board to secure better working conditions and the provision and improvement of amenities and incentives for rubber plantation workers. In order to achieve this objective, the Board implements a number of sub components in the component of labour welfare under the Human Resource Development Scheme. The schemes implemented to address the issues of safety, health and social security of the Labour Force include Educational Stipend Scheme, Merit Award Scheme, Housing Subsidy Scheme, Sanitary Subsidy Scheme, Housing and sanitary Subsidy Scheme for Scheduled Caste/Scheduled Tribe, Medical Attendance Scheme and Group Insurance cum deposit scheme. The total financial assistance under the above seven Labour welfare Schemes is estimated to be Rs. 30 million benefiting 23,000 workers annually. The implementation of the welfare schemes is properly monitored and verified by the Supervisory officers of the Board. The various schemes of the Rubber Board for labour welfare have contributed to the sustainable development of the labour force in the rubber plantation sector in India.

Content

1. Introduction

In India, the rubber plantation industry has recorded a steady growth over the past 60 years. Today India ranks first in terms of productivity, 4th in production and area among the rubber producing countries of the world. These significant achievements are attributed to the systematic R&D activities over the years.

Rubber was first received in India during 1878, from Sri Lanka and commercial cultivation started in 1902. Government of India through constitution of Rubber Board in 1947 provided institutional support for the rubber plantation industry. The post independence period showed a remarkable and rapid growth in the rubber plantation sector, aided by a number of favorable factors of which the most important was the Government support channelled through the Rubber Board in the form of various incentives, research and development support for cultivation, processing and marketing.

Systematic research on natural rubber (NR) started in 1955 with the establishment of the Rubber Research Institute of India (RRII). The broad research priorities viz., improvement in production and productivity, reduction in cost of production, achievement in quality competitiveness, and research and extension support were achieved over the years. The development of the most popular high yielding clone RRII 105, has substantially contributed to the viability of NR cultivation in India. The newly evolved higher yielding RRII 400 series clones are expected to further enhance the productivity significantly. Varghese *et al.*, 2009). Integrated approaches to reduce cost of production and improve quality of the product has resulted in the development of Discriminatory Fertilizer Recommendation based on soil and leaf analysis, effective plant protection schedules for major diseases and pests, suitable latex harvesting systems and appropriate processing technology for latex and dry rubber. Location specific agro technology has been evolved for rubber cultivation under sub optimal conditions prevailing in the non-traditional areas. (Varghese and Abraham, 2005).

Rubber plantations are a source of livelihood to many of the rubber growers as 86% of them are small growers. NR plantation is a self-sustainable ecosystem, which is a renewable non-polluting and environment friendly source of elastomer in contrast to synthetic rubber manufactured from depletable petroleum resources. The crop has a strong future in India, considering the ever-increasing consumption of NR in various rubber-based industries especially the automobile sector besides its uniqueness as a natural eco friendly product.

2. The profile of Indian Rubber Industry

Kerala and Kanyakumari District of Tamil Nadu together constitute the traditional rubber growing region in the country. The traditional region accounted for as much as 84 % of the total area of 6,35,400 ha. at the end of 2007-2008. Small holding sector, comprising 1.10 million units with the average size of 0.51 ha., dominate the production sector by sharing as much as 90 per cent of area and 92 per cent of production. Though size constrained, more than 93 per cent of the total area in small holding sector is occupied by high yielding cultivars and the sector is much ahead in adopting productivity enhancement measures.

Hevea being indigenous to the Amazonian rain forests of Brazil located at 5° longitude and an altitude below 200 m prefers a warm breezy humid weather and a fertile soil and hence performance is best under tropical conditions. However, this hardy perennial tree can grow well under less ideal conditions as well. Since there is no further scope for expansion of area in the traditional rubber-growing tract in Southwest India, cultivation has been extended to the non-traditional areas. The NE region has been identified as one of the most potential non-traditional tract suitable for expansion of rubber plantation industry. The agro-ecological relevance of this perennial plantation crop species for conservation of the ecosystem and socio-economic aspects for overall development of the region has also been recognized.

2.1 Gestation period

Rubber is a long duration crop with a gestation period of about seven years to attain maturity for commencement of tapping in the traditional rubber growing region in India. This period is referred to as immaturity period for rubber.

2.2 Plantation and the Worker

Plantation is defined as any agricultural undertaking, regularly employing hired workers and which is situated in the tropical or subtropical regions and which is mainly concerned with the cultivation or production for commercial purposes of coffee, tea, sugarcane, rubber, cinchona, cardamom etc. It does not include family or small scale holdings producing for local consumption and not employing hired labour (ILO, 1958)

2.3 Conditions of Employment

Conditions of labour include wage rates, dearness allowances, hours of work, overtime, leave, holidays with pay, residential accommodation, superannuation benefits like gratuity, provident fund and pension, grading, promotion, retirement, dismissal, and procedures for strike, lockout, lay- off etc. The most important legislation regulating the conditions of work in plantations and providing for the welfare of labourers is Plantation Labour Act, 1951 (Iype, 2000). There are provisions in the act for assuring the workers reasonable amenities like supply of drinking water, suitable medical and educational facilities, canteen, crèches and sufficient latrines and urinals. Housing accommodation is also to be provided. The act regulates the working hours and leave with wages of workers employed in plantations.

3. Labour Requirement in the rubber plantations

Rubber plantations in India are mostly situated on sloppy and undulating areas. On hilly land soil conservation measures are necessary. Since June-July is the planting season in S. India, preparations for planting like land clearing, lining, cutting terraces, pitting and filling are to be completed before the season. (Punnoose and Lakshmanan, 2000)

3.1. Clearing: A light burn after felling and drying may be done to ensure removal of light brushwood and branches of trees.

3.2. Lining: in flat or slightly undulating areas, square or rectangular planting may be adopted. Contour lining is done on undulating and hilly lands by marking out the planting points in contour lines across the slopes.

3.3. Terracing: In hilly areas cutting terraces is advisable to aid soil conservation.

3.4. Drainage: proper drainage is essential especially in low lying lands.

3.5. Silt pits and contour bunts: Silt pitting is practised on undulating land to check soil erosion and to facilitate rain water infiltration. Construction of stone pitched contour retaining walls is another effective method to restrict surface run off.

3.6. Pitting and refilling: In order to provide favourable conditions for the early establishment and growth of the young plant, a pit (standard size 75 cm^3) is dug at the planting point and refilled with fertile top soil.

3.7. Planting and after care: the planting density recommended is 420-500 plants per hectare. Poly bag plants are the most popular planting material. Stump plating and seed at stake planting are also practiced occasionally.

After planting the plants should be inspected regularly and only one vigorous shoot allowed growing. Pruning at regular intervals need to be carried out to remove any side shoots developing up to 2.5 m from the ground level.

3.8. Establishment of Cover Crops: leguminous cover crops are established and maintained for conserving the soil and for improving or maintaining the soil structure and fertility by fixing atmospheric nitrogen.

3.9. Mulching: Mulching nurseries and basins of young plants with dried planting materials and other mulch materials is done, before the onset of summer season, to reduce soil temperature and conserve soil moisture.

3.10. Weed control: Since weeds compete with rubber plants for light, moisture and nutrients, particularly, during the initial years, proper control of weeds is essential to achieve normal growth of the plants.

3.11. Inter cropping: During the initial years of a plantation, when the interspaces receive plenty of sunlight, a variety of intercrops can be cultivated to generate some income during the **unproductive phase of rubber.**

3.12. Manuring: immature and mature rubber trees: Rubber responds well to systematic manuring. The manorial requirements vary during the three important stages of growth, viz. Nursery, immature and mature stages. Manuring is done based on specific recommendation based on requirement.

3.13. Disease management: timely plant protection operations against major diseases ensure healthy growth and economic production

3.14. Harvesting by tapping: Latex is harvested by tapping the bark, a process of controlled wounding of the bark to cut open the latex vessels by regularly removing a thin shaving of bark from the surface of the tapping cut at specified intervals. Tapping is done to cut open the latex vessels in the case of trees tapped for the first time or to remove the coagulum which blocks the cut ends of latex vessels in the case of trees under regular tapping. The tapping cut should have a slope of about 30° and 25^0 to the horizontal for budded and seedling trees respectively. Since the latex vessels in the bark run at an angle of 3-5° to the right, a cut from high left to low right of the tree trunk, will open maximum number of vessels. The depth of tapping should be within 0.5 mm of the cambium to get optimum yield without injuring the cambium and regeneration of latex vessels. Rubber tapping, being a precision work, can be done by only trained tappers.

3.15. Rain guarding: During rainy season tapping can be carried out by fixing a rainguard above the tapping cut

3.16. Processing of the crop: latex, the main crop from the rubber tree can be processed and marketed as 1. Sheet rubber, 2. Crepe rubbers 3. Preserved field latex and larex concentrates and 4. Block rubber.

4. Labour Management in rubber plantations

The management of labour is crucial in any labour intensive enterprise like rubber plantation. In India around three- fourth of the development cost of rubber plantations and 60 per cent of the cost of mature plantations are accounted for by labour alone. Around 60 per cent of the labourers are tappers, while the rest are general field workers.

4.1 Immature Phase

4.1.1 Small holding

Normally labour requirement for purposes such as boundary protection and night watching/ security is significantly lower in small holdings, while that of manuring is higher due to the popular practice of applying cow dung. Among small holdings,29 percent of the labour requirement during the immature phase is met with family labour of which 14 per cent is female labour.

4.1.2 Estates

The estate sector mainly depends on permanent labour on roll and the share of female labour in plantation development operations ranges from 25 to 35 per cent. Normally permanent workers are engaged for tapping and related jobs while seasonal general field operations are carried out with casual labourers. Any casual worker engaged for 240 days or more in 12 calendar months will acquire the status of a regular worker and will become eligible for benefits under the various labour statutes.

4.1.3 Non-traditional areas

In the non-traditional areas, the labour requirement for operations such as clearing, terracing and weeding is significantly higher, since the terrain is not usually ideal for rubber. In the dry areas, additional labour for lifesaving irrigation is required especially during the initial years. Similarly, the labour requirement in non-traditional areas for fencing and vacancy filling is also higher (Joseph and Rajasekharan, 1991).

4.2 Mature phase

The annual labour requirement during the mature phase depends mainly on the tapping system followed, system of processing, adoption of rain guarding, application of stimulants and panel protection activities. In a mature rain-guarded plantation under 1/2 S d/2 system of tapping, the annual requirement of labour per ha is around 180 man-days. Female labour can be substantially involved in all the activities including tapping.

Table 1: Annual labour requirement during the mature phase

Item of work	**Number of man-days required (per ha)**
Weeding	10
Manuring	5
Spraying (Copper oxychloride)	2
Other plant protection activities	2
Tapping and processing (1/2 S d/2 system)	150
Rain-guarding	4
Panel protection	5
Others	2
Total	**180**

4.2.1 Small holdings

In the smallholdings, since the tapper himself processes the latex or carries the material to the collection centre of processing factories, there is no need of separate labour for processing. The tapper requirement per unit area is higher compared to that of estates due to higher tapping intensity. Around 23 per cent of the small growers utilize family labour for tapping and in northern Kerala it is up to 44 per cent (RRII, 1997). Due to the reduction in the size of the holdings, there is the peculiar situation of a tapper working for different growers. Utilization of family labour for tapping would in future prove ideal due to obvious sociological and economic factors.

4.2.2 Estates

The daily tapping task size ranges from 300 to 400 trees per tapper. The number of tappers employed by estates depends on the number of tapping tasks with an additional five per cent reserve so that tapping days will not be lost due to labour absenteeism or availing of leave by permanent tappers. The tapper requirement depends on the stand under tapping, task size and tapping intensity. An increase in the tapping task with cash incentive for additional volume of latex collected (based on DRC) reduces the total tapper requirements, increases the earnings per tapper and significantly reduces the cost of production. The estates require additional labour for processing depending upon the type of processing.

4.2.3 Non-traditional areas

In the non-traditional regions one of the major difficulties is the shortage of experienced tappers. Larger holdings and estates in these areas even go to the extent of employing tappers from the traditional belt. However efforts are made to train the local workers including the tribals in tapping and other skilled items of work.

5. Labour cost – heads

The heads under which labour can be accounted at different stages are enumerated below:

5.1 Up to planting stage include

Clearing of land, terracing, lining, pitting, filling of pits, budding/nursery management and field planting

5.2 During immature phase

Filling of casualties, mulching of plant bases, cover crop establishment and maintenance, shading and propping, branch induction, and thinning out of weak plants

5.3 During mature phase

Harvesting the crop by tapping, processing, protection of tapping panel, application of stimulants and raingaurding the trees

5.4 Labour cost heads recurring annually or seasonally

Application of manures and fertilizers, weeding, white washing, fencing, firebreak preparation, plant protection, irrigation, soil conservation and maintenance of roads, buildings, boundary protection etc

Altogether 827 man days per hectare are required in the first seven years of planting of which 329 man days are to be engaged during the first year itself.

The operation wise labour requirement may vary widely depending upon the terrain and topography as well as the previous crop status of land.

6. Wages, salaries and other benefits

The conditions of workers in the organized sector are governed by the provisions of the Plantation Labour Act of 1951 which is applicable to all plantations admeasuring, 5 ha and employing 15 or more workers. The wage rates are fixed through tripartite agreement under the provisions of the Minimum Wages Act 1948 (The Act, 1948). The minimum wages shall consist of a basic rate of wages and dearness allowance fixed on the basis of the cost of living index. And it shall be reviewed and revised, if necessary, at such intervals not exceeding five years. The payment of wages shall be fixed as per rules prevalent in each state.

In the Unorganized sector, the wage rates often show a tendency to rise with the price of rubber. The wage rates in the unorganized sector are fixed informally and are higher compared to the notified minimum wage rates. But the number of working days in the smallholdings is lower. The tappers in the smallholdings are paid on per tree basis, which also includes remuneration for processing.

In the non-traditional areas, generally the wage rates are lower compared to those in the traditional region. Payment on piece-rate basis and daily wages are practiced for indigenous tappers while experienced tappers from the traditional belt are paid monthly salaries often with free accommodation.

In the organised sector, the Government may fix the number of working hours for the schedules employment. A day of rest in every week is allowed to all employees. The tappers are paid daily wages (with a task ranging from 300 to 400 trees) and cash incentives depending upon the crop collected. A range of welfare measures covering basic amenities at work place, paid holidays, annual leave, medical care, canteen, residential quarters, educational facility for children, etc. are obligatory under the rules. The central and state legislations pertaining to minimum wages, industrial disputes, provident funds, accidents, gratuity, bonus, etc. are also applicable in the organized sector.

6.1 Bonus: is a cash payment made in addition to wages as a stimulus to extra work and efficiency by labour. Payment is bonus is made on the basis of profits, production or productivity, and matters connected there with are governed by the provisions of Bonus Act, 1965.An employer is bound to pay a minimum bonus of 8.33 per cent of the wage earned by the employee during the accounting year.

6.2 Provident Fund: The Employees Provident Fund Act 1962 is applicable to plantations with 20 or more employees. The contribution payable by the employee shall be at the rate of 10 per cent of the basic wage and dearness allowance, which is equal to the contribution by the employer. A worker is entitled to withdraw full amount in his credit at the time of retirement.

6.3 Gratuity: Is essentially a retirement benefit earned by giving service. It is a reward for good, efficient and faithful service rendered for a considerable period. The payment of gratuity Act 1972 provides for payment of gratuity to employees engaged in plantations to do any skilled, semi skilled or unskilled, manual, supervisory, technical or clerical work. For every completed year of service or part thereof in excess of six months the employer shall pay gratuity to an employee at the rate of 15 days, wages based on the rate of wages last drawn by the employee.

6.4 Pension Scheme: A pension fund is created from and out of contribution payable by the employer under section 6 of the Employees Provident Fund Scheme. The pensionable service of the member shall be determined with reference to the contribution received on his behalf. An employee on superannuation is entitled to pension. A person retiring after rendering 20 years of service will also be entitled to pension. Also a person who has rendered eligible service of 10 years or more, but less than 20 years shall also be entitled to short service pension.

6.5 Maternity Benefits: According to Maternity Benefits Act, 1961, a women worker is eligible for maternity benefits for the six weeks immediately preceding the date of her delivery and six weeks after the delivery at the rate of average daily wages of the preceding three months. For eligibility of maternity benefits, the woman worker should have worked for 80 days in the 12 months immediately preceding the date of her expected delivery.

7. Labour Welfare Measures

7.1 Canteen: Subject to rules made by the State Government, in or near every plantation, wherein 150 or more workers are engaged, the employer shall arrange a canteen with facilities for sale of tea, coffee and snacks for workers on a no profit basis.

7.2 Crèche: In every plantation where 50 or more women workers are employed or where the number of children of women workers is 20 or more crèche are to be provided and maintained at conveniently accessible places for use of the children of women workers.

7.3 Housing: It is the duty of the employer to provide and maintain accommodation for the workers and their families according to the standards fixed by the state Government, without charging any rent for the house.

7.4 Weather Protective: Once in a year the employer shall supply to every worker a woollen blanket, or an umbrella or a rain coat or a hat of suitable quality as approved by the Chief Inspector of Plantations.

7.5.Welfare Officer: A plantation wherein 300 or more workers are employed shall appoint a welfare officer to ensure the timely provision of all the welfare measures contained in the Plantation Labour Act.

7.6 Health and safety

7.6.1 Health care: The rules framed in Kerala provide for two types of hospitals, viz. Garden hospital and group hospital. The garden hospitals are intended to deal with out patients and inpatients not requiring elaborate diagnosis and treatment. Group hospital shall be capable of dealing with all types of diseases normally encountered, but not for routine treatment. Admission to a group hospital shall be on the recommendation of a garden hospital doctor, except in emergency.

7.6.2 Safety: The factories Act 1948 deals with provisions relating to safety of factory workers is applicable to factory workers in plantations also.

7.6.3 Compensation for injury by accident: The Workmen Compensation Act, 1923 provides for payment of compensation to workmen for injury by accident

8. Institutional Support – Labour Welfare Schemes

The Rubber Board implements a number of labour welfare schemes for the benefit of rubber plantation workers and their families in the rubber plantation sector. Since the major share of rubber planters are small holders with less than 5 ha. of land coming under the un organized sector, and are not entitled to the provisions under the Plantation Labour Act, the Rubber Board has been implementing a set of welfare schemes for them consisting of group insurance, housing subsidy, medical care and educational stipend to the children of workers.

The Schemes implemented to address the issue of safety, health and social security of the workers include, Educational Stipend Scheme, Merit Award Scheme, Housing Subsidy Scheme, Sanitary Subsidy Scheme, Housing and Sanitary Subsidy Scheme for SC/ST Plantation workers, Medical Attendance Scheme and Group Insurance cum Deposit Scheme.

8.1. Educational Stipend Scheme

This Scheme is intended to provide financial assistance from class VIII onwards, including professional courses, as lump sum grant and hostel/boarding fee to the children of tappers in the small holdings and children of tappers/general workers /non supervisory staff /field supervisors of the large sector holdings and the children of workers of factory situated in the rubber plantations. The tappers employed in an area of not less than 0.40 ha. in the small holding sector are eligible for the assistance. In the NE Region, stipend in the form of lump sum grant, school uniform allowance and hostel/boarding fee is being paid from class I onwards. This assistance helps the tappers/workers to reduce their financial burden to a certain extent for the education of their children. The assistance benefits around 11,000 workers annually in the large and small holding sector in rubber plantations.

Table 2. The various courses of studies and assistance given

	Category	Yearly Stipend
1	Class VIII to XII	Rs. 500/
2	Degree Courses	Rs. 1000/
3	Post Graduate Courses	Rs. 1500/
4	Professional/Technical	
	a) Certificate Courses	Rs. 750/
	b) Diploma Courses	Rs. 1000/
	c) Degree Courses	Rs. 2000/
	d) Post Graduate courses	Rs. 2500/

Under the scheme hostel fee is also reimbursed to children studying in Class VIII, IX and X @ Rs:200/- per month and for other courses @ Rs:300/- per month for a maximum period of eight months in an academic year.

In the North Eastern Region, Educational Stipend and Uniform Allowance at the rates noted below are being granted for children of rubber plantation workers from Class I onwards.

Table 3. Lump sum grant given for education

Name of Course	Lump sum grant per year	Hostel/ Boarding fee per month	Uniform Allowance Per year
Class I to IV	Rs. 300/-	Nil	Rs. 300/
Class V to VII	Rs. 500/-	Nil	Rs. 300/
Class VIII to X	Rs. 750-/	Rs. 200/-	Rs. 400/
Class XI to XII	Rs. 1000/-	Rs. 300/-	Rs. 500/
Other courses	As applicable in the traditional area		

8.2 Merit Award Scheme

Merit Award is given as an incentive for encouraging performance by the children of rubber plantation workers who pass out their academic courses meritoriously. Children of rubber tappers in small holdings and also children of tappers/general workers /non supervisory staff /field supervisors of the large sector holdings and the children of workers of factory situated in the rubber plantations, who meritoriously pass examinations of recognized courses, are eligible for this award.

This Scheme provides financial assistance to the children who pass with 80% and above marks for SSLC or equivalent and 60% and above for other courses. The Merit Award ranges from Rs.1000/- to Rs.5000/- for various courses. On an average this scheme benefits about 260 children of tappers/plantation workers of the large and small holding sector annually who perform excellently in their course of studies.

8.3. Housing Subsidy Scheme

This scheme is for assisting tappers of rubber small holdings and tappers/general workers /non supervisory staff /field supervisors of the large sector holdings and the children of workers of factory situated in the rubber plantations to construct their own houses and thereby attain one of the basic minimum necessities of life i.e., shelter. As per this, the applicant constructing a house is entitled for a subsidy of Rs. 12, 500. The eligibility of a tapper to apply under the scheme is that he or she should be employed in a holding of not less than 0.75 ha. for a minimum period of 5 years. When such a tapper constructs a house in his own/his spouse‘s land in the prescribed manner as stipulated in the rules of sub component, a maximum amount of Rs.12500/ or 25% of the estimated cost whichever is lower would be granted as subsidy.

In the North Eastern Region the scheme is implemented to plantation workers with certain modifications adopting the local technologies and an increased amount of subsidy. For houses built with split bamboo walls and GI Sheet roof, half mud walls with split bamboo walls etc with or without wooden frames and roofed with GI sheet, the maximum subsidy would be Rs.15000/-or 50% of cost of construction whichever is low.

The officials of the Board after inspecting the employment and the construction of the house of tappers recommends subsidy, if they are eligible. Hence the benefit goes directly to the needy and it acts as an incentive to the tappers and other workers to continue their employment. Around 900 workers of small holding and large sector plantations are recipient of the scheme annually.

8.4 Sanitary Subsidy Scheme

The scheme aimed at promoting hygienic habit in the living conditions and environment of tappers is applicable to the rubber tappers in the small holding sector. The tappers should have 5 years employment experience in an area of not less than 0.50 hectares and not covered by the Plantations Labour Act, 1951. Financial assistance to cover 75% of the cost of construction is given to the tappers to build latrine in their own residential premises, as per the plan and estimate prescribed by the Board. Approximately 700 tappers from the small holding sector plantations are benefited by the scheme annually.

8.5. Housing and sanitary subsidy scheme for SC/ST workers

This scheme implemented in the un- organized sector with the involvement of the rubber producers' societies is meant exclusively for tappers in the SC/ST communities who are employed in the small holding sector. Assistance under this scheme is granted, for construction of a house with latrine, to the extent of Rs.21,000/- or 25% of total cost of construction based on the recommendation of the Field Officer of the Board after due verification.

In case the applicant constructs a house alone, the assistance will be Rs. 15000/- or 25% of the cost of construction whichever is low and in case the applicant constructs the latrine alone, the assistance will be Rs. 6000/ or 75% of the cost of construction of latrine whichever is low. The sub component act as an incentive to SC/ST tappers to construct a house with latrine in their own land and about 130 of them from the small holding sector plantations have annually benefited by the scheme.

8.6 Medical Attendance Scheme

The Scheme provides reimbursement of medical expenses incurred for the treatment of tappers under allopathic, ayurvedic and homeopathic system of medicines, to an extent of Rs.2000/- each, per year. Tappers undergoing expensive treatment for major/terminal diseases are also reimbursed an amount of Rs.10000/- once in their life time. This scheme is implemented for the tappers in the small rubber holdings. The applicants must be employed in an area not less than 0.40 hectares and have worked at least 90 days during the preceding 12 months of the date of submitting the application. The bills relating to purchase of medicines, diagnosis etc. should be produced in original with the prescription in support of the claims within 3 months of the date of commencement of treatment or date of discharge from the hospital.

Under the Medical Attendance Scheme around 1500 tappers from the small holding sector are benefited annually.

8.7 Group Insurance cum Deposit Scheme

This scheme is an important social security measure implemented for the safety of the tappers in the unorganised sector against death and injuries caused by accidents. At the same time they are encouraged to develop the habit of savings on a long term basis. It is applicable only to those who are employed in the small holdings having an area of not less than 0.40 ha. The scheme is contributory from the tappers and Board‘s side. The contribution of a tapper is Rs.250/- per year and the Board‘s annual contribution for a member under the scheme is Rs:150/- and after deducting the premium for the insurance, balance contribution is deposited in appropriate funds with an objective to benefit the tappers on completion of the 10 year period of the scheme. The Insurance coverage is for an amount of Rs.50,000/-. The Group insurance scheme enrols tappers in every year and each year is considered as a phase and it shall be renewed annually.

This sub component provides compensation against death and injures in the accidents including compensation for temporary total disablement of the members. The savings portion of the insurance scheme is distributed on completion of 10 years, in proportion to the number of renewals made by the members in the scheme.

Tappers employed in the small holdings are totally insecure of their continuous employment. They are not safeguarded from injuries and death due to accidents. There are no legislations to safeguard the rubber tappers in the small holdings. In this context the group insurance cum deposit scheme provides safety and savings among the tappers. Since the scheme is in operation for a period of ten years the enrolled tappers are thereby persuaded to continue their employment. As and when they are not in the employment the benefits provided under the scheme are frozen for the period and after reemployment they can renew the policy. Hence the scheme acts as a binding force among the tappers to continue their employment. Under the Group Insurance Cum Deposit Scheme around 10,000 tappers from the small holding sector are benefited annually.

The total financial assistance under the above seven Labour Welfare Schemes is estimated to be Rs.3 crore (Rs.30 million) benefiting 23,000 workers annually. The subsidy is granted on the basis of the recommendation of the Rubber Board field officers after due field verification.

9. Women and Tribal Development

The Rubber Board has been implementing special programmes for the benefit of tribal people. The most successful of the various schemes has been the economic rehabilitation programmes implemented jointly with the state Governments. In a north eastern state of Tripura, a block plantation project is being implemented for tribal shifting cultivators in the land allotted to them, engaging them as wage earners during the immaturity period. The project, with an integrated approach, aims at an overall development. By the end of 2008-'09, an area of 3405 hectare were planted covering around 3088 families. Similar projects are being implemented in other non traditional areas like Orissa, Andhra Pradesh, and Karnataka and also in Kerala. The plantations have already entered tapping phase and the Rubber Board is providing further support by forming Rubber producers' Societies and assisting them in community processing and marketing with the required infrastructure.

Rubber being a long duration crop, requiring about seven years to come to yielding, the tribal families have to be supported during the immature phase. To supplement the income derived through wages, additional income generation activities were provided to the tribal families involving women by forming Self Help Groups (SHGs) in Tripura under the World Bank Assisted Rubber Project. About 7869 families were assisted through these activities and the scheme has been very successful besides income generation activities, emphasis is also given to education, health, savings etc.

In the traditional region also, programmes for women development have been implemented aimed at additional income generation and improving health and sanitation to women small growers/spouses of small growers and women workers in the small holding sector. In Kerala, five SHGs have been supported by creating infrastructure for making rubber wood handicrafts and the units attached to the RPSs are working well. These efforts are aimed at the development of the small holding sector in general and empowerment of the women and tribal workers in the rubber plantation sector in particular. Such activities have been aimed at making rubber plantation development more sustainable by not only increasing the net family income but also by improving the quality of life.

10. Conclusion

The various labour welfare schemes implemented by the Rubber Board, Government of India, have gone a long way in ensuring the sustainable development of the labour force in the rubber plantation sector in India.

Today the rubber plantations are a source of livelihood to many of the rubber growers including the resource poor tribal small growers in the marginal and non traditional rubber growing regions in the country. The crop has significant socio-economic relevance, as about a million growers are involved in the plantation industry in India, with a small grower predominance of 91% in production and 90% in total area under rubber, besides providing about 4,00,000 jobs in the plantation sector. Added to this, from an agro – ecological point of view, rubber is an eco-friendly tree species and reproduces a stable ecosystem similar to natural forest.

References

ILO, (1958). Conditions of employment of plantation workers. International Labour Organization, Report.No.VIII(1), 40th session,1958

Iype, V. (2000). Plantation legislation . Plantation management in Natural Rubber: Agro Management and crop Processing. (Eds.) George, P.J and Jacob,C.K). 539-554.

Joseph,T. and Haridasan,V. (1992). Resource Use in Rubber Small Holdings. *Indian Journal of Natural Rubber Research*, 6 (1&2) : 43-49

Joseph, T., Haridasan,V. and Cyriac,J. (1989). Economics of Rainguarding: A Comparative Analysis. . *Indian Journal of Natural Rubber Research* . 2(2): 125-130

Joseph, T. and Rajasekkharan, P. (1991). Status report on the rubber small holdings of Tripura. Rubber Board Bulletin,26 (4):16-24

Pothen,J., Joseph,T. and George, K.T. (2000). Plantation management in Natural Rubber: Agro Management and crop Processing. (Eds. George, P.J. and Jacob,C.K.) 521- 538.

Punnoose and Lakshmanan R. (2000). Nursery and field Establishment. Plantation management in Natural Rubber: Agro Management and crop Processing. (Eds. George, P.J. and Jacob,C.K.) 129-147

RRII, (1997). Operational Efficiency of Rubber Small Holdings In Kerala During 1997. A Sample Survey of 500 House Holds, Rubber Research Institute of India (un published)

Rubber Board, (1997). Indian Rubber Statstics, 22: 4,67

Rubber Board, (2008). Standing Committee on Labour- Report, pp 10-15.

Rubber Board, (2010): Rubber Growers' Companion 2010. 9- 44

Varghese, Y. A. and Abraham, S.T. (2005). Rubber (*Hevea brasiliensis*). In: *"Handbook of Industrial Products"* (Eds. V.L. Chopra and K.V. Peter). The Haworth Press Inc. NY, USA. pp. 403-458

Varghese Y. A., Mydin, K.K. and Meenakumari T. (2009). Performance of the RRII 400 series and certain Prang Besar (PB) clones in various locations in India – A Report , Rubber Research Institute of India, Kottayam, Kerala. 80 pp

Quality of employment for older workers and social cohesion in the European Union

João Dias
ISEG/Technical University of Lisbon and UECE

Ilona Kovács
ISEG/Technical University of Lisbon and SOCIUS

Maria da Conceição Cerdeira
ISCSP/Technical University of Lisbon, SOCIUS and CAPP

Abstract

Demographic pressures and the sustainability of the social protection systems ensure increasing the percentage of older workers in employment is at the top of the EU political agenda. Recent data demonstrate that increased employment among the 55-64 age group has been one of the most dynamic aspects of the EU labour market, rising 7.8 percent between 2000 and 2007. However, there is widespread ignorance about the quality of jobs held by this age group. Early retirement is often underpinned by discourse blaming older workers for not being able to adapt to technological and organizational changes. Sharp asymmetries in older worker employment rates between European countries refute simplistic explanations based on stereotypes suggesting, rather, the importance of the different national approaches to active ageing. In this paper, we challenge some highly diffused ideas that encourage discriminatory practices against older members of the workforce and analyse the quality of older worker employment in European Union countries.

Content

1. The context of ageing workforce employment

A key aspect of sustainable development involves the ability of societies to promote greater social cohesion. Over the last decade, the social and economic consequences of demographic changes have become a serious challenge for European policymakers. The decrease in fertility rates and increasing longevity lead to a decrease in young adults and a rising proportion of older workers (aged 55 and over) in the workforce, as well as a substantial increase in old-age dependency ratios. This trend tends to become more prominent in the decade ahead and implying serious problems in terms of the sustainability of pension systems and the labour force of European countries. It is no coincidence that raising the rate of older workers in employment and the sustainability of the social protection system are European Employment Strategy priorities (European Commission, 2007; Molinié, 2003). The EU active ageing policy deals with the consequences of demographic changes and sets targets for 2010: increasing the elderly employment rate to 50% and the retirement age to 65 years of age. EU countries are developing different measures to retain older workers in work, such as reducing pensions for those who exit earlier, introducing more limitations on early retirement and promoting financial incentives for gradual retirement schemes.

Although demographic changes require the growing employability of older workers, competitive pressures on businesses point in the opposite direction. Increasing competition, reducing costs, innovating and diversifying products, adapting to technological and market changes all imply companies undertake flexible rationalization processes such as lean-production and reengineering approaches and high performance working organizational practices (Bauer, 2004; Ramsay *et al.*, 2000; Oeij *et al.* 2002; Kovács, 2006). These processes demand a high performance workforce more capable of generating high-value outputs by deploying advanced cognitive and learning capacities, adapting to changes, initiative and proactive behaviour. Human resource management (HRM) practices for older workers are frequently based on negative perceptions, such as their alleged resistance to change and difficulties in dealing with technology, particularly computer technology. For these reasons, older workers experience discrimination in recruitment processes and have fewer opportunities for learning/training and promotion. These discriminatory human management practices weaken the overall employability of older workers. Indeed, older workers have become an adjustment variable recomposing the active population, backed by negative and positive stereotypes according to convenience. In times of low demand, they are deemed stagnant and obsolete and therefore must be removed from the labour market. In the 1970s and 1980s, age based discriminatory policies were based on negative views about older workers and their inadequacy when faced with the imperatives of technical/economic changes and a widespread culture of early exit developed (HRM practices stimulating early retirement). On the contrary, in periods of high demand, older workers are considered loyal and committed workforce with specific skills through accumulated work experience.

In this paper, we challenge some of these ideas and the grounds for discriminatory practices against older workers in carrying out comparative analysis of the quality of employment of this group of workers across 31 European countries.

2. Controversies and perspectives around older workers in employment

One of the social representations most commonly portraying older workers, and that supports discrimination practices based on age, is the presumption of a gap between wages and productivity. The idea is that ageing reduces the ability to work as older workers may be less healthy or experience cognitive difficulties in learning and adapting to change. Thus, a positive relationship between age and low productivity is deemed to exist as well as between age and a failure to adapt to technological and organizational change. In contrast, as a consequence of career progression mechanisms inherent to internal labour markets, older persons tend to receive higher wages than other age groups. However, these assumptions have been the subject of great controversy in recent decades. While some findings identify the existence of a negative relationship between age and productivity, others support precisely the opposite view (OECD, 2000). Furthermore, some works claim that individuals develop 'compensatory strategies' over their life cycle to overcome the difficulties of age (Volkoff, Moliné & Jovilet, 2000; Volkoff & Thébaud-Mony, 2000). Aubert and Crepon (2004) emphasize that productivity increases up to 40-45 and thereafter tends to stabilize. Friedberg (2003) raises objections to the supposed handicaps of the more senior workers to cope with technological and organizational changes. Regarding the relationship between salary and age, Gautié (2004) found positive correlations in the case of the highly qualified, but negative in the case of unskilled workers, especially in the private sector.

Some societal approach based studies show there are close links between national institutions and the quality of employment. In accordance with the most important typologies, quality of employment is closely linked to industrial relations systems (Calmfors & Driffll, 1988; Bassanini & Duval, 2006), models of production and work organisation (Piore & Sabel, 1984; Boyer & Durand, 1993) as well as social protection models and education and training systems

(Lane, 1989; Esping-Andersen, 1990; Ferrera, 1996; Regini, 1997; Ebbinghaus, 1999; Gallie & Paugham, 2000; Esping-Andersen & Regini, 2000; Shmid, 2002; Schmid & Gazier, 2002; Ditch & Roberts, 2002; Boeri, 2005; Barbieri, 2007; Maloutas, 2007; Zambarloukou, 2007). Other studies emphasize the types of capitalism (Hall & Soskice, 2001; Amable, 2003).

To summarize, we can conclude that stereotypes about some reduced working capacity of older workers are highly questionable. In our view, differences in productivity and job performance result from the interaction between individual resources (functional capacity and health, basic skills and vocational and educational level, values, attitudes, motivation and job satisfaction), working conditions and work organization. Therefore, the use of individual resources cannot be optimal when the conditions generated by the working environment and social institutions are not appropriate. Work organization, working conditions and social institutions shape the quality of work, employment and the position of older people in the labour market. Consequently, job quality is a key issue to the maintenance of older workers at work and to the sustainability of our societies.

3. Ageing worker job quality

In this empirical section, we consider only workers aged 55-64 years. In order to analyze job quality, we constructed eight aggregate indicators defining four quality dimensions, using the Fourth European Working Conditions Survey (EFILWC, 2005). As is well known, this survey enabled the construction of a large database on 31 countries across more than three hundred questions (variables), concerning various aspects namely those specifically related to the physical environment, health and safety, working hours, income and so forth. From this set of variables we constructed, for each country and each variable, a basic indicator using a weighted scheme, based on the importance attributed to each item by the respondents. The four quality dimensions and the eight defining aggregate indicators are presented in Figure 1.

In this section, we present the results for each quality dimension in graphical form, putting one component of this dimension in each axis. In all cases, the standard used for comparison is the value obtained for the set of 31 countries, that is, E31. The acronym for each country may be checked in figure 5, setting out our global job quality indicator. Due to a lack of space, some details concerning indicator construction are omitted and only a few comments will follow results presentation.

Of course, a cautionary note is necessary here. We are aware that our results are based on data obtained ahead of the current economic and financial crises and

Figure 1. Four job quality dimensions

it is entirely feasible that the position of countries may be different (for example in the cases of Ireland and the United Kingdom) in any after-crisis survey.

3.1 Quality of work

There is a clear division in the way this European working age group views the quality of work. In fact, around half of respondents record a positive view, both for the *intrinsic quality of work* (related to aspects such as work content, autonomy or organization) and the *communication/participation* component of this indicator. But there are sharp differences between European countries. For ten countries, we return a better than average judgement on both components, particularly strong in the case of Denmark, Sweden, Switzerland, Finland, Netherlands, Norway and Luxemburg.

On the other hand, we have a large number of countries with values below that of the E31 results for these two components. This is particularly the case for Portugal, Spain, Turkey and Italy but this group also includes some of the most advanced European countries such as Germany and France.

Figure 2. Quality of work

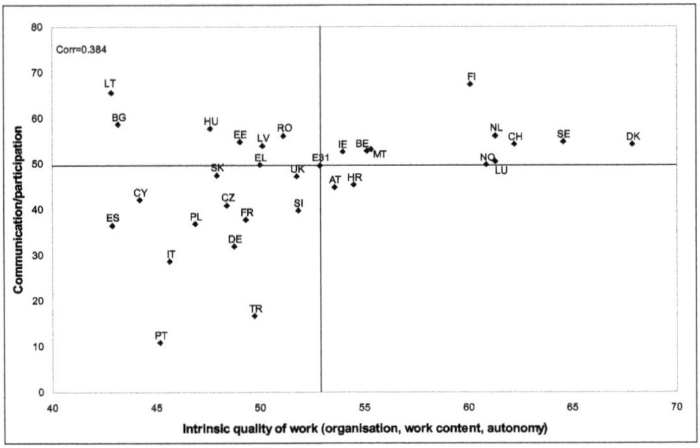

3.2 Working conditions and health and safety

The evaluation of European aged workers of their *working conditions* and *health and safety* is, in general, much more positive than the previous case of quality of work. For the set of 31 countries, the score is around two thirds for each component.

Figure 3. Working conditions and health/safety

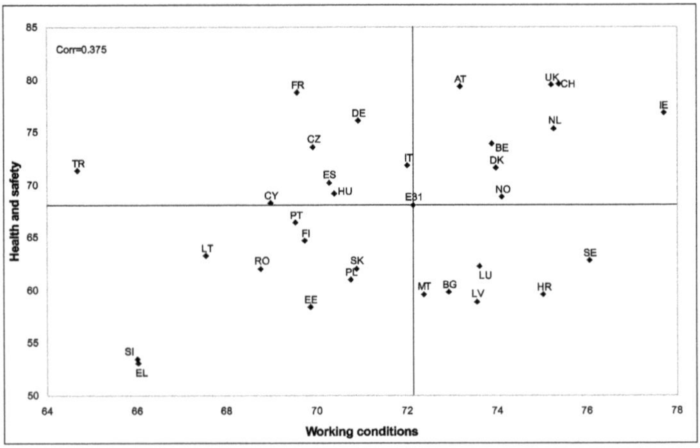

But there are, again, significant variations between European countries, particularly in relation to the *health and safety* component. Nevertheless, we do now record a more even distribution for each case (above or below E31). The "best" group (both above E31) now contains eight members: Ireland and UK, Switzerland, Netherlands, Austria, Belgium, Denmark and Norway. In the "worst position" we have a group of nine countries and the distance from E31 is particularly strong for Greece and Slovenia. Turkey appears at the greatest distance in terms of *working conditions* but above average in terms of *health and safety*. France has a strong position in terms of *health and safety* but returns a below average score for working conditions. In contrast, Sweden and Croatia register good scores for working conditions but are below average in terms of the other indicator.

3.3 Job satisfaction and job security

For the set of 31 European countries, we have a mixed situation concerning this aggregate indicator. In terms of job security, there is the relatively high score of almost eighty per cent (77.2%) for job security but a rather lower value (51.7%) for job satisfaction. Interestingly enough, the correlation coefficient between these two dimensions is relatively high and, in fact, we observe a concentration of the countries into two broad groups: those with above average scores and those with below average scores in both indicators.

Figure 4. Job satisfaction and job security

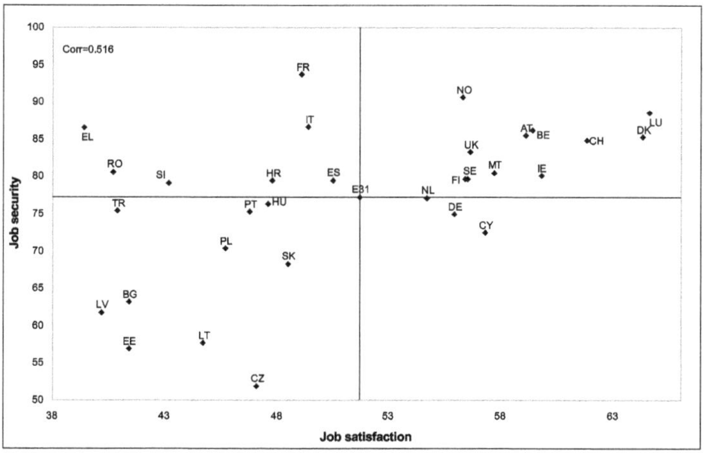

From the first group, Luxemburg, Denmark and Switzerland stand out, but the group includes eight other countries. For the second group, Latvia, Bulgaria, Estonia, Lithuania and Switzerland take the lowest positions. Turkey, Portugal and Hungary are also below average in terms of job satisfaction but not far from E31 on job satisfaction. Greece is also below average for job satisfaction but above average in terms of job security.

3.4 *Working time and work-life conciliation*

For our final dimension, *working time and work-life conciliation,* we record a relatively high score for the set of 31 European countries. However, once again, we have quite distinct situations for each country and also observe a relatively high correlation between the two components: *work-life conciliation* and *working time.* As such, the countries broadly cluster into two groups: those above average in both components and countries with a lower than average score for both *work-life conciliation* and *working time.*

Figure 5. Working time and work-life conciliation

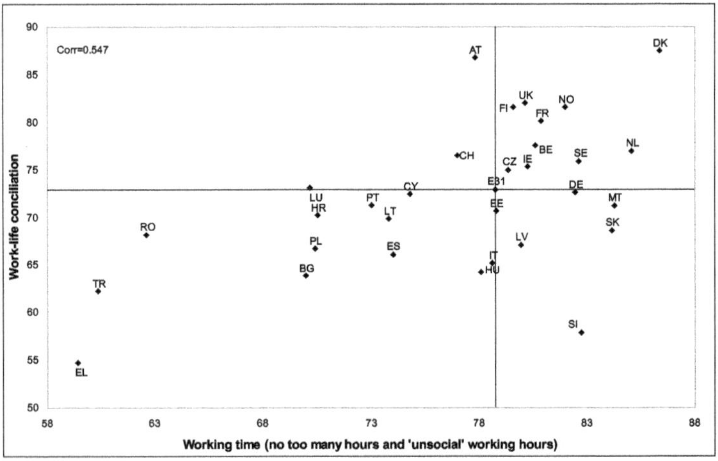

The first group has ten members and Denmark clearly stands out with the highest score for both components, with a result approaching 90%. Norway, Sweden, Netherlands, the United Kingdom, France and Finland also present high values. On the opposite side, Greece is lowest, followed by Turkey, Romania and nine other countries.

3.5 Global indicator of job quality

Concerning our global indicator of job quality, the score obtained by the set of 31 European countries (67%) is at two thirds of the maximum (100%). All countries are well above 50%. Yet there is a significant gap between the leading and the lagging countries. The first group is headed by Denmark, followed by Switzerland, Sweden, Netherlands and Norway. Clearly, Nordic countries appear among those countries with the highest scores.

Figure 6. Global indicator of job quality

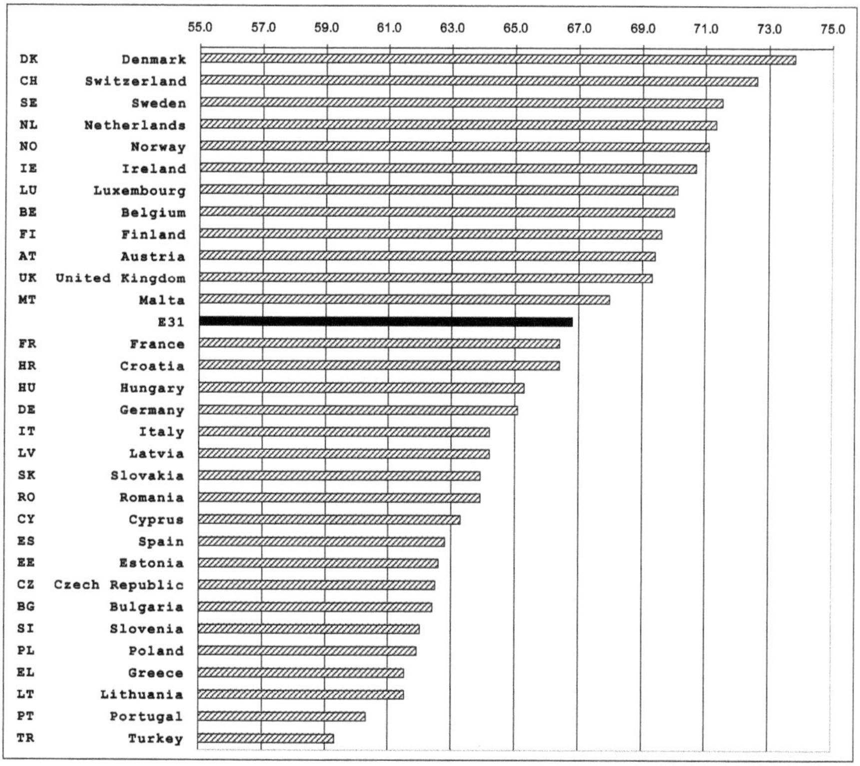

In contrast, Turkey and Portugal return the lowest values for this global indicator. Greece and Spain also belong to this group as well as all Eastern European countries.

3.6 Job quality and employment rate

In figure 7, we plot the values obtained for our global job quality indicator against the employment rate for the same group of aged workers. Comparing this with the E31 average, we encounter a diversity of situations (particularly in terms of employment rate), with countries above or below the E31 score for both variables or below and above in only one dimension.

Figure 7. Job quality and employment rate

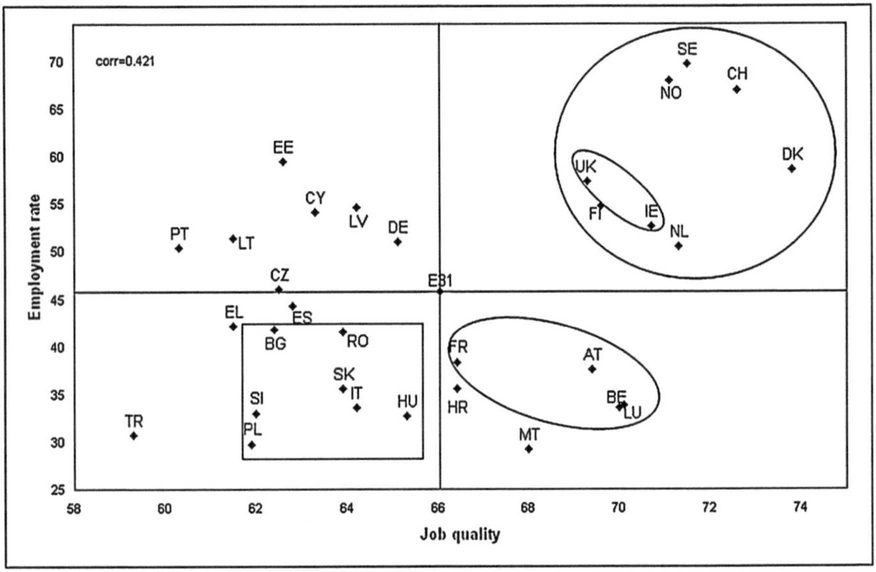

We now briefly comment on some cases. Scandinavian countries return above E31 scores for both job quality and the employment rate. Switzerland, Netherlands, United Kingdom and Ireland complement the group of countries with above average values in both cases. In contrast, that is, countries with below average values for job quality and rate of employment, we find a group of Eastern European countries along with Turkey, Greece and Spain. Some Western European countries (France, Austria, Belgium and Luxembourg), have a high value in terms of job quality but below average scores for the employment rate. On the contrary, seven other countries have high employment rates but lower than average values of job quality.

4. Conclusions

We did not identify a single trend related to quantitative and qualitative aspects in the employment of this older segment of the workforce. On the contrary, there are substantial differences among European countries. We detected a strong contrast between the group of Nordic countries and countries in Eastern and Southern Europe. Nordic countries (Denmark, Sweden Norway, Finland) have the highest employment rates and highest job quality for older members of the workforce. On the contrary, the majority of Eastern European countries (Poland, Slovenia, Bulgaria, Slovakia, Romania, Hungary), but also some Southern European countries (besides Turkey, Greece, Italy and Spain) register the lowest employment rates and lowest job quality indicators. Countries belonging to the Anglo-Saxon group (United Kingdom, Ireland) are characterized by relatively high employment rates and high employment quality. Western European countries (Austria, France, Germany, Luxembourg, Belgium) hold intermediate positions with low employment rates (except Germany) and high to medium levels of job quality. However, there are also some countries with high employment rates and low job quality for ageing workers (Portugal, Cyprus, Estonia and Lithuania).

The results of our study suggest there is a significant relationship between employment quality and the activity rate on the one hand and between the employment quality of older workers and the institutional context of the various countries, on the other. The social model prevailing in Nordic countries (Denmark, Sweden, Finland and Norway) is characterised by a coordinated market economy, universal welfare, strong trade unions, centralised collective bargaining, dialogue and participation. These countries were pioneers in introducing changes in the retirement system and the implementation of active employment policies with the purpose of promoting a career throughout the life cycle. Moreover, they have fostered forms of work organization and job design, based on ergonomic studies, especially adapted to older workers.

In contrast, the social institutional context of Eastern European countries is characterised by highly flexible and unregulated labour markets, weak trade unions and individualised employment relationships generating high insecurity. This institutional context is unfavourable both to retaining older workers in employment and to enhancing job quality. In turn, the institutional context of South European countries is characterised by contentious labour relations, weak trade unions, partial labour market deregulation, segmented protection and low levels of workplace democracy. This context is also not favorable to improving job quality and encouraging the retention of elderly workers in employment. Although the United Kingdom and Ireland present both relatively high employment rates and job quality indicators, they also display strong segmentation and high rates of poverty produced by the institutional context of these countries (flexible job markets, weak trade unions, decentralised bargaining and low protection).

The experience of the Nordic countries might serve as a benchmark for active ageing policies. This is the great challenge facing contemporary society in terms of sustainable development, greater justice and social cohesion. The objective of improving the employment rate among older workers, as defined by the European Employment Strategy, without linking the measures to promoting motivation and job satisfaction through improving the quality of working life, engenders the risk of producing new constraints on older people. Should the integrated policies that aim to make staying longer in the labour market attractive remain limited to the Nordic countries, there is the risk of reinforcing the aforementioned existing inequalities between the groups of countries. An active ageing policy that meets the objectives of sustainable development is possible only by breaking with the prevailing orientation of competitiveness driven employment policies, which lead to rising unemployment, the destabilisation of employment practices and undermine job quality with inequalities increasing at both the national and European levels.

Thus, there is a corresponding need to introduce changes in human resource management practices in order to increase the employability of human resources. This requires the development of a qualifying work organization, creating opportunities for learning and training with better career prospects and taking into account the satisfaction of older workers in terms of working conditions and wages. In human resource and organization management practices, special attention must be given to some other aspects, particularly: increased autonomy at work, allowing decision making by workers themselves and by teams over division of tasks, reduced working intensity and ergonomics strains, improved participation in decision making on work related problems and changes in work organisation.

References

Amable, B. (2003). *The Diversity of Modern Capitalism.* Oxford: University Press.

Aubert, P. & Crépon, B. (2004). La productivité des salariés âgés. Une tentative d'estimation. *Économie et Statistique*, 368, 95-119.

Barbieri, P. (2007). Atypical employment and welfare regimes. *Policy Paper. Equalsoc, Economic Change, Quality of Life & Social Cohesion*, 1, 1-23.

Bassanini, A. & Duval, R. (2006). Employment Patterns in OECD Countries: Reassessing the Role of Policies and Institutions. *OECD Social, Employment And Migration Working Papers,* 35.

Bauer, T. (2004). High performance workplace practices and job satisfaction: Evidence from Europe. *IZA Discussion Paper,* 1265, [online], retrieved 15 March 2008, Available at: ftp://ftp.iza.org/dps/dp1265.pdf.

Boeri, T. (2005). Reforming Labor and Product Markets: Some lessons from two decades of experiments in Europe'. *IMF working paper,* WP/05/97, pp. 1-27.

Boyer, R. & Durand, J.-P. (1993). *L'Après-Fordisme.* Paris: Syros.

Calmfors, L. & Driffill, J. (1988). Bargaining structure, corporatism and macroeconomic policy. Economic Policy, 6, pp. 13-47.

Ditch, J. & Roberts, E. (2002). Integrated approaches to active welfare and employment policies. Luxembourg: Office for Official Publications of the European Communities.

Ebbinghaus, B. (1999). Does a European Social Model Exist and Can it Survive?. In G, Huemer, M. Mesch, & F. Traxler (Eds), The Role of Employer Associations and Labour Unions in the EU (pp. 1-26). Aldershot: Ashgate.

EFILWC (2005). *Quality in Work and* Employment. Luxembourg: Office for Official Publications of the European Communities.

Esping-Andersen, G. (1990). *The Three Worlds of Welfare State.* Cambridge: Polity Press.

Esping-Andersen, G. & Regini, M. (Eds) (2000) Why deregulate labour markets?, Oxford: Oxford University Press.

European Commission (2007). *Employment in Europe 2007.* Luxembourg: Office for Official Publications of the European Communities.

Ferrera, M. (1996). The "southern model" of welfare in social Europe. *Journal of European Social Policy,* 6, 17-37.

Friedberg, L. (2003). The impact of technological change on older workers: Evidence from data on computer use. *Industrial and Labor Relations Review,* ILR Review, ILR School, Cornell University, 56, 511-529.

Gallie, D & S Paugam (2000): The Experience of Unemployment in Europe: the Debate. In D. Gaillie & S. Paugam (Eds.): *Welfare Regimes and the Experience of Unemployment* (pp. 351-374). Oxford: Oxford University Press.

Gautié, J. (2004). Les marchés internes du travail, l'emploi et les salaires. *Revue Française d'Économie,* 18, 33-63.

Hall, P. & Soskice, D. (2001). Un Introduction to Varieties of Capitalism. In P. Hall & D. Soskice, *Varieties of Capitalism: the Institutional Foundations of Comparative Advantage.* (pp.1-68) London: Oxford University Press.

Kovács, I. (2006). Novas formas de organização do trabalho e autonomia no trabalho. *Sociologia, Problemas e Práticas,* 52, 41-65.

Lane, Ch. (1989). From Welfare Capitalism to Market capitalism: A Comparative Review of Trends towards Employment Flexibility in the Labour Markets of Three Major European Societies. *Sociology,* 23, 583-610.

Maloutas, T. (2007). Socio-Economic Classification Models and Contextual Difference: The European Socio-economic Classes (ESeC) from a South European Angle'. *South European Society & Politics*, 12, 443-460.
Molinié, A.-F. (2003). *Age and working conditions in the European Union*. Dublin: European Foundation for the Improvement of Living and Working Conditions.
OECD (2000). *Reforms for an Ageing Society*, Paris: OECD.
Oeij, R. Auer, P. & Wiezer N. M. (2002). *New work organization, working conditions and quality of work: towards the flexible firm?*. Luxembourg: Office for Official Publications of the European Communities.
Piore, M. & Sabel, C. (1984). *The Second Industrial Divide: Possibilities for Prosperity*. New York: Basic Books.
Ramsay, H.; Scholarios, D. & Harley, B. (2000). Employees and High-Performance Work Systems, Testing inside the Black Box. *British Journal of Industrial Relations*, 38, 501-531.
Regini, M. (1997). Social Institutions and Production Structure. The Italian Variety of Capitalism in the 1980s. In C. Crouch & W. Streeck (Eds.), *Political Economy and Modern Capitalism: Mapping Convergence and Diversity* (pp. 102-16). London: Sage.
Schmid, G. & Gazier, B. (2002). *The Dynamics of Full Employment: Social Integration Through Transitional Labour Markets*. Cheltenham: Edward Elgar.
Schmid, G. (2002). Employment insurance in critical transitions during the life-course. In P. Auer & B. Gazier (Eds.), *The future of work, employment and social protection*. Geneva: ILO/IILS.
Volkoff, S. & Thébaud-Mony, A. (2000). Santé au Travail: l'inégalité des parcours. In A. Leclerc, A. Fassin, H. Granjean, M. kaminski & T. Lang (Eds.), *Les inégalités sociales de santé* (pp. 349-362). Paris: La Découverte.
Volkoff, S., Molinié, A-F. & Jolivet, A. (2000). *Efficaces à tout âge? Vieillissement démographique et activités de travail*. Paris: Centre D'études de L'emploi.
Zambarloukou, S. (2007). Is there a South European Pattern of Post-Industrial Employment? *South European Society & Politics*, 12, 425-442.

Chapter 6: Public Employment & Employee's Participation

The Development of Employee Involvement in China's State Owned Enterprises[1]

Siyan Wu
(Post-Doctoral Research Center of Shanghai Pudong Development Bank and Fudan University, Shanghai, PRC, 200002)

Yiming Zhang
(Business School of Nankai University, Tianjin, PRC, 300071)

Jianying Tang
(College of Economics and Management, Nanjing University of Aeronautics and Astronautics, Nanjing, PRC, 210016)

Jiaojiao Qu
(Business School of Nankai University, Tianjin, PRC, 300071)

Abstract

The paper traces the historical development of employee involvement (EI) in China's state owned enterprises (SOEs) from the planned economy to the market economy with the analysis of the social and economic backgrounds. The origin of the SOEs' employee involvement is the planned economy. At that period, the government had a decisive impact on the forms, process and contents of employee participation. The SOEs' EI practices had a strong political characteristic, which was established on the basis of ensuring the people's role as the owners of the country and spread from the top to bottom under the authority of the government. The SOEs' EI practices in the transition period to market economy still remain the traditional ways under the influence of the path dependence of institutional development. Meanwhile, the democratic management institutions which depend on the employees' owner status experience heavy collapse. In the period of transition to market economy, the SOEs' EI practices presents the features such as the path dependence of EI development, the management authority's dominance, the utility orientation of EI policies and so on. The effects and consequences of EI practices depend more and more on the values and strategic choices of SOEs' management.

Employee involvement (EI), sometimes also named organizational democracy in China, refers to employees involving in the management and decision process in the organization with a certain kind of participatory forms. Through the interaction between the employees and managers, employees could increase the influence upon their jobs and organizational policies to some extent. Employee involvement not only could effectively reflect employees' appeals, but also bring motivation, job enrichment and positive performance. Therefore, it can serve as a win-win solution to achieve the goal of both the organization and the employees, and play an important role to establish and maintain the harmonious labor relations.

In China, the government, employers and employees all regard employee involvement as an important strategy to coordinate corporate labor relations. As the form of "workplace democracy" or "industrial democracy", employee involvement arouses the government and legislature's special at-

---

1 The research is supported by the National Natural Science Foundation of China(No. 70702015).
Correspondence author: Siyan Wu, wusiyan@gmail.com, +8613611897668

tention since it could rebuild the corporate governance structure. With the strong push of the government and the automatic actions of the enterprises, the development of SOEs' employee involvement not only retains the traditional characteristics, but also experiences many new changes. As North said, path dependence means history is important, which can make us understand today's choices better. Tracing the development process of SOEs' employee involvement from the planned economy to market economy could help to explore its evolution path more clearly, understand the root causes of the formation of its operating mechanism and follow-up development trend, and analyze the "development" and "un-development." As an important part of human resources management and labor relations, employee involvement operates in the specific context of the economics, management and labor relations. This paper tries to review and commend on the historical development of China SOEs' EI practices from the planned economy to the market economy with the analysis of the social and economic backgrounds.

Keywords: State owned enterprises; employee involvement; historical development

Content

SOEs' employee involvement in the period of planned economy

The socio-economic and labor relations background

The period of planned economy was from PRC's establishment in 1949 to the year 1978. In the 50 years of the 20th century, the new country faced a terribly bad environment, such as heavy industrial pressure, serious resource shortages, inimical international political and economic context, and so on. Under these circumstances, the country naturally chose a strong government-led development model. This requirement combined with the Chinese Communist Party's socialist goals, drove China moving onto a road of single public ownership and planned economy. The planned economy had achieved great success in the poverty-stricken early stage. But with the economic development, it gradually exposed the flaws difficult to overcome.

In the planned economy period, the government completely controlled the state-owned enterprises in the fields of income, expenditure and distribution. The market mechanism and the role of the law of value were restricted to a minimum. The country dominated the production, exchange, consumption and distribution of all the economic activities. Without the enterprises' independent economic interests and managers' operational autonomy, the SOEs essentially operated directly by the government were once named as the "state-run enterprises."

According to the theory of labor relations, the employers or managers and the wage-earners are two parties of the employment relationship. But in the period of planned economy, the two parties hadn't come into being. The nature of SOEs' industrial relations was labor administration relations. The enterprises did not have independent economic interest and the right of self management, neither did the employers' status. On the other side, the workers did not have independent labor ownership and the right of freely choosing jobs. They must obey the job distribution of the country. The labor relations were established in term of the predetermined rules set by the government. There was no room for consultations and negotiations. Therefore, the labor relationship of state-owned enterprises during this period was not an employment relationship, but a top-down administrative subordinateness relationship.

The situation of SOEs' employee involvement

The government played an important role in the SOEs' democratic management. The Government decided the forms, degrees and effects of employee involvement. With the ultimate manifestation of government's leading role in the planned economy, employee participating in the management model shows the characteristics of political mobilization.

Ideology for the political mobilization was of extraordinary significance. It also was followed by the communist party. The communist party and the government attached great importance to the ideology of socialism, which was to ensure the working class leadership, reflected the status of ownership, emphasized on "relying on the working class all heart and soul", "everything for the people, all relying on the masses" and "from the people, to the people". According to the cognition in the planned economy period, democratic management of enterprises was an important part for the construction of socialist democratic politics; if workers worked and administrative personnel dominated management, two antagonistic classes would come into being, which was not socialism. Only when workers began to be truly absorbed in the decisive solution of managerial problems of labor organization, production and social relations, and these issues became the common problems of all the workers, which would be the socialist.

To reflect the working class' leader status, the Communist Party gave full play of its strong political mobilization, so that SOEs' worker participation in the planned economy period largely demonstrated a strong political characteristic.

Firstly, worker participation had a strong political mobilization. SOEs' employee involvement reflected the concept of "people are the masters of the socialist", therefore, it was complemented as a political mission required through the governments' administrative channels from top to down. In the early days of new China, the public and private enterprises all carried out democracy movement, which was known as the "second revolution after the liberation". In 1950, the CPC Central Committee and Administration Council put forward a democratic reform movement of the old suppressive system left by old China. In the state-owned enterprises, factory- workshop- team three tier of production management system was generally set up. The factory management council and workers representatives meeting were also established to implement democratic enterprise management. In 1957, according to the central directives of CPC, the factories and enterprises began to carry out rectification campaign to make the workers launched into advising, the enterprises listening to public criticism and correcting their behaviors. This kind of democratic movement had a strong political nature, which could make all the workers participate in enterprise management in a very short period of time.

Secondly, the employees participated in management activities with assault. Democratic participation was often regarded as an important role to encourage the workers to work energetically to complete the production tasks quickly. When production task was not yet completed at the quarter end, or needed over fulfilled, or when the government launched various production movements, participatory management would be used as a magic weapon to improve workers production activity and encourage them to make suggestions in increasing production and innovating techniques.

Thirdly, employee involvement was lack of persistence. Owing to participatory management did not exist as an institution, but as a main form of political activity, therefore the time participatory activities continued depended on whether the goal was achieved. When the political movement ended or a phase of the production task was completed, the democratic participation was also going to the end. But some activities, such as labor competition, reasonable proposal and increasing production movement, gradually transformed into a regular activity.

Fourthly, the participation was driven by the government. In order to "let the people participate in the management", to harmonize the conflict between managers and workers, and to exert workers' "enthusiasm, initiative and creativity," the participatory management in this period was mostly driven by the central government and the trade union by country-wide massive "democratic management" movement. For example, labor competition or reasonable proposal activity were pushed by the central government from top to down and the enterprises and workers positively responded.

"Angang constitution" was a typical representative of the political mobilization. In the 1950s, the large and medium-sized state-owned enterprises imitated the managerial system of "one-man leadership" in "Maanshan Iron & Steel Constitution" of the former Soviet Union. The core administration principle of SOEs was the chief executive totally in charge of the company. Its advantage was to effectively organize and direct the workers to complete the production target in a short time. But its defect is also obvious, such as to make people revolt against the bureaucratic behaviors, to make solutions with out respect of science, and run into grandiloquent and reckless in production. Therefore, there was an urgent appeal for China to establish a democratic managerial model to fit the specific context. Under this circumstance, the "two participate one reform" first implemented by Jinan Chengji Mill Factory, was paid great attention by the central government. In 1958, it was named as "Angang Constitution" and promoted heavily in the nationwide by Mao Zedong, chairman of China. Its main contents are summarized as "two participation one reform three combinations", which meant the managers participated in labor, workers participated in management; reformed the unreasonable rules and regulations; working people, leading cadres and technical personnel combined together. Angang Constitution could be regarded as an important exploration of the democratic management or employee participation, but with the background of "Great Leap Forward", it was a typical representative of politics arrogating economy and state controlling society in the period of planned economy. Thus, Angang Constitution became a political tool in using politics during the implementation and generalization process. It took some extreme approaches such as politics in command, mass movements, abandon of rules and regulations and so on. It was no longer a simple enterprise management method, and brought a variety of confusions and problems inevitably.

Worker and Staff Representative Congress is a main form of democratic management of state-owned enterprises, which experienced a rough passage in the planned economy period. It was established in the early days after the foundation of new China, but repealed with the implementation of "totally charge of one chief executive" in the early 1950s. It was re-established in the middle and latter half of the 1950s, and was damaged even more seriously in the period of the

"Cultural Revolution" from 1966 to 1976. During the period of planned economy, except the special period of "Cultural Revolution", what most state-owned enterprises in China implemented was the factory director responsibility system and the Worker and Staff Representative Congress system under the leadership of Party committees. In other words, under the leadership of CPC committees, Worker and Staff Representative Congress and factory director responsibility system constituted the two parallel enterprise management systems. As a result, corporate administration and employee participation began to be separated institutionally. Worker and Staff Representative Congress complied with the requirements of enterprises' democratic management at micro level, which was a method to resolve the problems brought by "one-man leadership". It adapted to the political demands at the macro level, concerting with the system of People's Congress as an extension of political system to enterprises. But this institution was not implemented practically in the period of planned economy.

In the planned economy, the forms of employee involvement were relatively simple, mainly concluding reasonable suggestions, the labor competition for a new higher production record, Worker and Staff Representative Congress and Factory Management Committee, etc. The direct employee involvement forms mainly played a role of contributing ideas and suggestions. The authorized self-management teams were barely organized. The main form of indirect employee involvement was Worker and Staff Representative Congress, whose biggest contribution was to establish the important role of democratic management.

The typical feature of democratic management in the planned economy period was that workers had no individual rights and personal interests. In theory, employee involvement was based on the principle that workers were given the "enterprise's owner" or "the masters of their company" status. And democratic management was a form for the Communist Party to activate the initiative, creativity and enthusiasm of the people. Thus, the workers participated in the managerial process on behalf of the overall identity of the working class, rather than independent individuals. They had no voice to appeal for their individual interests or rights. The democratic management was at the expense of individual interests to some extent.

The intrinsic motivation of employees to participate in democratic management is mainly the strong sense of responsibility with their owners' status. The extrinsic motivation is the enforceable guidance and heavy pressure generated by political movements. The economic profit making motive is not obvious during the period of planned economy (Liu, 2008, p.212). When the political and economic management system had not created good operation and development conditions for the development of democratic management, it was difficult to get rid of the political influences. Therefore, this democratic experiment based on the moral – political mobilization run counter to the communist's industrial democracy idea finally, owing to politics super session of economy, leaders overriding the institutions, and the public blind following.

SOEs' employee involvement in the period of transition to market economy

The social economy and labor relations backgrounds during the period of economic transition

The state-owned enterprise is the central part of Chinese economic reform. Through briefly reviewing the course of SOEs' reform, we can generally outline the institutional background of the labor relations' changes and employee involvement development path.

The purpose of state-owned enterprise reform is to strengthen SOEs' economic function, to improve their business efficiency and to make profitability. The reform of more than 30 years can be divided into three phases.

The reform stage of expanding SOEs' autonomy by decentralization (1979-1984)

The theme of SOEs' reform in this stage was decentralization, giving some autonomy rights and profit to the enterprises. Some measures were adopted, such as changing allocation of funds into loans, changing profits to tax and so on. During this period, SOEs' managerial system is chief executive responsibility under the leadership of the Communist Party Committee. The decentralization reform was essentially enlarging the power of leaders, especially the members of CPC.

There was some reform measures closely related with the labor relationship problems in this stage. Reward and piece-work wage system began to be complemented. The enterprises' managerial autonomy rights became to be enlarged and they were given some rights of recruitment and stuffing. The government tried to break the "iron bowl" or "eating from the same big pot" employment system which had been carried out for more than 20 years.

The reform stage of separating the ownership and management rights (1985-1992)

"Two rights" separation by means of contracting was the national reform measure in the second stage of SOEs' reform to constrain budget, strengthen the managers' responsibility and managerial authority. Under contract responsibility system, managers' power was further increased, while the protections of workers' rights were weakened. The main reform of labor relationship institutions mainly focused on "breaking three irons", which fundamentally shook the traditional labor relations. The implementation of labor contract to all the SOEs employees contributed to break the "iron rice bowl" of life-time employment. The "iron pay salary" was broken by giving SOEs certain autonomy rights to decide salary distribution and implement job-skill wage system. And the "iron lifetime post" was broken by abolishing life tenure of office cadres and allowing enterprise cadre to compete for positions. The breaking of "three irons" began to really touch almost all employees' vital interests.

The stage of establishing modern corporation system and strategic restructuring (1993-)

The debate on the "socialism" and "capitalism" ended in this period. Socialist market economic system was establishing gradually. The basic aim of SOEs reform was set to break through constraint of the existing national institutions, to transform the SOEs' role, employees' identity and the measure of resource allocation according to the market economy principles, and to improve SOEs' efficiency through management system reforming.

In coordination with Labor and employment reform including lay off and reposition redundant personnel by downsizing for efficiency, a series of social security policies and regulations have been put forward successively, leading labor relation changing from enterprise guarantee to social security. On the basis of clearly established ownership and well-defined rights and responsibilities, the government no longer interfere SOEs' management affairs directly. Labor control based on strict rules and regulations has been gradually established.

With the economic reform, labor relations were significantly transformed. The management and employee become two parties in the employment relationship and labor relation has changed from the labor administrative relationship in planned economy period to the market employment relationship. With the enlargement of SOEs' autonomy rights, the power of managers' labor control has been increased gradually. The status gap between managers and employees is increasingly broadened.

The development of SOEs' employee involvement during the economic transformation period

The main forms of SOEs' employee involvement during economic transition period are workers' congress, openness of factory affairs, employee directors and supervisors, democratic appraisal of managers, reasonable suggestions, quality circle and so on.

Workers' Congress

Workers' congress is a basic form of Chinese SOEs' employee involvement. Its development path is an epitome of the SOEs' democratic management (Liu, 2004, p.209).Other EI forms such as openness of factory affairs, democratic appraisal of managers, employee directors and so on, are all based on workers' congress.

In July 1981, Workers' Congress in State-owned Enterprise Provisional Regulations was announced by the CPC and State Council. Workers' Congress was affirmed to be the basic form of democratic management and required to be established in all the SOEs. Since then, the institution of workers' representative congress, which had been completely damaged by "cultural revolution" in 1966-1976, was fully recovered.

On September 15 in 1986, Factory Director Working Regulations, Enterprise Organization Working Regulations and Workers' Congress Regulations were set down. The SOEs' management system changed from "director responsibility system under the leadership of Party committee" into factory director (manager) responsibility system. The communist party committees in SOEs were in charge with workers' ideology and supervision of administrative work. Workers' congress was the basic form of democratic management, with the five rights of proposing, motion passing, decision making, appraising and supervising, electing and recommending. The original intention of implementing the three Regulations was to solve the relationship between the CPC and government job in SOEs, and separate the ownership and management rights. However, the actual subsequence was that the company's chief executive began to substitute the CPC's dominance. The chief executive was the company's CPC secretary at the same. This arrangement emphasized the authority of managers at the expense of employees' voice. The workers' congress was increasingly ignored inevitably.

Since 1994, the SOEs' reform has entered into the stage of establishing a modern corporation system. The leadership system of SOEs started to be regulated in accordance with the governance structure of corporations. The horizontal division of powers among CPC committee, director (manager) and workers' congress began to be shaken and substituted by the vertically empowered models of decision-making, executive and supervision body composed by shareholders' meeting, board of director, managerial level and board of supervisors, which were independent from each other and constrained each other. As a result, it brought the conflict between the 'New Three Boards' (shareholders board, directors' board and supervisory board) and the 'Old Three Boards' (CPC committee, workers' congress and trade union). In their conflicts and clashes, the property basis gradually replaced labor rights basis, management rights gradually covered supervision rights, and the 'New Three Boards' obtained the legal and policy supporting. The 'Old Three Boards' were gradually substituted, especially the power of workers' congress and trade union, in that their functions got increasingly reduced to only a formal setting without practical power.

In practice, since 'iron wages' and 'iron rice bowl' had not been completely broken in 1990s, the interests of the employees were still protected by the government, the role of Workers' Congress was to supervise and constrain managerial rights rather than appeal for employees' interests. After 1990s, the supervision power of workers' congress has been gradually weakened. With the implementing of labor contract, lying off and reposition redundant personnel, the status of employees in labor relation become much weaker. Workers' congress and trade union began to seek the representatives of the employees' interests appeal. However, due to existing rigid institution and strong dependence on enterprises, workers' congress and trade union couldn't represent and protect employees' interests well. With the implementation of Trade Union Law and related policies, the government begins to actively promote the trade union reforms, but there is still a long way for workers' congress and trade union to transform from SOEs' affiliation to employees' organization in market economy.

Employees Directors and supervisors

Employee representatives entering into the board of directors and supervisors could increase the level of EI and reflect workers' voice in SOEs' management decision-making, and also consistent with the background of establish modern corporation system in SOEs. Therefore, employee directors and supervisors are highly emphasized in China. The Corporation Law in 1993 clearly stipulated that the board of supervisors should contain the representatives of shareholders and appropriate proportion of workers representatives in all kinds of corporations; the board of directors in SOEs should contain the representatives of employees. Since then, SOEs' employee directors are confirmed in law. Generally speaking, who enters into the board of directors and the board of supervisors are always the president or vice-president of trade union.

Due to incorporated in the "Old Three Board" and the "New Three Board", the institution of the employee directors and supervisors combines the CPC's ideology of relying on the people. Almost all SOEs have set up the directors of employees system under the push of the government. In the year 2006 and 2009, SASAC set down two regulations about employee directors in pilot SOEs owned by the central government. The proportion, nomination, election, job specification, rights and obligations and working conditions of employee directors are stipulated. With the enforcement of government institution, employee directors will get further development in SOEs.

Openness of company affairs

In the middle and latter half of 1990s, openness of company affairs became a new government institution focus to regulate SOEs' democratic management, which is an important EI form in Chinese SOEs.

In1994, Tiantong Tractor Factory Group Ltd. in Shijiazhuang identified 8 basic channels to open company affairs to workers: holding workers' congress regularly, company situation meeting, party joint committee, monitoring system of workers' congress, appeal system, reasonable suggestion, prosecution boxes, managers' mailboxes and so on. It was not strange for most SOEs, but they haven't integrated these measures into one complete mechanism. The public investigation reports about Tiantong Ltd. caused CPC's attention. In 1998, Chinese Federation of Trade Union, Commission for Staff Working and Discipline Inspection, and the Organizing Department of CCCPC jointly held a seminar. After that, openness of company affairs began to be a national wide SOEs' employee involvement form required by the government. The National Investigation Group for Openness of Factory Affairs was established to implement and supervise the practice of openness. In 2002, the General Office of the CPC Central Committee and General Office of the State Council addressed a notification on implementing the openness of factory affairs system in depth in the SOEs to especially emphasized that major decisions should not be implemented without deliberating by Federation and workers' congress have rights of deciding and denying the major affairs involving vital interests of the employees.

Reasonable suggestions

Reasonable suggestions, also called as the suggestion system, or suggestion involvement, is the most common form of direct participation in the practice of employee involvement in the world. It is the most typical and most common forms of the employees' direct participation in Chinese SOEs, too, which aims to improve productivity, increase the economic efficiency, reflect the staff's 'master' status, and motivate employees' working enthusiasm.

During the planned economy period, the contents of the Reasonable Suggestions mainly were the proposals of increasing revenue and cutting expenditures and technological innovation in production (Li, 1991). In 1985, the government advocated the workers to take part in suggestion involvement in the processes of companies' pre-production information, decision-making, development, production, service and so on. This meant that suggestion involvement could be applied into the almost every aspect of company business. The involvement form began to change 'production style' to 'management style' (Zhang, 1995).

Quality circle

To more effectively improve product quality in the industrial enterprises, State Economy Commission decided to carry out total quality control in 1980. Since then, the quality circle as the basis for implementation of TQC, began to be widely applied in SOEs. It is an important form of employee direct participation.

The State Economic And Trade Commission distributed The Approaches For Quality Management Circle Activities in 1997. It made specific provisions about the organization and management of QC circle, such as the organizing of QC circle should fit actual conditions, whether voluntarily or administrative organized; QC circle could be organized in one's own working team, workshop (department), as well as cross team or workshop (department); the main types could contain 'field work type', 'tackling key problems type', 'managing type' or 'service type' according to specific context; the workers, technicians and managers should combine together; the appropriate number of a circle is from 3 to 10, etc.

Conclusions

Employee involvement in SOEs during the economy transition period has presented many new features on the basis of continuing the planned economy practice.

Path dependence in the evolution of employee involvement in SOEs

From planned economy to market economy, Chinese economic system reform represents a progressive feature (Wang, 1999), with a strong path dependence characteristic. SOEs are the core part of economic system reform, and employee involvement is an important part of labor relation of SOEs, therefore, they all lay a deep imprint of foretime under the effect of path dependence.

The most typical form of employees' indirect involvement is workers' congress, while the typical direct one is suggestion involvement. Almost all the EI forms derived from planed economy. The effects and consequences come down in a continuous line of the tradition in the past.

Different kinds of participation practice in SOEs more or less have formalistic problems. Driven by the government institution rather than enterprises' free will, SOEs carried out democratic management by procedural response. Actually, the practical implementation effects of a system, not only is determined by the external policies, but also a synthetic outcome of many factors including business environment, organization structure, cultural tradition, value of the managers and employees, etc.

Almost all workers' congresses and trade unions depended on the corresponding systems of traditional SOEs. Although the stratum structure or class structure of participants are very different now, the original influence of planned economy still exists. This phenomenon of desynchronized between the participant structural change and institutional change, reflected the typical phenomenon of 'path dependence'. It is also showed that some of the traditions can support the new employee democratic participation mechanism.

The counter-balance of managers' authority and employee involvement

Employee involvement is a sharing of management rights. No matter Whether employee involvement level is divided into those kinds such as informative participation, consultative participation, associative participation, administrative participation, and decisive participation, or divided into ostensible participation, semi-participation and full participation, the control degree of managers' authority is reducing with employee involvement deepening. There is a counter-balance relationship between managers' authority and employee involvement.

The goal of Chinese SOEs' reform is to strengthen SOEs' economy function to pursue the objective of profit continuously. In order to achieve this goal, SOEs' leadership system changed correspondingly. From 'one-man leadership' in planned economy to director responsibility system under the leadership of CPC committee, then to the contract responsibility system and later to the modern corporate governance system, with the increasingly strengthened managerial authority, the status gap between employees and managers has been increasingly broadened. Managers access to the full control over employees through breaking the so called 'iron wage' of the average distribution system and 'iron rice bowl' of lifelong employment system.

The increasing of managers' control rights, have an expulsion or extrusion effect on employee involvement to some extent, which is fully reflected in the operation and development of workers' congress. Under the planned economy system, companies had a strong political function rather than making profit. Driven by the mass line of CPC and the employees' 'Master Status' policy, workers' congress once had a very big power to determine production and operations, appointment and removal of managers and directors. In the economic transition period, the organization and the form of workers' congress are almost unchanged, but its power, activity contents, status and function mechanism are fundamentally changed with the strengthening of SOEs' economic function.

In the market economy, the government and society no longer exaggeratively emphasize on the employees' 'owner' status in property and management system, 'owner' has become a spirit or ideology, remaining in the spiritual connotation of the employee's responsibility sense and positive initiative, while it is no longer dominant management guidelines or principles in SOEs. Therefore, when political goals give place to economic objectives, the managers' authority lay pressure on employees' democratic participation, so that workers' congress and trade union are difficult to play the practical role at present.

The complementation of government enforcement and SOEs' spontaneity

The reform of SOEs in China is oriented by institution reforming. Employee involvement in SOEs, either direct or indirect, is both driven by the national policies. In the reform carried out by government, SOEs are not the subjects who choice the institutions, but the actual executants and operators of new institutions. Since SOEs lacked of spontaneous behaviors, they always perfectly followed the enforceable government policy in forms and procedures, but barely did their actual practice and performance. Therefore, there is a strange phenomenon that almost all the SOEs establish a complete and perfect participatory management channel, but the actual operational effectiveness is quite limited.

However, there are still many spontaneous forms of employee participation in SOEs. Under the influence of the modern management theory and practice, SOEs initiatively adopt some EI forms, such as self-management teams, employee opinion survey, suggestion boxes, BBS, etc.

With government reducing intervention on SOEs' business and management, the administrative features of labor relations will be reduced. More and more SOEs will take diversified EI practice on their own will, while the leading role of government will be weakened.

Formalism and pragmatism coexisting

The popularization of most EI practices in SOEs is driven by government policies, which results in many formalist behaviors taken by many enterprises to cope with to the policies. The formalist and ineffective phenomenon exists in all the EI forms, whether direct or indirect.

Contrary to the formalist EI behaviors, managers in SOEs begin to actively provide opportunities for employees to participate in management to increase performance and improve employees working attitudes. To earn profit in market economy, enterprises need to arouse employees' enthusiasm and initiative, improve the scientificity of decision-making, increase economic performance, and maintain harmonious labor relation. The managers realized employee involvement is an effective solution. Thus, from the pragmatism orientation, the enterprises carried out EI practice as needed to help accomplishing the economic goals. Direct involvement forms are more popularized and regarded as an important HRM practices, such as self-management teams, suggestions, quality circle and so on. While those indirect involvement forms, such as workers' congress and employee directors, are not supported or paid little attention by managers in that these EI forms threaten their managerial authority or constrain their behaviors.

Generally speaking, since the reform and open-up, the formalism and pragmatism of employee involvement in SOEs come into be coexisting. Driven by the enforceable government institution, SOEs respond the policy with corresponding procedural behaviors, leading many involvement forms superficial and could not play their due effects.

The effects and consequences of EI depend more and more on the value and strategic choice of SOEs' management. As is known, actors' concept plays a key role in the process of institution changing. From planned economy to market economy, SOEs' employee involvement forms are set up and promoted by government policy initially, but the real operational results are determined by the actors' ideology and behaviors.

With the deepening of market reform and enhancement SOEs' autonomy, managers' authority is strengthened at the expense of employees' negotiation power, which causes the transformation of SOEs' labor relations. In the swirl of this transformation, employee involvement is changing accordingly: government policy is still dominant, but is weakening gradually; employees' 'owner' status is limited to the spirit of moral content, no longer the dominant idea of SOEs; employee involvement on the purpose of economic performance continued to be strengthened. The 'development' and 'no development' of employee involvement in SOEs coexist. Many traditional employee involvement practices were retained and followed, but the effects and consequences are changing quietly.

References

Li, G.(2001). The historical development, characteristics and problems of reasonable suggestions in China. JiangHan Forum, 8, 70-75

Liu, J.L.(2008).The humanistic management of China's state owned enterprises. Beijing: China Economic Press.

Liu, Y.W.(2004). The adaptation and deviation: research on worker democratic participation in modern China. Beijing: Chinese Labor and Social Security Press.

Wang, Q.B. (1999). The progressive reform path of state owned enterprises: from the perspective of the whole reform. Management World, 4, 120-128
Zhang, L.G. (1995).An effective method for employee participate in management: reasonable suggestion activities. Shanghai Enterprise, 8, 13-15

Sustainable Measures to stabilise Labour Markets during the Crisis: the Role of Short-Time Work in Germany

Sabine Gensior
Brandenburg University of Technology Cottbus

Lothar Lappe
Berlin Institute for Applied Social Research (BIS)

Abstract

In the Federal Republic of Germany too, international speculation on financial and subprime markets coupled with the economic crisis has caused severe problems. Nevertheless, the spill-over-effects of the current crisis on labour markets have been mitigated by various initiatives and measures to combat unemployment, and especially by the implementation of short-time work.

If short-time work is also implemented in those economic sectors (mechanical and electrical engineering, automotive industry etc.) which have to cope with empty order books, this might be a means of stabilising employment and labour markets in a sustainable way.

We say that short-time employment is sustainable because (a) it safeguards jobs for workers and employees, and is backed by transfer payments from public employment services (short-time allowances) that secure an acceptable income level, and because (b) it can offer companies a secure supply of qualified and trained workers for the future. Furthermore, as a certain part of the wage costs remain in the company, these residual costs of short-time labour also offer a certain inducement to companies to renounce layoffs and bridge the crisis through temporary reductions of working hours. Thus it also offers a means of avoiding labour mobility and migration.

Content

1. Introduction

To combat the financial crises and the following economic crises various employment promotion policies have been introduced in many countries: A number of emergency mechanisms or monitoring measures have been developed by policymakers and other institutions and groups. We term such policies 'sustainable human resource management'.

In the Federal Republic of Germany the short-time working allowance is a relatively seasoned instrument of labour market policy-making used for cushioning the impact of unemployment. The short-time allowance is designed to prevent redundancies at least on a temporary basis in companies faced with a reduction in the number of working hours. Book III – Promotion of Employment – of the German Social Code (SGB III) distinguishes between three types of short-time work:

1. **Seasonal short-time work** due to lost working hours due to adverse weather conditions; this mainly affects the construction industry during the winter months;
2. **Transfer or structural short-time work** as a knock-on effect of enterprise restructuring measures (sizing-down, closure or partial closure of enterprises) associated with permanent loss of work; and
3. **Cyclical short-time work** due to a major short-term unavoidable reduction in working hours due to economic reasons or unavoidable circumstances (Crimmann & Wießner, 2009; Deeke & Ohlert, 2009).

Over the past few decades short-time work and the short-time allowance was primarily a tried and tested instrument for mitigating the impact of seasonal weather conditions.

However, the introduction of the *structural short-time allowance* together with structural short-time work in the 1988 Employment Promotion Act (*Arbeitsförderungsgesetz*) created the possibility of continuing in employment for a limited period of one to two years even though the job would be irrevocably lost after that time.

Widespread use was made of this instrument in the post 1990 period immediately following German reunification, particularly in the new east German Länder so that in the 1990s this instrument may be said to have had its 'baptism of fire' under conditions for which it was by no means created to meet:

"At that time the main point was to buffer the effects of job losses across the lame duck industries of East Germany." (Crimmann & Wießner, 2009, p. 3) In the first year following reunification a total of 6 million jobs were shed in the East German enterprise sector.

As Fig. 1 shows, in 1991 up to 2,250,000 people (in East Germany) were on short-time work.

> "However, an employment market instrument designed to cope with a temporary loss of working hours could only provide very temporary relief to the massive wave of redundancies. It proved inadequate to prevent a sharp increase in unemployment in the new Länder." This was a clear indication that while short-time work can provide temporary relief to the employment market, it is unable to solve problems of a structural nature." (Crimmann & Wießner, 2009, p. 3)

As Fig. 1 also shows, after a long period in abeyance (1997 – 2008), short-time work is once more strongly in demand. This time, however, the rise in short-time work – given the current financial crisis and its negative impact on the economy – bears the heavy imprint of cyclical elements.

Since August 2008 there has been a steady increase in the number of enterprises which have put their workforce on short-time due to a downturn in the economic cycle (see Fig. 2). Most companies applied for short-time work for a period of six to eight months when they foresaw a temporary lack of work. (Crimmann & Wießner, 2009, p. 2)

The development of the number of people benefiting from the short-time allowance (or Kug to give it its German abbreviation) is a compelling illustration of the high value this employment market instrument has for people in short-time employment (Fig. 3). In March 2009 nine out of ten people on short-time work or some 1.1 million people were receiving a cyclical short-time allowance." (Crimmann & Wießner, 2009, p. 2)

"To date German companies have indeed succeeded in building a bridge of employment over the crisis." (Süddeutsche Zeitung, 20 September 2010). Yet whether short-time work can provide a way out of a more drastic and more prolonged economic downturn, only the future will show.

In our paper we wish to discuss the ways and means of short-time work and the short-time allowance; we seek to explain who pays the short-time allowance, who benefits from it and in what ways and which professional training measures are particularly associated with it.

2. How the Short-Time Allowance actually works

Basically, short-time work in Germany is financed by the Federal Employment Agency (*Bundesagentur für Arbeit* – BA). But companies too play their part. Although they do not pay wages and salaries for lost working hours, they do have to carry part of the personnel expenses known as "residual costs". (Bach & Spitznagel, 2009) As such costs play an important role in the decision to make use of such an instrument, we must consider what costs – but also what advantages – fall to companies when they take up a short-time work scheme as a means of avoiding redundancies. In a short-time scheme company labour costs do not fall proportionally to lost working hours since part of the incidental costs continue to be paid. These residual costs can make up 24 or 35 percent of the usual standard wage costs depending on the extent to which social insurance contributions are reimbursed. If companies are bound by collective agreements to pay top-ups to short-time allowances, residual costs turn out higher. In the extreme case of a guaranteed net salary of 90 percent, for instance, they can be as high as 37 or 48 percent. These new regulations mean than companies are now in a better position than they used to be. Without reimbursement of social contributions, residual costs amount from 46 to 59 percent of wage costs. With the short-time programme companies are spared the costs of layoffs and staff reappointments while employees on short-time accept cuts in income in order to safeguard their jobs. Thus both sides play a part in assuring employment security. Residual costs also serve to counter deadweight effects and structural rigidity as companies will be mindful to introduce short-time work only where absolutely necessary in an effort to give safe passage to those jobs for which land is once more in sight.

So far Germany has coped well with the economic crisis but even so the German economy is not yet out of the woods. The past few months have shown that the short-time working programme is the proper and long-term response to the crisis. The short-time allowance enables companies to weather difficult times without having to resort to redundancy measures. Hundreds of thousands of jobs have been saved, two thirds of them alone in the small and medium sized enterprise sector. This means that companies can retain valuable know-how so that once the order intake situation improves, a skilled workforce can be instantly activated without companies having to embark on a long and costly search for new qualified personnel. On top of this, periods of short-time work can also be used to give employees further training in the sense of life-long learning. The Federal Employment Agency of Germany pays part of the further training costs and reimburses the full amount of social insurance contributions from the beginning of the training programme and for its entire duration. All this helps people keep their jobs and also gives them the chance to develop perspectives for the future. At the same time it can also help companies emerge from the recession without being unduly weakened with no blunting of their international competiveness.

3. Current regulation of short-time allowances – attempts to master the crisis through short-time work

Basically employees receive 60 percent of their former net salary as a short-time allowance (Kug). If their household includes a child, 67 percent is paid. The amount of the short-term allowance is calculated by the employer and paid to the employee. The local Employment Agency then reimburses the employer for the amount of the allowance.

3.1 New aspects of the short-time allowance

The maximum period for which the short-time allowance can be paid has been extended to 18 months. This ruling applies to all employees whose claims date from 1 January 2010. In the first 6 months of the short-time allowance, Employment Agencies reimburse employers for 50 percent of social insurance contributions. From month seven of short-time work Employment Agencies reimburse employers for 100 percent of social insurance contributions. This new ruling applies to all the companies owned by an employer if the employer has introduced a six months period of short-time work in at least one of their companies from 1 January 2009. The full amount of social insurance contributions can be covered from the start of training for those employees who take further skills training during short-time work. Proof of a wage loss of over 10 percent is sufficient for an application for the short-time allowance for one or more employees. On application by the employer, the condition that at least one third of the workforce must be affected by such a wage loss can be waivered and when making application, employers themselves can decide whether they want to make use of the new ruling or of previous law. Employers can also claim that in the event of a suspension of short-time working hours for a period of 3 months or longer during the period already specified for the short-time working allowance, they do not have to make renewed application for resumption of short-time working hours to the local Employment Office. In such cases the period specified for the short-time working allowance continues to run without interruption for the whole of the specified duration. "Working hour accounts" do not have to drop into negative territory before short-time working allowance can be claimed. Due to employment security agreements, the temporary changes to working hours that came into force from 1 January 2008 have no negative effect on the amount of the short-time working allowance. Short time working hours equally apply with no restrictions to employees of temporary employment agencies, and funding is also available for extensive further training measures for employees during periods of short-time work.

3.2 What does the employer pay?

In financial terms too, short-time working hours and professional skills building are the best alternative to layoffs and redundancies. The Employment Agency compensates for the loss of working hours with the short-time working allowance while employers must only pay the salary for public holidays and holidays. On top of this, there is a 20 percent reduction in social insurance contributions for working hours lost by short-time work whose costs are equally shared by the Employment Agency and the employer. From month seven onwards these costs are assumed in full by the Employment Agency which also from the beginning of the course reimburses all the social insurance contributions of employees participating in further training programmes.

3.3 Support for companies of all sizes

Companies of all sizes and from all economic sectors are eligible for short-time working allowances. No matter whether they be a graphics agency with a staff of five, an automotive supplier with a workforce of 500 or a major construction company with 50,000 employees on its payroll, each of these companies can benefit from short-time work. The main pre-condition is that the works' council (*Betriebsrat*) agrees to the introduction of short-time working hours. In companies with no works' council and no collective agreement regulation on short-time working hours, the short-time working programme may be applied for if all the employees concerned declare their agreement and if the appropriate preconditions are met. The process for applying for the short-time working allowance at the local Employment Agency has also been considerably simplified and streamlined during the current crisis with the aim of delivering rapid, unbureaucratic, efficient assistance.

3.4 Eligibility for the short-time working allowance

The short-time working allowance may be claimed if the loss of working hours is due to economic reasons or an unavoidable event; at least one third of the workforce has experienced a drop in salary of over 10 percent **or** if the company is no longer in a position to pay at least one employee his or her full salary in which case a drop in earnings of over 10 percent for this employee is deemed sufficient. Inevitable loss of working hours means when all other means to prevent the loss of working time like the taking of credits on working time accounts have been invoked. Further preconditions are that the company expects that the economic outlook will improve in 18 months time at the latest so that regular weekly working hours may be resumed, and that the reduction of working time has been reported to the appropriate Employment Agency.

3.5 Offsetting salaries with the short-time working allowance

If the hours worked by employees are cut back, the company only pays for the hours actually worked. Thus if weekly working time is reduced from 40 to 20 hours, the salary is also cut by half, reducing the financial burden borne by the company. To offset the loss of income, employees receive the short-term working allowance (Kug) which covers 60 percent of the lost net wage. Employees with a child receive 67 percent. The short-time working allowance is not subject to earnings tax but is governed by the provision concerning progression. Both components of the wage packet – the salary for reduced working hours and the short-time working allowance – are paid by the company to the employees. The social insurance contributions from the wage are borne by the employer and employee jointly. The Employment Agency reimburses the company for 50 percent of the short-time working allowance and its social contributions and the Agency reimburses 100 percent of costs from the seventh month onwards. Full social insurance contributions are reimbursed for employees taking part in skills building programmes during short-time work from the beginning of their training.

4. Qualification programmes during short-time work

In boom-times companies frequently have no time to give their employees further vocational training as they all indispensable on the job. Thus the period of short-time work offers an excellent opportunity for skills building. The Federal Employment Agency carries part of the costs involved in such programmes. Furthermore, upon application it can also assume costs for the full social insurance contributions paid by employees on their short-time working allowance from the first month they start on a further training period. The Federal Employment Agency is funding a wide range of further training opportunities up to the end of 2010. These can range from a course in technical or business English to certification as a forklift driver. Such measures benefit not just the company but the company employees as well who can refresh and extend their professional qualifications through a skills building programme and thus enhance their own individual career opportunities. For the company this is also an investment in its own future since a well qualified, highly skilled workforce improves company competiveness while at the same time raising employee satisfaction.

5. Qualification programmes outside of short-time working hours

It's not only during periods of short-time work alone, however, that further training measures can pay dividends. The Federal Employment Agency offers numerous skills promotion programmes which do not involve short-time work. Further training programmes, for instance, were specially conceived with older and poorly qualified workers in mind, and can now be used by all workers whose last occupational or training took place more than four years ago. The Federal Employment Agency assumes all the training costs and pays a share of the social insurance contributions of workers with low qualifications. Like the short-time working model, this makes the further training programmes a suitable instrument to effect a temporary reduction in wage costs while it also qualifies workers for subsequent tasks and duties.

6. Conclusions

In the Federal Republic of Germany too, international speculation on financial and subprime markets has exacerbated the impact of the economic crisis to cause serious upheaval. Even so, the spill-over-effects of the current crisis on labour markets have been mitigated by a set of initiatives and measures to combat unemployment, in particular the introduction of short-time work. Whether these will be more than short-term measures depends on what political actors decide.

The present situation in Germany is marked by a reduction of full employment and part-time work as well as by an expansion of temporary work managed by temporary employment agencies. At the same time we can observe – with regional differences – a modest increase in the unemployment rate which is certainly a result of the implementation of measures for short-time work.

If short-time work were also to be introduced to those economic sectors like mechanical and electrical engineering or the automotive industry which are already having to struggle with empty order books, this might be a means to stabilize employment and labour markets for the long-term.

We say that short-time employment is sustainable because a) it safeguards jobs for workers and employees, is reinforced by transfer payments from public employment services (short-time allowances) and thus secures an acceptable income level, and b) because it can offer a secure supply of qualified and trained workers for the future. As a certain part of wage costs remain in the company, these residual costs of short-time employment also offer a certain inducement to companies to renounce layoffs and bridge the crisis through temporary reduction of working hours. This is also a way of avoiding labour mobility and migration.

References

Bach, H.-U., & Spitznagel, E. (2009): Betriebe zahlen mit – und haben was davon. In: IAB-Kurzbericht, No. 17

Crimmann, A., & Wießner, F. (2009): Verschnaufpause dank Kurzarbeit. In: IAB-Kurzbericht, No. 14

Deeke, A., & Ohlert, C. (2009): Qualifizierungsmaßnahmen während Kurzarbeit nach endgültigem Arbeitsausfall. In: IAB-Kurzbericht, No. 3

Gensior, S., Jacobsen, H., Mendius, H.G. (2010): Kapitalmarkt, Gütermarkt, Arbeitsmarkt – beißen den Letzten die Hunde?, in: Gensior, S., Jacobsen, H., Mendius, H.G. (Hg.): Zeitschrift „Arbeit“, SAMF-Schwerpunktheft, H. 3, forthcoming

Herzog-Stein, A., Seifert, H. (2010): Stabile Beschäftigung durch flexible Arbeitszeiten, in: Gensior, S., Jacobsen, H., Mendius, H.G. (Hg.): Zeitschrift „Arbeit“, SAMF-Schwerpunktheft, H. 3, forthcoming

Walwei, U. (2010): Folgen der Finanzkrise: Wie robust ist der deutsche Arbeitsmarkt?, in: Gensior, S., Jacobsen, H., Mendius, H.G. (Hg.): Zeitschrift „Arbeit“, SAMF-Schwerpunktheft, H. 3, forthcoming

Psychological ownership of employees: A perspective from the nature of human capital properties

Fengqi Yang
PHD student at Nankai university, Tianjin city

Abstract

The nature that human capital vastly belongs to the individual and could only be entitled to that very person makes it almost impossible to impel the employees without proper motivation. Based on the psychology of mine, with its theoretical core of possession, psychological ownership was thought to be derived from three distinct while complementary routes: control, intimate knowing and investment of the self. More importantly, according to its theory builders, the psychological ownership of employees might be recognized in the absence of legal ownership. By one questionnaire survey, the author verified the existence of psychological ownership in the context of several Chinese workplaces and found it correlates positively with work control, autonomy and feedback from work. Then the implication was discussed, utilizing an inductive reasoning approach.

Content

Introduction

Since Schultz (1961) proposed the notion of human capital, more and more scholars inclined to recognize it as a very important source of incomes in modern society. Further, Rosen (1985) pointed out that the human capital should only be entitled to the very person who embodied it. Even Karl Marx had noticed such phenomena that the aptitude belongs to the individual and basically people are not equally gifted. Also, Qiren Zhou (2004) reasoned, following the above mentioned clues, and reached a conclusion which emphasized the uniqueness of the nature of human capital in light of property rights. Besides, his main proposition was much similar to that the aptitude belongs to the individual and could only be utilized through appropriate motivation.

Meanwhile, Zhou cited a research concerning the economy of slavery that was implemented by Barzel (1977) to concrete his opinions. It is clear that even in a slave society, the 'full-fledged property' could win their freedom in the sense of realizing their human capital property rights. The main reason is the unaffordable high cost of surveillance and policing which is obvious to the authority. As a derivative, Zhou argued that the unique nature of human capital property rights would inevitably influence the attitudes and behaviors of employees in workplaces in China, in contrast with other form of capitals', although literally all property rights are incomplete to some degree. In addition, the author of this article would rather believe the individuals whose rights have been jeopardized will simply 'shut down' their outputs, resulting in the nullification of the human capital assets. Furthermore, even compelled to do their routine jobs, the individuals could still possibly sabotage or boycott. It is almost impossible to supervise the work of top talented people without causing a great loss of time, energy, money and so on.

While in contemporary motivation theories, especially in the field of human resource management, there are hypotheses such as 'economic individual', 'sociable individual', 'bounded rationality', and 'self-actualization', except 'individual with discretion' or 'initiative individual'. Zhou (2004) acutely recognized the gap among these hypotheses and declared it is very hard to comprehend the motivation theories regardless of the nature of human capital property rights.

The Emergence of Psychological Ownership and Insider Control of Enterprises

Pierce et al. (2001, p.299) defined psychological ownership as a state in which individuals feel as though the target of ownership (material or immaterial) or a piece of it is "theirs" (i.e., "It is MINE!"). And this state consists of affective elements as well as cognitive elements, meanwhile, this is "part attitude, part object, part in the mind, and part real" (2004, p.509). In contrast, Avey, Avolio, Crossley, and Luthans (2009, p.174) argued that there should be two unique and independent forms of ownership which are prevention-based ownership and promotion-based ownership. In addition, according to Pierce, there should be three roots conducive to psychological ownership: control, intimate knowing and investment of the self, originating from another three profound motives which are home, efficacy and effectance, and self-identity respectively.

The connotation of control in Pierce's theory about psychological ownership is somewhat similar to the concept of insider control of enterprises or managers as discussed by Qiren Zhou. Specifically, Zhou (2004) considered the practice of motivation as a set of de facto property rights. In detail, the entrepreneurs or managers who are not entitled with adequate residual claims are compensated with vast insider control of the enterprises, compared with their entrepreneurship and contributions. Based on the case study of a certain conglomerate in Zhejiang province of China, Zhou later commented that in state owned enterprises, this gap is typically represented by hierarchical prerogatives which Steve Cheung (2009) named as hierarchical rent. So, it is easy to infer that the insider control exerted by entrepreneurs, managers or their counterparts will greatly influence the transition phase from state owned enterprises to private owned enterprises.

The author believes one typical entrepreneur or manager always deserves a stage to show his/her talents as well as expertise. And it is absolutely necessary to leave some 'gray area' in the labor contract to emancipate his/her entrepreneurship. Also according to Zhou, another explanation might be reasonable as well. That is the proprietors of the enterprises may be compelled to relinquish their control to the entrepreneurs or managers under the dual pressure of market and information ultimately.

Later on, the author realized that in addition to insider control, intimate knowing and investment of the self may interact with the discretion that the entrepreneurs or managers may have. As Herbert Simon said, 'management is to make decisions, sometimes, very hard decisions', so it is a prerequisite to have access to all kinds of information, especially subtle and critical hints. There is no doubt that this requires the intimate knowing on the whole. Besides, the author valued the high involvement of the decision makers, rather than a detached stance.

As a good example, Zhou (2004, p.168) used to quote the remarks of a general manager, 'It is necessary to have a share of the enterprise for all levels of managers, in order to be responsible for their daily decisions about the operations. And it is absolutely intolerable for me to hold a relatively small sum.' However, in view of the author, there should be many obstacles, no matter legislative or institutional, to overcome before ensuring the control and discretion of the entrepreneurs or managers in most of the Chinese enterprises and organizations as yet.

A View of Three Distinct Rights and the Development of Hypotheses

Since the property rights are multidimensional in essence, on one hand, it should be viewed as a consummate concept, including disposal, transfer, usage and so on. On the other hand, it could be regarded as a structural concept as well, such as the combination of different sub-rights. Generally recognized, this is the cornerstone of property rights theory. The author tends to believe that the rights of usage should overlap with the insider control in Chinese enterprises and organizations, and benefaction should cover residual claims. In general, property rights are the rights that can benefit or dis-benefit somebody.

In China, wide discrepancy between the east and the west, especially the urban area and the rural area, does exist. Great discrepancies also lie in the aspects of natural resources, economic development, and social customs. Hence, it is very hard to draw one single conclusion, considering China as a whole. While, we may analyze the vast enterprises and organizations in China from a perspective of human capital property rights which typically consists of residual claims, insider control and psychological ownership. In view of the author, the state or central government, municipality or province, and entrepreneurs or managers well represent such a cascade of stratum (see Figure 1). Meanwhile, these three entities resemble virtual personality, quasi-personality, and true personality respectively. As a result, these entities may have different portfolios of appeals concerning residual claims, insider control, and psychological ownership.

Figure 1. The portfolio of three distinct rights for three stratums

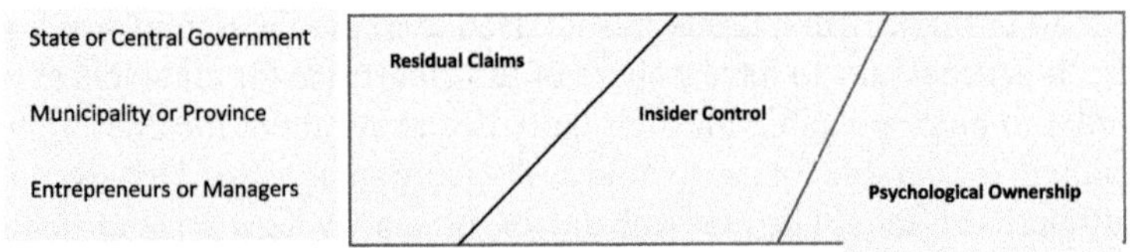

Specifically, the state or central government acquires residual claims by means of taxation, rent of land, in addition to various administrative fees. Possibly, the municipality or province, in addition to the entrepreneurs or managers may have their shares of residual claims which are relatively small. For instance, the municipality will exert taxation according to its authority as well. And usually a minor or null portion of the margins will be paid to compensate the entrepreneurship in state owned enterprises and organizations. In contrast, most of the net profit after tax and interests goes to the proprietors in private owned enterprises. So, it is obvious that the importance of residual claims does vary according to different entities such as the state or central government, municipality or province, and entrepreneurs or managers, in addition to among different types of enterprises and organizations. Restricted by the current compensation system and historical event in China, especially in state owned enterprises and organizations, it is very hard to remunerate the entrepreneurs or managers properly in accordance with the 'rule of demand and supply' and the scarcity of their talents. Hence, the author believes the entrepreneurs or managers in private owned enterprises should be able to acquire much more residual claims than their counterparts in state owned enterprises or organizations.

Focusing on the phenomena of insider control, the following inference might be true. Firstly, the initiative of active surveillance for the principal as well as the endeavor of the trustee will diminish along with the expansion of the state owned enterprise or during the process of state capitalism. As a result, the propensity of insider control will be more salient in local enterprises, coupled with the indirect influence of the central government. However, it might be the same or even worse in some oligarchies, especially those protected by the central government. Secondly, based on the same reasoning, the control by entrepreneurs or managers will be much higher than that of the local government, the equivalent of municipality or province. It will be extremely the case especially in private owned enterprises. Therefore, the author derived Hypothesis 1: the insider control by the entrepreneurs or managers in private owned enterprises is much higher than that in state owned enterprises and organizations.

Except for Zhou's calling for long period control at least by one outstanding entrepreneur that will induce sound performance, other psychologists such as Dixon & Street (1957), Rochberg-Halton (1980), Sartre (1943/1969), Tuan (1980), and White (1959) all agreed on the notion that control on tangible or intangible objects will foster psychological ownership in the end. In one of Parker's studies (1997), he empirically tested and found that control significantly elevated psychological ownership in self-managed teams. Hackman & Oldham (1975, p.162) used to consider autonomy as an objective job design attribute, which reflected "the degree to which the job provides substantial freedom, independence, and discretion to the employee in scheduling the work and in determining the procedures to be used in carrying it [the work] out". According to the author, autonomy should vastly overlap with the concept of insider control in enterprises in China. Besides, White (1959) commented control over one's environment will induce self-efficacy and delight in essence. Similarly, McClelland (1951, p.301) asserted, 'objects that can be controlled become regarded as part of the self'. Pierce et al. (2001) also held the view that higher autonomy entailed higher controlling in one's job.

So, it might be prudent to consider work control and autonomy simultaneously when studying psychological ownership in the workplace. Empirically, Mayhew, Ashkanasy, Bramble, and Gardner (2007) found autonomy positively correlated with psychological ownership in a large scale accounting company in Australia, taking advantage of dyadic samples by a questionnaire survey. In a similar way, Pierce, O'Driscoll, and Coghlan (2004) have tested and verified controlling positively correlated with psychological ownership among seven for-profit businesses in New Zealand.

Regarding the three distinct routes which will induce psychological ownership, the author believes control will play a significant role, especially in China, since the feeling of possession is vary based on control. In another word, control should be always on the first priority, considering the formation of psychological ownership. Tentatively, the author continues to derive Hypothesis 2: the autonomy that entrepreneurs or managers have in private owned enterprises is higher than that in state owned enterprises and organizations. And Hypothesis 3: the psychological ownership that entrepreneurs or managers have in private owned enterprises is higher than that in state owned enterprises and organizations. However, the author does not think the magnitude of psychological ownership will roar in absence of intimate knowing and investment of the self, even authorized by legal ownership.

Further, the author proposes autonomy and feedback from work will foster intimate knowing and in turn, enforcing the investment of the self into their jobs. Implicitly, Pierce, O'Driscoll, and Coghlan (2004, p.529) postulated that eventually, "employees who had developed feelings of ownership for their jobs were likely to develop feelings of ownership towards the organization" in which the jobs were embedded. By the way, they called for future research to test the mediating effects of job-based ownership in the relationship between control and organization-based ownership. Therefore, it is worthy to test and verify the positive correlations among work control (a proxy of insider control), autonomy, and feedback from work, in relationship with psychological ownership in the workplace. While it should be noted and argued that in private owned enterprises, especially a start-up, the job-based psychological ownership and organization-based psychological ownership would be the much same. Only in very large enterprises and organizations, the difference of these two concepts could be easily distinguished.

Since the reality of residual claims in enterprises in China is very hard to measure in one questionnaire survey, in addition to the lack of sound scales, the author did not probe the residual claims which should be better investigated longitudinally. Finally, the author arrived at the following hypotheses. They are Hypothesis 4: the work control of entrepreneurs or managers positively correlates with their psychological ownership in the workplace; Hypothesis 5: the autonomy of entrepreneurs or managers positively correlates with their psychological ownership in the workplace; and Hypothesis 6: the feedback from work for entrepreneurs or managers positively correlates with their psychological ownership in the workplace.

Questionnaire Survey and Results

Sample

The questionnaire survey was carried out in the enterprises and organizations in Beijing, Tianjin, Shanghai, Xi'an, Jinan, Qingdao, and Zhaozhuang of China. Taking advantage of the author's social network, for instance, by the aid of his friends, workmates, and part-time students, the author successfully persuaded the participants to fill out the questionnaires seriously and honestly, since the author did not urge for more questionnaires and it is up to them to ascertain the appropriate number of the questionnaires to be answered. Some of the questionnaires were mailed by post office and the rest were sent by e-mail boxes that constituted a rough ratio of 1:3. Altogether 127 questionnaires were retrieved with a response rate of 89%. Notably, it was a highly diverse sampling which consisted of more than 30 units of enterprises and organizations, resulting in an average participant number of around 4 for each unit.

The demographic of the participants were as follows, male 53.5%, female 46.5%; single 32.3%, married 67.7%; age below 23 5.5%, 23-30 years old 43.3%, 31-40 years old 39.4%, 41-50 years old 11.1%, and age above 50 0.8%. Among them, the education levels were college or university 70.9% and master or higher 26.0%, which constituted the very majority of the participants. Considering the rank and tenure, they were ordinary employees 48.8%, first line managers 22.0%, middle managers 21.3%, and top managers 7.9%. Meanwhile, people whose tenure was less than 3 years were 37.0%, 3-6 years 22.1%, and more than 6 years 40.9%. All of them worked in industries like manufacturing, IT hi-tech, trade, wholesale and retailing, finance and consulting services.

Scales

The author measured organization-based psychological ownership using a 7-item inventory that Van Dyne & Pierce (2004) developed. This inventory exemplified excellent psychometric properties in their prior studies as well as in one of Lv F. X. & Gu S. S.'s (2007) studies in the Chinese context.

Meanwhile, the author measured autonomy and feedback from work by using two separate 3-item sub-inventories respectively, which were all excerpted from Hackman & Oldham's (1975) Job Diagnostic Survey, modified by Idaszak & Drasgow (1987). Finally, the author measured insider control using a 22-item instrument developed and validated by Dwyer & Ganster (1991), hoping it should be a good proxy of insider control because it covered a wide span of control in the workplace.

Results

Results supported Hypotheses 1, 2, and 3. The descriptive statistics and independent t-tests showed that (see Table 1 and Table 2) the insider control (measured by Dwyer & Ganster's work control inventory), autonomy, and psychological ownership that the entrepreneurs or managers had in private owned enterprises were significantly higher than that in state owned enterprises and organizations. Specifically, their means were $3.50>3.13$, $p<0.001$; $4.98>4.32$, $p<0.01$; and $3.81>3.20$, $p<0.001$; significant at two tails.

Table 1: Statistics of psychological ownership, work control and autonomy

	Proprietorship	Sample Size	Mean	S.D.
Psychological Ownership	State Owned	71	3.20	0.76
	Private Owned	56	3.81	0.82
Work Control	State Owned	71	3.13	0.48
	Private Owned	56	3.50	0.54
Autonomy	State Owned	71	4.32	1.38
	Private Owned	56	4.98	1.41

Notes: N=127.

Table 2: Independent samples test of psychological ownership, work control and autonomy

		Levene's Test for Equality of Variance		t-test for Equality of Means		
		F	Sig.	t	df	Sig. (2 tailed)
Psycho-logical Ownership	Equal variances assumed	0.721	.398	-4.372	125	.000
	Equal variances not assumed			-4.332	113.8	.000
Work Control	Equal variances assumed	0.395	.531	-4.047	125	.000
	Equal variances not assumed			-3.995	111.6	.000
Autonomy	Equal variances assumed	0.051	.821	-2.646	125	.009
	Equal variances not assumed			-2.640	117.2	.009

Notes: N=127.

Considering the correlations between work control, autonomy, feedback from work and psychological ownership, the results supported Hypotheses 4, 5, and 6. (see Table 3) which meant the work control, autonomy, and feedback from work of entrepreneurs or managers positively correlated with their psychological ownership in the workplace. In detail, the correlations between psychological ownership and work control, autonomy, and feedback from work were all statistically significant ($r=0.384$, $p<0.01$; $r=0.279$, $p<0.01$; and $r=0.317$, $p<0.01$).

Table 3: Correlations of psychological ownership, work control, autonomy and feedback from work

		Entire Database			State Owned			Private Owned		
	Cron-bach's α	②	③	④	②	③	④	②	③	④
Psychological Onwership	.818	.384**	.279**	.317**	.272*	.129	.168	.323*	.317*	.297*
Work Control	.924		.656**	.504**		.610**	.493**		.657**	.391**
Autonomy	.827			.616**			.692**			.459**
Feedback from Work	.732									

Notes: **p<0.01, *p<0.05, N=127.

The above results were based on the entire database (127 cases), including employees from all levels. However, according to the results of three field studies, Van Dyne & Pierce (2004) were optimistic about the implications of psychological ownership, especially for managers. So, the author selected cases that met the requirement of 'first line manager, middle manager, or top manager' and obtained a database of 65 cases, in contrast with the former entire database. Still, the work control, autonomy, and psychological ownership that the entrepreneurs or managers had in private owned enterprises were significantly higher than that in state owned enterprises and organizations (see Table 4 and Table 5). The comparison of means were 3.64>3.27, $p<0.01$; 5.32>4.64, $p<0.05$; and 3.94>3.31, $p<0.001$; significant at two tails. Again, for managers only, Hypotheses 1, 2, and 3 were supported. Further, the author tested the relationship between psychological ownership and work control, autonomy, and feedback from work only for managers, and found all the correlations were higher than that of the entire database (see Table 6). For instance, the correlations were $r=0.387$, $r=0.319$, and $r=0.445$ respectively, all significant at $p<0.01$ level.

Table 4. Statistics for managers

	Proprietorship	Sample Size	Mean	S.D.
Psychological Ownership	State Owned	38	3.31	0.64
	Private Owned	27	3.94	0.71
Work Control	State Owned	38	3.27	0.48
	Private Owned	27	3.64	0.42
Autonomy	State Owned	38	4.64	1.22
	Private Owned	27	5.32	1.04

Notes: N=65.

Table 5. Independent samples test for managers

		Levene's Test for Equality of Variance		t-test for Equality of Means		
		F	Sig.	t	df	Sig. (2 tailed)
Psychological Ownership	Equal variances assumed	0.377	.541	-3.750	63	.000
	Equal variances not assumed			-3.685	52.5	.001
Work Control	Equal variances assumed	1.012	.318	-3.271	63	.002
	Equal variances not assumed			-3.346	60.2	.001
Autonomy	Equal variances assumed	0.603	.440	-2.352	63	.022
	Equal variances not assumed			-2.419	61.0	.019

Notes: N=65.

Table 6. Correlations for managers

		Managers		
	Cronbach's α	②	③	④
① Psychological Onwership	.771	.387**	.319**	.445**
② Work Control	.916		.676**	.544**
③ Autonomy	.798			.723**
④ Feedback from Work	.767			

Notes: **p<0.01, *p<0.05, N=65.

Dividing all the cases according to the proprietorship, the author obtained two separate databases which were private owned (56 cases) and stated owned (71 cases). More interesting was that in state owned enterprises and organizations, only work control positively correlated with psychological ownership ($r=0.272$, $p<0.05$; also see Table 3). The correlations between autonomy, feedback from work and psychological ownership were not significant ($r=0.129$, $r=0.168$; lower than that of the entire database) anymore. While the situation in private owned enterprises are almost the same with that of the entire database ($r=0.323$, $r=0.317$, $r=0.297$; all significant at $p<0.05$ level). In another word, psychological ownership positively correlated with work control (a good proxy of insider control), autonomy and feedback from work in private owned enterprises. However, in state owned enterprises and organizations, psychological ownership only positively correlated with work control.

Discussion

Although the emerging theory supports work control, autonomy and feedback from work as the antecedents of psychological ownership, it is hard to prove this relationship only in one cross-sectional study. Besides, more empirical evidences are needed, better in longitudinal or time-lagged models. Concerning the research of residual claims in enterprises or organizations, the author believes that field study should be a better choice. However, due to the large quantity of the research units (more than 30), it is very hard to adopt such a strategy in the current study. Moreover, the view of three distinct rights which covers residual claims, insider control and psychological ownership should be more carefully examined and a more robust nomological network is extremely needed.

As one of the most important attributes of human capital, the aptitude belongs to the individual and could only be utilized through appropriate motivation makes it necessary to enhance autonomy in various types of enterprises and organizations in China. The fact that entrepreneurs deserve stages requires the guarantee of insider control and autonomy to cope with the constantly changing environments. Unfortunately, there are only three items to measure the concept of autonomy, even tested as a sound scale. In the Chinese context, one possible criticism might be its generality, compared with Spector & Fox's 10-item factual autonomy scale.

Again, as one cross-sectional questionnaire survey, the suspect of common method bias is still a potential threat to the results. In future studies, dyadic sampling as well as two wave questionnaire survey may be an alternative. Thus, the common source bias of the data should be primarily eliminated.

Answering the question of whether it is acceptable or possible to obtain psychological ownership in the absence of legal ownership, the author believes they should cohabit with each other, especially scrutinized in a long time window. Figuratively, the psychological ownership of employees is sort of a kind of 'shadow property rights' or you may want to call it 'virtual property rights'. So, generally speaking, legal ownership should interact with psychological ownership intimately, varying in the same direction. This notion is against the forecast of Van Dyne & Pierce (2004) which declared psychological ownership could exist in the absence of legal ownership. The questions are how long you would watch these two concepts simultaneously and how could you successfully transform psychological ownership into legal ownership legitimately.

Taking the traditional principal and agent problem, at least in China, the covenants are mainly arranged by the central government or local government who merely embodies a virtual personality. Consequently, the residual claims are not transferrable, but betrothed to the government only. In turn, this restricts the options that the principal might use to curb the agent to some extent. The government officials or leaders who have authority to select the general managers or entrepreneurs are not entitled to ask for any residual claims, therefore, they are at the danger of taking a bribery or 'economic rent', especially when they are obsessed by avarice or personal influence. If certain negotiation mechanisms are in existence, which mean that the entrepreneurs or managers are allowed to negotiate with their supervisors or administrative superiors, even at the cost of compensating one kind of property rights with another (i.e., compensating residual claims for legal ownership or vice versa), it will contribute to the economic performance somewhat. The point is whether the residual claims of the entrepreneurs or managers would trigger a higher efficiency of utilizing the resources in our society and to what degree.

In the next, the author surmises that residual claims should shed some light on psychological ownership as well as insider control of the enterprises or organizations. Although it is almost impossible to gather some data about residual claims in one cross-sectional survey, based on common sense and reasoning, the author still believes the direct effect of residual claims on psychological ownership and insider control. While, the causality should be carefully examined, concerning the independent variable and the dependent variable or the reciprocity. In another sense, the puzzle of low efficiency in Chinese state owned enterprises and organizations might be mitigated by adopting such a policy which recognizes the residual claims of the entrepreneurs or managers. As a matter of fact, in western countries such as U.S.A., Germany or France, the private capitals are allowed to participate in the competition of key industries such as energy, electricity, transportation, and sometimes even the military business. That may be helpful to alleviate the above mentioned puzzle in a more broad way.

In the end, the author calls for more well-designed researches in wider areas of China, covering more industries and more important enterprises and organizations, since this study has a small sample size which is 127. Anyway, a questionnaire survey embedded in a field study should be on the first priority.

References

Carlla S.S., John T., Susan E.H., & Robert A.S.(1997). The measurement of job control. Journal of Organizational Behavior,18,225-237.

Eugen S., Ghada E., & Mike L.(2003). Differentiating work autonomy facets in a non-Western context. Journal of Organizational Behavior,24,709-731.

James B.A., Bruce J.A., Craig D.C., & Fred L.(2009). Psychological ownership: theoretical extensions, measurement and relation to work outcomes. Journal of Organizational Behavior,30,173-191.

Jon L.P., Michael P.O., & Anne-Marie C.(2004). Work environment structure and psychological ownership: the mediating effects of control. The Journal of Social Psychology,144(5),507-534.

Jon L.P., Tatiana K., & Kurt T.D.(2001). Toward a theory of psychological ownership in organizations. Academy of Management Review,26(2),298-310.

Linn V.D., & Jon L.P.(2004). Psychological ownership and feelings of possession: three field studies predicting employee attitudes and organizational citizenship behavior. Journal of Organizational Behavior,25,439-459.

Melissa ,G.M., &Neal,M.A., Tom B., & John G.(2007). A study of the antecedents and consequences of psychological ownership in organizational settings. The Journal of Social Psychology,147(5),447-500.

Lv, F.X,& Gu.S.S.(2007). Correlation analysis of the psychological ownership and organizational citizenship behavior. Management World,5,94-103.

Zhang,W.C.(2009). China's economic system. Beijing: Zhongxin Press .

Zhou,Q.R(2004). Property Rights and Institutional Change – An Empirical Study of China's reform (an enlarged revision. Beijing: Peking university Press.

Local Agenda 21 in the City of Osnabrück: Opportunities for a sustainable development on a local level – an example

Birgit Vogelsang
University of Osnabrueck, Germany

Abstract

„Think global, act local" – Following the UN Conference of Rio de Janeiro in 1992, this headline summarises the strategy for the Local Agenda 21 process of a sustainable development on a local operating platform.Local municipalities, which itself have undergone significant structural changes in Germany since the early 1990s, shall act as the political responsible party and the major player in this process. Another important actor is "the" economy, as represented by different actors – and they have operationalised "sustainability" for themselves over the last years.Economy has demonstrated only a marginal disposition for engaging in a Local Agenda 21 process, whilst this process is also impacted by different set ups in each municipality.This paper asks for underlying reasons of the absence of a wide consensus [to implement and to maintain a Local Agenda 21 process] despite the common postulate to act under a sustainable development scenario. The paper also addresses the various ways by which economic actors have attempted to comply with the public request to integrate sustainable development criteria within economical acting. In this context, the City of Osnabrueck and its Local Agenda 21 process (which commenced in 1998) are an example for emblazing structures as well as actors and their actions.From a social scientific point of view, this paper discussed the discrepancy between the idea of a Local Agenda 21 process and the chances to actually implement the models developed in this process; it also highlights the opportunities that can be explored given the openness of its general approach and the absence of an imperative given "one best way" – finding again new approaches to the aim of sustainable development.

Content

1. Introduction

„Sustainable development" – this is the leading record from the Rio Summit in Rio de Janeiro in June 1992. It is an action program aiming to solve global problems at a local government level. In chapter 28 of the Agenda 21 charta, communal administrations are requested to act as agents and to take political responsibility for a sustainable development on a local level. The communal administrations were assigned the duty to develop strategies in collaboration with citizens, local organisations and local companies to achieve the targets of the Agenda 21 by implementing a Local Agenda 21.

Of particular importance for implementing the Agenda 21 are business companies. In the early 1990s, the Business Council for sustainable Development noted the ambitious mission of the economic system as a whole and gave a conclusive evidence for the possibility to realise sustainable development in a fair way (cf. Schmidheiny, 1992). Every city and borough is free to find its own way of sustainable development. The background and main focus are such were different – in most cases it was not considered to involve local companies and to reach a consensus on the economic development in a sustainable way. On the other hand, there exist a few examples of business companies that found their own way of being economical and environmental sustainable – without being involved in the Local Agenda 21 process.

Nations, governments, administrations, business companies and other organisations are all part of a social paradigm shift in the sense of sustainable development. In view of this it is obvious to identify environmental motivated changes in society by implementing the theories of organizations. The theory of structurations, developed by Anthony Giddens, as well as the strategic analysis of organisations, developed by Crozier and Friedberg, are the basis for the comprehension of organizations, developed by Günther Ortmann. Organization structures are constantly constituted and reproduced within and through the actions undertaken by the actors. This approach not only allows to analyse the actions of different organzations which were active in a Local Agenda 21 process and the Local Agenda 21 itself, it also allows to analyse certain "ad hoc" or "urgent" developments which might appear rather illogical and even contradictory to the underlying intentions of sustainable development.

Definition „Sustainability“

„Sustainable development meets the needs of the present without compromising the ability of future generations to meet their own needs.” This is the definition that the 1987 Earth Summit gave in line with the Brundtland report to capture the term “sustainability”. Accordingly, the term of sustainability was not focused on environmental matters, but extended into social and economic dimensions.

2. Sustainability and Local Agenda 21 at the municipal administration level –communal planning between continuity and constant changes

In a direct response to the obligations which the German government assumed by signing the final communiqué of the conference of Rio de Janeiro, German cities and communities commenced sustainable action programs in the 1990s, which went by the name of “Local Agenda 21”. Germany did not roll out a specimen or predefined program, there was no one best way for implementing Local Agenda 21 processes. Every community and city is free to develop its own way for a sustainable development. However, over the last years, some doubt has risen in the public opinion about the overall effectiveness of finding new strategies in meeting future challenges, and who should address environmental, economical and social questions in an equal way.

Due to the fact that the Local Agenda 21 process is politically and administratively linked with the constitution of local government in Germany, it requires political decisions to be made, resolutions to be promulgated, and administrative structures to be set up. As a consequence, all these activities shall serve the general public welfare. However, this seemed to be increasingly complicated since the early 1990s which saw significant changes in the set up of German municipal administrations due to the modernization of administration and the increasing trend of privatisation of previously public businesses and the discharge of services that were provided by the local administration to private service providers (cf. Bogumil/Holtkamp, 2006). However, on the one hand, many authorised-regulating instruments and proceedings remained part of the municipal administration affairs – like the local nature conservation authority, which is responsible for maintaining compliance with legal requirements of environment. On the other hand, the municipal administration is impacted by structural changes, changes of interests and the likely imponderabilities with regards to new actors who were added to the local structure, and their respective activities.

Modernisation trends have an effect to the municipal system of political governance. At the same time, the municipal administration has the mission to run a Local Agenda 21 process – a process that is based on consensus with its citizens to solute problems in a sustainable way.

It remains within the discretion of the local policy makers to formulate and to enact a Local Agenda 21 strategy and process. Experience shows that the municipal administration appointments the office of city planning or to environmental agency to run the process (cf. Kuhn, 1998). The assignment of this responsibility is usually conditioned by past municipal development. E.g. if there had been a notable engagement for climate protection in the past, this would likely be the link for a Local Agenda 21 process. The Local Agenda 21 process in Osnabrück is notable wirth regards to its structure and its approach.

3. The economic view about sustainability

The need to operationalise "sustainability" – in particular in terms of economy – was was noted early on and proposals for solutions were made (cf. Simonis, 199; Weizsäcker, 1989; Weizsäcker, 1995). The need for interaction of sciences, politics and economics was highlighted. Business economics and political economics kept and keep busy on this subject (cf. Burschel,2004; Pfriem,1995;Minsch/Meier/Schneide-wind, 1996). In this context, "PANTA RHEI" a highly sophisticated eco-economic model with high business granularity was developed for Germany to evaluate the potential effects of a green tax system in Germany (cf. Meyer, 2008).

At the same time, international chief executives realised that public confidence and the society's respect the company′s environmental commitment is essential for their companies' future (cf. Schmidheiny, 1992, p. 37 ff.). The management philosophy, R&A activities, production and distribution were earmarked distinguished for further review to implement sustainable approaches. At the same time, environmental management systems were initiated as an instrument for developing a change of business strategies.

The international environmental management standard ISO 14001 and the Eco Management and Audit Scheme (EMAS) developed by the European Union are only two of the most established an comprehensive environmental management systems. Aside of them there are other environmental management systems like ÖkoProfit, that was designed in Austria and especially focuses on small and medium-sized enterprises.

Many companies decided to define their own way of sustainability in addition to the implementation of environmental management systems. Different environmental label, for example by the textile industry, are due to this development. There exist institutional labels, like “Öko-Tex Standard 100” or “eco proof”, but also company specific labels that were created as marketing tools for sales promotion purposed, e.g. Britta Steilmann invented her collection under the lable “it's one world” or “future collection”, the store brand of Otto, a German mail order company.

Integration of economics in the Local Agenda 21 process

A Local Agenda 21 process links itself with existing structures and with the actors who were already engaged in them. Change and continuity are signs for a process, which is appointed by complexity. This can described by means of the theory of structuration.

4. Theoretical approach

In his theory of structurations, Anthony Giddens abolished the separation of actors (agents) on one hand and society, organisation and their structures on the other hand. Giddens puts recursivity of action and structures at the centre of consideration. “Structure is both medium and outcome of social life. Structure enters simultaneously into the constitution of the agent and social practices, and “exists” in the generating moments of this constitution.” (Giddens, 1979, p. 5)

Looking at the Local Agenda 21 process by consideration of recursivity, one can see that this process is linking with other established organisations and their process. Nothing starts from scratch. The agents, who almost act inside their structures, now also take an active part in the organisational structures of Local Agenda 21. Because of this, new structures build up.

However, structures and actions by the involved organisations determine the action inside the structures of the Agenda. This means that actions based on the Agenda-process affect other organisations through their agents, who are involved in the Local Agenda 21 process. But the impacts are not predictable as it is not possible to clearly determine the causal connection to the Local Agenda 21 process. And this is the next point – the figure of contingency.

In Giddens' opinion it is important to recognise that in any particular context of interaction there will be a certain contingency. For agents, occurrences are unpredictable or unintended. “Social live is in many respects not an intentional product of its constituent actors, in spite of the fact that day-to-day conduct is chronically carried out in a purposive fashion” (Giddens, 1984 p. 343). Thus information in organisations is not neutral, but it is itself an important power resource. Because of capability, the agent may seek to use the resource – but he or her also can fail to do it. Thus results of actions are sometimes different from the original intention. This also is very close to the idea of "path dependencies" and "lock in". By this, a set of decisions is limited by the decisions being taken in the past. It is important, that the past circumstances, that were relevant for this decision in the past, may be no longer relevant for the new decision. Because of this, there decreasingly exist action alternatives. In worst cases, these processes can end in a "Lock-in"-situation.

To translate this into the Local Agenda 21 process: decision-making only can happen step-by-step. And for an agent, every step might bring him to new frontiers. Thus, he has to re-orientate himself for every next step. This stands for a great effort and a lot of time. However, this is the only possible way for finding a consensus – the ambitious aim of a Local Agenda 21 process.

5. Local development cooperation and local climate defense – the fundament for the Local Agenda 21 process in the City of Osnabrück

In the 1980s especially NGOs were promoting the idea that the city of Osnabrück should engaged itself more and more for climate protection. The bureau of environment founded by the citycouncil of Osnabrück in 1991 was an important actor in this case. At the time of its foundation the bureau of environment of Osnabrück was one of the biggest environmental bureaus in Germany. The reason for the new and more sustainable way was political change, and the new political power of the Green Party in the city council of Osnabrück up to 1992. Even in 1992 the city of Osnabrück signed the "Alianca del Clima". In the core of this paper is the idea "thinking global-acting local" as well. By the decision of being member of the "Alianca del Clima", the city of Osnabrück assumed a responsibility to reduce its carbon dioxide by 50% until 2010 (this term was changed a few years later: now the reduction target is 50% till 2030). In connection to this, the bureau of environment was assigned to balance the carbon-dioxide output in Osnabrück and to build up a concept for reducing the carbon dioxide emission (the core of this strategy shall be a lasting change of the production and consumption of energy. Only 40% of the recommendations of the conception are realized yet. In the opinion of the city council and the city administration the reason for the delays are opposition from political and economical forces.)

In order to achieve the carbon-dioxide reduction target, the city-council of Osnabrück decided in 1994 to set up a Working Group which went by the name of "Round Table Carbon-Dioxide". This round table is in session until today – but its meetings are not public. Members of this round table are members of the city council, different social groups of Osnabrück, members of different local companies, the Chamber of Commerce and Industry, and the Chamber of Crafts. It is the task of this working group – as an actor – to search for possibilities to reduce the carbon-dioxide emission in city of Osnabrück and to reduce the energy-consumption.

Until 2009, the city of Osnabrück was the biggest base for the british Rhein-Army after the second world-war out of Great Britain. Since the late 1940s, actors of the city council of Osnabrück tried to develop and to take care of contacts to different communities – first in Europe, and then all over the world. Next to this, many citizens of Osnabrück started to develop an intensive network of different and global north-south relations. In 1968 the German office of "terre des homes" was founded in Osnabrück. Especially during the 1970s and 1980s many citizens were engaged in questions about development policies. There have been many activities about these questions by different actors – like the university, the church, NGOs and private people. Because of this, the city council commanded the administration to prepare a balance sheet about all these activities. This paper was called "Third-world-Bilance of Osnabrück". All these results were published in 1995. In September of 1995 the city council decided that the working structures which were built up during this process, should be the base for a Local Agenda 21 process in the city of Osnabrück.

6. Local Agenda 21 in the city of Osnabrück: History

In February 1996, the city council of Osnabrück ratified the "Charta of Aalborg". By this contract, the local government assumed the responsibility to commence a Local Agenda 21 process in the City of Osnabrück. During the following two years, the structures for a local Agenda 21 process crystallised. The environment administration started its work for Agenda 21 in February 1998. At the same time, the bureau of local development cooperation continued its work as its members already had previous experience with working in the LDC related projects in the City of Osnabrück. It was their joint responsibility of to coordinate and to build up the Local Agenda 21 process. One key responsibility was looking after the social affairs and target groups, whilst the other focused on environmental affairs and economic management. Both took part in different working groups of the administration. During the next months, they developed, in cooperation with different actors, a proposal to organize the process. In July 1998, the local government approved the proposed structure.

The environmental administration office was looking for different work-groups, in particular energy, city-planning, and economic affairs.

It also was the duty of the two coordinators to take care for the development of aims and key-notes for the Local Agenda 21 process. Thus in 1999, the agenda-forum created these key-notes. During this time, both bureaus organized different events for the public, e.g. an agenda-market held at a central place in the city-center or presented different projects – like the agenda-21-house – inside of the chamber of crafts.

Since its formation in 1998, the workgroup „economy“ comprised about ten to twelve members. Representatives from the communal business development, the Chamber of Crafts, the Stadtwerke Osnabrück as a communal-based company, representatives from individual companies as well as owner of craftsman's establishments attended by the workgroup-meetings. Most of these participants were also members of different networks with a similar background – like the “Round Table CO^2”. A few of the representatives, like the Chamber of Industry and Commerce and several company-representatives

were recalled by decisions made by executive positions, which were based on the reason of lacking labour efficiency. The role of the work-group-speaker, who was an important key player in cooperation with public opinions and policy makers. was given from public figures with good connections to the local economic life to persons who had much less valuable personal contacts. In 1998 and 1999, two attempts were made by the workgroup coordinator to set up an ÖkoProfit project that would be able to build up a local economic network focused on environmental and economical sustainability; however, at every time, the members of the economic-workgroup did not approve this proposal.

In 2001, the bureau for city-planning and civic-participation became responsible for the Local Agenda 21 process. At this time, there was also a change in the overall structure of the process, and a number of working groups changed as well.

The green city-map of Osnabrück was the last project of the economical working group.

This was in 2008 – after they settled this project in 2007, the remaining members of the workgroup jointed the work group “energy, building and housing”.

7. Examples of Companies in Osnabrück and their individual ways for a sustainable development

There are a number of companies in and around the City of Osnabrück who developed their own ideas of "sustainable development inside the economy", and put these into practice. This was not coactively related to the Local Agenda 21 process. In the following, I want to present a summary view of the individual ways that theses companies took on their wary of a sustainable economy within their operating businesses.

Hellmann Worldwide Logistics

Founded in 1871 as a one-man-firm, Hellmann Worldwide Logistics today is a globalised logistic-enterprise with 213 offices in 47 countries. Hellmann employs 8,652 staff worldwide. The company's motto is "Thinking ahead, Moving forward"

Active environment is an important part of Hellmann's philosophy. Hellmann was the first logistics company in Germany be certified according to the international norm for environment management systems (ISO 14001), and received this certificate for its office in Osnabrück in 1996. In the meantime, all German branches have been certified along with those in Lichfield, Hong Kong and Miami. In order to publicise the environmental activities to the general public and to specialist circles and studies at various institutions, Hellmann carries out its own events under the banner of "traffic and environment".

It is the aim of Hellman to actively apply and dedicatedly itself to the subject of sustainability and thereby advances the interaction of economy, ecology and social responsibility. Examples for this are: Hellmann adopted using biodiesel for its trucks; Hellmann's headquater is built nature-orientated (for example green roofs) and they use renewable energy for heating their new bureau-building; Hellman sponsors environmental projects, e.g. they sponsored a school project of a professional school. Hellmann's environmental commissioner financed and helped planting a special sort of trees near the river "Hase".

Hellmann uses regenerative energy for its digital community center.

Stadtwerke Osnabrück AG .

The Stadtwerke Osnabrück AG has a long corporate history and evolved from several different entities. The core of today's Stadtwerke was the company formerly in charge for the street-lightning in the city of Osnabrück. In 1858, the first gas works was founded to supply the city's street-laps with gas. In 1890, the gas and water works became responsible for the water-supply. In 1905, the administration of the City of Osnabrück became responsible for the electricity works; and in 1906 the first public traffic for persons started with 16 tram-cars.

In 1926 the first open air swimming-pool opened its doors. First, the swimming pools as sport facilities were part of the communal administration. Since 2003 the swimming pools in the city of Osnabrück have been incorporated into the Stadtwerke.

Today, Stadtwerke Osnabrück is a communal based company for gas and water as well as a provider for local public transport, for sewerage and road building. Stadtwerke Osnabrück is also a shareholder of different enterprises, like the airport Münster/Osnabrück. Stadtwerke Osnabrück currently employs circa 1,100 employees.

For a long time, Stadtwerke Osnabrück has a considerable know-how in caring for the environment and climate. Areas of competence stem from their experience: in public transportation, the supply of energy and energy, water procuring etc.

It is the aim of the Stadtwerke to combine and to intensify these activities and to start new activities under the umbrella of a new entrepreneurial initiative called "KUK" (KompetenzUmweltKlima). The motto for the "KUK" is "We are doing well, but we can do better". There shall be a living environmental sense inside and outside of the enterprise – for the well-being of the city and the citizens of Osnabrück.

There exist different KUK-projects, for example repowering (installing wind energy converters on a hilltop near to the city), new environmental-saving busses, and environmental education. The Stadtwerke Osnabrück and 25 other local utility providers work in a project called "Green GECCO". The first project is an onshore wind energy project in Scotland. The first low energy consumption office-building in the city of Osnabrück was built by Stadtwerke Osnabrück. Last but not least, the public swimming pool "Nettebad" got certified for its very low energy consumption. It is one of the goals of the Stadtwerke to be a role model for other companies, and to promote rethinking livestyle choices of its customers. On the other hand, customers and employees receive a positive impression about the decisions the management made concerning the local commitment for environmental and local economic development.

Kromschröder (part of Elster Limited)

Kromschröder was founded in 1865 in the city of Osnabrück. The company produces different typs of gas-meters for private households and for companies, and control gears for heating systems.

In the 1970s, the company relocated from the city of Osnabrück (that is part of Lower Saxony) to a suburb about 10 km away named Lotte-Büren. This suburb is already part of the state of Northrhein Westfalia. Due to this relocation, Kromschröder management is subject to other state and local government conditions than the companies that are based within the city of Osnabrück.

The Kromschröder management addresses the local community administration of the city of Steinfurt. The administration of Steinfurt started a local Agenda 21 project that was financially supported by the state. This project is called "ÖkoProfit". It is an environmental management tool similar to ISO 14001, but it's less complicated. In 2004, the environmental commissioner of Kromschröder decided to take part in this program. Since then Kromschröder have taken part in every second year. It is the aim of Kromschröder's management to get certified in order to demonstrate that the management conforms with the instructions given by the local administration and the state. In addition, Kromschröder management can use the certificate for marketing purposes. Beyond the participation in the Öko-Profit-poject, Kromschröder as a company does not otherwise engage in the Local Agenda 21 process of Steinfurt.

8. Conclusion and Future prospects

The different aspects of sustainable development on a local level which have been discussed in this paper, revealed the heterogeneity within the whole process. Possible approaches to analyse and understand a Local Agenda 21 process include "Recursivity", "Contingency" or "Reflexive monitoring of action", "Lock in" and "Path dependencies" as well as different aspects of "Collaborative planning" – an approach by city-planning; Local Agenda 21 process – as these approaches particularly capture the marginal co-operation of economic actors.

In 2010 the city of Osnabrück implemented the "ÖkoProfit" project as well. The CUT – a part within the communal business development and the administration of the City of Osnabrück – was able to win 10 companies to take part in this project for a year. The bureau of economic advancement promotes this project. The most important reason for all companies to participate in this project was to identify possibilities to realise economies by implementing environmental-friendly technologies and processes. In addition, the participating companies want to set up a network for enquiring into the economic side of a sustainable development in the City of Osnabrück. The group started on March, 11th this year. A business consultant will coach the process. It will be interesting to understand what answers this process will find – answers to the questions of the companies that participate in the ÖkoProfit-process, answers to the questions from the public opinion, and answers to the questions from the local policy makers. The appraisal of results might be an important step for the sustainable development process in the City of Osnabrück.

References

Bogumil, Jörg/Holtkamp, Lars (2006): Kommunalpolitik und Kommunalverwaltung; Wiesbaden.

Burschel, Carlo et al. (2004): Betriebswirtschaftslehre der nachhaltigen Unternehmung; München.

Giddens, Anthony (1979): Central Problems in Social Theory; London.

Giddens, Anthony (1984): The Constitution of Society; Cambridge.

Giddens, Anthony (1992): Die Konstitution der Gesellschaft – Grundzüge einer Theorie der Strukturierung; Frankfurt/New York.

Hamedinger, Alexander et al. (2008): Strategieorientierte Planung im kooperativen Staat; Wiesbaden.

Kuhn, Stefan et al. (1998): Was ist eine Lokale Agenda 21. – in: ICLEI: Lokale Agenda 21 Deutschland; Berlin, Heidelberg.

Meyer, Bernd (2008): Wie muss die Wirtschaft umgebaut werden? Frankfurt am Main.

Minsch, Jürg /Meier, Bernhard/Schneidwind, Uwe (1996): Mut zum ökologischen Umbau; Basel, Boston, Berlin.

Ortmann, Günther et alt. (1997): Organisation als reflexive Strukturation. in: Ortmann, G.: Theorien der Organisation; Wiesbaden.

Ortmann, Günther (2009): Management in der Hypermoderne- Kontingenz und Entscheidung; Wiesbaden.

Pfriem, Reinhard (1995): Unternehmenspolitik in sozialökologischen Perspektiven; Marburg.

Schmidheiny, Stephan (1992): Kurswechsel; München.

Simonis, Udo Ernst (Edit.) (1991): Ökonomie und Ökologie – Auswege aus einem Konflikt; Karlsruhe.

Weizsäcker, Ernst Ulrich von (1989): Erdpolitik – ökologische Realpolitik als Antwort auf die Globalisierung; Darmstadt.

Weizsäcker, Ernst Ulrich von (1995): Faktor vier. Doppelter Wohlstand, halbierter Verbrauch; München.

Chapter 7:
The Role of Education and Research

Mobilizing Labour for Sustainable Development and Women Empowerment

A Case for Social Initiative in the Context of a Successful Experiment in the Indian State of Kerala

Varghese M. Mathunny
Former Principal, St. John's College, Anchal, Kerala, India

Abstract

Sustainable development is development that meets the needs of the present without endangering the interests of the future. Women empowerment refers to increasing the spiritual, political, social and economic strength of women. Social initiatives can play a crucial role in achieving the twin goals of sustainable development and women empowerment. This is particularly relevant in less developed countries where unemployment among women is widespread. It has been the experience in India that social initiatives with government support in different States have made significant progress in promoting self employment among women. This has resulted in bringing women from the less privileged sections into the mainstream of social and economic development. This paper gives an account of one such successful experiment in the State of Kerala in the Indian Union. Known as Kudumbashree (Prosperity of Family) this project was launched by the Government of Kerala in 1998 for wiping out poverty from the State through concerted community action. The Programme is women oriented and participatory in nature.

Content

Introduction

Labour plays a vital role in the life of a nation. It is the basic resource required for economic development. In less developed countries where labour is in excess supply unemployment is a major social and economic issue. The problem gets aggravated when the large majority of them are unskilled labourers. The society finds it difficult to offer adequate employment opportunities to the growing work force. The solution lies in employing them in socially necessary and useful occupations. There are many such opportunities available particularly for women who do not have any formal education. By converting the social needs into business opportunities the twin objectives of development and empowerment can be achieved.

The concept of development may be viewed from macro and micro level. The macro issues are those pertaining to growth of the output at the national level and micro issues are those relating to the local level development. Though treated at distinct levels the two approaches are interrelated. At both the levels, different dimensions such as economic, environmental, cultural, religious and gender affect and are affected by development. The main focus of the present discussion is the environmental and gender issues in relation to sustainable development and women empowerment. In the process role of socio- economic initiatives in development will be reviewed.

Sustainable Development

The concept of sustainable development received global attention in early 1980s when the United Nations constituted a World Commission on Environment and Development (WCED), popularly known as the Brundtland Commission. The report of the commission titled 'Our Common Future' defines sustainable development in the following words: "Sustainable Development is the development that meets the needs of the present without compromising the ability of future generations to meet their own needs" (WCED 1987) .The sustainability of development may be viewed from three different dimensions: economic, environmental and social.

Economic

An economically sustainable system must be able to produce goods and services on a continuing basis, to maintain manageable levels of internal and external debt and to avoid extreme sectoral imbalances which damage the agricultural or industrial production

Environmental:-An environmentally sustainable system must maintain a stable resource base, avoiding over exploitation of renewable resource systems and depleting non-renewable resources only to the extent that investment is made in adequate substitutes. This requires the conservation of plant and animal species and minimization of the adverse impacts on the quality of air, water and other natural elements so as to sustain the eco system's overall integrity.

Social:-A socially sustainable system must achieve distributional equity, adequate provision of social services including health and education, gender equity and political accountability and participation.

In the context of the multidimensional approach, sustainable development may be viewed as a process of change in which the exploitation of resources, the direction of investment, the orientation of technological development and institutional change are all in harmony and enhance both current and future potential to meet human needs and aspirations.

Women Empowerment

The social dimension of sustainable development is particularly relevant in less developed countries. Development that is sustainable has to address the problems of the vulnerable sections of people who suffer from social and economic deprivation. The worst sufferers of deprivation are women and children. It is therefore necessary that development plans are focused mainly on empowerment of women. The empowerment of women will have a cumulative effect on development through its impact in the family and society.

In traditional society women plays a crucial role in economic and social development. They control most of the non money economy through bearing and raising children and providing much of the labour for household maintenance and subsistence agriculture. Women also make important contribution to the money economy by their work in formal and informal sectors.

Everywhere in the world women have two jobs – in the home and outside it. Women's work is generally undervalued and the additional burden development imposes is usually unrecognized. They just remain silent players in the development process. This approach towards women's role in development was questioned by social activists in early 20th century. The debate that followed was instrumental in highlighting the 'invisibility' of women's contribution to the economy and the need for integrating them into the development process. The United Nation's declaration of 1975-85 as the 'Decade for Advancement of Women' further emphasized the need for treating women on an equal footing with men in economic activity. Women gradually made their entry into several areas of economic activity till now dominated by men. But women in less privileged sections in the third world countries remained unaffected by these developments. This calls for social initiatives for empowering women.

"Women's empowerment and their full participation on the basis of equality in all spheres of society including participation in the decision making process and access to power are fundamental for the achievement of equality , development and peace" (Beijing Declaration, para 13,1995)[1]. The Declaration further asserted that women's rights are human rights. Women empowerment refers to increasing the spiritual, political, social and economic strength of women. Empowerment makes women confident about their capabilities. It helps women to develop positive thinking about their ability to make change and to exercise assertiveness in collective decision making.

Relevance of Social Initiative

The unskilled or semi skilled women from less privileged sections can be brought to the mainstream of development by providing opportunities for employment. In many developing countries social initiatives with government backing have played a pioneering role in this direction. This paper gives an account of one such successful experiment known as Kudumbashree in the state of Kerala in the Indian Union. It is appropriate that we present a brief profile of the state of Kerala before we highlight the major features of the experiment.

5. A brief profile of the State of Kerala

Kerala is a relatively small state in the south west corner of the Indian Union. Bordered by the Arabian Sea in the west the state has a coast line of 600 kms extending from the south to the north. With an average rainfall of 300 cms and an average temperature of 32 degree Celsius the state is fertile and perennially green. The total area of the state is 38863 sq kms which is 1.3% of the total area of the country. According to 2001 census the population of the state is 32 million which is 3.43 % of the population of India. The density of population in the state is 819 persons per sq km as against 324 persons per sq km for the Union. The state has the highest literacy rate in the country .94% of men and 88% of women in the state are literate. This is far above the national average of 54.16. The life expectancy in the state is 74 years;

1 This declaration was adopted at the Fourth World Conference on Women held in Beijing from 4-15 September 1995.

71 for men and 76 for women. The infant mortality rate is 13 per1000 compared to 55 per 1000 for the country as a whole. A unique feature of Kerala's population is the sex ratio which is favorable to women with 1058 females for 1000 males. When these social indicators present a picture of high level of social advancement, growing unemployment is a serious problem which the state has to tackle in the economic front. There were 4.5 million job seekers in the state in 2009.A peculiar feature of Kerala's unemployment situation is that women outnumber men seeking employment through employment exchanges (Government of Kerala 2009a).

Kudumbashree

Kudumbashree meaning prosperity for the family is a Poverty Eradication Mission launched by the government of Kerala in 1998. The project is intended to ensure economic wellbeing of the family by eradicating poverty through concerted community action. The programme is women oriented and participatory in nature. The local self governments[2] provide necessary leadership for the social initiative at the local level. Kudumbashree is today the largest women empowering project in the country. The programme has 370,000 members and covers more than 50% of the households in the state. Started as a government programme Kudumbashree has assumed the nature of a people's movement and its presence is very much felt in the social fabric of the state.

Kudumbashree differs from conventional poverty eradication programmes in that it perceives poverty not as a function of income. A high income does not necessarily guarantee a high standard of living. The poor are poor not because of their fault. Their poverty is a direct or indirect consequence of the society's failure to establish equity and fairness as the basis of economic and social relations. This, in other words means that the society has a responsibility to ensure equality of opportunity to all sections of the people. Inequality of opportunity is deprivation. Viewed from this perspective poverty is a denial of basic human rights. Poverty violates one's dignity.

Built around three critical components – micro credit, entrepreneurship development and women empowerment, the Kudumbashree initiative has been designed to ensure a more dignified life and better future to the less privileged women. The goals set for the purpose may be listed as follows:

Network women into community based organizations across the entire length and breadth of the state.

---

2 Kerala has three types of local self governments – Corporations in Metropolitan cities, Municipalities in Urban areas and gramapanchayats in rural areas.

Bring women to the forefront of local development
Develop the capabilities of women to become agents of socio-economic change.
Find innovative and sustainable solutions to the root causes of poverty.
Help restore the voice and dignity of the less privileged sections.

Organizational Structure

The Kudumbashree functions through a three tier Community Based Organization (CBO). At the bottom are the Self Help Groups (SHGs) called Neighborhood Groups (NHGs) consisting of 10 to 20 women from Below Poverty Line (BPL) families. At the middle level there are the Area Development Societies (ADS) which is a federation of 10 to 15 NHGs. The ADSs in a local self government area are grouped into Community Development Society (CDS), which functions as the apex body in the three-tier structure. At present there are 194,000 NHGs, 17,000 ADSs and 1061 CDSs in Kudumbashree (Kudumbashree Annual Report 2008-2009). An important component of the Kudumbashree structure is its association with, and backing from local self governments and bureaucracy at the ADS as well as CDS levels.

Distinctive Features

Bottom-up Approach

Kudumbashree employs a bottom-up approach in its organizational structure and decision making. Its programmes are formulated at the grass root level in the NHGs. The NHGs provide a social forum for the less privileged women to present and discuss their problems and to collectively search for solutions. In the process they come up with micro plans which suit their local conditions. These micro plans will be integrated at the ADS level into a mini plan. The mini plans evolved by the ADSs will be integrated into a plan at the CDS level. This will in turn be adopted as the sub plan of the corresponding local self government area and one-third of the total fund for development plans in the gramapanchayat or municipality will be set apart for its execution. In this planning process which commences at the lowest level the local needs get priority and resources are accordingly earmarked.

Micro Credit

Micro credit scheme is a unique venture adopted by Kudumbashree for the mobilization of resources for employment generation. The thrift and credit societies set up at the NHG level promote thrift among the poor and provide them with cost effective credit. They work as informal banks of the poor women at their doorstep. The poor women bring in their savings, pool them together and form the corpus. Loans are disbursed to members from this corpus. The amount of loan and the priority of disbursement are decided by the NHGs. A member can avail of loan up to a maximum of four times her savings. The repayment is made at the regular weekly meetings of the NHG. The savings mobilized by the NHGs in the State under the scheme amounted to INR 11.76 billion and the loan provided to members amounted to INR 30.20 billion as on 31 March 2009. (ibid)

The thrift and credit societies play a vital role in enhancing the financial status of the less privileged women in the state. The micro credit scheme has developed the habit of thrift among the poor women in the State. They could avail of loans from their own savings in times of need. In most cases, the loans availed have been utilized for starting income generating self-employment projects. This arrangement has made them free from the clutches of money lenders. The thrift and credit operations require a formal bank account operated by the President and Secretary of the NHGs. In rotation, all members of the NHG get the opportunity for familiarizing with the banking functions. This gives them self confidence, build self-esteem and make them aware of their rights.

Linkage Banking

There is also a scheme under which the NHGs are linked to co-operative /commercial banks to augment the resources mobilized at the local level. The National Bank for Agricultural and Rural Development (NABARD) provide the finances required under the scheme known as linkage banking. Once the NHGs are linked with the banks they will be eligible for financial assistance from the banks. The assistance so received can be utilized by the NHGs for internal lending and for starting micro enterprises. As on 30th March 2009, an amount of INR 554.6 million has been disbursed to NHGs under linkage banking and 92978 NHGs are found to have availed of the assistance (ibid).

Bhavanashree –Micro Housing Scheme

The Kudumbashree has also designed a scheme to provide for the housing needs of the economically weaker sections. Under the scheme known as Bhavanashree arrangements are made to disburse micro housing loans to members of NHGs. So far an amount of INR 1.99 billion has been disbursed by the banks to the low income families for the construction of 40683 houses.

Micro Enterprises

From its very inception, Kudumbashree has been promoting micro enterprises run by women. An industrial unit with an investment ranging from INR 5000 to INR 250000 falls in the category of micro enterprises.

These enterprises which use local resources and skills provide gainful employment to women in BPL families in urban and rural areas. The project has the twin advantage of exploiting enterprising spirit among women and improving their income and standard of living. There are 25000 vibrant individual micro enterprises and 1000 group enterprises with minimum 10 women in each group functioning in the state (Government of Kerala 2005, p.157).Obviously, these small industrial units have gone a long way in promoting entrepreneurship among women and making them economically independent. It also implies development of managerial skills, productive skills and marketing skills. The activities undertaken under the scheme include direct marketing, IT units, soap making, production of paper cups and bags, catering service, canteen, dairy units, coconut oil extraction, ethnic delicacies, hotels and garment units. A unique venture taken up by Kudumbashree is the production of a take home food supplement for children below the age of three to improve their nutritional status. The product is named Amrutham and has a wide market throughout the state.

Human Resource Development

Over the years Kudumbashree has evolved a built in mechanism for human resource development in its fold. There is an in house faculty engaged in the preparation of curriculum and conduct of training programmes for the members. The training programme consists of three modules of which, the third one is exclusively on functional aspects of micro enterprises such as entrepreneurship development, personal management, production and marketing. Special attention is given to capacity and capability building at the grass root level.

New Areas of Intervention

Balasabha (Children's Forum)

Poverty eradication needs a holistic approach .With this end in view in 2002-03 Kudumbashree started organizing children of the BPL families into groups called Balasabha. The motto behind this programme is to prevent inter-generational transmission of poverty. Balasabha provides an ideal forum for children to develop their innate talents and to make them conscious of their rights and duties. With this end in view regional and state-level conferences of children are organized periodically.

Ashraya -Destitute Identification, Rehabilitation & Monitoring programme

Ashrya means to depend on. Over the years Kudumbashree has emerged as an agency on which the the poorest of the poor and the destitutes can depend on for economic and social security. Poverty eradication in their case is not an economic question alone. It is more a question of lifting them up to a dignified state of life. Kudumbashree has formulated a specific project called Ashraya for the destitute families. Under this scheme the destitutes and the downtrodden through out the state are proposed to be identified and rehabilitated. Their social and economic conditions are constantly monitored. The project was launched in 2002-03 and during the year it was implemented in 179 gramapanchayats at an estimated cost of INR 740 million. Gradually it was extended to several other gramapanchayats and municipal areas. The project envisages addressing the various deprivations faced by destitute families such as lack of food, health problems, and educational facilities to children, shelter, sanitation, drinking water, skill development and employment opportunity. 58389 people of 745 local self government areas have benefited from this programme till date.

Santhwanam – Project for Detection of lifestyle diseases

This is a project for the detection of lifestyle diseases like hypertension and diabetes implemented in collaboration with an NGO, Health Action for People. The financial support for the project is provided by State Bank of India, a public sector bank. Kudumbshree volunteers trained for the purpose visit the households in selected areas and conduct the screening tests. Till date santhwanam volunteers have identified 50,000 cases of diabetes and 75,000 cases of hypertension. This programme for the health care of the people launched by the Kudumbashree has been widely acclaimed

Lease land Farming

In spite of the fact that Kerala is a thickly populated state and that there is shortage of land, large areas of cultivable land are kept idle in the state due to waning interest in agriculture. At the same time, there are people from the weaker sections of the community who are ready to turn to cultivation as a means of livelihood but landless. When rice farming became non-lucrative, farmers in the State left the fields fallow. Kudumbashree found this as an opportunity. Neighborhood groups of the Mission were encouraged to cultivate rice by leasing in the land left fallow by farmers. This programme which was started in 2002-03, was successfully extended to 870 gramapanchayats. 44,883 NHGs consisting of 30,098 families have participated in this programme and 74,301 hectares of land was brought under cultivation.(Government of Kerala 2009a, p.322).Lease land farming has been beneficial to both the landless poor families and to the landlords who ceased to cultivate rice fields. The land owners could retain their land under rice farming without loosing the ownership rights. The initiative shown by Kudumbashree has helped to arrest the drastic decline in rice cultivation in the state. Cultivation of other crops such as bananas and vegetables also is undertaken by the NHGs in the land leased in under the scheme known as Harithashree .Loans are made available to NHG groups from banks for meeting cost of cultivation.

Cost effective alternatives for plastic bags

Extensive use of plastic bags has been a serious environmental menace both in the rural and urban areas of the state. Recently the state government has banned the use of plastic carry bags of less than 30 micron strength. Utilizing this opportunity Kudumbhashree units have been encouraged to start production of cloth and paper bags which could replace plastic carry bags.

S3 (Self Sufficient, Self Reliant. Sustainable) Panchayats

While addressing the multiple deprivations faced by the poor families it has been the experience of Kudumbashree that poverty reduction will foster economic development and economic development will lead to sustainability and prosperity. Taking cognizance of this fact Kudumbashree has evolved a project to build a model of total economic development in selected grmapanchayats. The project focuses on self sufficiency, self reliance and sustainability.[3] Kudumbashree has initially introduced this programme in three gramapanchayats, one each in the southern, the central and the northern regions. As a second phase this programme was extended to 14 districts in the state.(one in each district). It is proposed to further extend the project in more gramapanchayats in the state.

3 The project envisages addressing the problems relating to the following sectors:
Child development
Mentally and physically challenged
Adolescent care
Enterprise development
Agriculture/Animal husbandry/Dairy development
Revamping and repositioning of traditional sectors
Destitute identification and rehabilitation.
Basic minimum needs: Land for house, Shelter up gradation, Drinking water, Safe sanitation facilities, Electrification.

Clean Kerala Business – A project for solid waste management

Converting waste into wealth is the idea behind the project. Solid waste is a serious menace in urban and rural areas in the state. Kudumbashree has initiated an innovative enterprise namely 'Clean Kerala Business' to tackle this problem in an organized and planned manner. Under this programme, members from NHGs are engaged in the collection of segregated waste from households and its transportation to dumping yards. This project provides a unique example of community participation in handling a social menace. At present there are about 2500 women engaged in collection and transportation of waste in 28 Urban Local Self Governing Areas in the state.

Responsible Tourism

Kudumbashree joined hands with the State Tourism Department in implementing a project titled Responsible Tourism in the tourist centers in the state. Under the tie up the Kudumbashree groups supply locally produced vegetables and food items to the hotels in the tourist destinations. Handicrafts and eco friendly products produced by SHGs are also promoted through this channel. The basic purpose of the project is to make tourism industry environment friendly and socially committed with local support and cooperation.

Samagra – Holistic approach to Development

Samagra means holistic. The hallmark of Kudumbashree Mission is the holistic approach to development. An integrated approach has been adopted in preparing projects for different sectors such as agricultural crops, animal husbandry and fish farming. Measures are also adopted for productivity improvement, quality enhancement, product diversification and market promotion. This strategy has been successfully adopted by Kudumbashree in banana and vegetable cultivation in Trivandrum district in the state. The technical support provided by the Agricultural University and assured market in and around the district made the venture profitable. The same strategy adopted in enhancing milk production in the district also was successful. The involvement of official and non official agencies in the planning and implementation of the various programmes made it possible to identify the opportunities available and exploit them successfully. he asme strategy adopted in enhancig milk production in the district also was successful.

Kudumbashree as State Urban Development Agency (SUDA)

Kudumbashree has been declared by the state government as the State Urban Development agency. It also works as the nodal agency for the urban poverty alleviation programmes and employment guarantee schemes sponsored by the Union government. In this context the role played by Kudumbashree in the implementation of Mahatma Gandhi National Rural Employment Guarantee Scheme (MNREGS) in Kerala is worth mentioning. From enrolment and job card registration to work identification, maintaining muster rolls and participating in social audit, Kudumbashree covers the entire ambit of activities. Kerala is the only state where the task of work supervisor and site manager has been entirely entrusted to women.

Kudumbashree and Human development

Three important aspects which make the Kudumbashree a unique programme merit mention here. First, contrary to most welfare or social security schemes, in Kudumbashree the decision making authority rests with the elected representatives, who are poor women themselves, rather than bureaucrats or politicians. Second, it has a dual advantage which no other existing welfare programme possesses: a functional dynamism which is found among non governmental organizations as well as a strong interaction with and backing from local self governments. Third, in addition to the regular poverty alleviation programmes, Kudumbashree conducts a range of programmes with specific objectives, such as awareness and educational programmes on women empowerment and entrepreneurship development, just to name two. These aspects make Kudumbashree a unique and rewarding programme in which poor women become active and informed agents of human development and social change.

Kudumbashree Accounts and Audit Service Society (KAASS)

Kudumbashree has evolved a system to ensure financial accountability of its activities. Its accounts from the grass root to the apex level are audited by an audit team consisting of commerce graduates drawn from NHG families. The members in this audit team are trained and guided by professional chartered accountants.

Political Empowerment of Women

Kudumbashree has been instrumental in politically empowering the women in the State. This has been amply demonstrated by their involvement in the decentralized planning process in the State. In the elections to the Local Self Governments held in 2005 as many as 968 women who were part of Kudumbashree missions for varying periods of time have been elected to the local administrative bodies in the State.(The Hindu, English daily, dated 06.10.2005).These women who now form part of the administrative machinery at the local level would be able to work as facilitators of development. They can also act as watch dogs in the administration of development programmes specially meant for the poor. A democratic polity buttressed by a free press and active civil society in which vulnerable groups have a voice make it almost impossible for government and others not to take quick action (UNDP 2000, p74) The successful experiment in women's participation in the administration of local self governments has made the State government in Kerala to increase women's reservation in local bodies to 50% from 33%.This will come into force in the elections due at the end of this year.

Conclusion

Kudumbashree is an experiment in participatory development and women empowerment. The poor and the downtrodden are brought into the main stream of development by their involvement in poverty eradication programmes and participation in local governance. The Kudumbashree women have acquired skills and self confidence by participating in self help groups at the grass root level. The thrift and credit operations and micro enterprises have enhanced their economic status. The progress in women's education has further contributed to their social advancement the impact of which is reflected in the remarkably high level of social indicators in the State. Being a women oriented movement, Kudumbashree has contributed significantly to the empowerment of women. Women empowerment can positively influence the lives not only of women themselves, but also of men and of course those of children (DREZE and SEN 2000, p.18). Moreover, a Women's agency can work as a catalyst and bring about rapid socio-economic changes. Women's decisions and actions can have profound influence on other members of the family and on the society as a whole. In the process deprivation is checked in a big way and fruits of development reach the vulnerable sections of society.

References

Chaudhary S.N.(ed) (2005) :Human Rights and Poverty in India vol.1, Concept Publishing Company, New Delhi.

Dreze, Jean and Sen, Amartya (2002) India Development and Participation, Oxford university Press, New Delhi.

Devika J and Thampi, V.Binitha (2007) Changing Regimes of Empowerment and Inclusion in the Public: Women and the Kudumbashree in Contemporary

Kerala in Oommen M. A ,(ed), A Decade of Decentralization in Kerala , Experience and Lessons, Institute of Social Sciences, New Delhi.
Dey, Dipankar (2007) Sustainable Development Perspectives and Initiatives, Icfai University Press, Hyderabad.
Eapen, Mridul (2007) Gender Budgeting and Decentralized Planning in Oommen, M.A (ibid).
Government of Kerala (2005) Human Development Report Kerala, Planning Board, Trivandrum,
Government of Kerala (2009a) Economic Review, Planning Board, Trivandrum
Government of Kerala (2009) Report of the Committee for Evaluation of Decentralized Planning and Development
Kudumbhashree (2005) Kudumbashree, Concept, Organization and Activities, Mimeo.
Kudumbashree: Annual Report 2008-2009.
Kumar, Ashok, (ed) (2005) Women and Development, Institute of Sustainable Development, Luknow.
Oommen M.A (2007) Kudumbashree of Kerala: An Appraisal, Kudumbashree Office, Trivandrum.
UNDP (2000) Human Development Report, Oxford University Press, New Delhi.
Vijayan, Aleyamma (2007) A decade of Gender Mainstreaming in Local Governance in Kerala in Oommen M.A.,(op.cit)
World Commission on Environment and Development (1987), Our Common Future, Oxford University Press.

Employment and sustainable development: education, training and R&D in the regulation of the labour market

Ilona Kovács
Professors of the ISEG, School of Economics and Management, Technical University of Lisbon

Margarida Chagas Lopes
researchers at SOCIUS – Research Centre in Economic and Organizational Sociology

Abstract

Sustainable development has been considered in various discourses as the answer to the economic, social and ecological crisis. However, its principles are far from being implemented. The dominant model of society, which gives priority to financial capital and short-term profitability in the context of globalisation and market deregulation, involves social disinvestment, increasing inequalities and exclusion, that is to say, non sustainable development. We argue that sustainable development requires an orientation towards human needs, social and ecological sustainability and consequently a break with the prevailing model of society and learning and knowledge sharing within modern societies.

In the first section we confront the "market-driven work society", which is embedded in the neo-liberal paradigm, with the alternative model of the "humanized work society", which aims to dignify work, enhance quality of working life and skills development. The next sections focus on the long-run and new forms of labour market regulation and the roles successively played by education, vocational training and – desirably – innovation in that regulation process. We stress that sustainable development implies an effective upgrading of work and skills, requiring adequate structural education, training and R&D policies.

In other words, progress towards labor and sustainable development will impose the need for global socio-cultural transformations. Therefore, in order to meet that major goal, 21st century societies should face important challenges and no lesser risks which we will address as a final summing up remark in the Conclusions.

Content

Introduction

The economic crises and current recession are manifestations of failure in pursuing the objectives set by the United Nations (Millennium Goals) in 2000 with respect to eradicating extreme poverty and hunger and achieving environmental sustainability. There is also a failure to accomplish the objectives set in 2000 by the Lisbon Strategy (Kovács, Casaca, 2007). While the financial sector can extract high profits from the real economy, several EU countries face increasing difficulties, including fiscal deficit, rising socio-economic inequalities, unemployment and poverty, and growing indebtedness of the countries and families. The source of these social problems and serious environmental problems is the profit-oriented economic system, which is governed according to neo-liberal principles and ignores human and social needs. Sustainable development has been considered in various discourses as the answer to the crisis. However, its principles are far from being implemented. On the contrary, market principles prevail, and the search for short-term profit has led to the aggravation of social, economic and environmental problems. The objectives of sustainable development – such as ecological equilibrium, reducing inequalities globally and nationally, and the promotion of gender equality – are not compatible with the market-driven society; they require an orientation towards human needs, and social and ecological sustainability. Moreover, they certainly require a break with the prevailing model of learning and knowledge sharing within modern societies. This means a major challenge to education, training and work systems to progress towards a de facto inclusive learning society, instead of settling for the present outcomes of the "most competitive knowledge societies"...

Employment and antagonistic social models

1.1 The market-driven work centred society

The market-driven work centred society embedded in the neo-liberal paradigm, with its pursuit of high profitability, increased liberalisation and growing deregulation, is presented by its advocates as the only trend of evolution. The liberalisation of markets and the intensification of competition are understood to be powerful mechanisms for the competitive capacity of economies, which lead to economic growth. This model is based on the primacy given to the economy, free market principles and profit, competition, and individualism. Information and Communication Technologies (ICT) are considered the driving forces in the free market economy, leading to a new era of growth, competitiveness and innovation, (Sahlman, 1999). Globalisation – the universalisation of the market – is presented as an inevitable process that will bring greater well-being to humanity as a whole. Accordingly, the mission of governments is to promote the adaptation of the national economies to the demands of the global market and to leave the task of guiding societies entirely to the market and the private sector. Social rights, the protection of workers, social regulation and trade unions are seen as archaic obstacles to competitiveness and the new order. Social rights are changed into profitable commodities. Reforms are promoted the world over in order to open markets, deregulate the economy, privatise strategic sectors and public services, liberalise the labour market, reduce social protection, and hold individuals responsible for their own labour market situation and security. Therefore, good public management has to remove all regulations that may hamper the free market game.

Hegemony and liberalisation of the financial markets, the increase of speculative behaviour, financial investor pressure, and shareholder value orientation are the principal factors leading to the replacement of a long-term orientation by short-term profitability. The maximum profitability rates required to fulfil investor interests in rapid and high returns call for the minimisation of labour costs and the maximisation of productive efficiency in companies. This is the reason for centring on the greatest value-generating key activities (core business) and subcontracting by increasingly delocalising other activities to low wage countries. (Castillo, 2003; Kovács, 2002). This is also the reason for the simplification and decentralisation of business structures throughout flexible rationalisation processes, such as lean production and re-engineering, all of which aim to produce more, better and faster, with less. Company restructuring enabled by ICT and driven by global competition results in the spread of a new form of organisation of production based on decentralisation, fragmentation and geographic dispersion of productive activities that are integrated into networks by ICT (Castells, 1998).

The constant search for more profitable places to produce outsourced activities leads to underinvestment and prevents the creation of jobs. The growth of an underpaid workforce encourages low road competition through a reduction of labour costs, instead of promoting high road competition by way of technological and organisational innovation. With neo-liberalism, management practices are increasingly resorting to individual responsibility at work, the individualisation of pay, career, training, information / communication, and assessment of personal potential. But these practices, rather than providing greater autonomy, undermine the individual by leading to insecurity and weakness of social ties (Fitoussi and Rosenvallon, 1997; Linhart, 2002). Within the context of high differentiation, the defence of interests related to work is increasingly left to individual level negotiations. Trade unions are being undermined and the defence of worker interests at the transnational level is poor or non-existent. The neo-liberal objective seeks to transform the employment contract from one based on the status of the employee (collective identity), which grants a series of social rights, into market contracts in favour of individual negotiations. In these negotiations, the upper hand tends to belong to the employer, who defines the terms of negotiation and justifies changes as inevitable due to impositions of technology and market conditions. This context leads to deterioration in wages, employment and living conditions.

The increase in unemployment and precarious employment is not merely a consequence of economic failure and firms' loss of market share. Companies with good results may end up closing when the return on financial investment is less than that generated by other companies. The economy becomes a prisoner of the "impatient capital" (Harrison 1994; Sennett, 2005). We face a new form of income economy, a set of financial capitalism set only on reducing production costs and forgetting to invest. This hypertrophied financial head dominates an anaemic body, undermining its healthy growth (Peyrelevade, 2008).There is a trend to rising social inequalities between those who have relatively strong positions in the labour market and those who find themselves in situations of unemployment and precarious employment. The new organisation of production in the context of the global competition condemns growing segments of the population to unemployment, unstable employment, precariousness and poverty, with the risk of their being subjected to a spiral of ever greater fragility and instability (Beck, 2000; Boltanski and Chiapello, 1999; Castel 1995; Castells 1998; Castillo 1994, 2003; Grupo de Lisboa, 1994; Harrison, 1994; Kalleberg, 2003; Kovács and Chagas Lopes, 2009; Paugam, 2000).

There is a brake on upward-social mobility. For a substantial proportion of employees, i.e. those finding themselves in a disadvantaged labour market position, it seems extremely difficult to set about improving their employability. These are, in the main, females, in younger and older age groups with low levels of schooling. Their mobility (lateral) tends to be limited to poorly qualified positions within the same company, or when swapping one company for another, to positions that perpetuate their labour market fragility, specifically the lack of opportunity for training and promotion (Kovács, 2005).

In conclusion, we can say that this model, based on the maximum release of market mechanisms of social regulation, subordinates society to the market laws, which aim to raise high economic dynamism. This model involves the diffusion of multiple unstable forms of employment, job insecurity, and deterioration of job quality, and consequently the failure of social integration through work. It also involves the destruction of social regulation built to conceal the market economy and social cohesion. Unemployment, instability and insecurity are permanent risks.

1.2. The model of renewed and humanised work centred society

An alternative model – the "humanised work centred society" – aims to dignify work, and enhance the quality of working life and skills development. This model implies democratic and socially responsible governance by means of systematic dialogue, participation and negotiation in order to reconcile social and economic goals. From our point of view this is the only model able to encompass sustainability. This alternative is based on the idea that work will continue to structure and provide coherence in an individual's life. There is no evidence that paid work or employment is losing any of its centrality. Furthermore, various studies have concluded that there has been an effective increase in working time as well as in the intensification of work (Reich, 2000; Schor, 1991). The main problem is not the end of work (Gorz, 1998; Méda, 1995; Rifkin, 1995), but the wealth of work that is devoid of quality and, in so being, it fails to live up to the expectations of people or gives little or no guarantee of stability of income and/or working conditions to enable them to enjoy a decent life. Work remains a central reference, not only in economic aspects, but also for the psychological and cultural. The vast majority of people are employed and working time remains long. There are not fewer employees, but workers more exposed to insecurity and unemployment. Work does not disappear, but becomes increasingly invisible since the present ways of producing hide the place where it is produced (Castillo, 2003). Contrary to the ideas proposed by those proclaiming the end of work, employment remains a central feature of our societies; it is the source of individual and collective identities, social cohesion and integration (Schnapper, 1998). The humanised work centred society is able to provide sustainable development (equality, social cohesion and ecological equilibrium) in contrast with the features of the market driven work centred society, as shown in the following table:

Table 1.2.1: Antagonistic models of work centred society

Market-driven work centred society	Renewed and humanised work centred society
Society subordinated to economy and market regulation driven by interests linked to financial capital	Social regulation of market economy by socially responsible and democratic government aiming for sustainable development

Deregulated labour market aiming for flexibility (free use of work as source of competitiveness)	Regulated labour market with institutional protection of work and full employment orientation
Corporate government aiming for shareholder value orientation by flexible rationalisation	Democratic and socially responsible corporate government articulating economic and social objectives and human centred technical-organisational options (humanised flexibility)
Short-term orientation	Long term orientation
Work: cost to be reduced	Work: activity to be transformed into meaningful activity providing autonomy, satisfaction and professional development
Individualistic values, individual responsibility for employability and security	Articulation between emancipator individualisation and social values
Long working hours and intensification of work	Reduction of working time

A high road to economic development based on improving efficiency and innovation is understood; i.e., through economic gains there are also wage gains, improvements in the quality of working life and the social conditions safeguarding workers' rights and promoting adequate social protection standards. In other words, there is an institutional protection of work. According to the human and social oriented economic system, a long-term orientation prevails. The renovation and humanisation of a work centred society involves the redistribution of socially useful work, the reduction in working timetables, flexibility without precariousness. Socially responsible and democratic government through dialogue, negotiation and participation at all levels allows the conciliation of economic and social objectives. Work retains its centrality but the reduction in working time opens up the space for other activities (cultural, civic, etc.). A shorter working week can help to respond to a range of interlinked problems such as over-consumption, high carbon emissions, entrenched inequalities and ill-being associated with long working hours, unemployment and the lack of time to live sustainably, to be active citizens, to care for each other and simply enjoy life (Coote, Franklin, Simms, 2010).

The promotion of working life quality requires the transformation of work into an interesting and meaningful activity, capable of providing autonomy, satisfaction and social integration. ICT are able to bring about simultaneous improvements to productivity, employment and quality of life whenever a human-centred or humanised flexibility perspective prevails in the technological and organisational options taken (Kovács, 1998; 2002; Oeij and Wiezer, 2002). Flexible forms of employment associated with social and individual objectives can enable greater individual control over time, better conciliating work and family life, and other activities. The following table compares the two models of society in regard to its implications on employment, quality of work life and social rights:

Table 1.2.2: Social implications of antagonistic models of the work centred society

Market regulated work centred society	Renewed and humanised work centred society
Increasing inequality, insecurity and risk of social exclusion	Promotion of equality and social inclusion by humanised work
Flexibility with precariousness	Flexibility without precariousness
Weakness of social ties and vulnerability of individuals	Strong social ties, conciliation of individual and collective interests
Strong employer position and debility of trade-unions	Dialogue, multiple forms of participation, negotiation
Spiral downturn in wages and working conditions Commoditisation of social rights Weakening of social cohesion by unemployment, precariousness and poverty Deepening of ecological crises	Improved quality of working life and of life in general Social rights associated with renewed/humanised work Identity and integration by humanised work Environmental sustainability

Such a renewal of the work centred society needs to create new regulatory forms and functions that extend beyond national level regulation. There have to be effective mechanisms for the implementation of decent work principles or core labour standards (ILO) in the defence of worker interests on a truly global scale (Santos, 1998) within a different type of globalisation that focuses on the reduction of inequality and economic, social and ecological imbalances. Therefore, the renewed and humanised work centred society implies the need for labour market regulation in order to enhance work institutional protection, to promote the articulation between economic and social objectives, to contribute to humanised technological innovation and mainly to create the conditions for sustainable knowledge and professional/occupational development. Nevertheless, labour market regulation has not followed a straightforward pattern over time and nor does it encompass a unique one model fits all. In the following sections we deal with the leading developments in labour market regulation and set the main challenges imposed by globalisation today.

The long-run trend in Labour Market Regulation

With the labour market crises and the end of "employment for life" it became clear that new forms of regulation of the labour market were needed since it had proved unable to return to equilibrium by itself. Employment precariousness and the recurrence of unemployment spells even among some of the most qualified workers made education and training part of the new regulation tools. The need to take into consideration the "demand side" of the labour market appeared inevitable: given that being qualified would no longer guarantee access to and maintenance of a job, greater attention began to be paid to innovation's and technology's shorter cycles, to the specificities of the skills demanded by the organisations and most of all to the ability of workers to be flexible in order to be employable.

That is why lifelong learning has been increasingly called upon to perform the role of a labour market regulator or, at least, to reinforce the action of other regulation mechanisms, such as labour law. At the same time, there has been increasing pressure for schools to share their previous role as the unique source of knowledge with other learning institutions, notably firms and other organisations. In that light, for most reference authors the dynamics of individual learning processes would combine formal learning in school with work experience acquired during the successively performed jobs, allowing for "human capital" depreciation during separation spells (Willis 1986; 1987). Obsolescence would inevitably take place, the longer the separation and the higher the depreciation rate, unless some form of adequate training were undertaken. Likewise vocational training and education acquire a prominent role in promoting (re)employability. And, as has always happened in face of the failure of market mechanisms, governments and public funding were called to support this new strategy. Labour market policies were then applied to the utmost, either in the form of active labour market policies or as unemployment subsidies and other public transfers (Heijke & Muysken 2000). Education and vocational training are undoubtedly public (or semi-public) goods, but it is only when the market fails and ideological suspicion towards public intervention lessens that they acquire prominence, in this case as remediation strategies. The functionalist approach towards education and training was emerging again… Actually, by not intervening to promote (re)employability and new skills throughout vocational training, governments would face even larger pressure on the public budget in the form of passive labour market policies and among all unemployment subsidies.Left to market uncertainties and to the absence of strategic alignment for long periods, training has been increasingly marked by severe vicious circles and strong bottlenecks: training markets are generally tailored for high dimension businesses, training programmes are mostly attended by the already qualified and most mobile workers and the outcomes of training frequently fail to meet the organisation's needs (Chagas Lopes 2004; Chagas Lopes 2006; INE 2009). That is why great emphasis has been placed on other forms of ALMP since the nineties in most international fora, like the OECD. In the same vein, the European Union's essay of integrated regulation has increasingly insisted on the need for "activation". This is especially so since the Lisbon Summit and the Second Phase of the European Employment Strategy (Heintz, 2006).

The reinforcement of the economic and social crises in the transition to the new millennium placed new pressure on public budgets with important restrictions to the funding of labour market policies. Education and training certainly retained their role as regulators of labour markets but they proved to be increasingly inefficient even under the form of lifelong learning strategies. Once again the labour market had to seek new forms of hetero-regulation. Of these, flexicurity was among the most prominent, together with important alterations to labour market legislation, which led towards greater flexibility (Wilthagen 2008). By clearly allowing for unemployment spells, even for the more qualified and trained workers, flexicurity induces an important divide between the employment relationship and the supply of skilled work that is in total opposition with the neo-classical approach. In fact, new theoretical perspectives began to predominate, among which life cycle theories were considered one of the most important critical alternatives.This does not mean that flexicurity deliberately proposed a break with the functionalist perspective, only that education and training were no longer powerful enough. Hence, they were to be supplemented by Social Security: the latter should intervene additionally during unemployment spells to ensure a minimum income and to help finance training and/or education to foster (re)employability. We will not pursue this subject but just emphasise its external nature relative to the labour markets which it was supposed to help regulate. In fact, labour market regulation performed an outward trajectory over time which was driven by theoretical revision and undoubtedly by the main impact of the employment and labour crises.

The present need for (new forms of) Labour Market Regulation

With globalisation, labour markets have met with new forms of disequilibria which originate either within each country's labour market or as an outcome of the global interaction.

The struggle for competitiveness leads resourceful countries to permanently push the technological innovation frontier onwards. Hence, technology cycles become even shorter and maturity peaks are reached at a faster pace as if in some sort of perpetual movement until a crisis like the present one hits this wealthier part of the world. For technology dependent countries this circular auto-feeding movement means the reinforcement of the dependence in which they got caught by trying to keep a position in the global trade to survive. Actually, besides their increasing losses in competitiveness, they also face severe distortions in the labour markets: the qualification systems remain intrinsically national in terms of the values and skills they promote and they rarely adjust easily to innovation especially when it comes from abroad. Likewise in these countries an increasing divide between the organisations' demand for skills and the supply of qualifications takes place and becomes difficult to eradicate.

Less dependent countries also face distortion and disequilibria. For most of them, precariousness stemming from external labour market flexibility has increased along with the struggle for competitiveness and alleviation in the labour laws. As a result they face a rising mismatch between the duration of labour contracts – which tend to follow the shorter productivity patterns – and the need to improve qualifications throughout labour market experience. Lower rates of return for investment in learning and increased free-riding flows then appear as obvious consequences, with further qualification and training efforts proving to be inefficient to overcome these bottlenecks (Chagas Lopes 2006).

Distortions like the latter often become powered by the rigidity of the structure of the demand for labour: the economic structure proves unable to absorb the medium and high-level skills it so urgently requires. This paradoxical behaviour has sometimes been called the 'chimney effect" and it induces severe underutilisation of skills and competencies, as depicted by the following Figure:

From the above Figure, three main traits are clear:

- the incapacity of the demand for labour to absorb higher skills, which leads to their unemployment and to brain drain;
- the occupational downward trend, which results in a meaningful share among the higher skilled being offered only poorly qualified jobs;
- the eviction effect of the less skilled workers, thereby reinforcing the probability that the outsiders will remain excluded for longer periods.

Figure 1: Historical dimensions of short-time work: Persons (Crimmann & Wießner, 2009)

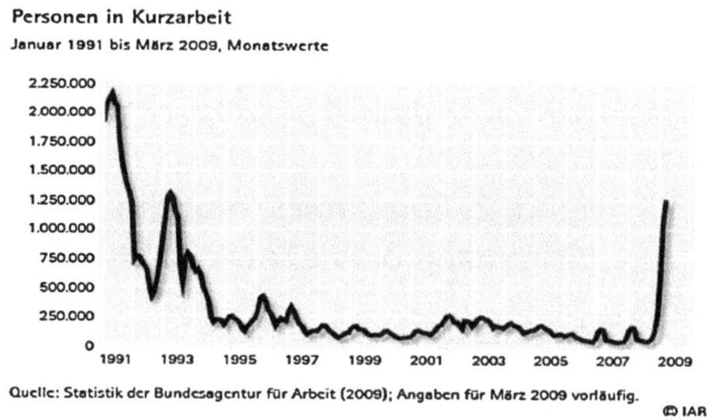

These sorts of bottlenecks tend to be reinforced whenever the economic strategy and education and training policies are kept separate, thus precluding articulation of the corresponding decision making. It would appear then that the need for regulation in the labour markets is consensual nowadays. Nevertheless, we can distinguish among several regulation approaches, in particular between the one which the European Union has been trying to adopt and the OECD's perspective.

Although aware of the modest ability of the "European model" to raise employment and foster competitiveness, the European Commission seems to overlook the kaleidoscopic nature of the European Union most of the time. Actually most European official documents stress the need for a (global and unique...) regulation model, which should be able to foster "(...) fair and decent working conditions and labour standards to all workers in EU and protect workers against overexposure to the whims of the market (...)" (European Parliament 2007). It would seem that at least the neo-classical pro-free market penchant has been overcome, although perhaps not for good As a matter of fact European labour markets behave quite differently even when the economic conjuncture is stable. These differences have been persistent over time and are deeply rooted in structural reasons, leading us to systematically distinguish among the diverse pieces of the "European mosaïque". Reflecting on the new forms of labour market regulation, the OECD's approach mostly emphasises the role of "(...) good domestic policies ... supported by well designed employment protection legislation (...)" (OECD 2007: 3) in order to foster (re)employment opportunities. It stresses the crucial role which labour market regulation should play in shifting jobs from declining to expanding occupations, in 'making work pay' and in promoting skill development opportunities for the less educated in order to limit low pay traps

(OECD 2007).Unlike the EU, the OECD does not have to deal with integrated decision making and perhaps for that political reason it does not neglect the role that national decision making should play in labour market regulation. Accordingly, we argue that country specific R&D and Innovation policies must play a leading role in today's hetero-regulation of the labour markets (LM). In doing so, they complement education, training and other policies' regulatory capacity by enhancing an upward move in the demand for skills:

Figure 2: Companies, monthly (Crimmann & Wießner, 2009)

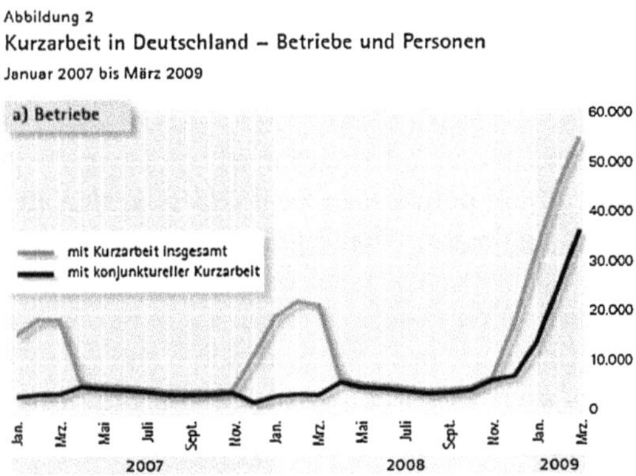

Besides the inevitable split up due to lack of a global regulation model, in each country's labour market R&D policies should be called to intervene and upgrade the demand for skills so that the underutilisation of the qualifications supplied should be minimised. From our point of view, EU centrally decided Innovation and R&D policies risk glossing over each country's specificities and as a result they may contribute little to reinforcing the EU's ability to absorb higher qualifications. In the next section we shall explore the intervention of R&D and Innovation as labour market regulators in more depth.

R&D and Innovation in the Regulation of Labour Markets

A great number of analyses rely upon R&D output indicators – such as the proportion of graduates and post-graduates in the specific fields of Engineering and Science – to illustrate the ability each country has to foster R&D and Innovation.

Notwithstanding, this kind of information is quite limited as it gives us no sign of the capacity of the economic structure to absorb the high and medium-high qualifications upon which it so much depends to enhance productivity. Nor do such indicators inform us on the rate of "human capital" underutilisation. Most reference authors on learning methodologies, like Kolb, define (experiential) learning as "the process whereby knowledge is created through the transformation of experience" (Kolb 1984: 23). Accordingly we cannot disregard occupational experience – and employment status – when analysing the broad process of skill and competency development. It becomes clear that, together with differences in individual learning styles, the unequal distribution of job opportunities strongly affects the ability to foster and reap the fruits of innovation. This underlines the importance of the context for which innovation is designed: to neglect that context, inner aspirations and decisions will lead to misunderstanding of the innovation processes.

In the context of the globalised world, knowledge is increasingly shared unevenly, and this leads to inequalities in labour market opportunities and working conditions. Economic policy should set as its leading target the promotion and dissemination of knowledge as a common good able to meet the collective interests related to sustainable development. This would imply reducing inequalities in the production, sharing and access to information and knowledge as well as in the international division of labour, as illustrated in the next Figure:

Figure 3: Persons/Employees, monthly (Crimmann & Wießner, 2009)

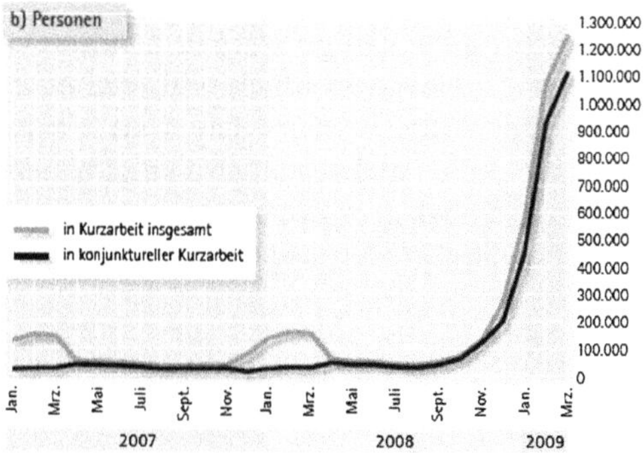

In order to access how far R&D and innovation are embedded into production activities, become (or not...) more evenly shared and effectively contribute to the regulation of labour markets, we need other kinds of indicators that complement the ones relative to outputs in higher education and advanced studies. The relative capacity of absorption of high-skilled workers is one of the more relevant indicators. Data for EU-27 depicts a quite heterogeneous context from this point of view, with some of the countries absorbing in 2006 no more than half of the EU-27 average employment in high and medium-high-technology manufacturing (EU 2009). Even in knowledge intensive services, where larger gains in productivity have been obtained in today's economies, the divide (here among European countries) clearly appears. For some specific countries, data for the gross expenditure in R&D relative to GDP would not lead us to expect such poor final outcomes. This inconsistency indicates that there are still important difficulties in transforming R&D into effective innovation, another major caveat that economic policy should tackle. Organisational models, managers' competencies and skills, entrepreneurial values and inherited culture also exert an influence on the ability to innovate. They severely affect knowledge, technology diffusion, the demand for skills and organisational innovation. In some countries, despite the appreciable results displayed by in-house product and process innovation, even among small and medium enterprises, cooperative and networking ties among innovators are very weak or practically absent (Parvan 2007). Accordingly, sustainability will be at stake.

These results alert us to the importance of the context and to the impact that national specificities exert upon innovation processes. They also shed light on the strong articulation that exists between the employment structure and labour market opportunities and R&D and innovation efforts. Education and training will no longer be able by themselves to regulate labour market disequilibria and they may even operate towards the reinforcement of bottlenecks if innovation in the economic structure does not take place. In a sense, striving for competitiveness and valorising human capital can go hand in hand provided that adequate R&D policies translate into innovation which will lead enterprises to steadily absorb the medium and high skilled workers they need to raise competitiveness. R&D policies will enhance skilled and sustainable employment and contribute to foster inclusion and citizenship when reforms are taken to develop a renewed and humanised work centred society, breaking with the neo-liberal policy framework.

Conclusions

Employment and sustainable development, as a major target to be met by 21st century societies, undoubtedly require their ability to face important social challenges and no lesser meaningful risks.

From our point of view, the driving force of this process of global change should be sought in the domains of politics and culture. A progress towards sustainability will become possible only by breaking with the neo-liberal policies of the market driven society and by promoting policies able to develop a society oriented towards human needs and social and ecological equilibrium. As we have previously referred, a whole change in the dominant way of living will be at stake: this will call for a radical move from high profitability, increased liberalisation and growing deregulation to an inclusive society where employment stability, access to learning and knowledge and, most of all, to an equitable sharing of the "fruits of development" will become the norm. Likewise, one of the leading global challenges is the eradication of the increasing divide which is taking place between the "new North" and the "new South" knowledge within the actually asymmetric globalization of economy. In addition to that polarization, a major risk is the worsening of social and ecological problems due to the lack of global regulatory institutions. Actually, the present financial crisis and the disequilibria of the global economy, as a whole, severely point to a big default: neither are there global regulatory institutions powerful enough to redress the global system to the – old or new – order, nor the shy attempts to reform old regulators, as the IMF, seems to convey to any meaningful reordering processes. For the European Union in particular, a profound challenge must be meet as well: the need to overcome the political temptation of proposing unique solutions as they are completely at odds with its inner and profound heterogeneity.

Regarding the full and decent employment targets, the Governing Body of the International Labour Office calls for an "employment oriented" response to the global economic crisis. "It is time to apply the same efforts and policy creativity to create jobs and support enterprises that were deployed in saving banks and rescuing the financial system," said Director-General Juan Somavia in Davos (ILO, 2010).

And then we come to the very point: it became common sense that sustainability within labour markets could only be achieved throughout the development of labour force's skills and competencies. But if left to (un)regulation, with no strategically designed articulation to economy, another kind of risk becomes dominant: the severe underutilisation of skills and competencies, mostly the highest qualified ones, who will be strongly exposed to brain drain or durable unemployment. Actually, education and training continue playing an important role as labour market regulators and likewise structural reforms in these two domains remain necessary. But fostering sustainability becomes now more demanding: it requires a steadily upgrading in the structure of the demand for skills which will allow a systematic matching with the supply side outcomes. In other words, it requires Innovation and R&D to become effectively embedded into production activities instead of remaining mostly confined to Higher Education and Government Agencies. That is to say, it requires institutional innovation as well, pledging for effective interaction among innovation players and requiring practical networking amongst the innovative entrepreneurs. In a nutshell, it requires cultural change, most of all.

References

Beck, Ulrich (2000), Brave new world of work, Cambridge, Polity Press.

Boltansky, Luc e Chiapello Éve (1999), Le Nouvel Esprit du Capitalisme, Paris, Éditions Gallimard.

Castel, Robert (1995), Les métamorphoses de la question sociale. Une chronique du salariat, Paris, Fayard..

Castells, Manuel (1998), La era de la información economia, sociedad y cultura, la sociedade red, vol. 1, Madrid, Aliança Ed.

Castillo, Juan José (1994), "La qualificación del trabajo y los distritos industriales", in: Economia y Sociologia del Trabajo nº 21-22

Castillo, Juan José (2003), Los estragos de la subcontratación (La organización del trabajo como factor de riesgo laboral), UGT Madrid.

Chagas Lopes (2004), "Formação Profissional e Crise do Emprego", Cadernos Sociedade e Trabalho, IV, Lisbon, DEEP/MSST

Chagas Lopes (2006), "O Desenvolvimento dos Recursos Humanos em Portugal nos Últimos 20 Anos", In António Romão (org., 2006), A Economia Portuguesa 20 Anos Após a Adesão, Edições Económicas, II Série, nº1, Coimbra, Almedina.

Coote, A.; Franklin, J.; Simms A. (2010), 21 hours Why a shorter working time could help us all to flourish in the 21th century, NEF, www.neweconomics.org.

EC (2009), Sustainable Development in the European Union – 2009 monitoring report of the EU sustainable development strategy, Luxembourg: EUROSTAT.

EU (2009) Europe in Figures – Eurostat Yearbook 2009, Luxembourg: EUROSTAT.

European Parliament (2007), Alternative Progress Indicators to Gross Domestic Product (GDP) as a Means Towards Sustainable Development, Brussels.

Fitoussi, Jean-Paul e Rosenvallon, Pierre (1997), Nova Era das Desigualdades, Celta, Oeiras.

Gorz, André (1998), Misères du Présent. Richesses du Possible, Paris, Édition Galiée, 1997.

Grozelier, Anne-Marie (1998), Pour en finir avec la fin du travail, Paris, Éditions de l'Atelier.

Grupo de Lisboa (1994), Limites à competição, Lisboa, Publicações Europa-América.

Harrison, Bennett (1994), Lean and Mean, The Guilford Press, New York, London.
Heijke, Hans & Muysken, Joan (2000), Education and Training in a Knowledge Based Economy, Palgrave, Mc.Millan.
Heintz, James (2006): Globalization, Economic Policy and Employment, Employment Strategic Papers, Genebra, ILO.
ILO (2010), http://www.ilo.org/jobspact/lang--en/index.htm
INE (2009), Aprendizagem ao Longo da Vida –Inquérito à Educação e Formação de Adultos 2007, Lisbon, National Institute for Statistics.
Kalleberg, Arnel (2003), "Flexible Firms and Labor Market Segmentation", Work and Occupations, May, pp. 154-174.
Kolb, D.A. (1984), Experiential Learning: Experience as the Source of Learning and Development, New Jersey, Prentice Hall.
Kovács, Ilona (1998), "Trabajo, cualificaciones y aprendizaje a lo largo de la vida", Sociologia del Trabajo, Madrid, nº 34, Otoño, pp .3-25.
Kovács, Ilona, (2002), As Metamorfoses do Emprego. Ilusões e Problemas da Sociedade da Informação, Celta, Oeiras.
Kovács, Ilona, (2005), Flexibilidade de emprego – riscos e oportunidades, Oeiras, Celta.
Kovács, Ilona y Casaca, Sara Falcão (2007), "Flexibilidad y desigualdad en el trabajo: tendências y alternativas europeas", Sociología del Trabajo, nº 61, Otoño 2007, pp. 99- 124.
Kovács, Ilona and Chagas Lopes, Margarida (2009), "Alternativas à crise do emprego: desafios à educação/formação e novas formas de regulação", Calouste Gulbenkian Foundation: "Próximo Futuro".
Linhart, Danièle, (2002), "Los assalariados y a mundialización. El caso Francés", Sociologia del Trabajo, nº 45, pp. 53-68.
Méda, Dominique (1995), Le travail: une valeur en voie de disparition, Paris, Aubier
OECD (2007), Employment Outlook, Paris: OECD.
Oeij, R. A. P. and Wiezer N. M. (2002), New work organization, working conditions and quality of work: towards the flexible firm? European Foundation for the Improvement of Living and Working Conditions, Dublin.
Parvan, S.-V. (2007), Statistics in Focus, nº 116 .
Paugam, S., "La salarié de la precarité. Les nouvelles formes de l'integration profissionnelle, Paris, PUF, 2000.
Peyrelevade, J. (2008), O Capitalismo Total, Ed. Século XXI, Lisboa
Reich, Robert (2000), The Future of Successs – Working and Living in teh New Economy, Alfrede A. Knopf, New York.
Rifkin, Jeremy (1995), The end of Work: The Decline of the Global Labor force and the New Post-Market Era, New York, Jeremy P. Tacher; G.P. Putnam's Sons.

Sahlman, A. William (1999), "The New Economy is Stronger Than You Think", Harvard Business Review, November-December, pp. 99-106.
Santos, Boaventura de Sousa (1998), Reinventar a Democracia: Entre o pré-contratualismo e o pós-contratualismo. Lisboa, Gradiva.
Schnapper, Dominique, Contra o fim do Trabalho, Lisboa, Terramar, 1998.
Sennett, Richard (2005), The Culture of the New Capitalism, New Haven, Yale University Press.
Schor, J. B. (1991), The overworked American. The unexpected decline of leisure, Basic Book.
Willis, Richard (1986),"Wage Determinants: a Survey and Reinterpretation of Human Capital Earnings Function" In Handbook of Labour Economics, Ashenfelter&Layard (org), Amesterdam, North Holland.
Wilthagen, Ton (2008): Mapping out Flexicurity Pathways in the European Union, Tilburg, Tilburg University.

The reality of corporate social responsibility in Brazil and Portugal

Maria João Santos
Department of Social Sciences, Higher Institute of Economics and Management – Technical University of Lisbon and researcher at SOCIUS – Economic Sociology and Organizational Research Centre
Carla Montefusco de Oliveira
University of Fortaleza, and research internship at SOCIUS at Federal University of Rio Grande do Norte

Abstract

Besides analyzing the multiple theoretical and conceptual interpretations that the term corporate social responsibility (CSR) gives rise to, it is also important to understand the social, economic, cultural and symbolic contexts which are at the heart of social responsibility practices within the business world. It is this scope that this paper focuses upon, given that it seeks to analyze the similarities and asymmetries between corporate social responsibility practices in Brazil and Portugal. Portugal, due to its European Union membership, is profoundly influenced by many of the Union's principles and guidelines due not only to the greater relative geographic proximity of Portuguese companies but also due to the institutional context and the predominance of the European Union regulatory business framework, which takes CSR into consideration. In the case of Brazil, companies have historically operated closely tied to the state structure thus generating a culture of state dependence. This only started to change as from the 1980s when it became effectively possible to identify a feeling of responsibility for national development in the Brazilian business class.

Content

Introduction

There are a number of analytical perspectives based on the role that companies have historically played in economic and social development, thus leading to interpretations of varied types regarding this phenomenon. Companies can be considered, from the diachronic viewpoint, as the privileged focus of conflict between capital and labour, and in this case they are considered as economic units the sole function of which is to increase the economic advantage to their shareholders. Alternatively, they may be considered as players that interact with the social framework and are involved in creating social value.

Since there is no one way of defining the role of the company in society, the concept of Corporate Social Responsibility (CSR) is also subject to various interpretations. Thus, theoretical conceptions regarding companies, and more specifically CSR, are not built on homogeneous explanations on the theme, but rather present numerous ways to interpret the constructs of CSR, depending on the focus given to the various aspects which make up the relationship between the company and society.

Besides the many theoretical and conceptual interpretations which arise, it is also important to understand the social, economic, cultural and symbolic contexts which are at the heart of CSR practices. Therefore, in addition to the differences that exist conceptually, it is essential to also understand the context underlying measures taken by companies as part of their social responsibility.

It is in this context that this work seeks to discuss and analyze the level of similarities and asymmetries between the reality of corporate social responsibility in Brazil and Portugal. The two countries selected as the object of this research, besides having a long history of trade relations and cultural exchange which stretches over centuries, were selected due to the possibility of carrying out a comparative study on CSR practices in Brazil and Portugal via the exchange of experience and research carried out by the authors of the study.

CSR: the need for a context

The theme of CSR has been a source of great controversy for several decades, and even amongst those who defend its importance, it is possible to find the same terminology used with different meanings. (Rego et al, 2006). This situation is not a problem in itself but suggests the need for some convergence in conceptualizing the concept (Ashlye, 2001), so that it becomes clearer to see the actual implications for the company of adopting social responsibility practices.

As Garriga and Mellé (2004) argue, when constructing a map of the theoretical conceptions of CSR one is faced with a great challenge to overcome the limitations of the approaches which tend to focus on a single aspect, thus presenting very reductionist views. To quote Garriga and Mellé (2004) further, the theories most often used are focused on four main aspects: finding long-term profit objectives; using the power of business responsibly in relation to society; including social needs within business, and contributing to social well-being by doing what is ethically correct.

A further point which is also relevant in this debate is the need to take into consideration the various socioeconomic phenomena, namely the multiple aspects of the relationship which is established between the company, society and the government, which are always present when we seek to explain CSR. If we consider the argument put forward by Polanyi (2000) that markets are immersed in the social context of which they form part, one may presume that the conceptions and practices within the scope of CSR do not originate exclusively from movements within companies, but are indeed the result of interactions that the company has developed with other social actors (the government, NGOs, civil society in general). Those interactions include, amongst other elements, the individual and/or collective interests of the parties involved in the process, social norms, institutional rules, organization profiles, and also the social expectations created with regard to companies.

In this sense, as the economy is part of society, companies interact in this context in many ways and not simply in terms of sales and purchasing relationships. Trade transactions are also social relationships, which means that understanding the role of companies in society is of fundamental importance, as is the need to take into consideration the social, cultural and symbolic aspects which make up the company/society relationship, in addition to the economic definitions.

According to Davis (1976), economic activities are so bound up with the whole social system that everyone is affected if companies fail to show social responsibility in their operations. Business has activities which are so connected with the whole of society that this makes social responsibility inevitable.

The decentralization of the discussion of social responsibility to beyond the company includes adopting a perspective directed towards the sustainability of the concept itself, since it exposes the need for a real network of business which incorporates the multi-dimensional concept of social responsibility in all relationships with the stakeholders associated with that business network. (Ashley et al., 2000, p.05)

Companies, when analyzed within the context of interactions of which they form part, may certainly be understood in terms of their primary function of producing goods and services, but also as a result of the multiple social relationships that take place within this process of production. This covers not only relationships between capital and labour, but also all the socioeconomic, cultural and subjective interactions that are established and which, to a greater or lesser extent, may determine configurations in the methods of doing and managing business.

At the centre of debates involving CSR are the nature and limits of the responsibilities that the company should have towards society. Here it is important to point out that decisions and actions related to business management are influenced, amongst other factors, by the conception that managers have of the company's role in society. Furthermore, the methods of social pressure and the expectations that created with regard to companies are also the result of how the organizations and society in general understand the role of the company.

CSR in the Brazilian context: appearance and evolution

If we look at the peculiarities of the Brazilian reality, one can note that it is only possible to see the real formation of a national business class from 1930 on. Up until that time business activity in Brazil was embryonic and the economy was based on agro-exports. It was following events such as the First World War, the economic crisis of 1929 and the 1930 Revolution that a rupture with Brazil's colonial past gained pace, thus favouring the process of national industrialization (Brum, 1991).

From the 1950s on, with the establishment of the Juscelino Kubitschek Government, the process of industrial acceleration began to be seen as a fundamental element in the creation of new levels of development within the country. At the same time, the regulatory mechanisms which governed economic interactions in Brazil during the Juscelino government favoured foreign capital, placing Brazil in a position of dependence in relation to larger-scale international economies and resulting in national business elites, to some extent, reproducing this relationship of dependence and expecting the Brazilian State to intervene to promote the national companies to the same levels of competitiveness as those of the foreign companies.

Hence, it can be seen that historically Brazilian companies developed with close ties to the state structure, such that up until the initiation of democracy in the 1970s, the Brazilian private owner showed no concerns regarding the role he could play in social development. On the contrary, he relied on State support and even for investments in infrastructures.

Therefore, having developed under the protection of the State, the Brazilian business class eventually took on a role only in occasional philanthropic and heterogeneous actions, and (...) particularly from the 1980s on it is possible to identify business social activity with the expectation of participating in the social development of the country. (Rico, 2004, p. 2)

Gradually, entrepreneurs and executives operating in Brazil have been made aware that these perverse conditions of the socioeconomic structure of the country heavily restrict the prospects for their businesses to be profitable. Such barriers may be even stronger regarding expectations for the internationalization of companies that are seeking a significant position in the globalized economy. (FISCHER, 2005, p. 8)

The very formation of the Brazilian business class, and the history of the political, cultural and economic constitution of the country is heavily laden with traditions of authoritarianism and patronage, to such an extent that the process of democratization of the country is still in its infancy, which means the effectiveness of relationship channels between companies, the State and civil society is a process which is continuing to mature.

Hence, it is only from the 1990s on that the discussion on CSR began to gain ground in Brazil, motivated simultaneously by the work of academics, the strength of social and environmental movements and the creation of bodies such as the Institutes, Foundations and Companies Group and the ETHOS Institute.

Within this perspective, Cappellin and Giffoni claim that in the early 1990s the expansion of the CSR agenda in Brazil became much stronger by means of corporate donations to projects and bodies outside the company and that, in the context of the restructuring of production, one of the strategies of which was the downsizing of staff and increased employee turnover, it led the business community to defend deregulation of many of the employee rights that had thus far been won. According to these authors, in the second half the same decade, the possibilities for understanding CSR were magnified by factors such as the Child and Adolescent's Statute, the Consumer Protection Code, the Federal Law for the Promotion of Culture and, indeed, the motivation coming from the government of Fernando Henrique Cardoso which, in 1994, launched the Programa Mãos à Obra Brasil (Hands to Work Brazil Programme), reorganizing and stimulating partnerships between the State and Society in the construction of social development.

With regard to the current situation in Brazil, according to data from the last survey conducted by IPEA (2005), between 2000 and 2004, the proportion of companies[1] carrying out some kind of social action grew 10%, from 59% to 69%, which represents a total of 600,000 companies already involved in CSR projects. 50% of the total number of companies that stated that they were involved in some kind of social project were located in the South East, while 29% were in the South, 10% in the North East, 8% in the Central West and 3% in the North (this data corresponds to the actual distribution of companies throughout the different regions of the country).

---

1 According to this research 58% of Brazilian companies are currently located in the South East, 30% in the South, 9% in the Central West, 9% in the North East and 4% in the North (IPEA, 2005).

Given the sheer size of Brazil in geographical terms, as well as the particular characteristics under which the economy of each region develops, it is not possible to treat social responsibility as an unambiguous theoretical and practical construct in the Brazilian reality. However, one can point out that, even if we set aside the differences, the issue of CSR has gradually been occupying more space both in academic studies and in the sphere of business discussions. This reflects a breakthrough since, according to Swift and Zadek (2002), many strategies for sustainable development and an increase in the competitive power of regions and / or countries can gain greater potential if they are developed in partnerships between government, civil society and business.

CSR in the Portuguese context: the existence of different realities

In Portugal, the theme of social responsibility is framed within the context of worldwide agreements and the strategies defined within the European Union. As part of the European Union, Portugal is profoundly influenced by many of its principles, since these are closer to the reality of Portuguese companies, not only in terms of geographic proximity, but due to the institutional context and the predominance of trade agreements established in this region, where CSR is becoming an inescapable presence.

Following the guidelines of the European Commission, in 1998 the Portuguese government introduced the National Plan for Economic and Social Development (PNDES 2000-2006) and in 2007 the National Strategy for Sustainable Development (ENDS 2015), as well as the respective Implementation Plan (PIENDS). This establishes guidelines and measures for sustainable development, with implications for the promotion of social responsibility. Despite a strong institutionalization that reflects the direct involvement of the Portuguese government, the progressive movement towards affirming social responsibility has been triggered mainly by the business sector, not only in the context of large companies (both due to the weight of their history as public companies with a strong public service tradition, and the need to fall in line with a trend followed by their multinational counterparts, mainly European and North American ones), but also in the context of small and medium-sized enterprises (SMEs), which despite not having heightened awareness, have adopted some of these practices as principles of good management.

This movement towards the affirmation of CSR, considering the way it has recently been viewed (from the perspective of management strategy aimed at promoting sustainable development), is quite recent in Portugal, and public awareness of the issue dates mainly from the beginning of this century. In order to better understand the position of Portuguese companies regarding the adoption of CSR practices two studies were carried out. One of these focused on the reality of large companies (Santos et al, 2005) and another on small and medium enterprises (Santos et al, 2006), as it was felt that, as stated in the first part of this article, the context has a strong influence on the actions of companies and there are profoundly different realities and frameworks.

The research carried out on large national companies (Santos et al, 2005) showed that there has been a growing commitment to the principles of sustainable development and social responsibility. This movement is, however, quite recent, with the first sustainability reports only being published after 2000, with a noticeable lag in relation to the movement seen in many other multinational companies, particularly in the European Union. However, despite the lack of a formalized policy of sustainability, the fact that many of the larger companies analyzed were public companies in the past means that the principle of the public good was already a part of the culture of some of these companies and they therefore already engaged in social responsibility practices. Nevertheless, these actions are mostly diffuse in nature and not sufficiently systematic, not having been managed strategically.

The developments noted are in the sense of greater inclusion of sustainability in the organizational strategy and efforts to define an appropriate governance framework that reflects a coherent and consistent vision of a responsible company. Linked to this position there has also been a demand for greater organization and systematization of the various practices adopted. The extension of these principles to subcontractors or suppliers and, above all, the development of community oriented actions present themselves as the main thrust in the establishment of a practice of corporate social responsibility that is progressively extending nationwide.

Despite the attempt to frame strategic CSR within the corporate mission and vision, the importance of philanthropy is still apparent in external social responsibility, in some cases with CSR being reduced to little more than cash donations or support to social projects developed primarily by other agents. These actions are often to promote the company's image and have limited impact on the community to which they are directed. While there are some symbolic social responsibility projects at the national or even local level, there is not a corporate culture that considers the social role of the company beyond the creation of value. A culture of citizenship and direct involvement in the community is rare. By way of an example we may consider the reduced level of Corporate Volunteering in Portugal, which is often the chosen form for more direct involvement of the company in the exercise of citizenship.

Regarding CSR actions aimed at employees, it appears that there still remains a strategy which is heavily focused on the training of technical skills geared towards exercising the profession and, in the case of large companies, some of which are traditionally linked to the public sector, there is a strong emphasis on social support provided to employees. However, actions to promote employability, work / life balance, gender equality, support for minorities and social cohesion are still greatly lacking. At the environmental level, eco-efficiency and the use of alternative energy are efforts which should be mentioned, in addition to the commitment to improving the quality of products and services and the expansion of SR to the value chain by the imposition to select suppliers that incorporate principles of social and environmental responsibility.

For small and medium-sized enterprises CSR presents a different challenge (Santos et al 2006). Since these are often overwhelmed by time constraints, money and resources, CSR is essentially linked to effective management: increased motivation of employees, reduction in energy consumption, improved customer relationships or explanation of product characteristics. Corporate social responsibility thus appears in SMEs appears implicitly and in an unstructured fashion. It is a result of the search for greater efficiency in the management of resources, and a focus on business benefits that can be generated through increased efficiency. The focus is oriented towards the adoption of simple, inexpensive and practical gains. Many companies know almost instinctively that their success depends heavily on good communication with customers, providing support services or, for example, establishing a good relationship with the local community of which they are a partMoreover, due to increasingly aggressive global markets many multinational companies impose a set of social and environmental rules on the management of SMEs, requiring them to incorporate some of these principles. In this case, the prior establishing of a set of practices for subcontractors in their value chain means that the exercise of social responsibility in SMEs is also the result of ideologies imposed from the outside, which do not always correspond to an attitude which is truly at the company's heart.

To corroborate this fact it may be pointed out that, according to the 2003 Corporate Responsibility Index published by Accountability, Portugal is in 21st place in the ranking, after the other 14 EU countries, with the exception of Greece, and just below Japan and the USA. Moreover, Portugal is at the bottom of the list of the EU-15 in some important indices such as income per capita, productivity, level of education, lifelong training and number of fatal accidents at work. In areas such as education, the country is also behind all the new EU partners. This situation makes even more evident the reduced impact that certain business practices have had, especially in areas such as the prevention of accidents at work, equality in income levels and non- discrimination in relation to gender, among others, these being areas where companies have a strong impact and, consequently, a lot of work to do.

Final Considerations

To sum up, one can state that both Brazil and Portugal have seen a growing commitment to the principles of sustainable development and CSR. In general the inclusion of a notion of citizenship and concern for the principles of economic, social and environmental sustainability is visible. Linked to this position, there has been a systematization of the CSR practices adopted. There has also been an attempt to minimize environmental impacts and an affirmation of the exercise of citizenship embodied in the implementation of various social projects established in partnership with various organizations of the civil society. The extension of these principles to subcontractors or suppliers and, above all, the development of community oriented actions present themselves as undeniable strengths in the establishment of a practice of corporate social responsibility that is progressively being felt in both countries.

However, the incremental nature of this process should also be highlighted and the need to systematically search for improvements in performance in each of these areas. This is because, despite the importance that CSR has taken on in the business context, the actions carried out are still at the micro level. The initiatives appear to be fragmented and often disconnected from the core business of companies. They are often the result of isomorphic actions with a low level of commitment, where the importance of philanthropy is still strong. The predominance of an ideology of sporadic action has prevented social responsibility from being considered strategically as a means of achieving higher levels of global sustainability.

Without undervaluing the important advances in terms of socially responsible behavior that have been seen in many businesses and organizations in both countries, the fact is that in general this ideology of micro policy has had very limited impact. In this sense, the actions carried out address specific problems but do not solve structural problems. This is due, among other factors, to the predominance of an understanding of the role of business which does not call into question the principle that corporate profit is the ultimate goal but ought instead to include / take into consideration the people that make up the human framework of the corporate structure, the community where the company carries on business and with which it interacts (creation of social value) and the preservation of the environment.

References

Ashley, P.; Soares, T & Macedo (2001). Um Modelo Conceitual para a Incorporação da Responsabilidade Social à Governança das Relações Negócio-sociedade. Texto apresentado ao ENANPAD 2001, Área: Teoria das Organizações e publicado em Resumo dos Trabalhos – ENANPAD 2001 sob a codificação TEO185.

Brum, A. (1991). O Desenvolvimento Econômico Brasileiro. Petropólis – RJ: Vozes, Ijuí – RS: FIDENE.

Cappellin, P. & Giffoni, R. (2007). A Responsabilidade Social no Norte e no Sul. In Dossiê Globalização e Trabalho: perspectiva comparativa entre Norte e Sul. Caderno CRH, Vol. 20, N. 51, Salvador, Set/Dez,.

Fisher, M. (2005). Estado, Mercado e Terceiro Setor: uma Análise Conceitual das Parcerias Intersetoriais, in Revista Administração, São Paulo, v.40, n.1, Jan./Fev./Mar., p. 5-18.

Garriga, E. & Melé, D. (2004). Corporate Social Responsibility Theories: Mapping the Territory. Journal of Business Ethics, 53, 51-71,

Instituto de Pesquisa Econômica Aplicada. (2005). Pesquisa Ação Social das Empresas. Disponível em www.ipea.org.br, acesso em 29/10/05, (IPEA).

MORI. (2000). "The first ever European Survey of Consumers' attitudes towards Corporate Social Responsibility", November.

Observatory of European SMEs (2002). "Report 2002/No 4 – European SMEs and Social and Environmental Responsibility". Observatory of European SMEs.

Pinto, G. (2004). Corporate Social Responsibility, State of Art in Portugal 2004. CSR/SME – Promoting Social Responsibility in Small and Medium Size Enterprises Report. CECOA.

Rico, E. (2004). A responsabilidade social empresarial e o Estado: uma aliança para o desenvolvimento sustentável. São Paulo em Perspectiva, Vl.18, N.4, São Paulo, Out/Dez,.

Rego, A.; Cunha, M.; Costa, N.; Gonçalves, H.; Cabral-Cardoso, C. (2006). Gestão Ética e Socialmente Responsável. Lisboa, Editora RH.

Santos, M.; Silva, J.; Santos, A. & Pereira, E. (2006). Responsabilidade Social nas PME – Casos em Portugal. Lisboa, RH Editora.

Santos, M.; Eusébio, C.; Almeida, J.; Lopes, P., & Sampaio, J. (2005). Desenvolvimento Sustentável e Responsabilidade Empresarial, Oeiras, Celta Editora.

Swift, T. & Zadek, S. (2002) Corporate Responsibility and the Competitive Advantage of Nations. The Copenhagen Centre and Accountability.

Zadek, S. (2001). The Civil Corporation: the new economy of corporate citizenship. London, Earthscan Publications Lda.

Labour & Sustainable Development

György Széll

"Workers and their trade unions can make a significant and positive difference to the sustainable management of the environment and ecosystems. Workers are social agents directly associated with the production chain. Meanwhile, workers are all too often among the first victims of environmental damage."
(UNEP, 2007, p. VI)

Abstract

The Copenhagen Summit on a Post-Kyoto regulation of Climate Change in December 2009 demonstrated the urgency of action to be taken to save our planet from many more man-made disasters (UN 2009). At the centre of the environmental problems, which were created by modern capitalism and industrialisation, is the production process, i.e. labour. The responsibility lies in the decision-making process about *who*, decides *what, when, how, where* and *for whom* products and services are made (Széll 1994 a, b). Henceforth, for a sustainable future all stakeholders have to be involved. Environmental problems are global ones, however, manifest themselves on the local and regional level. Therefore the need for coordinated action of science, civil society, business and politics on these levels to stop further degradation and develop sustainable alternatives.

For this purpose innovation – not only technological but foremost social innvoation – is necessary. To promote innovations education and research are at the forefront. Better education for the biggest possible number and research, which is truly interdisciplinary, are preconditions. Education and research are first of all public goods. Their privatisation and commercialisation have led to ignorance about environmental problems, focussing largely on growth and profitmaking. Instead the public sector has to be strengthened – preventing at the same time widespread corruption – to allow sustainable education and research.

Corporate Social Responsibility (CSR) is another important issue. CSR means social *and* environmental responsibility. In this context trade unions and works councils have a special duty, not only in formulating sustainable business strategies, but especially in implementing them.

China has recently become the third biggest national economy in the world, and will certainly – with its ongoing high growth rates – soon overtake Japan and the USA as well to become number one. However, its boom over the last three decades has been highly paid with large environmental destruction. Some of its cities and regions are amongst the most polluted ones in the world. A central role for sustainability – like in many other Third World countries – plays the informal sector, which by its definition is unregulated – not only socially, but also environmentally. A specific challenge in this regard is migration. China has even officially some 225 million migrant workers, who are suffering from and at the same time producing environmental hazards (ITUC 2010; Széll 2010).

China's future will decide about the future of our sustainability and by it of the future of humankind. Therefore to hold this important congress in Peking – at one of its most prestigious universities and its very enlightened school of labour and human resources – is a privilege and at the same time a unique opportunity.

Content

Some Basics

I will start with a citation from the United Nations Environmental Programme agency:

> "Labour and the Environment have long been perceived as an issue vested with highly conflicting interests. Most of the world population relies on natural resources and the environment for wages, if not simply for survival. Many workers share the fear that strengthened environmental policies will lead to job losses. However, perceptions of conflicting interests have evolved over the years. A number of studies, as well as practical experience, have made it clear that changing production and consumption patterns and adopting new techniques and methods – which are among the alternative ways out of the current environmental crisis – will foster job creation. Protecting our natural resource base and the environment will actually contribute to protecting employment and fighting poverty." (UNEP, 2007, p. VIII)

To remember: labour is the only value creating activity (cf. Adam Smith, Karl Marx, David Ricardo etc.), and we are living in really existing capitalism as the dominant mode of production. However, at the same time in many countries – mostly in the Second and Third World – the informal sector has become the largest. Besides these two sectors there survives still in many places the subsistence economy. Actually this kind of economy, which respects nature, has been for thousands of years a sustainable way of reproduction for humankind.

After all, what is sustainable development? Actually the concept derives from forestry in the late 19th century. It has been reintroduced on a more general level by the so-called Brundtland-Commission, i.e. the commission for environment and development of the United Nations with its famous report "Our Common Future" (1987), which led to the first *United Nations Conference Environment and Development* in Rio de Janeiro in 1992, producing the Agenda 21.[1] The main idea of sustainable development is that we should leave the planet at least in a situation, as we found it, or even in a better shape. Sustainability means in this understanding that it is ecological as well as *social*, as the Social Agenda 21 demonstrates!

Already in 1972 the alarm was ringing with the first report "Limits to growth" by the Club of Rome. Since then many international conferences followed, leading amongst others to the Kyoto Protocol in 1997, however, definitely the destruction of the environment has not really been stopped since then. Therefore a moral radical change is needed. Since a couple of years a number of scientists propagate factor 4, 5 or even factor 10 (Weizsäcker et al. 1997; 2010; Bleischwitz 2002). That means that with the same input of energy and resources you reach an output four, five times or even ten times higher. So, besides prevention of waste and unnecessary production as well as consumption, higher resource effiency is the main target for sustainibility. This approach of *Sustainable Production and Consumption* has been convincingly presented by Peter Hennicke, the successor of Ernst Ulrich von Weizsäcker as president of the Wuppertal Institute, in his keynote during the China's Social Sciences and Humanities Forum 2010 and also before (Hennicke 2009; 2010)

1 Agenda 21 is one of five agreements adopted at the 1992 UN Conference on Environment and Development (UNCED) in Rio de Janeiro. "These [agreements] establish governing principles and commit governments to a range of post-Rio processes, centred upon the provision of national reports which may be compared internationally and against a limited set of goals established. Agenda 21 forms the general guiding document for pursuing sustainable development and initiates significant institutional changes" (Grubb and others, 1993, p. xiii). Chapter 29 of Agenda 21 focuses on strengthening the role of workers and their trade unions in sustainable development activities. "[Its] main concern is 'poverty alleviation and full and sustainable employment, which contribute to safe, clean and healthy environments ...' Tripartite collaboration between governments, trade unions and employers' organizations should be established, particularly on the implementation of Agenda 21. ILO conventions on workers' freedom of association and on the right to organize should be ratified and implemented. Environmental policies should be jointly developed by workers' and employers' organizations. Workers and trade unions should have access to relevant information. Education, training and retraining programmes, particularly on the working environment, should be strengthened. Other trade union activities should focus on participation in sustainable development activities of local communities and on regional and international organizations." (Grubb and others, 1993, pp. 139-40) The complete text of Agenda 21 is available on the UN Division of Sustainable Development site (www.un.org/esa/sustdev/documents/agenda21).

This approach is the answer to'All power to the market!', which has been proclaimed by neo-liberals over the last thirty years, and which had led not only to the ecological and social mess, in which we are right now, but also to the recent world-wide financial and economic crises – the worst in over eighty years. As we should have learnt previously the market is not and can never be objective: Interests and psychology come in, so perfect markets as taught in business manuals are never possible; especially the labour market has its own rules, and after all no long-term effects can be seriously calculated, e.g. with the costs of nuclear waste. So short terminism is dominant – as also in the practices of bonuses for managers. Therefore for sustainability we need a *Stakeholder Democracy* instead of *Shareholder Dictatorship*. And its fundamental base remains the civil society, including science, notably social sciences.

The challenges

The main challenges are twofold: the environmental and the decent work challenges. UNEP has summarized the main points in the following two boxes:

Box 1: The dual challenge in numbers

Environmental challenge
• Climate-related disasters: 262 million people affected annually over the period 2000-2004 • Water shortages: 1.8 billion expected to suffer from fresh water scarcity by 2025, mostly in Asia and Africa • Environmental refugees: 50 million people potentially forced to become environmental refugees by climate change over the next few years • Displacement by flooding: 330 million people increasingly exposed to flooding in coastal areas, flood plains of rivers and small island States • Food shortages and malnutrition: currently affect 180 million people and threaten to affect 600 million people by 2080 • Pollution: 2 million premature deaths globally each year due to indoor and outdoor air pollution
• Loss of biodiversity: the great majority of well-studied species are declining in distribution, abundance or both. Biological products and processes make up 40 per cent of the global economy. Poor people, especially those living in areas of low agricultural productivity, depend heavily on the genetic diversity of the environment.

Decent work challenge
• Working poor: 1.3 billion in the world with earnings too low to lift them and their dependants above the poverty threshold of $2 per day (more than 43 per cent of the global workforce) • Unemployed: 190 million globally • Young job seekers: over 500 million additional job-seekers over the next 10 years • Insecurity: 5.3 billion people without access to any social security coverage • Access to energy: 1.6 billion people without access to modern energy (almost 1 in 4 humans living today) • Adequate housing: 1 billion slum dwellers in poor housing lacking essential facilities such as clean water and sanitation.
(UNEP, 2008, p. 2)

State of the art

Checking the different institutions, I arrived at the following results, which present the main initiatives to cope with the challenges presented above:

The Green Jobs Initiative

is a partnership established in 2007 between the United Nations Environment Programme (UNEP), the International Labour Organization (ILO), and the International Trade Union Confederation (ITUC). The International Organization of Employers (IOE) joined the Initiative in 2008. Its programme is described as follows:

"Workers and trade unions are among the largest and most important major groups of civil society, with increasing interaction with UNEP's activities and policy dialogue since 2002. According to Chapter 29 of Agenda 21, 'workers and trade unions should play an active role in the sustainable development activities of international and regional organizations, particularly within the United Nations system.' UNEP's current initiative to build a partnership on labour and the environment is an extension of its efforts to engage *major groups and stakeholders* in its work and to establish a meaningful dialogue with civil society, as key stakeholders in the international environmental policy arena.[2] The objectives of the initiative were:

2 See the UNEP Major Groups and Stakeholders Branch website (www.unep.org/civil_society/major_groups).

(i) to reinforce the social and labour dimension of environmental conservation and sustainable development,
(ii) to strengthen the relationship between UNEP and the world of labour in addressing the integration of an equitable industrial development and environmental protection,
(iii) to address the gap in representation of workers and trade unions in international environmental processes, as they can uniquely stimulate debate around the social aspects of sustainable development while at the same time contributing to the debate on economic and environmental dimensions.

The process of engagement has been initiated in June 2005, in close consultation and collaboration with the workers and trade unions, in an attempt to build greater ownership of the engagement process into the trade union movement. This process has yielded, among other activities, the Trade Union Assembly on Labour and the Environment / WILL 2006 and this publication." (UNEP, 2007, pp. X-XI)

UNEP's Labour & Environment Initiative

"aims at strengthening the role of international labour communities in areas related to environmental development in particular and sustainable development in general. It also aims at promoting the active participation of workers and their trade unions in decisions on the design, implementation and evaluation of national and international policies and programmes on environment and development."

Making the environment a focus of collective bargaining

"One year after the Trade Union Assembly on Labour and the Environment / WILL 2006, the United Nations Environment Programme presented the publication *Labour and the Environment: A Natural Synergy* during a side event on the occasion of the 24th Session of the UNEP Governing Council and Global Environmental Ministerial Forum on 5th February 2007. *Labour and the Environment: A Natural Synergy* is a joint publication by UNEP, the International Labour Organization (ILO), the World Health Organization (WHO), workers and trade unions through the International Trade Union Confederation (ITUC), and the International Labour Foundation for Sustainable Development (Sustainlabour). [It] addresses critical issues such as the importance of providing for just employment transitions. It reports on initiatives adopted throughout the world to reduce pressures on natural resources and the environment while leading to job creation. This publication will contribute to a common understanding of the nexus between labour, the environment and sustainable development, and of the need to build partnerships and alliances to forge an environmentally sustainable global economy.

The publication pictures examples of the application of technical expertise, of workplace participation, and of tools that promote workers' health and safety to problems that extend beyond the workplace into areas such as environmental protection, public health and the accountability of employers. Examples are cited of the incorporation of environmental matters in collective bargaining and in agreements at the workplace, nationally and internationally. One key message of the publication is that broad evaluation of development alternatives and integrated policies is of fundamental importance if we are to avoid perpetuating traditional trade-offs between social, environmental and economic objectives. It is clear that environmentally related changes (such as those resulting from or responding to climate change, and the necessary transformations of production and consumption patterns) will have socio-economic impacts on labour. Protecting the environment and ecosystem services, and ensuring decent jobs and just transition, must be treated as common sustainable development policy objectives. Workers and trade unions need to support and contribute to the necessary shift in post-modern industrialization and its models. Beyond new employment opportunities, moving towards a more environmentally friendly and sustainable global economical model represents an opportunity to contribute to poverty reduction and to tackle related issues, such as how the benefits of free trade are distributed. What is required, trade unions say, is a shift to participatory management of change, which values worker innovation, empowerment and responsibility, and an acceptance of fundamental rights and freedoms.

UNEP, ILO, WHO, ITUC, and Sustainlabour seized the opportunities to outline areas of cooperation for further implementing the Resolution of the Trade Union Assembly on Labour and the Environment / WILL 2006. Partners agreed to jointly implement a project proposal on "Strengthening trade union participation in international environmental processes." The overall objective of the project will be to improve engagement of workers and trade unions in the development and implementation of environmental policy, e.g. at UNEP, MEAs, and other UN constituencies, with a view to improve environmental and sustainable development policies. The project will focus on Africa, Asia Pacific and Latin America and the Caribbean, and on capacity building – looking to other areas of mutual interest including training and educating on the latest developments in international environmental law in areas such as the newly adopted chemicals treaties; awareness raising; and adaptation/replication of selected case studies presented at the Assembly. In addition further areas of research such as "Green jobs, employment and environment: Environment and employment opportunities" were identified.

Sustainlabour

"Sustainlabour was founded and has grown with the belief that workers can play a fundamental role in the route to a sustainable world. Trade unions are in a unique position to stimulate the social aspects of sustainable development while at the same time can contribute to the economic and environmental dimensions. Workplaces are at the centre of production and consumption, therefore they should be central locations in any effort aimed to change production and consumption patterns at local, national and international levels. We envision a world which is just and egalitarian for the present generation and for the generations to come, where finite resources are fairly distributed and sustainability is ensured, where environmental and social needs are taken into account as much as the economic ones, where human rights- including workers' rights and the environment are universally respected.
... To involve Trade Union in environmental debates
... To integrate labour issues in the environmental agenda
... To engage workers in defence of the environment
... To encourage changes that are in favour of the environment and workers
To reinforce the labour movement, we aim to:
Promote sustainable development by strengthening its social and labour dimension.
Encourage the participation of workers and their organizations in sustainable development policies at local, regional and international levels. This should be done by addressing worker and trade union needs and gathering the benefits of their roles, skills, resources and along with possible contributions.
Support the engagement of trade unions in Sustainable Development through a variety of innovative worker actions.
Quite simply, it is common sense for us to pull together, and revitalize our struggle for the protection of a healthy resource rich environment for all of us along with the unborn generations to come.
The current model of development is socially unfair and environmentally unsustainable. This means the world must and will change. It also means that our production and consumption models will undergo a deep transformation. Understanding these changes and its consequences for workers and their communities is one of the major challenges the Trade Union movement needs to address. Therefore, we, the workers and the Trade Unions, should organise and strategise a debate and decide on our courses of action.
We at Sustainlabour firmly believe a sustainable and fair development requires broader labour rights along with environmental protection. The creation of decent and environmentally responsible jobs is the only way to guarantee the livelihoods of the millions of workers that live today on this planet. Workers and their Trade Unions can play a fundamental role on the path to a Sustainable World, a more central and active role than the one they have played so far. Integrating the environmental dimension in the trade union agendas is a real challenge but also a necessity that must be faced by Trade UnionsTo advance towards the trade unionism of the 21st century, we must integrate the environment in our policies. Otherwise, we won't be able to ensure our coherence as a social movement, and to guarantee to devise and elaborate an economic development based on justice. To facilitate/guarantee the participation and intervention of workers at workplaces and also at local, regional and international level, it is necessary to:
count on capacity building mechanisms,
have access to training materials and facilities, and
develop technical assistance systems as working tools. Sustainlabour wants to facilitate training and technical assistance for Trade Union organisations.

'Partners of Sustainlabour' is a structure created in 2005 to integrate organizations willing to develop strategic alliances with Sustainlabour. Objectives:
To build a network to advice for trade unions,
to receive advice on activities and programs,
to obtain financial support,
to spread word of Sustainlabour's objectives and activities receiving advice on activities, programs and initiatives.
Sustainlabour will only approve partnership from non-for-profit organisations which have objectives that are consistent with the Foundation aims of promoting human and labour rights and sustainable development"

South Centre

The South Centre is another initiative, which cares much about migration. Actually concerning the relationship of labour and sustainibility demography has to be taken into account. One side is the demographic increase of human population, although it has been everywhere slowed down – notably in China with its on-child policy, but also in most rich countries, and even in South Korea and Taiwan – world population is still forecasted to grow until the year 2050 up to 9 billion people. And there with our lifestyle the sustainibility of the earth for humans is nearly reached.[3]

"The issue of migration across international borders, primarily for work purposes, is structurally linked to the issue of global development. Existing global development inequities, especially between North and South, and the inability of many developing countries to provide adequate and decent employment opportunities for their people as a result of these inequities, contribute greatly to cross-border migration flows. Migration, therefore, has a synergistic relationship with the South's development prospects. It can provide positive developmental benefits but also, if not harnessed well, may result in further developmental challenges. …

Today's migration flows reflect the basic structural inequalities that exist in the current global economic system. People without decent livelihood opportunities in their home countries often have no other choice than to risk everything and seek such opportunities in a foreign country, away from home and family. Migrant workers most often come from developing countries that are unable to provide their people with adequate livelihood opportunities. This inability to do so by many developing countries is often the result of structural economic deficiencies that have not yet been effectively addressed. While doing so is primar-

3 Specialists argue that with the energy of the sun and based on a vegetarian lifestyle the maximum population on earth is between 12 to 15 billion people. But this would already demand a fundamental revolution of lifestyle for every human being, and not taking into account the ongoing deterioration of our climate.

ily a national responsibility, the global community also has the responsibility to cooperate and assist developing countries put in place the policies and measures needed to remedy such deficiencies, develop their economies sustainably, and enable developing countries to provide adequate economic livelihood opportunities for their people. The development of developing countries should be the primary policy objective upon which migration initiatives must be based. Only through the achievement of development and the creation of adequate employment opportunities at the national level can migration be made a choice rather than a necessity. The ability of migrant workers, their families, and their home countries to benefit from remittance flows must be enhanced and facilitated.

The human rights of migrant workers, including their freedom of association and to benefit from labor legislation in their home and host countries, should be promoted and protected. The brain drain caused by the outflow of skilled workers from developing countries needs to be addressed in a creative way so as to ensure that the human capital, skilled labor pool, and the productive and service provision capacities of developing countries are not lost. In order to do this, developing countries should be able to exercise policy flexibility individually and in collaboration with their international development partners so as to ensure that the best conditions possible for their migrant workers are made available overseas while at the same time creating jobs at home. Cooperation at the national and international levels among governments and all other relevant stakeholders is needed.

In this regard, the High Level Dialogue is therefore an important forum that developing countries need to engage in insofar as migration issues are concerned. In that forum, the linkage between development and migration must be highlighted. Developing countries need to ensure that the migration debate is centered on the need to promote the development of developing countries rather than on "end of pipe" approaches (e.g. border control or immigration and employment policies) that tend to be favored by developed countries."

The International Labour Organisation

The best summary for the 2007 ILO's stance on the topic is the Director-General's introduction to the International Labour Conference 'Decent work for sustainable development':

> "1. A balanced approach to sustainable development
> I believe that an overarching issue that we are facing, at the national and international levels, is to reach agreement on much more effective ways of implementing a well-balanced approach to sustainable development, within which its social, economic and environmental pil-

> lars are fully integrated. In the ILO, we need to anchor the vision of sustainable development as the overriding policy paradigm within which the Decent Work Agenda can make its key contribution to development.
> We should recall that, at the Johannesburg World Summit on Sustainable Development in September 2002, a commitment was made to "promote the integration of the three components of sustainable development – economic development, social development and environmental protection – as interdependent and mutually reinforcing pillars. Poverty eradication, changing unsustainable patterns of production and consumption and protecting and managing the natural resource base of economic and social development are overarching objectives of, and essential requirements for, sustainable development". This built on Principle 4 of the Rio Declaration on Environment and Development of 1992, which states that: "In order to achieve sustainable development, environmental protection shall constitute an integral part of the development process and cannot be considered in isolation from it."

What economists call market failures are really policy failures. They have created serious imbalances, with attendant social and political reactions that can be measured in polls, observed in elections and, increasingly, seen in the streets. Together with the many benefits that certain categories can be seen to have gained in all countries, the World Commission on the Social Dimension of Globalization has warned us that the "current process of globalization is generating unbalanced outcomes, both between and within countries. (…) These global imbalances are morally unacceptable and politically unsustainable."

The ILO's tripartism has its feet well planted on the sound governance of the labour market with a view to achieving fair, productive and competitive market economies. I therefore believe that it can play a central role in defining the convergence of public policies and market mechanisms that is needed to achieve the balances that are essential for sustainable development. The discussion on the promotion of sustainable enterprises at the Conference this year is therefore particularly timely. Promoting sustainable enterprises is about strengthening the institutions and governance systems which nurture enterprises – strong and efficient markets need strong and effective institutions. It is also about ensuring that human, financial and natural resources are combined equitably and efficiently in order to achieve innovation and enhanced productivity. This calls for new forms of cooperation between government, business and society to ensure that the quality of present and future life (and employment) is maximized, while safeguarding the sustainability of the planet.

The ILO is able to inject more energy into the drive for a fully integrated approach to sustainable development because it is in workplaces that the social, economic and environmental dimensions come together inseparably. I am also convinced that, to ensure the progress of our Decent Work Agenda, we will have to situate it more clearly in a framework of sustainable development. We need more and better jobs, especially in societies suffering from widespread poverty, but they must also have the quality of sustainability. What does that mean?

In social terms, such jobs must be open to all equally and the related rewards have to be equitable. Inequality and discrimination provoke frustration and anger, and they are a recipe for social dislocation and political instability. In economic terms, jobs have to be productive and able to compete on a competitive market. And, environmentally, they must involve the use of natural resources in ways that conserve the planet for future generations, while being safe for working women and men and for the community. Social inequality within and between nations, exacerbated by the uneven distribution of the benefits and costs of globalization, is a serious threat to sustainable development. Open markets are leading to an intensification of competition on domestic and export markets, thereby creating the need for enterprises throughout the world to maintain a constant improvement in their performance or to risk going under. Shifting our consumption of resources to much less environmentally destructive patterns will create many opportunities for poverty reduction through decent work, and will also drive significant adjustments in enterprises and employment.

Sustainable lives for people, sustainable enterprises and a sustainable environment for the planet are interlinked; they have to be built through collective action from the local to the global levels. We have to start thinking further ahead than the preoccupation with day-to-day survival in the market. Sustainability in all its three dimensions places the ILO's tripartite constituents under the obligation to plan how opportunities are to be taken and adjustments managed in an equitable manner.

> Market-driven economies, without effective public policies and strong social partners, do not automatically promote social inclusion, nor do they create enough routes to productive and decent work for the disadvantaged. Nor do unregulated markets internalize environmental costs or reflect them in price structures. If we are to anticipate the impact of the accelerating rate of social, economic and environmental transformation that has been set in motion by the opening of national economies to stronger international and domestic competition, and to establish appropriate policies, it is necessary to strengthen the capacity of States for action and the capacity of tripartism for cooperation. Sustainable development requires a strong and generally agreed public framework of rules and regulations. The aim, however, must be to avoid the burden of an overly centralized and bureaucratic State, with all the attendant risks of stifling innovation and competition. Tripartism is one of the most promising routes for the development of a strong social infrastructure, in which employers' organizations and trade unions can promote the dialogue and trust needed to ensure compliance with generally agreed rules, thereby reducing the need for costly mechanisms of state enforcement." (ILC 96-2007/ Report I (A), pp. 7-9)

The ILO has also ordered a quite important report by Lene Olsen "The Employment Effects of Climate Change and Climate Change Responses: A Role for International Labour Standards?" in 2009.

Child labour [4]

One of the main issues in the context of labour and sustainable development is the issue of child labour, because it harms our future directly, if children are exploited and their health and safety destroyed. The worst forms of child labour are defined in the Worst Forms of Child Labour Convention, 1999 (No. 182) they are:

> "(a) all forms of slavery or practices similar to slavery, such as the sale and trafficking of children, debt bondage and serfdom and forced or compulsory labour, including forced or compulsory recruitment of children for use in armed conflict;
> (b) the use, procuring or offering of a child for prostitution, for the production of pornography or pornographic performances;
> (c) the use, procuring or offering of a child for illicit activities, in particular for the production and trafficking of drugs as defined in the relevant international treaties;
> (d) work which, by its nature or the circumstances in which it is carried out, is likely to harm the health, safety or morals of children. Recommendation 190, accompanying Convention No. 182, provides further guidance."

Zero Emission Research Initiative/ZERI

One of the most interesting initiatives in the field of business and sustainability has been ZERI, which was created by a Belgian business man, Gunter Pauli, in 1994 together with the United Nations University in Tokyo. (Kuehr 2007a; Kühr & Széll 1997) Because I still consider it – although it had to face major problems in the past – as one of the most fascinating and promising initiatives. I will give here space for its own self-description, because it cannot be presented better:

> "ZERI has demonstrated that it is possible to increase productivity while creating new jobs. ZERI's founder, Gunter Pauli, has observed that economists tend to focus on the productivity of labour and capital, and on producing more with less people and less risk capital. But by including the productivity of raw materials, ZERI can change that paradigm; for, by using waste and unused resources, we can generate more income as well as more jobs while also reducing levels of pollution. ... Africa should be proud of its leadership in this area. Indeed, the ZERI initiative has also become an important platform for North-South co-operation.' (Kofi Annan, Secretary-General of the United Nations)

---

4 including in the following instruments, documents and events:
- ILO Minimum Age Convention, No. 138 (1973);
- UN Convention on the Rights of the Child (1989);
- Copenhagen Declaration on Social Development (1995);
- International Child Labour Conferences in Amsterdam and Oslo (both 1997);
- ILO Declaration on the Fundamental Principles and Rights at Work (1998);
- ILO Worst Forms of Child Labour Convention, 1999 (No.182);
- World Fit for Children (2002), outcome document of the 2002 UNGASS on Children;
- Global Action Plan against the Worst Forms of Child Labour (2006)
- ILO Declaration on Social Justice for a Fair Globalization (2008).

'These are exciting concepts, which point towards a more holistic view of sustainable development than anything debated to date.' (Paul Scott, Tomorrow Magazine)
'Zero Emissions, industrial clustering and the other concepts and practices associated with them represent a crucial link in the gradually emerging network of ideas that can lead us out of our crisis.' (Fritjof Capra, Physicist, Systems theorist and author of 'The Web of Life')
'As we search for new ways to control our impact on the world's environment, it is important to set ourselves demanding targets. While at first sight the goal of Zero Emissions, which is examined in this book, may seem beyond our reach, I believe it has importance in focusing our quest for solutions to a complex problem.' (Rodney Chase, Deputy Group Chief Executive, BP International Limited) 'The goal is zero: zero accidents, zero waste, zero emissions.' (Edgar S. Woolard Jr., Former Chairman, DuPont)
'With early success stories from Fiji, Namibia and Colombia highlighted in this book, Gunter Pauli demonstrates that it is not anymore a question if Zero Emissions works or not, but rather when it will be implemented all around the world.' (Sarwono Kusumaatmadja, Chair, UN Convention on Biodiversity, 1996)
'Zero Emissions will be the standard for industry in the 21st century.' (1996 White Book on the Environment, The Environment Agency, Japan)
'These are exciting concepts, which point towards a more holistic view of sustainable development than anything debated to date. The current case studies centre on projects in the tropics- important enough in view of the increasing environmental and social impacts in the developing world. More significantly, if they are shown to work they might help change the industrial mindset in the developed world.' (Tomorrow magazine) 'Pauli's treatise is compelling ... [he] clearly knows his stuff, and serves up new concepts and terminology every few pages. But woven through are inspiring stories of enterprises in a variety of countries that have prospered by creating closed loop systems.' (The Green Business Letter, n.d.) 'The discussed cases show that not only can pollution and waste be reduced to zero, but at the same time income and amount of jobs can be increased. The whole of society will benefit from it.' (International Journal of Environment and Pollution, n.d.)"

Upsizing: The Road to Zero Emissions, More Jobs, More Income and No Pollution

" 'Zero Emissions' has become a definitive term in the debate on sustainable development. While considered a utopian target by some, the concept describes what business and industry of the future must aim to achieve: no pollution and no waste. This volume presents findings from the research work of over 2000 scientists undertaken under the banner of ZERI (Zero Emissions Research Initiative), a business foundation working jointly with UNDP (United Nations Development Programme) in a number of developing countries. Gunter Pauli feels that if we are serious about creating jobs, generating more income and eliminating pollution, we have to build on the assets we have instead of continuing to analyze the problems we face. The volume examines how the adoption of Zero Emissions concepts not only reduces pollution and waste but can contribute significantly to the generation of income and jobs – specifically for those who need them most – the rural poor in less developed countries." (Pauli 2000)

The European Union

One of the main actors in the field is the European Union, which through different initiatives tries to be the leader for greening the planet. Within the Lisbon Agenda from 2000 sustainability got a very prominent place (Széll, Kamppeter & Moon 2009). The most recent position is summarized as follows:

> "The Renewed EU Sustainable Development Strategy was adopted by the European Council in June 2006. It is an overarching strategy for all EU policies which sets out how we can meet the needs of present generations without compromising the ability of future generations to meet their needs. The Sustainable Development Strategy deals in an integrated way with economic, environmental and social issues and lists the following seven key challenges:
> Climate change and clean energy, Sustainable transport,
> Sustainable consumption and production, Conservation and management of natural resources, Public health, Social inclusion, demography and migration, Global poverty."

The European Foundation for the Improvement of Living and Working Conditions

is a tripartite European institution, created in 1977 and composed of representatives from employers, trade unions and governments, headquartered in Dublin, Ireland, which had been present also during our congress. As its name indicates it has as target the improvement of living and working conditions, which are apparently very closely related to our topic. Many relevant publications have appeared in the past, also their homepage fuses with important data.

On national levels we have a great number of specific initiatives for the promotion of sustainability and labour, which would be to too vast to be handled here appropriately. One exemplary case may be, however, cited: The German *Stiftung Arbeit und Umwelt (Foundation Labour and Environment)*, which has been created by the industrial trade union for mining, chemistry and energy (IG BCE) in 1994 and is promoting sustainability through many activities to overcome the bad image and practice of this sector. It is a good example of cooperation between employers and unions, the so-called social partnership, enhanced by codetermination.

Other Issues

Let us move to some other issues, which are worthwhile to be discussed here. Although we speak of de-industrialisation in the rich, the OECD countries, which actually is largely compensated by delocalisation to less developed countries, these countries still produce more and more waste and emissions. The so-called knowledge-based society is nearly as energy and resource hungry as the industrial societies. The paperless office – as forecasted in 1980 by Siemens, one of the biggest companies in the world – for the year 2000 has remained a pious dream. Although the computerisation of the world – business and private – has revolutionised our work and private life, however, we print not less, but much more than in the decades before, continuing to destroy large forest areas. In the meantime toxic waste from the IT-sector has become one of the main environmental issues (StEP).

Another technology, which is essential for labour and sustainability, is the transport sector. Transport is today one of the main polluters, and largely related to labour. There have been initiatives like telework to reduce transportation to and from work, but – although it has been successful namely in the IT-sector or within science and consultation – the percentage of this kind of work on the global level is only around 1 %, within the OECD-countries it is already about 5 %, maybe with further potential, but definitely not solving the problems of sustainability.

Within the service sector tourism grew to one of the most important businesses in the world, called 'white industry' in contrast to the black, polluting, traditional industrial sector. However, as it is linked by definition to transport, it is quite polluting and not sustainable, if it is increasing as it does still today. Although there are projects of environmentally friendly tourism, these remain so far the exception and are definitely not compatible with mass tourism. But not only transportation of people and goods linked to tourism are not sustainable, but also the destruction of natural habitats for species and plants, the changes of landscapes through buildings and roads are quite harmful.

The other most polluting source is energy for power generation, including heating and cooling. Innovative, intelligent technologies, environmentally sound technologies (EST) can be partly an answer to these challenges, like Zero emission housing, Zero emission transport, the above mentioned factors 4, 5 and 10. (ZERI; Kuehr 2007b) However, technology alone cannot be the answer for the problems created by technology itself.

Water is probably the most central issue for sustainability, because without proper water no life is possible. Without water all living creatures die within a short period. The control of water resources has become therefore a source of environmental conflicts, but also for business monopolies (Széll 2005).

Linked in some way to this issue is health and safety of labour. Sustainability depends on healthy people. Although medicine has made great progress over the last couple of decades, increasing the life expectancy all over the world enormously, however, there are also now setbacks to be seen. Especially in former socialist countries – due mainly to pollution – the life expectancy is decreasing. The same holds true for large parts of Africa,[5] some countries in Asia (namely Indonesia), and Latin America (Brazil), where the destruction of nature for industry, cattle raising etc. has increased the number of hungry people by factor two. The care sector is another economic and social activity, which has been increasing due to the increasing life-expectancy. However, in many cases the quality of artificially extended life is not always sustainable.

Finally, everybody knows or should know by now – except the majority of US-Americans and the newly rich in the Third World – that the American way of life is not sustainable. China has become recently the second most polluting nation in absolute figures, not yet per capita, closely followed by India. The Third World, first of all China – although to speak of China as a developing country is certainly partly misleading –, India, Africa, Latin America and notably the oil-producing countries strive for a kind of American dream.[6] For how long and at which price?

Conclusions and perspectives

What conclusions can be drawn from the arguments presented until now? And which are the perspectives for humankind? From Rio (Agenda 21) to nowhere? Peter Hennicke argued two years ago (Hennicke 2009) that we have a window of opportunity of ten years more to change course as Schmidheiny already asked for for the Business Council for Environment and Development during the Rio Conference in 1992 (Schmidheiny 1992). So there are only eight years left. The forthcoming UN-Cancún summit on the environment in November 2010 will be over, when this book will be published. Already the pre-conference in Bonn in May 2010 was not very promising. So, the prospects, when I write these lines in July 2010, are not good at all.

However, on the other side there are worthwhile initiatives. E.g. the Japanese government is propagating and preparing for a Low Carbon Society in 2050

5 For sure, also HIV is another main reason for declining life expectancy in a number of countries.

6 In all Third World countries we have to a bigger or lesser degree a "First World", i.e. a population, which already lives an American lifestyle, as we have in the First World bigger or lesser parts of a Third World.

(NIES).[7] But will it not be too late by then? More promising in the short and mid term perspective are initiatives like a sustainable company, sustainable enterprises (ILO 2009b); an important step into this direction has been Corporate Social *and Ecological* Responsibility (Széll 2006). CSR is based on stakeholder democracy – as mentioned above –, it needs active participation of all social actors. After all, sustainability is about the quality of life and working life (Széll & Széll 2009), based on democratic participation. Sustainability is a public good, therefore the role of politics, of law, and of regulations is a central element for it. As ecological and social destruction do not know any borders, the regulations have to be international. And they have to be based on transnational cooperation. The international trade union research network GURN should be an important partner in this endeavour. Scientific co-operation in the same vein is practiced since more than thirty years within the Research Comittee 10 "Participation, Organisational Democracy and Self-Management" of the International Sociological Association, which has been a co-organizer of this congress – as in the past of other RLDWL-events.

The eighth congress of our RLDWL-network on "Regional and local sustainable development", which will hopefully take place in Bhubaneswar, Orissa, India – the second most populated country in the world, probably even overtaking soon China – in December 2012 will be the occasion to make an assessment and report on progress of labour and sustainability.

References

Bleischwitz, Raimund (2002), *Cognitive and institutional perspectives of eco-efficiency: a new research landscape towards Factor Four (or more)*. Wuppertal, Wuppertal Institut für Klima, Umwelt, Energie (Wuppertal papers 123).

Brundtland, Gro Harlem et al. (1987), *Our Common Future, Report to the United Nations*. Oxford, Oxford University Press.

Engels, Friedrich (2009), *The Condition of the Working Class in England*. Oxford, Oxford University Press [1844].

European Commission (2009), *Mainstreaming sustainable development into EU policies: 2009 Review of the European Union Strategy for Sustainable Development*. Brussels COM(2009) 400 final.

The European Foundation for the Improvement of Living and Working Conditions, http://www.eurofound.eu.

Global Unions Research Network/GURN, http://www.gurn.info/en/.

7 Cf. Also the business initiative: Dialogue Forum Low Carbon Society, http://www.low-carbon-society.org/?pg=contact&lang=en

Grubb, M.; Koch, M.; Munson, A.; Sullivan, F. & Thomson (1993), *The Earth Summit Agreements: A Guide and Assessment. An Analysis of the Rio '92 UN Conference on Environment and Development.* London, Royal Institute of International Affairs & Earthscan.

Harrisson, Denis; Széll, György & Reynald Bourque (eds.) (2009), *Social Innovation, the Social Economy and World Economic Development. Democracy and Labour Rights in an Era of Globalization.* Frankfurt/M. et al., Peter Lang.

Hennicke, Peter (2009), 'Increasing Resource Productivity: A Win-Win Strategy to Protect Resources, Climate and Jobs?', in György Széll & Ute Széll (eds.), *Quality of live and working life in comparison.* Frankfurt/M. et al., Peter Lang, S. 39-54.

Hennicke, Peter (2010), *Employment, people's livelihood, and sustainable development.* Keynote lecture at the China's Humanities and Social Science Forum 2010, Beijing, Renmin University, 12 June 2010.

ILO (2004), *A fair globalization: Creating opportunities for all*, report of the World Commission on the Social Dimension of Globalization (Geneva).

ILO (2007a), *Equality at work: Tackling the challenges.* Global Report under the follow-up to the ILO Declaration on Fundamental Principles and Rights at Work, Report of the Director-General, Report I(B), International Labour Conference, 96th Session, Geneva,.

ILO (2007b), *Decent work for sustainable development.* ILC 96-2007/Report I (A). http://www.ilo.org/wcmsp5/groups/public/---dgreports/---cabinet/documents/meetingdocument/wcms_085092.pdf.

ILO (2009a), *Guide to the new Millennium Development Goals Employment Indicators including the full set of Decent Work Indicators.* http://www.ilo.org/wcmsp5/groups/public/---ed_emp/documents/publication/wcms_110511.pdf.

ILO (2009b), *The promotion of sustainable enterprises.* Geneva.

ITUC (2010), *Internationally Recognised Core Labour Standards in the People's Republic of China.* Report for the WTO General Council Review of the Trade Policies of the People's Republic of China (Geneva, 10 and 12, May, 2010).

Japan/National Institute for Environmental Studies (NIES), *Japan Low-Carbon Society Scenarios toward 2050.* http://2050.nies.go.jp/

Kuehr, Ruediger (2007a), 'Towards a sustainable society: United Nations University's Zero Emissions Approach', *Journal of Cleaner Production* 15: 1198-1204.

Kuehr, Ruediger (2007b), 'Environmental technologies e from misleading interpretations to an operational categorisation & definition', *Journal of Cleaner Production* 15: 1316-1320.

Kühr, Rüdiger & György Széll (eds.) (1997), *Zero Emissions Research Initiative Kongreß Osnabrück. Dokumentation.* Osnabrück, Universität Osnabrück.

Lan, Xue; Simonis, Udo E.; Dudek, Daniel J. et al. (2007), *Environmental Governance for China*. Berlin, WZB (Discussion Paper P 2007-001).

Marx, Karl (1973), *"Grundrisse". Foundations of the critique of political economy (1857-1858).* Harmondsworth/Penguin & London/New Left Review.

Meadows, Donella et al. (1972), *The Limits to Growth.* Club of Rome. Harvard, MIT Press.

Mehte, Wolfgang (1984), *Ökologie und Marxismus.* Hannover, SOAK Verlag.

Olsen, Lene (2009), *The Employment Effects of Climate Change and Climate Change Responses: A Role for International Labour Standards?* Geneva, GURN. http://www.gurn.info/en/discussion-papers/no12-nov09-the-employment-effects-of-climate-change-and-cliamte-change-responses-a-role-for-international-labour-standards.

Pauli, Gunter (2000), *Upsizing: The Road to Zero Emissions, More Jobs, More Income and No Pollution.* Greenleaf Publishing (UK).

REN21 Renewable Energy Policy Network (2005), *Renewables: 2005 Global Status Report* (www.ren21.net).

REN21 (2006), *Renewables: 2006 Global Status Report* (www.ren21.net).

Schmidheiny, Stephan (1992), *Changing Course – A Global Perspective on Development and the Environment.* Harvard, MIT.

South Centre (2006), *Migration: Is it for development?* Geneva. http://www.southcentre.org/index.php?option=com_content&view=article&id=400%3Amigration-is-it-for-development&catid=70%3Alabour-migration-and-development&Itemid=67&lang=en

StEP – *Solving the e-waste problem*, http://www.step-initiative.org/index.php.

Stiftung Arbeit und Umwelt, http://www.arbeit-umwelt.de/

Sustainlabour, http://www.sustainlabour.org/

Széll, György (1994a), 'Technology, Production, Consumption and the Environment', *International Social Science Journal* # 140: 215-225.

Széll, György (1994b), 'High-Technology, Industrialization, and Problems of Development', in D'Antonio, William V.; Sasaki, Masamichi S. & Yoshio Yonebayashi (eds), *Ecology, Society & the Quality of Social Life*, New Brunswick & London, Transaction Publishers, pp. 149-168.

Széll, György (1999), 'Umwelt – Entwicklung – Frieden: Lösungsbedürftige Probleme aus der Sicht der interdisziplinären Wissenschaften', in Klaus Bosshardt (ed.), *Problembereiche interdisziplinärer Forschung*, Bern et al., Peter Lang, pp. 151-168.

Széll, György (2000), 'Arbeit, Bildung und Demokratie', in *Jahrbuch Ökologie 2001,* München, Beck, pp. 174-182.

Széll, György (2005), 'Environmental Conflicts as a new Dimension of Peace Research', in University of Hiroshima, School of Development Studies (ed.),

[The prevention and solution of disputes over the use of resources], November, pp. 21-32.

Széll, György (2006), *Corporate Social Responsibility in the EU & Japan*. Frankfurt/M. et al., Peter Lang.

Széll, György (2010), 'Changing Labour Relations in China', *Indian Journal of Industrial Relations*, April: 554-565.

Széll, György; Bösling, Carl-Heinrich & Ute Széll (eds.) (2008), *Education, Labour & Science – Perspectives for the 21st Century*. Frankfurt/M. et al., Peter Lang.

Széll, György & Gian-Primo Cella (eds) (2002), *The Injustice at Work: An International View on the World of Labour and Society*. Frankfurt/M. et al.: Peter M. Lang.

Széll, György; Kamppeter, Werner & Woosik Moon (eds.) (2009), *European Social Integration – A Model for East Asia?* Frankfurt/M. et al., Peter Lang (in the series *Labour, Education & Society # 14*).

Széll, György & Ute Széll (eds.) (2009), *Quality of Life & Working Life in Comparison*. Frankfurt/M. et al., Peter Lang.

Széll, György & Ken'ichi Tominaga (eds) (2004), *Environmental Challenges for Japan and Germany – Interdisciplinary and Intercultural Perspectives*. Frankfurt/M. et al., Peter Lang.

Trade Union Assembly on Labour and the Environment/Workers' Initiatives for a Lasting Legacy (2006), *Labour and the Environment: A Natural Synergy* Nairobi. http

United Nations (2009), *UN Climate Change Conference 2009*. http://www.denmark.dk/en/menu/Climate-Energy/COP15-Copenhagen-2009/

UNEP (2002), *Global Environment Outlook (GEO-3)* (www.unep.org/geo/geo3).

UNEP (2003), *Enhancing Civil Society Engagement in the Work of the United Nations Environment Programme*: Strategy Paper (UNEP/GC.22/INF/13) (www.unep.org/civil_society/PDF_docs/Enhancing_Civil_Society_Engagement_In_UNEP.pdf).

UNEP (2005), *One Planet, Many People: Atlas of our Changing Environment* (http://na.unep.net/OnePlanetManyPeople/index.php).

UNEP (2007), *Labour and the Environment: A Natural Synergy*. http://www.unep.org/labour_environment/.

UNEP, (2008), *Green Jobs: Towards Decent Work in a Sustainable, Low-Carbon World. Policy messages and main findings for decision makers*. Nairobi.

United Nations Framework Convention on Climate Change, http://unfccc.int/2860.php.

Vargá, Martin & Ruediger Kuehr (2007), 'Integrative approaches towards Zero Emissions regional planning: synergies of concepts', *Journal of Cleaner Production* 15: 1373-1381.

WRI (World Resources Institute) (2005), *The Wealth of the Poor: Managing Ecosystems to Fight Poverty* (www. wri.org/biodiv/pubs_description.cfm?pid=4073)

Weizsäcker, Ernst von; Lovins, A.B. & L.H. Lovins (1997), *Factor Four – Doubling Wealth, Halving Resource Use – A Report to the Club of Rome.* London, Earthscan.

Weizsäcker, Ernst von; Hargroves, Karlson 'Charlie'; Smith, Michael H.; Cheryl, Desha & Peter Stasinopoulos (2010), *Factor Five – Transforming the Global Economy through 80% Improvements in Resource Productivity.* London, Earthscan.

Zero Emmission Research Initiative, http://www.zeri.org/.

Arbeit, Bildung & Gesellschaft
Labour, Education & Society

Herausgegeben von Prof. Dr. György Széll, Prof. Dr. Heinz Sünker, Dr. Anne Inga Hilsen und Dr. Francesco Garibaldo

Bd. 1 György Széll (ed.): Corporate Social Responsibility in the EU & Japan. 2006.

Bd. 2 Katja Maar: Zum Nutzen und Nichtnutzen der Sozialen Arbeit am exemplarischen Feld der Wohnungslosenhilfe. Eine empirische Studie. 2006.

Bd. 3 Daniela De Ridder: Vom urbanen Sozialraum zur kommunikativen Stadtgesellschaft. 2007.

Bd. 4 Heinz Sünker / Ingrid Miethe (Hrsg.): Bildungspolitik und Bildungsforschung: Herausforderungen und Perspektiven für Gesellschaft und Gewerkschaften in Deutschland. 2007.

Bd. 5 Anja Bastigkeit: Bildungsbiographie und elementarpädagogische Bildungsarbeit. 2007.

Bd. 6 Antônio Inácio Andrioli: Biosoja versus Gensoja. Eine Studie über Technik und Familienlandwirtschaft im nordwestlichen Grenzgebiet des Bundeslandes Rio Grande do Sul (Brasilien). 2007.

Bd. 7 Russell Farnen / Daniel German / Henk Dekker / Christ'l De Landtsheer / Heinz Suenker (eds.): Political Culture, Socialization, Democracy, and Education. Interdisciplinary and Cross-National Perspectives for a New Century. 2008.

Bd. 8 Francesco Garibaldo / Volker Telljohann (eds.): New Forms of Work Organisation and Industrial Relations in Southern Europe. 2007.

Bd. 9 Anne Marie Berg / Olav Eikeland (eds.): Action Research and Organisation Theory. 2008.

Bd. 10 György Széll / Carl-Heinrich Bösling / Ute Széll (eds.): Education, Labour & Science. Perspectives for the 21st Century. 2008.

Bd. 11 Francesco Garibaldo / Philippe Morvannou / Jochen Tholen (eds.): Is China a Risk or an Opportunity for Europe? An Assessment of the Automobile, Steel and Shipbuilding Sectors. 2008.

Bd. 12 Yunus Dauda: Managing Technology Innovation. The Human Resource Management Perspective. 2009.

Bd. 13 Jarmo Lehtonen / Satu Kalliola (eds.): Dialogue in Working Life Research and Development in Finland. 2009.

Bd. 14 György Széll / Werner Kamppeter / Woosik Moon (eds.): European Social Integration – A Model for East Asia? 2009.

Bd. 15 Benedicte Brøgger / Olav Eikeland (eds.): Turning to Practice with Action Research. 2009.

Bd. 16 Till Johannes Hoffmann: Verschwendung. Philosophie, Soziologie und Ökonomie des Überflusses. 2009.

Bd. 17 Denis Harrisson / György Széll / Reynald Bourque (eds.): Social Innovation, the Social Economy and World Economic Development. 2009.

Bd. 18 Werner Weltgen: Total Quality Management als Strukturierungsaufgabe für nachhaltigen Unternehmenswandel. 2009.

Bd. 19 György Széll / Ute Széll (eds.): Quality of Life and Working Life in Comparison. 2009.

Bd. 20 Francesco Garibaldo / Volker Telljohann (eds.): The Ambivalent Character of Participation. New Tendencies in Worker Participation in Europe. 2010.

Band 21 Richard Ennals / Robert H. Salomon (eds.): Older Workers in a Sustainable Societey. 2011.

www.peterlang.de

www.ingramcontent.com/pod-product-compliance
Ingram Content Group UK Ltd.
Pitfield, Milton Keynes, MK11 3LW, UK
UKHW021830100926
8556IPUK00004B/253

9 783631 617311